Media Selling, Fourth Edition

FOURTH
EDITION

Media
Selling

Television
Print
Internet
Radio

CHARLES WARNER

A John Wiley & Sons, Ltd., Publication

This edition first published 2009
© 2009 Charles Warner

Edition history: Blackwell Publishing Ltd/Iowa State University Press (3e, 2004)

Blackwell Publishing was acquired by John Wiley & Sons in February 2007. Blackwell's publishing program has been merged with Wiley's global Scientific, Technical, and Medical business to form Wiley-Blackwell.

Registered Office
John Wiley & Sons Ltd, The Atrium, Southern Gate, Chichester, West Sussex, PO19 8SQ, United Kingdom

Editorial Offices
350 Main Street, Malden, MA 02148–5020, USA
9600 Garsington Road, Oxford, OX4 2DQ, UK
The Atrium, Southern Gate, Chichester, West Sussex, PO19 8SQ, UK

For details of our global editorial offices, for customer services, and for information about how to apply for permission to reuse the copyright material in this book please see our website at www.wiley.com/wiley-blackwell.

Library of Congress Cataloging-in-Publication Data

Warner, Charles, 1932–
  Media selling : television, print, the Internet, and radio / by Charles Warner. – 4th ed.
    p   cm.
  Includes bibliographical references and index.
  ISBN 978-1-4051-5839-8 (pbk. : alk. paper)
  1. Selling–Broadcast advertising.   2. Advertising, Newspaper.   3. Internet advertising.   4. Advertising, Magazine.   5. Advertising, Outdoor.   I. Title.
  HF5439.B67W37 2009
  659.13068′8–dc22

                              2008055192

A catalogue record for this book is available from the British Library.

Set in 11 on 13pt Dante by SNP Best-set Typesetter Ltd., Hong Kong
Printed in Singapore

01   2009

This book is dedicated to my wife, Julia, whose loving care and support enabled me to write it, and to my daughter, Crickett, from whom I learned a great deal about courage.

Contents

Contributors

Charles Warner is the Goldenson Professor Emeritus at the University of Missouri School of Journalism. He teaches graduate courses at The New School in New York in the Media Management Program in the Media Studies and Film Department. He is also an active blogger at www.mediacurmudgeon.com. He is the author of the first edition of *Broadcast and Cable Selling*, the classic text in the field. He was a Vice President of America Online Interactive Marketing from 1998–2002. He has been actively involved in consulting and training for such companies as ABC, CBS, NBC, Fox, ESPN, MTV, Turner Broadcasting, A.H. Belo, Viacom, Clear Channel, AOL, and MSN. Before entering academia in 1981, he was Vice President and General Manager of WNBC-AM, WMAQ-M and WKQX-FM, WWSW-AM and WPEZ-FM, and CBS Radio Spot Sales. He attended Dartmouth College, earned his BFA from the School of Dramatic Arts at Columbia University, and earned his MS in journalism from Southern Illinois University.

Roger Baron is Senior Vice President, Director of Media Research for advertising agency DRAFTFCB. He received a BA in Communications and Public Policy at the University of California, Berkeley, and an MA in Telecommunications at the University of Southern California. His professional experience includes five years at Leo Burnett as a media researcher and media supervisor on the Kellogg cereal account. He spent 12 years at D'Arcy Masius Benton & Bowles, San Francisco, the last four as VP/Media Director. He is a past president of the Media Research Club of Chicago and today is active in the Advertising Research Foundation. He serves as DRAFTFCB's representative to the AAAA Media Research Committee, the Media Rating Council and other industry groups. He is co-author with Northwestern professor Jack Sissors of *Advertising Media Planning*, 6th edition, the largest selling college text on the subject.

Ken Foster has 30 years of marketing and media experience, having worked on the agency, media, and client sides of the business. He has written four educational marketing books and taught Marketing Communications and Media Analysis at the University of Utah for 21 years. He served in the administration at the University of Utah for 20 years and was in charge of Marketing and Public Relations until he retired in 2001 to consult with private industry and educational institutions. He has worked extensively with organizations of all sizes all over the USA in both the public and private sector.

Phil Frank was formerly VP, new business development at Time, Inc.'s Corporate Sales and Marketing Department. He was a VP and National Sales Manager of AOL Interactive Marketing and before that a media supervisor at Ogilvy & Mather and a Senior Vice President and Group Media Director at Ammirati Puris Lintas. He earned his BA from Lehigh University.

J. William Grimes is a widely known media professional who has been President/CEO of four major media companies, including Univision Multimedia Inc, Zenith Media, and ESPN (1981–1988) where he was the recipient of the *USA Today* Sports Executive of the Year and the Gallagher Report's Television Executive of the Year. He is also a former Senior Vice President of CBS. He taught a graduate Media Economics course in the Media Studies and Film Department at The New School in New York and was coordinator of the department's graduate Media Management Program. He earned his BA from West Virginia University, and studied Law at St John's University.

Tim Larson is Associate Professor of Communication at the University of Utah and co-director of its Integrated Marketing Communication Certificate Program. He is the director of the New Media Sequence at the University of Utah and teaches media policy, management and IMC courses at the undergraduate and graduate level. Prior to coming to the University of Utah, he was on the staff of the Wisconsin Governor's Blue Ribbon Cable Task Force. Dr Larson earned his PhD from the University of Wisconsin.

William Redpath is a Vice President of BIA Financial Network, Inc., Chantilly, Virginia. Prior to joining BIAfn in 1985, he was an auditor with the Cincinnati office of Arthur Andersen & Co.; Assistant Financial Manager of WISH-TV, Indianapolis; on the internal audit staff of ABC in New York; and a Senior Financial Analyst with NBC in New York. Mr Redpath earned a BA degree in Economics and Political Science from Indiana University and an MBA from the University of Chicago. He is a Certified Public Accountant (Virginia), a Chartered Financial Analyst, an Accredited Senior Appraiser in Business Valuation in the American Society of Appraisers, and holds the Accredited in Business Valuation designation from the American Institute of Certified Public Accountants.

Ron Steiner has had a 41-year career in broadcast television as a television station general sales manager, a television station general manager, a consultant to television station group owners, and a consultant and seminar leader for numerous state broadcast associations. He is the founder of Broadcast Sales Training, the leading sales training program utilized by television stations. He created the Broadcast Sales Academy, the most respected training program for television salespeople. He is also the creator and lead trainer for the New York State Broadcasting Association Sales Certification Program and creator and founder of www.tvsalespro. com, a multi-media sales training program "TV Sales Pro," delivered on the Web and via satellite.

Thomas J. Stultz is a 35-year newspaper veteran who has held a variety of executive positions in the industry including, most recently, President and CEO of Triple Crown Media, Inc. He has held senior management and marketing positions with Multimedia Newspaper Company, Inc. in Greenville, SC, Suburban Newspapers of Greater St Louis, and Harte-Hanks Communications, Inc. He began his newspaper career as a reporter in Ashland, KY. Today he serves as Senior Vice President and Managing Director of IMG College, a division of IMG Worldwide, Inc. and is based in Lexington, KY where he leads the company's collegiate sports marketing rights and its association management businesses. He earned his MBA from Georgia State University.

Paul Talbot is Vice President of Sales, SportingNews.com and before that was Vice President of Sales for Sporting News Radio. He was Senior Vice President and Market Manager for the Infinity Broadcasting (now CBS Radio) radio stations in Phoenix, AZ, and sales manager for that station group prior to being promoted to run the group. He was also National Sales Director, Interactive Marketing, with AOL and before that a regional sales manager with AOL.

Vincent Thompson is founder of Middleshift LLC, an Internet consulting company that has worked with Facebook.com, Break.com, Streetfire.net, TVGuide. com, and Spark Networks. Middleshift has also represented the original content of Michael Eisner's Vuguru.com and Rob Barnett's MyDamnChannel.com to marketers. Prior to his consultancy, Vince spent seven years at AOL where he was the Regional Vice President of Sales in the Southwest. Earlier in his career he worked in sales and business development for Third Age Media and before that managed local television station sales forces. He is the author of the best selling business book, *Ignited: Managers, Light up Your Company and Career for More Power, More Purpose, and More Success.* He holds an undergraduate degree in Communications from the University of Southern California's Annenberg School of Communications and a Masters in Business Administration from Pepperdine University's Graziadio School of Business.

Preface and Acknowledgments

Media Selling, 4th edition is an update of *Media Selling*, 3rd edition, which I wrote with another author. I wrote all the chapters of the fourth edition unless otherwise noted. Media convergence, fragmentation, the growth of online advertising, especially Google and search advertising, the difficulties of cross-platform selling, and the decline of newspapers, magazines, and radio necessitated a revision.

The third edition chapters on Media Research, Newspapers, Television, Radio, Cable, Magazines, and Interactive have been rewritten to reflect the current marketplace and media environment. The Interactive chapter has been renamed "The Internet" in order to reflect current usage. Chapter 7 of the third edition, "Skills: Effective Communication, Effective Listening, and Understanding People," has been shortened to eliminate much of the information on communication theory. National selling has been emphasized and local selling somewhat de-emphasized (except in radio), based on comments from professors who used *Media Selling*, 2nd edition. Chapters on Yellow Pages, Outdoor, and the Future of the Media have been eliminated. I realized that the third edition's predictions for the future were so far off that it was a waste of my and readers' time to attempt to predict the next big thing.

Focus of the Book

Media Selling focuses on several basic concepts:

- Selling after the advent of Web 2.0 and Google's AdWords has changed irreversibly. There are now two basic types of selling: (1) Personal, face-to-face selling, on which this book focuses because it is the most prevalent type of selling done by television, newspapers, magazines, radio, and Web sites and portals that feature display, rich media, and video advertising. (2) Computerized selling done on the Internet by means of an auction, as pioneered by Google's

AdWords, in which search advertising is sold. This type of advertising and its ramifications will be covered in more depth in Chapter 20, "The Internet."

- Personal selling without tricks or manipulation – with authenticity – in order to build and maintain long-term relationships based on trust.
- The imperative of honesty, integrity, and ethics in selling in this era of corporate misdeeds and erosion of confidence in the media, and in this new era of transparency in which it is virtually impossible to erase the digital footprints of misdeeds.
- Attitudes control successful sales performance, and attitudes are controllable by using sound goals and objectives to motivate salespeople and help them achieve their dreams.
- Developing emotional and social intelligence – self-awareness, self-management, social awareness, and relationship management – are necessary for success in selling.
- Understanding of the basic principles of persuasion and influence is important for today's media salesperson.
- Solutions selling, meaning selling solutions to marketing and advertising problems.
- Because a majority of media business is conducted through negotiating, today's media salespeople must be expert negotiators.
- Understanding the concepts of marketing and advertising in order to develop appropriate solutions.
- Understanding the strengths and weaknesses of all of major media is important in an era of cross-platform selling.

Unique Features

The fourth edition of *Media Selling* has several unique features:

- A fully integrated and organized selling system – AESKOPP – that enables salespeople and sales managers to organize and evaluate sales efforts.
- A strategic personal selling approach that emphasizes solving customer problems by developing trusting, long-term relationships using the wisdom of emotional intelligence and the principles of persuasion and influence.
- Definitions of the six steps of personal selling that focus on discovering and understanding customer needs and wants, solving advertising and marketing problems, and getting results.
- Tips on organizing, writing, and delivering major presentations to groups at key accounts.
- A thorough section on negotiating and closing.
- Tips on effective sales organization systems, To-Do lists, and time management.

- A Web site (www.mediaselling.us) that contains sample presentations, blank forms, outlines, a success case study, and helpful articles.
- A Web site (www.mediaselling.us) that contains a companion book, *Media Sales Management*, that is available free.

Most books on personal selling tend to assume a salesperson sells a product with a fixed price, and once a salesperson overcomes objections, an order will follow at that price without negotiating. Television, cable, online, and radio prices have traditionally been fluid and negotiated, while newspapers and magazine prices have traditionally been more rigid. However, today newspapers' and magazines' rates are being negotiated more often, especially on a corporate or group basis. Closing becomes a part of the negotiating process and stresses getting commitment rather than trying hard closes, because old-fashioned closing techniques do not work with today's sophisticated media buyers and customers.

Style of the Book

I and the other contributors have tried to write the book in a relatively informal, personal style. Incidentally, I have used the term salesperson throughout this book instead of sales representative or account executive or account manager just to be consistent, because they all mean the same thing.

Media Sales Management

A complete, thorough companion text to *Media Selling*, titled *Media Sales Management*, is available for free downloading on www.mediaselling.us.

Media Sales Management includes chapters on how to hire the best people, training exercises, sales management case studies, an in-depth performance coaching system, a discussion of sophisticated pricing strategies that will increase shares of business, and much more. It is designed to be used along with *Media Selling* in a college course on Media Sales and Sales Management and for working media sales managers and ad directors.

Acknowledgments

Special thanks go to Elizabeth Swayze, who has been a superb and patient professional, and all of her colleagues at Wiley-Blackwell, especially Margot Morse, who have worked so hard to make this book possible. Thanks go to a hall-of-fame group of chapter authors in order of appearance: William Redpath, Tim Larson, Ken Foster, Roger Baron, Bill Grimes, Ron Steiner, Tom Stultz, Vince Thompson, Paul Talbot and Phil Frank. The book was guided by the thoughtful reviews of several of my academic colleagues, and I would like thank them for their efforts and encouragement.

Updating the 3rd edition of *Media Selling* has been difficult for several reasons, mostly because of the rapid changes in the media industry, especially the Internet. It is virtually impossible to keep up with accelerating change and this book, like the previous edition, is sure to be out of date before it is published. With that in mind, I have tried to give readers the URLs of Web sites and industry newsletters and blogs where they can go to get updated information.

In the middle of revising the 3rd edition, in the fall of 2006, I became quite ill and informed my editor, Elizabeth Swayze, that I would not be able to finish the book. However, my patient, perfect wife, Julia, nursed me back to health and encouraged me to finish the book and subsequently put up with my foul moods as I trudged along. If readers find this edition useful, then thanks go to Julia. It could not have been finished without her encouragement.

Charles Warner
New York, March 2008

Part I

The Marketing/Media Ecology and Personal Selling

1

The Marketing/Media Ecology

Charles Warner

The media are integral elements of America's economy and of the marketing process that is vital to that economy's vigor. Consumer demand (and spending) are what drives the economy, and it is marketing and advertising that fuel consumer demand. Advertising is a major component of marketing and it is through the media that consumers receive advertising messages about products. If any one of the three elements (marketing, advertising, and the media) is not healthy, the other two cannot thrive. This chapter will examine the interdependent relationships among marketing, advertising, and the media.

What Is Marketing?

In his influential book, *The Practice of Management*, Peter Drucker, "the Father of Modern Management," presented and answered a series of simple, straightforward questions. He asked, "What is a business?" The most common answer, "An organization to make a profit," is not only false; it is also irrelevant to Drucker. If we want to know what a business is, we have to start with its purpose. "There is only one valid definition of business purpose: to create a customer," Drucker wrote.

Drucker pointed out that businesses create markets for products: "There may have been no want at all until business action created it – by advertising, by salesmanship, or by inventing something new. In every case it is a business action that creates a customer." Furthermore, he said, "What a business thinks it produces is not of first importance – especially not to the future of the business and to its success." "What the customer thinks he is buying, what he considers 'value,' is decisive – it determines what a business is, what it produces and whether it will prosper." Finally, Drucker said, "Because it is its purpose to create a customer, any business enterprise has two – and only these two – basic functions: marketing and innovation."[1]

Notice that Drucker did not mention production, manufacturing, or distribution, but only customers. That is what marketing is – a customer-focused business approach. The production-oriented business produces goods and then tries to sell them; the customer-oriented business produces goods that it *knows* will sell, not that *might* sell.

Another leading theorist, former Harvard Business School Professor Theodore Levitt, wrote an article in 1960 titled "Marketing myopia" that is perhaps the most influential single article on marketing ever published. Levitt claims that the railroads went out of business "not because the need [for passenger and freight transportation] was filled by others . . . but because it was *not* filled by the railroads themselves. They let others take customers away from them because they assumed themselves to be in the railroad business rather than in the transportation business."[2] In other words, they failed because they did not know how to create a customer; they were not marketing-oriented. Where would makers of buggy whips be today if they had decided they were in the vehicle acceleration business or in the transportation accessory business instead of being in the buggy whip business?

Levitt cited the problems Detroit's car manufacturers were having in 1960 and would have in the future – they were too production oriented. When American automobile makers researched the needs of their customers, they merely found out customers' preferences among existing products. Japanese automobile makers did the *right* research in the 1970s and gave these customers what they really wanted and still are doing so today, as evidenced by the fact that Toyota has become the world's number-one car manufacturer.

As a result of the customer-oriented, marketing approach espoused by Drucker, Levitt, and other leading management and business writers, many companies asked themselves the question, "What business are we in?" and subsequently changed their direction. They began to have a heightened sensitivity to customers and began to change the old attitude of "Let's produce this product because we've discovered how to make it."

In today's economy the customer rules and any company that does not put their customers on a pedestal and make raving fans of them will disappear from the business landscape as fast as so many of the dot.coms did.

Some Brief Economic History

From the beginning of the eighteenth century to the latter part of the nineteenth century, America had little or no mass-production capability. People devoted their time to producing agricultural goods, building manufacturing capacity, and developing commerce. They concentrated on inventing and manufacturing products. It was the *era of production.*

By the beginning of the twentieth century, the population had spread out from the East Coast, manufacturing had become efficient, and surpluses had developed. The basic problem shifted from one of production to one of distribution – getting the plentiful goods to people. Thus, in response to the new challenge, businesses developed new distribution systems: mail-order houses (the beginning of Sears, Roebuck and Company), chain stores, wholesalers and distributors, and department stores. It was the *era of distribution.*

When the 1920s came roaring in, the problem changed from one of supply to one of demand. Mass production and mass distribution were in place and an abundance of goods was produced and distributed. The problem now was to convince consumers to buy what was available. Enter the *era of selling,* as businesses attempted to create a demand for the products they had produced and distributed with more intensive selling techniques and advertising. Manufacturers made deceptive and extravagant promises about products, and high-pressure selling tactics were common, especially during the Depression in the 1930s as businesses became more desperate to sell their products.

After World War II, businesses had no trouble selling whatever was made. Consumers released their pent-up demand for goods built up during the years when manufacturing capacity was directed toward supplying the war effort. However, by the 1950s, consumers were beginning to be particular and to demand more choices; they wanted what *they* wanted, not what manufacturers happened to want to produce. The *era of marketing* had begun. Those businesses, such as IBM and General Electric, that recognized the shift in consumer attitudes adopted a consumer-driven approach and survived; those that did not, such as the Pennsylvania Railroad, disappeared.

As has been widely reported, we are now in the *era of information.* Those businesses that can provide, distribute, organize, access, and create information are the ones that are growing rapidly. Google is an information era company that, by creating popular search technology, has more market capitalization than General Motors or Ford, older production-oriented companies. The Internet is the ultimate distribution channel for information and has become an integral part of most companies' marketing efforts.

The Marketing Concept

The fundamental concept underlying marketing is that of *consumer orientation*; however, just because a business is consumer oriented doesn't automatically ensure its competitive survival. Two other ideas must accompany consumer orientation for the marketing concept to be complete: *profit* and *internal organization*.

To continue to be sensitive to consumer needs, a business must also stay in business by making a profit. Although Drucker pointed out that profit is not the purpose of a business, profits are still the fuel that keeps the machines of business running; thus, profits are a necessary ingredient in the marketing concept.

To serve consumers, businesses must be organized internally to do so. The efforts of a number of functional areas or departments have to be coordinated so that all of them have the same goal – to create customers by serving the customers' needs.

When the marketing era evolved in the 1950s, many marketing-oriented companies, such as Procter and Gamble (P&G), realized they had to change their internal organizational structure to accommodate their change in corporate strategy from production orientation to marketing orientation. They went from an organizational structure based on function (manufacturing, engineering, sales, and distribution) to one arranged by product (Tide, Jif, Crest, and so on).

Thus, a marketing-oriented company will typically organize around its marketing effort and put those functions that relate directly to marketing under the organizational wing of marketing – departments such as sales, product design, consumer research, advertising and promotion, and customer service, for example.

The efforts of marketing-oriented departments are directed toward customer satisfaction, and more important, customer loyalty. Profit is the reward a business reaps from satisfied, loyal customers.

You might have noticed that we have been using the terms "customers" and "consumers" interchangeably. It is time to clear up that confusion and accurately define the terms. A customer buys a product, a consumer uses a product. Sometimes a customer and a consumer are the same person, for example, the man who buys an electric shaver for himself and uses it. Sometimes they are different people, for example, the girl who says she wants an iPod Nano and her mom who buys it for her. P&G's customers are retailers and their consumers are people who buy Crest. By advertising to consumers and creating demand for Crest, P&G pulls the product through the distribution system. Some manufacturers do not advertise their products but sell them to wholesalers who they hope will sell the product to retailers and, thus, push it through the distribution system. In the media advertising business, the customer is the advertiser and the consumer is the viewer, reader, or listener.

You will find a more detailed discussion of marketing and marketing strategies in Chapter 15, because media salespeople must have a deeper understanding of marketing than is provided here in this introductory section in order to be effective problem solvers and solutions sellers.

What Is Advertising?

Harvard Business School professor Theodore Levitt changed the direction of marketing with his 1960 article "Marketing myopia," and he changed the perception of advertising ten years later with his article "The morality (?) of advertising." Levitt wrote that "In curbing the excesses of advertising, both business and government must distinguish between embellishment and mendacity." He presents a philosophical treatment of the human values of advertising as compared with the values of other "imaginative" disciplines.[3]

Levitt defended advertising against critics who would constrain advertising's creativity, who want less fluff and more fact in advertising. Many critics of advertising come from high-income brackets in business and government whose affluence was generated in industries that either create (advertising agencies) or distribute (the media) advertising, in industries that have grown through the use of effective advertising, or by using advertising to promote themselves (politicians). Thus, advertising's critics must look carefully at their own glass houses when throwing stones at advertising.

Also, advertising's critics, Levitt claims, often view the consumer as a helpless, irrational, gullible couch potato, which is far from the truth. As David Ogilvy, the advertising genius and practitioner *par excellence*, wrote to his advertising agency copywriters in his book, *Confessions of an Advertising Man*, "the consumer is not an idiot, she's your wife."[4] Obviously, when Ogilvy made the comment in 1963, most copywriters were men, which is no longer the case.

Levitt, too, believed that "most people spend their money carefully" and are not fooled by advertising's distortions, exaggerations, and deceptions. He writes that rather than deny that distortion and exaggeration exist in advertising, these properties are among advertising's socially desirable purposes. Levitt goes on to say "illegitimacy in advertising consists only of falsification with larcenous intent." Levitt's thesis is that advertising is like poetry, the purpose of which is "to influence an audience; to affect its perception and sensibilities; perhaps even to change its mind." Advertising, like art, makes things prettier. "Who wants reality?" Levitt asks. When most people get up in the morning and look at reality in the mirror, they do not like what they see and try to change it by shaving, using hair gel, or applying makeup. These things give people hope that they will be better accepted, more attractive, and thus happier. The goal of the poet, the artist, and the composer is similar to the goal of an ad – creating images and feelings. Most advertising, especially on television, is about feelings and emotions. It is about trying to make people feel good about a product. Levitt writes that "Advertisements are

the symbols of man's aspirations."[5] So, Madison Avenue (as the advertising industry is often referred to), like Hollywood, is selling dreams, and dreams and hope
are essential to people's well-being.

Google extended the definition of advertising to include search, or keyword,
advertising, that is limited to two lines of copy underneath a link to a commerce
Web site on which people can buy a searched-for item or get more information.
No image making or branding is involved, yet it is still considered advertising.

Furthermore, advertising develops mass markets for goods, and mass production reduces the cost of producing these goods. Thus, advertising is a major con-
tributor to reducing manufacturing costs, search costs, and, ultimately, retail
prices. Products such as personal computers, digital video disc (DVD) players,
video cameras, iPods, and personal digital assistants (PDAs) steadily come down
in price as the market for them grows larger and as manufacturing savings are
passed on to consumers in the form of competitive pricing. Consumers get information about these reduced prices through advertising, by the way, not via smoke
signals.

Advertising is not only an important part of the nation's economy, but also, as
the nation's population increases and products proliferate, advertisers and their
agencies will continue to invest more money in the media to reach these consumers. You will find a more detailed discussion of advertising and advertising strategies in Chapter 17, because media salespeople must have a more in-depth
understanding of the principles of advertising than is provided here in order to be
effective sellers of advertising.

The Media

Advertising is one of the integral elements of the marketing process, just like sales,
product design, promotion, and customer service are. We might look at advertising as the mass selling of a product. Where is advertising seen or heard? In the
media. What business is an advertising agency in? In the advertising creation
and placement business. What business is the media in? *The advertising delivery
business.*

When people talk about the media, they are referring to the distributors of
news and entertainment content – television, the Internet, newspapers, radio, and
magazines. However, newspapers are not in the news business, magazines are not
in the fashion business, and broadcast and cable television are not in the entertainment business. All of these media are supported entirely or in part by advertising
and are, therefore, in the advertising delivery business.[6] The media are dependent
on advertising, and advertising, as an integral part of a larger marketing system,
is co-dependent on the media. Without the media to reach large numbers of
consumers with an ad or a commercial, marketers would have to go door-to-door

and try to sell their goods one-on-one through personal selling or consumers would have to wander from store to store wondering which sold the product they needed – both very expensive undertakings. Advertising agencies would not exist if there were no media to run the ads they created.

The reason marketers and advertisers are dependent on the media is because the media are pervasive and popular with consumers (viewers, readers, listeners) and are their link to the global village. People love their media and depend on their media – their favorite television program, such as "American Idol," their favorite Web site, such as MySpace.com or Facebook.com, their favorite magazine, such as *People*, their favorite Country music radio station, or their favorite newspaper, like the *Wall Street Journal*. Because of this affection and dependency, the media are actually the most powerful business in the country – more powerful than the industries, celebrities, and politicians they cover, expose, and glorify.

It is because of this enormous power coupled with a perception that the media emphasize negative news, poor-quality, user-generated video, or sex and violence that people probably have such a low opinion of the media. Americans seem to blame all the ills of society on the media. It is for this reason that we have devoted a separate chapter in this book to ethics. Chapter 3 emphasizes the importance for salespeople to deal with customers ethically, because the reputation of the media is at stake, and that reputation needs to be improved.

The role of the media is to expose consumers to advertising, not to guarantee sales or results to advertisers. The media are just that – a medium, a connection between advertisers and customers. There are signs in radio station KOMC/KRZK in Branson, MO, for example, that read "Our purpose is to bring our audience and advertisers together," which is exactly what Google's search advertising does. When asked in an interview in a national business magazine what the radio business was all about, Lowry Mays, founder of Clear Channel Communications, replied, "To help people sell more Fords." These signs and statements reinforce the notion that the media are in the advertising delivery business.

In most of the world's countries, the media are supported and controlled by government; however, the media in the United States are kept free from government control and interference because of advertising support. The mass media from which the American public gets the vast majority of their information and entertainment are free or relatively inexpensive because they are supported by advertising. If Google were not supported by advertising, people would have to pay a few cents for each search. A daily newspaper that costs 50 cents at a newsstand would cost $6 or $7 were it not for the advertising, plus the newspaper would be much less desirable and useful for consumers if it contained no classified ads, no movie listings, or no bargains for price-conscious shoppers.

Finally, in spite of a love–hate relationship between the public and the media, or perhaps because of it, most media companies are profitable. Many of the great fortunes in the world have been built in the media. Even if new products do not survive in the marketplace, the media still receive the advertising dollars invested to introduce the product, just as the media get the advertising revenue from political candidates who eventually lose. The profit margins in the media are, as a rule, higher than in most other industries, except for the software industry, perhaps. Top-rated radio and television stations in major markets often have profit margins of 50 percent or greater. Newspapers in large markets are usually monopolies or close to it because joint operating agreements and profit margins often reach or exceed 20 percent, although these margins have been declining in recent years. Popular national magazines often have similarly high profit margins, although smaller magazines are having problems making a profit after the recent increases in postal rates. Websites and portals such as Google, Yahoo!, and AOL are quite profitable.

The reason for these high profit margins is because in an advertising-supported medium such as radio, television, newspapers, magazines, and Web sites, the cost of putting in an extra ad has no or very low incremental costs involved. For example, in television, the time for commercials is baked into most programming, so if a commercial is not scheduled in a commercial pod, a promotion or public service announcement will run. A television station does not expand the programming time if it does not have commercials to run. Thus, at a television station, it costs nothing to add a commercial – there are no incremental costs involved. On the other hand, if an automotive manufacturer sells a car, it has to build one with all of the concomitant costs involved (labor, materials, transportation, etc.). Once a radio or television station has sold enough advertising to cover its cost of operations and debt payment, if any, all additional advertising sold is virtually 100 percent profit. In newspapers and magazines, which have an additional revenue stream, that of subscriptions, once the cost of operating is recovered, the incremental cost of adding a page of advertising is very low in comparison to the cost of an ad to an advertiser.

What this profitable economic model means for salespeople is that advertising revenue is extremely profitable and, therefore, there is more money to distribute to salespeople in the form of compensation than in less profitable industries. Media salespeople are among the highest paid of any industry.

Test Yourself

1 In the era of marketing, what is the primary focus?
2 Why are consumer orientation, profit, and internal organization important to the marketing concept?
3 What is the difference between a customer and a consumer?
4 Is advertising distorted and exaggerated? If so, what do you think Theodore Levitt might say about this contention?
5 What business is the media in?
6 Why are the media potentially so profitable?

Project

Make a list of all of the local media in your market: radio stations, television stations, cable systems, newspapers (daily, weekly, shoppers, suburban, ethnic, etc.), local magazines or journals (e.g., local business journals), outdoor companies, bus or subway posters, Yellow Pages, and local Web sites that sell advertising. Interview one or two sales managers or advertising directors of some of the media that have revenue in addition to advertising (newspapers subscriptions or a Web site's e-commerce, for example) and get a rough estimate of what percentage of revenue comes from advertising and what percentage comes from other revenue sources. Then write some notes about what surprised you in this exercise.

References

Kenneth Blanchard and Sheldon Bowles. 1993. *Raving Fans: A Revolutionary Approach to Customer Service*. New York: William Morrow and Company

Peter Drucker. 1954. *The Practice of Management*, New York: Harper & Row.

Theodore Levitt. 1960. "Marketing myopia," *Harvard Business Review*, July–Aug.

Theodore Levitt. 1970. "The morality (?) of advertising," *Harvard Business Review*, July–Aug.

David Ogilvy. 1989. *Confessions of an Advertising Man*, 2nd edition, New York: Atheneum.

Resources

www.adage.com (*Advertising Age* online)
www.onetvworld.org (Cable Television Advertising Bureau online)
www.editorandpublisher.com (*Editor and Publisher* online)
www.mediapost.com (daily updates about all of the media and media research)
www.iab.net (Internet Advertising Bureau online)
www.newspaper-industry.org (newspaper industry information)
www.oaaa.org (Outdoor Advertising Association of America online)
www.rab.com (Radio Advertising Bureau online)
www.tvb.org (Television Bureau of Advertising online)

Notes

1 Peter F. Drucker. 1954. *The Practice of Management*. New York: Harper & Row.

2 Theodore Levitt. 1960. "Marketing myopia," *Harvard Business Review*, July–August.

3 Theodore Levitt. 1970. "The morality (?) of advertising," *Harvard Business Review*, July–August.

4 David Ogilvy. 1989. *Confessions of an Advertising Man*, 2nd edition, New York: Atheneum.

5 Levitt. "The morality (?) of advertising."

6 HBO is on cable television but is not supported by advertising, but by a monthly subscription fee. Therefore, HBO, and other premium cable service, are not in the advertising delivery business, but in the subscription television business.

2

Selling: Assumptions, Approaches, and Types of Selling

Charles Warner

The first sale I ever made was for a television station in South Carolina in 1957. The owner of the station had called up a local florist and suggested to the proprietor, Mr Parrott, that his shop purchase a spot next to a popular CBS network program. The owner of the television station explained that the Florists Delivery Service (FTD) was a regular sponsor of the highly rated program, "Person To Person," and that a lot of people would be watching. The flower-shop owner could buy a commercial linking him to the prestigious network program and its national sponsor.

The station owner called me into his office and told me to run down the street and sign up Mr Parrott. I did precisely as I was told. I ran down to the florist shop with a sales contract in my hand and had the following conversation:

"Hi, Mr Parrott. I'm Charlie Warner. Mr Brown sent me down here to pick up an order for an adjacency next to 'Person to Person.'"

"A what?"

"An adjacency – a commercial next to Edward R. Murrow's program 'Person to Person.'"

"Oh, yes. Well, I told him I'd try it. How much is one?"

"Here's our rate card. Would you like an ID or a chain-break?"

"A what?"

"A 10-second or a 20-second spot?"

"Oh. Let's see, the 10-second one is cheaper. I'll take it."

"Would you like to buy more than just one?"

"No, not now. I'll try it this first time out. How much?"

"That will be $28.44."

"OK."

"Great. Let me fill in this contract here for you to sign. Oh, by the way, there's a charge of $10 for us to make a slide for you."

"A what?"

"A slide. You know, a picture to go up on the TV screen."

"Oh, yes. A picture is extra?"

"Of course. We have to charge for production."

"Oh, a picture is production?"

"Yes. I'll have our promotion man design one and get back to you with the artwork." (Long pause while filling out the contract.)

"Sign here, Mr Parrott."

"Well, OK, I guess . . . I never watch television myself. I hope it works."

"Thanks. I'll be back in a few days with your slide."

A station artist made a 35-mm slide, the client approved it, and the brief, static commercial ran next to "Person to Person" on Friday night. I returned to see the florist the following Monday afternoon and had this conversation:

"Hi, Mr Parrott. Did you see your spot?"

"No."

"Oh, er . . . well, would you like to buy it on a regular basis? I can give you a discount if you sign up for thirteen weeks."

"I don't believe so."

"Why?"

"I didn't get any results. Nobody has called today."

"Well, that's . . ."

"No. I can't afford it anyway. TV is too expensive."

"OK. Well, thanks anyway."

What went wrong with this sale? If you answered "everything," you would be correct. First, the owner of the station was concerned with selling his product, not with satisfying his customer's needs; he was product-oriented, not customer-oriented. He apparently did not inquire about what the customer wanted, or if he did, he did not communicate it to me. The instructions were to "get an order," not to "find out what Mr Parrott wants and needs." Second, the owner took a very short-range point of view; he was not interested in creating a repeat customer, or in developing a long-range relationship and partnership, only a one-shot sale.

If the owner was initially at fault, I, as rookie, compounded the errors tenfold. First, I made no attempt to prepare for the call or to consider a strategic approach.

Second, I used jargon; I failed to put things in the prospect's language. Next, I did not ask any questions to determine what his advertising goals and problems were; I just handed the florist a price sheet (rate card). I did not control the interview by using probing questions, and the questions I asked were the wrong ones, ones that easily could be answered in the negative. I did not pick up cues about the prospect's expectations ("I'll try it this first time out") or, most important, try to control his expectations.

Instead of explaining the production charges earlier, I presented them as an add-on after I told him the price. I not only told him to sign a contract for just a small amount but also asked him to wait while I filled it out in front of him. In addition, the client had to ask me what a slide was and I probably made him feel ignorant. Because I was not listening attentively, I did not catch the prospect's doubts ("I hope it works"). I failed to try to build a relationship by developing rapport or being empathetic. I had no skills in understanding objections and then dealing with them. Finally, I *told* the prospect to sign ("Sign here . . .") and I made no attempt to make the customer feel good about his purchase and reinforce his good judgment.

When I eagerly returned the following week, I began by asking the wrong question, got a predictably negative answer (which I did not handle well), and went immediately to a weak close based on a price concession. Finally, I gave up too easily. I realized by that time I had done everything wrong; but even so, I still gave up too easily.

This book is about doing it right, about selling media with an in-depth, customer-oriented, solutions-based, partnering approach. This book is for people who hope to have or who have already begun sales careers in the media.

Assumptions

Three assumptions form the foundation of the media sales theories and methods proposed in this book.

Assumption 1: People are complex and basically trustworthy

Each person is a unique and complex individual who cannot be described adequately by simple, one-word, personality-type labels. People are enormously complicated and understanding them requires much more than snap judgments based on first, or even second, impressions. Understanding people requires emotional intelligence, which will be covered in Chapter 6. It also requires effective listening skills, caring, fairness, and respect, which will be covered Chapter 7.

The assumption that people are basically trustworthy gives us a workable model for our actions. Think what the world would be like if we made the opposite assumption – that no one could be trusted. We could not tell anyone the truth and we would have no idea if what people told us was true.

In order to have a functioning society we must act on the principle of reciprocity, especially in regards to being straightforward, telling the truth, and trusting people. If we act on the principle that we get from people what we give them and, thus, offer the first gift of trust, the odds are that we will receive a reciprocal gift of trust in return. There will always be an occasional aberration in which someone does not return your trust and tries to deceive you, but that is life – nothing is perfect – and we cannot act as though no one can be trusted.

Assumption 2: Personal selling is a worthy craft

This statement includes several important concepts. First, personal selling is about dealing with people – the most fascinating, complex, challenging, and fun type of selling there is because people are fascinating, complex, challenging, and fun.

Second, selling is a craft. Selling contains a body of knowledge and techniques that can be learned, but can only be perfected through practical experience, which makes it a craft. The craft of selling is expressed and exercised primarily through understanding people.

Third, selling is an expression of worthy values – freedom and independence. Selling affords people freedom in dealing with the most complex subject, people, and selling allows you the freedom to express yourself. Selling also gives you the independence you need to have control over your own actions and work habits and, therefore, to have an exciting daily challenge. In addition to freedom of movement, action, and independence to work at your own pace and in your own way, selling also gives you the opportunity to earn an excellent living if you are good at it.

Fourth, selling is worthy because you are helping other people – you are helping them get what they want, helping them to be successful. You help advertising agency buyers get what they want for their clients and you help advertisers get results as they define them and sell more goods. In a sense, you are helping fuel the economy.

Fifth, selling fosters optimism, self-confidence, and the belief in the inherent rationality and goodness of people. Selling encourages, virtually forces, people to have a positive view of the future, of themselves, and of others – to have a healthy outlook on life. You cannot face selling, day in and day out, if you do not believe in your ability to help your customers solve their marketing and advertising problems. There is great personal satisfaction in helping your customers get results, sell more products, and be successful.

Assumption 3: The media are highly visible, important, and under attack

The media, including Web sites and blogs, are ubiquitous and powerful, and they transmit advertising, political, cultural, social, and moral messages (either intended or unintended) to a mass audience. Also, because radio and broadcast television stations operate on airwaves owned by the public and cable television operates on common-carrier-like technologies, these media are subject to a complicated web of government regulations.

Because of the complex and fuzzy combination of show business and public service, the media will continue to be loved and hated, praised and vilified, regulated and deregulated, and given credit or blamed for everything from keeping our nation free to poisoning the minds of our children. Salespeople in the media must learn to deal with all types of extreme reactions and to accept the fact that they, as representatives of their medium, will have to face these often highly emotional, reactions on a daily basis.

The good news is that, as a salesperson, you will have easy access to clients. The bad news is that your medium will be blamed for everything from a client's sore back to the nation's economy, and you will have to listen to the reasons for your medium's and all of the media's failures – people tend to lump all the media together as a target for their anger, so it does not matter if you're selling for a Web site, a television network, or a newspaper, you will probably get comments about how awful the media are. You will have to learn to listen good-naturedly and non-defensively, and to take it.

The media industry is changing at an accelerated rate in terms of both technological advances and the audience's tastes and needs. As America continues its transition from a production-oriented to an information-oriented industrial system, consumers become more particular and selective. This creates a shifting emphasis for salespeople – from that of selling and getting an order toward one of building relationships and solving problems. Meanwhile, there is less time available for preparation, planning, and negotiating as advertising schedules run for shorter and shorter periods of time and buyers wait until the last minute to place schedules.

In the past, the media enjoyed virtually guaranteed profits, but today the media are becoming increasingly fragmented. Too many media are chasing smaller and smaller market segments and profits are declining in many of the more traditional media. This means that as the competition for advertising dollars increases, the need for effective salespeople increases, because, to quote an old saw, nothing happens until someone sells something.

The ultimate goal of a business is survival, and profits are critical for a business to survive. Profits are what are left over after subtracting expenses from revenue. There are only so many expenses that accountants and bean counters can cut from a company's budget before cutting through muscle and deep into the bone, thus crippling the business. A more effective way to assure profits is to grow revenue, which requires salespeople, not accountants. Consequently, sales are critical to a company's survival and growth, which is why salespeople are usually the last personnel to be cut during a business slowdown.

There have never been so many opportunities for competent salespeople in the media; and yet, selling is more difficult, complex, and competitive than ever before. To succeed, you must be better trained, better prepared, and better motivated than was the case in the past, which is why you are reading this book.

With these assumptions in mind, let's look at several approaches to successful media selling and several types of selling, and define some terms.

Approaches

The AESKOPP approach

Media Selling presents an approach that will help you organize your personal selling efforts and not only get you off to the right start, but also, if you follow the approach, keep you on that track to success. The question most asked by beginning salespeople is, "Where do I start?" The answer is: "Start with the AESKOPP approach."

AESKOPP is a mnemonic that will help you remember the following elements of successful selling:

Attitude
Emotional Intelligence
Skills
Knowledge
Opportunities
Preparation
Persistence

We will look at each piece of the AESKOPP approach more closely in Chapter 4.

A relationship, non-manipulative, solutions approach

A relationship approach   Media selling is about establishing relationships and then *getting customers and keeping them*. Getting customers and keeping them involves a process by which salespeople help buyers get the products they want – it does not mean manipulating people to do things they do not want to do. The best way for salespeople to get what they want is to help buyers get what they want by building trusting relationships, guided by *three basic relationship rules*:

1 *Do unto others as they would have others do unto them.* This is a slight twist on the Golden Rule from the Bible, which assumes that everyone likes to be treated the same as you do – not necessarily so. It is better to observe people carefully and discover how they prefer to be treated without making any prior assumptions.
2 *People like and trust people like themselves.* People have an affinity for people similar to themselves – call it tribalism or elitism – but it is a reality that salespeople must learn to contend with.
3 *People don't care how much you know until they know how much you care.* In other words, shut up, listen carefully, and give people signals that you care about them as people, not merely as potential sources of revenue.

A non-manipulative approach   Tony Alessandra and colleagues introduced the concept of non-manipulative selling in his well-organized and thoughtful book of the same name, *Non-Manipulative Selling*, in 1992. Along with sales experts and trainers such as Larry Wilson, Alessandra taught a new form of selling that did not rely on old-fashioned tricks and manipulation techniques. His approach was that of creating long-term customers and managing relationships. The next iteration of selling was the consultative selling approach, which was a further customer-oriented refinement of non-manipulative selling. Neil Rackham's excellent book, *SPIN Selling*, best articulates the consultative selling approach. However, the latest maturation of the non-manipulative, consultative sales approach is a global trend toward *solution selling*, the ultimate customer-focused, non-manipulative approach, on which this book focuses.

A solution-selling approach   A relationship, non-manipulative, solutions-oriented approach to selling advertising in the media means helping buyers invest in advertising that provides solutions to marketing and advertising problems and that gets results.

Some definitions   *Buyers* are divided into three types: *prospects*, *customers*, and *partners*.

Prospects are people who have not bought a product for a variety of reasons, ranging from never having heard of it to disliking it; prospects require *developmental selling*. In the media, prospects might be those people who (1) have never before advertised because they have an established business that they feel does not need advertising; (2) have never advertised because they are starting a new business; (3) advertise but not in your medium; or (4) advertise in your medium but do not use your network, station, Web site, newspaper, cable system, or magazine.

Customers are people who have either decided to buy a product or who have already bought a product and are going to buy it again. Customers require *outrageous service that will make them "raving fans."*[1]

Partners are customers who have joined with a media company to conduct business based on mutual trust and, in a sense, to help each other to be more successful by cooperating in discovering innovative solutions that connect a partner to a medium's audience in a way that delivers partner-defined results and jointly builds the brands of both companies.

Products are either tangible or intangible. *Tangible* products are goods you can see and touch, such as automobiles, personal computers, or cosmetics. *Intangible* products are services that cannot be seen, touched, or tested in advance, such as insurance, banking and financial services, or advertising.

Tangible products can be experienced and they are usually easy to demonstrate – product features and benefits are apparent before a purchase. However, even tangible products have some degree of intangibility, as pointed out by Theodore Levitt:

> You can't taste in advance or even see sardines in a can or soap in a box. This is common for frequently purchased moderate- to low-priced consumer goods. To make buyers more comfortable and confident about tangibles that can't be pre-tested, companies go beyond the literal promises of specifications, advertisements, and labels to provide reassurance.[2]

Packaging is one common tool used to make the intangible elements of products more tangible in a customer's mind – for example, putting pickles in a glass jar so purchasers can see them. Advertising is another tool used to communicate advance assurances that a product is what it says it is.

It is harder to keep customers satisfied with intangible products than with tangible ones. The biggest problem with intangible services – such as advertising, insurance, or banking services – is that customers are usually not aware of the full range of services they are getting until they no longer get them. Therefore, they rarely appreciate the positives, and the negatives tend to be blown out of proportion. This situation means that intangibles require more service and greater efforts on the part of salespeople. From now on all products and services will be referred to as *products*, whether they are tangible or intangible.

Interactive advertising has changed the nature of servicing intangible products as dramatically as it has changed the nature of selling. Advertisers can now receive detailed information about their schedules online, without communicating with a salesperson, which changes the servicing role of a salesperson, as will be covered in Chapter 13.

A systematic approach: the Six Steps of Selling

One of the many mistakes I made on my first sales call to Parrot's Flowers was that I immediately went into a presentation and close without identifying Mr Parrott's problems. I didn't follow the *six steps of selling*:

1 Prospecting
2 Identifying problems
3 Generating solutions
4 Presenting
5 Negotiating and closing
6 Servicing

We will go over each step in depth in the chapters that follow, but it is important to keep these steps in mind as you read this book and make sales calls. In the meantime, following are some definitions to start you off on the right foot

Prospecting. Prospecting is finding potential customers – identifying people who have the money to advertise, who pay their bills, and who are a logical fit with your medium.

Identifying problems. After you find someone who is a prospect, you have to identify what their advertising problems are and why they might need your medium.

Generating solutions. Once you have identified a prospect's problems, you must do some intelligent digging and research and come up with solutions. Next, you put your solutions into an arresting, believable, and winning proposal that puts them in the best possible light. Finding solutions to customer problems is the most creative and satisfying part of a salesperson's job. Creativity is largely a matter of solving problems and then presenting them in new and different ways, so you must fully understand your customers' marketing and advertising problems *and* have a full understanding of the capabilities of your medium in order to solve a customer's problems and present your solutions creatively.

Presenting. Presenting is presenting your solutions convincingly, persuasively, and dramatically one-on-one or to a group of people. A successful salesperson must be comfortable and expert at presenting to individuals and to large groups.

Negotiating and closing. All media selling is based on negotiation, even Google's AdWords online-auction is an online, automated negotiation. The object of negotiating is to close a deal, to get an order, so negotiating and closing are one step.

Servicing. Selling is getting customers and keeping them. Servicing is the step of selling that keeps them.

As you go forward in this book, the Six Steps will give you a framework to begin thinking about selling in a structured, strategic, organized, and disciplined way.

The road to success in selling starts by taking one step at a time and in the proper order.

A strategic approach

A strategic sales approach includes a hierarchical set of concepts: Purpose, mission, objectives, strategies, and tactics. Like any military or business organization and their people, a sales department and salespeople must understand these five concepts and follow their precepts in order to have a consistent and meaningful sales approach.

Purpose   The *purpose* of a media sales department or division is to maximize revenue by getting and keeping customers. In many organizations the head of sales has a title of Chief Revenue Officer. That title says it all and clearly states the purpose of a sales organization.

Mission   The *mission* of a media sales department or division must be the same as its parent company's mission, and should be meaningful and uplifting, and present everyone in an organization, including salespeople, with a model they can act on daily. Go to www.charleswarner.us/articles/ESPNMSN.html to view ESPN's mission statement, one of the best ever written. Google's corporate mission is a simple and powerful mission statement that guides the company's actions: "To organize the world's information and make it universally accessible and useful."

Objectives   The four *objectives* of a media salesperson in order to fulfill its purpose to maximize revenue and get and keep customers are:

① *To get results for customers.* Results must be defined by customers – increased sales, reduced distribution costs, increased profit margins, return-on-investment (ROI), increased awareness, or improved corporate image, for example. Salespeople must *put customers first* – not themselves, not their company, but customers. If customers do not get results, they will not renew their advertising schedule. Thus, salespeople must take a long-term view and create renewable, replicable business.

② *To develop new business.* That is, to turn prospects into customers. Salespeople must continually develop new business not only to replace accounts that are lost each year due to normal account attrition but also to ensure growth. The most important reason for constantly developing new business is to create demand, because it is demand that largely determines the price of media advertising. Salespeople who do not continually seek out new accounts are like sailors who have fallen overboard and are treading water – they get nowhere.

③ *To retain and increase current business.* Servicing business properly to keep accounts satisfied and getting renewals are vital, yet even more important is to continually pre-sell and provide clients with solid evidence, reasons, and, especially, ideas, for them to *increase their investment* in your medium. Advertising is not an expense, it is an investment – an investment in future sales and profits. Your best prospects are your current customers, and continually showing them the benefits of your medium and getting an increased investment from them is vital for growth. On every service call, *always* present customers with ideas that will lead to an increased investment and will reinforce the value of their current investment. Remember that advertising is an intangible product that requires more reinforcement, servicing, and reassurance than a tangible product would. Customers require constant attention if you are going to retain and increase current business.

④ *To increase customer loyalty.* If you are going to put customers first, get results for customers, and get all-important renewals, then you are going to have to keep customers' satisfaction levels high and increase customers' loyalty – make customers partners. Like the ex-Mayor of New York, Ed Koch, you have to continually ask, "How am I doing?" in order to keep a relationship going, to keep your partners happy and loyal. More and more sales organizations of major companies such as IBM and Hewlett-Packard are evaluating and compensating their salespeople based on levels of customer satisfaction. That means that salespeople must not only make a sale, but also keep partners happy through excellent service after the sale – provide absolutely outrageously good service and not only make them happy, but make them raving fans. Chapter 13 covers the techniques of providing customers excellent service.

Strategies   Strategies are long-term, overall operating concepts and principles that guide actions toward stated objectives. In order to achieve the above sales objectives, salespeople should follow these sales *strategies*:

① *Sell solutions to marketing and advertising problems.* Computer manufacturers and retailers learned the hard way that the majority of consumers do not understand or care about hardware (although geeks care) – for example, how many memory chips a computer has or how many bytes are stored on a disk. What the ordinary consumer cares about is what a computer does – what writing or accounting or design problems the software was able to solve – and how easy it is to use. By the same token, potential advertisers do not care about a broadcast station's power or antenna height, a cable system type of commercial insert equipment, a Web site's underlying architecture, or a magazine or newspaper's press size or color-separation ability. What prospects care about is how advertising is going to help them solve marketing or advertising problems. Therefore, salespeople must learn to position their offerings in such a way that they always answer prospects' question, "What's in it for me (WIIFM)?" as is covered in depth in Chapters 9 and 10.

② *Reinforce the value of advertising and of your medium.* The migration of marketing dollars from advertising to promotion after the 1970s hurt the growth rate of advertising. Salespeople who sell advertising must continually reinforce advertising's positive long-term effects and the value of advertising to build brand image and sell products. In Chapter 8 you will learn in more detail what the dangers of promotions and the benefits of advertising are. Salespeople must continually reinforce the benefits of their medium in order to reinforce the value of advertising and try to put the brakes on the migration of advertising dollars to promotion.

③ *Create value for your product.* A salesperson's most important job is to create a positive perception and image of their product in a prospect's mind. A kids' toothpaste is (1) a toothpaste that is blue and tastes like bubble gum or (2) a revolutionary new product that is a glistening, bright, cool, deep blue color that shimmers with flecks of silver, making it interesting, exciting, and fun for children to push out of a dispenser that is easy for small hands to manipulate. Its foaming action in the mouth is new and different; it is thicker and foamier, as if something important is really working in kids' mouths to fight cavities and to make their breath smell great so their mommies will know they really did brush their teeth. When the kids first taste their very own type of new toothpaste that is *not* for adults, they experience a taste sensation unlike any other. It is not toothpaste; it is *bubble gum!* Kids cannot wait to brush their teeth several times a day. They are likely to say after lunch, "Well, I think I'd better go brush my teeth."

Which of the above two descriptions of the new kids' toothpaste creates more value for the product? Which description is more likely to make the sale? The second description creates value for the product, which is positioned according to its benefits to the kids.

You must also create value for your product so you will not have to lower your price to get an order. You will find a much more thorough discussion of the many ways to create value in Chapter 8, because in order to be successful in selling solutions to advertising problems you must be able to create value effectively for your medium.

④ *Become the preferred supplier.* Salespeople must establish, maintain, and improve relationships with both a customer and that customer's advertising agency. It is a certainty that clients will eventually change advertising agencies, so salespeople *must* establish relationships at the client level. Advertising agencies will often tell you not to see a client, because they believe the client is *their* client. Well, the client is *your* client – the client's name is on the ad or commercial in your medium, not the agency's name. In order to become the preferred supplier, or partner, salespeople must provide more and better information and service than any other salesperson from any other medium so the customer will think of them first when they need information or want to buy advertising.

⑤ *Innovate.* Every medium must continually introduce new ideas: new packages, new promotions and contests, new content, new community affairs projects, new special sections, new functionality, new ways to access information, and new events. New products and opportunities such as those mentioned give salespeople a reason to make another call on a customer or agency, they create excitement, and they provide new ways to solve marketing and advertising problems.

Key functions   A salesperson has three *key functions* to help them carry out their strategies and every day tactics of selling:

① *To create a differential competitive advantage in a buyer's mind.* Salespeople who cannot find ways to create *differential competitive advantages* for their product are merely order takers or clerks who wait on customers and process transactions, and they will not build a long-term career in the highly competitive environment of media selling.

② *To manage relationships.* A relationship must be built on mutual trust and respect; salespeople must take the long view. The relationship between a salesperson and a customer does not end when a sale is made; it is just beginning of the relationship from the customer's point of view. The relationship should intensify over time and help to determine a customer's buying choice the next time around. Thomas J. Peters and Robert H. Waterman, Jr. emphasize in their book, *In Search of Excellence*, that the most important element the companies examined in the book shared was being *close to the customer.* Managing a relationship means recognizing that your most important task is building and maintaining a long-term relationship by getting and staying close to the customer.

③ *To solve problems.* Salespeople must be creative in solving advertising problems so as to get results for clients. The goals of a salesperson begin with getting results for clients and a salesperson's key functions end with solving problems for clients. You cannot get results for clients unless you learn to discover and then solve problems – this is what solutions selling, the basic approach recommended in this book, is.

Related functions
① *To obtain and process orders.* Not only to solve problems and get orders but also to make sure that the orders enter the operational system so they can be executed properly and on time. Sloppy paperwork will kill customer relationships and, therefore, will bury most salespeople.

② *To provide customer service.* To be certain that each account's advertising schedules are handled properly and that the billing and production details are correct, to communicate new market information to customers, to communicate new benefits and advantages, to increase revenue from accounts, and to work on establishing long-term relationships.

③ *To manage accounts.* To set objectives for revenue and service, to plan the execution of management's specific sales strategies as they relate to your accounts, and to become knowledgeable about your accounts' industries, business, marketing goals, and marketing and creative strategies.

④ *To monitor the marketplace.* To provide information to your management and other salespeople about competitors in all media – their prices, strategies, content or format changes, management and ownership changes, advertising and promotion strategies, and sales strategies and tactics. Competitive intelligence is vital to your management in determining your company's competitive strategy.

⑤ *To recommend tactics.* To recommend pricing changes, new packages, promotions, and changes in selling approaches to your management as a result of what you learn on the street about what your competitors and other media are doing.

⑥ *To cooperate.* To help other salespeople in your department learn from each one's experiences – successes and failures; to help the sales department meet its strategic selling objectives; to cooperate in completing reports, expense accounts, and contracts accurately and on time; to help with promotions, parties, and events; and to cover for other salespeople who are absent. Departments in which the mode of operating is cooperative are more productive than those in which the operating mode is competitive, according to Alfie Kohn in his book, *No Contest: The Case Against Competition.*

These are the key and related functions of salespeople. Their responsibility is to *demonstrate an intelligent effort* (DIE) in carrying out these functions. In other words, not only must salespeople do what they are supposed to do to carry out these functions, but they must also let their management and their customers know that they are doing it diligently – that they are carrying out their functions and implementing the strategy and tactics which management has designed to reach the company's objectives.

Types of Selling

Now that you have a foundation consisting of the assumptions about and approaches to media selling, you need to know how to apply them to several types of selling.

There are two basic types of selling, *missionary selling* and *service selling*. Successful salespeople must apply a non-manipulative, strategic approach to whichever type of selling they are engaged in. Often salespeople are described as *hunters* or *farmers* depending on the type of selling they do.

Hunters are usually salespeople who have the personality, motivation, experience, and preference to do missionary selling (also referred to as development selling), which involves developing new business – finding new customers to a medium (e.g., television, online) and to a media outlet (e.g., a station or a Web site) – and typically involves calling on customers, including local retailers, not on advertising agencies. This type is selling is commonly referred to as *direct selling*.

Some media companies call their top missionary salespeople "evangelists," an appropriate title for a missionary salesperson. But whatever the title, missionary/development selling typically involves direct selling.

Farmers are salespeople who have the personality, motivation, experience, and preference to do service selling (also referred to as transactional selling), which includes calling on, servicing, and getting increased business from current customers, and typically involves calling on advertising agencies.

Both types of selling require the ability to build relationships with different types of customers.

Two types of customers

In their *Harvard Business Review* article "Make sure your customers keep coming back," F. Stewart DeBruicker and Gregory Summe identify two types of buyers: inexperienced generalists and experienced specialists. In media selling, examples of inexperienced generalists are smaller customers, often retailers and others called on direct (those who do not have an advertising agency), who are new to advertising in a medium. Examples of experienced specialists are advertising agency media buyers. DeBruicker and Summe point out that strategies for selling and creating value to these two types of customers must be different.

Inexperienced generalists typically do many jobs in their businesses. For example, a small, owner-run retailer might keep the books, set up displays, and do personal selling as well as place advertising. If this retailer, who we will call Jane, is unfamiliar with radio, for instance, she wants to know how to buy it, how to schedule it, how to write copy, and how to best position her store to appeal to her target customers. Jane is more interested in expert marketing and advertising advice and in results (selling more goods) than in price; therefore, a salesperson must provide expert advice in those areas in which she needs help.

Experienced specialists typically specialize in one activity. For example, an agency media buyer does only one thing, placing media buys, and is an expert in that activity. If this buyer, who we will call John, is making a television buy in a market, he is interested only in price and service – fast, responsive service. John is not interested in marketing or advertising advice or in advice about writing effective copy; he is interested in a different type of results – ratings, circulation, cost-per-points, cost-per-thousands, reach, and frequency, all of which you'll learn about in Chapter 14 – but John is mostly interested in price.

As inexperienced direct accounts gain experience, their needs shift from asking for marketing and advertising advice to asking for responsive service and competitive prices. However, one thing direct accounts, especially retailers, will always focus on is sales results, which will always be more important to them than ratings, circulation, or research data. In the following sections of this chapter, you will learn more about strategies for calling on direct accounts and on agencies.

Salespeople who sell the Interactive medium find that the majority of their prospects at both direct accounts and agencies are inexperienced in the medium and need expert advice. Unfortunately, as in other media, after salespeople go to the considerable effort and invest a lot time in teaching customers about their medium, the clients become experienced and more interested in price. So, the selling strategy must change accordingly.

Missionary selling

Missionary selling most often involves calling on the principal owner, the CEO, or director of marketing or advertising of an account. Calling directly on an account and not on the account's advertising agency, if the account has one, is referred to as *direct selling*. Often, direct selling, particularly in local media, entails calling on retail businesses. The information that follows is for calling on retail businesses, but it also applies to most direct selling.

The retail business Retailers bridge the gap between manufacturers and consumers, and advertising plays an important role because retailers sell their goods and services in a highly competitive environment. Few businesses that start up survive; two out of every three new retail businesses will fail within one year. Changes in the nation's demographics and lifestyles have caused many of the more traditional retailers to rethink their strategies. Single-brand loyalty has declined, and mass-marketing techniques have been developed to accommodate the proliferation of new products. Consumer groups that used to share homogeneous tastes have now splintered into many groups, all demanding different products to meet their different and changing needs.

Retailers have had to change their ways of doing business to satisfy and attract consumers who are generally older, better educated, more cynical of product claims, and more demanding of quality. To entice these consumers, advertising and promotion have become more important than ever before; retailers now use new media technologies such as the Internet and new media combinations such as Interactive, catalogues, and data-based marketing.

Retailers must keep pace not only with the changing demands of their customers but also with the number of products and with the discounts, rebates, and promotions associated with these products. At the same time, they must create an image for their stores and create traffic for the brands that are advertised by manufacturers and are typically available at many other retail outlets. This results in an ambivalent relationship between manufacturers and retailers. Manufacturers, also known as vendors, want consumers to buy their brands, but they do not care where they buy their products; retailers want consumers to shop in their stores, but they do not care which brand is purchased.

Getting products off a manufacturer's shipping department shelves, off a wholesaler's warehouse shelves, and off a retailer's shelves and onto the consumer's shelves is an enormously complex marketing process of which advertising is only a relatively small part, as you will learn in Chapter 15 "Marketing."

Selling to retailers   Retail is a broad category for which there is no standard definition; stores (hard goods, soft goods, food), services (insurance, banks, dry cleaning), entertainment (theaters, clubs, DVD rental), and restaurants all normally come under the general classification of retail. In this book, all types of retail establishments and sellers of services are referred to as *stores*. The most appropriate way to differentiate between types of accounts is according to their orientation – results-oriented or numbers-oriented. For example, those that are results-oriented should be designated as retail clients, or retail *accounts*, and have missionary salespeople call on them. A retailer may have an advertising agency that buys according to the dictates of a store owner who cares only about results and who directs the agency to buy in a particular pattern that has proven to be successful in the past. This kind of agency and account should be called on by a retail specialist.

Retailers care about results, not about the size of a medium's audience, so the best way to appeal to them is with a return-on-investment (ROI) analysis, which will be covered in Chapter 8.

A retail salesperson must be patient and not always seek a fast sale, a quick close, a high share of budget, or a high price. These tactics are best suited for a numbers-oriented agency-selling situation. It may take much longer to sell to a retailer who is trying to fit advertising into a complex marketing and merchandising mix than to an advertising agency that is merely trying to make an efficient media buy.

Co-op advertising   Co-op advertising occurs when a manufacturer, or vendor, underwrites all or part of an ad, commercial, or banner that a local retailer places. See Chapter 19, "Newspapers," for a more thorough description of how co-op advertising works.

Caveat   Occasionally a retailer or direct account will ask media salespeople to recommend an advertising agency. The natural tendency for salespeople is to recommend an agency on their account list or a friend on whom they call. Do not do this – always recommend several agencies (a choice of three is best) for two reasons: (1) If other agencies find out a salesperson recommended someone else, they will be justifiably upset and might stiff the salesperson on future buys; and (2) if the client does not like an agency the salesperson recommends, the client will blame the salesperson. If you are asked to recommend an agency, say, "Here is a list of three agencies that I think could do a good job for your size and type account. You pick the one you like best."

On the other side of the coin, sometimes agencies will ask salespeople to send them clients in order to solidify the relationship with the agency. Do not do this because if you have other agencies on your list and they find out you are favoring one agency over another, you will be in trouble.

Service selling

Service selling entails calling on existing customers and partners, and most often involves calling on advertising agencies, which, of course, is referred to as *agency selling*.

The advertising agency business   Advertising agencies came into existence in the 1880s when they sprang up as sales representatives for newspapers and magazines. As sales representatives for the media, they kept a 15 percent commission on the amount of money advertisers spent with them in the media they represented. Thus, an advertiser might spend $1,000 for ads in a magazine and the agencies would keep $150 and give $850 to the magazine. As time went on, the agencies got close to their advertisers and began to create advertising for them and to decide in which media to place it. The agencies maintained the practice of keeping 15 percent of the amount the advertisers spent in the media. The structure of the advertiser–agency–media relationship was set and has remained virtually unchanged to the present day.

Agencies also make money by adding a 15 percent commission to the material, services, and production they purchase for a client, a practice that is referred to *as grossing up* a charge. For example, if an agency purchases $850 worth of photography for a client, it would gross it up 17.65 percent (or multiply $850 by 1.1765) and charge the client $1,000. (You may recall from basic high school math that you cannot take a 15 percent discount off the price of some product and then multiply the discounted price by 1.15 to get the original number; the two values will not be equal. For example, 15 percent less than 100 is 85, but 1.15 times 85 equals only 97.7.)

Fee arrangements. Advertising agencies are service businesses and their expenses are mostly for people: copywriters, artists, media buyers, media planners, account management people, and so forth. Advertising agencies have to do virtually the same amount of work to produce an ad in a small newspaper as for one in the *New York Times* or to produce a commercial for a local television station in Nashville as for one on the NBC television network. So if a client needs a great deal of work done and is not buying enough media to produce sufficient commissions to compensate the agency adequately for its efforts, the agency might charge the client a fee. The fees are typically based on the following: (1) a monthly retainer fee against which media commissions are credited, (2) an agreed-upon charge per hour for work performed, or (3) a complex formula related to the amount of work the agency performs for a client as a percentage of the agency's total overhead. The fee arrangement is growing in popularity, as both agencies and clients perceive it to be more equitable than the straight 15 percent commission on media purchases and more in line with the actual amount of work done for a client. By the year 2000, almost 70 percent of the advertising agencies in the US worked on some type of fee arrangement, rather than a straight 15 percent commission, with their clients. One reason that the fee arrangement is preferred by many advertisers is that they do not want their agency's income to depend on how much money they spend in the media. Advertisers want to make sure the agencies place their money as efficiently as possible and that the most effective, not necessarily the most expensive, media are purchased.

A trend that has developed in recent years is that more agencies are merging with each other or are being bought out by large international publicly owned conglomerates. This trend has put pressure on agencies to produce higher profits. As the push for bottom-line performance has increased, some advertisers have become concerned that the more expensive and easily purchased media such as network television might be favored over the less expensive media such as radio and Interactive, which are more time-consuming to purchase.

Agency structure. Advertising agencies vary in size from large conglomerates with more than 25,000 employees in offices throughout the world and with media billings in the tens of billions of dollars to local, one-person agencies in small towns.

Basic functions The work in the typical agency is broken into three basic functions: *account management, creative,* and *media.* These functions are supported in larger agencies by plans groups and by research, production, traffic, and accounting departments.

The account management function is carried out by account executives, account supervisors, and management supervisors, who are the primary contact people between agency and client. The account management team usually solicits the clients and services them once they are signed up.

The creative function is handled by artists, copywriters, and creative directors (or supervisors) who create advertising Typically, the account executive will present a client's advertising problem to the creative group, normally an art director and a copywriter, who will mull it over and then recommend an overall campaign or a single ad or commercial approach. Ideas are often the result of brainstorming among art directors, copywriters, account people, and media people in the agency. The account executive then will present the idea to the client. If the client accepts the approach, the creative people will proceed to write detailed storyboards (for television) and arrange for the production of the commercials.

The media function is carried out by media planners, media buyers, and media directors (or supervisors) who evaluate and place advertising. Planners recommend what media and how much of each should be used. Media buyers select which networks, stations, newspapers, magazines, or Web sites to buy; and they are the people on whom media salespeople typically call. However, in recent years planner have become more important in the evaluation process and salespeople, especially magazine salespeople, have been calling on planners more often.

Media departments are organized in various ways depending on the agency. Some are organized by product, and buyers buy all markets around the country for a certain product or brand. Other agencies organize on a regional basis and have buyers specialize in buying one or more markets for all of the agency's products. Most large agencies have gone to this regional organizational approach because they feel it gives them more in-depth knowledge about the constantly changing rates, ratings, and circulation data in markets; it also gives them better leverage in negotiating, particularly if they buy for a number of products. Furthermore, large agencies usually have buyers who specialize in a particular medium: network television buyers, spot television buyers, radio buyers, print buyers, and Interactive buyers, for example.

The support functions in larger agencies are handled by a number of groups.

The plans groups (sometimes called the strategy group) consist of the top account, creative, and media management people who meet to discuss the overall long-term strategic plans the agency will recommend to each client.

The research department keeps up to date on economic, population, media, advertising, marketing, and other relevant research information and provides it to the account management, creative, and media departments in an agency.

Production departments produce ads and commercials by overseeing all the myriad details that go into getting advertising in front of viewers, listeners, or readers.

The traffic department in an agency sees to it that the right ads or commercials get to the right newspaper, magazine, or television or radio station at the right time, with instructions on when, where, and how often to run them.

The accounting department bills clients, pays media, does an agency's payroll, and produces financial reports.

To complicate matters further, some agencies' media departments serve as the *agency of record* for large multiple-product advertisers, such as Procter & Gamble (P&G). The giant consumer-products company has dozens of products on which it invests millions of dollars in advertising. To keep track of all of its advertising for all of its brands and to make sure that it is taking advantage of all possible media discounts, one agency is designated as the agency of record. This agency gathers and coordinates all the information about all media buys from all of P&G's various advertising agencies.

House agencies. Some advertisers establish their own in-house advertising agencies. Instead of paying a 15 percent commission or a retainer fee to an outside advertising agency, they want to keep the money within their own company. Such advertisers hire people to fill the creative and media buying functions and produce and place their own advertising, usually under a separate agency name. Often the savings realized from house agencies do not offset the disadvantages of having less than superior advertising execution. Full-service agencies can support top creative and media people with the income from several accounts, whereas house agencies typically do not have the funds or diversity of interests to attract excellent people.

Boutiques. A *boutique* is an agency that sells various agency functions on a piecemeal, or modular, basis. Some boutiques sell only their creative services, some specialize in doing only media planning and buying, and some do only research. Boutiques often can offer advertisers topflight talent they might not otherwise be able to afford. For example, a highly regarded art director and a top copywriter in a large agency may get tired of the bureaucratic environment and decide to set up their own small creative boutique to serve just a few clients. Of course, if the boutiques produce excellent advertising, they soon grow larger. Many successful large agencies started out as boutiques. Clients of boutique-type agencies usually deal with several agencies, each with a specialty, simultaneously.

Digital agencies. A *digital agency* is one that specializes in creating and placing advertising in the online media. Large, multi-national, conglomerated agencies, such as WPP, typically have divisions that specialize in online advertising. Often these divisions consist of people who started a digital agency that was purchased by the large conglomerate. Buying Interactive advertising, including search advertising, is quite complex and requires special, often highly technical, expertise.

Trade deals and buying services   One of the characteristics of broadcast time is that it is instantly perishable; lost revenue from an unsold spot can never be recovered. Many years ago, enterprising entrepreneurs discovered they could make a profit by bartering goods for unsold time on radio and television stations at a very favorable exchange rate and then reselling the time to advertisers.

Here is how a typical barter arrangement, or *trade deal*, might be made: Entrepreneurs form a barter advertising agency, sometimes referred to as a *barter house*, and contact radio and television stations. They then negotiate to give the stations something of value in return for time. A barter house might send a catalogue of merchandise (television sets, stereos, athletic equipment, or whatever) to a station. The merchandise is offered at full price – at retail cost or above.

The barter house then negotiates with the station for time, often referred to as a *bank* of spots, at a favorable exchange rate – $2 worth of spots for every $1 worth of merchandise, for instance (a two-for-one trade deal). Stations willing to make such an arrangement would run the spots contracted for with the barter house only if they have no paid advertising to fill up their time. Thus, the station is able to get something of value in return for the commercial time that would have had no value.

The barter house builds a bank of spots on as many stations in as many markets as possible and then calls on advertisers, offering to sell them advertising at large discounts on the stations with which they have contracts. They might have gotten the spots at a 50 percent discount from the two-for-one trade deal. They then resell the spots to advertisers at a 25 percent discount off the station's rate card, with the understanding that the spots might not run at the best times, namely, only in unsold time periods. The barter house makes a tidy 25 percent profit on this resale. It also makes money on the other end by buying merchandise in volume or otherwise heavily discounted and trading with a station for spots based on the full price of the merchandise.

Several barter houses became successful at convincing advertisers they could place media schedules for them for less, and they persuaded the advertisers to let them handle their media buying. The barter houses soon discovered that by taking tough negotiating stances and by acquiring extensive market and station knowledge, they could often outperform media departments at traditional agencies. In the late 1960s, the general function of these services changed from being primarily barter houses to being boutique-type *buying services* staffed by professional media directors, planners, and buyers who did not handle barter and who performed a straightforward media-buying service. Media-buying services typically operate on a fee basis, with an incentive built into their fee for bringing in a media buy at targeted rating-point levels for less than the allocated budget.

Television bias   In most large- and medium-sized agencies, there is a bias in favor of television in general and network television in particular. A typical large national advertising agency might place 40 percent of its total US media dollars in broadcast network television, 25 percent in spot television, 16 percent in cable, 10 percent in magazines, 4 percent in radio, 2 percent in newspapers, 2 percent in Interactive, and 1 percent in out-of-home media. The reason advertising agencies try to sell the benefits of letting their agency handle the advertising for large users of network television (both broadcast and cable) is because if clients can afford the networks, they will generate large commissions or fees. The media department likes to buy network television because it can spend and administer huge amounts of money with fewer people. Because the size of each order is so large, two or three people can easily spend and keep track of $50 million on the television networks. The same amount spent in radio might keep a media department of ten people busy most of the year.

Moreover, creative people do not get higher-paying jobs by producing beautiful newspaper ads or banner ads; they move up the ladder to become high-paid creative directors by developing a reel of award-winning television commercials.

Finally, agencies keep accounts by doing what their clients want, and clients are typically enamored with the traditional national media, especially with network television. Agencies may recommend new creative approaches or nontraditional media, but they normally do not push very hard if their client is not disposed toward what they are recommending.

Selling to agencies Advertising agencies are typically ratings-oriented and require a service-oriented salesperson who understands ratings and is experienced in operating in a numbers- and negotiation-oriented selling environment. Most advertising agency buyers do not care much about results – they are experienced specialists who are mostly interested in the type of audience a medium has and the price.

Agencies depend on the media for their existence. Their incomes are based to some degree on how much advertising they buy; conversely, the media depend on agency buying decisions for much of their income. As a result, agencies and media continually perform a ritualized, arm's-length waltz: agencies try to buy at the lowest prices possible, and the media try to sell at the highest prices possible. This is a good example of an ambivalent, co-dependent, love–hate relationship.

A further complication is that agencies tend to be defensive because of the tenuousness of agency–client relationships. Although clients and agencies have contracts that normally spell out the financial details of relationships, rarely is a long-term commitment involved. Agencies continue to serve their clients because of an advertiser's trust, faith, and, and too often, whim. Agencies sell a service even more intangible than media advertising – they sell their abilities to create good advertising and place it efficiently and effectively. There are not many ways to measure the creative and buying effectiveness of an agency. For example, did sales go up because the advertising was great or were prices cut? Did sales go down because of a poor ad campaign or was the product awful? It is often easier for a client's product managers to blame an agency for their failures than to blame themselves.

Advertisers might drop an agency for a number of reasons: advertiser personnel changes (a new person at the client wants to make a change); new personnel at the agency (the client does not like an agency's new creative director); agency plunder (agencies target other agencies' clients); or competitive media grumbling (a disgruntled salesperson from a medium goes to a client and criticizes an agency). Salespeople who call on agencies must learn to deal with the complex needs and behaviors of agency people, particularly of media buyers.

Media buyers are in the bottom echelon of an agency's media department. They are typically overworked, unappreciated, and underpaid. They are the agency's infantry troops slogging through mountains of media research and media proposals. There is little wonder that buyers tend to be defensive, given the pressure under which they work. They are particularly touchy about salespeople calling on their clients.

Calling on clients. Some media salespeople, especially those from magazines and television networks, frequently make sales calls on both the advertising agency and the agency's clients with the blessing, or at least the grudging cooperation, of an agency. Generally, the larger the agency, the more secure it is with its relationship with clients, or at least so it seems because the loss of one client does not threaten the agency too much. The higher the position of a person in the agency hierarchy, the less that person usually objects to media salespeople calling on the agency's clients because they hope the salesperson can convince the client to increase the client's advertising budget. However, buyers, who are far down on the organizational ladder, normally do not like salespeople calling on their clients, especially if it is to complain about a buy or to make waves of any sort.

If you feel it is necessary to stir things up to get your message across to a client, and a buyer has told you not to call on the client, then sell your way up through the agency's media department (through the associate media director to the media director to the vice president in charge of media). All along the way, tell your medium's story; tell the agency why you want to see its client and exactly what you are going to tell the client. Someone higher up will finally give you permission to see the client because he or she will realize that, in the final analysis, the agency cannot keep you away if the client agrees to see you, plus, you might get the client to invest more in advertising.

The secret of getting agencies' permission to call on their clients is to keep the agencies involved all along the way and to go over your proposals with them so they will be assured you are not going to make them look bad.

Numbers: the security blanket. As mentioned previously, agency selling is numbers-oriented selling, as opposed to direct selling, which is usually results-oriented. Since an agency's performance is difficult to measure, anything that has a number associated with it is eagerly grasped as a measurement device. In broadcasting and cable, ratings are used as a tool to evaluate an agency's media-buying performance. Online, impressions are currently the quantitative criteria and in magazines and newspapers circulation is generally the quantitative criterion. Evaluating these numbers after a campaign has run is called a *post-buy analysis.*

An agency's television and cable media buyers make decisions based on ratings information that is three months to one year old at the time the buy is made. When the ratings for the time period that the advertisements ran are published, agencies compare the actual audience size and costs to those that they had projected at the time the buy was made. This analysis is usually done on a computer, which also checks all the advertising that actually ran against invoices. This process of *posting* is used, more than any other variable, in evaluating the performance of agency television and radio buyers.

When media outlets fail to reach a projected audience in an original buy (that is, they fail to *post*), agencies may pressure for make-goods. In many cases stations, networks, and Web sites offer ratings or impressions guarantees and will schedule make-goods to meet their audience guarantees.

If a buyer can bring in a campaign on budget for the desired audience level, the agency and the buyer have a way of quantifying their performance to their clients. The agency and their clients feel secure with the numbers because they are tangible evidence of the fact that the agency performed its service and exercised good buying judgment. Therefore, do not expect agencies and their clients to give up their security blankets. You have to play the game using their rules, and their rules place emphasis on numbers, not on results.

Still, if agencies and their clients take refuge in the security of numbers and make their media buys based on ratings, impressions, and circulation, you might well ask how a salesperson makes a difference and emphasizes quality. It is because numbers are so absolute and finite that salespeople *can* make a difference. In fact, in a numbers-oriented selling situation, salespeople are the only difference, because a 10 rating is a 10 rating is a 10 rating. Buyers continually need reassurance that what they are buying will turn out to be what they hoped for. In their hearts, they know that numbers do not walk through doors and buy products, but that people do. They know that ultimately they will be judged by their clients on the overall effectiveness of their advertising campaigns. If they buy very efficiently in media that have the wrong demographics or to which no one pays attention, then their campaigns will not be successful. So, agency buyers depend on media salespeople to keep them thoroughly informed about the various media: demographics, attentiveness levels, programming and content changes, rate changes, personnel changes, and anything that will help them evaluate the media better and make better buys – to give them excellent, responsive service.

For more information about selling a national medium (network television, non-local Web sites and portals, and magazines) see Appendix A, "Selling Magazines to Agencies." Although the title indicates it is about selling magazines, the techniques apply to virtually all national media, but I recommend you read it after you have read Chapters 3 through 24, so you will be more familiar with the terminology, techniques, and tactics included in it.

Sales Department Structures

In order to apply a systematic, strategic selling approach to the different types of selling – missionary and service, direct and agency – media sales organizations use a variety of organizational and management structures. For more details on sales department structures see Chapter 2 of *Media Sales Management* on the *Media Selling* Web site (www.mediaselling.us/MSM_Chapter2-Structure.pdf). But before we discuss sales department structure, we need to look into what a sales department does.

A media sales department is responsible for the advertising revenue of a medium. The sales department, often referred to as the advertising sales or just advertising department in magazines and newspapers, is responsible for sales planning, which includes setting policy, establishing procedures, and determining strategies. The sales department is responsible for hiring and training salespeople. It communicates appropriate sales information to other departments and passes on appropriate information about other departments to its sales staff. It is also responsible for supervising the activities of salespeople, for controlling inventory and sales expenses, and for evaluating the performance of salespeople.

Theorists in organizational structure have an axiom that "structure follows strategy," which means that a sales department's structure should reflect its sales strategy, and in most cases, this axiom holds true.

Many media outlets in larger markets (newspapers, radio and television stations, and cable systems) structure their local sales organizations so there are two divisions: agency and retail. National media often divide their sales staffs by category, or *verticals*. Such categories might be: Financial, Consumer Package Goods (CPG), Technology, Communications, Entertainment, Automotive, Music, and Retail. Category sales specialists must have in-depth knowledge of the verticals they call on and they often have both direct selling and agency selling responsibilities.

Management structures of sales departments range from a small-market radio station in which the general manager of the station is also the sales manager to whom three salespeople report, to a large-market newspaper in which there is a director of advertising sales (who reports to the publisher), a national sales manager, a retail sales manager, a classified sales manager, category sales managers, and a sales staff of perhaps 150.

However, no matter what the structure is, the purpose of a sales department is to maximize revenue by organizing its sales staff to carry out systematic and strategic approaches to selling.

Why a Systematic, Strategic Approach Is Necessary

The International Radio and Television Society (IRTS) conducted a time buyer survey among important media buyers in New York City several years ago. The buyers were asked to name and rank the characteristics they thought were most important for a salesperson to have. The following list resulted from the study:

1   Communication skills – clarity and conciseness, not oral skills or flamboyance, were ranked as most important
2   Empathy – insight and sensitivity

3　Knowledge of product, industry, and market
4　Problem-solving ability – using imagination in presentations and packaging
5　Respect
6　Service
7　Personal responsibility for results
8　Not knocking the competition

More recently, a major radio station group commissioned research in seven major markets of advertising time-buyers and media executives to find out what they wanted from salespeople. The results were similar to the IRTS study. Here is what buyers wanted from salespeople:

1　Ideas – especially in the area of added value and how to sell their client's product better
2　Communication – clear, concise communication, not long-winded, exaggerated sales pitches
3　Respect for their time
4　Run as ordered
5　Responsiveness – return calls *fast*, be available at all times, get schedules confirmed quickly and correctly

In 2008, *Advertising Age* reported the results of an Advertising Perceptions study. The author of the article wrote, in part:

> In addition to brand knowledge, media buyers and planners are also looking for good communication skills, professionalism and an understanding of marketers' needs and priorities. The least important characteristics in a sales rep identified by marketers were sales presence and entertainment. Only eight percent of respondents said going to dinners, shows and sporting events with sellers was important . . . "Most people probably aren't going to own up to the fact that they really love being entertained."[3]

Much of the remainder of this book will be spent helping you develop the attitude, emotional intelligence, skills, knowledge, opportunities, preparation, and persistence necessary to become a salesperson who will make raving fans of agency buyers and customers who want the above qualities from salespeople.

In the classic *Harvard Business Review* article, "What makes a good salesman?" David Mayer and Herbert Greenberg point out that the two essential qualities for a salesperson to have are *empathy and drive*. Empathy is the ability to feel as another does. Being empathetic does not necessarily mean being sympathetic. A salesperson can know what another person feels without agreeing with that feeling; but, as Mayer and Greenberg point out, "a salesman simply cannot sell well without the invaluable and irreplaceable ability to get a powerful feedback from his client through empathy."[4] This quality or attribute will covered in more detail in Chapter 5. Drive is a particular type of ego drive "which makes him want and need to make the sale in a personal or ego way, not merely for the money to be gained."[5]

This book can help you learn the systems, approaches, and techniques to improve your empathy and drive, but it cannot imbue you with these two essential qualities – they must come from within. In essence, this means that to be successful in selling, you must genuinely like people and crave to be successful.

Test Yourself

1   What are the three assumptions that this book makes about selling?
2   What are the elements in the AESKOPP approach to selling?
3   What are the three rules of relationships?
4   What are the three types of buyers and what are the differences among them?
5   What is the difference between tangible and intangible products?
6   What are the Six Steps of Selling?
7   What is the purpose of a sales organization?
8   What are the objectives, strategies, key and related functions of a salesperson?
9   What is the difference between missionary and service selling?
10 What are the two types of customers and what are some of the differences between them?
11 What are some of the differences between direct and agency selling?
12 Explain what a trade deal is.
13 Name two types of sales department organizational structure.

Project

Make an appointment with the person responsible for purchasing advertising at a large advertiser in your market (not at an advertising agency). This person might be the sales manager of a large automobile dealer or the head of marketing at a large hospital. Interview this person and ask him or her what is expected of salespeople, what attributes he or she would like to see, and what kind of service is preferred. Make a list of these answers and compare them to the answers that professional buyers gave in the two surveys in this chapter. Are there any differences? What are they? What did you learn from this exercise?

References

Tony Alessandra, Phil Wexler, and Rick Barerra. 1992. *Non-Manipulative Selling*, 2nd edition. New York: Fireside Books.

Kenneth Blanchard and Sheldon Bowles. 1993. *Raving Fans: A Revolutionary Approach to Customer Service*. New York: William Morrow and Company

F. Stewart DeBruicker and Gregory L. Summe. 1985. "Make sure your customers keep coming back." *Harvard Business Review*. January–February.

John Phillip Jones. 1995. *When Ads Work: New Proof that Advertising Triggers Sales*. New York: Lexington Books.

Alphie Kohn. 1986. *No Contest: The Case Against Competition*. Boston: Houghton-Mifflin.

Theodore Levitt. 1983. *The Marketing Imagination*. New York: Free Press.

David Mayer and Herbert Greenberg. 1964. "What makes a good salesman?" *Harvard Business Review*. July–August.

Thomas J. Peters and Robert H. Waterman, Jr. 1982. *In Search of Excellence: Lessons from America's Best Run Companies*. New York: Harper & Row Publishers.

Neil Rackham. 1988. *SPIN Selling*. New York: McGraw-Hill.

Resources

www.mediaselling.us/media_sales.html (*Media Sales Management*)

Notes

1 Kenneth Blanchard and Sheldon Bowles. 1993. *Raving Fans: A Revolutionary Approach to Customer Service*. New York: William Morrow and Company.

2 Theodore Levitt. 1983. *The Marketing Imagination*. New York: Free Press, p. 95.

3 Megan McIlroy. 2008. "Media buyers single out top ad sales reps." *Advertising Age*, January 15.

4 David Mayer and Herbert Greenberg. 1964. "What makes a good salesman?" *Harvard Business Review*. July–August, p. 120.

5 Ibid.

3

Sales Ethics

Charles Warner

The Sales Executive Council (SEC) is a private membership-based research consortium serving approximately 300 of the world's largest sales organizations, including IBM, Coca-Cola, GE, McGraw-Hill, Microsoft, and Walt Disney. The SEC is a division of the Corporate Executive Board and its mission is to assist executives in enhancing the effectiveness of their sales strategy and operations, from sales productivity and strategic account management to sales training and compensation. The SEC's primary tool is conducting research on sales problems their members face and producing case studies of best practices companies use to solve these problems.

One of the SEC's reports dealt with sales force retention and motivation. In one survey that was a part of this report, it asked 2,500 senior sales executives in major industries worldwide to rank the attributes, from most important to least important, that they felt were necessary to be successful as a salesperson and sales manager.[1]

The most important attributes, by far (63 percent inclusion versus 50 percent inclusion for the second ranked attribute) were honesty and integrity. See Exhibit 3.1 for details. The SEC conducted this survey in the year 2000 before the scandals involving Enron, WorldCom, Adelphi Cable, AOL, Wall Street, and the sub-prime mess. One can only guess how high the scores for honesty and integrity would be today.

How does one know how to be honest and act with integrity? What are the rules for honesty and integrity? In business the rules usually come from codes of standards or codes of ethics.

Exhibit 3.1 Importance ranking of 40 leadership competencies by sales leaders

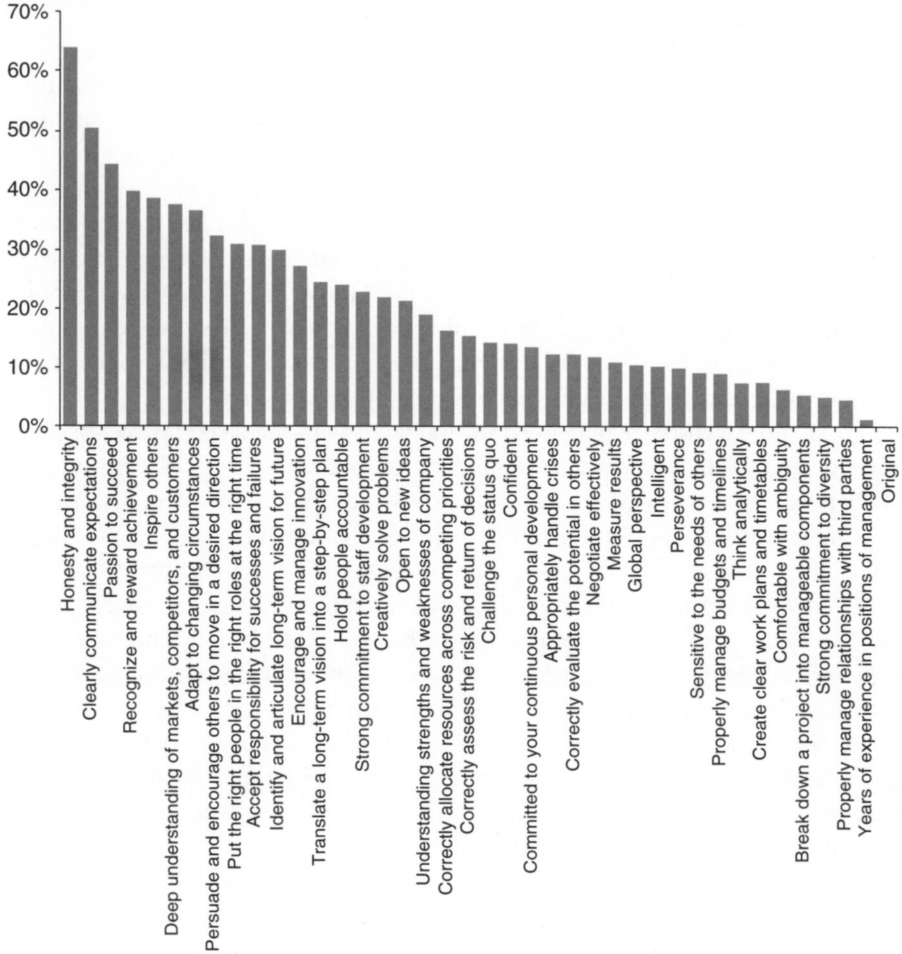

Source: Corporate Leadership Council research.

Sales Ethics in the Advertising-Supported Media

A ballad made famous in the late 1930s by Jack Teagarden, titled "A Hundred Years Today," has been used by countless young men to woo their dates and to convince them not to wait to give out their kisses (and more), because who would ever know what they had done in a hundred years? It was a pitch for a one-night stand, not a long-term relationship. It was probably an effective short-term tactic because two people were not going to live another hundred years and were more than likely able to keep their actions secret if they wanted to.

However, clever short-term tactics are unwise for corporations for three reasons: (1) corporations, by charter, are immortal – they last forever – and, therefore, they want to do business a hundred years from today, (2) corporations have multiple relationships with customers and suppliers making it highly unlikely that they can keep details of these relationships secret for very long, and (3) in the age of transparency[2] created by the Internet, "Information is like a toddler: It goes everywhere, gets into everything, and you can't always control it."[3] These reasons are especially important for large public corporations that file detailed reports with the Securities and Exchange Commission. Some of these reports contain information on contracts with key strategic partners and are available to the public from www.sec.gov/edgar.shml – an example of transparency.

These three factors are magnified several times with media companies because their revenue depends on maintaining long-term trust of their advertisers, subscribers, and audiences. Major advertisers provide the lion's share of revenue for most media businesses. Furthermore, major advertisers such as GM, P&G, IBM, and Coca-Cola not only have long memories, but they will also be around in a hundred years. As Warren Buffett, the country's most astute (and wealthy) investor, has said, "Trust is like the air we breathe. When it's present, nobody really notices. But when it's absent, everybody notices."[4] It is not smart business to undo a trusting relationship and bite the hand that will feed your company in future years. If salespeople lie, cheat, gouge, or over-promise and under-deliver in order to make short-term numbers, they jeopardize revenue far into the future. Simply put, advertisers do not buy from someone they do not trust – they are not looking for one-night stands; they prefer marriage.

There is also a good chance that if you deceive any of these large customers, they will tell others, especially your competitors and the press. The press loves stories about corporate bullies, liars, and cheats, and as Dov Seidman writes in *How*, "Corporate scandals, celebrity breakups, political corruption: Each day's news – delivered instantly via television, radio, Web site, cell phone, RSS feed, and BlackBerry – exposes the transgressions of the icons of the day . . . once we've gotten a taste of scandal we can't seem to get enough."[5] The public has become scandal addicted.

It seems that many corporations and people today do not either know about or care about business rules, standards, or ethics. Perhaps they go along with unethical behavior because of group pressure or peer pressure or perhaps they rationalize to themselves "everyone does it," "it's standard practice in this business," or "no one will know; I won't get caught." Maybe they think, "My manager said to do what it takes to make the quarter," or "If I don't take their money, someone else will." Such callous rationalization of lying, cheating, and stealing is typical sociopathic behavior.

Within the last two years, I know of a salesperson for a major media company who forged a client's name on a contract. The salesperson was certain the customer would eventually sign the contract, and the salesperson wanted to start the campaign early in order to meet his quota and, thus, make more money. When the advertiser got the first invoice, the surprised reply was, "What's this, we never bought anything or signed anything?" Why did the salesperson forge a signature? Was there pressure from management to close business early or did greediness motivate the salesperson? What was the root cause of this unethical behavior? Of course, being a sociopath or a narcissist clearly can lead to unethical behavior, but people not suffering from these personality disorders sometimes behave unethically. Why?

Reasons people don't follow the rules

There are many reasons for unethical behavior, but here are the four most common. (1) People have a strong tendency to bow to authority and follow orders from higher-ups, giving them the excuse that "I was just following orders." (2) People have a strong tendency to bow to the social pressure and conformity of their peer group, perhaps a left-over tendency from their teenage years, leading to the excuse of "everyone does it." (3) Unethical behavior is often due to an absence of clearly defined and communicated rules of behavior, standards, or codes of ethics in a peer group, organization, company, or an industry, particularly for salespeople, allowing people to say "nobody told me." (4) They are unaware that "Every keystroke on your computer is there, forever and ever"[6] in the age of transparency and the likelihood of getting caught is exceedingly high. (5) Corporate cultures that encourage employees to wink at their company's code of standards or mission statement can justify their actions by saying, "no one will know; I won't get caught."

While people who bow to authority may have to give up their individual free will and autonomy for the sake of a company, they do not have to turn their conscience and their self-esteem over to someone else. "Just following orders," as we learned in the Nuremberg trials, is not a valid, acceptable excuse for doing the wrong thing. On the other hand, people who cave in to peer pressure to conform negate their own free will and autonomy and hand over their conscience and individuality to the crowd. "Everybody does it" is not an acceptable excuse for breaking the rules or for unethical behavior. An absence of clearly defined standards and codes of ethics can lead to unethical behavior because people can use the cop-out "nobody told me." This excuse is hollow because ethical behavior is implied and assumed in all of our daily social interactions. For example, we do not go around killing people because nobody said "Don't kill anyone today." We all know what we are supposed to do and not to do.

Groups, organizations, and companies must create and communicate ethical standards to guard against these abuses and, even more importantly, to follow up with practices and behavior at the highest levels of the organization that adhere to stated corporate standards. Unfortunately "Do as I say, not as I do," can be as effective on employees as it was on me as a teenager when my father told me not to smoke cigarettes as he puffed away on one of his 40 Chesterfields a day. For example, Enron had a clearly defined code of conduct that it communicated to everyone in the company and posted on its Web site. Enron's top executives obviously viewed this code as public relations, not as a set of rules they should follow, thinking arrogantly and cynically, "No one will know."

Employees of an unethical company whose executives do not follow the rules should strongly consider leaving the company and looking for another job rather than becoming a whistle-blower. Tragically, whistle-blowers are too often perceived to be "rats" or "squealers" by potential employers rather than as the heroes they are. Leaving an unethical, corrupt company is probably in your long-term self-interest because when the company's ethical problems come to light, your pension fund or 401(k) plan will be worthless if it is invested in company stock and your reputation will be tainted in the job market. Therefore, select the companies you work for very carefully and choose one that will enhance your reputation, not detract from it.

What Are Ethics?

Ethics are clearly defined standards and norms of right and wrong that are expressed as guidelines for behavior. There are three general types of ethical standards. First, most organizations, companies, and professions have written codes of ethics or standards of conduct. Next, are accepted beliefs and modes of conduct among various social and ethnic groups. Finally, individuals have their own standards of right and wrong that they use to make daily judgments, which are based on a combination of deep-seated personal values and beliefs inculcated from the first moment parents say 'bad boy" or "bad girl."

Why Are Ethics and Rules Important?

With heightened press coverage of corporate, government, and Wall Street scandals, the public has become increasing concerned about the ethical behavior of the representatives of our important institutions. Therefore, if ever there was a time when ethical behavior for business and for salespeople was important, it is now. And it is vital to the health and credibility of American business to do the right thing rather than to do things right. Companies should perceive ethical behavior as enlightened self-interest because it preserves a company's long-term reputation, which is its greatest asset.

Five Ethical Responsibilities for Media Salespeople

1   Responsibility to consumers

As defined in Chapter 1, consumers use a product and the consumers of the media are the audiences as readers, viewers, or subscribers.

If a media outlet does not put the interests of its consumers or audience first, the audience will gravitate to sources of information and entertainment that do. It is amazing how most people tend to give their loyalty to those who look after them and have strong values. If a media outlet does not tell the truth, withholds important information from consumers, sells shoddy products, or erodes consumers' values and sense of self-esteem, these consumers will eventually turn to information, entertainment, and opinion sources that provide what they want, and that they find truthful, useful, interesting, and convenient. In other words, they will find someone else to partner with.

Audiences want something in which they can believe. Therefore, the media should not transmit false or misleading advertising. General rules for media salespeople should include not accepting advertising for products that are unsafe. People do not like to be deceived, especially by the media. Thus, when a medium lies to its audience and loses its credibility, it eventually loses its audience, and can no longer be advertiser supported. Putting the consumers first is at the heart of the marketing concept, and is the essence of ethical behavior in the media.

2   Responsibility to their conscience

All salespeople are responsible to themselves for doing what they believe is good or bad, right or wrong and is based on their own conscience or moral standards. John Wooden, the legendary UCLA basketball coach, said that there is no pillow as soft as a clear conscience. Purposely acting unethically will erode a salesperson's self-esteem. By acting ethically, salespeople increase their self-esteem, self-image, and self-confidence and do the same for their company. They develop a long-term perspective, which benefits their mental health and their company as well as the customers and consumers.

Unfortunately, some salespeople and sales organizations are more motivated by greed, in making money or "getting the stock price up," than in building a highly respected personal or company reputation. Such greed inevitably produces cheating, which is a cancer that erodes a person's or a company's reputation and eventually will kill the company. Those who conduct business unethically know they are doing so, but they continue doing the wrong thing because they believe they will not get caught. However, they are playing an ethical lottery in which the odds of being discovered are high, as we saw with Enron and WorldCom. Practicing ethical behavior every business day is the only sure way of maintaining a reputation, and self-esteem grows as the result.

3   Responsibility to customers

Customers do not buy from or partner with media companies and salespeople they do not trust. Thus, media salespeople should concentrate on building trust and managing relationships for the long term, not merely selling for a one-shot deal. For example, Time Warner corporate policy, as articulated by former CEO Richard Parsons, is to "under-promise and over-deliver."

Customer-oriented rules for media salespeople – the Don'ts

- Don't lie to advertisers.
- Don't sell anything that customers do not truly need.
- Don't allow clients to feel like they lost in a negotiation.
- Don't be unfair to advertisers.
- Don't sell something customers cannot afford.
- Don't use bait-and-switch tactics (selling something that they know is not available just to get the money in the door).
- Don't recommend or accept advertising that is in bad taste or that will harm a client's image.
- Don't accept false or misleading advertising.
- Don't give kickbacks (a euphemism for bribes) to customers. Kickbacks often come in the form of unauthorized rebates or other cash payments given by salespeople from their own pockets. Kickbacks are illegal, and there are serious consequences to violating the law, including fines and imprisonment.

Customer-oriented rules for media salespeople – the Dos

- Do represent your clients. Media salespeople's responsibility is to transmit or publish the best possible advertising for their clients and to try to get the clients the best, fairest deal they are entitled to according to a medium's official pricing and positioning policies. Many companies today employ customer ombuds-men to represent customers' interests to its sales organizations.
- Do keep privileged information confidential. Salespeople must keep privileged information to themselves, including details about advertisers' strategy, budgets, creative plans, special sales, and media plans until the campaign has

broken and the information is readily available from outside sources. When a client or advertising agency requests competitive information, salespeople should not give it out before the campaign starts. If salespeople have done their selling job properly, they have sold themselves as solutions providers, which implies a privileged relationship, such as that between a doctor and patient. Customers have a right to assume that salespeople are experts whose recommendations are given with their best interests in mind.

- Under-promise. It is salespeople's responsibility not to promise what advertising by itself cannot deliver. The media can deliver potential exposure to an audience. But the media cannot be certain of generating sales results, so should not promise results to advertisers. Rather, salespeople should promise only what they can deliver.

4   Responsibility to the community

The word community has many meanings, but in this context, it is limited to four: (1) The global community, (2) the general business community, (3) an industry community, and (4) a local community.

- *The global community*. Each corporation and individual ultimately has a responsibility to the world community. We owe it to society to act in a way that provides the greatest good for the greatest number of people, that enhances the environment, that improves the human experience and condition, and that, in the words of the Hippocratic oath, does no harm. To answer questions about our social responsibility, we should always ask ourselves the question, "Suppose everybody did this?"[7]
- *The business community*. As members of the free-market business community salespeople must behave responsibly so that investors, regulators, and the general public have faith in our capitalistic system. All companies have, or should have, published rules, codes, or standards that prohibit unethical behavior such as selling stock based on inside knowledge, shredding documents or deleting computer files to avoid prosecution, and cooking the books to inflate revenue. In business, as well as in society, salespeople must ask: "Suppose everybody did this? Would the regulators, investors, and the public maintain their faith in the free-market system and in business?"
- *An industry community*. The media have a special responsibility to the public, because the media deliver the news. The public also forms many of their social values, beliefs, attitudes, and opinions from the print, electronic, interactive, and entertainment media. This enormous power makes it more imperative that the media wield that power responsibly.

    As a country, we altered our aggregate opinions about racial prejudice, about the war in Iraq, and about women's rights while we watched images of these issues mesmerize, indoctrinate, and change us. The advertising messages between these images guaranteed the freedom of the press that bigots, the government, and non-egalitarian people might not want us to have. If any one of these groups had controlled the media, we might not have been exposed to these issues and the truth would not have worked its torturous way into our collective consciousness.

Therefore, media companies and their salespeople have the responsibility of keeping the media and the press free by fueling it with the advertising revenue it needs to remain so. Without a free, advertising- or subscriber-supported media, there cannot be a free exchange of ideas. This exchange of ideas leads to an informed electorate, the foundation of US democracy. As a salesperson, you might say, "The high-minded notion of protecting democracy is fine if you're selling '60 Minutes' or CNN or the *Huffington Post*, but I'm selling commercials on a Rock 'n' Roll radio station." But no one program, no one news story, or no one medium is more important than another, rather it is the free-market, advertising-supported system. By selling within that system, media salespeople are sustaining a market for advertising that supports all information and entertainment content.

Salespeople must be ethical and play by the rules not only because public attention is focused on corporate ethics, but also because attention is intensely focused on the media. The believability of the media in general and journalism specifically has been eroding recently, and advertising has never been at the top of the list in the public's esteem. Thus, the media must attempt to turn around the image, esteem, and credibility of its product (information, entertainment, and opinion) and its supporting buttress, advertising, if the media hope to thrive.[8]

- *A local community.* All companies, organizations, and people have a responsibility as citizens to act responsibly and ethically towards their neighbors in the community where they live and work. The simple rule is, "Don't foul your own nest. Don't cheat your neighbor." The local media must first serve their communities, for without local support, local media cannot thrive or even exist. Remember that broadcast media are given licenses based on their promise to serve their communities, so their obligation is not only a moral, social one, but also a regulatory one.

5   Responsibility to a company

Media salespeople represent their companies to their customers and because they are selling an intangible product, they become the personification of, the surrogate for, their product. Salespeople are often the only contact a customer will have with anyone from a company. Therefore, they have to face the kill-the-messenger attitude many people have about the media. Because of this unique situation, a company's credibility depends on its salespeople's credibility, which to a large degree depends on their personal conduct and integrity.

Salespeople must be law abiding, respectful of civil liberties and actions or statements that are potentially offensive to others and be moderate in their personal habits. It is the responsibility of salespeople to build and maintain customer relationships based on dependability, reliability, believability, integrity, and ethical behavior.

Salespeople must give their job their full attention, not steal company's assets, not waste its resources (which includes efficient and reasonable use of entertainment and transportation money), not file false expense reports, and not offer special deals to get business away from others within their own organization.

Salespeople have a responsibility to their company to maximize revenue by getting the highest possible and reasonable rates, selling special promotions and packages, attaining the largest possible and reasonable orders, and reaching the highest possible budget shares. There are times when the responsibility to a company to maximize revenue can come in conflict with a salesperson's duty to his or her customers, to his or her conscience, and to the various communities. When such conflicts occur, salespeople should remember the hierarchy of responsibilities and that their company is at the bottom of that hierarchy, because it is in its best long-term interest to be last. Good companies know that what goes around, comes around; that good karma returns home; that ethical behavior is good business; and that employees are happier working for ethical companies.

Great media companies understand that, if they take care of their audience, usage, readership, and ratings will go up resulting in increased revenue. Also, if advertisers trust salespeople and their companies, most advertisers will pay higher rates for better service from these trusted partners. If salespeople do the wrong thing, it results in lost customers, expensive employee turnover, high lawyers' fees, large court costs, and, perhaps, even time in jail.

Unfortunately, many companies set up rewards for salespeople that unwittingly reinforce doing the wrong thing. These include compensation systems that reward getting an order regardless of what's best for the customer, contests that reward selling special promotions or packages regardless of advertisers' needs, and bonuses for making sales budgets regardless of what is reasonable.[9] Beware of CFOs and top management that recommend accounting practices that "preserve a company's assets": they often have the wrong assets in mind. A company's and a salesperson's most precious asset is an excellent reputation, which is preserved by always doing the right thing all of the time.

All large media corporations dream of having a respected publication write something positive about their company. On October 9, 2002, the *New York Times* ran an article in its business section with the headline, "Viacom is planning a multimedia campaign against AIDS," which read, in part:

Viacom plans to focus its various media properties on a single public service campaign with an AIDS-awareness and education effort. The campaign, scheduled to begin in January, will use unsold advertising time on Viacom's CBS and other television networks, and on its television and radio stations, as well as outdoor billboards, for messages about AIDS. But the company, which plans to announce its plans today, says the effort will go beyond traditional public service announcements to weave messages about AIDS into the scripts of television programs, and possibly films.[10]

Viacom, which is now CBS, conducted the AIDS campaign not only to serve the public, but also to enhance its own and the television medium's reputation. This example demonstrates how salespeople can enhance their company's reputation by focusing on the five levels of ethical responsibility in the order of their importance. Salespeople can remember these levels by thinking of the Five Cs:

The Five Cs of ethical responsibility

Consumers
Conscience
Customers
Community
Company

An Ethics Check[11]

Is it legal? When salespeople conduct an ethics check, the first question to ask is: "Is what I am considering doing legal?" The term "legal" should be interpreted broadly to include any civil or criminal laws, any state or Federal regulations, any industry codes of ethics, or any company policy. If salespeople do not know or have any doubts about the legality of what they are doing, they should ask their boss and the company's legal department.

Is it fair? Is it rational, as opposed to emotional, and balanced, so that there are no big winners and big losers? Is it fair to all: to both sides, to the consumer, to the salesperson, to the advertiser, to the various communities, and to the company? If the company had an open-book policy, would all of its customers think everyone got a fair shake? Are all customers getting fair rates, placements, rotations, and make-goods? To test for fairness, ask yourself the question, "Suppose everybody did this?"

What does my conscience say? Salespeople should ask themselves, "How would I feel if what I am doing appeared in the *Wall Street Journal* or the *New York Times*? How would it make me feel about myself? According to my personal moral standards, is what I am doing OK?"

A company's and a salesperson's most valuable assets are their reputations and their relationships with their customers. Reputations and relationships are built by consistently doing ethics checks on the way you do business, by taking a long-term view and not doing anything that would put you or your company in jeopardy, even a hundred years from today. As Dov Seidman writes in *How*, "As reputation becomes more perishable [because of the age of transparency] it's value increases. As it becomes more accessible, it becomes a greater asset – and liability."[12] Never take a chance that could lead to ruining your or your company's reputation and making it a liability.

Test Yourself

1   What are the five rationalizations some people use for their unethical behavior?
2   What are the four reasons why people are inclined to behave unethically?
3   What are the Five Cs of ethical responsibility for media salespeople?
4   What are the Don'ts for media salespeople?
5   What the Dos for media salespeople?
6   What are the three rules of the Ethics Checklist?

Project

Go to the Web and search the Web sites of several major media companies and see if you can find any statements about ethical behavior, standards of conduct, corporate citizenship, or corporate responsibility. Then, go to the Web sites of major advertisers such as GM, P&G, Ford, GE, IBM, or McDonalds, and see if they have any statements about ethical behavior, standards of conduct, corporate citizenship, or corporate responsibility. What did you discover?

References

Kenneth Blanchard and Norman V. Peale. 1998. *The Power of Ethical Management.* New York, William Morrow.

Keith Davis, William C. Frederick and Robert L. Blostrom. 1980. *Business and Society: Concepts and Policy Issue.* New York: McGraw-Hall.

Howard Gardner, Mihaly Csikszentmihalyi and William Damron. 2001. *Good Work: When Excellence and Ethics Meet.* New York: Basic Books.

Dov Seidman. 2007. *How: Why How We Do Anything Means Everything – in Business (and in Life).* New York: John Wiley & Sons.

Resources

www.lrn.com/index.php (Dov Seidman's LRN corporate Web site.)
www.sec.gov/edgar.shtml (Securities and Exchange Commission Public Company
filing.)

Notes

1 "Voice of the sales leader." 2001. *Leading the Charge.* Washington, DC: Sales Executive Council, p. 13.

2 Dov Seidman. 2007. *How: Why How We Do Anything Means Everything – in Business (and in Life).* New York: John Wiley & Sons.

3 Ibid., p. 34.

4 Ibid., p. 158.

5 Ibid., pp. 36–37.

6 "Tell-all PCs and phones transforming divorce." http://www.nytimes.com/2007/09/15/business/15divorce.html. Accessed September 15, 2007.

7 Keith Davis, William C. Frederick and Robert L. Blostrom. 1980. *Business and Society: Concepts and Policy Issue.* New York: McGraw-Hill.

8 Howard Gardner, Mihaly Csikszentmihalyi and William Damron. 2001. *Good Work: When Excellence and Ethics Meet.* New York: Basic Books.

9 Jensen, Michael. 2001. "Corporate budgeting is broken – let's fix it," *Harvard Business Review,* August.

10 "Viacom is planning a multimedia campaign against AIDS." 2002. *New York Times,* October 9, p. C11.

11 Kenneth Blanchard and Norman V. Peale. 1998. *The Power of Ethical Management.* New York: William Morrow.

12 Dov Seidman. 2007. *How: Why How We Do Anything Means Everything – in Business (and in Life).* New York: John Wiley & Sons.

4

The AESKOPP System of Selling

Charles Warner

Let's return to those years of yesterday when I made my first sales call and ask what I did wrong. The answer is easy – everything. But everything is not a helpful response, so we will put the responses into a context of a selling system to help you understand the elements of a successful sales call and a successful sales system.

To begin with, I did not plan my call properly, did not have a framework or method for breaking down the sales call into component parts in order to analyze it. The AESKOPP system of selling provides such a framework.

The AESKOPP system is a generalization, a simplification of some underlying, universal sales principles and provides a framework for coaching, planning, and evaluating sales thinking and action. It posits that successful selling requires Attitude (A), Emotional Intelligence (E), Skills (S), Knowledge (K), Opportunities (O), Preparation (P), and Persistence (P):

$$A \times E \times S \times K \times O \times P \times P = Success$$

Notice that each element in the above formula is multiplied by the others. Just as in a mathematical formula, if any one of the elements is not present, then the result is zero success; any element multiplied by zero is zero. Thus, all of the elements must be present for a successful result – getting customers and keeping them.

Before making a sales presentation to a prospect or customer, salespeople should get into the habit of asking themselves the seven AESKOPP questions, and they should also evaluate their overall sales approach and performance by regularly asking themselves these questions. In addition, managers should continually ask these questions about their salespeople and their performance in order to coach them effectively.

The Seven AESKOPP Questions

1. Do I have the right mental Attitude to solve problems and get results for my customers?
2. Do I have the Emotional Intelligence to understand people and build rapport with them?
3. Do I have the Skills necessary?
4. Do I have the Knowledge necessary?
5. Do I have the Opportunities?
6. Do I have sufficient Preparation?
7. Do I have the Persistence to never, never, never, never give up?

If the answer to all of the above questions is yes, you will make lots of sales. However, if you put a priority on closing a sale above all else, you put establishing and maintaining relationships, solving problems, and getting results in a subordinate position. This means that sooner or later your customers will know you care more about yourself and your income than about their problems and their desired results.

The AESKOPP System

In the remainder of this book, we will examine the AESKOPP system in detail. Chapter 5 goes into more depth about how an optimistic attitude can help you create a positive future. Chapter 6 covers emotional intelligence and provides you with details about how to improve your emotional intelligence. Chapters 7 through 13 concentrate on skills. Chapters 14 through 23 cover knowledge. Chapter 24 covers opportunities, preparation, and persistence.

Following are definitions of each of the seven AESKOPP elements.

Attitude is having the desire and motivation to be a salesperson and having the proper mind-set to do it. If you have the skills, the knowledge, and the opportunities to sell but have no desire to do so, you will not be successful.

Emotional Intelligence is the ability to understand yourself and others so you can develop empathy and rapport with people and manage relationships successfully.

Skills are the ability, improved through practice, to use your knowledge of techniques, methods, and tools. For salespeople, it is understanding the techniques of prospecting, identifying problems, generating solutions, presenting, negotiating and closing, and servicing.

Knowledge means knowing the product you are selling in depth – knowing more about it than your customers do so you can educate them. For salespeople, it means having information not only about their product, but also about research, about marketing and advertising, about customers' businesses, and about competitive media.

Opportunities are the circumstances in which you can use your tools. Even if you have the tools and know how to use them, you cannot accomplish anything unless you have opportunities to put them to use. Salespeople may know how to solve problems and have a storehouse full of product, marketplace, and competitive knowledge, but if they do not make sales calls and find prospective customers, they will lack the opportunities to put their skills and knowledge to work.

Preparation is getting organized to solve customer problems. Even if you have the attitude, emotional intelligence, skills, knowledge, and opportunities to sell, you will not solve problems or make many sales if you forget your presentations and if you do not know anything about clients' businesses or personalities.

Persistence means never giving up. Salespeople need to continue working on prospects past any initial uninformed "no" they might encounter.

Core competencies of the AESKOPP system

Each of the seven elements of the AESKOPP system is made up of a group of core competencies – building blocks – that, linked together, lead to successful performance on that element. The core competencies are subject to change, depending on the media selling job involved. Some sales positions, such as in a large-circulation national magazine – *People*, for example – require a high level of knowledge, especially about national advertising, the product, and magazine research, plus very strong relationships with major advertising agencies and advertisers. Other sales positions, such as in a local television station, might require an understanding of retail businesses – an automotive dealership, for example – and skills in negotiating with advertising agencies.

Exhibit 4.1 shows a list of core competencies for each of the elements of the AESKOPP system. The most effective way to use this list of core competencies is to download it from the book's Web site (www.mediaselling.us) and use it as a coaching instrument.

Each of the seven AESKOPP elements will be defined and explained much more thoroughly in subsequent chapters.

Exhibit 4.1   Salesperson core competencies

Attitude (12%)	Missionary selling
Honest	Service selling
Positive/Optimistic	Persuasion
Committed	Negotiating/closing
Confident	Servicing
Courageous	Team leadership
Competitive	*Knowledge* (20%)
Coachable (open/non-defensive)	Financial/economic/business/category
Self-motivated	Marketing/advertising/research
Assertive	Market
Flexible	Product (your medium)
Cooperative	Competitors
Nurturing	Competitive media
Emotional intelligence (20%)	Pricing
Self-awareness	Sales process
Self-management	Contract terms
Social awareness	*Opportunity* (8%)
Relationship management	Prospecting/getting appointments
Internal	Identifying problems (discovery)
External	*Preparation* (12%)
Skills (20%)	Generating solutions (research)
Communicating	Strategic thinking
Internal	Creativity/problem-solving
External	Organization
Listening	Planning
Understanding people	Time management
Presenting	Creating presentations
Individual	*Persistence* (8%)
Groups	Determined/never giving up
Creating value	Follow-up

The next step in effectively using the AESKOPP system is to evaluate yourself based on your degree of expertise on each of the core competencies listed above. I have assigned a percentage to each of the seven AESKOPP elements according to my perception of the importance each contributes to a salesperson's ultimate success. These AESKOPP elements and their corresponding core competencies will change with the type of media selling job as will the percentages I have assigned, but the AESKOPP elements and core competencies in Exhibit 4.1 are a good place to start in order to define and evaluate a media salesperson's job. I recommend that salespeople and sales managers go over the list together and add or delete core competencies and put weights on each according to the needs of the medium they sell and the company they work for.

Then, salespeople should study their modified and weighted list, evaluate themselves, and then develop a plan to improve those competencies in which they lack experience or have a deficit.

Note the title "Salesperson core competencies." The term salesperson is used because it is inclusive of a wide variety of titles that salespeople in the media are assigned by their organizations: sales representative, account executive, account manager, sales consultant, radio marketing consultant, business development director, director of new business, and many more. The preferred title is account executive or account manager, which implies managing customers' accounts, schedules, and campaigns according to what is best for a customer. Titles that include "consultant" should be avoided because customers need results more than advice. In this modern age of solutions selling, results generator might be a suitable title. But this euphemism is akin to calling a janitor a maintenance engineer, so account executive or account manager are more appropriate titles. However, in this book, to avoid confusion, salesperson will be used in order to encompass all titles.

The AESKOPP system of selling provides salespeople an excellent way to keep track of their strengths and opportunities for improvement (a positive way to say weakness or shortcoming). It is also a valuable tool for managers because, by using a modified and weighted core competencies checklist, they will have an excellent coaching tool, a snapshot of a department's strengths and weaknesses, and an indicator of who has high potential to become a manager.

Test Yourself

1 What do the various letters in AESKOPP mean?
2 Do all of the seven AESKOPP elements have to be present for successful selling?
3 Name five core competencies in the Skills element.
4 Name five core competencies in the Preparation element.
5 How can a salesperson use the core competencies rating system to improve performance?
6 Name two ways a sales manager can use the core competencies rating system.

Project

Rate yourself on all of the core competencies, make a list of the five you need to work on most, and then assign yourself some learning goals – for example, "to improve my market knowledge by reading Chamber of Commerce material and Census data."

Resources

Michael Corbett. 1999. *The 33 Ruthless Rules of Local Advertising*. New York: Pinnacle Books.

Philip Kotler. 1999. *Kotler on Marketing: How to Create, Win, and Dominate Markets*. New York: The Free Press.

Don E. Schultz, Stanley I. Tannenbaum and Robert Lauterborn. 1994. *The New Marketing Paradigm: Integrated Marketing Communications*. Chicago: NTC Business Books.

Part II

Attitude, Emotional Intelligence, and Skills

....

5

Attitude and Goal Setting

Charles Warner

We have been using the word attitude in this book in a positive context. You might hear sports commentators say that a particular athlete has an "attitude," which translated into everyday, non-sports speak means that the athlete has an aggressive, nasty, or arrogant attitude. However, the word attitude is not a singular noun as in sports-speak, but is an aggregate concept that encompasses all types of mind-sets, both positive and negative.

In this chapter we will answer the following questions about attitude:

1   What is attitude?
2   Why are attitudes important in selling?
3   Can I control and change my attitudes?
4   How can I motivate myself to maintain a positive attitude?

What Is Attitude?

An attitude is a point of view, either negative or positive, about an idea, situation, or person. We develop favorable attitudes about those ideas, situations, or people that are associated with positive rewards and benefits and unfavorable attitudes toward those that are associated with penalties or dislikes. An attitude is also an outlook on life or a mind-set about something.

An attitude has three components: what you think, what you do, and what you feel.

To change your attitudes you can change the way you think, act, or feel. But changing the way you think and act is easier than changing how you feel, because attitudes have a strong emotional component despite being supported by varying degrees of fact. Thus, by correcting misconceptions or adding facts, you can change your attitude and those of others. For example, you can learn to like someone about whom you had a negative first impression by thinking about a positive attribute or characteristic and acting friendly at the next encounter, despite lingering negative feelings. Also, acting and thinking positively helps you begin to change the feelings part of your attitude.

Why Are Attitudes Important in Selling?

Attitudes are important in selling because performance in a job depends on a person's attitudes and attributes – see the definition of attributes further on in this chapter. Performance in selling is like performance in sports; it is a synchronization of mind, body, and action. Many of the characteristics of successful athletes and successful salespeople are similar, as is the jargon of selling and sports – both use the terms, "superstars," "heavy hitters," and "rookies."

Performance in any endeavor starts with a dream of successful accomplishment. Scientist/philosopher Buckminster Fuller said that people can accomplish anything they can imagine; but first they must have the courage and confidence to believe in their imaginations and to dream. We translate our dreams into objectives and goals, and these objectives and goals are born in our minds as the result of the interaction of our mental attitudes.

You might think that performance comes about as the result of attitudes; to the contrary, we tend to form attitudes because of how well we do things, because of our actions. Research has indicated that performance, which is a series of successful behaviors, often precedes attitudes. In other words, if we do something well, we tend to have a favorable attitude toward it. For example, if you are successful at a job, you are likely to have a favorable attitude about the company for which you work. In contrast, having a positive attitude about your company does not necessarily mean you will perform any better, because what determines job performance is mostly your internal drive or motivation to perform well, not external factors such as a pleasant work environment or company picnics.

Attitudes represent the mind portion of job performance and, more importantly, performance in selling. Attitudes can be useful in helping salespeople perform better because they can be changed, controlled, and directed from counterproductive attitudes to productive, objective-oriented ones to help improve performance. Thus, your actions can lead to a feeling of success, which, in turn, leads to a positive attitude.

Attributes are somewhat like attitudes in that they have a significant impact on job performance, as well. Attributes are inherent talents, characteristics, or qualities of a person. You are born with attributes, but you develop attitudes as you experience life. You can change attitudes, but you can only improve or enhance your attributes, you can't change them. I include attributes in the Attitude section of the list of core competencies in Chapter 4 (p. 58). For the purpose of this book, we are combining the concepts of attitudes and attributes into one broad concept – attitude – to avoid confusion and so that the AESKOPP mnemonic is no longer than seven letters.

The following quote explains why attitude is the first element in the AESKOPP system of selling.

> The longer I live the more I realize the importance of attitude on life. Attitude, to me, is more important than facts. It is more important than the past, than education, than money, than circumstances, than failures, than success, or what other people say or do. It is more important than appearance, giftedness, or skill. It will make or break a company . . . a church . . . a home. The remarkable thing is we have a choice every day regarding the attitude we embrace that day. We cannot change our past . . . we cannot change the fact that people will act a certain way. We cannot change the inevitable. The only thing we can do is play on the one string we have and that is attitude . . . I am convinced that life is 10 percent what happens to me and 90 percent how I react to it. And so it is with you . . . we are in charge of our attitudes. (Charles Swindoll)[1]

Attitude control and enhancement in sports is an obvious example of the importance of mental attitude. Experts estimate that sports performance is determined by about 75 percent inherent ability and about 25 percent attitude, with ability consisting of such inherent elements as size, speed, coordination, quickness, and endurance. Attitude is the head, or mind, portion of sports performance. Sales performance is also determined by ability and attitude, but, unlike sports, is split equally between ability and attitude.

While skills and knowledge are vital in selling, the following attitudes from the Core Competencies in Chapter 4 are even more important. Successful media selling requires the following attitudes:

Honest. Being *honest* is technically not an attitude, it is an attribute – it means behaving with integrity and in an ethical, straightforward, morally upright, and truthful way. You trust honest people and feel that their word is their bond. Because so much media business is conducted by verbal agreements and not by signed contracts (contracts sometimes do not get signed for weeks or months after an advertising campaign has started), being honest in media selling is of primary importance, which is why it is listed first.

Positive/optimistic. You cannot sell successfully if you do not have a *positive outlook* on life and, thus, have an *optimistic* attitude. An example of a positive attitude is Albert Einstein's comment that "In the middle of difficulty lies opportunity"[2] – the glass-is-half-full attitude. On the other hand, negative people are downers, to themselves and others. Optimism is also directly related to self-esteem and confidence. People with high self-esteem and confidence believe they can affect the future and make things come out right. As Helen Keller said, "Optimism is the faith that leads to achievement. Nothing can be done without hope and confidence."[3]

Committed. Being *committed* means you have absolutely no doubts and will give everything in support of an undertaking or a cause without turning back. As Myer Berlow, former President of AOL Time Warner Global Marketing Solutions, says: "When you're eating ham and eggs for breakfast, the chicken was involved but the pig was committed."[4] Generals have been known to burn bridges behind their troops to make retreat impossible and, thus, force their soldiers to be totally committed and to fight for their lives.

Another dimension of commitment is passion for the cause and the task. Louis Gerstner, ex-CEO of IBM wrote in his book, *Who Says Elephants Can't Dance?*, which describes his incredible turnaround of IBM, that "personal leadership is about passion."[5] He means a passion for or commitment to winning. Being committed also means that people accept responsibility and hold themselves accountable for their successes and failures.

Confident. Feeling *confident* is vital in selling. Without confidence, or belief, in yourself, your product, and your offer, you cannot generate the enthusiasm required to reflect a positive image of your product to buyers. All training, all knowledge acquisition, all practice, all planning should be aimed at one thing – making you feel more confident about what you are selling.

Courageous. Being *courageous* is a vital attribute for salespeople; it does not mean you have no fear, it means you have the ability to overcome fear. You need courage to stand up to managers and others who might pressure you to do the wrong thing or to be dishonest. You need courage to set out every day to make 10 calls when you know you will probably face 10 rejections. You need courage to tell your boss the bad news that you did not get an order on a piece of business you had been working on for months. You need courage to be honest and tell the truth to your customers and to your management.

Competitive. Being *competitive* means having a strong desire to win. However, the drive and passion for winning must be channeled into two areas – being *self-competitive* and being *externally competitive*. When you are self-competitive, you compete with yourself, pushing yourself to improve. In his book, *Who Says Elephants Can't Dance?* Louis Gerstner refers to this self-competitiveness as "restless self-renewal," or the motivation to constantly improve.[6] Self-competition is a prerequisite for improvement, which the Japanese call *kaizen*, meaning constant improvement in small increments, which lead to huge improvements in the long run, as Toyota practiced religiously on the way to becoming the world's largest car maker.

Being externally competitive means having a strong desire to beat the competition, those direct competitors in your medium and competitive media. If you are a television station salesperson, you want to beat the salespeople from other television stations to get higher shares of business and get higher rates, while pulling advertising dollars away from newspapers, radio, Yellow Pages, and outdoor. Being externally competitive means winning by playing the game fairly and by the rules and not becoming overly competitive either within or out of your own company, which can lead to dishonest and unethical behavior, as described in Chapter 3.

This attitude is probably better described as being *ethically competitive, externally competitive,* and *self-competitive,* and is exemplified by being a member of a 400-meter relay race in the Olympic Games. You cooperate with other team members in passing the baton, as you perfect your own running technique and set increasingly lower lap-time goals, while your overall goal is for the team to win the race.

Coachable (open/non-defensive). Being *coachable* means that you are open to feedback and coaching in the form of an evaluation or criticism without becoming defensive. Being *open* and *not defensive* is directly related to your self-esteem and self-confidence. People with low self-esteem and self-confidence take almost anything said to them in a negative way, as a criticism or slap in the face. Being coachable and not defensive will help you improve and grow and will make you more valued by your management.

Self-motivated. Being *self-motivated* means that you do not depend on others to spark your drive to achieve but have the discipline and courage to set your own goals and to improve yourself. Being self-motivated means you have a strong desire to work, to do a good job, to achieve, and to improve. Managers often refer to people who are self-motivated and self-confident as being *low-maintenance.*

Assertive does not mean aggressive. It means being firm in expressing your ideas, thoughts, and feelings. One need not be pushy; quiet determination and resolve can result in being heard, included, and recognized.

Flexible means being willing to change your plans, your attitudes, opinions, and your feelings about people and situations. It allows you to be less rigid, open to new ideas and ways of doing things. Flexibility is an attribute that you were either born with or not, but it can learned with practice.

Cooperative. Being *cooperative* means being a good team member, willing to help others and work towards company goals. The best analogy for cooperation I have ever read is, "We are all angels with only one wing, and the only way we can fly is by embracing each other."

Nurturing. Being *nurturing* means caring for others, wanting to help and mentor. Having a nurturing attitude is vitally important for media salespeople so that they will not forget about their customers after a sale and will care about getting results. This attitude helps salespeople overcome a tendency to hit-and-run after making a sale. Paperwork and production need to be completed properly, the schedule placed properly, and the customer contacted frequently and serviced after an ad or commercial runs.

Can I Control and Change my Attitudes?

Attitudes can be changed and controlled, but you must have the will power and discipline to practice relentlessly. Making any changes within ourselves takes self-discipline and practice. Techniques used by sports psychologists can help you control, manage, and change your attitude.

① *Positive framing.* This technique is based on the concept that verbal or written communication creates images, or pictures, in our heads that we cannot erase with mere language. If you tell people "do not think of a tree" and then ask them what kind of a tree popped into their mind, they will invariably tell you they had an image of an oak, Christmas, or a palm tree. They simply cannot think of a no tree, zero tree, or nothing tree, as instructed. Because we think visually, in pictures, you want to put positive pictures in your and your customers' minds.

Imagine if, after losing a basketball game, a coach uses a negative frame and says to his team, "Do not miss free throws! We lost the game because we missed too many free throws! You're a bunch of bums!" The team will get a picture implanted in their heads of missing free throws and will continue to miss free throws. On the other hand, if the coach were to say "Make your free throws. Free throws win ball games," it would form a positive image.

Always use positive frames in your inner dialogues with yourself and in external dialogues with others. When you use a positive frame, you put a positive spin on things and you create optimism in yourself. An example of a positive frame would be an offer by a gas station of a "cash discount" instead of informing consumers of a "credit card surcharge." Positive framing is a very valuable sales tool as we will see later in Chapters 11 and 12.

② *Visualization and mental rehearsal.* To use visualization, mobilize all of your senses and imagine a future sales call, down to how prospects will look and act while viewing your presentation. Visualize your prospects' reaction to your presentation – a big smile and a nod of the head. Next, mentally rehearse your presentation, including how you will overcome objections, and rehearse silently your proposals. Visualize the ideal outcome of your presentation and your reaction when your proposal is accepted. Will you jump up and click your heels? If so, practice this in your mind. Rehearse your presentation word for word, out loud, over and over, visualizing prospects' reactions and your responses to their questions. Constant practice of visualization is a key to success and is an excellent confidence booster. While visualization has been referred to as *instant replay*, Spencer Johnson and Larry Wilson, in their best-selling book, *The One Minute Sales Person*, call this technique "The One Minute Rehearsal."

Another dramatic example of the incredible power of visualization was seen in the 40-minute IMAX film set in the 1998 NBA finals. The film featured Michael

Jordan explaining what makes him so good; why he demands the last shot of the game, no matter what is at stake. Michael Jordan's rules are:

1   Learn to love the game before you learn to master it.
2   Past failures are irrelevant to the task at hand.
3   If you can visualize winning, you won't fear losing.
4   Strength of heart [attitude] is more important than strength of body.[7]

Visualization also includes the notion of hearing a sound in your head. The great cellist, Zara Nelsova, visualized the phrase "Seamless lines of sound join the eternity between one note and the next"[8] so she could be consistent in her magnificent playing and performances.

③ *Do the right thing.* Behave ethically at all times. Integrity and honesty are not only good business practices that will help you manage relationships and build trust effectively over the long run, but also they are good for your soul. Conducting business with integrity improves your self-esteem, self-confidence, and health because you know that you are doing the right thing.

Using these three techniques requires mental discipline. Just as the dream of an Olympic gold medal helps athletes push their bodies to their physical limits time and again, they must channel their minds toward positive attitudes. Sales success requires the same persistence and mental discipline.

How Can I Motivate Myself to Maintain a Positive Attitude?

People's motivational drive comes more from internal forces than from external ones. While people who fail in sales often blame external elements, such as a company or its management, the vast majority of these people lack sufficient internal motivation to succeed. People who are successful in sales and in most other endeavors crave success and are, thus, high achievers.

High achievers

People who have strong internal motivation and drive to be successful are high achievers. Research has identified some common characteristics of high achievers:

1   They set goals and objectives.
2   They enjoy solving problems.
3   They take calculated risks.

4   They like immediate feedback on their performance.
5   They take personal responsibility for achieving their goals and objectives.

Looking at these characteristics, we feel solution selling is an ideal occupation for high achievers, who are more likely to satisfy their needs in sales jobs because of the nature of the tasks required in sales, especially in media sales. Selling requires a continual goal-setting process. High achievers like selling and are motivated by it because it gives them the opportunity to use their self motivation to work to its peak while satisfying their needs to solve problems, take risks, and receive immediate performance feedback.

Goal Setting: Theory and Practice

Peter Drucker popularized the importance of setting goals and objectives in his classic book, *The Practice of Management*, published in 1954. While there is still some question about who first used the term "management by objectives" (MBO), it is generally conceded that the initial push came from Drucker, who attributes it to Alfred P. Sloan, the managerial and organizational genius who is credited with building up General Motors.

In the 1960s, Edwin A. Locke published a series of articles that detailed his research on goal setting and on how this motivates people. He not only explained why goals work but also proposed some basic rules for setting them. While Drucker, Locke, and most other goal-setting theorists put their work in a managerial context, these theories also apply to individual goal setting where competence and confidence grow as you get better at your own objectives and goals.

Goal-setting theory

Goals and objectives have a significant effect on performance if they have the following attributes: *clarity, difficulty,* and *feedback.* A goal has a time horizon of more than one year and an objective has a time horizon of less than a year. Therefore, one would set several short-term objectives to reach a long-term goal.

Goal clarity is the single most important element of setting goals. Goals and objectives must be specific so they can be measured. A general objective of increasing the number of prospecting calls next month is vague, nonspecific, and virtually useless. A more specific objective would be to average two prospecting appointments per day for the next month.

Goal difficulty. Increasing the *difficulty of goals and objectives* generally amplifies the challenge, which, in turn, raises the effort to meet the challenge. This concept of goal difficulty creates confusion and is where defining the difference between goals and objectives becomes important. Because *goals* have a long-term time horizon, it is useful to set goals, and, thus, expectations, high. In the best-selling book, *Built to Last*, Collins's and Porras's research shows that one of the things that highly successful companies have in common is that they set BHAGs – Big, Hairy, Audacious Goals. The authors write: "A BHAG should be so clear and compelling that it requires little or no explanation. Remember, a BHAG is a *goal* – like climbing a mountain or going to the moon – not a 'statement.' If it does not get people juices going it's just not a BHAG."[9] One of the 18 built-to-last companies examined by Collins and Porras was Merck. Its BHAG was "to become the preeminent drug maker worldwide, via massive R&D and new products that cure disease."[10]

On the other hand, short-term *objectives* set by management should be set to make people feel like winners, a deep-seated need. Unfortunately, management often set BHAGs, or "stretch" short-term objectives, believing that they motivate people. Exhibit 5.1 shows the relationship between motivation and objective difficulty. Setting a very low objective has no motivating effect. On the other hand, setting an objective too high demotivates people because they give up the moment they realize that the objective is unachievable. Working hard to achieve an impossible objective creates cognitive dissonance, so people quit making an effort in order to bring thinking and action into internal harmony.

As you can see from Exhibit 5.1, the best objectives are moderately difficult, yet provide a challenge because they are perceived as attainable and are, thus, motivating. Contrary to what many managers believe, the trick in setting objectives is to set them on the low side of the moderately difficult peak to ensure

Exhibit 5.1   Goal difficulty and motivation

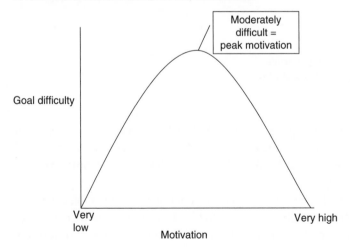

that they can be reached with a strong effort and, thus, allow people to feel successful. Unfortunately, too often managers set objectives on the high side of the moderately difficult peak and unintentionally reduce people's motivation.

Interestingly, people with low self-esteem often set unrealistically high goals because they expect failure. Already viewing themselves as losers, they are more comfortable reinforcing this view in advance. Claiming that "the objective was too high," allows them to quit before trying rather than attempting something difficult that they think they are bound to fail at.

The ideal is to set a series of moderately difficult objectives that get progressively more challenging as each objective is achieved. This series of realistic step-by-step, increasingly more difficult objectives will lead you to your BHAG.

This is an art. It takes work, analysis, thought, and luck, especially when faced with an unpredictable future.

Goal feedback. You need to get *feedback* – a reading on how you are doing. You receive feedback from yourself by successfully solving problems and closing sales, and analyzing what you did right, or by failing and analyzing what you did wrong. For example, analyzing statistics about your ratio of total calls to successful calls will give you feedback on how you are doing. We will offer you more specific advice about methods for organizing yourself and analyzing your productivity in Chapter 24. Furthermore, you should get feedback on your goals from your manager on a regular basis. You have the right to know how you are doing and what your manager thinks you can do to improve, but remember, be self-motivated and low-maintenance.

Objective-setting practice

Sound individual objectives must be:

1 Measurable
2 Attainable
3 Demanding
4 Consistent with company goals
5 Under the control of the individual
6 Deadlined.

Here is a mnemonic for setting objectives – MADCUD. I will provide you with more details about using and prioritizing the MADCUD objectives on a daily and weekly basis in Chapter 24. But for now, here are the elements' definitions:

Measurable. The *measurable* criterion relates to the concept of clarity. Objectives and goals must be specific enough to be measurable, for example, "to increase sales by 15 percent" or "to increase your number of face-to-face presentations from a current average of 10 per week to an average of 15 per week." Notice that objectives always begin with "to," which implies an action you are going to take.

Setting specific, measurable, revenue objectives is not generally a good idea, although it is common practice. Rather than setting the final objective as a revenue objective, it is more productive to set a series of specific, measurable, smaller objectives that will help you reach a desired monthly revenue level. In the chapter "A Bias for Action" in *In Search of Excellence*, Thomas J. Peters and Robert H. Waterman, Jr. quote the president of one of these successful companies who says he has his managers focus on a few important activity-based objectives. If they have this task-oriented focus, he says that "the financials will take care of themselves."[11]

Attainable. Set moderately difficult but *attainable* objectives. If objectives are reasonable, challenging, and attainable, they are motivating. If people perceive goals to be unattainable, they will not work hard to achieve them. It is important to give time and thought to setting realistic, attainable goals so that when you accomplish them you will feel successful.

Demanding like *attainable*, is related to difficulty. As seen in Exhibit 5.1, an objective has to be not only attainable but also sufficiently demanding to be challenging. High achievers are particularly motivated by goals that challenge them. For high achievers the big payoff is the conquest and feeling like a winner, more so than any money that might be involved.

Consistent with company goals. Individual objectives should be *consistent with company goals and objectives*. For example, broadcast salespeople sometimes work at cross-purposes to their sales departments by concentrating on selling rates that are too low or by "cherry picking" inventory, which means only selecting the highly rated advertising slots or special low-price offers to sell. Such practices would be inconsistent with an overall company goal of maximizing revenue, for example.

Under the control of the individual. Another seemingly self-evident criterion for sound objectives states that they must be *under the control of the individual*. Instead of setting a revenue objective, set objectives for the number of calls you will make or for the number of presentations you will give. These are activity goals. Too often, the concept of setting activity objectives is overlooked, especially by beginning salespeople. For example, objectives that would not be under the control of salespeople would be "to increase revenue next month by 25 percent." But what if that next month's ratings on your television station went down 30 percent or last month was the bottom month in a yearlong advertising slowdown. You cannot control ratings, circulation, or the general economy; you an only control how hard you work and your own activities.

Deadlined. Your goals must be *deadlined*; they must have a due date. Without clear deadlines, objectives become amorphous. Here is an example of some objectives a radio salesperson might write: "Next month I will increase my average rates from last month by 10 percent; I will increase the number of prospecting calls I make in the average week from 10 to 15; and I will make 25 percent more face-to-face presentations." These goals are measurable, attainable, demanding, consistent with company goals, under the control of the person, and deadlined. Notice the phrase "a radio station salesperson might *write*." Objectives that are not written down are worthless. A further way to increase your commitment to your objectives is to give your manager a copy of your written objectives.

Remember to keep your objectives flexible. If they are carved in stone and unchangeable, your objectives can lose their motivating effect particularly if they turn out to be either too high or too low. In addition, new opportunities might arise that require a priority change.

Take full responsibility for your Cycle of Success

High achievers set goals and objectives, enjoy solving problems, take calculated risks, want immediate feedback on their performance, and take personal responsibility for their own Cycle of Success (see Exhibit 5.2).

The Cycle of Success is an ongoing cycle of ever-more demanding objectives and goals that lead to ever-increasing success. But just as the AESKOPP formula for success was multiplicative in the sense that if any of the seven AESKOPP elements were not present, success could not be achieved, so with the Cycle of Success, all of the elements are inextricably linked.

Exhibit 5.2   The Cycle of Success

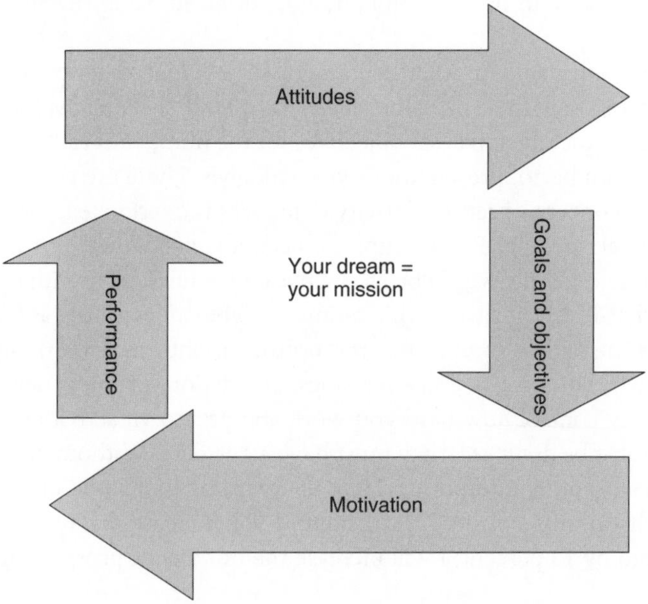

The Cycle is your cycle. You own it and must take full responsibility for keeping it moving. What drives it, the motor for this cycle is your dream. Remember the words of Buckminster Fuller earlier in this chapter, if you can dream it, you can do it. Walt Disney said the same thing, and, in fact, all great people started with a dream of being great.

Your dream, your mission

You cannot win an Olympic gold medal if you do not or cannot dream of winning one. Dennis Waitley in his inspirational book, *Empires of the Mind*, writes about the dreams of accomplished people like Antonio Stradivari, Andrew Lloyd Webber, Sandra Day O'Connor, Michael Jordan, Jacques Cousteau, Jonas Salk, and Bill Gates. He suggests writing a personal mission based on your dream to help you realize it. Write it down, keep it in your wallet or purse, and let it drive your Cycle of Success.

Test Yourself

1   What is an attitude?
2   What is the difference between a value and an attitude?
3   What is the difference between an attitude and an attribute?
4   Which comes first, attitude or performance? Why?
5   What is the difference between a goal and an objective?
6   What are the six criteria for sound objectives?
7   What are the elements in the Cycle of Success?

Project

(1) Choose a task, such as writing a term paper or a sales presentation, or an activity, such as dating, and write a MADCUD objectives statement that will help you complete the task or activity successfully. (2) Then, write a BHAG for yourself – several years in the future – and then write a personal mission statement that will help you focus on and achieve your BHAG, your dream.

References

Peter F. Drucker. 1954. *The Practice of Management.* New York: Harper & Row.

Charles A. Garfield with Hal Zina Bennett. 1984. *Peak Performance: Mental Training*

Techniques of the World's Greatest Athletes. New York: Warner Books.

Louis V. Gerstner, Jr. 2002. *Who Says Elephants Can't Dance? Inside IBM's*

Historic Turnaround. New York: Harper Business.

Spencer Johnson and Larry Wilson. 1984. *The One Minute Sales Person*. New York: William Morrow and Company, Inc.

Edwin A. Locke. 1966. "The ubiquity of the technique of goal setting," *Behavioral Science*, Vol. 2.

Edwin A. Locke. 1968. "Toward a theory of task motivation and incentives," *Organizational Behavior and Human Performance*, Vol. 3.

Edwin A. Locke.and J.F. Bryan. 1967. "Goal setting as a means of increasing motivation," *Journal of Applied Psychology*, Vol. 51.

Edwin A. Locke, Norman Cartledge, and Claramae S. Kerr. 1970. "Studies in the relationship between satisfaction, goal setting and performance," *Organizational Behavior and Human Performance*, Vol. 5.

Thomas J. Peters and Robert H. Waterman, Jr. 1982. *In Search of Excellence: Lessons from America's Best Run Companies*. New York: Harper & Row Publishers.

Dennis Waitley. 1995. *Empires of the Mind*. New York: William Morrow and Company, Inc.

Resources

www.lessons4living.com (Lessons For Living Web site.)

Notes

1   www.lessons4living.com/attitude. htm. November 3, 2002.

2   Tal Ben-Shahar. 2007. *Happier: Learn the Secrets to Daily Joy and Lasting Fulfillment*. New York: McGraw-Hill.

3   Helen Keller. 1903. *The Story of My Life*. New York: Bantam Classics, reissue edition 1991.

4   Personal conversation, October, 2002.

5   Louis V. Gerstner, Jr. 2002. *Who Says Elephants Can't Dance? Inside IBM's Historic Turnaround*. New York: Harper Business, p. 236.

6   Ibid., p. 214.

7   Ed Adams. 2002–2003. "Coach's eye." *Sailing World*, December–January, p. 58.

8   Personal conversation with Daniel Gold, nephew of Zara Nelsova. October, 2002.

9   James C. Collins and Jerry Porras. 1994. *Built to Last: Successful Habits of Visionary Companies*. New York: Harper Business, p. 111.

10 Ibid., p. 113.

11 Thomas J. Peters and Robert H. Waterman, Jr. 1982. *In Search of Excellence: Lessons from America's Best Run Companies*. New York: Harper & Row Publishers, p. 154.

6

Emotional Intelligence

Charles Warner

When I returned from the final sales call in 1957 on Parrott's Florist as described at the beginning of Chapter 2, my general sales manager asked, "How did it go? Did you close him?"

"No. He said he didn't get any results," I replied sheepishly.
"That's a common objection," replied my sales manager. "You should have asked him a bunch of questions that led him to the answer you wanted him to give you and then sold him sizzle!"
"Sizzle?"
"Yeah, you know, 'sell the sizzle, not the steak!' My sales manager always spoke in exclamation points. It was his way of showing that he was enthusiastic.
"Enthusiasm, enthusiasm! Enthusiasm is what gets orders! Always sell the sizzle!" And with that, he reached back to his small bookshelf, took out a book, and handed it to me. "Read this!", said my sales manager, "it's by Elmer Wheeler and it's called *Sizzlemanship!* It's the greatest book ever written about selling! Memorize it!"

Old-Fashioned Models of Selling

In 1957, books on selling, such as *Sizzlemanship!*, Frank Bettger's *How I Raised Myself from Failure to Success in Selling*, and Og Mandino's ode of humility, *The Greatest Salesman in the World*, preached a model of selling that was developed in the 1920s, 1930s, and 1940s, as described in Chapter 1. Books on selling urged the use of techniques and tricks that were relatively successful for products that could be sold in one encounter, that were often low-cost, and which people could be badgered into buying, often just to get rid of the salesperson.

These outmoded selling models used a simple mnemonic to guide salespeople, AIDA, which stood for Attention, Interest, Desire, and Action. The old-time practitioners urged outrageous, often silly, techniques for getting a prospect's attention. They advocated manipulative techniques such as "sizzlemanship" to get interest and create desire (usually by overselling and over-promising). And they advocated a number of techniques that pressured prospects to act immediately, allowing the salesperson to slam down a one-time sale. While there is nothing wrong with the AIDA mnemonic, these old-fashioned, manipulative, hard-sell techniques, which include the "tell and sell" model, are largely responsible for the bad reputations that salespeople are often saddled with today.

Old Models Don't Work Today

Carl Zaiss and Thomas Gordon point out in their excellent book, *Sales Effectiveness Training*, that old selling models do not work in today's highly competitive, interactive, and sophisticated business environment. This is due to increased competition, the increased need for stronger customer loyalty and long-term relationships, the increased cost of developing new business, and the current trend in business toward solutions selling.

Rather than being seen as the manipulators and hard closers of the past, salespeople want to be perceived as trusted and respected partners who get results for their customers. Unhappy with the pressure and grind of one-shot sales, today's media salespeople prefer long-term relationships.

While many experts on selling have helped shift the focus from the oldfashioned, hard-sell approach to a gentler needs-based and consultative approach, four men stand out in the field. They are Larry Wilson with his Counselor Selling Program and training seminars and books, Mack Hanna with his Consultative Selling Program, Tony Alessandra and colleagues with their book *Non-Manipulative Selling*, and Neil Rackham with his book, *SPIN Selling*. While the consultative selling approach has now evolved into a solutions-selling approach, I still recommend reading the Alessandra and Rackham books.

Solution Selling as the Current Model

Buyers and customers of the media are hypersensitive to the tricks and manipulations of the past. With complex alternatives and problems, buyers need established and ongoing relationships based on mutual trust. This is the first step for successful solutions selling and requires *emotional intelligence*.

Emotional intelligence

The term, emotional intelligence, was popularized by Daniel Goleman, a Harvard-educated PhD in psychology, in his best seller, *Emotional Intelligence: Why It Can Matter More Than IQ*, which expanded on the work of the world-renowned educational psychologists, Howard Gardner, Robert Sternberg, and others.

Gardner, Sternberg and others questioned accepted definitions of intelligence and began to look beyond a number or IQ (intelligence quotient). After exploring the topic thoroughly, they realized that what IQ tests measured was only a person's ability to take an IQ test and was not the enormously complex construct that had been referred to in the past as "intelligence."

While Howard Gardner broadly defined intelligence as "the ability to solve problems or to create products that are valued within one or more cultural settings," in his influential book, *Frames of Mind: The Theory of Multiple Intelligences*, he identified seven facets of intelligence. These are linguistic, logical-mathematical, musical, bodily-kinesthetic, spatial, interpersonal, and intrapersonal. In his later book, *Intelligence Reframed: Multiple Intelligences for the 21st Century*, he added three more facets of intelligence: naturalist, spiritual, and existential.

Daniel Goleman concentrated his research on the importance of the personal intelligences, which he labeled *emotional intelligence*. Beginning in *Emotional Intelligence*, published in 1995, and in three subsequent books, *Working With Emotional Intelligence*, *Primal Leadership: Realizing the Power of Emotional Intelligence*, and *Social Intelligence* Goleman has continued to refine and simplify his construct of emotional intelligence (EI) and social intelligence. In *Working With Emotional Intelligence*, Goleman defined emotional intelligence as the "capacity for recognizing our own feelings and those of others, for motivating ourselves, and for managing emotions well in ourselves and in our relationships."[1] His book, *Primal Leadership*, written with Richard Boyatzis and Annie McKee, lays out an expanded definition that includes four dimensions of EI (See Exhibit 6.1).

How important is emotional intelligence in selling?   Goleman makes the case that, contrary to previously held theories, intelligence or IQ might not be an accurate predictor of life success. "At best IQ contributes about 20 percent to the factors that determine life success, which leaves 80 percent to other forces. As one observer notes, 'The vast majority of one's ultimate niche in society is determined by non-IQ factors, ranging from social class to luck.'"[2] A study of Harvard graduates in the fields of law, medicine, teaching, and business found that scores on entrance exams, a surrogate for IQ, had zero or negative correlation with eventual career success.

A study initiated in 1968 by the Stanford Graduate School of Business reinforced the importance of EI for success in business. It conducted in-depth interviews with the members of its graduating class, which examined the students'

Exhibit 6.1   Emotional intelligence domains and associated competencies

---

Personal competence: These capabilities determine how we manage ourselves.
  Self-awareness
- *Emotional self-awareness:* Reading one's own emotions and recognizing their impact; using "gut sense" to guide decisions.
- *Accurate self-assessment:* Knowing one's strengths and limits.
- *Self-confidence:* A sound sense of one's self-worth and capabilities.

  Self-management
- *Emotional self-control:* Keeping disruptive emotions and impulses under control.
- *Transparency:* Displaying honesty and integrity; trustworthiness.
- *Adaptability:* Flexibility in adapting to changing situations or overcoming obstacles.
- *Achievement:* The drive to improve performance to meet inner standards of excellence.
- *Initiative:* Readiness to act and seize opportunity.
- *Optimism:* Seeing the upside in events.

Social competence: These capabilities determine how we manage relationships.
  Social awareness
- *Empathy:* Sensing others' emotions, understanding their perspective, and taking an active interest in their concerns.
- *Organizational awareness:* Reading the currents, decision networks, and politics at the organizational level.
- *Service:* Recognizing and meeting . . . client or customer needs.

  Relationship management
- *Inspirational leadership:* Guiding and motivating with a compelling vision (for media salespeople this would translate into creating value with an inspiring vision for your medium and your media outlet).
- *Influence:* Wielding a range of tactics of persuasion.
- *Developing others:* Bolstering others' ability through feedback and guidance.
- *Change catalyst:* Initiating, managing, and leading a new direction.
- *Conflict management:* Resolving disagreements.
- *Teamwork and collaboration:* Cooperation and team building.

Source: Daniel Goleman, Richard Boyatzis, and Annie McKee. 2002. *Primal Leadership.* Harvard Business School Press. Used with permission.

academic records and grades, their extra-curricular and social activities, and their reputation among their fellow students. The school kept track of the graduates' careers and levels of success with re-interviews in 1978 and in 1988. When the school published the findings of its 20-year study in 1988, it concluded that the only two things that the most successful graduates (top 5 percent in title, position, money, for example) had in common was that all of the most successful graduates were in the bottom half of their class in grades and all of them were popular. In other words, relationship skills were more important for success than grades.

A major element of EI and success is optimism. A study of salesmen at Met Life by Martin Seligman revealed that

> Being able to take a rejection with grace is essential in sales of all kinds, especially with a product like insurance, where the ratio of nos to yeses can be so discouragingly high. For this reason, about three quarters of insurance salesmen quit in their first three years. Seligman found that new salesmen who were by nature optimists sold 37 percent more insurance in their first two years on the job than did pessimists. And during the first year the pessimists quit at twice the rate of the optimists.[3]

Media salespeople sell an intangible product similar to what insurance salespeople sell, but media salespeople do not have quite the same rejection rate, which makes media selling more desirable and satisfying. However, the above research reinforces the importance of optimism in selling. Optimism is defined in terms of how people explain to themselves their own successes and failures. People who are optimistic believe failures are the result of something that can be changed so that they can be successful the next time around. Pessimists take personal blame for failures, blaming them on some inherent characteristic they are helpless to change.[4] Pessimists also often blame their parents or their bosses or even the weather for their failures. Their attitude is that they expect failure; therefore, they create failures and a disastrous future. On the other hand, optimists expect success, and therefore create a successful future.

Do I have emotional intelligence?

Socrates said that all knowledge begins with "Know thyself." Self-knowledge is the keystone of EI. It is the awareness of one's feelings as they occur. Self-awareness is a non-reactive, nonjudgmental attention to one's inner states and feelings. To find out if you have emotional intelligence you have to ask yourself the following questions and answer them honestly.

1　Do I motivate myself to stick doggedly to tasks and practice or am I too easily distracted?
2　Am I critical, condescending, and inhibited or am I socially poised and cheerful?
3　Am I unexpressive and detached or am I outgoing and easily committed to people and causes?
4　Am I prudish, uptight, and uneasy with new experiences?
5　Do I tend to be anxious and handle stress poorly or am I comfortable with myself and how well do I handle stress?

(For the following questions, see Exhibit 6.1.)

6 How self-aware am I and how honestly am I able to assess my own strengths and weaknesses?

7 How is my emotional self-control and how well do I control my impulses?

8 How transparent am I? In other words, can people tell I am honest and believe I am trustworthy, that I am not hiding things?

9 Am I flexible and do I adapt easily to change or in overcoming obstacles?

10 Do I have a drive to achieve and to improve my performance to meet my inner standards of excellence?

11 Am I ready to grab the initiative, to act, and to seize opportunities as they present themselves?

12 Am I generally optimistic and do I see the upside in events?

13 How well do I sense others' emotions, understand their point of view, and take an active interest in their concerns?

14 How well do I read the currents, decision networks, and politics in my organization?

15 How good am I at recognizing and satisfying my customers' needs?

16 How good am I at creating value by communicating an inspiring vision for my medium and my product?

17 How persuasive am I?

18 Am I a catalyst for change in my organization?

19 How good am I at confronting problems, conflicts, and disagreements and resolving them?

20 How good am I at cultivating and maintaining a web of relationships?

21 How cooperative am I and how good a team member am I?

Hopefully your answers to the above questions placed you more than half-way toward the side of possessing EI, which means that you know you have an opportunity for improvement. This is a positive frame for the concept of deficiency and your first lesson in the use of framing.

People are sometimes tempted to use personality tests to determine their EI, but most of these tests, developed in the 1960s and 1970s, do not have much value in predicting success, uncovering motivation, and understanding yourself and others. Instead, they attempt to pigeonhole people into types such as "feeling" or "thinking" or "expressive." Most psychological tests are not designed to find EI. Psychological tests are often used by companies to screen job applicants, or are designed to diagnose psychological disorders, and are poor predictors of motivation and how people will manage relationships.

Can I learn emotional intelligence?

Goleman feels that emotional intelligence can be learned. In *Working With Emotional Intelligence* he writes:

Unlike IQ, which changes little after our teens years, emotional intelligence seems to be largely learned, and it continues to develop as we go through life and learn from our experiences – our competence in it can keep growing. In fact, studies that have tracked people's level of emotional intelligence through the years show that people get better and better in these capabilities as they grow more adept at handling their own emotions and impulses, at motivating themselves, and at honing their empathy and social adroitness. There is an old-fashioned word for this growth in emotional intelligence: maturity.[5]

Some of the things you can do to improve your EI are:

1 Work on controlling your impulses – "there is no psychological skill more fundamental than resisting impulses."[6]
2 Work on developing a positive, optimistic, hopeful outlook and a belief that you are the master over the events in your life and can meet the challenges as they come up, as you learned in the previous chapter.
3 Work on improving your communication and listening skills. Chapter 7 covers more about how to acquire and practice these vital skills.

How can I apply emotional intelligence to selling media?

Now that you have learned about what emotional intelligence is and how EI can help you improve your relationships, the next step is to relate EI to selling. Using the Three Golden Rules of Selling is the optimum way to apply EI to selling.

Rule 1: Do unto others as they would have others do unto them   Unlike the Bible's Golden Rule, this does not make the assumption that others like the same things that you like. Modern psychology and EI indicate that it is better to recognize people's diversity and differences and to value their needs, wants, desires, or preferences. Empathy requires that you find out how others feel, what they like, what they want and then base your response to them according to how they want to be treated.

Rule 2: People like and trust people exactly like themselves   This rule reinforces the notion that people are most comfortable with other people who are similar, a fact we observe every day as people gather in groups and cliques.

Rule 3: People don't care how much you know until they know how much you care   This rule reminds us that feeling and communicating a sense of caring for another person comes first in any relationship. In other words, you put another's concerns before your own.

These rules should be applied in the following steps:

Step 1   Just before sales conversations or meetings, ask yourself how you feel at that moment and then pause, *exhale*, and proceed. It is important to exhale because when we are nervous or tense, we tend to hold our breath, which tightens us up and makes fluid movement difficult. Exhaling is a sports training technique in which athletes release tension and improve performance. Taking time to recognize your feelings, to relax, and to exhale will allow you to manage your emotions consciously, and to control and use your emotions and your tensions to help you.

Step 2   Sense the mood and the emotional climate of the person or group you are meeting with. Beginning salespeople are usually nervous and anxious when they meet with customers, particularly the first time, and are unaware that customers are probably as nervous, anxious, and uncomfortable as they are. Effective leaders, politicians, and entertainers develop a knack for sensing the mood of a crowd or audience and playing to it. Salespeople must develop similar radar.

Step 3   Set the mood, the emotional tone and climate, for the meeting. Emotion is contagious, so by taking charge and energetically exuding a sense of confidence and enthusiasm (yes, "enthusiasm!" like my first sales manager often repeated) you infect the others with your contagious enthusiasm and positive vibes. Enthusiasm does not have to be the loud, excited, highly demonstrated type we often associate with back-slapping, broad-grinning used-car salesmen, but honest enthusiasm can come through in a restrained, calm, confident way that is in harmony with the emotional state of the other person or people in a meeting.

As Goleman points out in *Emotional Intelligence*:

> We transmit and catch moods from each other in what amounts to a subterranean economy of the psyche in which some encounters are toxic, some nourishing. This emotional exchange is typically at a subtle, almost imperceptible level; the way a salesperson says "thank you" can leave us feeling ignored, resented, or genuinely welcomed and appreciated. We catch feelings from one another as though they were some kind of social virus.[7]

Make sure the viruses you transmit are positive, caring ones.

Step 4:   Let the person or people you are meeting with know that you care. The best way to accomplish this step in a first meeting with a person is to begin by being very open about yourself. The goal is to reach out with personal details about yourself to enable the other person to get to know you. At that point you can ask the question, "How about you?" to learn more about the other person. People will normally reciprocate with openness and talk about themselves, their families, their hobbies, and interests. As they are talking, you must search for common interests and associations, such as being married, having children, or loving sports. This is an application of Golden Rule #2 of Selling: people like and trust people exactly like themselves, and your job is to talk about and emphasize those things in each of your personal lives that are similar. By showing a genuine sense of caring about their personal interests, they will know that you care. After the meeting, write down all the personal details for future reference.

Be prepared to encounter different responses from men and women, for as Goleman writes, men generally "take pride in a lone, tough-minded independence and autonomy" and women generally "see themselves as part of a web of connectedness."[8] These gender differences are pointed out to encourage you to be aware of your own tendencies and to know what you might expect in an initial encounter with someone, so that you can try to be more like them and to build rapport. You can and probably should change these gender generalizations and initial stereotypes once you have had the opportunity to get to know someone better.

Also, when meeting with a group of people for the first time, it pays large dividends to research their personal backgrounds and interests prior to your meeting.

Step 5:   Listen with "emotional synchrony," as Goleman calls it. "The degree of emotional rapport people feel in an encounter is mirrored by how tightly concentrated their physical movements are as they talk . . . One person nods just as the other makes a point, both shift chairs at the same moment, or one leans forward as the other leans back."[9] This type of synchrony is a major way to transmit a "social virus" or emotional state or mood. It is also makes you more similar to the other person in the conversation, gets you closer, and makes them feel that you care.

Having learned about the importance of emotional intelligence in building relationships in this chapter, in the next chapter you will learn how to put your EI knowledge to work in communicating with people, listening carefully to them, and understanding what makes them tick.

Test Yourself

1   Why don't old-fashioned sales techniques work in today's media selling environment?
2   What is emotional intelligence?
3   Why is EI more important for success in business and other fields than IQ?
4   What are the four major elements of EI?
5   Why is optimism important in selling?
6   What are the three EI rules of selling?
7   What are the five steps in applying the EI rules?

Project

Select a week in your life (next week might be good) in which you commit yourself to taking notes on encounters you have with people during the week whose job it is to serve you and be pleasant: waiters in restaurants or retail salespeople, for example. Take notes in two columns. In the first column, note the type of or lack of emotional intelligence you observe in each of the service people you encounter. Did the person try to connect with you, did the person cause you to leave the encounter feeling put off, angry, dissatisfied, happy, or pleased? In the second column, makes notes on your feelings and your ability to control your emotions in reaction to those encounters. You might copy into your notebook the EI elements in Exhibit 6.1 and use it as a guide. At the end of the week, look over your notes and see if you picked out those people who displayed EI and how they were different from those who did not display EI and if you were able to recognize your emotions.

Resources

www.danielgoleman.info/blog (Daniel Goleman's Web site and blog)

www.eqatwork.com (EQ at Work Web site – Emotional Intelligence training and certification)

www.eiconsortium.org (The Consortium on Emotional Intelligence in Organizations at Rutgers University)

References

Tony Alessandra, Phil Wexler, and Rick Barerra. 1992. *Non-Manipulative Selling*, 2nd edition. New York: Fireside Books.

Howard Gardner. 1983. *Frames of Mind: The Theory of Multiple Intelligences*. New York: Basic Books.

Howard Gardner. 1993. *Multiple Intelligence: The Theory in Practice*. New York: Basic Books.

Howard Gardner. 1999. *Intelligence Reframed: Multiple Intelligences for the 21st Century*. New York: Basic Books.

Daniel Goleman. 1995. *Emotional Intelligence: Why It Can Matter More Than IQ*. New York: Bantam Books.

Daniel Goleman. 1998. *Working with Emotional Intelligence*. New York: Bantam Books.

Daniel Goleman. 2006. *Social Intelligence: The New Science of Human Relationships*. New York: Bantam Books.

Daniel Goleman, Richard Boyatzis and Annie McKee. 2002. *Primal Leadership: Realizing the Power of Emotional Intelligence*. Boston: Harvard Business School Press.

Neil Rackham. 1988. *SPIN Selling*. New York: McGraw-Hill.

Robert J. Sternberg. 1988. *The Triarchic Mind: A New Theory of Human Intelligence*. New York: Viking Penguin.

Carl D. Zaiss and Thomas Gordon, PhD. 1993. *Sales Effectiveness Training*. New York: Dutton.

Notes

1   Daniel Goleman. 1998. *Working With Emotional Intelligence*. New York: Bantam Books, p. 317.

2   Ibid., p. 34.

3   Ibid., p. 89.

4   Ibid., p. 88.

5   Ibid., p. 7.

6   Daniel Goleman. 1995. *Emotional Intelligence*. New York: Bantam Books, p. 79.

7   Ibid., p. 114.

8   Ibid., p. 139.

9   Ibid., p. 116.

Skills: Effective Communication, Effective Listening, and Understanding People

Charles Warner

Following is a review several things we have covered so far.

The three *Golden Rules of Selling* are:

1   Do unto others as they would have others do unto them.
2   People like and trust people exactly like themselves.
3   People don't care how much you know until they know how much you care.

Next, are the *determinants of success* in the AESKOPP system:

1   Establish and maintain relationships with prospects and customers.
2   Solve advertising and marketing problems for them.
3   Get results for them (as they define results).

The most important skill in selling is dealing with other people, and the most important knowledge you can have is knowledge of people and how to build relationships. Understanding your customers' business, your product, and its capabilities are secondary because if you cannot get people to like and trust you, you will never get to the point of being able to discover what their problems are, let alone solve them.

Exhibit 7.1 shows a schematic conception of what is involved in building and maintaining relationships.

Communication is the fuel that keeps a relationship going. Without communication, both verbal and non-verbal, a relationship does not go anywhere. The

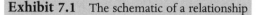

Exhibit 7.1 The schematic of a relationship

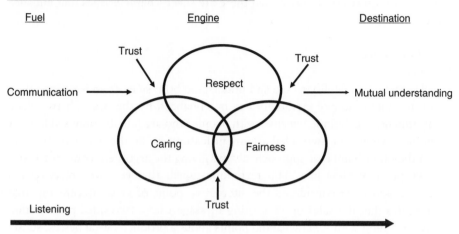

foundation on which the relationship rests, the road on which it travels, is *listening*. Without listening, you do not know where communication is going and there can be no progress in a relationship. The engine that drives the relationship consists of equal parts of *respect*, *caring*, and *fairness* that must constantly mesh and work hard together. It is kept running smoothly, with a minimum of friction, oiled by *trust*, which leads to the final objective of a relationship – that of *mutual understanding*.

How different this approach of mutual understanding is from the old-fashioned "tell-and-sell" school of selling that urged "Always Be Closing!" (exclamation point courtesy of my first sales manager). This new approach to selling says that in order to sell something, you must understand people, you must have respect for them and respect their feelings, you must establish a relationship based on trust and reach mutual understanding before you try to solve problems, you must first listen to the other person's point of view, you must restate the other person's viewpoint, and, finally, you must change yourself in a positive direction and meet the other person more than half way. These rules do not include "Always Be Closing," or "tell and sell."

Communication

Source

Communication begins with a *source*, the initiating origin of information in the communication process. The credibility of the source of information is its most important characteristic. Source credibility is multidimensional and, therefore, weakness in one dimension, or characteristic, can be offset by strength in another. Communication research has shown there are seven characteristics that enhance source credibility:

1   *Trustworthiness.*
2   *Competence.*
3   *Objectivity* – the ability to see and understand both sides of an issue, position, or argument. Source credibility can be enhanced by the use of a two-sided argument, a technique effective with people who are initially opposed to your point of view. The two-sided argument features an on-the-one-hand this and on-the-other-hand that approach, always giving the argument counter to your own point of view first. This technique signals that you are objective and candid and have considered the alternative point of view. Recent research indicates that if a sales or advertising message uses a two-sided presentation by beginning with several candid points about a product's weaknesses, subsequent points about the product's strengths are much more likely to be believed. Initial candor is a powerful tool for enhancing objectivity. Salespeople should remember this technique.
4   *Dynamism.* The more dynamic, energetic, and enthusiastic sources are, the more credible they are. It follows that if people are enthusiastic others are likely to say to themselves, "Well, if she believes in it so much, it must be a good product."
5   *Expertise.*
6   *Physical attractiveness.* Of course, beauty is always in the eye of the beholder, but communications research has clearly shown that people generally perceive a source of information to be more credible if the source is physically attractive, according the beholder's standards of beauty. This fact probably explains why we rarely see ugly people delivering the news on television and why network television anchors and reporters are often chosen first for their good looks and cute personalities and second for their journalistic expertise. Salespeople can enhance their physical attractiveness by good grooming. How many customers have scruffy beards, goatees, green hair, dreadlocks, visible tattoos, or body piercing and how many don't? Think about it and go with the numbers.
7   *Similarity.* Recall Golden Rule of Selling #2 that "people like and trust people exactly like themselves"? People are simply more comfortable with people like themselves in age, gender, race, cultural background, and tastes and interests.

How do you use the seven characteristics of source credibility to enhance your ability to build a relationship and reach mutual understanding? As mentioned earlier, these characteristics are multidimensional and they work together in an intricate and complicated way. Some characteristics might be more important to some people than others are. You must observe and listen to the prospect or person with whom you want a relationship, understand what characteristics are important to them, and then emphasize your strengths in those areas.

For example, if you are a young female salesperson, you might not have similarity between you and an older male customer from a different cultural background. In this situation, you would emphasize your *competence* in how you present your case; your *expertise* in the medium you are selling; your *dynamism/enthusiasm* for your product and how it can solve the customer's problems. Finally, you would demonstrate your *objectivity* by using a two-sided argument and presenting some drawbacks of your medium first before presenting its many strengths. These positive attributes can go a very long way toward overcoming your lack of similarity.

Message

The second element in the communication process is the *message*. After establishing your source credibility, you want to work on the strength of your message. Because it is critical that customers comprehend the information you are communicating, what you communicate should be kept relatively simple and easy to understand. *Repetition* is a key factor in the strength of information and its comprehension; during a conversation or presentation, you must find ways to repeat your important points. For example, regularly summarizing the three major points you are trying to make in a conversation or in either written or oral presentations is an excellent way to repeat your points and make them more memorable. The notion of repeating *three* points is an important one. Just as repetition is effective in advertising, it is also effective in conversations and presentations.

Ordering effects can have an impact on your message's comprehension and make it more memorable. There are two ordering effects: *primacy and recency*. People tend to remember best those elements they see or hear first (primacy) in a conversation, television newscast, or sales presentation and what they see or hear last (recency). Recency effects are especially important when people have to consider carefully and weigh all information in a sequence. Thus, arrange your material with your most important points first and repeat them at the end of a presentation in a concise summary.

Channel

Channel effects are the third element in the communication process. The most effective channel of communication for simple messages is face to face, the second most effective is sight-plus-sound (such as film, television, or videotape), the third is sound only (for instance, radio, audiotape, or telephone), and the last is sight only (newspapers, magazines, and all printed materials). However, exactly the reverse is true when dealing with complex messages and material. Thus, complex presentations that contain a large number of facts, statistics, and complicated logical arguments have a much better chance of being comprehended and remembered when they are in writing. The lesson here is that simple messages and presentations that tend to appeal to the emotions are best remembered when presented on video. Complex sales presentations are best remembered when they are in writing, as a PowerPoint presentation or comb-bound booklet or both, supplemented by a face-to-face discussion that engages people emotionally and that reinforces the major points of your sales presentations. Always keep in mind the KISS rule – keep it short and simple – and eliminate extraneous points and material from your presentation.

Receiver

There are two characteristics of a *receiver* in the communication process that are important – intelligence and self-confidence. People who are not very intelligent and suffer from low self-confidence tend to be slower in comprehending the benefits and advantages of your product, but, on the other hand, they have a greater tendency to accept and to yield to your attempts to persuade them. If you have intelligent and self-confident customers, they are likely to understand the material you present, but will require from you a good deal of source credibility, objectivity, expertise, strong evidence, and message strength to get them to accept your proposal. Remember, that while intelligent people might comprehend your points better and faster, they will also come up with a greater number of hard-to-answer counterarguments and objections. Know your customers' needs so you can position your presentations effectively.

Listening

Listening is the single most important sales skill, as it is the foundation on which relationships are based and is the road to mutual understanding. Listening is the basis for Golden Rule #3, "people don't care how much you know until they know how much you care," which requires that you not only listen but also observe. You are listening to gain understanding of what is being communicated verbally, but we know that non-verbal communication and body language contain a great deal of the meaning of any message. This is why observing is included in listening – you listen for verbal clues and messages and you observe non-verbal messages and body language.

Inevitably, the most effective and successful salespeople are those who have mastered the skills of good listening and observing. Unfortunately, as much as I and other sales trainers and authors such as Larry Wilson, Huthwaite & Company (the firm that teaches SPIN Selling) write and teach about the primacy of listening in the sales process, and as many times as I have done sales training seminars over the years, I still see too many salespeople nod their heads when they hear about the importance of effective listening and then go right on talking too much, trying to sell as prospects desperately try to get a word in edgewise. Perhaps this unfortunate situation comes about because people who like to talk a lot are attracted to selling and are unable or unwilling to change their behavior.

In over 50 years of being a salesperson and managing and training salespeople, the most successful salespeople I have known have been world-class listeners and live by the adage: "Nature has given us one tongue, but two ears so that we hear from others twice as much as we speak." In Exhibit 7.2 you will see what world-class listeners do and what they do not do.

Exhibit 7.2 The Dos and Don'ts of world-class listeners

What world-class listeners do

They adopt the proper attitude. They are optimistic; they tell themselves that they are going to like the person they're calling on and that they are going to have a positive outcome. They are positive, confident, friendly, open, and intensely curious.

They shut up and listen.

They are conscious of their body language. World-class listeners are conscious of their posture and how they sit when they listen to someone. They try to make sure their body language indicates they are fascinated and eager to learn more – often leaning forward.

They respect the other person's point of view. World-class listeners are able to put themselves in another person's shoes. They see both sides and respect others' views; they don't denigrate or belittle others' views.

They listen and look for emotional cues. World-class listeners observe how someone says something and look for clues that reveal underlying feelings. People often say things that try to cover up how they are really feeling. World-class listeners listen and observe carefully and with empathy and understanding for how the person is feeling. World-class listeners look for nonverbal clues as to how other people feel and what they really mean to say. World-class listeners listen for *how* people say something, not so much *what* they say.

They listen for and look for buying cues. They watch very carefully for any little sign or movement that indicates another person has made a decision to agree with them or to buy – a slight leaning forward, a tiny nod of the head, a sudden tension that signals an intent to buy and a desire to begin negotiating.

They match speech, listening patterns, and movements to the speaker. World-class listeners let the other person set the pace. They talk and listen at the other person's pace, not theirs. They do the adapting by speeding up or slowing down to match; they don't make other people adjust to them. This type of listening is referred to academically as synchronic listening or listening in synchrony, and it merely means being "in synch" with someone

Exhibit 7.2   The Dos and Don'ts of world-class listeners (cont'd)

else (not the singing group). By being in synch, world-class listeners show respect for the other person, for their style and even cultural differences.

They are patient. They know that if they listen patiently and courteously to everything others have to say, without interrupting, others will reciprocate and give them a courteous hearing.

They pause often. World-class listeners pause after someone says something to make sure the other person is finished. Like any good interviewer, they know that a pause often prompts others to talk more – often revealing more than they intend to.

They listen actively (see Exhibit 7.3 for details).

They ask how they can help. Once they have gathered information, they don't start selling immediately; world-class listeners ask how they can be of help.

They summarize well. Periodically through a discussion, they pause and summarize the points of agreement. Brief summaries not only make points memorable through repetition, but they also focus the discussion and get it back on track if it has wandered.

They listen with authenticity. World-class listeners are authentic; they don't try to emulate someone else, they are themselves. Others can tell when someone is insincere. Being insincere is manipulative and does not build trust.

What world-class listeners don't do

They don't listen judgmentally (see Exhibit 7.3 for details).

They don't interrupt and step on sentences. The biggest giveaway of poor listeners is that they constantly step on other people's sentences – interrupt or finish a statement for others. They cannot wait to be heard. These people spend their time during a conversation thinking of what *they* want to say and are more concerned with their need to express themselves than with listening. Poor listeners don't let the other person finish what they are saying, especially if the other person talks slowly. World-class listeners don't make these errors.

They don't think of a rebuttal. Allied to stepping on sentences is thinking of what the next comment or rebuttal is going to be while someone is talking. We often have a tendency to do this while we are listening to a speech or lecture to which we cannot respond; we engage ourselves mentally in the game of forming a reply to a particular point. This is a nonproductive game to play. World-class listeners pay full attention to the speaker and concentrate on listening carefully to every word without thinking of their comeback or rebuttal.

They don't respond too soon. World-class listeners let others finish a discussion and make as many points, as many objections, as they feel inclined to do. They let people get all the negatives out on the table before responding. By responding too soon, they know they look defensive and may even be interrupting.

They don't react emotionally. We learned about the importance of self-management in Chapter 6. World-class listeners understand that an excellent place to practice self-control is while they are listening. In Chapter 10 we will go into more detail about negotiating and how sometimes manipulative negotiators will purposely try to get people angry so emotions will kick in and they will make a bad – emotional – decision. World-class

Exhibit 7.2 The Dos and Don'ts of world-class listeners (cont'd)

listeners know the best way to counteract an attempt to make them angry or to get a rise out of them is to stay calm and never react emotionally – that is the way they turn the tables on others who try to manipulate them.

They don't become distracted. Too often people do not concentrate on looking at the person who is talking; they allow their attention to be diverted to other things. They doodle, look out the window, glance at some attractive person in the next office, or conduct other discourteous and disconcerting behavior. Some people keep their cell phones and pagers on and, worse, answer them, which gives the speaker the silent message that they are not interested in the speaker. World-class leaders focus intently on speakers, look them in the eye, and turn off their cell phones and pagers.

They don't respond to negatives. World-class listeners know better than to respond too quickly to negative statements because they understand it makes them look defensive and that they might give some credence to the negatives. They ignore negatives and reinforce positive statements or compliments.

They don't ask leading questions. They don't try to use manipulative questioning and selling techniques or try to trick people into saying things they don't intend to say.

They don't take notes. In 45 years of selling and watching Hall of Fame media salespeople sell, I've rarely seen any of them take notes. They prefer to focus intently on the other person and do their best to build empathy and rapport, which note-taking makes difficult. Taking notes is a distraction from rapport-building. Of course, the Hall of Famers were all very bright and had memories good enough to remember what was said in a conversation. These great salespeople typically made detailed notes on important calls after a call was over. Times when note-taking is a good idea is during the discovery process when you are learning a great many facts – more than can be remembered – and during complicated negotiations over schedules, prices, and contract conditions. By the time negotiating starts, though, you should have built sufficient rapport and know your customer well enough be able to take notes. The rule on taking notes is: Don't take notes unless you have to in order to remember complicated factual details and, even then, keep them as brief as possible.

An article in *Fortune* magazine, "America's Best Salesmen," describes the sales technique of securities salesperson Richard F. Greene when having a meeting with a prospect:

Greene is an instinctive expert on human psychology, the article states.

"If you talk, you'll like me," he explains. "If I talk, I'll like you – but if I do the talking, my business will not be served. Now this fellow is the same as everyone else. His wife doesn't listen to him – and he doesn't listen to her. When he goes to parties, the person he's talking to is looking over his shoulder to see what else is going on in the room. Then all of a sudden he goes to breakfast with me. He starts to answer a question. *And he doesn't get interrupted.*" Before the eggs have cooled, Greene has won another client.[1]

Another type of communication is *nonverbal communication*. Research has shown that as much as 65 percent of communications between people can be nonverbal. In other words, *how* people say something is often more important than *what* they say. Part of the process of listening entails being sensitive to all the nonverbal, often unconscious, hints people give you about how they feel about you and your medium or product. People's posture and body movement, their facial expressions, their eye contact and movement, their tone of voice and pitch, and their pace of talking usually tell more about how they feel than the content of their messages do. Salespeople must develop skills not only in picking up nonverbal messages but also in using nonverbal communication to give messages.

When selling, look for the attributes and postures described below that might indicate how the other person is receiving your message. Keep in mind that these attributes and postures do not give universal messages that have the same meaning for everyone. Body language, tone of voice, gestures, and facial expressions are unique to each person and communicate consistent meaning only for them. As you get to know your prospects better, you will learn to understand their nonverbal language as well as you understand their words.

Use gestures, space, enthusiasm, openness, and other body language to help you emphasize your sales points and to show customers that you care about them and are interested in them, but make sure your gestures are in synch with the person with whom you are talking. Of course, you can overdo the use of gestures. You can become too excited and animated with a shy, inhibited, quiet prospect, for instance. One particular gesture to avoid is finger pointing. This gesture implies "I'm telling you what to do" or "Shame on you" or other authoritarian messages that impede open communication.

Feedback　To be an effective listener, you have to close the feedback loop in the communication process. You must listen actively and give *responsive feedback*. You must give both verbal and nonverbal feedback, including gestures and expressions, and communicate the appropriate enthusiasm as you actively encourage people to open up. The most important single thing you can do in giving responsive feedback is to *smile*. A smile says, "I like you; I care about you; I'm interested in what you're saying; I'm glad I'm here with you; I approve of you." Nodding your head in agreement is another effective feedback mechanism. Use it often.

Techniques for Effective Listening

All knowledge, all learning about a customer begin with a question such as, "How's business?" or "How can I help you?", "What are your marketing goals?" or "How about those Raiders?" Therefore, all effective listening techniques begin with a question. These techniques work in a business or a personal conversation,

---

Exhibit 7.3 Techniques for active, non-judgmental listening

---

1 *Ask a question.*
2 *Listen to the answer carefully, actively.* For example, wave your hand toward yourself, which gives the message, "tell me more." Notice what gestures the people you are listening to use. Are they very expressive and do they motion with their hands a lot? Use their gestures. Are they calm and analytical? Do they lean back and ponder things with their fingers intertwined and their chins resting on their folded hands. Get in synch with them.
3 *Respond non-judgmentally.* Non-judgmental listening is non-defensive listening. Don't argue or defend your point view. Nod, smile, and encourage them to continue talking.
   - *Develop a non-threatening, non-confrontational approach.* You want people to feel *secure* in opening up, revealing personal information.
   - *Offer personal information first.* People will reciprocate by giving you personal information.
   - *Find something you have in common.* Similar interests such as kids, sports, or pets, for example.
   - *Similar interests create common bonds.* Common bonds create openness, honesty, and trust.
   - *Vary your responses.* Otherwise your responses become monotonous and recognizable as technique and not authentic.

---

but it is a good idea to practice them often at the beginning in personal situations, with family and friends, and become comfortable and adept at these listening techniques before attempting them with customers. Here are guidelines and exercises that will help you become a world-class effective, non-judgmental listener.

Use all of the techniques for effective listening to achieve the goal of becoming a *trusted advisor* to your clients. Keep the concept of being a trusted advisor in the back of your mind as you progress through conversations with customers and always return to the question, "Am I behaving and listening in a manner that my customer believes I am a trusted advisor and am not merely trying to sell something?"

Exhibit 7.5 provides you with an effective listening exercise that you should practice as often as you can until you become comfortable with variations on the feel–felt–found technique and are an expert in becoming a trusted advisor. You can download all of the exhibits in this chapter, which appear in one file titled "Effective Listening" from www.mediaselling.us. By downloading these exhibits, you can have them all in one packet to make them easier to study and review. I know of many salespeople who put these files on their PDAs so they can review them before making important calls.

Exhibit 7.4   Barriers to active, non-judgmental listening: Nine "Nevers"

1   *Never ask "why?"* "Why?" questions are challenging to someone. When you ask "Why?" you sound like you doubt what they are saying or are testing them. "Why?" questions send bad emotional vibes.

2   *Never ask leading questions.* Leading questions like "Have you stopped beating your wife?" or "Are you still paying those outrageously high newspaper rates?" are challenging and produce frustration and anger.

3   *Never minimize a problem.* This response seems natural, as though you are trying to help someone feel better, that things are not as bad as they seem. However, you are being judgmental and making an assumption than you know more than the person complaining does. Furthermore, you are there to help solve their problems, and the bigger the problems are, the more you can help, so don't minimize problems. Finally, some people love to complain, so do them a favor and let them – "feel their pain."

4   *Never cheer up or reassure.* These responses make you seem happier or more knowledgeable than the person who is speaking. It may be counterintuitive, but telling someone to cheer up may be unrealistic. It's better to share their misery; develop empathy and demonstrate your supportive feelings.

5   *Never advise or teach.* These responses make you seem superior and makes the other person feel inferior. You may come across as arrogant. You want to be "a trusted friend," not a teacher.

6   *Never criticize or moralize.* These responses are highly judgmental and frustrate and anger other people.

7   *Never argue or defend.* These responses are completely counterproductive and move a conversation backward, not forward. The moment you become defensive, you lose control of the agenda of a conversation and lose rapport and credibility – you are seen as not being objective (and you aren't).

8   *Never be aggressive.* Aggressive responses make you appear competitive instead of cooperative and look as though you are trying to get what you want instead of what the other person wants.

9   *Never respond with "you" statements.* "You" responses are those that begin with "you," such as "you shouldn't be paying those high rates on other stations." "You" statements appear to be accusatory or seem to be telling other people what they "should" do. Never, never use the word "should" in a response, it is completely judgmental.

Source: Many of the "Never" responses are based on suggestions in Carl D. Zaiss and Thomas Gordon. 1993. *Sales Effectiveness Training*. New York. Dutton.

Exhibit 7.5	Effective listening exercise

1   *Listen carefully, actively to the objections, questions, or statements of your customers.*
2   *Repeat or rephrase their objection.*
    "Let me make sure I understand your position . . . you feel our rates are too high?"
    Put the burden of understanding on yourself. By repeating or rephrasing an
    objection, you let your customers know that you are listening and that you heard
    what they were saying – they like that.
3   *Get their agreement that you understand.*
    "*Is that correct?*" This is a powerful step in the process you are getting their
    agreement that you understand their objection and that you are on their side. You
    are encouraging them to say "yes," a habit you want them to get into. If they say,
    "no" then you must follow up and clarify their objection, and keep doing so until
    you get it right and they agree that you understand.
4   *Respond with a form of an "I understand" statement (vary your responses).*
    "I understand how you feel; other advertisers have felt the same way, but they have
    found that our rates are based on market demand and the size of our audience.
    We have the largest audience in town and the largest number of advertisers of any
    station in the area, and those advertisers are paying our rates and getting great
    results." The feel–felt–found responses are incredibly powerful: with the "feel"
    response you are acknowledging your customer's feeling and respecting them; the
    "felt" response reinforces and legitimizes their objections so they don't feel silly, out
    of line, or alone; the "found" response gives you the opportunity to mention the
    benefits and advantages of what you are offering in the context of the success
    enjoyed by other advertisers – comforting knowledge for a prospective advertiser.

Understanding People

If you are an effective, world-class listener, that is great, but what are you listening
for? Are you listening to find out what makes people tick and to understand them
as human beings, or are you listening to them as targets in a business game?
In order to understand people we must know what makes people behave as
they do.

The personality-type approach

One way we can try to understand people is with a personality-type approach.
There are several well-known personality-type descriptive methods; probably the
most recognized is the Myers-Briggs Type Indicator (MBTI) which divides people
into four classifications and then into two preferences within each classification.
The classifications are:

1   How people direct their energy: Extroversion (E) or Introversion (I)
2   How people prefer to process information: Sensing (S) or Intuition (N)
3   How people prefer to make decisions: Thinking (T) or Feeling (F)
4   How people prefer to organize their life: Judgment (J) Perception (P).[2]

Myers-Briggs personality types are then defined by a combination of these four preferences, such as an ISTP (perhaps a journalist) or an ENTJ (perhaps a business executive).

Perhaps the personality-type approach most widely used in business today is the Persogenics-style approach, which was developed in the 1960s by Dr Ford Cheney. The current management of Persogenics claims that their personality profiling method produces more accurate results than Myers-Briggs tests do. Persogenics trains people to identify their own style (by taking a self-administered test) and to identify the style of others using detailed descriptions of the behavior of four types of people. The four types of styles Persogenics identifies are:[3]

1   The Dominant – assertive, outspoken, controlling, task-oriented, driving for results.
2   The Expressive – assertive, highly responsive, forceful, demonstrative, people-oriented.
3   The Analytical – not assertive, less responsive, task-oriented, disciplined, more interested in information than people.
4   The Amiable – not assertive, not forceful, people- and team-oriented, peacemakers.

Persogenics suggests that if you follow their program, you can adjust your behavior to match customers' styles. Persogenics suggests that people have a primary and secondary style. Therefore, you might be Expressive/Dominant and a customer you are meeting with might be Dominant/Analytical. With this customer, you would tone down your Expressive enthusiasm and focus quietly on a logical, fact-laden presentation with lots of data for the customer to analyze. Persogenics is a good enough system for helping salespeople communicate and build rapport with customers because it builds on the similarity principle. But like any commercial service or system, it requires time, professional training, test taking, and money. The tests and training are not inexpensive, especially for one person.

How can we identify someone's personality type or style without having them take a test or you going through potentially expensive training? And are personality-type and personal style descriptions the best way to understand people?

While personality type and personal style descriptions are interesting and often fun to talk about, they are a relatively simplistic description of the way people behave. In fact, they almost sound like stereotypes, and depending on stereotypes to gain deeper understanding of people can be shallow and foolish. Also, describing how people behave does not give us much insight into why they behave that way, or what their needs and motivations are.

The needs–motivation approach

Why do people behave as they do? What are the underlying reasons for their actions? What drives their personality or style? Psychologists, psychiatrists, and other scientists try to answer these questions in order to understand, predict, and help people change their behavior. Likewise, salespeople must try to understand and predict customers' behavior.

Behavior is the outcome of a process that begins with needs, which impel motives, which lead to behavior. Behavior is the only portion of this process that is observable. We cannot see people's motives or the underlying needs that lead to motives, but we can observe their behavior and try to infer why they act as they do. Needs are not only unobservable but they are also usually unconscious. Even though people act to satisfy their needs, they may not be consciously aware of these needs. Exhibit 7.6 shows the needs–motivation–behavior process.

People have multiple needs that are swirling around in their unconscious psyche trying to get recognized and be satisfied. Some of the stronger needs push and impel, or motivate, behavior. Needs are a vague, indefinable itch in the psyche, motives are the semiconscious desire or semiautomatic reaction to scratch, and behavior is the physical act of scratching. Because we can only see them scratching, we infer people have an itch (whereas it might just be a nervous habit). Needs can be uncovered but they cannot be created. People either have a need (itch) or they do not; salespeople cannot create needs because those needs have been formulated early in prospects' personality development.

It is much more difficult to make a list of motivations, or motives, than to create a list of needs because motives tend to be impelled by the force of a cluster of complex needs that are unique to every person and to every situation. Some people have a small cluster of needs that drive their behavior; other people have multiple needs that interact in a complex way. After we look at the different needs that people have, we will examine more about motivation later in this chapter.

Exhibit 7.6   The needs–motivation–behavior process

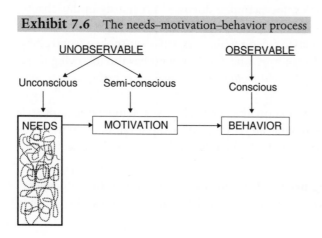

Human needs

Psychological research has shown that people are so enormously complex that it is virtually impossible to generalize about any need's hierarchy that fits all people. After the basic existence needs (physiological needs and safety and security needs) are satisfied, one person may feel a strong need for self-fulfillment, another person may feel a strong need for achievement and recognition, and yet another person may sense a huge urge for social acceptance. People tend to take care of the basic, lower-order needs first.

Salespeople must understand that people do not have simple motivations or needs and that understanding people requires a complex analysis of their unique, individual combination of needs.

Henry Murray developed a needs theory in the 1930s and 1940s that he called the "Manifest Needs Theory," which has been used subsequently as a starting point for many researchers, sales trainers, and authors. Murray thought that people should be classified according to the strengths of various needs and believed people possessed a number of divergent and conflicting needs.

Murray believed that needs are learned, not inherited, and are activated by cues from the external environment (a sales discussion, for example). He did not arrange his list of needs in a hierarchical fashion, but his longer list of specific human needs is useful in describing people and in helping us understand them.

List of human needs   Below is a list of human needs I have adapted from a list of Murray's needs and combined with a list of Murray's needs adapted by theorist Douglas N. Jackson, and combined with a list by Joseph Thompson. I have added a few needs to those of Murray, Jackson, and Thompson based on my experience.[4] As you read the list of needs, try to visualize a person you know who you think displays behavior that might be driven by one or more of the needs.

Using the needs–motivation approach   The personality types (ENTJs, for example) and styles (Amiables, for example) discussed previously in this chapter are attempts to describe or paint a word portrait of a person's cluster of needs. For instance, the Dominant style person who is assertive, outspoken, controlling, task-oriented, and results-driven might be a person who has the following needs from the list in Exhibit 7.7: achievement, aggression, control, dominance, endurance, and order.

So, while you do not need to know the personality type, temperament, or style of people to understand them, you can create your own portrait of them using the 26 colors in your palette (needs in the Human Needs list) by careful observation.

Guidelines for identifying needs   Current research has found that, in general, needs tend to be stable over time. As needs swirl around in the psyche, pushing

Exhibit 7.7 Human needs

Need	Brief description
Achievement	Need to overcome obstacles and challenges. To aspire to accomplish difficult tasks; to maintain high standards. To work hard to achieve goals. To respond positively to competition. To put forth extra effort to achieve and maintain excellence.
Affiliation	Need to form friendships and associations. To enjoy being with friends and people in general, and to accept people readily. To cooperate. To enjoy joining and being with groups.
Aggression	Need to belittle, harm, blame, ridicule, or accuse another. To start arguments. To be willing to hurt others to get one's way. To have a tendency to "get even." To be overly competitive. To be sadistic.
Autonomy	Need to resist influence or coercion. To break away from restraint, confinement, or restrictions of any kind. To enjoy being free, unattached, and not tied to people, places, or obligations. To resist authority. To seek independence.
Competition	Need to be involved in competitive activities. To win. To beat someone else. To do anything to win.
Conservativeness	Need to hold on to what one has. To refrain from losing what has been gained. To avoid change because it is change. To stick with tradition and past values, beliefs, opinions, and practices.
Contrariness	Need to act differently from others. To hold unconventional views. To be contrary. To take an opposite stand from others merely for the sake of being different. To argue just for the sake of arguing.
Control	Need to have control over as many things as possible that affect one's life. To avoid delegating responsibility or tasks to others. To keep work, information, and decision making under one's control. To control all possible variables in an attempt to make life predictable and free of surprises.
Cooperation	Need to cooperate. To be a team player. To help others. To be fair. To seek win–win agreements. To build consensus.
Creativeness	Need to seek and enjoy aesthetic impressions and experiences. To be artistic and imaginative. To enjoy the creative process and building or designing things. To enjoy participating in and experiencing music, dance, theater, or art. To enjoy problem solving.
Defensiveness	Need to defend oneself against any blame or real or imagined belittlement. To justify one's actions. To offer excuses and explanations. To resist probing. To interpret other people's comments, no matter how innocent, in the most personal, negative way possible.
Deference	Need to admire and willingly follow a superior or another person. To cooperate with a leader. To serve gladly. To defer to others in most things.

Exhibit 7.7 Human needs (cont'd)

Need	Brief description
Dominance	Need to seek power. To attempt to influence and control others. To persuade, prohibit, or dictate. To lead or direct. To express opinions forcefully. To try to organize and lead groups. To be political and gain power through political means.
Endurance	Need to work long hours. Not to give up easily on problems, even in the face of great difficulty. To be patient and unrelenting in one's work habits.
Entrepreneurism	Need to start something new. To build from the ground up. To take big risks in order to win big.
Exhibitionism	Need to attract attention to one's self. To excite, amuse, shock, or thrill others. To be dramatic or funny.
Impulsiveness	Need to act on the spur of the moment and without deliberation. To make decisions too quickly. To give vent readily to feelings and desires. To speak freely – may be volatile in expressing emotions.
Insecurity	Need to be emotionally insecure. To have low self-esteem. To seek aid, protection, or sympathy. To constantly seek advice, affection, attention, and reassurance. To be dependent and to feel insecure or helpless. To confide difficulties and insecurities to a receptive person.
Novelty	Need to seek new experiences. To change for the sake of change. To seek variety and excitement. To prefer things because they are new and/or different.
Nurturance	Need to nourish, aid, or protect someone else. To give sympathy and comfort. To assist whenever possible. To give a helping hand readily and to perform favors for others.
Order	Need to arrange, organize, and put away objects. To be tidy and clean. To be scrupulously precise and orderly. To be interested in developing methods to keep materials and effects methodically organized.
Play	Need to relax, to amuse oneself. To seek diversion and entertainment. To have fun and play games. To laugh and joke.
Recognition	Need to receive praise and commendation. To receive attention and to gain approval. To crave appreciation. To earn praise. To seek and display symbols of status.
Risk-avoidance	Need to avoid failure, shame, or any possibility of loss. To take precautionary measures. To cover up anything that looks like a failure and often to have an unreasonable, obsessive fear of failure.
Risk-taking	Need to enjoy taking risks for the hope of big rewards. To gamble on long-shot odds with large payoffs. To court danger, live near the edge. To be a daredevil.
Understanding	Need to analyze and understand many areas of knowledge. To be intellectually curious. To be fascinated with ideas. To desire to have all the facts and gain as much knowledge on a subject as possible.

out into consciousness in an attempt to get satisfied, over time the same cluster of needs tend to appear in people. But the rank order of this cluster of needs changes continually. For example, achievement might be someone's primary need one day, but if the person wins a marathon race the next day, that need bubbles down and recognition may bubble up to the top.

Keeping the above concepts in mind, here are some guidelines for identifying needs:

1   *Don't try to be a psychiatrist.* Your function is to recognize customers' needs and adjust your behavior accordingly. Your job is not to try to change people or tell them what they should do. For instance, if a customer has a high need for dominance and aggression and terrifies employees, it would not be a good idea to tell the customer that this behavior is destructive.
2   *Deal in the present.* The only thing you can be certain about is that peoples' needs swirl around and change in priority. What their primary needs were one week ago may not be the same the next week. Deal with the moment during which you are having a discussion and make adjustments accordingly. Always remain flexible.
3   *Recognize situational influences.* When a customer responds unfavorably to you, it may have nothing to do with you or your presentation but with other external, situational influences. You may be the fifth salesperson the customer has seen that morning, and the customer may be thoroughly frustrated, confused, and bored; or you may be making your presentation during a busy season in which the customer is constantly being interrupted by calls and questions. The customer may be reacting to the frustration and confusion of the situation and not to you. Take these situational influences into consideration when you try to identify needs.[5]

With practice, careful observation, and concentrated listening, salespeople can learn to infer their customer's needs. With careful observation, salespeople can recognize the few dominant needs that seem to motivate their customers' actions. Make a copy of the list of human needs in Exhibit 7.7 and put it in a handy place where you can refer to it easily – download it to your personal digital assistant (PDA). After making a call, review the human needs list, create a needs-based portrait (more about this later in this chapter), and put the portrait in your account file. Chapter 24 will cover account files and sales organization systems. As you get to know your customers better, you can review your account file and your needs-based portrait to verify your observations. If you have perceived your customer's needs correctly, you have gained a powerful tool to position yourself and your product to have a competitive advantage.

For example, when calling on a customer, scrutinize the customer's office. Is it filled with pictures of them being chummy with famous and powerful people (such as the car dealer shaking hands with a baseball star or the state governor)? This customer has a need for recognition. Position your product so that it appeals to this recognition need: "You and your dealership will both become well known and credible if you do your own commercials," for example.

Does a customer keep you waiting for 20 minutes for a scheduled appointment and then interrupt your discussion by taking phone calls? This customer has a need for dominance. Show respect for and defer to this customer but do not back down easily or seem to be weak. People who have a need for dominance and power over others do not like wimpy people. Position your product according to the customer's desire to beat the competition, to achieve success, to accomplish marketing and advertising goals.

Does a customer ask intelligent, probing questions and want to learn as much as possible about your business? This customer has a need for understanding. Position yourself, your medium, and your product as offering solutions to advertising problems with detailed presentations containing lots of facts and figures.

Is the customer's desk bare: no reports, no folders, or no piles of papers? This customer has a need for order. Position yourself as a tidy, orderly salesperson who takes care of all the little details involved with getting an advertising campaign up and running.

Does a customer talk about goals and challenges? Does the customer use sports analogies or talk in terms of winning or attaining excellence? This customer has a need for achievement. Position your medium and your product as a means for the customer to win, to beat the competition, to achieve success, to accomplish marketing and advertising goals.

A needs-based portrait   Now that we have identified 26 colors/needs, we can now create a needs-based portrait of someone using a mixture of five, six, or seven colors. The chances are pretty good that if we tried to name our portrait, we would come up with a name something like "The Achiever," "The Expressive," or "The Idealist" – types used by other descriptive systems. Each portrait will be as unique as each person is and much more complex and informative than just the title. But what about motivation?

If you identify a cluster of five, six, or seven needs that seem to drive a person's behavior, then you have enough information to help you position your medium and your product to align with those needs and you do not have to worry about motivation. It does not matter why someone does something (greed, pride, lust, love, or revenge, for example), what matters is that you have identified several needs that drive that motivation.

Some people will have a relatively small number of primary needs that drive their behavior, others might have multiple needs. Also, people often have a different cluster of needs and motivation in business than in they do in non-business situations. It is important to get to know your customers well enough so that you can paint two needs-based portraits of them because it can be extremely helpful in maintaining relationships.

For example, some people might have needs primarily for achievement, control, and dominance, and those needs drive their behavior. In business situations they might be competitive and stingy. In a non-business, family environment, they might be cooperative, nurturing, and generous. Some people might have needs for achievement, affiliation, cooperation, creativeness, exhibition, recognition, play, and understanding. In business situations they might be friendly, somewhat disorganized team players who crave being well liked. In a non-business environment they might take acting or painting classes for their own pleasure and growth and not care what people think.

Exhibit 7.8 shows how a personal needs-based portrait of a customer might look.

Note in Exhibit 7.8 that Jane Doe's needs are not arranged in alphabetical order, they are arranged in the order of their perceived (by the salesperson) priority. When you identify needs, you are making an educated guess. You know your perception of Jane's needs are not precise and are subject to change, but your intuition tells you that she clearly is not a risk-taker and is very defensive – during the last four times you have called on her, she has consistently behaved in ways that would indicated her risk-avoidance and defensiveness. She always asks for cost-per-thousand price guarantees and wants to buy something safe. She reacts very defensively about what she has bought on other Web sites. You are pretty sure that risk-avoidance and defensiveness are the two needs that tend to be the strongest and motivate her buying behavior.

When you create a needs-based portrait of someone, try to pick out one or two needs that seem to dominate and then try to arrange the rest of the needs you identify in order of priority. This arrangement will help you when it comes to positioning your product.

Exhibit 7.8 Customer personal needs-based portrait

Customer: Jane Doe, Dewey, Cheatham, & Howe Advertising Agency

Personal needs (business situations)	*Personal needs (non-business situations)*
Risk-avoidance*	Affiliation*
Defensiveness*	Novelty
Recognition	Recognition
Control	Deference
Competition	Play
Autonomy	Nurturance
Contrariness	

* Most dominant needs

Personal needs versus business needs

The needs we have been discussing up to this point have been *personal needs*. There are two types of needs, personal needs, and *business needs*. Personal needs are primarily governed by emotions and could just as well be labeled *emotional* needs. Business needs are mainly governed by reasoned, problem-solving behavior and could just as well be labeled *rational needs*. Personal needs, as discussed earlier, include the need for recognition, achievement, or dominance. Business needs are the reasons people give for their purchases – the rational justifications.

Sterling Getchel, who was an enormously successful advertising copywriter, observed that people buy for emotional reasons and then support their purchase decision with rational reasons. He became wealthy writing advertising based on this belief. Sales trainer and author Tom Hopkins writes that "seldom do people buy logically."[6] At the other end of the heart-versus-head spectrum are those who claim that people are basically rational beings whose behavior consists of a series of attempts to solve problems to satisfy their needs. Even though both emotional and logical needs interact in varying degrees of intensity in all customers at all times, you will be substantially more successful if you assume that personal, emotional needs outweigh business, rational needs in people's decision making by two to one – go with Sterling Getchel.

Positioning your product to align with personal needs   As a salesperson, you will be expected to meet and satisfy, for the most part, customers' business needs as a minimum requirement for getting an order. The majority of media salespeople focus on and are adept at satisfying business needs. The big win, the home run, for salespeople is the ability not just to satisfy business needs, but to *position* their medium and their product to appeal to the emotional, personal needs of customers. You want to understand your customers so well that you can position your offers in such a way that your customers will buy because they like you and because your offer meets their personal needs – so they will justify making an emotional decision with logical reasons.

Remember the second core function of a salesperson from Chapter 2 is *managing relationships*. The first step in managing any relationship is getting the other person to like you; the best way to accomplish this, to a large degree, is to understand and then align with their personal needs.

Test Yourself

1   What are the three equal elements that make up the engine that drives a relationship?
2   What is the goal of a relationship?

3   What are seven characteristics that enhance source credibility?
4   Name two ordering effects and what do they mean?
5   What are the four steps in the effective listening exercise?
6   What do people rely on more to make decisions, rationality or emotions?

Project

Get together with three or four friends and each create a customer needs-based portrait of a person not in the group whom all of you know reasonably well. Then, compare the portraits you have created and discuss them. How many of you had the same dominant needs? How many had similar lists? If there were differences, what were they? Finally, after the discussion, reach consensus on a single list of six or seven needs.

References

David Maister. 2002. *The Trusted Advisor.* New York: The Free Press.

Carl D. Zaiss and Thomas Gordon. 1993. *Sales Effectiveness Training.* New York: Random House.

Notes

1   Monaci Jo Williams. 1987. *Fortune,* October 26. pp. 122–134.
2   www.teamtechnology.co.uk. Accessed January 20, 2003.
3   www.persogenics.com. Accessed January 20, 2003.
4   Henry Murray. 1938. *Explorations in Personality.* New York: Oxford University Press, used with permission; Douglas N. Jackson. 1974. *Personality Research Form Manual.* Port Huron, MI: Research Psychologists Press, used by permission of Sigma Assessment Systems, Inc.; Joseph Thompson. 1973. *Selling: A Managerial and Behavioral Science Analysis,* 2nd edition. New York: McGraw Hill.
5   Material in this section is adapted from Gary M. Grikscheit, Harold Cash, and W.J.E. Crissey. 1981. *Handbook of Selling: Psychological, Management, and Marketing Bases.* New York: John Wiley, pp 184–185, used with permission.
6   Tom Hopkins. 1980. *How to Master the Art of Selling.* Scottsdale, AZ: Champion Press, p. 46.

8

Skills: Influence and Creating Value

Charles Warner

When I made my first sales call on Parrott's Flowers, the first question Mr Parrott asked after he figured out what I was trying to sell him, was, "How much is it?" The how-much-does-it-cost question is typically the first one people ask when they are considering a purchase. If they are inexperienced buyers, they often ask the price question defensively because they do not want to go over an arbitrary price limit they have set. If they are experienced buyers, they often ask the price question because they want to react negatively in an attempt to scare the seller and keep the price as low as possible. Experienced buyers also try to convince sellers that they are selling a commodity.

A *commodity* is a product that is interchangeable with other products, widely available, and, therefore, undifferentiated – differentiated only by price. Because commodities are interchangeable with other products and are undifferentiated, meaning there are many substitutes, it is difficult to charge a higher price than other similar products charge. Because commodities are widely available and, thus, a supply surplus exists, it is even difficult to maintain price levels. Because commodities are products that are differentiated only by price, commodities are sold to the highest bid among low bids. Examples of commodities are wheat, corn, and soybeans, which are typically sold in commodity markets such as the Chicago Board of Trade.

Advertising agency media buyers and price-conscious advertisers naturally want to convince media salespeople that they are selling undifferentiated commodities and, invariably, start price negotiations as quickly as possible and with a low offer. In fact, media buyers' primary objective is to try to lower media prices; therefore, they want media salespeople to believe they are selling a commodity and to sell based exclusively on price.

The hallmarks of weak or inexperienced media salespeople are that they do not know how to position their products effectively, that they readily accede to buyer demands, and that they sell based only on price. The sales pitch of weak salespeople is "I have the lowest price," a technique that does not add value. Companies do not need salespeople who can sell based only on low prices; employers can hire hourly-wage order-takers to handle commodity-like transactions or can use an online auction service such as Google's AdWords, which disintermediates salespeople.

World-class media salespeople do not sell their product as a commodity or on online auctions, and they do not lower their rates except in extreme circumstances. One of the main reason world-class salespeople do not discount their rates is because lower prices affect their income – less revenue equals lower commissions or bonuses. Instead, they position themselves and their products persuasively and they create value before they mention or discuss price.

In this chapter, you will learn more about some persuasive techniques that can influence people, discover why creating value is important, and learn how to create value for your medium, for your company, and for yourself.

The Psychology of Influence

In 1984 Robert Cialdini wrote an extremely influential book, *Influence: The Psychology of Persuasion*. In 2001 he published the fourth edition of the book, re-titled, *Influence: Science and Practice*. Perhaps he dropped the word persuasion from the title because it has a negative, manipulative connotation.

The concept of persuasion somehow indicates that people are persuaded to do something they would rather not do or that is against their better judgment. This book advocates non-manipulative selling; therefore, the concept of persuasion is dealt with gingerly to emphasize ethical persuasion in order to be consistent with the book's approach to selling. I will advocate that any attempt at persuasion should be viewed as *influence*, suggesting that people are being tilted or swayed to consciously, willingly do something, which is more suitable for the relationship-based, solution-selling approach advocated in this book.

Cialdini studied compliance practitioners and professionals such as salespeople, fund-raisers, and advertisers. He studied compliance using participant observation and gained experience in organizations that practiced persuasion techniques, such as organizations selling encyclopedias, vacuum cleaners, portrait photography, and dance lessons – some of the worst examples of manipulative persuasion techniques. Over a three-year period, Cialdini observed thousands of different tactics that compliance practitioners employed to produce a yes, and he found the majority fell into six basic categories. "Each of these categories is governed by a fundamental psychological principle that directs human behavior, and in so doing, gives the tactics their power."[1]

| **Exhibit 8.1** Principles of influence |

1   Automatic responses
2   Reciprocation
3   Commitment and consistency
4   Social proof
5   Scarcity
6   Liking and authority

Source: Robert B. Cialdini. 2001. *Influence: Science and Practice.* Boston: Allyn and Bacon.

I have modified Cialdini's list of six principles by combing two, liking and authority, and have added one, which I call automatic responses, which was not on Cialdini's original list. I believe this modified list makes it easier to understand, to remember, and to use.

Exhibit 8.1 shows a modified list of the six principles of influence.

Let's now look at each of the six principles of influence separately. While you are reading the descriptions, think of ways that you might use them to honestly and ethically influence people.

Automatic responses

Being trained in psychology, Dr Cialdini begins his research by looking at animals, fish, and insects. He writes about the many animals that have instincts that cause them to act in certain fixed action patterns that involve intricate sequences of behavior, such as in mating rituals. Cialdini refers to these instinctual behaviors in animals as pre-programmed tapes and believes that humans, too, have pre-programmed tapes that can trigger unconscious, automatic responses of compliance, sometimes at the wrong times.[2] An example that Cialdini uses to support his thesis is research conducted by social psychologist Ellen Langer and her colleagues, which reinforces the "well-known principle of human behavior that says when we ask people to do us a favor we will be more successful if we provide a reason."[3]

Langer demonstrated this need for a reason by asking a small favor of people waiting in line to use a copy machine: "Excuse me, I have five pages. May I use the Xerox machine *because* I'm in a rush." Langer reports that this request plus a reason was successful 94 percent of the time, compared to the 60 percent success rate of the request "Excuse me, I have five pages. May I use the Xerox machine?" In another experiment Langer used another "because" phrase that added no new or even any logical information to a request: "Excuse me, I have five pages. May I use the Xerox machine because I have to make some copies?" The result was 93 percent compliance. There is no logical explanation for the high compliance rate;

therefore, a "because" explanation must trigger an instinctual response that, as human beings, we have been pre-conditioned to make.

There are many automatic responses or inherent assumptions that we can use to influence people. Many of these inherent assumptions are culturally based and may not be valid in all circumstances. For example, most Americans have the expensive-equals-good assumption and its opposite, an inexpensive-equals-bad assumption. As Cialdini points out, " in English, the word cheap doesn't just mean inexpensive; it has come to mean inferior, too."[4] Therefore, when we combine this expensive-equals-good inherent assumption with a material self-interest assumption that people want to get the most and pay the least for their choices, our sales tool becomes more powerful when we mix in the concept of *perceptual contrast*.

We see the use of the perceptual contrast principle daily in automotive sales, retail clothing sales, and real estate sales. An example would be the new car salesperson who tries to sell us a $22,000 car and then adds on, one at a time, options that seem to be a minor expense when contrasted to the $22,000 price of the car. But the options add up, and soon the car costs $30,000. Another example would be a real estate salesperson who shows prospective buyers three houses that are dumps and then shows them a reasonably clean house that looks spotless in comparison. In the retail clothing business, salespeople are taught to show expensive items first so that subsequent, lower priced items seem like a bargain in comparison. If customers say they are interested in several items, say a suit and some socks, salespeople are taught always to sell the most expensive item first, in this case the suit, then to show them expensive cashmere socks. Why? Because cashmere socks, when compared to regular socks, would seem expensive; but compared to what a suit costs, the socks are not perceived to be overpriced. Many prospective buyers are not perceptive enough to see the effects of the contrast principle working.

Another example Cialdini uses is one from a student. He relates that while waiting to board a flight at O'Hare airport, the student heard a gate attendant announce that the flight was overbooked. In an attempt at humor, which some airlines encourage, the gate attendant announced that anyone willing to take a later flight would be compensated with a voucher worth $10,000. Because people waiting at the gate knew it was a joke, they all laughed, but when the attendant then offered a $100 voucher, no one took it. Why? Because compared to $10,000, $100 seemed measly. No one took a $200 or $300 voucher either and the attendant had to raise the ante to $500 to get any takers. Had the attendant started with a ridiculous $5 joke offer, there probably would have been many takers for a real offer of $100 because, compared to $5, $100 would have seemed generous – a good deal.

Thus, the perception of a good deal is based on several things, including inherent assumptions and contrast. The broadcast television networks use these principles of influence effectively when they price commercials in their top-rated programs such as the Super Bowl, the price of which is usually announced in July. One reason for announcing high Super Bowl pricing in July is to make prices for commercials purchased during the television scatter market, which breaks in September, seem reasonable at $300,000 to $600,000 each.

Used appropriately, the contrast principle is a legitimate method of positioning your offers when selling media. For example, compare the price of your offers to much more expensive prices of competitive media. Or, make your first offer or proposal unreasonably high so that the second one seems reasonable, regardless of its actual value. Or, make your first offer very low and refer to it as cheap, which will imply not only a low price, but low quality, and then show that subsequent offers, each more expensive, are better, of higher quality.

Reciprocation

Noted archeologist Richard Leakey ascribes the essence of what makes us human to the principle of reciprocation. The rule of reciprocity is that *we must provide to others the kind of actions they have provided to us*. We learn reciprocity as the major motivation for cooperation, which is essential to the functioning of society. It creates a web of indebtedness that allows for the division of labor, the exchange of diverse forms of goods and services, and the interdependence that binds people together into workable units, groups, and cultures.[5] The concept of indebtedness, or *future obligation*, allows people to exchange goods without fear of loss and to build sophisticated systems of aid, gift giving, defense, and trade.

We are taught from early childhood that if someone gives us something, we have an inviolable future obligation to return the gift or favor, no matter how small, whether or not we asked for the favor. The rule of reciprocity is overpowering. "The rule possesses awesome strength, often producing a yes response to a request that, except for an existing feeling of indebtedness, would surely be refused," writes Cialdini.[6] People who do not reciprocate are held in the lowest possible esteem and are seen as welshers or moochers.

According to Cialdini, a researcher sent Christmas cards randomly to people the researcher did not know, had never met, and who were unaware of who the researcher was. The researcher got almost a universal response. Everyone felt obligated to send the researcher a Christmas card the next year. Probably the most notorious abuse of the rule of reciprocity occurs with the Hare Krishnas when they solicit donations by first giving a target person a gift of a book, a flower, or a magazine. Even if targeted passerbys are initially repulsed by the look of the Krishnas, when they have flowers given to them or pinned to their lapels, and say, "No, thank you," they are told that the gift cannot be taken back, that "It is our gift to you." That is when the overpowering rule of reciprocity kicks in and the vast majority of people feel obligated to make a reciprocal gift because refusing it would be against our nature. It is an automatic, uncontrollable response. There are two overwhelming obligations involved: to accept a gift and to reciprocate. So, of course, people take the flower and then feel obligated to make a contribution.

We can see the reciprocity rule used in a myriad of circumstances. Waiters who leave a gift of a candy mint know that it will increase tips, grocery stores that offer free samples of food know that sales will increase significantly, and marketers that give away free samples of their products know trial and future use of a product will increase.

The reciprocity rule works both ways. Not only is there an obligation to reciprocate when someone gives you a gift or does you a favor, but also there is an obligation for the gift giver to provide an opportunity for the gift receiver to repay the dept or return the favor. A socially satisfactory closure only occurs when a gift has been given and the receiver's reciprocation is accepted. "Thank you" must be followed by "You're welcome."

This rule applies to concessions also, and it is called the rule of *reciprocal concessions*. Imagine that I am heading our college class fundraising drive and I call you up, introduce myself, and then say, "How are you doing today?"

You respond by saying, "Just fine, thanks, Charlie."

"We have a huge big fundraising goal this year. Can you pledge $500 because I want our great class to win the competition for raising the most money?"

You decline by saying, "Gee, that's a lot. I just can't afford it now."

"So $500 is a little steep?"

"Yes."

"I certainly understand; a lot of our classmates are in a similar position. Could you give $10, then we stand a good chance of winning the competition for the highest percentage of participation, and could you volunteer for three hours a week to help me solicit our classmates on the phone?"

How can you not give $10 and three hours of your time, during which you will raise more than $500 using the same technique I used on you: I asked for something, you felt a little guilty but declined. I then came back with a lower ask, a concession to my original ask, to which you felt obligated to reciprocate with a concession – a small gift of money and time.

In Chapter 12, we will show you how to use reciprocation tactics to your advantage in negotiating and closing – not unfairly, of course – but to help you counteract people's tendencies of material self-interest (getting the most for the least amount) and receive a fair price for your product.

Commitment and consistency

Cialdini reports on a study of people placing bets on horses at a racetrack. They were much more confident of their horses' chances of winning after placing a bet than before. The same thing happens with voters; they believe much more strongly that their candidate will win after they vote than before they vote. The need for our beliefs to be consistent with our actions lies deep within us and directs our actions with quiet power. As Cialdini writes: "Once we make a choice or take a stand, we will encounter personal and interpersonal pressures to behave consistently with that commitment."[7]

But in order for people to be consistent, they must take a stand – have something to be consistent about. Commitment comes first. There are several techniques to get people's commitment. Telemarketers and fundraisers understand the power of commitment when they call and ask, as I did in the conversation above, "How are you doing today?" or "How are you feeling?" If you say, "Fine," or something similar, you are responding to the apparent concern about you that has been expressed and you will find it difficult to be subsequently grouchy or stingy. Other ways to intensify commitment is to *get people to say yes to small things first*, to give a small amount of money or to volunteer or both. This works even better if you can *get people to write something down*, put a check mark in a box, or sign their name to a petition. The third way to strengthen commitment is to *get people to tell someone else*. All of these techniques are powerful ways to increase commitment.

One of the best illustrations of the principles of commitment and consistency comes from research by psychologists Jonathan Freedman and Scott Fraser. They reported on the results of an experiment in which a researcher, posing as a volunteer, went door-to-door in a residential California neighborhood. They first asked people if they were in favor of driver safety, and, if so, to sign a petition. Everyone signed. Who could be against safe driving? Then the researcher asked if the homeowners would put a small sign on their lawns that read BE A SAFE DRIVER. It was such a trifling request that nearly everyone agreed to it. Two weeks later the "volunteer" returned and said that speeding on local streets had not diminished and asked if people would put up a very large, poorly lettered sign that read DRIVE CAREFULLY. The sign almost completely obstructed the view of their house from the street. Seventy-six percent of the people who had put up the small sign agreed to put up the ugly, massive sign. Even the researchers were amazed at how well the consistency principle worked. Once people committed to being involved in a safe driving campaign, they went all out.[8] This technique of getting people to agree to a small request and then to larger and larger ones is called *the foot-in-the-door technique*.

In a follow-up experiment, the researchers went to another neighborhood and asked homeowners if they supported safe driving. If the answer was yes, they showed pictures of the houses with the huge, ugly DRIVE CAREFULLY signs on the lawns, and asked homeowners if they would be willing to put the signs up. Interestingly, only 17 percent said yes, which not only demonstrates the power of the foot-in-the door technique, but also shows the importance of getting an original commitment to safe driving.[9]

The researchers then went to another neighborhood and tried a different procedure. First, they asked homeowners to sign a petition that favored "keeping California beautiful." Naturally, nearly everyone signed it because everyone believes in maintaining the quality of the environment. Two weeks later, the people who signed the "keep California beautiful" petition were asked to put the big DRIVE CAREFULLY sign on their lawn. The response of the homeowners astounded the researchers; over 50 percent of those asked said yes. Freedman and Fraser finally realized after examining the data that when people signed the beautification petition, they changed their view of themselves to public-spirited citizens who acted on their civic principles and who supported good causes.[10]

If Freedman and Fraser had first gone to homeowners and asked them if they supported safe driving, and, if they said yes, then asked them to put a huge DRIVE CAREFULLY sign, the results would have been different. The majority of the homeowners would have refused them. And, if the researchers had returned in two weeks and asked homeowners to put up a smaller 4 ft by 3 ft sign, they might have received over 75 percent compliance using this *door-in-the-face* technique.

Finally, the technique of making a public commitment is an important one to amplify commitment. For example, if you want to stop smoking, tell everyone you know that you have stopped. Cialdini writes that Chicago restaurant owner Gordon Sinclair lowered his no-show rate for reservations from 30 percent to 10 percent by simply changing "Please call us if you change your plans," to "Will you please call us if you change your plans" and then waiting for a response. When people responded with a yes, they were publicly expressing their commitment.[11] The pause was the key to this technique. Public commitments work especially well with people with high levels of pride, self-esteem, or public self-consciousness because their egos are involved.

For media salespeople these lessons are important ones to keep in mind when you make present proposals and offers. We will discuss some of these techniques in more detail in Chapters 11 and 12.

Social proof

According to Cialdini, the principle of social proof states that *people determine what is correct by finding out what other people think is correct*. The principle applies especially to the manner in which we decide what constitutes correct behavior. "We view behavior as correct in a given situation to the degree that we see others performing it."[12] Whether it is when to laugh in a movie, how to eat chicken at a dinner party, or whether to help someone lying on a sidewalk, the actions of others are what guides our behavior.

Examples of compliance practitioners using social proof are all around us – street performers who salt their empty fiddle case with a $5 bill and public radio and television stations during pledge weeks that constantly give us the names of people who contribute. This technique tells us that "everyone is doing it, so it must be the right thing to do." Evangelical speakers, such as Billy Graham, seed their audiences with ringers so they will come up and give witness and donations at the proper time. Nightclub owners will keep a long line waiting outside even when there are plenty of seats inside to increase the perception that it is a hot place. Advertisers inform people that their product is "the fastest growing" or "number one" because they do not have to convince us directly that that their product is good; they need only to tell the public that others think it is good.

Social proof has particularly strong influence under two conditions: *when we view others to be similar to ourselves* and *when people feel unfamiliar or insecure in a specific situation*. In other words, in the first instance monkey see, monkey do, but not when a monkey sees an elephant do it. And in the second instance of monkey see, monkey do, the monkey copies if the monkey is not sure what to do. Therefore, in media selling, give evidence of what other people who are similar to a customer have done, and always give evidence or social proof to people who seem insecure or lacking in confidence.

Scarcity

For media salespeople, the scarcity principle is probably the most important principle and the one they will use most often. Cialdini states the scarcity principle as: *opportunities seem more valuable to us when they are less available*. We are familiar with this principle because we see it operating in everyday life in collecting baseball cards, in scalping tickets outside a big game, in choosing wine, in the dating game. Everyone knows that when you tell people they cannot have something, that something becomes even more desirable.[13]

However, there are several interesting corollaries to the basic scarcity principle. The first one is that people are more motivated by the thought of losing something than the thought of gaining something of equal value. The threat of a potential loss looms especially large under conditions of risk and uncertainty. So, when people are faced with a great deal of risk or uncertainty about the future, they worry about loss and do not think of a possible gain.

For this reason, Cialdini suggests the limited-number tactic is particularly effective. When people are informed that there are only a *limited number* of tickets or shares of stock left to purchase and they are then urged to make a decision quickly, they invariably make an immediate decision and say yes. This tactic is so powerful that unethical salespeople often use it even when it is not true. Keeping with the spirit of this book, we urge media salespeople to use the limited number tactic only when it is true, but when it is true, use it, because it works.[14] You are doing a service to your buyers and customers to inform them that a desirable opportunity such as the Super Bowl, special Web site content, or the last episode of a hit television program has only a few slots left. If you have done your job of creating value, they will be motivated by fear of losing it.

In addition to time, *information*, particularly if it is scarce, can be valuable. Businesses know that information is their most valuable resource, and information is more valuable if it is scarce, that is, if very few have it. And having exclusive information is even more precious, more powerful, and, therefore, provides greater opportunities for misuse and corruption, as seen in the continuing insider trading scandals on Wall Street.

What kind of information can media salespeople use ethically with customers in order to influence decisions? Certainly not inside information about a competitor's advertising before it runs, as we pointed out in earlier in Chapter 3. You also cannot lie to customers and tell them that competitors are interested in something the customers are considering if it is not true. Also, do not promise customers exclusive information for their eyes only. On the other hand, it is your responsibility to tell customers if others, particularly their competitors, are considering buying the same thing. The rule is simple, always play it straight and be honest. You must be fair to everyone and make any relevant information available to everyone.

What you can share with your customers is non-exclusive and non-proprietary information that they might not be aware of, such as information about advertising trends, information in blogs and trade journals about new products, or information about new creative approaches that customers would find valuable. It takes time to dig for this kind of information, but it is worth the effort. Give it to customers, and they will appreciate it and you will take a big step toward becoming the preferred supplier.

The final corollary to the scarcity principle is that limited resources become even more valuable when other people are competing for them. Frantic bargain basement shoppers grab up merchandise when they see others competing for the same merchandise and the ardor of an indifferent lover surges with the appearance of a rival, for example. So, when competition does really exist for a scarce resource that you are selling, make sure everyone knows about the competition.

Liking and authority

The liking principle is straightforward and comes as no surprise: *we prefer to say yes to people we know and like,*[15] which is similar to the second Golden Rule of Selling: people like and trust people exactly like themselves. Dale Carnegie's book, *How to Win Friends and Influence People*, was first published in 1937 and became the best-selling self-help book of all time. Even though the book is simplistic, Carnegie's essential point was that the best way to influence people is to get them to like you. This is an effective approach if you are a likable, credible, caring person, but it does not work if you are insincere or not authentic.

Cialdini refers to the principle of authority as *directed deference*. The great power of the authority principle is that for a society to function, we must obey the rules of that society and, therefore, obey its designated authority figures and symbols. Thus, we are trained from childhood on to obey the commands and requests of legitimate authority figures: our parents, police officers, firefighters, government officials, judges, tax collectors, and presidents.

There are many symbols that communicate authority: titles, clothes, and trappings.[16] Titles are important, they communicate status, prestige, success, power, and authority. When I was a Vice President in AOL's Interactive Marketing Division in 1998, I remember the constant battles our top management had with AOL's inflexible HR department attempting to get the regional sales managers and business development salespeople titles of Vice President. The sales managers and business development salespeople used the valid argument that they called on CEOs and Senior VPs of Marketing and Advertising and that these high-level people wanted to deal only with correspondingly high-level executives, not merely salespeople. Although HR held firm for several years, the regional managers and business development salespeople had a simple solution; they called themselves Vice Presidents on their calling cards. It worked and it became easier to get appointments with top executives. Unfortunately, what this title-consciousness leads to is title inflation and eventually everyone is a Senior Vice President calling on Senior Vice Presidents. But title inflation is rooted in the basic principle that people do tend to defer to authority.

Clothes are another symbol of authority, status, and power. Clothes, like titles, can trigger compliance. A police offer's uniform, a doctor's coat, and a pilot's uniform are all symbols of authority. Slightly more subtle, but no less authoritative, are colored shirts with white collars and white cuffs. Add a Hermès scarf or Ferragamo tie and Gucci loafers, and you have an outfit that reeks with authority and commands respect. Trappings of authority such as Rolex watches, huge offices and desks, and luxury cars all add to the cachet of authority and power in some circles, particularly in urban centers such as New York. In Silicon Valley, black turtle necks and jeans might be the symbols of power. But salespeople must be sensitive to these subtle displays of power fashion and keep in mind the second basic rule of selling that people like and trust people exactly like themselves, including people who dress like they do.

There are two reasons to learn about the principles of influence, offensive and defensive. Offensively, it is a good idea for you to use the principles of influence when it is appropriate in order to influence people legitimately. But be mindful of the *law of instrument*, which was defined by Abraham Kaplan in *The Conduct of Inquiry*, as "give a small boy a hammer, and he will find that everything he encounters needs pounding."[17] In other words, now that you know a little about the theory of influence and the power of automatic responses, reciprocity, commitment and consistency, social proof, scarcity, and liking and authority, do not use them as a hammer in every sales situation. However, do use them when appropriate to position your proposals and product effectively to create added value for them.

I strongly recommend that you read Robert Cialdini's book, *Influence: Science and Practice*, study it carefully, and become an expert at using and recognizing the tactics of influence. By being an expert on these principles you can defend yourself against others who use them. Customers and buyers in their attempt to get more for less will often use one or all of these principles to get you to give them more, lower your prices, give them better position, say yes to a deal that is good for them, or to defer to their power and authority. The defense against the use of these principles of influence is to recognize them for exactly what they are and to stop before you respond automatically, to name the tactic ("that's reciprocation," or "the buyer is using social proof to try to influence me"), and then to respond appropriately and rationally.

Creating Value

Creating value encompasses salespeople's main purpose of creating customers and keeping them, their four objectives, their five primary strategies, and their three key functions as they go through the six steps of selling. In the following section you will learn why creating value is important and you will learn five steps to help you create value.

Why creating value is vital

Remember why it's important not to sell media advertising as though it was a commodity – an undifferentiated product that is sold only on the basis of price? Because if price is the only consideration, a product, including advertising, can be sold by means of an online auction on Google or eBay. This online auction model disintermediates salespeople – puts them out of a job. A company that sells on a commodity basis doesn't need salespeople. Therefore, if you want a long-term career in sales, you must learn how to differentiate a product, how to create value for it. Here are two more reasons for learning how to create value.

1   Creating value addresses sales objectives, strategies, and key functions during the six steps of selling   Let's review sales objectives, strategies, key functions, and the six steps of selling:

FOUR PRIMARY SALES OBJECTIVES

1   To get results for customers
2   To develop new business
3   To retain and increase current business
4   To increase customer loyalty

FIVE PRIMARY SALES STRATEGIES

1   To sell solutions to advertising and marketing problems
2   To reinforce the value of advertising and your medium

3   To create value for your product
4   To become the preferred supplier
5   To innovate

THREE KEY FUNCTIONS OF A SALESPERSON

1   To create a differential competitive advantage in a buyer's mind
2   To manage relationships
3   To solve problems

THE SIX STEPS OF SELLING

1   Prospecting
2   Identifying problems
3   Generating solutions
4   Presenting
5   Negotiating and closing
6   Servicing

2   Creating value addresses buyer's needs   If we review the results of two time buyer surveys from Chapter 2, as shown below, we see that they provide a virtual road map for creating value. In other words, if you give buyers what they ask for, you will create value. Note in the lists below of what buyers want, "a low price" is not one of the answers. This fact reinforces the notion that buyers will always asks for a lower price than you first offer, but they do not necessarily expect to get a lower price. It is their job to ask; it is material self-interest at work.

International Radio-Television Society (IRTS) Time buyer survey of what buyers want:
   (1) Communication skills – clarity and conciseness, not oral skills or flamboyance, were ranked as most important; (2) Empathy – insight and sensitivity; (3)
   Knowledge of product, industry, and market; (4) Problem-solving ability – using
   imagination in presentations and packaging; (5) Respect; (6) Service; (7) Personal responsibility of results; and (8) Not knocking the competition.
Major radio station group buyer survey of what buyers want: (1) Ideas – especially in
   the area of *added value*; (2) Communication – Clear concise communication,
   not long-winded, exaggerated sales pitches; (3) Respect for their time; (4) Run
   as ordered; and (5) Responsiveness – return calls *fast*, be available at all times,
   and get schedules confirmed quickly and correctly.
Advertising perceptions study reported in Advertising Age:

   In addition to brand knowledge, media buyers and planners are also looking for
   good communication skills, professionalism and an understanding of marketers'
   needs and priorities.

The least important characteristics in a sales rep identified by marketers were sales presence and entertainment. Only eight percent of respondents said going to dinners, shows and sporting events with sellers was important . . . "Most people probably aren't going to own up to the fact that they really love being entertained."[18]

ADDED VALUE

Please note the phrase "added value" associated with answer (1) in the survey above. Added value to buyers means additional value that a medium gives at no charge. What buyers want is something free: bonus spots, bonus banners, free promotions, free event tie-ins, free merchandise, or free opening and closing bill-boards, among other things. The push for added value has become so pervasive in some media, especially in radio, that many buyers claim they will not place an order without something free thrown in the deal. To salespeople a request for added value should not be seen as a problem, but as a negotiating opportunity. In Chapter 12, when I cover negotiating and closing, I will show you how to use requests for added value to your advantage by using contrast, social proof, and other principles of influence. However, for the time being, suffice it to say that creating value for your medium and your company does not mean giving stuff away free.

3   Creating value addresses companies' needs   Creating value also addresses sales management's needs because if salespeople can create the perception of value for their product and, therefore, keep prices up, they will help accomplish their company's primary purpose for a sales department: *to maximize revenue.* Top management of media companies today must look at both the top line (revenue) and the bottom line (profits). The best way for media companies to grow is to manage the top line and increase revenue, for which they depend on salespeople who sell advertising. Advertising is responsible for the majority of revenue for most media companies. Thus, maximizing revenue is management's mantra for media sales departments.

The push for maximizing revenue is understandable, but it creates a dilemma for media salespeople. On the one hand, they must please management (and keep their jobs) by maximizing revenue. On the other hand, they must consider the needs of their customers and follow the tenet of their number-one objective, getting results for customers. How do they resolve this dilemma? By creating value. It is often difficult to create value in and to hold rates. The only hope sales-people have of keeping their rates is to be creative and innovative in differentiating their product and creating value.

Additional reasons for creating value

1   Creating value reinforces the value of advertising, of your medium, and of your product   Customers and buyers often look for reasons to cut back on their advertising, to look for a less expensive placement in your medium, to look for less expensive media, or to ask you to lower your prices in order to keep the business you have. If you call on a customer who is considering cutting back on advertising, go to www.mediaselling/downloads.html.us, download the presentation "Advertising Strategies in a Slowdown," and show it to the customer. The presentation gives facts, based on research conducted during recessions in the past, that show when companies cut advertising, they lose market share, often for five years, while competitors who continue advertising gain share. It also shows that market share, once lost, is extremely difficult and expensive to gain back

2   Creating value enhances your credibility and builds trust   In the process of creating value, you display your expertise, which builds your source credibility. You demonstrate that you understand your customer's business, their marketing goals and problems, your product, your market, media trends, the buyer's and customer's business needs (as indicated in the above buyer surveys), and the buyer's personal needs. All of these elements build trust.

3   Creating value can forestall and minimize future objections, especially the price objection   Before you make a specific proposal that includes prices, if you invest time in creating value for your product, you forestall, or answer beforehand, many potential objections that might come up during a discussion of your proposal. During the creating value process, you justify your pricing.

4   Creating value reinforces your solutions-selling approach   During the process of creating value, you can show customers that you are taking a solutions-selling approach and that you are trying to help them solve their advertising and marketing problems. By taking this approach, you are able to demonstrate that your primary objective is to help them get results, not necessarily to sell them something.

5   Creating value helps you avoid commodity selling   By creating value, you reinforce your product's worth. An old adage says, "There are people who know the price of everything, but know the value of nothing." In other words, price and value do not mean the same thing, as you will see in the next section of this chapter. During the process of creating value, you differentiate your product and its features, benefits, and advantages and make it worth more to your customers so that they will be willing to pay a fair price. In creating value you want to reinforce the inherent assumption that expensive equals good.

6   Creating value helps you control your customers' expectations   When people contemplate investing in advertising, they do so with the expectation that their business will increase. And because their hopes are high, their expectations usually rise to meet them. In other words, there is a natural tendency for people to expect too much. Part of creating value is creating *realistic value* in the minds of customers, which means lowering your customers' expectations. The lower you can set their expectations, the more pleased they will eventually be with their results, as they define them.

What is value?

The perceived value formula The formula for perceived value is:

$$\text{Perceived Value}(PV) = \frac{\text{Quality}(Q) + \text{Results}(R) + \text{Service}(S)}{\text{Price}(P)}$$

In order to increase the *Perceived Value* to a customer, you must increase the value of the numerator in the above equation (quality, results, and service) and not lower the denominator (price). In fact, if salespeople are expert in creating value and increasing the perception in a buyer's mind of the value of quality, results, and service, then they can increase the price.

Quality is a subjective concept. Like the concept of beauty, quality is in the eye of the beholder. Perceptions of quality are defined by several attributes of a medium. For example, a magazine might be perceived to be high quality because of glossy paper stock, beautiful four-color photographs, a pleasing layout and design, and eye-catching, tasteful graphics. A newspaper might be perceived to be high quality because of the upscale demographics of its audience and because of the many Pulitzer Prizes it has won. A radio station might be perceived to be a high-quality station because it plays classical music. A television station might be perceived to be a high-quality station because its season kick-off parties and presentations are eye-popping, expensive, and include television stars. A Web site might be perceived to be a high-quality site because of its design, its uncluttered look – Google's site would be a good example. The more attributes that a medium and its salespeople can promote to create a perception of quality, the higher perceived quality is, the higher prices the medium can charge.

Results in a media context means, primarily, does advertising in that medium get an acceptable return on investment and get results as defined by the customer? Customer-defined results vary a great deal by media and by customer. In some cases, results can mean beautiful reproduction and display of four-color ads. At other times, results can mean sales. With some clients, results can mean recall of specific product claims in an ad or commercial. With others, results can mean return on advertising investment as measured by increased stock price. And with other clients, results mean an increase in market share.

With advertising agencies, results might mean fast response times to request for avails (availabilities) or RFPs (requests for proposals), proposals that meet their buying criteria, excellent service, and follow-up.

By understanding a customer's definition of results, salespeople can demonstrate how their medium in general and their specific media outlet can improve results.

Service is a product attribute that is becoming more and more important in our economy. In fact, with many products, especially those that are either highly undifferentiated or intangible, customers consider service to be the most important differentiator. Also, as an industry matures, customers migrate from being inexperienced generalists to being experienced specialists. Inexperienced generalists are interested in learning more about a product, understanding how to use it, and figuring out how to buy it, and because of the FUD factor – fear, uncertainty, and doubt – will often be predisposed to pay a premium price in order to gain experience. On the other hand, experienced specialists, such as agency media buyers, know a product well. They know how to use it and how to buy it, and price and responsive service are most important to them. To experienced specialists, who have multiple substitutes for virtually all mass media, the single most important differentiator, after price, is service.[19]

By emphasizing the importance of quality, results, and service, salespeople can divert the discussion away from price and get customers and buyers to focus on these other attributes.

Value is a perception Every person or potential buyer places a different weight on the relative importance of the quality/results/service mix and, thus, has a different definition of the value of that mix. Therefore, *value is a perception* that is unique to each individual. Thus, the price people will pay for a product is a result of their unique solution to the perceived value formula. For example, a commercial on a local television station news program may be worth $1,000 to one advertiser based on how many adults between the ages of 18 and 49 the newscast reaches. On the other hand, it might be worth $2,000 to another advertiser who wants to have the company's name associated with a station's newscast or sports segment within that newscast, who desires to reach mature, male business decision-makers, and who likes an association with sports. Therefore, paying a premium for sponsoring a sports segment that features a brief opening *billboard* such as "Sports brought to you by Warner Ford," makes economic sense to that advertiser.

Value signals Value signals reinforce the perception of value. Here is a list of some value signals:

1 *Company image and reputation*. Does a company's management have a track record of success and a philosophy that stresses dedication to excellence and high business standards? Apple has an excellent reputation, Haliburton a horrible one, for example.
2 *Media outlet reputation*. *Time* magazine has an excellent reputation; the *National Inquirer*'s is not so good.

3   *Ethical practices.* Does the media outlet have a reputation for treating its customers fairly? Is its word its bond? Do advertisers trust it?

4   *Awards and prizes.* How many awards for excellence or Pulitzer Prizes has a media outlet amassed? Awards and prizes are the best proof of quality.

5   *Cumulative advertising and promotion.* Coca-Cola is the world's most recognized brand because it has consistently advertised its product for almost 100 years.

6   *Content.* Editorial or programming content. The *New York Times*, the *Washington Post*, Slate.com, and National Public Radio (NPR) are perceived to have high-quality reporting and content.

7   *Sales promotion material.* Slick, well-designed, tasteful, informative sales brochures speak volumes about an organization.

8   *Continuity.* The number of years a company has been in business, the number of years a television news anchorperson has been on the air, the number of years a Web site has been in existences, or the tenure of a magazine editor all impart a perception of value.

9   *Advertisers.* The presence of well-known, prestigious advertisers gives a medium credibility and value – they reinforce the idea that "you are known by the company you keep," an example of social proof.

10 *Audience or reader quality and quantity.* High-income readers of *Smithsonian* magazine or the huge audience of Yahoo.com or a Super Bowl telecast, for example.

11 *Price.* The higher the price of a product, the higher the perceived value (expensive equals good). Patek Philippe watches are perceived to have more value than Casio watches, for example.

12 *Management.* The better the reputation of top management and the more visible managers are in the business community, the more favorably a company is viewed.

13 *Production values.* Well-produced YouTube.com videos, slick magazine ads, and well-produced radio and television commercials add value to a medium.

14 *Sales presentations.* Well-written, problem-solving, and graphically arresting proposals and presentations not only help make a product tangible, they also add value. See Chapter 10 for guidelines for generating winning proposals and presentations.

15 *Salespeople.* One survey asked media buyers what first came to mind when the call letters of a radio or television station were mentioned. Seventy-five percent of all buyers gave the name of the salesperson who called on them. Thus, salespeople are the surrogate for the product and can make tangible intangible media advertising and add value.

16 *Ideas for added value.* Promotion or event sponsorships, community service project tie-ins – see the list of creating value ideas at the end of this chapter in Exhibit 8.9.

17 *Creative approaches.* Ideas for arresting ads, banners, or commercials can add value for direct clients without advertising agencies. Agencies usually do not

appreciate suggestions for creative approaches in copy and art because they see creative execution as their prerogative.

Positioning value

Positioning is creating a unique perception of your product to have a differential competitive advantage in the mind of your customers. As marketing guru Philip Kotler says, "Having a competitive advantage is like having a gun in a knife fight."[20]

When you position your company and your product to have a competitive advantage, a competitor's image is as important as your own image, if not more so, because you are positioning your product against the image of your competitor's medium and product. If you position properly, you can accomplish two things: You position your product to have an advantage and you position your competitors' products to have a disadvantage.

You must clearly establish a differential competitive advantage in the minds of potential customers for your medium, your company, and your product. To do so, you should begin the positioning process by asking yourself the following questions:

1 What position, if any, does my product already occupy in the mind of my customer? Of course, the best way to find out is to ask. In Chapter 9 (p. 160) there is a list of Discovery Questions you can use that will help answer this question.
2 What position do I want to occupy? It must be unique and concise. It must have an easily definable competitive advantage that clearly makes a difference; if it takes too long to explain, customers will not stick around or stay awake long enough to find out how good it is.

When you position your company, your medium, and your product, you should use the right words to paint a positive, colorful picture. For example, you do not sell advertising; instead, you present a traffic-building ad campaign. You do not peddle banner positions; instead, you offer profit-producing advertising. You do not sell advertising; instead, you sell the opportunity to influence prospective customers. Advertisers do not buy ads, banners, or spots; they buy the most effective and efficient way available to generate sales. Always use phrases that color your offer green – the color of profits.

Create value in both types of selling

No matter what type of selling you are engaged in – missionary/development selling or service/transactional selling – you must always find ways to create value. In missionary selling creating value comes by generating practical creative solutions to marketing problems and creating arresting, exciting presentations. In service selling creating value comes by giving outrageously excellent service, as detailed in Chapter 13.

Six steps for creating value

One of the oldest rules of selling is, "Don't mention price until you are ready to negotiate and close." Before you get into a discussion about price, you should position your product to create the perception of value, and the best way to increase the value of what you are selling is to follow the five steps for creating value. As part of the creating value process, it is a good idea to have a general presentation (GP) for your media outlet. Many media organizations have a GP, which is an introduction to their product that reinforces the product's history, reputation, and combination of quality, results, and service advantages and benefits – without mentioning price. To see an example of a GP, go to www.mediaselling.us/downloads.html and look at the presentation for the *DeSoto Times*, a small community newspaper.

The six steps of creating value parallel a salesperson's six primary sales strategies.

1   Reinforce your expertise as a problem solver.
2   Reinforce the value of advertising.
3   Reinforce the value of your medium.
4   Reinforce the value of your product (your Web site, your network, or your television station, for example).
5   Position the benefits and advantages of your product.
6   Include a return-on-investment (ROI) analysis, if appropriate.

1   Reinforce your expertise as a problem solver   You want your prospects to consider you as a marketing and advertising expert who can solve their advertising and marketing problems. In order to demonstrate your expertise, you should demonstrate your broad-based knowledge of national and international economic and business trends, economic and business trends in your market, economic and business trends in the media and in your medium, and economic and business trends in your customers' businesses. There are two major benefits of having up-to-date information in these areas: (1) You will be welcome at top-management client levels and (2) you will be welcome at all client and agency levels because you provide updated information to your customers and buyers.

Other examples of some of these trends can be found in the "Creating Value for Television" presentation on www.mediaselling.us/downloads.html.

Also, demonstrate your knowledge of marketing and advertising – the goals, strategies, and tactics not only of your customers and their competitors, but also of your own competitors.

Finally, provide your customers with the latest research available. Do not just present reams of data, but put research information in a concise, summarized, easy-to-read format. Customers will appreciate and reward you for your consideration and respect for their time.

Your goal in providing all of this information is to become your customers' preferred supplier – the salesperson and organization your customers would most like to do business with, and, more important, the salesperson they will always call first when they want information.

2   Reinforce the value of advertising   In most cases, especially with advertising agencies, you do not have to reinforce the value of advertising. However, at times you will find an organization that is not advertising in the mass media. It may be hard to believe, but there are a still a few holdouts. For example, it was not until recently that hospitals became major advertisers in many communities. Or an organization may be investing its marketing dollars primarily in promotion. Or an organization might be considering investing less money in advertising and more in promotion.

In all of these cases, it is necessary to sell the value of advertising and reinforce the first principle of creating value, that *advertising is not an expense, it is an investment.* You must continually reinforce this concept throughout all of your sales presentations and sales conversations. For example, never ask someone, "How much do you spend in advertising?" Ask, "How much do you invest in advertising?" When you submit a proposed schedule or campaign, never show a total cost, refer to it as a total investment.

Also, as pointed out in Chapter 2, you must reinforce the value of advertising as opposed to the costs of promotions. Remember that in 1978, 60 percent of all marketing dollars were spent in advertising, 40 percent in promotion. In 2006, it was estimated by some experts that about 60 percent of all marketing dollars were spent in promotion, 40 percent in advertising. The migration of marketing dollars from advertising to promotion hurt the growth rate of advertising over those years. You must continually reinforce advertising's positive long-term effects and the value of advertising to build brand image and, thus, try to reverse the shift of advertising dollars to promotion. Exhibit 8.2 shows seven problems with promotions that you can discuss with your customers that will help stem the tide of advertising dollars being switched to promotion.

Furthermore, the majority of promotions involve some inducement for consumers to act immediately and purchase a product. Inducements invariably involve a price reduction in some form such as rebates, coupons, or free merchandise, for example.

Examples of promotions that have hurt the profit margins of entire industries are the costly rebates American automotive manufacturers offer.

These losses due to rebates – essentially a price cut – back up and reinforce the claim that "the cost to a manufacturer of a 1-percent reduction in price is always far greater than the cost of a 1-percent boost in advertising expenditure."[21] Do

Exhibit 8.2   The seven problems with promotions

Problem	Description
1 Short-term effects	There is overwhelming evidence that "the consumer sales effect is limited to the time period of the promotion itself." Contrary to some marketers' belief, there is no residual effect of a promotion. Consumers do not turn into long-term customers. "When the bribe stops, the extra sales also stop."[1]
2 Promotions mortgage future sales.	By encouraging consumers to take action immediately, a promotion brings forward sales from a future period and, therefore, future sales are lower than forecast because of problem #1 above.
3 Promotions encourage stockpiling.	Savvy consumers stock up on low-priced promotion items, which cannibalizes future full-price sales and lowers margins.
4 Promotions train consumers not to pay full price.	Price-conscious consumers are aware of continual promotions and wait for them – they become trained never to pay full price – which lowers profit margins.
5 Promotions devalue a brand's image.	Continual promotions create a low-price, even "cheap," image and often appear to be desperate measures of a sinking brand in trouble. If consumers believe price cuts come from an oversupply, they will often wait for an even lower price.
6 Promotions are addictive.	Marketers become dependent on more and more quick fixes in a vicious circle of more and more promotions at lower and lower prices at shorter and shorter intervals. Unilever describes this circle as "promotion, commotion, and demotion."[2]
7 Continual use of promotions leads to retaliation.	Promotions "fuel the flames of competitive retaliation far more than other marketing activities."[3] Competitors join the price war to defend their position. The long-term result of price wars can lead to the elimination of both retailers' and an entire industry's profit margins.[4]

[1] John Phillip Jones. 1990. "The double jeopardy of sales promotions." *Harvard Business Review.* September–October. Reprint 90505. p. 5.
[2] Ibid., p. 7.
[3] Ibid., p. 7.
[4] Shuba Srinivasan, Koen Pauwels, Dominique Hansses, and Marnik Dekimpe. 2002. "Who benefits from price promotions?" *Harvard Business Review.* September–October. Reprint F0209C. p 2.

your customers want to increase sales? Recommend that they raise their advertising investment and do not reduce their prices.

Of course, all of these reasons why cutting prices is not a good idea for customers doubly reinforce why media salespeople should not cut their rates.

3   Reinforce the value of your medium   In many cases, you may not think you have to sell the value of your medium to a current advertiser who is a heavy user. However, keep in mind that competing media salespeople are calling on your advertisers and doing their best to switch your customers' advertising to their medium. It is a good idea to reinforce the value of your medium, and you can do this in three ways with current advertisers:

- At yearly renewal times, or at mid year, make a *stewardship presentation* that shows the ads or commercials an advertiser ran during the previous year and what results they got, and remind them of the excellent service they received from you.
- Ask advertisers for testimonial letters or, better, ask them to participate in a success case study. Go to www.charleswarner.us/advcase.html to read a paper titled "How to Write an Advertising Success Case Study." Helping you write a success case study reinforces an advertiser's excellent judgment in buying your medium.
- Invite advertisers to your industry's trade association presentations. Association such as the Television Bureau of Advertising (TVB), the Interactive Advertising Bureau (IAB), the Cabletelevision Advertising Bureau (CAB), and the Radio Advertising Bureau (RAB) regularly make presentations touting their medium in cities around the country. It is the job of these associations to sell the value of their media and they do it very well.

You should also make presentations to advertising agencies, especially to media planners, on the value of your medium if you sell for a medium other than television. Agencies have prejudice in favor of television, as covered in Chapter 2. If you are not selling television, selling the value of your medium to agencies is important in the long term even though it is not likely to produce an immediate order.

Another reason for reinforcing the value of your medium to both agencies and clients is to attempt to get them to invest more dollars in your medium – increase the size of the advertising dollar pie. You should sell the value of your medium first and worry about your share of the pie later. In many markets, there are radio or television station associations that cooperate in an attempt to get new advertisers into their particular medium and away from another, usually newspapers. For example, a team of television station sales managers will call on a major department store that invests all of its advertising dollars in the local newspapers and try to convince the department store to invest some that money in television.

4   Reinforce the value of your product   One of the best examples of a company that positions itself superbly is Patek Philippe, the Swiss watchmaker. Go to the company's Web site at http://patek.com/patek-philippe.html, click on "The Manufacture," "Values," and "History" links, and see how the company promotes its values, its history, its patents, its customers, and its complicated watches. Notice that while price is never mentioned for any of their watches, some of the famous people who have bought them are listed, such as Charlotte Brontë, Queen Victoria, Marie Curie, and Albert Einstein. After seeing how Patek Philippe positions itself and creates value for its watches, ask yourself if you would like own one and if you would rather sell these watches as a commissioned salesperson than sell Casio watches.

Just as the Patek Philippe Web site reeks of quality, you want your customers to get the same sense of quality when you talk about your product. One way to create the perception of quality is to repeat the word, to use it in every possible context, such as "We have a quality news Web site and quality bloggers," or "We have a quality production department that produces the highest quality commercials."

Remember, you are trying to position the quality, results, and service of your product to have a competitive advantage. After quality come results; stress that your medium gets results, and the best way to reinforce this concept is with advertising success case studies. These cases studies are not only good for positioning the value of your medium with an advertiser who is involved in developing the case study with you, but they are also powerful sales tools. An example of excellent success case studies can be seen at www.msn.com. At the bottom of MSN's home page there is an "Advertise" link, click on it and then click on the "Research Library" link. Also, on www.mediaselling.uss/downloads.html you will find a success case study titled "Aladdin Resort and Casino." Download and read this case study and set a goal of writing several success case studies for your medium. You will find case studies are an effective proof of performance that your medium gets results for advertisers.

Another way to reinforce the value of your product and communicate an image of being responsive to customer needs is to present a *value proposition* to customers. Here is an example of a value proposition for a television station:

> We are committed to partnering with our advertisers (and their agencies) by providing innovative solutions for connecting them to our audience in a way that delivers advertiser-defined results and jointly builds both of our brands.

The above value proposition states that you want to do more than sell your customers something. It means that you want to partner with them, you want to get results for them, and you want to create a win–win situation.

5 Position the benefits and advantages of your product Too often inexperienced media salespeople sell on the basis of the *features* of their product and do not place enough emphasis on *advantages* and *benefits*. Here are the definitions of these elements:

Features are descriptive. Features are facts and information about your product and its various parts. The features of a radio station, for example, are its tower, its transmitter, its programming format, its personalities, its coverage, its audience, and its ratings. The features of a newspaper are its presses, its delivery methods, its editorial stance, its comics, its editors and reporters, its special sections, and its circulation. Features describe what you have to sell, but they do not indicate or imply if the features are good or bad or why a customer should care about them. Customers do not buy solely based on product features.

Advantages. Advantages are comparative. They describe why the features of your product are better. Customers are interested in a feature's advantages and consider these advantages when they make a purchase (or in the case of advertising, an investment) if they feel the features are relevant. Use the contrast principle when you present advantages. Also, you must present the advantages of your product as customers go through each phase of the buying decision process.

In his classic book, *Major Account Sales Strategy*, Neil Rackham, describes the *buying decision process*. Rackham suggests that people go through three initial phases when making a buying decision:[22]

Recognition of needs. With consumers, this phase might come when they discover their old car has broken down and they need new one. With advertisers it might come when they have planned a sale event and want to advertise it and call salespeople and ask them to present schedules. Or, with an agency buyer, it might come when they send out a request for an RFP to the media they are considering buying.

Evaluation of options. In this phase buyers ask: "What are my choices?" "Should I buy what I did last time?" "Should I look for alternatives or for a lower price?" It is in the evaluation of options phase that product advantages become critical because it is during this phase that buyers narrow down their choices by eliminating those products that are considered less desirable or to be of lower quality.

Resolution of concerns. In this phase buyers look carefully at the few products they are considering and ask themselves: "What happens if the car breaks down; does it have a warranty or service guarantee?" "Which one has the best quality-to-price ratio?" It is in this final stage that benefits are of critical importance, and we will get to benefits shortly.

You must position your advantages so they are clear in your customer's minds when they reach the evaluation of alternative phase of the buying process. The best way to accomplish this positioning is *always to show comparative advantages and dramatize them.* Exhibit 8.3 shows five examples of how a television station might display the ratings of its evening newscast in a sales presentation. The first four examples are for station WAAA-TV, the fifth example is for station WBBB-TV.

Exhibit 8.3 Ratings of a TV newscast

Poor WAAA-TV display of ratings

	Adults 25–54 Nielsen ratings WAAA-TV
Early news	6.0

Fair WAAA-TV display of ratings (shows a comparative advantage)

	Adults 25–54 Nielsen ratings WAAA-TV	Adults 25–54 Nielsen ratings WBBB-TV
Early news	6.0	4.0

Good WAAA-TV display of ratings (quantifies a comparative advantage)

	Adults 25–54 Nielsen ratings WAAA-TV	Adults 25–54 Nielsen ratings WBBB-TV	WAAA-TV difference
Early news	6.0	4.0	+2.0

Best WAAA-TV display of ratings (dramatizes a comparative advantage)

	Adults 25–54 Nielsen ratings WAAA-TV	Adults 25–54 Nielsen ratings WBBB-TV	WAAA-TV advantage
Early news	6.0	4.0	+50%

WBBB-TV counterproposal display of ratings (minimizes a comparative disadvantage)

	Adults 25–54 Nielsen ratings WAAA-TV	Adults 25–54 Nielsen ratings WBBB-TV	WBBB-TV disadvantage
Early news	6.0	4.0	–33%

Notice the WBBB-TV proposal. WBBB-TV saw a copy of WAAA-TV's proposal that claimed WAAA-TV had a 50 percent lead over WBBB-TV, which is accurate. However, WBBB-TV showed in its counterproposal that things weren't all that bad – that it only trailed WAAA-TV by 33 percent, which is also accurate. The lesson here is to learn how to use numbers to compare, maximize, and dramatize your advantages and to minimize your disadvantages.

Benefits. Benefits are reasons why the features and advantages of your product solve customers' problems. Benefits are what you should concentrate on selling because that is what customers buy. Peter Drucker explained succinctly that people do not buy quarter-inch drill bits, they buy quarter-inch holes. Every time you state a feature or advantage of your product or proposal, customers ask themselves the WIIFM question, "What's in it for me?" Benefits answer that question. You must never let a customer ask the WIIFM question out loud, you must answer the question by attaching a problem-solving benefit to every feature you mention.

6   Include a return-on-investment (ROI) analysis, if appropriate   Bill Grimes was CEO of ESPN during its major growth years in the 1980s. In the early 1990s he was CEO of Multimedia, Inc., which owned radio and television stations and newspapers, and produced and distributed syndicated television programs, including "Sally Jesse Raphael." He wrote the about how to use an ROI analysis effectively in Chapter 21 of the previous edition of *Media Selling*.

At one point in my career . . . I had responsibility for a group of television stations and newspapers. The economy was weak at the time in many of our key markets and advertising budgets were not increasing. Thus, driven by a desire to preserve my comfortable employment, I began seeking a more intelligent way to sell advertising than packaging the best combination of CPMs, reach and frequency. To begin, I made the assumption that the most interested person at any client company should be its owner or chief executive. Next, I asked my sales managers and myself: why do companies advertise and why should they? The simple answer was that companies advertise to acquire and maintain customers for their business. Then I recognized that attracting new customers was not an economically sufficient reason. What company needs new customers if it loses money because of the cost of attracting them? The profit that a company achieves from the new customers generated by an advertising expenditure on my stations and newspapers must exceed the cost of the advertising. Note that I said profit, not sales.

It then occurred to my increasingly excited team of television and newspaper sales managers that the cost of advertising is a business expense to companies and that the same money spent in advertising its products or services could also be spent – or better, invested, as you have learned elsewhere in this book – on other projects or assets that could increase a company's profits. For example, the company could hire more people; it could open new stores or offices, it could buy other businesses, or it could simply take the money allocated for advertising and return it as a dividend to its shareholders if it were a public company.

Then it became clear to us all that advertising expenditures were indeed a business expense, but more importantly an investment. When companies make investments of capital they expect a return on their investment (ROI).

At last we sensed a breakthrough. What if we could demonstrate to the client some estimated ROI that he or she might find believable – an ROI estimate both believable and financially acceptable? Would that not lead to making the client very happy? And would that not lead to even more advertising? From that revelation I was determined to develop a ROI model for a large client of one of our stations or papers. To do that, I needed lots of information about that company's business and then I would need to test the ROI model with our salespeople.

The prospective client we selected was a large supermarket chain in St Louis where we owned the leading television station. To gather the necessary information about its business that could not be found through our researching efforts at the station, I called the company's CEO who arranged for a meeting with his senior managers. In preparation we read the company's annual report and gathered as much information from local market sources that we could. At the beginning of the meeting I told the client that we were not there to talk about our station but to learn about their business and then determine whether we could help improve profitability. "No media peddler has ever said that to me," the CEO stated. "Ask your questions."

First we learned that the company owned eleven supermarkets in the St Louis market which generated $200 million in sales and that its market share was 25 percent. Total sales annually in the market were therefore $800 million. The company's management also said that their market share rank was third among the six competing supermarkets. Its operating or pre-tax profit margin was three percent (about average for the supermarket industry) which meant that after paying all operating expenses – cost of goods sold, salaries and benefits, rent, and marketing costs – the company had three percent of revenues remaining before paying taxes. Also, we were told that the lifetime of a customer of the company was a little over three years. This meant that the supermarket chain's customers remained loyal customers for that period of time. Finally, and importantly, we learned that the shares of the company's stock were selling for 12 times the company's pre-tax profits.

We thanked management for the information; assured them that we would use it in confidence; and, that we would return with a recommendation to invest in advertising on our station only if we believed we could increase their profits and their shareholders' value. Note the words "invest," "increase," and "profits."

Back at the television station, I asked our team the key question: did we believe that with a substantial expenditure of advertising on our station over a sustained period – at least a year – the supermarket chain could increase its share of market? And, if we believed that our station could grow the supermarket chain's business enough for it to have a positive and competitive ROI, could we convincingly present this to the client? Our salespeople, citing several success stories of how several station advertisers had experienced solid market share increases, stated strongly their belief that with an expenditure of $1 million over the course of the year and with maximizing the commercial placement of the client's schedule, and with a solid creative approach, the supermarket could attain a two percent market share increase. With each market share point worth $8 million in total sales in the market (one percent of $800 million total market supermarket sales) and with our client's 25 percent market share; that meant each share point increase was worth $2 million in sales for our client. It seemed to me that we could make a strong case that our supermarket client could likely receive a compelling ROI with an investment on our station.

We decided to build our ROI model on the client gaining a one percent market share increase – not the two percent our people felt achievable – because it would obviously be more believable to the client. With the one percent of market sales worth $2 million annually for our client we now had to estimate what the incremental costs associated with our recommended program would be. First, there was the $1 million in additional advertising invested by the client on our station. We then assumed for the eleven stores to generate $2 million in additional sales, it would not require much additional operating expense. It seemed unlikely that the stores would have to stay open more hours a day. Therefore, essential non-personnel costs such as rent, lighting and heating expenses would not increase. We did build into our model $200,000 for several new checkout counter personnel and another $300,000 in miscellaneous expenses since we did not know as much about the supermarket business as our client did and because we wanted as few of our assumptions challenged by the client as possible.

Exhibit 8.4 shows the way the economics of our ROI program for our client now looked.

A 50 percent return on investment was almost 17 times the three percent ROI the supermarket chain was currently receiving on its shareholders' investment. Therefore, we knew the client – if he accepted our assumptions in our ROI model – would acknowledge that the ROI was more than acceptable. But I knew that there was one more vital piece of missing information that our client would find even more appealing.

Because we had learned that the equity value of the company was currently based upon a multiple of 12 times the company's pre-tax profits, we could now provide a believable estimate for the increase in the enterprise value of the supermarket chain company. This information is readily available on the Internet for all publicly traded companies and can be determined for private companies relatively easily by any financially trained person. Therefore, multiplying $500,000, the incremental pre-tax profit the investment in advertising with our station produced by 12, the pre-tax multiplier the stock market had placed on the company's share price resulted in an increase of $6 million in the market value of our supermarket chain. Assuming that there were 50 million shares outstanding, the price per share of the company's stock would increase about 12 cents. This is this kind of information that CEOs like to hear. See Exhibit 8.5 for the potential effect of the advertising investment on share price.

We added one more assumption to our ROI model that gained the attention and approval of the client's management team. We assumed that half of the incremental sales revenue, or $250,000, generated by the advertising on our station would come

Exhibit 8.4   Advertising return-on-investment analysis

A	Investment in TV advertising	$1,000,000	
B	Investment in 8 check-out personnel	$200,000	
C	Miscellaneous expenses	$300,000	
D	Total investment	$1,500,000	D = A + B + C
E	1% market share increase realized from TV advertising	$2,000,000	
F	Increased pre-tax income	$500,000	F = E − D
G	ROI	50%	G = F / A

Exhibit 8.5   ROI impact on share price analysis

A	Return on $1,000,000 advertising investment	$500,000	
B	Equity value of company multiple	12	
C	Increase in company market value	$6,000,000	$C = A \times B$
D	Outstanding shares of stock	50,000,000	
E	Increase in value per share	$0.12	$E = C/D$

from current customers spending more money per shopping visit. The other half we assumed would come from new customers. Since the client had told us before that new customers remain with stores on average three years, we then estimated that our advertising program would also add $250,000 more in profits during the two years following the advertising campaign on our station even if the $1 million advertising investment was not continued. This additional pre-tax profit also increased the already high ROI on the $1 million investment and it would positively impact the share price in the following two years as well.

It is important to note here that we did not attempt to persuade the client to allocate any of his current advertising budget to our $1 million proposal. We believed that if we proposed that any of the dollars the client was currently spending on media in St Louis, including investment on our station, were re-allocated, the client may well argue that his current share of market sales could be offset to some degree. We knew that our ROI proposal had to be judged on its own merits as a new and incremental investment opportunity and to suggest switching any of its current advertising investment to our proposal would lead to a debate on existing market share and possibly upon existing relationships the client may value.

Two meetings later we had the sale. Two wonderful other things happened. The salespeople had reason to believe that advertising on our stations or in our newspapers meant a lot more than cost-per-thousand and cost-per-point. Advertising was a very valuable investment made by a company, and discussing ROI with senior management was a smart way to build a really deep relationship with a client. And that leads to the next wonderful thing that happened: the CEO of the supermarket chain wrote and said, "Never before have I worked with media people who knew something about business, finance, and corporate value. Your team was a combination of the best consulting firm and investment banker we have used."

Position benefits according to business and personal needs

As mentioned before, there are two types of needs: business needs and personal needs. You must position benefits so that they directly address business problems (it is better to refer to them as *challenges* when you make presentations to customers) and business needs and how your proposed solutions help customers get what they want – achieve their marketing and advertising goals and get results as they define results. There is also a subtle subtext involved that you should master. You must also position the benefits of your product and solution in such a way that it appeals to customers' personal needs.

This type of subtle, indirect positioning according to personal needs is where it gets difficult. You can hardly say to a customer, "My proposal to run commercials just before the Super Bowl on my television network will not only help you achieve your marketing goals of reaching the largest possible male audience and lock out your competitors from this valuable position, but it will also appeal to your huge, oversized ego to be in the Super Bowl." Or, "My proposal to run remnant space on my newspaper's Web site when it is available will not only help you achieve your goal of making your advertising investments as efficient as possible, but it will also appeal to your obsessive, miserly fear of losing money."

No, you have to be careful and practice subtly positioning your benefits to meet personal needs. Creating a needs-based portrait, as discussed in Chapter 7, is the first step in positioning benefits according to personal needs. The next step is to develop a Benefits Matrix, as seen in Exhibit 8.6. You can download a blank Benefits Matrix from www.mediaselling.us/downloads.html.

You will notice in the Benefits Matrix that the statements that position the benefits reinforce the benefit in terms of both business and personal needs. For

Exhibit 8.6   Benefits Matrix

Customer	Business challenge	Personal needs	Feature	Benefit	Position the benefit
Beer	Increasing market share	Risk taker; likes to dominate competitors; motivated by greed.	Sports on television	High reach in target audience.	"High up-side potential." "Buy now, beat the competition."
Financial services	Increase share of mind and share of market	Likes to play it safe; conservative; motivated by fear of loss.	News on radio	Ideal environment to improve brand image; credibility.	"We're a safe buy." "No one will criticize you for buying my station – it's number one in news."
HMO	Perceived as hindering choice	Goal oriented; likes to have friends, be liked; motivated by pride.	Health Web site	Associated with positive concept such as health and wellness; image enhancement; accurate information.	"Help you achieve your goals." "You'll look good."

example, in the first row, the "High up-side potential" statement could refer to investing in commercials in a Super Bowl telecast that might feature a dramatic match-up that could attract a huge audience. This benefit not only has a practical, business advantage of achieving higher-than-expected reach in an advertiser's target audience, but also a personal, emotional advantage of appealing to the customer's risk-taking nature and greed. The "Buy now, beat the competition" statement has the practical advantages of investing before all the spots are gone, but also it appeals to the customer's need for domination and competitiveness.

The home-run secret

The most important skill in media selling is being able to subtly position the benefits of your product according to personal needs – without being obvious, as shown in the Benefits Matrix. You should create a Benefits Matrix for your key customers and buyers and you have to practice saying the right words to hit their hot buttons. However, if you can master the art of positioning benefits in this manner, it is the biggest home run in selling media and, in fact, in all personal selling.

Two don'ts in creating value

Don't promise results. The first principle of creating value is: *Advertising is not an expense, it is an investment.* The second principle is: *Under-promise and over-deliver.* One of the main things you accomplish when you create value is that you embed and, thus, control your customers' expectations. Do not be guilty of setting unrealistic expectations in your customer's minds; it is the fastest way to lose credibility, create a furious client, and guarantee no renewal. You will have happy customers if you lower their expectations and then, as their advertising runs, if they have better results than they expected, you will get an enthusiastic renewal. Conversely, you will have an unhappy customer if you raise their expectations by hinting at or promising unreasonable results. If they have worse results than they expected, you will get an angry cancellation and possibly even a lawsuit.

Unfortunately, you cannot promise or even predict results with confidence or accuracy because there are many other marketing variables that affect customers' sales that you have no control over, as seen in Exhibit 8.7.

Don't knock the competition. The third principle of creating value is: *Don't knock the competition.* Its corollary is: *Don't even mention the competition.* Perhaps the best reason for not knocking the competition is because, as shown in the survey mentioned at the beginning of this chapter, buyers do not like it. Unfortunately, in some highly competitive industries such as radio and magazines, weak, unprofessional salespeople habitually sell negatively. Exhibit 8.8 shows the reasons why not to knock or mention the competition and gives you some ways to deal with competitors when asked about them.

Exhibit 8.7   Marketing variables that affect sales

Variable	Description
Competitors' offers	Competitors might offer contests, sweepstakes, rebates, free delivery, cash back on purchases made elsewhere for less.
Competitors' advertising activity	No matter how much an advertiser invests, if a competitor invests substantially more, especially in the same medium, it's difficult to gain market share
Competitors' creative approach	Competitors' effective and attention-grabbing creative approaches can blunt your customer's attempts to gain market share. Bud Light buried Miller Light over the years, not only with heavier advertising weight by also with consistently brilliant, funny commercials that young men loved.
Customer's backend	Advertisers may have great creative and sufficient advertising weight, but if their backend cannot process orders efficiently or deliver on time, they lose customers and sales.
Competitors' backend	If competitors' have highly efficient backend systems, they might steal customers with faster delivery cycles, better after-purchase service.
Competitive pricing	No matter how much an advertiser invests, if competitors' prices are lower for similar quality, it is very difficult to increase sales.
Competitors' innovations	New, improved product lines and models from competitors can slow your customer's sales.
Purchasing cycle	No amount of advertising can change a product's historic purchasing cycle. No advertiser can sell bikinis in the middle of zero-degree cold spells in January.
Interest level, novelty	Some products are ho-hum products – they have low consumer interest. Household products such as toilet paper do not elicit a lot of interest from consumers. New, novel products like the Apple iPod create interest. An advertiser with a ho-hum product can see sales fall when competitors introduce exciting new products.

Creating value ideas

To wind up this chapter, in Exhibit 8.9 you will find a list of creating value ideas. These are just a few of hundreds of ideas that can help you add value for your product, reinforce the perception of quality, results, and service for your company and your product, and help you become a world-class media salesperson.

Exhibit 8.8   Reasons for not knocking (or mentioning) the competition

Reason	Description
1 Buyers hate it.	How would you like it if every conversation you had during a business day was negative, nasty, and mean spirited. You would probably become depressed. Buyers feel the same way.
2 You tear down the image of your medium.	After buyers hear how bad several competitors are, they begin to have a negative impression of the whole medium. Knocking the competition is destructive to your medium.
3 You waste time.	Customers' and buyers' time is limited; you usually have just a few minutes to get their attention and make a presentation. If you spend time knocking the competition, you waste valuable time. Remember the old adage, "You can't sell what your competitors don't have." You can only sell the benefits of what you have to offer, so get on with it.
4 You lose credibility.	When you knock the competition, you are not perceived as being objective. Buyers say to themselves, "Of course you're badmouthing the competition; you're trying to sell me something. Why should I believe you?" Therefore, when you knock competitors, you lose credibility.
5 You lower your image.	Selling negatively puts your down in the gutter with other negatively selling salespeople. Stay above it; refuse to throw dirt. Buyers will appreciate your positive approach and like you better for it.
6 You can touch hidden sore spots.	You may not know if a customer or buyer has invested in advertising with a competitor (in your medium or another medium), so if you knock a competitor a buyer has invested in, you are insulting the buyer's judgment. When this happens, buyers become defensive and entrenched, and they vigorously defend their past decisions. Also, a buyer may like a salesperson (may even be dating the salesperson) and when you knock that salesperson's medium, you are knocking the salesperson and the buyer will become very defensive and defend their friend's product (and dislike yours). Remember, the media are an intangible product and, thus, salespeople become the surrogate for their products – *are* the products in the minds of buyers.
7 You build competitors' importance and image.	Did you ever see an ad in a magazine for Rolex that had a headline "We're better than a Timex?" *Never* mention the competition below you in rank position; all you do is elevate them to your level. If you mention competitors under you in rank position, buyers' reactions are "Why is this salesperson talking about that competitor? What is the salesperson afraid of?"

Exhibit 8.8 (cont'd) How to respond when asked about competitors

Response	*Description*
1 Compliment competitors.	Use a two-sided argument. The first side is to compliment your competitors (remember, you do not know who your buyer knows or likes at your competition). By complimenting, you boost the image of your medium and come across as a positive, nice person. For example, if a buyer asks, "I understand *US News* has lowered its circulation base rate. Is this true?" you might respond with something like: "I've heard that, too. It's a shame. *US News* is a solid news magazine with an excellent editorial product and sales staff."
2 Talk about your strengths.	Do what politicians do, do not answer the question directly, answer the question with information about the benefits of your product. For example, if a buyer says, "WAAA-TV's late news had a 20 percent drop in women 18–49 ratings," you might respond with "My station, WBBB-TV's, late news had a 2 percent increase in that demo even though it was a summer book and viewing levels were down."
3 Expose generic weaknesses.	The second side of the two-sided argument is an exposure of your competitor's generic weakness – weaknesses that are not specific to that individual competitor, but to a type or genre of products. For example, you might add to your response #1 above to the question, "I understand *US News* has lowered its circulation base rate. Is this true?" the second side of the argument: "All news magazines are suffering from the advertising slowdown and are looking to cut expenses. Cutting subscriptions is one way to do this. Also, general news magazines are suffering mass circulation erosion because of people getting their news online."

Exhibit 8.9 Creating value ideas

1 Show audience demographics by ZIP codes.
2 Show Simmons, MRI product-usage data to advertisers.
3 Provide customers with information from their trade journals.
4 Assign category sales specialists.
5 Conduct seminars on strategy for advertisers, for example, "How Retailers Can Use Television," or "How to Use Cable Television to Reach Upscale Viewers," or "How to Get Results Using Online Advertising."
6 Offer business breakfasts once a quarter for local business leaders featuring well-known, expert speakers.
7 Create a buying spectrum graphic that includes your competitors and shows a continuum of values ranging from price to quality, with quality entailing better placement and position and your medium at the quality end of the spectrum.

Exhibit 8.9 Creating value ideas (cont'd)

8   Sponsor a kids' fair or bridal fair at a local convention center or fair ground.

9   Develop a system for the sales staff for presenting a predetermined number of speculative ads or speculative commercials per week.

10   Sell production packages to advertisers. For example, mat services in newspapers or jingle packages in radio.

11   Create SWAT teams of salespeople by category and have the team develop category presentations for the use of the whole sales staff.

12   Have exhibition booths at relevant industry trade shows such as truckers' conventions, retail trade conventions, or Comdex (yearly computer industry trade show).

13   Conduct seminars for advertisers and advertising agencies on how to plan and buy your medium.

14   Conduct creative execution seminars for advertisers and advertising agencies.

15   Offer joint promotions with a charity group, an advertiser, and your company.

16   Sponsor city association luncheons honoring advertisers and advertising agencies and present creative awards.

17   Create fun carnival days to promote your medium at local trade association or civic organization meetings.

18   Offer reciprocal trade arrangements for retail shelf space.

19   In broadcasting, offer remote broadcasts to advertisers; call them marketing opportunities.

20   Distribute magazines and newsletters about your company in both print and e-mail versions.

21   In broadcasting and cable, offer special weeks on the air, similar to a newspaper or magazine advertising section, such as a week featuring furniture styles and values. In print, offer these types of special sections.

22   Develop a "Little Things Mean a Lot" list: Top management follow-up calls; thank-you notes and birthday cards in invoices; Rolodex-shaped calling cards for salespeople with business, home, and cell phone numbers and e-mail addresses on the cards; framed success letters (on your walls and on your customers' walls); and shopping bags for stores imprinted with your logo and theirs.

23   Develop a total customer responsiveness (TCR) mentality throughout your company, especially by those who answer the telephone. Distribute to the entire staff the "Close to the Customer on the Telephone" paper found on www.mediaselling.us.

24   Provide copy-testing research.

25   Offer premium prices for a guaranteed position or placement.

26   Provide advertisers with several advertising success stories in their category.

27   Provide advertisers with marketing research by category.

28   Conduct media auctions for a charity to establish the value of your advertising rates. Donates space or time and then the charity auctions it off to advertisers, who use the time; the money goes to the charity.

29   Look for advertising agency account synergy opportunities for two or more accounts at an agency to share in an idea, promotion, or advertising.

30   Have an area on your Web site through which someone interested in advertising with you can contact you. Also, have access to case studies and other research material on the Web site. See www.msn.com for an example.

Exhibit 8.9   Creating value ideas (cont'd)

31   Conduct shopping mall research among a store's customers asking them why they shop at competitors' stores.
32   Provide a list by category of your advertisers over the last year.
33   Use Reception Referrals, a system at your reception desk where you put on file detailed information about advertisers, the products they promote or stock, and dates of their sales so if people call and ask about a commercial they heard on your station, the receptionist can give them complete details.
34   Conduct brainstorming sessions. Invite clients to your offices and let the sales staff create ideas for that client, not ideas why a client should purchase you, but ideas for promotions, positioning, slogans, for example.
35   Spend time in a customer's business. For example, bag groceries, wait on tables, or clean up a showroom.

Test Yourself

1   What are the six principles of influence outlined in this chapter?
2   Discuss what the meaning is of the two terms foot-in-the-door and door-in-the-face.
3   What is the definition of a commodity?
4   What are the five reasons for creating value?
5   Give an example of an advertiser's positioning strategy as seen in an ad or a commercial.
6   What are the five steps of creating value?
7   What are the seven problems with promotions?
8   What are the differences between features, advantages, and benefits?
9   What are the three principles of creating value?
10   What are seven reasons for not knocking the competition?

Project

Project #1: Select a week in your life (the same week that you do the project at the end of Chapter 6 would be a good one to choose, then you can combine the two projects) in which you commit yourself to taking notes on encounters you have with compliance practitioners during the week, waiters in restaurants, telemarketers, retail salespeople, or fundraisers, for example. Take notes in two columns. In the first column, note which one of the six principles of influence, if any, the compliance practitioner used. In the second column, note whether the attempt to influence you was effective or, if the person did not use a principle of influence, which one might have been appropriate. At the end of the week, look over your notes and see: (1) If you identified different principles of influence and (2) if those principles of influence were effective in influencing you and if not which principles might have been used.

Project #2: Go to a local radio or television station, a local cable system, a local newspaper, or local Web site and ask for a copy of a general presentation. If they do not have a general, introductory sales presentation, ask for a copy of a sales presentation to a specific account. Assure them that you are requesting the presentation for a class project and will not show it to competitors. Using what you have learned in this chapter about creating value, critique the presentation – make notes on how it could be improved to create more value. As part of this project, craft a value proposition for the organization and include it in the presentation.

References

Tony Alessandra, Phil Wexler, and Rick Barrera. 1992. *Non-Manipulative Selling.* New York: Fireside Books.

Michael T. Bosworth. 1995. *Solutions Selling.* New York: McGraw-Hill.

Robert Cialdini. 1984. *Influence: The Psychology of Persuasion.* New York: William Morrow.

Robert Cialdini. 2001. *Influence: Science and Practice.* Boston: Allyn and Bacon.

Jay Conger. 1998. "The necessary art of persuasion." *Harvard Business Review.* May–June.

Mack Hanan. 1999. *Consultative Selling.* New York: AMACOM.

Stephen E. Heiman and Diane Sanchez with Tad Tuleja. 1998. *The New Strategic Selling.* New York: Warner Books.

John Phillip Jones. 1990. "The double jeopardy of sales promotions." *Harvard Business Review.* September–October.

John Phillip Jones. 1995. *When Ads Work: New Proof That Advertising Triggers Sales.* New York: Lexington Books.

Philip Kotler. 1999. *Kotler on Marketing.* New York: Free Press.

Charles U. Larson. 1986. *Persuasion: Reception and Responsibility.* Belmont, CA: Wadsworth.

Neil Rackham. 1989. *Major Account Sales Strategy.* New York: McGraw-Hill.

Al Ries and Jack Trout. 1981. *Positioning: The Battle for Your Mind.* New York: McGraw-Hill.

Al Ries and Jack Trout. 1986. *Marketing Warfare.* New York: McGraw-Hill.

Jack Trout with Steve Rivkin. 2000. *Differentiate or Die.* New York: John Wiley & Sons, Inc.

Resources

www.mediaselling.us (this book's Web site with useful downloads)
www.msn.com (Microsoft's Network Web site with case studies)
www.patek.com (Patek Philippe's Web site)

Notes

1   Robert Cialdini. 2001. *Influence: Science and Practice.* Boston: Allyn and Bacon, p. x.
2   Ibid., p. 4.
3   Ibid., p. 4.
4   Ibid., p. 4.
5   Ibid., p. 20.
6   Ibid., p. 22.
7   Ibid., p. 53.
8   Ibid., p. 65.
9   Ibid., p. 66.
10 Ibid., p. 67.
11 Ibid., p. 74.
12 Ibid., p. 100.
13 Ibid., p. 205.
14 Ibid., p. 206.
15 Ibid., p. 144.
16 Ibid., p. 188.
17 Abraham Kaplan. 1964. *The Conduct of Inquiry.* Scranton, PA: Chandler Publishing, p. 28.
18 Megan McIlroy. 2008. "Media buyers single out top ad sales reps." *Advertising Age.* January 15.
19 F. Stewart DeBruicker and Gregory L. Summe. 1985. "Make sure your customers keep coming back." *Harvard Business Review.* January–February.
20 Philip Kotler. 1999. *Kotler on Marketing.* New York: Free Press, p. 94.
21 John Phillip Jones. 1995. *When Ads Work: New Proof That Advertising Triggers Sales.* New York: Lexington Books, p. 53.
22 Neil Rackham. 1989. *Major Account Sales Strategy.* New York: McGraw-Hill, p. 4.

9

Skills: Prospecting and Identifying Problems

Charles Warner

Solution Selling

This chapter covers the first two steps of solution selling. You will learn techniques to improve your skills on these two steps and you will learn a system called the Money Engine that will help you organize your efforts for each step.

The six steps of solution selling

1 Prospecting
2 Identifying problems
3 Generating solutions
4 Presenting
5 Negotiating and closing
6 Servicing

The Money Engine

The Money Engine is a system for not only getting customers, but also keeping them. It is a system that will help you organize your time during the above six steps, as seen below in Exhibit 9.1.

Exhibit 9.1   The Money Engine

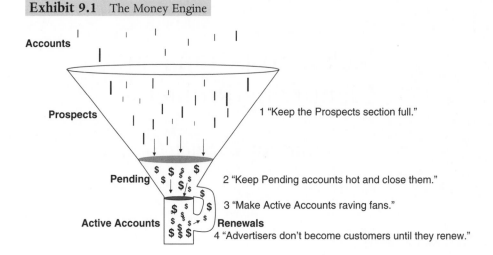

The model for the Money Engine was suggested by the Sales Funnel in *The New Strategic Selling*[1] and by Ron Steiner, who ran the annual Broadcast Sales Academy and teaches the sales funnel model. You will notice in Exhibit 9.1 that at the top of the Money Engine there are number of perpendicular lines. These lines represent all of the accounts that are on your *account list*.

Generally, media companies provide salespeople with some type of account list, which sometimes include hot prospects and even a few *active accounts*. The Money Engine will help you divide your selling efforts appropriately. If you are not given an account list and have to start from scratch knocking on doors and looking under every rock for someone to call on, the Money Engine model will work well for you, too. In either case, a typical account list might include 100 accounts – sometimes more in small or medium-sized markets and fewer in large markets or in national media where salespeople call primarily on advertising agencies.

Prospects are those accounts in the top part of the engine. While prospecting will be covered later in the chapter, it is imperative for you to understand the first principle of the Money Engine: *Keep the Prospects section full.*

Think of the Money Engine as a steam boiler that runs a revenue locomotive. You have to keep the top part – the tender, where all the fuel for the engine is stored – filled with prospects to make sure that you continually stoke the boiler fire. Out of a list of, say, 100 total accounts, 80 of them might have reasonable potential. You should spend enough time prospecting to make sure that about 40 of these accounts are bona fide prospects for your medium. Bona fide prospects are those whose target market (women 25–54, for example) your medium reaches. In other words, if there is a good fit between your medium's audience or readers and an advertiser's customers, that advertiser is a bona fide prospect.

Forty is an arbitrary number and in some sales situations, 60 might be a realistic number of prospects, and in others, 10. After a couple of months in a sales job you will know what an appropriate number is so that you can concentrate your selling efforts on legitimate prospects and not spin your wheels with those who will never buy anything.

The second section of the engine contains Pending accounts. This section is the boiler where prospects – the fuel – are heated up. Prospects become pending when, after you have qualified them, they are in the market to buy and have made a decision to invest in your medium. When salespeople get a request for a proposal (RFP) or call from an advertising agency buyer to make a proposal, the business is now pending.

This brings us to the second principle of the Money Engine: *Keep Pending Accounts hot and close them.* Once an advertiser or an agency buyer has decided to make a buy, you must stay right on top of the situation constantly, cover all the bases, and create a sense of urgency in order to get a commitment. You should shoot for having about 20 accounts pending at any given time, depending, of course, on your medium and market. In order to have 20 accounts always in the Pending section, you have to work hard to keep the Prospects section filled. You should always strive to achieve a closing ratio of 50 percent with accounts in the Pending section and, thus, move them to the Active Account section of the Money Engine.

The bottom section of the boiler is the Active Accounts section. Active Accounts are advertisers who produce revenue. If you have kept the Prospects section full, and if you have kept Pending accounts hot and have closed 50 percent of them, you should have 10 Active Accounts that are generating money for your company and for you. This brings us to the third principle of the Money Engine: *Make your Active Accounts raving fans.* Provide superb service and make sure your active accounts get results.

Note that there are accounts in a section of the Money Engine that looks like a handle that goes from the Active Accounts section back up to the Pending section. This is the Renewal section, which brings us to the fourth principle of the Money Engine: *Advertisers do not become customers until they renew* and its corollary: *Always sell for the second order, not just the first.* This second order will come if you under-promised when you were creating value and you over-deliver. In other words, you managed your advertisers' expectations properly and they got better results than they expected. The lower you can set their expectations, the higher their satisfaction with over-delivery will be.

The principle that advertisers do not become customers until they renew is important to remember because there is too often a tendency for salespeople to forget about accounts once they have been sold. Too many salespeople see their job as over once they make a sale. On the other hand, buyers believe a relationship is not a one-night stand but is just beginning when they make a buy. In local broadcasting and cable, attrition rates are often as high as a 60 percent from one year to the next, some of it from inattention. Attrition is lower in newspapers and magazines where the inverse is often the case. But whatever the case, it is vital to manage active accounts intensively and give them excellent service in order to reduce the amount of natural account attrition, as it is much easier to maintain and renew an account than it is to create a new one.

Prospecting

Prospecting is *creating opportunities to make a proposal*. The key to successful prospecting is working smart, which means learning how to find the right people to call on by using all of the methods of prospecting and then developing an organized system for setting up appointments and presenting to prospects. You should spend approximately 7.5 percent of your productive time each month prospecting, perhaps twice that if you are just beginning a job or you have no assigned account list. Chapter 24 covers techniques for developing and implementing an organized prospecting system.

Methods of prospecting

The first thing to do when you begin prospecting is to *select a method*.

1   By current advertisers in other media
2   By season
3   By category
4   By geographic region
5   By advertisers in your medium
6   By inactive advertisers
7   By current advertisers
8   By business, civic, or social organization

The obvious first place to start prospecting is in *other media*. Try to find businesses that are advertising but not in your medium. It is generally easier, and thus a more efficient use of your time, to try to sell prospects who already have an advertising budget than to have to start from scratch with someone and sell them first on advertising, then on your medium, and then on your product.

To prospect in other media, you should know something about their rates so you can estimate advertising budgets. In many larger markets, *newspaper checking bureaus* keep track of ads by client categories. Also, many markets have TNS Media Intelligence competitive media reports (CMR) online that radio and television station can subscribe to. Each month CMR publish details of all radio and television advertising schedules that ran the previous month. If your market does not have monitoring services available, you can ask advertisers or their agencies for rate cards of other media outlets in your market and you and your fellow salespeople can monitor other media on a systematic basis.

For national media such as broadcast and cable network television, magazines, and Web sites with national appeal, you can go www.adage.com, then go to the "Data Center" and click on "Leading National Advertisers Corporate Profiles" to get total spending levels by media and by the top 100 national advertisers.

Next, in your monitoring, you should try to pick out the creative approaches your prospects use, the images they are trying to project about their businesses, and their approximate target audiences for the advertising.

In a local market, the Yellow Pages, known as the Prospector's Bible, is the place to start because anyone in business who sells a product or service to the public will be in the Yellow Pages. It is the place to start and to go back to time and again when you prospect in a local market. However, today the best source of prospecting information is the Internet. If you are fortunate to have an auto dealer or two on your list, there are several places you can go on the Web to get a wealth of information. The Web site for the National Automobile Dealers Association, www.nada.org, has up-to-date news on auto industry trends and www.hoovers. com is a good resource to research companies and industries in general as is BusinessWeek.com, Investing and Stock Research – go to www.investing.business-week.com/research/company/overview/overview.asp.

If you get a job or work for a television station that is a member of the Television Bureau of Advertising (TVB), its Web site has some industry profiles.

There are other industry associations, such as the American Beverage Association, that have informative Web sites (www.ameribev.org). If you do not know whether or not a business or an industry association has a Web site, Google it.

If you sell broadcast, cable, or Interactive, *read newspaper ads* carefully, for they are the most fertile ground for other media. Look for a newspaper advertiser's selling points, image, creative approach, and target audience when you examine newspaper ads. If advertisers are continuously getting positions with low reader impact, such as bottom-left, back-of-the-section, or gutter positions (next to the fold), they might be ripe prospects for broadcast, cable, or Interactive.

If you sell for a local newspaper, radio station, or Web site, monitor television for commercials for local businesses. Television is vulnerable because it is expensive and many local businesses, especially car dealers, tend to over-invest in television.

Prospecting by *seasonal sales patterns* is a productive way to organize your prospecting efforts. Most advertisers have seasonal sales patterns; therefore, advertisers should be contacted anywhere from three to six months before their peak selling seasons begin. A salesperson should find out when advertisers set their annual advertising budget and make promotion plans and contact them at that time.

November is obviously too late to start selling advertising for the Christmas season.

Another way to organize your prospecting is by *category*. Select a business category, such as men's clothing, for example, and begin contacting as many of these companies as you can. Combine this category method with the seasonal one and choose a category that has a seasonal sales peak coming up. You will find that this category method is an excellent way to become an expert in a particular business category and helps you get referrals. As you get prospects to tell you about their advantages over their competitors, you will also learn how to approach those competitors. You can also go to www.adage.com in the "Data Center" and look in the Marketers/Advertisers section (click on READ MORE) for the advertising to sales ratios for over 200 business categories.

Many successful media salespeople have carved out profitable careers by specializing in one or two categories, such as telecommunications, supermarkets and food, automotive industries, and so on. There are many excellent resources on the Internet for prospecting by category.

Often it makes sense to organize prospecting efforts *geographically*. This is particularly the case in markets that are spread out physically, such as Los Angeles. Isolate an area of town that looks promising and start making phone calls to set up appointments. When you do get your appointments, you will save time and gas money by going to one general area. You can use the Internet to help you prospect in a new geographical area by going to www.mapquest.com or Google Maps at www.maps.google.com and get a map of the area, which you can download onto your cell phone.

You can prospect in *your own medium*. However, this type of prospecting tends to encourage parasitic behavior and leads to hordes of salespeople trying to carve up the same advertising pie, which, in turn, often leads to price cutting and overall lower rates. It is better to try to increase the size of the pie by developing new advertisers whenever possible.

Prospect internally by looking at *inactive account lists*. Go back several years through the files of completed contracts and look for advertisers who were once active but are not currently running. You might be amazed when you ask someone why they are no longer advertising with you and the reply is, "No one asked for my business again." This inactive account would be another easy sale for the disciplined, well-organized prospector.

Furthermore, do not overlook the obvious. Do not forget your *current advertisers*. While serving these customers, think of ways to get them to increase their schedule with you. Sell promotional packages, special events, longer schedules, or more ads, but do not fail to look at them as potential prospects for new revenue.

Finally, you can organize your prospecting efforts *organizationally*, by civil, social, or business clubs or by sports, church, or fraternal organizations. Insurance salespeople often prospect this way, and so can media salespeople.

Referral prospecting

You should never pass up the opportunity to ask a prospect, a customer, a friend, or an acquaintance to refer you to someone who might be a potential advertiser. The best referrals are from happy customers, so get in the habit of politely asking for referrals, because you have nothing to lose and sales to gain.

Prospecting is where selling begins. Good prospectors can always make a living; they do not have to depend on economic conditions, ratings, circulation, or rates. They can find new customers time and time again, year in and year out. Successful salespeople know how to organize themselves and to plan their time using the Money Engine to keep the Prospects tender full, to keep Pending Accounts hot and to close them, and to make Active Accounts raving fans.

Identifying Problems

The next step, after prospecting, in the solutions selling process is *identifying problems*. This step has two phases: *qualifying* and *identifying problems*.

Qualifying

After you have identified prospects and have made an initial appointment, qualifying prospects comes next. Qualifying is finding the *right* people to call on. According to Mark McCormack, author of *What They Don't Teach You at the Harvard Business School*, effective selling is more a matter of timing and the quality of the doors you knock on than it is the quantity of doors you knock on.[2]

Qualifying is an important part of the selling process because it is in this step that you *begin your relationship with your customers*. Qualifying is largely a matter of finding out if a prospective customer has the resources to advertise and if there is a fit with your medium so that you can get results for the prospect. Qualifying is when you begin to identify needs – both business and personal. You must carefully observe prospects' surroundings and behavior and learn to read the room and their desk.

Learning about your prospects   Harvey B. Mackay, Chairman of the Board of Mackay Envelope Corporation and author of the successful book *Swim With the Sharks Without Being Eaten Alive*, says that knowing your customer is not a cliché, it is the foundation of a sale.[3] In an article in the *Harvard Business Review*, Mackay wrote about a mythical conversation with a salesperson who cannot get a buyer, Bystrom of International Transom, to quit using Mackay Envelope's competitor,

Enveloping Envelope. Mackay looks at the account folder with the salesperson and says sternly: "Did you read his desk? Were there any mementos there that told you about him? How many plaques on the wall? What's his alma mater? If he's businesslike with you, what are his aspirations? How does he identify with company goals? You don't have in here a recent article or current analyst's report on his company." Mackay gets up from his desk and gesticulates as he paces to and fro and continues. "How well have YOU shown him that you know and admire his company; that you know how it fits in its industry? Do you know the strengths and weaknesses of Enveloping Envelope in terms of International Transom? Have you emphasized to Bystrom those strengths that we have almost exclusively, such as centralized imprinting?"[4]

You do not want to be in the same position as the hapless salesperson above. Make sure you qualify prospects thoroughly, read the surroundings, the office, their desk, and their behavior. The first appointment is essential for gathering information about your prospects so you can begin to create a needs-based portrait of their business and personal needs and motivations.

The qualifying appointment   On your first qualifying appointment, it is usually best not to take notes. Taking notes while your prospect is talking is similar to tape recording the conversation; it makes many people nervous and unwilling to open up. It also means you are concentrating on writing and not on the prospect. If you are conducting a lengthy, fact-gathering interview, you might need to take a few notes very quickly, but be careful not to do anything that might reduce the opportunity to establish rapport during the first interview. Immediately *after* you leave the appointment, take full notes while the details are fresh in your mind. Also, follow up the initial appointment with your prospect with more fact-finding interviews with people who work for the prospect. Learn the prospect's business thoroughly before you make a sales presentation.

Here are your goals for your first meeting:

① *To build rapport instantly: You never get a second chance to make a first impression.* You have about 15–60 seconds to create a favorable first impression. Prospects will continue to judge you based on this first impression and reinforce their judgment the remainder of the time they know you. Your initial goal from the moment you lay eyes on your prospects is to get them to like you, which requires using the emotional intelligence and influence skills you learned in Chapter 6. You must also use the communication, effective listening, and understanding people skills you learned in Chapter 7.

When you shake hands, do exactly what the other person does. If prospects have soft, limp handshakes, you reciprocate. People of this type are not prone to enjoying aggressive handshakes that involve a tight grip, firm squeezing, and vigorous pumping. In contrast, if people grab your hand, squeeze, and pump heartily, follow their energetic lead. Remember, people like and trust people exactly like themselves. As you do when you talk to prospects on the telephone, synchronize with their speech patterns in person.

② *To build trust.* The quickest way to build trust with people you do not know well is to find something on which you can agree and then agree 100 percent. In your conversations with prospects, you will touch on a number of subjects, many of which you will disagree on. On the other hand, do not be hypocritical and say something you really do not believe. Keep probing until you find something you can agree on and then say, "I agree 100 percent." Try to compliment your prospect on something specific, which usually gets prospects talking.

If prospects bring up any negatives about salespeople, your medium, or your company, honor them and compliment them for bringing up the point. People will trust you if you show confidence in yourself and in your product and are not afraid to deal with negatives, especially if you bring it up. Be totally candid. The two-sided argument is particularly effective at this time. For example, you might say, "There are some problems with using radio, Mr Jones. You can't demonstrate or show products on radio, but an effective creative approach can work wonders."

③ *To become a partner with prospects.* You must communicate your desire to become a partner with your prospects in solving their problems and making them successful. Sell yourself as a media expert and an advertising problem solver. By not trying to sell prospects anything while you are qualifying them, you plant the seed that you and your product might become the solution, instilling a sense of cooperation. You are beginning to cultivate a relationship, build a partnership.

④ *To qualify creditworthiness.* Qualifying also means that you must check a prospect's credit. There is no future for a salesperson who sells advertising to someone who will not or cannot pay for it. Many small- and medium-market media pay commissions on collections and not on billing. Thus, a salesperson who sells to prospects that have shaky credit ratings is taking time away from selling to prospects that will pay their bills and generate sales commissions.

Checking credit ratings is a task for a business manager and not for salespeople, particularly on the first call. Salespeople, however, should make it a point to know the results of credit checks. If a business office, for whatever reason, recommends getting cash in advance from a prospect whose credit has not yet been established, salespeople should ask for cash in advance very delicately, so as not to risk offending or insulting a potential customer. If a prospect gets upset, a salesperson can blame an overzealous business manager, who is paid to take the heat in situations such as this. This tactic leaves the door open for future contacts. By the way, all political advertising is cash-in-advance, and politicians and those who plan and buy their advertising understand this policy.

Most beginning salespeople find that qualifying is not an easy step to master. One reason for this difficulty is that proper qualifying requires salespeople to be tough-minded and to not waste time with people who are not good prospective advertisers or with people who are not in a position to make the final decision, no matter how pleasant they might be.

⑤ *To assess perceptual set and readiness.* Every person enters every situation with a *perceptual set*, which is a predisposition to perceive things in a certain way. People come to any encounter with values, attitudes, beliefs, and opinions about virtually everything. For example, they might not like salespeople in general or they might not care for either female or male salespeople. They might not like your medium. They might not like young people.

It is important for you to ferret out prospects' perceptual set so you can plan your sales strategy and set your selling priorities. For instance, you may recognize that a particular older male retailer does not seem to care to deal with young people or with females. If you are both, you will have to build source credibility with qualities other than similarity. Thus, you might concentrate on being especially businesslike and try to develop trust through your expertise and extensive product knowledge (but do not use industry jargon – talk in the prospect's language).

Readiness is the notion that people will learn what they want to learn and are able to learn. A wide variety of variables, such as educational level, emotions, ambitions, success, past experience, and selective perception condition people's readiness.

A prospect who has had a bad experience advertising in your medium is not willing to learn about what you are offering. You might have to focus your sales strategy on discussing several successful case histories of similar businesses in your medium just to get this prospect to listen to a presentation of the benefits you offer.

⑥ *To get an appointment for a discovery meeting.* Remember that the qualifying appointment is not to be a sales call; it should be a call in which you gain permission to learn more about your prospects' business, to ask a series of Discovery Questions so you can bring back an appropriate solutions-based proposal.

Identifying problems phase

The entire premise of solutions selling rests on the idea that a prospect has marketing and advertising problems – virtually no one is ever satisfied with the number of customers they have; they always want more. So, once you qualify prospects and find out they have the resources to advertise, and you believe your medium can legitimately help them, the next phase in the solution selling process is to get access to prospects' information so you can identify their problems. How do you do this detective work? You ask a lot of the right questions.

A quote by the artistic/creative genius, Pablo Picasso, pinpoints the vital importance of asking the right questions in a somewhat humorous light. He said, "Computers are useless. They only give you answers."[5]

There are three types of questions, or probes: *open-end questions*, *closed-end questions*, and *verification questions*. Start with open-end questions, such as "Tell me more about your business." You get a lot more information with open-end questions because you are not asking for specific information. Your prospects will often wander off in several directions and sometimes, even, give you more information than they intended. Remember, most people like to talk, so let them.

Closed-end questions are those that ask for a specific answer, such as "What is your advertising budget?" Think of your questioning technique as a funnel that starts out wide, with open-end questions pouring lots of information into the funnel, and as you learn more, you can be more selective and ask narrower and narrower, more specific, closed-end questions in order to get the information you want. The reason you start with open-end questions is that they build trust in the relationship, and once trust is established, the prospect is much more likely to give you informative answers to your closed-end questions.

A verification question is an efficient information-seeking question framed in a way that elicits a yes answer to verify information that you believe is correct. For example, "As advertising manager, you make the final decision. Is that correct?"

Discovery Questions Ask the 26 Discovery Questions shown in Exhibit 9.2 in a series of interviews with appropriate people in prospects' organizations. It may not be possible to ask all of the questions on one call – always be sensitive to the time constraints of your prospects. You might want to spread the questions out over several appointments and among several people.

Note that the first several questions are ones that you should know the answers to based on your research. This is perfect situation to use verification questions to make sure your information is correct and to show your prospects that you are knowledgeable about their business and industry.

As you can see from the list of Discovery Questions, the questions are quite thorough and are obviously not appropriate in every situation. I suggest using the questions in Exhibit 9.2 as a guideline and that you develop your own list of questions that are appropriate for your market and your medium.

Finally, the most important questions are follow-up questions. After you get an answer to one of the following Discovery Questions, ask "Why?" Also, when you are following up and probing, probe for feelings, not just for the company line. If you ask the right probing questions, you can get people to think about their problems from a new perspective and to think more deeply about their problems and potential solutions.

When you ask your Discovery Questions, the conversation should not be interrogative or manipulative, but should be relaxed and comfortable. In Chapter 6 we wrote that old models of selling do not work any more, which is a major reason why the solution-selling model evolved. Experienced advertising agencies media buyers have seen every trick. They know full well when a salesperson tries to manipulate them or tries to close them.

Some salespeople have been trained to ask manipulative questions that lead prospects to a conclusion that the salespeople want them to reach, regardless of what a prospect might want. Even though in Chapter 6 I recommended Neil Rackham's *SPIN Selling* because it contains some useful sales lessons, I do not recommend

Exhibit 9.2 Discovery Questions

1 Before making a call, you should research the following information about a prospect. Your first question should be a verification question to confirm that the information you have gathered is correct. For example, "Our research indicates that your revenue is $6 billion a year, your profit is $550 million, and that you have 11,000 employees. Are my assumptions correct?"

    A   Size
- Revenue (sales)?
- Profit?
- Number of employees?

2 In your research, you should also develop a profile of the company and find answers to the following questions. If you can't find the information, you should ask appropriate, closed-ended questions.

    A   How long have you been in business?
    B   Business structure? (For example, public company, privately held, corporation, partnership, sole proprietor, franchisor, franchisee)
    C   Number of locations/outlets?
    D   Distribution channel? (For example, retail, direct marketing, wholesalers, online, catalogues)
    E   Type of product/service? (For example: impulse purchase, planned purchase, high-priced, low-priced, middle-range, mass consumer, luxury)
    F   Peak selling season(s)?
- Percentage of yearly business at peak seasons
    G   Business cycle? (For example, purchase once a day, once a week, once a year, once in a lifetime)
    H   Five largest customers?
    I   How has your business changed in the past year?

3 Before making a call, you should research the following information about a prospect. Your next group of questions should confirm what you have learned.

    A   Total marketing budget?
- Direct selling?
- Advertising?
- Promotion? (% trade, % consumer; advertising/promotion ratio?)
- Cause marketing, corporate relations, PR budget?
    B   Total advertising/direct marketing budget in dollars?
- Advertising rank in industry? (Who is #1, #2, and #3?)
- National, national spot, and local budgets?
    C   Advertising as a percentage of revenue (sales) – ad/sales ratio?
- Ad/sales ratio rank in industry (who is#1, #2, #3)?
- Advertising rank in industry? ("What competitors spend more in what media?")

4 During the discovery process (which will take several calls at different levels of an organization), you should find answers to the following questions:

    A   "What research do you look at and what does it tell you?" (You need to know the answer to this question so that your eventual proposal doesn't contradict what they believe from their research.)

Exhibit 9.2 Discovery Questions (cont'd)

B   Who in the organization will make the final decision?
- A single decision maker (e.g., CEO, Senior VP, Marketing)
- The key influencers (e.g., CFO, Senior VP Advertising)
- Influencers (e.g. ad committee, consultants)

C   What is the organization's decision making process like (fast, slow, consensus, CEO only, consultants, e.g.)

5   "If I could wave a magic wand, and make three wishes come true for your company next year, what would you wish for?" (Examples: Increase profitability, reduce expenses, sell more product/service, introduce new products, increase share of mind (branding), increase stock price)

6   "What are your marketing goals?" Examples:

Introduce new product/service	Establish or re-establish image
Create demand	Increase profit margins
Introduce line extension	Build brand awareness
Change customer attitudes	Increase response level
Develop/increase traffic	Reinforce leadership position
Feature specialty products	Promote special sales
Maintain market dominance	Promote special events
Develop seasonal buying	Increase market share
Recapture old customers	Increase usage
Build destination	Move up one market rank
Expand target market (age, geography)	Expand size of pie (market)
Build private label	Dominate (own) a market

7   "What problems are you having in achieving those marketing goals?"

8   "What are your primary marketing strategies?" (For example, differentiation, focus/niche marketing, or low-cost producer)

9   "What are your secondary marketing strategies?" (For example, defense, offense, flanker brand, fighting brand, guerrilla marketing, ambush marketing)

10   "What is your current market position?" (For example, dominant leader, number one, close second, follower, last)

11   "Who are you trying to reach – who is your primary target customer?"

A   "What percentage of your business is done by your heavy users/big customers?" (For example 85% of product bought by 15% of customers.)

B   "Who are your secondary target customers?"

C   "Who are your most profitable customers?"

12   "Why do your customers buy from you – what is your major appeal?"

13   "What messages or creative approaches have been most successful for you in the past?"

A   "Who (organization) does your creative?"

B   "Who (organization) does your media planning?"

14   "What advertising media are you currently using?"

A   "How is your budget allocated among the media you use?"
- Does this allocation reflect current media usage by consumers?"

B   "How effective are the media you are currently using?"

Exhibit 9.2 Discovery Questions (cont'd)

C "How to you track the results/response to your advertising?"

D "What advertising problems are you having and which ones are you trying to solve?"

E "Are there any perceptions about your brand that you would like to change?"

15 "What do you want your advertising/direct marketing to do for you?"

A "What are your advertising goals?" (For example: sales/transactions, branding, awareness, information, persuasion, or reminding/reinforcing)

16 "Who are your three/five biggest competitors?"

17 "Why do your customers buy from each of your major competitors?"

A "What strategies do you have to capture share from your competitors?"

B "How are you differentiating yourself from your competitors?" (For example: price, quality, convenience, location, selection)

18 "What do you do better than your competitors?"

A "What do they do better than you do?"

19 "What do you think of my medium of advertising?"

"Who owns the search terms most valuable to your business and industry?"

- "Have you been monitoring your competitors' advertising activity, campaigns, and creative?"

B "Are there any specific goals you have in mind for your advertising?" (For example, low CPMS, low CPCs, promotions)

C "What advertising/marketing element has produced the best ROI for you?"

20 "What time of year do you (A) plan and (B) buy advertising?"

21 "Are there any co-op dollars available?"

22 "Do you use promotions – if so what kind?" (For example, sales, rebates, contests, sweepstakes, coupons, free samples)

A "Is your decision to purchase a medium based on doing a promotion?"

B "Do you create your own promotions or do you depend on the media or an outside agency or promotion company?"

23 "What are your criteria for judging the best proposal?"

A "What are your metrics for success?"

24 "What do you think of my company?"

A "What is the likelihood that you'd buy from us?"

25 "Is there anything I should have asked you, but haven't?"

26 "What questions do you have for me?"

using the technique of asking the SPIN selling questions. The mnemonic SPIN stands for four types of questions that salespeople should ask: Situation questions, Problem questions, Implication questions, and Needs-Payoff questions.[6]

Rackham chose an unfortunate mnemonic, unwittingly I'm sure, because SPIN has a pejorative meaning. Spin is a term that means spinning a news story that could be negative away from the underlying truth toward a meaning that is more favorable to the spinner. Spinning news or information is manipulative. Also, the book, published in 1988, was based on research conducted over several years before that, before solution selling became the modern model for selling, which means that SPIN selling is an outdated method.

The last two types of SPIN questions (Implication and Needs-Payoff questions) also tend to be manipulative, as Rackam suggests asking them. Using these types of questions is using the Socratic method.

If Socrates was the greatest teacher of all time, how could he be manipulative? In her book *I Only Say This Because I Love You*, author Deborah Tannen writes:

> The Socratic method, according to philosopher Janice Moulton, is frequently (though not accurately) identified as "a method of discussion designed to lead the other person into admitting that her/his views were wrong" . . . I use the term *Socratic method* to refer to a style of arguing in which you try to get others to admit they are wrong – and to agree with your conclusion – by getting them to agree to one after another step along the way, which [*sic*] the Greek philosopher Socrates (as we see in Plato's dialogues) posed a series of questions, the answers to which exposed others' ignorance or uncovered contradictions in their beliefs.[7]

We all know what happened to Socrates – he committed suicide by drinking hemlock rather than being exiled from Athens. Salespeople who try to manipulate and use tricks on savvy customers and media buyers will be exiled. When you ask Discovery Questions, do not ask leading questions; ask straightforward, authentic, non-manipulative questions.

Once you have asked enough questions to identify the marketing and advertising goals, strategies, and problems a prospect has, do a thorough diagnosis of the problems. Come up with solutions that are unique to your medium, and generate proposals that offer your solutions effectively – the subject of the next chapter.

Test Yourself

1 What are the four principles associated with the Money Engine?
2 What are the five prospecting goals?
3 What are the eight methods of prospecting?
4 What are the two phases of identifying problems?
5 What are the six goals for your first qualifying appointment?
6 Why is the Socratic method manipulative?

Project

Assume you are a salesperson for a Web site. Write a script for a prospecting telephone call to a local business in which you try to get an appointment. Assume the prospect you are calling answers yes to all of your questions. Rehearse reading your script several times, and then record yourself. Play back the recording. Did you sound friendly and confident? Would you give yourself an appointment? Make notes on how you could improve your telephone technique and try again. Repeat this exercise until you are satisfied that you sound effective, friendly, and confident.

References

Stephen E. Heiman and Diane Sanchez with Tad Tuleja. 1998. *The New Strategic Selling*. New York: Warner Books.

Harvey Mackay. 1988. "Humanize your selling strategy," *Harvard Business Review*. March–April.

Harvey Mackay. 1988 *Swim With the Sharks Without Being Eaten Alive*. New York: William Morrow.

Mark McCormack. 1984. *What They Don't Teach You at the Harvard Business School*. New York: Bantam Books.

Neil Rackham. 1988. *SPIN Selling*. New York: McGraw-Hill.

Deborah Tannen. 2001. *I Only Say This Because I Love You*. New York: Random House.

Resources

www.ameribev.org (American Beverage Association Web site)

www.hoovers.com (Web site containing financial information about companies)

www.iab.net (Interactive Advertising Bureau Web site)

www.nada.org (National Automobile Dealers Association Web site)

www.nna.org (National Newspapers Association Web site)

www.onetvworld.com (Cabletelevision Bureau of Advertising Web site)

www.rab.com (Radio Advertising Bureau Web site)

www.tvb.org (Television Bureau of Advertising Web site)

Notes

1 Stephen E. Heiman and Diane Sanchez with Tad Tuleja. 1998. *The New Strategic Selling*. New York: Warner Books.

2 Mark McCormack. 1984. *What They Don't Teach You at the Harvard Business School*. New York: Bantam Books.

3 Harvey Mackay. 1988. *Swim With the Sharks Without Being Eaten Alive*. New York: William Morrow.

4 Harvey Mackay. 1988. "Humanize your selling efforts." *Harvard Business Review*. March–April.

5 http://quotationspage.com/quotes/Pablo_Picasso/. Accessed November 11, 2007.

6 Neil Rackham. 1988. *SPIN Selling*. New York: McGraw-Hill.

7 Deborah Tannen. 2001. *I Only Say This Because I Love You*. New York: Random House, p. 80.

10

Skills: Generating Solutions, Proposals, and Presentations

Charles Warner

The third step in the solutions-selling process is *generating solutions* – the step in which you find an effective match between prospects' problems / challenges and solutions that you can provide. Then, you have to present these solutions in an arresting, dramatic, and winning proposal or presentation. The generating-solutions step of selling implements all five of the primary sales strategies: (1) selling solutions to advertising and marketing problems, (2) reinforcing the value of advertising and your medium, (3) creating value for your product, (4) becoming the preferred supplier (because you have offered solutions, which your competitors probably haven't), and (5) innovating (because you've come up with creative, unique solutions).

Generating Solutions

After you have identified a prospect's problems / challenges, you have to *brainstorm* to come up with solutions that are unique to your medium and to your media organization, and that take advantage of opportunities you can offer. The process of generating solutions is the most creative and satisfying step of selling and

Exhibit 10.1   Rules for brainstorming

1   *Everyone must contribute.*
2   *Let your imagination run wild.* You're after quantity of ideas, not quality of ideas. Calm down, relax and let your brain run free. The more ideas you have the better. There is no such thing as a bad idea. Don't worry about being silly. Have fun, get crazy, produce ideas. Here are some techniques that will help you expand your thinking:
   A   Think about the ideal or the perfect situation – suspend reality – think of the ultimate.
   B   Think of the wildest thing in the world – expand.
3   *Do not be judgmental at the beginning.* Make absolutely no judgments about your own or anyone else's ideas or suggestions. There is no such thing as a bad idea. Do not challenge or criticize anyone's idea in any way. On the contrary, encourage people to come up with more and wilder ideas. During the idea-generation stage of brainstorming, it is imperative that practicality or feasibility be thrown to the winds – don't be concerned if it can't work, out with it! The more ideas the better.
   A   Push extremes.
   B   Look for opposites.
   C   Use free-form word associations.
   D   Go off on tangents.
4   *Look for combinations.* Pause and look for combinations of words or ideas. Don't worry about whether the combinations make sense or are plausible yet. There is no such thing as a bad combination.
5   *Make connections.* See if any ideas or combinations of ideas connect to another idea or combination of ideas. Do the ideas connect to anything you can possibly think of?
6   *Modify.* Become more judgmental. Can you modify an idea to make it more feasible.
7   The facilitator should *write everything down* so the team can see the whole list.
8   *Select the best ideas.*

requires making innovative connections between a prospect's advertising problems / challenges and solutions that are unique to your medium outlet.

Exhibit 8.9 in Chapter 8 featured a number of ideas for creating value, and all of these can be used to generate ideas for solutions, depending on your medium. Another way to come up with ideas is to brainstorm with people in your organization. You want a diversity of people at all levels to participate in brainstorming sessions. It is often a 19-year-old receptionist or a multiply-pierced, tattooed, green-haired production person who comes up with the best ideas. You want to brainstorm with other salespeople, management, and, especially, content people (programmers, editors, etc. who really understand your content), in fact, anyone who can help you come up with new, innovative, unique solutions that no other media or no other media outlet can provide. See Exhibit 10.1 for the Rules of Brainstorming.

Creating Presentations and Proposals

In 1961, I was fortunate enough to have worked my way from being a rookie sales-person in Spartanburg, SC, to being an account executive for the number-one televi-sion station in the country – WCBS-TV, Channel 2, in New York. At the time the station was referred to as the "Big Deuce." It was the Mecca for media salespeople because it was in the number-one media market, it was an owned station of the number-one television network, CBS (known as the "Tiffany Network" at the time), and it was, by far, the most dominant television station in New York City.

The General Sales Manager of WCBS-TV, Norm Walt, was notorious in the media and advertising community for insisting that all of his salesmen (there were no women salespeople at that time) create a written presentation for every submis-sion. All of the Big Deuce's business at the time came from advertising agencies, and agency buyers would call the salesman assigned to them and request avails for one of the agency's accounts. Buyers just wanted to know what times were available on the station and prices for each avail. Other television stations' sales-men (all men in those days) often did just that, submit a list of avails and prices and let buyers select what they wanted to buy. Not Big Deuce salesmen.

To buyers' never-ending protestations, WCBS-TV salesmen would come in with thick presentations and proceed to go over every page. Salesmen who did not follow this procedure were fired by the flame-throwing Walt, so everyone slogged through their presentations. The presentations were prescribed to be comb-bound in white plastic, to have a thick, clear plastic outer cover over a deep, heavy-stock yellow-gold cover page with the famous black CBS eye in the bottom right-hand corner with a tastefully large, white Helvetica-font number two over the eye. It was an impressive and tasteful package and it reeked of quality and importance, which, of course, is what Norm Walt wanted.

The presentations had to contain information about the Big Deuce's complete dominance in the market – 48 out the 50 top-ranked time-periods and commercial breaks in the market, for example. The presentations were designed to overwhelm buyers with WCBS-TV's dominance and make them feel they would be lucky to be able to get on the station. Salesmen were chosen for their ability to communi-cate an image of complete confidence and domination. Most of them crossed over to arrogance.

Salesmen did not offer a list of avails and prices; after creating value for the Big Deuce, they offered packages of spots. Buyers could not buy individual spots within a package; they had to buy the whole package. I offered a package to the buyer for Griffin Shoe Polish that consisted of two Early Morning News spots, seven Late-Late Show spots (after1:00 a.m.), and one desirable spot, the "7:00 p.m. News with Robert Trout." When I presented the package, the buyer said, "You've got to be kidding! The only spot I want is the news spot. OK, I'll take it to get the news spot."

I jubilantly brought the order back to the station, showed it to Norm Walt who said, "Great order, Charlie. I can confirm all the spots but the 7:00 p.m. News. Go back and get the buyer to accept the change." That was the way it was back then and some salesmen were able to sell that way. I was not good at it.

WCBS-TV designed the whole system to create value and maximize revenue, and it did. But times have changed drastically as the television medium has been fragmented and no one station or network is dominant. Today, buyers are generally in the driver's seat, not stations or networks. However, the power of an excellent presentation has not diminished.

This topic of proposals and presentations brings up some questions. How excellent is excellent? What is the difference between a presentation and a proposal? How long should a presentation or proposal be?

How excellent is excellent?

An excellent presentation is one that wins, that beats the competition. If your competitors regularly bring three-page proposals to buyers who have placed request for a proposal (RFP) or asked for avails, you should bring five-page proposals. If your biggest competitor regularly makes 50-page presentations to major accounts for large, year-long partnership deals, you create a dramatic 75-page presentation that blows away the competition.

Never deliver avails, a one-page proposal, or a rate card only, no matter what buyers ask for. You do not want to be merely a clerk who processes transactions. *Always* include qualitative information about your advantages over the competition, and your benefits. You must create a differential competitive advantage for yourself and your product in order to avoid, whenever possible, discounting your rates. Your proposals and presentations are major building blocks in creating a differential competitive advantage and creating value. Remember if you are merely a delivery person, you will be disintermediated by an automated buy-sell process such as Google's.

Game theory

Game theory is currently a hot topic in economics, investing, politics, and international relations. The mathematical genius John von Neumann first developed game theory in 1928.[1] John Nash, the subject of the movie, *A Beautiful Mind*, won a Nobel Prize in Economics for his refinements to von Neumann's theories. Watching players bluff in a poker game in 1928 inspired von Neumann – godfather of the modern computer and one of the sharpest minds in the twentieth century – to construct game theory, a mathematical study of deception and competitive strategies.

At its most basic level, game theory posits that players of any game (Monopoly, poker, business, war, negotiating, or selling), should not make moves according to the probability of success, but based on the moves of their competitors. So, when you play poker, you do not play the odds of drawing a particular hand or card, but you play according to what the other players' tendencies and moves are. An excellent example of the use of game theory principles was in Super Bowl XXXVII when John Gruden's Tampa Bay Buccaneers whomped the Oakland Raiders. Gruden had been the coach of the Raiders the previous year and knew their tendencies. He knew that Raider quarterback, Rich Gannon, usually pumped one way and then threw the other way. Because the Buccaneers' defensive backs knew Gannon's tendencies, there were a record five interceptions. The Bucs played the game according to what moves they knew their competitor would make.

How excellent is excellent? Excellent is not an absolute term, it is a comparative term that measures how good you are compared to your competitors. So, excellent means excellent enough to win. There are never any excuses for not knowing what kind of proposals and presentations your competitors make, not knowing what kind of proposals your customers like, and, therefore, not doing better proposals and presentations than your competitors do.

Proposal or presentation?

What is the difference between a presentation and a proposal? A *presentation* is a structured communication about the features, advantages, and benefits of any one or all of the following elements: your medium, your company, and your product. A presentation can be verbal, written, or computerized (i.e. PowerPoint). It can be a simple two-minute elevator pitch, a brief e-mail, or it can be a 200-slide PowerPoint presentation accompanied by a 300-page, leather-bound printed book. Presentations can range from a general presentation (GP) that is an introduction to a medium and a company, to a customized, solutions-based recommendation for a partnership deal.

A *proposal* is a formal offer of available inventory (space, time, or banner slots) and corresponding prices. A proposal certifies that at the time the offer is made, the inventory is available at the price indicated.

Therefore, a presentation may or may not include a proposal. Generally, the first presentation you make to a prospect would be a GP and not include a proposal. The purpose of the initial GP is primarily to create value for your medium, your company, and your product. Subsequent presentations might include proposals, but *all* of them must include some creating value elements. To view a well-structured, thorough, informative GP, look at the AOL General Presentation (GP), 2000, at www.mediaselling.us/downloads.html. Even though the AOL GP from 2000 is out of date, you can learn a lot about how to structure and format a presentation.

Here are 10 good reasons for creating excellent, customized, solution-based presentations:

1   You cannot win without one and you can win even bigger with a good one.
2   You are compelled to do your homework and be thoroughly prepared.
3   They increase your confidence and commitment when you rehearse.
4   They show that you understand your prospects' businesses.
5   They are proof of your professionalism and trustworthiness.
6   They concentrate prospects' focus and attention on your solutions.
7   They provide permanent, tangible, memorable records for prospects.
8   They provide you with a permanent record.
9   They show your management how you sell.
10 They build libraries of presentations and best practices.

How complex should presentations be?

Exhibit 10.2 shows that the relationship between the complexity of a presentation and the dollars involved.

As you can see from Exhibit 10.2, the complexity of your presentation should increase as the dollars at stake increase. The dollars involved are relative to your medium and market, so an advertising proposal for a one-week schedule for a few hundred dollars need not be more than five 8½ × 11 inch pages (but always should be longer than all of your competitors' proposals and always should include some creating value elements that emphasize your benefits). On the other hand, a presentation to a major advertiser recommending a large $450 million investment in a partnership that includes not only advertising but also promotions, events,

Exhibit 10.2   Sales proposals and presentations

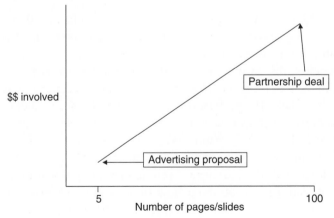

signage, and personal appearances, for example, might run 50 PowerPoint slides, accompanied by a 100-page hard copy with reams of data attached to it.

Planning Your Presentation

Begin your planning by determining your target (more about targets later in this chapter) and the presentation's style and then *develop an outline*. You must plan what benefits and solutions you are going to present and how you are going to price and order your proposals.

Develop your proposed advertising schedule before you create an outline and presentation because you want your presentation to lead up with clear, inescapable logic to an investment in one of the schedules you are going to propose.

Always include at least three proposals in a presentation. Including three or more proposals allows you to use effective ordering effects, such as foot-in-the-door or door-in-the-face. One of your proposals should be large (the optimal order you'd like to get), one (or several) medium, and one small (the minimal order).

Ordering tactics for proposals

The order of the proposals in your presentation depends on the characteristics of your prospect. Normally, you should put the smaller proposal (in dollar terms) first and then build up to the increased benefits and advantages of each of the larger ones. This ordering is effective because it does not intimidate prospects with a large investment at the beginning. You can build up slowly and logically to the reasons for investing more money and for giving you your optimal order. This tactic is particularly useful with prospects who might not be used to spending much money and with those new to your medium or to advertising and usually leads to a sale for the medium proposal or even the large one. This first ordering method is known as the *foot-in-the-door* technique. Remember Chapter 8?

On the other hand, if your prospects see themselves as important, big-spending clients, then starting with the large proposal can be effective in letting prospects know you think they can afford it. You can discuss all of the benefits of the larger proposal and then show how the medium and smaller proposals are not worthy of such an important client.

With some customers, putting the most expensive proposal first makes the following ones look inexpensive by contrast and is an effective tactic with a customer who always complains about high prices. This second method is known as the *door-in-the-face* technique; it presents an unreasonably large initial proposal that is sure to be turned down to make the next proposal seem more reasonable.

Whichever tactical or ordering decision you make, it should be a conscious one and one that best satisfies prospects' business and personal needs.

Putting prices in your proposals

Break costs into smaller units. "Just pennies a day" is an example of this tactic. Break your rates or schedules down to the lowest possible unit rate. Show the average unit rate of a schedule instead of the total weekly or monthly or total package price. An average of only $10 per ad unit sounds to a prospect like an easier amount to handle than $860 per month. If prospects ask for yearly totals, give them the yearly amount, but also show weekly, monthly, and average rates. Your objective is to minimize the impact of the dollar amount you are proposing. Learn to use modifying words that connote minimization, such as "only" and "just," when you refer to your costs or prices when you discuss them. *State costs as investments.* Advertising is not an expense; it is an investment in future profits. Therefore, on proposals, show "Total investment" *not* "Total cost."

Determine your presentation's style.

Exactly what reaction do you want and what would you like to sell the prospect? This information comes from your targeting and from your analysis of a prospect's needs. Your presentation's style – how you phrase and write your proposals and presentations – will depend on the style preferred by your prospects. Do you need to write very formally with lots of supporting figures for those who like precision, understanding, and expertise or less formally and more colorfully for a prospect who is impressed by media glitz and glamour and a casual approach? Do you need to write a short presentation for prospects who have short attention spans, bordering on attention-deficit-disorder (ADD).

Your presentation outline

After you have determined what solution is best for the client, what you have targeted to sell, and what the best style is, write an outline. You can review it and change it as you complete each step and evaluate it. Here are the guidelines for developing your outline:

1 *Aim your presentation at the right person* at the client or to an agency, to a buyer or to top management. Each group will require a slightly different approach, will need different facts, and will have different needs to be satisfied.

2 *Set priorities for the problems* you are trying to solve, and call them challenges in your presentation. Customers do not want to be reminded they have problems. Concentrate on solving the challenges that are uppermost in prospects' minds first.

3 *Be parsimonious with facts.* Do not try to overwhelm prospects with facts; give just enough to win. Some prospects, especially those who must be convinced of your expertise, might need more facts and data, but, generally, this is a wasteful, time-consuming approach.

4 *Avoid presenting your proposal costs (and cost-related statistics) until near the end of the presentation.* Always plan to include qualitative information and to provide facts that create value before you mention price.

5 *Anticipate the competition.* Know what your competitors are most likely to offer and to say about you. Position your strengths directly against their weaknesses and emphasize your strengths; point out, briefly, their generic weaknesses, but do not appear to knock them. Remember game theory and anticipate how complex competitors' presentations are and make yours better and longer – just longer enough to win.

6 *Remember the KISS rule, Keep It Short and Simple.* Often presentations ramble on with unnecessary detail. Present only as much information as you need to make an important point and to beat the competition. Show just enough to win.

7 *Be honest and accurate.* As you develop your outline, do not include anything that might be an exaggeration, give false information, or use numbers or figures for which you do not give a credible, reliable source. Always double-check your figures for accuracy. Mistakes and inaccuracies in your numbers and writing will destroy your credibility.

8 *Target what you want to sell.* Target the type of order you want to get, which will guide your outline and eventual proposal.

Targeting

Targeting is determining in advance the kind of order you want to get within the framework of an appropriate solution; it is *setting a goal* for yourself for each presentation. Targeting gives you something to shoot at, helps you select your selling tactics, and helps you develop and create your presentation. Your target is your destination and your presentation is the road map.

Targeting is the only part of the solution-selling process where the focus is on your company's needs. Without a clear, realistic target, you might get so wrapped up in satisfying prospects' needs that you forget about balancing their needs with your company's needs. While you want an order, you want the *right order* for both your prospect and for your company. The following *value proposition* shows how targeting can be good for both your advertisers and for your company.

We are committed to partnering with our advertisers and their agencies by providing innovative solutions for connecting them to our audience in a way that delivers advertiser-defined results and jointly builds both of our brands.

Target selection   In order to be coordinated with your overall sales strategy, targets should be selected based on the following elements:

① *A specific opportunity.* In this case, your target is to sell an advertiser a specific opportunity in your medium that is the right solution to an account's advertising or marketing problem. Examples of opportunities are: special programming (e.g., the Academy Awards) or a promotion (e.g., "Win a Vacation"), a special content area on a Web site (e.g., health), a special section in a newspaper (e.g., Home & Garden Sunday section), or a special advertising section in a magazine (e.g., New Technology).

② *Price.* In this case, your target is to get prices within a predetermined range. Examples are: In television to get no lower than $1,300 for an early news spot, in radio to get an average rate of no lower than a cost-per-point of $125, or on a Web site to get no less than a $20 CPM (you will learn about cost-per-points and cost-per-thousands in Chapter 16 "Media Research"). In these situations, your primary concern is to sell your product for the highest possible price, regardless of the overall size of an order, the type of order, or the share of an advertiser's budget. A price target might be used in situations, such as in broadcasting and cable, where you have limited inventory to sell, or in newspapers where moving advertisers up to a higher lineage commitment would increase their total investment in the paper.

③ *Size of an order.* Here, your target is to get an order for a particular dollar amount based on what you know advertisers' budgets are and how much investment it will take to get results, as they define and expect them. This type of targeting allows you to set goals for each order based on what it will take to achieve the results an advertiser expects. It also allows you to set minimum order-size goals for yourself so that you can manage your selling efforts to achieve your revenue targets. For instance, if you decide to restrict yourself to orders above a certain amount, you can avoid calling on prospects who do not have businesses large enough to support advertising at your minimum level. A combination of price and size targets works well.

④ *Share of budget.* In this case, your target is to get a predetermined share of a customer's advertising budget. This targeting is especially effective when you have abundant inventory available and when getting the highest possible price is not an issue. Used with the other three types of targets, the share-of-budget target can be the most profitable. For example: "I want to sell out the Super Bowl adjacencies at no less than $10,000 each as part of a package that sells for a minimum of $150,000 and that gets 45 percent of XYZ Company's first quarter television budget." This statement gives you a measurable, attainable, demanding, written, and flexible target as well as a good, solid goal.

Setting size-of-order and share-of-budget target requires good qualifying. You must know the total revenue of prospects' businesses and their advertising budgets. The type of target you choose will determine your sales strategy, which you must bake into your presentation from the very beginning.

Major Presentations to Key Accounts

At the upper ranges of the sloping line in Exhibit10.2 – toward the partnership deal end – you should create a winning presentation that will knock your prospects' socks off. And a dynamite presentation does not have to last for an hour and a half, or even an hour. The ideal length for a presentation is between 20 and 25 minutes, not including time for questions. Therefore, when you write a presentation, write one that the person can comfortably deliver in 20 to 25 minutes.

Here are some tips for creating such a presentation.

1   Appoint a prep team

Ask people who have expertise in different areas such as research, marketing, production, and creative to help you craft a major presentation and join your prep team.

2   Preparation

The prep team should meet in a room that contains flip charts or white boards on which to write. In this prep room, you will develop a maximum of 11 charts or subject areas – less for some presentations. Pick someone with good, legible hand writing to be the scribe and put information on the charts/whiteboards. The charts are:

- *Your prep and presentation team*. A list of who is on the team and each person's role, including the presenters.
- *Your purpose*. Concisely state the purpose of your presentation. For example, "To introduce solutions and get a commitment from the prospect to pursue a deal" or "To gain an agency's support for the proposed deal" or "To close a deal."
- *The prospect's objective and challenges*. A chart showing the prospect's marketing and advertising objectives, target consumers, and the challenges (do not call them problems) the prospect is facing in achieving those objectives with their target customers.

- *Your opportunities.* Write down all the relevant opportunities (promotions, packages, etc.) that might possibly be relevant to the prospect or be a potential solution.
- *Your target.* Determine your target – opportunities you want to propose and your dollar, size, or share-of-budget target.
- *An ROI analysis, if applicable.* An ROI analysis shows what the bottom-line effect is of a one-year advertising investment.
- *The timetable.* A time-line chart that shows milestone dates for key tasks (deliverables) and who does what and when they do it. Include in this chart tasks such as who does the setup of the room and who prepares and delivers copies of the presentation to the site. Also, plan something special for the setup, such as printed note pads with the prospect's name and logo on them, high-quality pens, such as Cross or Mont Blanc, to take notes with, small calculators they can take home if numbers are involved. Brainstorm to come up with some creative setup ideas.
- *The prospect's team.* A chart showing the key people who will be involved in making the decision – the decision maker and influencers who will be listening to and/or evaluating your presentation.
- *Ideas.* Brainstorm and come with an *idea pipeline* in five areas:
  - i   *The big idea.* A creative or promotion idea that meets the prospect's challenges (solves problems). The big idea may also be a way to present an existing product element or promotion as a solution.
  - ii   *A theme idea.* Come with ideas for a unifying theme that captures the essence of the big idea and of the presentation overall.
  - iii   *Evidence, examples, analogies, equivalencies, and stories.* Think of all the testimonials, success case studies, examples, analogies, equivalencies (definition and example later in this chapter), and stories that might be relevant to support and dramatize your benefits. Analogies and stories are especially effective. An analogy compares your product with something else.
  - iv   *Language.* Brainstorm to come with ideas on the most effective language – phrases and words – to use. You want your language to mirror the jargon, idioms, and slang the prospect and the prospect's target audience use.
  - v   *Wow! opening and closing ideas.* Creative opening and closing ideas plus a memorable and exciting presentation method or style that enhances the impact of a presentation will win big. It may mean opening or closing with a video clip from a *Spiderman* movie, balloons cascading down from the ceiling, a personal appearance by an "American Idol" contestant, a video clip from "The Daily Show," "The Colbert Report," or the hottest video from YouTube. Do not create a wow! opening or closing that you are not comfortable delivering, but if you are comfortable with a dramatic presentation style, it can be extremely effective.
- *Deal terms.* In some large deals there are terms and conditions such as payment schedules, exclusivities, content restrictions (no pornography, for example),

revenue sharing, or options to renew that are material. Material means that they are deal breakers – not getting these terms would prevent consummating a deal. It is best to put important terms and conditions that are different from standard media contract terms that advertisers are used to in your presentation and sell them aggressively because you want prospects to know what your terms and conditions are before you get into negotiations. If you spring terms and conditions on prospects after they have agreed to pursue a deal and while you are negotiating, prospects and their negotiators (sometimes lawyers) often become angry and negotiations stall. Introducing deal terms in your presentation will make negotiations go more smoothly.

Giving advertisers a deal term that includes the option to renew a contract at the end of a year at the same price originally agreed on is not a good idea because it precludes raising rates or taking a bid from a higher bidder.

- *A Benefits Matrix.* Develop a Benefits Matrix for your presentation.
- *Your offer and anchor.* When appropriate, have a chart that shows the details of the structure of your opening offer. Pricing your initial offer is probably the most important decision you will make, so spend plenty of time debating and crafting it. You will learn more about opening offers, called anchors, in Chapter 12, "Negotiating and Closing."
- *Follow-up* – Brainstorm on creative ways to follow up on your presentation. For example, if you give a presentation in your office, as the audience leaves your presentation, give people tickets to an opening of a movie. Have a top executive or celebrity greet them and thank them for their time. You could give them a T-shirt or baseball cap with your logo on it, or send something really cool to their offices the day after the presentation. A creative follow-up solidifies the relationship, makes them like you more, makes them feel that you care, reminds them of the terrific experience they had at your presentation, and reinforces the value of doing business with you.

3   Structure your presentation effectively

A winning presentation should have the following seven structural elements: Opening, Theme/Introduction/Purpose, Agenda, Main Body of content, Success Stories, Deal Terms, Summary, and Conclusion/Next Steps.

Opening   A relevant quote is a good way to open a presentation to focus, motivate, and even inspire an audience. A carefully chosen quotation can be the theme of your presentation. Here are some good quotes:

Problem solving. "Everything should be made as simple as possible, but not simpler," or "Imagination is more important than intelligence" (Albert Einstein).[2]

Major change. "If there's not a ripple at the bow you're drifting," or "If in the last few months you haven't discarded a major opinion or acquired a new one, check your pulse. You may be dead" (George Bernard Shaw).[3]

Motivation. "When you cease to dream you cease to live" (Malcolm Forbes). "If you can dream it, it is possible" (Buckminster Fuller). "Our greatest glory is not in never failing, but in rising every time we fail" (Confucius). "Failure is only the opportunity to more intelligently begin again" (Henry Ford)[4]

Marketing strategy. "Never interrupt the enemy when he is doing something wrong" (Rommel). An especially relevant quote: "For every complex problem there is invariably a simple solution – which is invariably wrong" (Lady Mary Wortley Montagu).[5] "The only functions of an enterprise: marketing and innovation" (Peter Drucker).

An excellent source for finding relevant quotes is www.quotationspage.com.

Theme/introduction/purpose   Near the beginning of a presentation you should state the theme of the presentation. A theme gives a presentation direction and focus. Examples of themes:

"Together into the Year 2009!"
"Making Burger King Number One!"
"A Global Solution for a Global Company!"
"Yahoo! and AT&T: Partnering for Solutions"

The introduction slide should state the purpose of the presentation, and the presenter's remarks should expand briefly on the purpose statement. An example might be, "The purpose of this presentation is to show how the Fox Television Network can provide you with effective and efficient solutions to your two biggest marketing challenges."

Agenda   The next slide after the introduction should list the main topics of the presentation. Like the old saw says, "Tell 'em what you're going to tell 'em." An agenda or Table of Contents tells your audience what to expect, prepares their minds, and sets their anticipation positively to receive your communication. Research shows that people like to know what's coming. An example of an agenda:

1   The economy and competitive landscape
2   AT&T's objectives
3   AT&T's challenges
4   Options in meeting those challenges
5   Recommended solutions
6   Terms and conditions
7   Summary
8   Conclusion/next steps

Main body of content   The main body of a presentation should flow logically from one topic to the next and from one solution or proposal to the next. Every feature, every statistic must be accompanied by a corresponding advantage (why it is better) and benefit (how it solves a specific prospect's problem). Numbers without comparisons are ineffective. Dramatic comparisons make the numbers memorable. See Chapter 8 for examples.

Make sure to include success stories or case studies that are relevant to the prospect's business and that give proof that you can get results. Use success stories, case studies, and testimonials in every presentation. A Web site that has good case studies is Microsoft's MSN at http://advertising.microsoft.com/advertising-case-studies. On the www.mediaselling.us Web site, there is an excellent success case study in the link "Aladdin Resort and Casino Case Study" that was prepared by the Infinity Broadcasting stations in Phoenix and tells a powerful story.

Each section of the presentation (as outlined in the Agenda at the beginning of your presentation) should come to a solid conclusion that points inescapably to the solutions you are offering.

Writing tips: When you create a presentation, it is imperative to start with an outline, then write the presentation following the outline.

After you have written the presentation that follows your outline, edit it to make sure that the headlines are clear, concise, and compelling. Good, short headlines are hard to write, but are the most important single element in a sales presentation – craft them carefully. When you edit your presentation, make sure there is a logical, cohesive flow that leads to an unavoidable conclusion. Make sure you back up each of your benefits with credible, fully sourced evidence. Credible evidence includes testimonials, success case studies, and analogies.

Keep numbers to a minimum in the body of the presentation. Instead of raw numbers, always try to use equivalencies. For example, if you are selling for a Web site for a station or newspaper in a town near Kansas City, instead of saying that your site has 73,000 unique visitors a month, say, "My Web site has more visitors than a sold-out Arrowhead Stadium holds." This statement makes the number 73,000 more concrete, dramatizes it, and gives your prospects something they can visualize in their minds. Put the dull, raw numbers and statistics in an Appendix that you leave behind.

Do not use convoluted or flowery language, but write positively and with enthusiasm. Write clearly, crisply, and concisely and with as few words as possible; ruthlessly edit out unnecessary words. Write in prospects' voice and use their industry language and jargon, not yours. Use simple everyday words. It is said that Ernest Hemingway had a small vocabulary of only 800 words, but he used those 800 words brilliantly.

You want to project through your writing that "we're here to make this easy for you." An overly wordy, complex proposal can cause prospects to think doing business with you is going to be too complicated or too hard. You want them to think that you are a salesperson or a team of experienced professionals who know how to make your recommendations work.

When you are satisfied with your presentation, write a script for yourself that contains examples, anecdotes, and stories that reinforce your major points and make your presentation memorable. Most people will remember your stories, particularly if they are good, longer than they will remember your solutions and the facts that support them. Make sure to actually write these stories and anecdotes in your script, as there is nothing worse than coming to a place in your script that reads, "Tell the St Peter joke," and you have forgotten the first line.

Success case studies and success stories. Include relevant case studies, success stories, or testimonials.

Terms and conditions. Include deal terms.

Summary: The summary is the most valuable, but often the most overlooked, part of a presentation. The summary ensures that prospects leave with key points you want them to remember. Too many summaries are too long – 15 points, for example. Remember the psychological rule of five plus or minus two, which means that the maximum number of things people can possibly remember is seven (Snow White and the eight dwarves? The nine wonders of the ancient world? Ten card stud?) Five is better for remembering than seven and three is ideal. If you can boil your summary down to three key points you want your audience to walk away with, you can be quite confident that those three points will stick with them.

Conclusions and next steps: One of the principles of maximizing a customer's experience is "finish strong." This point comes from the article, "Want to perfect your company's service? Use behavioral science," in the *Harvard Business Review.*[6] Your close should be creative, powerful, and memorable.

The conclusion is the close. It tells your audience what you want them to do. If you are offering proposed advertising schedules with prices included in the conclusion, make sure you order them effectively. Do not offer any price concessions or a Clincher Close at the conclusion of your presentation; save these for later, during negotiations (you will learn about Clincher Closes and negotiating strategies in Chapter 12). At this time, during the conclusion, hand out copies of the presentation, ask if there are any questions, and thank them for their time and attention, their intelligent questions and clarifications, and the opportunity to present your solutions. Finally, make sure to implement the follow-up your prep team has planned.

Create modular presentations

When you write presentations, write them in a modular form – that is, so you can use sections of them again within another presentation. Always keep an eye out for opportunities to write a section of a presentation in such a way that you can copy it and paste it into other proposals and presentations. You repeatedly use much of the information you convey to prospects and customers; this is especially the case with advantages and benefits, value propositions, positioning statements, research information, and competitive media information. Label and save these modular sections as separate PowerPoint and Word files that you can easily retrieve and insert into any presentation, document, or e-mail.

Checklist for Customized, Solution-Based Presentations

Exhibit 10.3 shows a checklist for major customized, solutions-based presentations that are appropriate for key accounts.

Exhibit 10.3 Checklist for customized solutions-based presentations

1 First slide with company's name, logo, and a catchy *theme* that communicates that you understand its challenges and suggests a partnership.
2 Second slide with a concise *Introduction* which includes a statement of the purpose of the presentation.
3 Next, a list of *agenda* items or a *Table of Contents*.
4 A list of the prospect's *marketing and advertising goals*.
5 A list of the prospect's *challenges* in achieving those goals.
6 A statement of the prospect's *current strategy* in achieving marketing and advertising goals (for example, differentiation, focus, low-cost producer).
7 A description of the prospect's *primary customers/target audience*.
8 An identification of *opportunities that are solutions* to the prospect's problems and challenges.
9 Present the *advantages of your solution* over your competition, but *don't knock the competition*.
10 Present *the benefits of your solutions* (for example, schedules, campaigns, packages, etc.) to the prospect's challenges.
11 Show specifically *how the solutions and recommendations will make their business more profitable*. Use an *ROI analysis* if appropriate.
12 Show relevant *success stories and case studies* from similar customers as proof of your ability to perform and get results.
13 Show *terms and conditions* if they are different from standard terms and conditions in your medium.
14 A concise *summary* of the main benefits and solutions
15 A *conclusion* or *next steps*, both for you and for prospects to implement the proposal and/or to advance the partnership, which is a *call for action or commitment*
16 An *appendix* containing numbers and supporting information

Note how the steps logically lead up to proposing solutions and follow with the advantages and benefits of those solutions. Without solutions, a presentation, other than an introductory GP, does not answer a prospect's WIIFM question, "What's in it for me?" Even an introductory GP should answer the WIIFM question in a general, overall, non-specific way (see the AOL GP at www. charleswarner.us/aolgp.htm). Solutions are the nutritious meat and potatoes of a presentation that make your business grow; without realistic solutions presentations are non-nutritious desserts that are unhealthy for the future of your business because prospects answer the WIIFM question by saying to themselves, "Nothing."

Test Yourself

1 What is the best way to generate a variety of solutions?
2 What is the difference between a proposal and a presentation?
3 How long should a presentation be?
4 What are the four different types of targets?
5 What are the seven elements in an effective sales presentation structure?
6 Give an example of an equivalency.

Project

Who is the largest advertiser in your market? Ask the local newspaper ad department and several local radio and television sales departments. Then select a local medium. Create the first three slides of a PowerPoint presentation to the largest advertiser for the medium you select. Use the Checklist in Exhibit 10.3 for your guide: A first slide with medium's name, your name and phone number, advertiser's logo and a catchy theme headline, a second slide titled "Introduction" and statement of purpose, and last a Table of Contents for your presentation.

References

Richard B. Chase and Sriam Dasu. 2001. "Want to perfect your company's service? Use behavioral science." *Harvard Business Review.* June.

Neil Flett. 1996. *The Pitch Doctor: Presenting to Win Multi-million Dollar Accounts.* New York: Prentice-Hall.

László Mérö. 1998. *Moral Calculations: Game Theory, Logic, and Human Frailty.* New York: Copernicus.

William Poundstone. 1992. *Prisoner's Dilemma.* New York: Doubleday.

Resources

www.charleswarner.us (author Charles Warner's Web site with case studies, presentations, and articles on advertising, marketing, managing, and sales)
www.gametheory.org (website about game theory)
www.mediasellng.us (this book's Web site with many useful downloads)
www.msn.org (the Microsoft Network Web site that includes case studies)
www.quotationspage.com (search for relevant quotations by famous person or by subject)

Notes

1 William Poundstone. 1992. *Prisoner's Dilemma*. New York: Doubleday.

2 Neil Flett. 1996. *The Pitch Doctor: Presenting to Win Multi-million Dollar Accounts*. New York: Prentice-Hall, p. 201.

3 Ibid., p. 202.

4 Ibid.

5 Ibid.

6 Richard B. Chase and Sriam Dasu. 2001. "Want to perfect your company's service? Use behavioral science." *Harvard Business Review*, June.

11

Skills: Presenting

Charles Warner

Presenting is what most people first think of when they think of selling – calling on prospects, customers, and buyers, educating them, and convincing them to buy your product. But you cannot begin selling without thorough preparation, as you have learned in previous chapters.

Media salespeople present to several different types of people involved in the buying process: prospects for new business, current customers for increases and renewals, and advertising agency media buyers for new and renewal business. For national media and in large markets, especially the top 25, the vast majority of media business is conducted with advertising agencies and that involves presenting to media buyers. As markets get smaller, more business, especially in newspapers, is conducted directly with customers and not through agencies. In this chapter, I will refer to prospects, customers, and media buyers as prospects to avoid confusion.

Furthermore, we have discussed selling solutions and putting solutions in the form of proposals that contain advertising schedules and prices. For the first section of this chapter, I will assume all your proposals and presentations are, in fact, solutions of some sort or other, and refer to them as proposals to keep things simple. For media buyers, a solution might well be a schedule that meets their marketing goals, reaches their demographic targets, and falls within their price range.

Presenting is personal selling to qualified prospects. Your overall goals in this step are: (1) To create a differential competitive advantage for your product with an overwhelming weight of evidence; (2) to create value for your product; (3) to build desire for your proposal; (4) to establish conviction that your proposal is the best one; and (5) to get a commitment. Commitment might be taking action and giving you an order, it may be an agreement to recommend your proposal to a client, or it might be having you make a presentation to a board of directors. Just as presentations get longer and more complicated as the amount of money involved increases, getting a commitment and closing a sale takes longer and is more complicated as the amount of money involved grows. Sometimes, with relatively small proposals and renewals, you can get a commitment and close on a single call. On the other hand, with major presentations to key accounts for large partnership deals, it can take weeks, even months to get a commitment.

In order to accomplish the above goals, the sales tactics you use during the presenting step of selling are designed to take prospects up the Sales Ladder as shown in Exhibit 11.1.

The Sales Ladder is based on the buyer-action theory proposed by Manning and Reece in *Selling Today: A Personal Approach*.[1] Exhibit 11.1 indicates which of the Six Steps of Selling move prospects up the Sales Ladder to commitment. Also, you will see that that the steps on the Sales Ladder are parallel to the customer decision process defined by Neil Rackham in *Major Account Sales Strategy*.[2] In addition, the sales ladder also parallels the objectives of advertising that are covered in Chapter 17 of this book. These parallel models depict the decision process that people go through when they buy, use, and repurchase products. Note, too, that people start out as prospects and do not become a customer until they repurchase.

Exhibit 11.1   The Sales Ladder

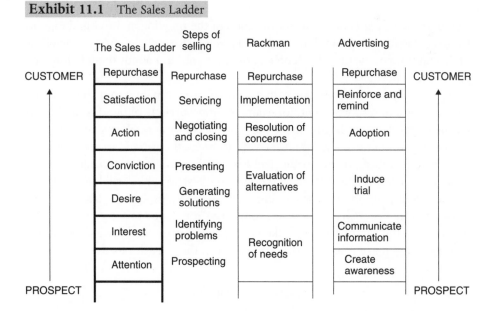

	The Sales Ladder	Steps of selling	Rackman	Advertising	
CUSTOMER	Repurchase	Repurchase	Repurchase	Repurchase	CUSTOMER
	Satisfaction	Servicing	Implementation	Reinforce and remind	
	Action	Negotiating and closing	Resolution of concerns	Adoption	
	Conviction	Presenting	Evaluation of alternatives	Induce trial	
	Desire	Generating solutions			
	Interest	Identifying problems	Recognition of needs	Communicate information	
	Attention	Prospecting		Create awareness	
PROSPECT					PROSPECT

Sources: Gerald L. Manning and Barry L. Reece. 1990. *Selling Today: A Personal Approach*. Boston: Allyn and Bacon; Neil Rackham. 1989. *Major Account Sales Strategy*. New York: McGraw Hill.

The Sales Ladder us useful in both one-on-one and group selling situations. I consider one-on-one selling to be presenting to one person or to small groups of two or three, and group selling to be presenting to groups of four or more. Typically, one-on-one presentations are for relatively (relative to the market and the medium) modest amounts of money and group presentations are for substantial deals.

One-on-One Presenting

In one-on-one presenting it is important to structure your in-person calls properly so you can take prospects up the Sales Ladder. Call structure allows you to set the agenda for a call and to keep your calls focused on selling, not extraneous matters.

Structure your calls as follows in order to keep you calls sales focused:

- Greeting
- New information
- Opening
- Recap and purpose
- Discussion
- Summary and close

Greeting

The purpose of a greeting is to set the tone of the meeting and to build rapport by first being friendly, complimentary, and positive. Keeping in mind Golden Rule of Selling #3, you want to let people know that you care about them before you get down to business.

It is usually best to start out with small talk: a comment about the weather, current news, or a sports event, for example. Appropriately phrased compliments are also a good way to begin; notice the office decor or desk photographs and say something complimentary. You are trying to break the ice and lower prospects' anxiety. Remember, prospects often feel anxious about meetings, too. On the other hand, some prospects dislike making polite conversation. You will know if this is the case from your observations during previous meetings. Limit small talk to one or two comments, such as, "How are you today?" or "Good to see you again." No matter what the circumstances, make your greeting warm and sincere. Whatever your greeting, make it brief so that you can keep the call sales focused.

New information

The next phase of a call provides your prospects with some relevant information and, better, *new* information, if possible. By giving relevant or new information, you add to your source credibility and your prospects' perception of your expertise. Examples of information you might give are: "I saw a new creative execution your competitor is using. Have you seen it? Do you like it?" When you give information, you turn the conversation from a discussion about personal matters as it was in the greeting phase to a focus on business.

Opening

Your opening should be a thoughtful, well-planned statement and not a casual, off-the-cuff remark. A good, solid opening piques your prospects' interest. Your prospects are already interested in what you are going to offer because they agreed to the meeting. You got their attention during your initial meetings when you gathered information in the Identifying Problems and Qualifying steps. During those meetings, you looked for business and personal needs, you made your first assessment of the prospect's intelligence and self-confidence, and you created a personal needs-based portrait (see Chapter 7). You also tried to determine prospects' perceptual set and readiness to hear your information. Your opening should take all of these factors into consideration and hint at the benefits of your proposal.

An example of an effective opening might be:

> YOU: "Mary, I know how much you love Woody Allen movies. Remember when he said in *Annie Hall* that he'd been going to psychiatrists for 15 years and still wasn't any better? He said he was so desperate he was thinking of going to Lourdes. Well, I've put together a proposal that I think will meet some of your challenges so you won't have to go to Lourdes."

On the other hand, there are times when a planned open is not appropriate, and you have to ad-lib. One of the best examples of a creative opening is one I call the Barbed-Wire Open that I learned from a 25-year-veteran radio salesperson named Mark in Fresno. He told me that he made a call one blistering hot day on a client who owned a men's clothing store. Mark had identified the owner's needs and problems and was returning to sell a radio campaign. He said that when he walked into the store, he knew the call was not going to a be good one. There was about an inch of water on floor, and as Mark slogged towards the owner on soggy carpeting he made the mistake of asking, "How's it going?"

> OWNER: "How's it going! How's it going! Can't you see it's a damned flood. The damn air conditioner broke. It's 102 degrees outside and 104 in here. There are no customers and it'll cost me a fortune!"
>
> MARK: "Gee, this is awful. I've never seen such a mess. You must be furious." He glanced up and saw a strand of barbed wire mounted on a wooden plaque above the back door. "Say, isn't that a Scutt Single-Clip 'H' Plate up there. I've seen picture of it but never seen a real one?"

OWNER (perking up): "Yes, it's very rare. How did you know? Are you interested in barbed wire?"

MARK: "Yeah, I've got a Kelly Thorny Common and a Jayne & Hill Locked Staples at home and, of course, some plain old Glidden Square Strand. Say, why don't you close down – you're not going to do any good sweltering in here. Let's go across the street to that cool diner, have a Coke, and talk about barbed wire."[3]

Mark knew his barbed wire, he was authentic, and he knew how to ad-lib. Most of all, he knew how to sell.

Recap and purpose

The next step in your call structure is to *recap* what challenges you are addressing and then state the *purpose* of the call. Your purpose statement sets the agenda for the call. Here are some examples:

YOU: "Mary, when you called for avails, you indicated you needed to buy a schedule that reached women 18–49, that achieved high reach in a two-week period, and that met your cost-per-point targets. The purpose of my call is to show you how my proposal meets your parameters and to reach an agreement today so I can book the order before the spots are sold to someone else – demand is running high." (Scarcity principle, deadline, and competition for limited supply.)

Or another one:

YOU: "Since the last time I saw you, Mr Hernandez, I've thought a great deal about how we might increase your traffic on Mondays and Tuesdays. The purpose of my call today is to show you mock-ups of some banners that I think will get results for you."

Your summary and purpose statements guide prospects into the discussion phase. Your wording depends on your earlier assessment of prospects' challenges and needs.

Discussion

The overall strategy for the *discussion* phase is to move prospects from *desire* for the solutions you present to *a conviction* that your proposal is the best one. The emphasis is on two-way communication in which prospects are partners. They learn through discovery that what you are offering will satisfy their business and personal needs. Their conviction will be stronger if they discover the benefits of your solutions rather than being told directly. Part of prospects' discovery process comes from asking questions or bringing up objections.

Dealing with objections   Body builders use the expression "no pain, no gain." Salespeople should use the phrase "no objection, no sale." To the novice, objections might seem to be negatives and barriers. On the other hand, to the experienced professional, objections are a welcome and necessary part of the discussion process; they are not negatives, they are requests for more information. Prospects do not ask questions and raise objections if they are not interested in what you have to offer.

Dealing with objections successfully is one of the most important skills a salesperson can learn. There are two types of objections: *figurative* and *literal*. A figurative objection is one that does not represent what prospects' words seem to indicate and should not be taken literally. Such objections have no real meaning, but rather represent other, hidden objections, which are often quick initial responses that represent defense mechanisms rather than real reasons. Figurative objections are often used as a buying or negotiating tactic by prospects whose motives are to put salespeople on the defensive and to gain an upper hand.

Literal objections are real reasons why prospects are seriously questioning your proposal, and must be answered with additional information in order to move prospects from desire to conviction. When you deal with literal objections, you should encourage prospects to answer their own objections, which is accomplished through the use of probing questions and restatements and the legitimate use of some of the principles of influence.

Following are several dialogues to help you. These should be used as examples and not as a script. You must sound natural and sincere when you are talking to prospects, not scripted. If you sound rehearsed, you convey the unintended message that you have pat answers that are not unique to their individual objections, and thus you are perceived as being manipulative. You will notice that the following techniques for listening to objections are the same as the effective listening techniques you learned in Chapter 7, but another step has been added, a trial close. Here are examples of some appropriate responses:

Probe to understand. Used open- and closed-end questions to be sure that you hear the full objection or concern and that you and your prospect have the same understanding of it. Discover exactly what the objection is so that you can give a thorough, intelligent answer.

Always listen rather than respond when prospects begin to express an objection and encourage them to continue. Never jump in with a counterargument. Sometimes a short response such as "Oh?" will provide additional information. For example:

PROSPECT: "ESPN is pretty good, but it doesn't have enough golf."
YOU: "Oh?"
PROSPECT: "Yeah, I like to watch golf and see the great players select their clubs."
YOU: "Oh?"
PROSPECT: "Yes, I know it's a personal preference. After all, I'm selling tires to everyone, not just the upscale guys who play golf."

YOU: "Oh?"

PROSPECT: "Yeah, my audience prefers auto racing as a sport. ESPN carries auto racing doesn't it?"

YOU: "Yes. It's the most popular spectator sport in the country." (Social proof.)

Compliment, restate an objection, and get agreement. Compliment prospects for raising an objection, for having such good insight. By giving them a compliment, you put prospects in a receptive frame of mind, not on the defensive, and you trigger an obligation for them to reciprocate by listening to your answer. Next, *restate the objection* and then get their agreement that you understand it.

PROSPECT: "I don't like your newspaper's editorials praising the mayor."

YOU: "That's a very good point, Mr Hernandez. I'm glad you brought that up. Let me make sure I understand your point; you don't like the mayor and don't think he's doing a good job. Right?"

PROSPECT: "Yes, that's right."

Empathize, reassure, and support. Empathize with prospects' objections (how they feel), then reassure them that their objection is not out in left field somewhere (reassure them), and, finally, support your position.

YOU: "I understand how you feel. A lot of my clients have felt the same way, but they have found that their ads still pull well no matter what stand our editorials take. By the way, why don't you write a letter to the editor? They'll probably print it. You express yourself very well and speak for a lot of people."

PROSPECT: "That's a good idea. I think I will."

Trial close. Next, get prospects to agree that you have answered their objection and ask for a commitment. You may not get one at this stage of the discussion, but it never hurts to try. The advantage of a trial close early in a discussion is that it elicits either a commitment or another objection, which is what you want.

Using trial closes is good way to bring out all of the objections prospects have. And once you have addressed them all, you will get a commitment. Let's continue the discussion above:

YOU: "Great, maybe your letter to the editor will run on the same day as your ad – that would be nice. Shall we go ahead, then?"

PROSPECT: "Well, before I say yes, I'd like a position up front in the first section."

Your trial close worked. Our prospect has, in effect, said yes, and you are now negotiating for position (and not price). Here is another example:

YOU: "Channel 32 is the area's top-rated independent television station."

PROSPECT: "That might be, but I hear that your ratings aren't that good."

YOU: "What kind of ratings are you referring to?" (Probe to understand)

PROSPECT: "The latest Nielsens. The network affiliates have much higher ratings."

YOU: "In all time periods?" (Probe to understand)

PROSPECT: "I honestly don't know the details. I just know that the affiliates tell me they have much higher ratings."

YOU: "What you seem to be concerned about is that you won't be able to reach as many people in your target audience on an independent station. Is that correct?"

PROSPECT: "Yes, that's right."

YOU: "You're right. The affiliates do have higher overall ratings at many time during the day, especially in primetime. So I understand how you feel. Your best customers are young women, right?"

PROSPECT: "Yes."

YOU: "My station is particularly effective in reaching young women 18–49 in early fringe. Here is a rating sheet that shows we have higher ratings among young women during the day than all of the affiliates do. If your commercial runs in that time period, you'll be along side Procter & Gamble, Colgate, Johnson & Johnson and many big national advertisers." (Social proof.) "I might be able to get you only one or two in early fringe next week; there is a lot of demand for that time period right now." (Scarcity, competition.) "Shall we go ahead?" (Trial close.)

Several additional techniques for dealing with objections follow. Each is effective in different situations. However, before you use these techniques, it is imperative to know what objections are common for your medium and product and be prepared to answer them. Ninety-five percent of the objections you hear should not be new to you.

The best sales organizations spend a great deal of time practicing how to deal with objections. Write down the most common objections for your medium and product and then craft intelligent, concise answers. Rehearse the answers repeatedly until you can deal with the most common objections in your sleep and with confidence. Find out from other salespeople in your organization how they answer these objections.

There are several reasons for practicing answers to objections. First, like a hitter in baseball, if you know what pitch is coming, you have an infinitely better chance of hitting it solidly. Second, rehearsing gives you confidence – nothing can puzzle you, and as we know, sometimes prospects throw out objections just to stump you in order to get an edge. Third, by practicing, you can craft answers that are logical and concise, which will allow you to move discussions forward more easily.

Once you have assembled a list of objections for your medium, you can practice using the following techniques to deal with them.

Forestall objections: Forestalling objections means to head them off, to anticipate and answer them before prospects bring them up. Early in your presentation, address the objections from the list of common objections that you have developed. Use a two-sided argument at the beginning of a presentation, which makes you appear to be more objective and candid, which, in turn, increases your credibility.

Here's an example of how, during the recap and purpose phase of a call, you might forestall an objection you know is going to come up.

> YOU: "Since the last time I saw you, Mr Hernandez, I've thought a great deal about how we might increase your traffic on Mondays and Tuesdays. The purpose of my call today is to show you mock-ups of some banners that I think will get results for you." (Same recap and purpose as above.) "You've also mentioned you didn't like our Web site's editorial position in regards to the mayor. A lot of people agree with you, especially in the Latino and African-American community. On the one hand, by advertising in my paper, you'd be supporting a newspaper whose editorial position you are opposed to, which I can understand why you'd be reluctant to do. On the other hand, you know that your customers who disagree with the paper read the paper, if just to get mad at it and reinforce their own views. Plus, your customers who agree with the paper will respect you for running an ad in spite of your opposition. You win both ways. Remember also that you've been a consistent advertiser and have run banners in the past even though you disagreed with our editorials." (Consistency principle.)

Use "Yes, but . . ." and compare. When prospects state an objection, first agree with them, and then state a benefit that compensates for the perceived shortcoming. This technique works well when it is combined with a comparison with competitive alternatives. For example:

> PROSPECT: "Wow. That's a lot of money to advertise on your cable network."
> YOU: "*Yes*, I can see how that might seem like a lot at first, *but* as a businessman, you know you get what you pay for." (Automatic response, expensive equals good.)
> PROSPECT: "There are so many channels on cable, how will my prospects ever see my commercial on only one or two channels?"
> YOU: "*Yes*, there are a number of choices on cable, and I can certainly understand your concern. *But*, because cable is much more selective than broadcast television, you don't have to pay high prices for coverage of down-scale audiences you're not interested in." (You are not knocking a specific competitor; you are pointing out a generic weakness.) "You can be selective. And commercials on any type of television have much more impact with sight, sound, motion, and emotion than advertising on radio or print ads do." (Contrast principle.)

Use case histories. When an objection comes up, respond by citing case histories of successful advertisers. For example:

> PROSPECT: "I don't want any nighttime spots."
> YOU: "I understand how you feel, a lot of advertisers feel the same way. Nighttime is not the highest-rated time period in radio. However, it is efficient. The Men's

Clearance Loft uses nothing but nighttime. In fact, it never runs advertising before midnight. The Loft has been on for three years and has increased its business more than 200 percent. The people there love nighttime radio because they can run a lot of spots and remind people over and over of their low prices. Also, they can afford to dominate a time period in nighttime radio." (Social proof and competition for a resource.)

Case histories of successes in a prospect's line of business are particularly effective. Often retailers are very competitive, and if you can sell one of them in a product category, others will follow.

Use "Coming to that . . ." Often in a presentation, prospects will raise an objection that you know you will answer later in your presentation. Simply tell them you are "coming to that." Also, use this response with minor or figurative objections you suspect are not really material or relevant.

While the general rule with most objections is to deal with them as soon as they occur, sometimes it makes sense to stall prospects, especially when the objections are minor or figurative. If you allow prospects to slow you down too much with nitpicking, you will never finish covering your major advantages and benefits. If an objection is real, literal, or important, prospects will certainly bring it up again. If an objection is literal and you use "coming to that," make sure you do not forget about it and actually come to it later. If you leave a literal, material objection unanswered, it remains a barrier to a sale and it looks like you are trying to dodge the issue.

Pass on objections. There will be times in discussion or presentation when it is best to ignore an objection by pretending a prospect had not mentioned it. Some books refer to this technique as *selling through objections*. This technique is effective when objections are so trivial that they really do not deserve the dignity of an answer. This technique also works with figurative objections. If you suspect that an objection is a reflex response, nod slightly, smile, ignore it, and keep selling benefits. For example:

YOU: "I can offer you a sponsorship of the new Green Grocer segment in our 'Sunrise News' program. This is the first day we have been allowed to offer it, and a lot of supermarkets are probably going to want it. I came to you first."
PROSPECT: "I don't know how anyone can stand that jerk of a weatherman of yours."
YOU (smiling slightly): "This sort of exposure should be perfect for your supermarkets because many shoppers are thinking about what fresh produce is available when they go shopping later in the day."

Dealing with the price objection. Finally, you will never be a successful media salesperson if you do not learn to deal with the price objection effectively. If you cannot deal with the price objection, you will find yourself selling a commodity. Commodities are not technically sold, but are bought in a reverse auction where the lowest bidder is awarded the business.

During your discussion, you should continually use the word quality to describe your product. By including the word "quality," you have emphasized value instead of price whenever you can. You have focused on results, service, demographics, and all of the things that create value. You should break down prices into smaller units and refer to your proposal as an investment rather than a cost.

When you create value, you try to forestall the price objection, but you cannot forestall it completely. By creating a perception of value you raise the floor of prospects' initial lowball offers (material self-interest). If you can raise the floor of an initial offer by, perhaps, 10 percent and the settlement is in the middle between your initial offer and a prospect's initial offer, then you have managed to raise your price by 10 percent.

The price objection is almost universal. There are a few products, such as a Rolls Royce or a Patek Philippe watch, where price is seldom an issue. The higher the price of these symbols of status and authority, the higher their value is. However, it is rare for the price of media to have status value for prospects. Advertisers might want their commercials to be in the Super Bowl or in a prestigious magazine, but they do not generally want to brag that they paid a higher price than anyone else. Therefore, count on hearing the price objection when you are selling media.

Getting a price objection is a good thing. When you finally mention price in your presentation and a prospect says, "That's a great price!" how would you feel? You would feel terrible because you would know that you have under-priced your offer. People's perception of a fair price has a great deal to do with their personal needs, motivations, and inherent assumptions. If you have identified these elements well, you will know what reaction to expect when the subject of price comes up. Excellent preparation is the best way to deal with the inevitable price objection.

Welcome the price objection because it signals that prospects want your product, are convinced that it is right for them, and are ready to take action if an agreement on price can be reached. If you hear the price objection, it is time to summarize and close, which will, more than likely, lead to negotiations.

Conditions   There is a difference between an objection and a condition. An objection might be, "Your price is too high." A condition would be, "Since I saw you last, my insurance rates have gone up so high I have to close my business." You can overcome an objection; you cannot overcome a condition. A condition is a valid reason for not buying or at least for not buying now.

As a general rule, you should discover conditions in the identifying problems and qualifying step, as it is the major function of the qualifying step. You must learn to *recognize conditions* so you do not waste time trying to overcome something that is impossible to overcome.

Even experienced salespeople who are good qualifiers sometimes let a condition slip by them in the initial steps and discover they have encountered one in the discussion phase. When you discover a condition that would stand in the way of a sale, you should use probing questions to determine if it is really a condition. Once verified, gracefully and politely stop and cut your losses. Even though you have invested time and effort in a presentation, do not waste any more time, be as pleasant as you can, and leave. After all, the condition might someday go away.

Discussion phase tactics   *Vary your style.* The longer your presentation is, the greater the chances are that your prospects' attention will wander. Following are some ways you can *vary your style* to keep them interested.

Use contrast in your presentation. People notice things that are brighter, bigger, or louder than what has come before, as well as sudden changes in intensity. Anything that is consistently too loud, too soft, or even too in-the-middle will begin to bore. Vary your style; talk louder, then softer. Do not be too emphatic or enthusiastic all the time.

Use movement in your presentation. If you are sitting, get up and walk around for a while, particularly to emphasize an important point. Use gestures to highlight your points.

Also, make prospects move if you can. Have prospects turn the pages of your proposal or hand them a pen and ask them to make notes in the margins. Ask them to figure a simple math problem for you on the desk calculator to make a point. Movement keeps prospects alert and attentive.

Use novelty. Something is novel if it is fresh, new, different, and unusual. As part of the media industry, you are in the news and entertainment business. Most people love to hear about and be associated with well-known media personalities such as bloggers, magazine editors, newspaper publishers, and television reporters. Even in many small and medium-sized markets, local television anchors and radio disc jockeys are often important celebrities. So, having lunch or their picture taken with one of these celebrities might be a novel and exciting experience for prospects, especially those who have a high need for recognition or status. (Authority principle.)

A few years ago, a national television salesperson in New York was about to make a call on a buyer who had just been discharged from the hospital. The day before the call, the salesperson contacted the people in the offices of the building directly across the street from hers and paid them to hang a sheet out of their windows. On the sheet was written, "Welcome Back, Jeannie!" in huge letters and the sign was unfurled just as the salesperson made the call. The salesperson got the buyer's attention and, of course, got a good order.

One salesperson in a medium-sized Texas market had been calling on a car dealer trying to crack the account and to get the dealership on radio. The salesperson had done research and knew that the prospect had a four-year-old boy. Each time the salesperson made a call, the salesperson brought along a new Matchbox series toy car. At the appropriate time in the presentation, the salesperson made a point about radio's ability to "move cars," at which time the salesperson produced the toy car and rolled it across the desk toward the prospect. This novelty gimmick became great fun for the prospect as the prospect began to look for the place in the presentation when the toy car would appear. The anticipation riveted the prospect's attention. The car dealer rewarded the salesperson with the biggest share of the dealership's advertising budget.

Use equivalencies to dramatize numbers. One way to help prospects remember the numbers that are inevitably included in a media sales proposal is to use equivalencies. An example of an equivalency would be to tell a prospect, "If the Cineplex movie theater in the mall sold out four showings of *Spiderman III* every day for an entire year, not as many people would see the movie as would see just one commercial on my station's 'News 6' at 10:00 p.m. on Sunday evening." Equivalencies dramatize numbers and make them understandable and tangible.

Narrow down objections and reconfirm. This tactic is also referred to as *questioning down.* Sometimes prospects have some objections that are not easy to overcome with the above techniques and require more discussion and negotiation. The goal in this phase of the discussion is to *narrow down* their objections until they have just one or two. Use trial closes as you go along to make sure you have narrowed down all of the objections to one or two, then *reconfirm* that these are the only objections left. When you overcome the only remaining objections that prospects agree exist, you have made a sale.

Change the basis for evaluation as a last resort. Changing prospects' basis for making a purchase evaluation is not always possible or even desirable. However, there will be times in a sales presentation when you find yourself faced with objections that you cannot overcome. Occasionally, it is possible to alter the evaluative basis, or norms, and to change the rules in your favor, but proceed slowly and deliberately. Use well-worded verification questions to let prospects change their own direction. One of the most common alterations in evaluation criteria would be to change from efficiency (overall cost and cost-per-thousand, or CPM) to effectiveness (impact, return-on-investment, attentiveness, message recall, for example) or to results (depending on prospects' definition of results). Examples of these alternatives are:

1   Salespeople for independent television stations might try to get prospects to evaluate schedules on the basis of return-on-investment while network affiliate salespeople might try to have schedule evaluation based on ratings.
2   Adult contemporary radio stations push the 25–54 demographic while rock stations push the 18–34 demographic as the primary basis for evaluation.
3   Both radio stations might try to get an advertiser who invests a lot of money in television to evaluate that investment based on a media-mix concept that optimizes the total number of people reached rather than just on the basis of

people reached by television alone. You will learn more about media mix in Chapters 16 and 17.

4 Cable salespeople might try to get buyers to evaluate their audience based on the exclusive, upscale, targeted audiences cable reaches rather than on the basis of overall ratings, whenever possible.

5 Interactive salespeople might prefer to have their proposals evaluated on sales results rather than on a cost-per-click or cost-per-thousand model, and might try to change the basis for evaluation accordingly.

Reassure doubts. Prospects may like what you are offering but have some doubts. Doubts are different from objections. When prospects doubt a benefit or an advantage, they have essentially accepted them but remain unsure about how it might apply to their business. The way to handle doubts is with *reassurances* about yourself, your company, and your medium. Prospects need an infusion and transference of confidence from you. The more knowledgeable, enthusiastic, and confident you are about your product, the more reassured prospects will be and the quicker they will accept your point. If they have doubts, they have not moved on to conviction.

Be patient with doubts, do not gloss over them, and do not try to close until they are resolved. Neil Rackham, as you can see in Exhibit 11.1, the Sales Ladder, refers to doubts as concerns. Rackham makes the point that you cannot resolve prospects' concerns for them, as concerns are their own internal conflicts. They might be political issues, such as how the boss will like it, how it will affect their careers if they make a mistake, or is it really better than other alternatives? Probe to find the real reason for the doubt or concern and use data and facts to reassure them, but do not pressure them, do not minimize their concerns, and let them work through them on their own. There are times when you will have to back off, and come back another time after they have dealt with their issues.

Evaluate prospects' reactions. As you go through the discussion phase, you must continually be aware of how your prospects are responding to each point you make. You must listen carefully and *be extremely observant for any possible feedback.* Make a mental note of those benefits prospects respond to most positively so you can use them in a summary later. Watch for signs of boredom or inattention and notice if anything strikes prospects negatively. Look for signs that prospects have shifted from interest to desire and from desire to conviction. Once you see signs of conviction, stop talking and close.

Summary and close

After you have dealt with prospects' objections and concerns and when you see indications of conviction – body language such as leaning forward or more rapid head nodding – it is time to close, to ask for the order. But, first, you should summarize your benefits, which reinforces those benefits. An example is:

YOU: "Well, Mary, you've agreed that my proposal concentrates on women 18–49 over two weeks and is very close to your cost targets. Can we go ahead?"

This last request was a simple trial close that probably will lead to further negotiations, which is one of the purposes of the summary and close phase. In the close, you're asking for action, or in some cases, you will ask what the next steps are. Next steps are a form of a close because you are asking for a commitment for action.

Exhibit 11.2 shows an outline of the all of the steps in a sales-focused call structure and overcoming objections. This outline is also available on

---

Exhibit 11.2 Call structure and dealing with objections outline

1 Greeting
2 New information
3 Opening
4 Recap and purpose
5 Discussion
  A Dealing with objections
    • Probe to understand.
    • Compliment, restate, and get agreement.
    • Empathize, reassure, and support (feel, felt, found).
    • Use trial closes.
    • Forestall objections.
    • Use "Yes, but . . ." and compare.
    • Use case histories.
    • Use "Coming to that . . ."
    • Pass on objections.
    • Dealing with price objections:
      a continually talk about quality.
      b break price into smallest possible units
      c talk value, not price
      d refer to investments, not costs.
  B Conditions
  C Discussion tactics
    • Vary your style:
      a contrast
      b movement
      c novelty.
    • Use equivalencies.
    • Narrow down objections and reconfirm.
    • Change the basis for evaluation as a last resort.
    • Reassure doubts.
    • Evaluate reactions.
6 Summary and close

www.mediaselling.us so you can download it into a PDA or cell phone and review it before making a presenting call. I also recommend putting a list of common objections you encounter and your responses in your PDA, cell phone, or Black-Berry for continual review and refinement.

How to use your proposal one-on-one

A great deal of business today is done via e-mail. It is often hard to avoid e-mailing proposals to clients and buyers, but you should do everything possible to give presentations and make proposals face to face. The following techniques are for face-to-face situations.

Communicating with buyers and prospects face to face is much more effective than communication by e-mail, as pointed out by Daniel Goleman in an article titled "E-mail is easy to write (and to misread)"[4] in which he writes:

> new findings [in social neuroscience] have uncovered a design flaw at the interface where the brain encounters a computer screen: there are no online channels for multiple signals the brain uses to calibrate emotions.
>
> Face-to-face interaction, by contrast, is information-rich. We interpret what people say to us not only from their tone and facial expressions, but also from their body language and pacing, as well as their synchronization with what we do and say.
>
> Most crucially, the brain's social circuitry mimics in our neurons what's happening in the other person's brain, keeping us on the same wavelength emotionally. This neural dance creates an instant rapport that arises from an enormous number of parallel information processors, all working instantaneously and out of our awareness.[5]

Stripping out the science mumbo-jumbo, the message clearly is that face-to-face communication is infinitely more effective (and persuasive) than e-mail or phone conversations. Sell face to face whenever possible.

When you make presentations to larger groups, you should use PowerPoint or other presentation software. But, when you present one-on-one or to small groups, showing people proposals in PowerPoint is often awkward and too impersonal. In these situations use a hard copy of a proposal.

One technique of handling hard copies of proposals is to put them unfastened into a folder and then to hand each page, one at a time, to prospects. This prevents prospects from jumping ahead and it focuses their attention, especially if they are in a hurry or are impatient. You can control the pace of your presentation and force prospects to stay with you. One of the drawbacks of this technique, though, is that prospects' desks become a jumble of pieces of paper. It can be awkward to try to put all the single sheets back together in order to leave prospects with a complete, well-organized copy of the proposal. When you use the *one-page-at-a-time technique*, bring along an extra copy or two to hand prospects when the call is over.

Another technique is to give a complete copy of your proposal to prospects and ask them to follow along with you as you go through it. Sometimes you can arrange the physical surroundings so that you can sit side by side with prospects. Give them a complete copy and sit with them as you both go over the presentation while they turn the pages, then say, "Here's a proposal I prepared. Let's go over it together. I'll highlight the important points for you. Don't hesitate to stop me if you have any questions." Bring along a couple of highlighter pens; give one to prospects and while you highlight important points, encourage them to do so likewise. Do whatever you can to get prospects involved, to ask questions, or to go back and forth in it. Paraphrase the written text as you go and point out the most salient points rather than reading word for word.

Control the physical environment so that you eliminate barriers that make developing rapport difficult. In general, you should work as close as possible without violating prospects' social space. Use emotional intelligence when evaluating the proper social space in which to work. By careful observation, you can find ways to connect with them; you will see where their social space is and not invade it. Often invading someone's social space is a matter of inches, so get as close as you can, but never too close. Be very sensitive to gender differences as well as differences when evaluating the proper social space in which to work. If you get too close, some people can become offended or take it the wrong way. Always work in what I call professional space.

A third technique is to give your prospects a complete bound copy of your proposal to look over and read while you follow along page by page to be ready to answer any questions. If you use this method, make sure that you tell your prospects, "Here's my proposal. Why don't you read it over and I'll answer any questions you have." If you use this technique, do not interrupt. Too often sales-people will go into prospects' offices, hand them a proposal, and then begin making a verbal presentation. The prospect's head bobs up and down as they try to read and listen at the same time. Prospects might also whip ahead to the price page and not hear your well-presented benefits. I do not recommend this technique, primarily because of the latter reason.

If you have to use e-mail to deliver your proposals and presentations, it is imperative that you meet the people to whom you are sending the proposal face to face at some time in order to get to know them, build rapport with them, and do a needs portrait of them. After you accomplish these things, your e-mails will have much greater impact.

Presenting to Groups

When presenting to groups where the stakes are typically bigger, the proposals are bigger in both size and dollar value, and therefore, it is more appropriate to refer to them as presentations.

Just as it is in your one-on-one calls, it is important to structure your discussion. The primary purpose of a presentation to a group of people is the same as a one-on-one presentation – to move prospects up the Sales Ladder from *desire* to *conviction* to *action*. You should use a PowerPoint presentation to a group of people because this more formal approach focuses the group's attention on your solutions and call to action. However, when you use a PowerPoint presentation, remember the cardinal rule of PowerPoint: *Never read the information on the slides*. Use the PowerPoint slides merely as an outline of the points which you want to expand; illustrate with stories, and reinforce by referring to hand-out material. PowerPoint slides should have the same relationship to presenters to a group as a person backstage prompting an actor on stage – prompting and reminding the performer, not becoming the performance itself.[6]

Next, structure your oral presentations as follows:

- Opening
- Theme
- Agenda
- Main body of content
- Summary
- Conclusion and next steps.

Objectives

Before you begin your preparation for a major presentation to a key account, you must clearly define your objectives. Often, when presenting to groups there will be several presentations during the sales process and you must set objectives for each presentation. The first one might be a stock general presentation (GP), the second to propose solutions, and the third to show solutions that have been altered to meet prospects' needs and to get a commitment. Initial presentations rarely result in a signed contract. Typically with bigger deals, a commitment leads to further negotiations on deal terms, contract conditions, payment terms, and pricing structure.

Preparation

Obviously, the first step in preparation is creating the presentation, as covered in Chapter 10. The next steps are deciding the who, where, when, and how questions.

① *Who?* Who in your organization should be the person to give a presentation? The rule of thumb is to try to match size and levels. In other words, have your CEO present to CEOs of large companies, your President (or equivalent) present to Presidents of large companies, your Senior VPs present to Senior VPs of large companies, and so forth.

Sometimes there will several people on your presentation team. It might include your CEO, a VP of Sales, yourself, and a marketing person. There should be no more than three, or, at most, four people from your organization on the presentation team, and everyone on the team should actively participate in the presentation and not merely be listeners. Too many people overwhelm and confuse prospects. If the leadoff person from your organization is a CEO, President, or Senior VP, then the primary salesperson on the account should be present and be introduced as the primary contact for the account in the future. The lead should deliver at least one-third of the presentation so prospects can get to know that person. In some situations, with an organization's largest accounts, a CEO might do the entire presentation talking to an account's CEO and promise the client their continued involvement in the account.

Who should receive a presentation? The first presentation to an account or agency should be to the most senior-level executives that you can gather so that you can introduce your organization and get agreement to pursue a relationship. You want to sell to VITO (Very Important Top Officers), as designated by Anthony Parinello in *Selling to VITO*, an excellent book that I strongly recommend.

② *Where?* If possible, give presentations in your offices because you get the home field advantage and can control the environment and timing. If you give a presentation at a prospect's location or at an agency, make sure you check beforehand to see if the there is an LCD projector that will take input from your computer. Also, offer to have food or refreshments delivered. Serve coffee and food before or after a presentation, but never during. Always arrive an hour early to give yourself plenty of time to set up.

③ *When?* You should give your presentation during prospects' advertising planning cycle. You must find this out during your discovery process and give your presentation at the beginning of the process, as it is a waste of time to give a presentation a few months after a major account and its agency have planned their media expenditures for the coming year. If you have a choice, it is better to give presentations in the morning when people are fresh and can more easily stay awake than later in the afternoon when they are often drowsy.

④ *How?* Even if you have given a particular type of presentation several times, and even if you have created a customized, solutions-based presentation before, always *write a script*. Type the script in large type (16 or 18 point bold sans serif) with only one sentence on a line, in small paragraphs that contain only one point per paragraph, with a space between paragraphs, and with emphasis marked: Read up /, read down \, or EMPHASIZE. Also, mark where your gestures go in a presentation and rehearse the gestures.

Use the slides in the presentation as the basis for your script, but do not read the slides. *Discuss* them and, most important, tell anecdotes, stories, and use equivalencies to illustrate and reinforce the points you are making on the slides.

A script gives you confidence; cues you for the anecdotes, stories, equivalencies and gestures, keeps you on track, and helps you avoid wandering off on tangents and rambling.

Rehearsal is imperative, no matter the size of the order. If the situation requires a presentation, then it requires that it be done professionally. In order to make certain that your presentation is better than your competitor's, you must rehearse. While you do not need the months of rehearsal that a Broadway play does, you need to rehearse once or twice in front of your prep team. It is a good idea to try to rehearse in the room where you will give the presentation so you will feel comfortable in that room. Rehearse walking around the room and talking to empty chairs, especially to the chair in which you want the decision maker to sit.

When you rehearse, keep a mental picture of the physical setup so you will be prepared and comfortable. You want to *work in as intimate space as possible* in order to develop rapport with your audience. Practice your movements in a space that is similar to the one in which you will be presenting. Rehearse everything in your script, including your examples, anecdotes, and stories. Rehearse your gestures, too. Time all your rehearsals so you know exactly how long your presentation takes. Use the same presentation aids, such as a laser pointer and a remote mouse, as you will use in the actual presentation.

As Timothy J. Koegel writes in his invaluable book, *The Exceptional Presenter*, "Those who practice improve. Those who don't, don't."[7]

These aids make your presentation look more professional and allow you to move around to make your presentation more energetic and dynamic.

Have plenty of handouts such as relevant articles, pictures of what you are offering and copies of the presentation. It is OK to hand out copies of your presentation beforehand along with reinforcing data and encourage people to take notes on the handouts. There are some drawbacks to handing out copies of a presentation at the beginning – often people skip ahead to an area in which they are interested. However, the positives of people being able to follow at their own speed and take notes reinforces the points you make, and in most cases the positives outweigh the negatives.[8]

Know your subject thoroughly. Rehearsal also allows you to hone your knowledge. You are the expert and must have the answers to all possible questions and objections prospects have. It is a good idea to give different areas of expertise to different members of your team. For example, assign operations/production to the person who is an expert, promotion to someone with that expertise, and research to an expert in that field. This arrangement not only relieves pressure on the main presenter, but also introduces other members of your team of experts. Rehearse transitions from one team member to the next in order to make them fast and smooth.

Understand your audience. Before going into a presentation, you should know in advance your audience's personalities, emotional needs, inherent assumptions, and motivations, especially those of the decision makers to whom you will direct your presentation. You should also have sense about their attitudes about your company and product.

Finally, plan in advance how you want to arrange the seating. An effective presentation begins with an *effective room setup*. Do not have alternate seating – a member of your team, then a prospect, then a member of your team. Give the prospects the best seats and put them all together in a row or in a circle at the end of a table so they have the best view of the projection screen. Sit the main decision makers in the middle so that they are always the center of your attention, although you will include others from time to time. Have your team sit behind the prospects or at the front of the table – your people do not need to have a good view of the presentation. The message you want to convey is that your focus and complete attention is on the prospects. Assign members of your team to watch a member of the prospect's team and take notes unobtrusively of their assigned prospect's reaction to different points in the presentation in order to give you accurate feedback in a debriefing.

Delivery

Nick Morgan in an article titled "The kinesthetic speaker: Putting action into words" in the *Harvard Business Review*, writes,

> Sure, presentations are about what a speaker says. But they're also about how a speaker moves. By making adroit use of your body and the space around you, you can create a physical connection with the audience that will earn trust and inspire action.

In the article Morgan writes the Dos and Don'ts of kinesthetic speaking, as seen in Exhibit 11.3.

Morgan writes that the alignment of a speaker's movements with his words reinforces the message he is trying to convey. Following are some tips that will make your delivery more effective.

Open   Before you begin your PowerPoint presentation, make opening remarks that relate to the *theme* of the presentation and that include an *agenda* of what you are going to cover. These should be memorable and demonstrate your confidence and your control of the situation. Timothy Koegel in *The Exceptional Presenter* recommends that you memorize the first two minutes of your presentation and practice it repeatedly until your remarks flow smoothly and naturally.

Also, opening remarks should deal with questions such as, "Should I take notes?", "Can I ask questions?", and "How long will the presentation take?" Opening remarks should also deal with how to handle questions as they occur in a presentation. One way is to take questions at the end of the presentation, another is to take them at any time, another is to take them at specific times during the presentation, or to take only important questions during the presentation and

Exhibit 11.3   The Dos and Don'ts of kinesthetic speaking

Do . . .

- identify individuals who can serve as proxies for the whole audience
- vary the distance between yourself and the audience, moving into the personal space of proxies to recount an anecdote or to make a plea
- ensure that your physical moves are in harmony with your verbal message
- prepare your own presentations so your physical moves don't betray inauthentic content
- read and respond to the nonverbal cues of audience members.

Don't . . .

- speak generally to the entire audience for long periods
- repeatedly move back and forth between podium or slide projector and the screen
- turn away from the audience to cue up your next slide while speaking
- fidget away your nervous energy
- count on the audience remembering more than one or two of your main points.

Source: Nick Morgan. 2001 "The kinesthetic speaker: Putting action into words." *Harvard Business Review*. April, p. 115.

others afterwards. Saving questions until the end will allow you to save time, but it creates a one-way presentation. While you maintain control, you limit interaction and leave some questions unanswered. Worst of all, it hurts the rapport you would like to build between you and the audience.

Taking questions any time during a presentation is very effective if you have relatively loose time constraints, because it gets the audience involved. But keep close track of time. If people ask too many questions, you will not finish the entire presentation, so give the problem to them by saying, "Time is in your hands. Our presentation runs 25 minutes and I have built in 15 minutes for questions, but please feel free to ask as many questions as you like, and we can extend the time frame." In this way you alert them to the need to keep track but that you can extend the time if they want.

Taking important questions during the presentation and the rest later is another good tactic. By saying in your opening remarks, "we have allowed time at the end of the presentation for questions, but, of course, feel free to ask any questions that help clarify our presentation," you encourage your audience to save questions while not muzzling them.

Your opening remarks should begin with a sincere "thank you" for giving you the time to make a presentation and should include a tidbit of knowledge about prospects and their companies that relates to the *theme* of your presentation. For example, before Matt Weisbecker, then of AOL Interactive Marketing, gave a presentation to Panasonic, he prepared himself by reading a book about the company's founder, Matsushita. He opened his presentation with a quote from the company's mission statement that Matsushita had written in 1936 and compared it to AOL's mission statement.

Find out what your audience's interests and hobbies are and relate your opening remarks to them. If you know the decision makers are big sports fans, open with a sports analogy or story that involves their favorite sport or team. Find out what their interests and hobbies are and relate your opening to those interests, if possible. You can also open with an amusing or insightful story, but make sure it is relevant. You do not want your prospects to lose the point of the presentation. *Bridge* your opening story or joke (make sure it is funny and *not off color*) with a statement like "with that in mind . . ." or " . . . which brings me to the purpose of our presentation." If you cannot make a bridge statement like these, then the story or joke is not relevant and do not use it.

One of the best opening stories I ever heard comes from James Burke's *Connections* and tells how at the battle of Agincourt a severely outnumbered (six-to-one) English army defeated the French by using long bows, which the French had never seen. The story highlights how disruptive technology changed forever the way armies waged war and is an analogy of how the Internet changed the way companies conduct business.

In the useful, informative book, *Krushchev's Shoe – And Other Ways to Captivate an Audience of 1 to 1000*, Roy Underhill writes that the features of a presentation or speech that people enjoy most are hands-on experiences.[9] He advocates using your opening to involve your audience in some way, perhaps to get them to perform some action. You might ask, "What is the biggest challenge facing your industry in the next five years?" and then let everyone answer. Or, a favorite of mine is to ask them to write down the five most important people in their company. When they have finished, ask them how many of them put their customers on their lists?

Another way to involve your audience is to ask them to build something. You might open a couple of sets of Lego blocks, dump them on the table, and ask people to build something in five minutes. When they have finished and shared what they have built with one another, tell them that your organization has a number of different packages, programs, and products that they can use to build a solution just as unique.

Your opening remarks give you the opportunity to make a favorable first impression. Therefore, the stronger the opening the better and more lasting the impression. Your opening sets the tone for the entire presentation, so open creatively and use props if you can. Because of the primacy and recency principles, discussed in Chapter 7, people will remember your opening and closing most vividly.

Main body of content   Exhibit 11.4 contains *delivery tips* for the main body of your presentation. Exhibit 11.5 shows an example of a story that touches an emotional chord.

Exhibit 11.4 Delivery tips

Tip		Description
1	Audience expectations	You should have a sense of your audiences' expectations and their preferred style: Conservative, formal, and straightforward or informal, humorous, and glitzy, for example.
2	Poise and confidence	Having poise and demonstrating a sense of confidence are critical for delivering a successful presentation.
3	Love your product	Be passionate about it and convey that passion to your audience with your physical movements and gestures.
4	Be concise	Don't ramble. Stick to your script and stay within the allotted time. Remember that the ideal length of time for a presentation is 25 minutes.
5	Remember WIIFM	Keep in mind that with everything you say your prospects are asking themselves, "What's in it for me (WIIFM)?" Therefore, with every feature or advantage you mention, relate its benefit.
6	Keep jargon to a minimum	In your written presentation you used your prospects' language and avoided jargon, so do not fall into using it during your oral presentation.
7	"We're number one" never sold anything	What prospects want are solutions, not chest-thumping numbers. Use equivalencies for numbers whenever you can and make sure the numbers you use are relevant to the solutions you are proposing. No one cares if you are number one if you cannot solve their problems.
8	No negatives	During your presentation never be negative and never knock the competition.
9	Don't be defensive	If you get a question, even a hostile one, do not panic. Repeat the question, say something like "good point," and answer it concisely, honestly, and directly or put it off until later in your presentation when you have an answer for it. Do not waffle or lose your confidence.
10	Smile	Inexperienced speakers are often frightened when they present in front of a group and forget to smile. Do not make that mistake; smile as appropriate and authentic throughout the presentation.
11	Establish eye contact with everyone	Move around and try to establish some eye contact with everyone, even though you will be concentrating most often on the decision maker.
12	Vary your voice	Vary your tone of voice, your pitch, and your volume. Modulate well; you do not want to lull people to sleep with a monotone. Rehearsal helps.
13	Use people's names	Direct your points to specific people and use their names: "Isn't this the solution you asked for, Jane?", for example.

Exhibit 11.4 Delivery tips (cont'd)

Tip		Description
14	Be careful about injecting humor	Unless you are funny and have knack for telling jokes and for humor, do not use it. Nothing falls flatter than a poor joke. *Never* insert off-color or inappropriate humor.
15	Involve the audience	People learn better when they participate than they do when they just listen. Bob Pittman was the best presenter I have ever seen in action. When he was President of America Online, he would use a variety of questions to get audiences involved. He would often say, "Raise your hands if you ever bought a Cuisinart machine. Now keep them up if you know what closet it's in. Come on now, be honest." Then he would make the point that AOL was not a gimmick, it was an everyday necessity.
16	Tap into the decision maker's emotions	Great speakers like Winston Churchill and Martin Luther King were able to touch the hearts of their audience. They tapped into emotions and feelings, and made these emotions work for them. When you do your homework about your audience in general and the decision maker in particular, find out what their passions are and then find stories that touch their feelings about their country, their business, or its founder. See Exhibit 11.5 for the kind of story that would elicit an emotional response. But remember to match your emotional fervor to the audience's ability to receive the message.*
17	Keep going	It takes listeners a long time to catch up to the fact that you have lost your place or gone to the wrong slide. Pause, collect yourself, and keep going. Never say, "I'm sorry" or point out a mistake because your audience more than likely will not notice a mistake unless you point it out. Keep on trucking.
18	Laugh it off	If something happens such as a projector breaks or a bulb burns out, so what? Keep on going. Your audience is with you and wants you to do well, so make them comfortable by handling a crisis with grace and humor without blaming someone – your assistant, the projector, or God. Laugh it off gracefully and keep on trucking.
19	Be yourself and have fun	Relax and be natural; rehearsals will help a lot to give you confidence and to relax enough to be yourself. You must be authentic because people will know if you are trying too hard or are phony and trying to sell them snake oil.

* Jay Conger. 1998. "The necessary art of persuasion." *Harvard Business Review*. May–June.

Exhibit 11.5 The Firefighter

Four months after the tragedy of 9/11, I heard a story that dramatically made a point. A Vice President for America Online, where I was working at the time, gave a presentation to the CEO of a key account. When the presentation concluded, the CEO asked for a substantial price concession.

The Vice President told a story of a weary New York firefighter who was returning home from working at Ground Zero several weeks after the tragedy. As he trudged along, he saw a homeless man holding a small American flag who asked the firefighter for money for a meal. The firefighter said, "I'll give you $10 for that flag." The homeless man replied, "I may be hungry and homeless, but this is my country's flag. No deal." The weary fireman nodded, stuffed a $10 bill into the homeless man's hand, and went on his way.

The Vice President then said to the CEO, "I understand you asking to get the best possible deal for your company – I'd probably do the same thing in your position. However, I cannot sell AOL at a discount because I'm passionate about and respect this company and our product and I will not undervalue or undersell it." The CEO did not mention price again and the VP got a commitment for a sizeable deal.

Summary   Most summaries are too long. I have seen presenters summarize 15 points at the end of a presentation. That is not a summary, it is a novelette. Use the Rule of Three and keep your summary to three points, because that is all your prospects will remember.

Conclusion and next steps   Richard B. Chase and Sriram Dasu, in an article titled "Want to perfect your company's service? Use behavioral science" in the *Harvard Business Review*, stress the importance of finishing strong. The authors indicate that, of the two ordering effects, primacy and recency, recency, or the last experience people have in an encounter such as a presentation, is by far the most important.[10] Therefore, not only is it important to have a dramatic, attention-getting opening, but it is even more important that your conclusion is memorable.

Ratchet up your passion in your conclusion. You want to make as emotional appeal as you can for why a deal between your company and a prospect's company is an ideal partnership. You are asking for the prospect's hand in marriage and you should make your closing remarks worthy of such a union. Widely regarded as the greatest speech in the English language, Lincoln's Gettysburg Address opens memorably with "Four score and seven years ago," but ends unforgettably with "and that government of the people, by the people, for the people shall not perish from the earth." I do not expect you will be able to write as moving, as unforgettable a finish as Lincoln did, but his stirring words are a good place to start when you think about your conclusion.

After your conclusion, ask for *next steps*, which is a nice, polite way to *close and ask for a commitment*. Next steps might include signing a contract or a letter of intent to do a deal, shaking hands on the deal, or having you present to a prospect's board of directors. Whatever commitment you want, never forget to ask for it. It is an unforgivable sin in selling not to try to close.

If you get no questions when you are finished with your presentation, you have done something wrong and are in trouble. A friend of mine who used to sell for IBM in the 1970s tells a story about a major presentation he made to the board of directors of a large regional insurance company. At the end of the two-hour presentation, when my friend asked if there were any questions, there were none. My friend said he was squirming and did not have a clue as what to do in the deafening silence. His boss, the regional sales manager, who had been an observer, said, "You didn't do a very good job of explaining the benefits of our solution. They didn't understand. Do the presentation again." My friend panicked for a moment, but did the presentation again as he was told. At the end there were lots of questions and an order followed.

This story points out that presenters must take responsibility for whether or not the audience understands a presentation. If there are no questions at the end of a presentation, it is your fault because you did not explain things well enough. You must take responsibility for clearly communicating the benefits of your solutions, which requires anecdotes, stories, equivalencies, good kinesthetic speaking, and audience participation.

Debriefing   In the first few days after a presentation, the presentation team must have a debriefing meeting. If possible, hold the meeting in the prep room where the charts are still visible. Go over each chart and ask if your preparation was on target and if prospects accepted your ideas and solutions. See Chapter 10 for the elements of an effective presentation.

You cannot learn by your mistakes unless you analyze them objectively. After every presentation be paranoid about losing the order and debrief. The only way to be certain you are better than the competition is to rehearse and debrief more thoroughly than the competition does.

Presenting effectively is a skill that, like acting, requires rehearsal and performance feedback in order to perfect your technique. Also, like the best actors, the best presenters come across as natural – "Their style is conversational, and they look completely at ease in front of any audience."[11] It is worth the time and effort you invest in rehearsal, because you cannot be successful unless you learn to present exceptionally well, naturally, and with confidence.

Test Yourself

1   What are the four goals of the presenting step of selling?
2   What are the seven steps of the Sales Ladder?
3   What are the six steps in a call structure?

4   What are some techniques for overcoming the price objection?
5   What are three methods of handling proposals one-on-one?
6   What are the 19 delivery tips for making a major presentation to a group?

Project

Write a presentation for a Web site to a major advertiser. Complete the presentation you started in the project at the end of Chapter 10, using the checklist at the end of that chapter as a guide. Print out the presentation and ask a friend to play the part of a prospect. Give the presentation using both the one-page-at-a-time method and the sit-side-by-side method. See which method you are more comfortable with and pay particular attention to social space and how close you can comfortably work (for you and the prospect). After you have made the presentation twice, write a script and rehearse delivering the presentation in front of a full-length mirror. Go over the delivery tips in this chapter before you deliver the presentation, and afterwards, see how you did. What did you remember to do and what did you forget to do?

References

Richard B. Chase and Sriram Dasu. 2001. "Want to perfect your company's service? Use behavioral science." *Harvard Business Review*. June.

Jay Conger. 1998. "The necessary art of persuasion." *Harvard Business Review*. May–June.

Roger Fisher and William Ury with Bruce Patton. 1991. *Getting to Yes*, 2nd edition. New York: Penguin Books.

Neil Flett. 1996. *The Pitch Doctor: Presenting to Win Multi-million Dollar Accounts*. New York: Prentice Hall.

Saul Gellerman. 1990. "The tests of a good salesperson." *Harvard Business Review*. May–June.

Timothy J. Koegel. 2007. *The Exceptional Presenter*. Austin, TX: Greenleaf Book Group Press.

Michael Maccoby. 2000. "Narcissistic leaders: The incredible pros, the inevitable cons." *Harvard Business Review*. January–February.

Gerald L. Manning and Barry L. Reece. 1990. *Selling Today: A Personal Approach*, 4th edition. Boston: Allyn and Bacon.

László Mérö. 1998. *Moral Calculations: Game Theory, Logic, and Human Frailty*. New York: Copernicus.

Nick Morgan. 2001. "The kinesthetic speaker: Putting action into words." *Harvard Business Review*. April.

Gerard I. Nierenberg. 1973. *Fundamentals of Negotiating*. New York: Hawthorne Books.

Anthony Parinello. 1999. *Selling to VITO: The Very Important Top Officer*. Holbrook, MA: Adams Media Corp.

Linda L. Putnam and Michael Roloff. 1992. *Communication and Negotiation*. Newbury Park, CA: Sage Publications.

Neil Rackham. 1989. *Major Account Sales Strategy*. New York: McGraw Hill.

Howard Raiffa. 1982. *The Art and Science of Negotiation*. Cambridge, MA: Harvard University Press.

Thomas C. Schelling. 1980. *The Strategy of Conflict*. Cambridge, MA: Harvard University Press.

James K. Sebenius. 2001. "Six habits of merely effective negotiators." *Harvard Business Review*. April.

G. Richard Shell. 1999. *Bargaining for Advantage*. New York: Penguin Books.

Edward R. Tufte. 2006. *The Cognitive Style of PowerPoint: Pitching Out Corrupts Within*. Cheshire, CT: Graphics Press LLC.

Roy Underhill. 2000. *Krushchev's Shoe*. Cambridge, MA: Perseus Publishing.

Bob Woolf. 1990. *Friendly Persuasion*. New York: Berkley Books.

Resources

www.barbwiremuseum.com (the Devil's Rope barbed wire museum Web site)

Notes

1   Gerald L. Manning and Barry L. Reece. 1990. *Selling Today: A Personal Approach*, 4th edition. Boston: Allyn and Bacon.

2   Neil Rackham. 1989. *Major Account Sales Strategy*. New York: McGraw Hill.

3   www.barbwiremuseum.com

4   "E-mail is easy to write (and to misread)," http://www.nytimes.com/2007/10/07/jobs/07pre.html?adxnnl=1&adxnnlx=1194734824-j+0H1TUQ4tBCQ/CngUsdZA. Accessed November 10, 2007.

5   Ibid.

6   Edward R. Tufte. 2006. *The Cognitive Style of PowerPoint: Pitching Out Corrupts Within*. Cheshire, CT: Graphics Press LLC.

7   Timothy J. Koegel. 2007. *The Exceptional Presenter*. Austin, TX: Greenleaf Book Group Press, p. 132.

8   Tufte. 2006. *The Cognitive Style of PowerPoint*.

9   Roy Underhill. 2000. *Krushchev's Shoe*. Cambridge, MA: Perseus Publishing, p. 1.

10   Richard B. Chase and Sriram Dasu. 2001. "Want to perfect your company's service? Use behavioral science." *Harvard Business Review*. June.

11   Koegel, *The Exceptional Presenter*, p. 121.

12

Skills: Negotiating and Closing

Charles Warner

Negotiating is one of the most researched and studied topics in business, law, politics, and international affairs. In June 2007, a search on Amazon.com for books on the subject of negotiating came up with 109,847 titles, including *Negotiating for Dummies* – obviously not a book for readers of this book. It is clear people are buying and reading books on negotiating, so you must assume that your prospects, customers, and buyers have read some of them and possess varying degrees of negotiating expertise. To assume otherwise is foolhardy because the uninformed and unprepared salesperson will lose when up against a knowledgeable negotiator. If you are calling on retailers, you must assume they are experts in negotiating because they negotiate every day with their vendors and customers. If you are calling on media buyers, their titles often include the word negotiator, especially at large agencies that purchase network television.

The majority of negotiating books are about how to negotiate in one-time situations in which long-term relationship are not important and negotiating for tangible goods, such as real estate. Negotiating in the media is different from most other types of negotiating and requires special skills for two reasons. First, media negotiating is not about winning at all costs in hard-nosed competitive battles over price and terms. The media does the vast majority of its business with long-term customers and agency buyers, and maintaining relationships with these customers and buyers is vital. Second, the media, especially broadcast and cable, sell a perishable product that, if not sold, goes to waste.

Furthermore, all media selling involves negotiating. A negotiation might be a simple three-step process such as, "My price is $100," "I'll give you $90," and "I'll take it." Or an advertiser might negotiate over the position of an ad with a newspaper that will not budge an inch on rates. Or television network executives and advertising agency negotiators might negotiate for a $50 million upfront deal. Or a major media conglomerate might negotiate with a major advertiser for a multi-million-dollar cross-platform deal on all of its media properties. But whatever the size of the deal, if you do not learn to be an effective negotiator, your chances of having a successful career in media selling are small, and your chances of being world class are zero.

Negotiating and closing are included in the same step of selling because the ultimate goal of negotiating is to reach a satisfactory agreement, to close a deal. Therefore, you should look forward to negotiating and not be apprehensive. Why? Because, when you enter into negotiations, prospects have reached the Conviction step on the Sales Ladder. They want to make a deal, and they are ready to take the next step, Action, if they can get what they perceive to be a good deal. It is your task in negotiating to see that customers perceive they get a good deal, which actually should be a good deal for both sides. *An exchange of satisfactions* best describes negotiating. In his classic book, *The Fundamentals of Negotiating*, Gerard Nierenberg writes, "All parties to a negotiation should come out with some needs satisfied."[1]

The Negotiating and Closing Process

The process of negotiating and closing is quite complex – it is full of many rules and a wide variety of tactics and choices. In this chapter only, I have organized and structured these rules, tactics, and choices in a numbered, outline-type format in order to make them easier to follow, especially if you download and print out the Negotiating and Closing Outline from the book's Web site, www.mediaselling. us/downloads.html.

> Rule: Don't negotiate until you've created value and created a differential competitive advantage for your product in the mind of a customer.

> Rule: Don't discuss price until you're ready to negotiate and close.

Many inexperienced salespeople make the mistake of negotiating too soon, before they have created value. The first question both experienced media buyers and inexperienced prospects often ask is, "What's the price?" For example, a prospect new to your medium might innocently ask "How much does an ad on your Web site cost?" Your response should be, "Well, that's like asking how much a car costs. Are you talking about a Hyundai or a Rolls Royce? The answer is 'It depends.' Let's find out what your needs are and then we'll see what the best type of ad or banner for you would be." If an experienced television buyer whom you have dealt with frequently asks, "What is your cost-per-point?" you should delay the answer until you have had a discussion about the value, benefits, and supply-and-demand issues concerning your product. Even with experienced buyers, always follow the first two rules above.

Some negotiations are not complicated and require minimal preparation. However, because 80 percent of your business will come from 20 percent of your customers, you will find that the majority of your business might involve complex negotiating with your more important customers and agency media buyers. In large markets and in national media such as magazines, portals (e.g., Yahoo!, AOL, MSN), and network television, virtually all business involves complex negotiating, which requires thorough preparation, as outlined below.

The five elements in the negotiating and closing process are:

1   Your negotiating approach
2   Preparation
3   Maneuvering for dominance and control
4   Bargaining
5   Closing and getting commitment

See the Negotiating and Closing Outline at http://www.mediaselling.us/downloads.html for a summary of the above five elements and for all of the rules of negotiating.

1   Your Negotiating Approach

Your approach to negotiating should be information-based, relationship-based, ethical, and flexible.

1.1   Information-based

It is often said that information is power, and in no situation is information more powerful than in negotiating. You should conduct research and gather information about the other side and their competitors, about your competitors, about the other side's cultural background, and about the other side's attitudes and bargaining tactics.

Information about your customers and their competitors The more information you can gather when you ask your Discovery Questions and afterwards about customers' goals, strategies, challenges, and business and personal needs (a needs portrait), the better chance you have to achieve your objectives in a negotiation. An information-based approach focuses on solid planning, careful listening to discover information about your customers' needs and interests, and recognizing signals the other side sends through its behavior and tactics during the negotiating process.

It is also important to gather complete information about the other side's competitors: the competitors' marketing and advertising strategies, their market position, their value proposition, their image, and their reputation. As we learned in game theory, your customers' strategies will be determined by their competitors' strategic and tactical moves, so you must have competitive information in order for you to position your offers in a way that helps your customers beat their competitors.

Information about your competitors In *The Art of War*, Sun Tzu, the legendary Chinese general, writes: "Spies are a most important element in war, because upon them depends an army's ability to move."[2] For "spies" substitute the modern concept of competitive intelligence, for "war" substitute negotiating, and for "army" substitute the word negotiator. The sentence now reads: Competitive intelligence is the most important element in negotiating, because a negotiator's ability to move depends on it. Another lesson from Sun Tzu that we must not forget is that the "the true object of war is *peace*."[3] Likewise, the true object of negotiating must be *agreement*, not victory.

Intelligence about your competitors is critical to your negotiating planning and to reaching a final agreement: intelligence about what prices your competitors will offer, intelligence about what concessions they will make, and intelligence about what tactics they have traditionally used in past negotiations. Having this information will help you determine your prices, your offers, and your tactics.

Information about the other side's cultural background The way people approach negotiating and their negotiating style is primarily based on their cultural background. For example, many people from the Middle East conduct business based on haggling over price, which is always negotiable. Some people in America believe in negotiating at every opportunity, others believe that negotiating indicates that they cannot afford something and, thus, do not negotiate to avoid looking cheap.

As an example, I gave a negotiating seminar to a group of magazine salespeople in New York several years ago and made the point that negotiating approaches are culturally based. A woman in the audience said, "Yes, I agree. My family never negotiated for anything." A salesperson sitting next to her said, "Wendy, you grew up in Greenwich, Connecticut. I grew up in the Bronx. My father sold garments on Seventh Avenue and the first two things he taught me were 'do not eat ham' and 'do not pay retail.'" Neither approach is right nor wrong; both are perfectly valid approaches. It is important for you to acquire information about the other side's approach so you can plan your negotiating tactics accordingly.

The attitudes and tactics of the other side   You might discover in your competitive intelligence research that the person you will be negotiating with tends to be an over-confident braggart who takes great pleasure in belittling others. Bob Woolf, in *Friendly Persuasion*, recommends adopting a self-effacing and non-blustering attitude, especially when you have an advantage or leverage. Woolf suggests that confidence in yourself, your plan, and your offer is vital, but he also recommends that you maintain a humble, agreeable attitude to keep the other side off guard, especially if the other side is overconfident.

Or, you might discover that the other side's lead negotiator has a habit of keeping people waiting for an hour or so before arriving at a negotiating session in order to get the other side angry. Many unethical negotiators will use various bargaining tactics to get the other side angry because they know that when people become angry, their emotional intensity rises and they will make irrational, emotional decisions instead of rational ones. Richard Shell writes in *Bargaining for Advantage* that "You must learn to recognize the hidden psychological strategies that play such an important role in negotiation."[4]

The Influence section of Chapter 8 covers many of these psychological tactics. Some negotiators will try to use the reciprocity principle against you by giving you a small concession and then asking for a big one in return. Sometimes clever negotiators will try to get you over-committed by threatening to buy from your competition in the hope that such a threat will create competitive bidding and lower prices substantially. If you do your research on the other side's typical attitudes and its tendency to use various tactics, you can plan your approach to respond accordingly and, therefore, gain an advantage.

1.2   Relationship-based

Successful negotiating is based on trust. And because media salespeople are selling an intangible service in which a salesperson becomes the surrogate for their product, most media selling is all about relationships. As I discussed earlier, to get trust, you must first give trust. However, do not give your trust unconditionally. The first time you negotiate with someone be skeptical. Being skeptical means delaying judgment about people until you learn from their behavior over time that they can be trusted. Initial wariness is important because you might discover eventually that you are dealing with highly competitive, unethical negotiators. However, in media selling you will find that the majority of the people you deal with take pride in being fair and honest, especially at large, reputable advertising agencies and clients. But you must establish a bond of mutual trust with these people. Once this trusting relationship occurs, you will find that negotiating is not necessarily contentious and competitive, but can be cooperative, challenging, and enjoyable.

1.3   Ethical

No matter what approach the other side takes, you must retain your integrity, be true to your convictions, and always act ethically – follow the ethical guidelines in Chapter 3.

1.4   Flexible

There is no one best way to negotiate. You must remain adaptable and be able to adjust to the needs of maintaining a relationship, to the urgency of the situation, to the complexities of a large deal, and to whether you are negotiating with a team or an individual. If you negotiate with people on a frequent basis, the rules and patterns of negotiating often become implicit, unstated, and comfortable. But always be alert, because they might take advantage of your comfort and change their mood, attitudes, style, and bargaining tactics in order to catch you off guard and gain an edge. You must be flexible in your approach and tactics, and you must *deal with each negotiation based on the situation at the moment* and not based on past patterns.

2   Preparation

The side that is best prepared and has the best-thought-out plan, comes out ahead in virtually every negotiation.

There are 10 preparation steps in negotiating:

2.1   Assess the situation.
2.2   Asses negotiating styles.
2.3   Identify interests, set objectives, and determine targets.
2.4   Assess leverage.
2.5   Estimate the ballpark, commit to walk-aways, and set anchors.
2.6   Determine bargaining tactics.
2.7   Decide when and how to open.
2.8   Determine frames.
2.9   Determine concessions and trade goals.
2.10 Plan your closes.

2.1   Assess the situation

The first step in planning is to assess the negotiating situation. One of the elements that distinguishes Richard Shell's *Bargaining for Advantage* from other books and seminars on negotiating and make the book applicable to media negotiating is his concept that there are four basic situations that require different strategies, as shown in Exhibit 12.1, The Situational Matrix

Balanced concerns   In media selling you will run into all four types of situations, but the majority of your negotiating will be in a *balanced concerns* situation in which both stakes, such as price and deal terms, and conditions, such as position in a publication or added value, are as important as maintaining a relationship. Because media negotiating is typically conducted with regular customers who will give you repeat business, you must not negotiate so aggressively and competitively that you win and your customers lose. You must have a balance between getting favorable prices and terms and maintaining a trusting relationship.

Relationship   You will rarely encounter a *relationship* situation in media selling in which maintaining future relationships are such an overriding concern that you will accommodate advertisers with generous terms or large discounts. Because

Exhibit 12.1   The Situational Matrix

Perceived conflict over stakes

	High	Low
High — Perceived importance of future relationship between sides	**I Balanced concerns** (Business partnership, joint venture, or merger) *Best strategies:* Problem solving or compromise	**II Relationships** (Marriage, friendship, or work team) *Best strategies:* Accommodation, problem solving, or compromise
Low	**III Transactions** (Divorce, house sale, or market transaction) *Best strategies:* Competition, problem solving, or compromise	**IV Tacit coordination** (Highway intersection or airplane seating) *Best strategies:* Avoidance, accommodation, or compromise

Source: G. Richard Shell. 1999. *Bargaining for Advantage*. New York: Penguin Books, p. 127. Used with permission.

the stakes in a media deal are often public knowledge, as they are in the upfront market or when large contracts between public companies are posted on the Internet, media companies are usually unwilling to give one advertiser a significantly better deal than they would give to another advertiser. On the other hand, many media deals and contracts include a *favored-nation clause* in which a media company agrees to give an advertiser the same low price if the media company ever charges another advertiser a lower price. In a businesses in which most advertisers have many competitors, advertisers and their agencies trust media companies not to give better deals to competitors. Most media companies maintain their integrity and attempt to treat advertisers fairly.

Furthermore, by overemphasizing a relationship, media companies are subject to relationship blackmail. In an article in the *Harvard Business Review* titled "Negotiation as a corporate capability," author Danny Ertel writes:

> Over the years, I have asked hundreds of executives to reflect on their business relationships and to ask themselves which kinds of customers they make the most concessions to, do more costly favors for, and generally give away more value to. Is it their good customers or their bad customers? The vast majority respond, with some chagrin, "The difficult ones, of course. I'm hoping to improve the relationship." But that hope is almost always in vain: once customers find they can get discounts and favors by holding a relationship hostage, why should they change? Without realizing it, many companies have systematically taught their customers the art of blackmail.[5]

It is important not to allow advertisers to blackmail you by threatening to take their business elsewhere if they do not get more than other advertisers get. Do not cave in; treat everyone fairly.

Transaction   In media selling you will occasionally run into a *transaction* situation in which stakes are much more important than relationships. These situations sometimes occur with new customers who try to make a large one-time deal and negotiate a very low price. But beware of someone who is not a regular customer, whose reputation you do not know, who makes big promises, and who asks for big discounts in return. Always remember that your regular customers are your best customers and vow never to make a one-time deal, no matter how big a promise, that you would not make with your regular customers.

Tacit coordination   You will also find that you will often be in *tacit coordination* situations. Tacit coordination occurs when two people pull up to a Stop sign at the same time or when two people simultaneously try to sit in a seat on an airplane. Negotiation is typically quick and unspoken; one person or the other will nod and accommodate the other and move on. Remember the 80/20 rule applies. Twenty percent of your customers who give you 80 percent of your business will typically be repeat ones who are familiar with your pricing, your terms and conditions, and the added value you offer, if any, and will renew with little or no negotiating involved. In these situations, trust is the key factor. If your clients have learned to trust you to give them the best deal available at the time of the negotiation, they will not haggle – a tacit coordination situation.

In broadcast and cable where inventory is limited and, thus, pricing is based on supply and demand, customers and buyers will usually negotiate to get the best prices available at the time they are making a buy. Some agencies will buy for an account on a weekly or monthly basis and those negotiations will be short and to the point. Your goal should be to develop strong relationships with your customers so they trust you to bring them the best available deals at all times. Mutual trust keeps negotiating to a minimum and makes tacit coordination possible.

An example of tacit coordination would be when customers indicate they do not want to negotiate. They might say, "Bring me your best deal and if I like it, I'll buy it," and mean what they say. In such cases, it is imperative that you know the attitudes of your customers before you enter a negotiation and bring these customers reasonable, fair prices and offers.

Once you have determined what type of situation you will be facing in an upcoming negotiation print out the Negotiating and Closing Planner from http://www.mediaselling.us/downloads.html, and fill it in. In fact, you may find it helpful to print out a planner and follow it as you read this chapter.

2.2   Assess negotiating styles

The next step in preparation and planning is to assess the negotiating style of the other side and to recognize your own negotiating style. Research on negotiating indicates that there are two primary negotiating styles, competitive and cooperative. Author Richard Shell reports that in one study of lawyer-negotiators, who one might expect to be competitive, instead he found that "65 percent of the sample of attorneys exhibited a consistently cooperative style of negotiation, whereas only 24 percent were truly competitive in their orientation. (11 percent defied categorization using these two labels)."[6]

Some of the people Shell uses as examples of highly competitive negotiators in *Bargaining for Advantage* are Donald Trump, Wayne Huizenga, and Henry Kravis. These famous businessmen appear to fit the personality classification of *narcissist*, as described by Michael Maccoby in his *Harvard Business Review* article, "Narcissistic leaders: the incredible pros, the inevitable cons." From my 45 years in the media business, I come to believe that many of the top executives in the media fit Maccoby's narcissistic label. i have included narcissist in the description of negotiating types in Exhibit 12.2 because I believe many of the 11 percent that defied classification in the study mentioned by Shell probably fall into that category, particularly in the media business.

Exhibit 12.2 Negotiating types and patterns of negotiation

Competitors. Favored outcome: "I win, you lose." These people are highly competitive; they focus on winning – often at any cost. They usually put winning in personal terms; they want to beat *you*. They typically pay close attention to the size of their piece of the pie. They are unconcerned about being fair; they want the biggest slice. Winning (and not getting a worse deal than someone else) is everything to them. They often see negotiating as a game and enjoy the process as long as they think they can win.

Accommodators. Favored outcome: "I lose, you win." Accommodators want to maximize the other side's gain; they want the other side to have the biggest piece of the pie. They want you to think they are fair at almost any cost to them. They want you to get the best deal for you – the relationship is the most important thing to them. They are rarely seen in media negotiations.

Narcissists. High probability of an "I lose, you lose" (no deal) outcome. Narcissists do not care about any outcome that does not give them exactly what they want. They want the whole pie. Driven by ego, pride, greed, and selfishness; narcissists are only interested in their own outcomes. They hate to compromise, which means they make threats and demands and then will not negotiate. When others refuse to deal on their terms, which is often the case, narcissists usually turn into fierce, ruthless competitors. This switch is progress because they can be bargained with, although with great difficulty because they tend to use unethical tactics.

Cooperators. Favored outcome: "I win, you win." Cooperators try to maximize joint gain, build trust, and enhance the relationship. They are concerned about being fair. Cooperators are often problem solvers who can increase the size of the pie.

One of your objectives in negotiations is to train the other side to cooperate by demonstrating that both sides can win, to show them that negotiating fairly and in good faith can produce an outcome that is beneficial for both sides. It is very difficult to change a person's negotiating style, so be prepared to be competitive if you have to.

Patterns of negotiations
Cooperators versus Cooperators. A good combination. If a problem can be solved and an agreement reached, it will be. Often increases the gain for both sides – the pie gets bigger.

Competitors versus Competitors. They understand each other; although there is a higher risk of a breakdown and the negotiation consumes more time and resources, this is not a bad combination. Rarely is there an increase in the size of the pie, however. In fact, when competitors try to maximize their own gain or share, the amount of the settlement usually decreases.

Cooperators versus Competitors. A dangerous combination. Most negotiating problems occur with this combination. The two sides do not speak the same language, do not have the same goals, and do not understand each other. Invariably the competitor takes advantage of the cooperator, who winds up with a small piece of the pie.

Exhibit 12.2 Negotiating types and patterns of negotiation (cont'd)

Cooperators' objectives	*Competitors' objectives*
1 Conduct self ethically	1 Maximize gain
2 Get a fair agreement	2 Win by outmaneuvering
3 Build trust	3 Relationships not important

Cooperator traits	*Competitor traits*
1 Trustworthy, ethical, fair	1 Dominant, forceful, attack
2 Courteous, tactful, sincere	2 Crafty, rigid, strategic, uncooperative
3 Fair minded	3 Carefully observes opponent
4 Realistic opening position	4 Unrealistic opening
5 Does not use threats	5 Uses threats
6 Willing to share information	6 Reveals information only strategically, gradually
7 Probes opponent's position	7 Willing to stretch facts

Cooperators are quintessential win–win negotiators – they can increase the size of the pie. On the other hand, competitors are win–lose negotiators – they do not care if the pie shrinks, as long as they get the biggest piece. Neither cooperators nor competitors are wrong, they just see the world differently. If you trust a competitor, you will be easily exploited. If you try to be pleasant and get along with or be well liked by a competitor, you will be seen as naive and weak and be taken advantage of. It is imperative to match the style of the other side. When in doubt, be skeptical and assume the other side is a competitor until proven wrong.

Just as it is vital to know yourself if you are to acquire emotional intelligence in order to be effective at establishing and maintaining relationships, it is equally important to know your negotiating style if you are to be an effective negotiator. You must also be flexible and change your negotiating style to match the other side's style. Changing styles is extremely difficult for many people; if you find it difficult to change your style, select a colleague on your side who has a style that matches the other side's style and let that person do the negotiating.

Rule: Match the other side's style (cooperative or competitive).

After you have identified your and the other side's negotiating style, complete the Negotiating Style section in the Negotiating and Closing Planner.

2.3 Identify interests, set objectives, and determine targets

Identify interests Media companies and advertisers set negotiating objectives in order to achieve their overall, long-term interests. In your negotiating planning process, you must identify both sides' interests before you can set your negotiating objectives, because the ideal outcome of a negotiation is an agreement that satisfies both sides' interests. For example, a beer advertiser might have an interest in acquiring sponsorships for all major league sports in the United States. Before the season begins, the beer advertiser might want to invest in an exclusive sponsorship of the Major League Baseball games broadcast on your radio station, KAAA-AM, and want to lock out other beer sponsors. Let us assume that your station's interests are not to be overly dependent on a small number of advertisers, are not to engage in exclusive sponsorship deals, and are to have several beer advertisers compete for a scarce resource (your baseball broadcasts). Once you have determined what both side's interests are, write them down in the Negotiating and Closing Planner.

Set objectives   Next, you should set your objectives based on your understanding of both sides' interests. Set MADCUD objectives (see Chapter 5) for each negotiating opportunity you have. For example, if you were negotiating for KAAA-AM before the baseball season started, your negotiating objectives would be much different from what they would be if you were a month into the baseball season and had no beer advertisers. Following are some examples of MADCUD objectives in negotiating situations:

Measurable: An example of measurable objectives for a negotiation would be: To get a minimum of a 13-week insertion order for at least three banner ads a week and to get a no-cancellation contract term.

Attainable: The above measurable objectives must be realistic and reasonable for the advertiser in question and, thus, reasonably attainable – not too much of a stretch.

Demanding: Richard Shell suggests you should set objectives based on your *highest legitimate expectations* (HLE). Research indicates that those who expect more, get more. As we learned in Chapter 5, reasonable but challenging objectives have the greatest motivating effect. Therefore, how you define the concept of more is critical to your success. If by more, you mean your highest legitimate expectations (HLE), your chances of being successful will be much greater.

Consistent with company goals: Too often media salespeople set objectives that meet their own selfish needs and are not consistent with the overall long-term goals and strategies of their companies. For instance, salespeople might set an objective of making a sale regardless of price in order to make the commissions on the sale or make their quota. Or salespeople might set an objective of getting a sizable order by promising exceptionally favorable positions in a magazine contrary to the magazine's policy guidelines of offering desirable positions only to the largest advertisers. When you set negotiating objectives, always keep in mind that your company's interests, not yours, come first.

Under control of the individual: In a negotiation, you cannot control the other side's attitude or behavior, but you can control your own. As in sports, the mental game in negotiating is more important than the physical game. Keep in mind Michael Jordan's rules for winning: (1) Learn to love the game before you learn to master it. (2) Past failures are irrelevant to the task at hand. (3) If you can visualize winning, you won't fear losing. (4) Strength of heart (attitude) is more important than strength of body. Often the strategy of the other side is to get you to lower your confidence and expectations. If you allow this to happen, you will be inclined to lower your rates, give away too much, and settle for much less than you deserve. Control your confidence and expectation during a negotiation and keep them high.

Deadlined: Deadlines in negotiating are based on the scarcity principle – the scarcity of time. When you are selling a non-perishable product such as a house, do not set a deadline for a settlement because having no deadline puts pressure on the other side to settle and increases the fear of losing, which gets more intense over time, thus giving an advantage to the seller.

The opposite is true when you are selling a perishable product such as seats on an airplane, hotel rooms, broadcast or cable time, a prime position on a Web site, or a special issue or section of a publication that has a firm closing date. Set a deadline for settlement, because without a deadline there is no pressure on the other side to settle before the product perishes (goes away). Without a deadline, crafty buyers will wait until the very last possible moment in hopes that sellers will reduce prices significantly rather than see what they are selling go to waste, thus giving an advantage to the buyer.

Setting deadlines on all of your offers counters delaying tactics by the other side. So, when you present a proposal, put a comment line under the line that shows your prices that reads: "These rates are good until December 1," when you know the schedule is planned to start December 7, for example.

Rule: When selling a perishable product, always set a deadline on your offers.

Determine targets You learned about targets in Chapter 10, and you should determine which of these targets is appropriate for an upcoming negotiation. To review, the four types of targets are: a specific opportunity, price, size of order, and share of budget.

Set your objectives and determine your targets for a negotiation and then write them down in the Negotiating and Closing Planner. Furthermore, once you set your objectives and targets based on your highest legitimate expectations (HLE), you must commit to them. The best way to increase your commitment is to write down your objectives and targets and then tell someone about them. For example, say to your boss, "I'm convinced I can get a 15 percent increase over what we got last year from this account, and here's the rate and terms I'm going to get."

Rule: Make a commitment to your objectives and targets, write them down, and tell someone about them.

2.4   Assess leverage

The next step in the planning process is to assess your and the other side's leverage situation to determine who has the stronger and weaker position. Leverage is based on how badly people want something and how fearful they are of losing it. As Bob Woolf writes in *Friendly Persuasion*, "Every reason that the other side wants or needs an agreement is my leverage – provided that I know those reasons."[7]

There are two kinds of leverage: positive and negative. You have *positive leverage* when you have something that the other side wants much more than you want to hold on to it. You have *negative leverage* when the other side is afraid of losing something you have. Both are powerful, but negative leverage is more powerful. Competition for a scarce resource increases negative leverage and often leads to *over-commitment*, which occurs when people invest their egos and a lot of time in negotiating. Their fear of losing after they have invested so much escalates to the point that they often become over-committed and make unrealistically high offers. For example, the television rights for NFL football became so expensive because of over-committed bidding in 1998 that by 2003 ABC, CBS, and Fox were all losing money televising NFL football.[8]

Media salespeople have more leverage than inexperienced salespeople may realize. Most businesses, except for very small ones, must advertise in order to attract customers, survive, and grow. If a business has competitors, it has to advertise more than its competitors advertise if it hopes to gain market share. Also, advertising agencies have to invest all the money their clients allocate to advertising because advertising budgets reflect the sales levels advertisers hope to achieve. Their ultimate goal is not to save money, but to get the optimum reach and frequency for the money they have allocated. This need to advertise gives media salespeople leverage if they are selling a medium or a product that is in demand or can provide a viable solution to an advertising problem.

Assessing both sides' leverage is critical in deciding your overall negotiating strategy and tactics. Once you have a sense of which side has the stronger leverage, there are four leverage tactics that will help you strengthen your leverage or weaken the other side's leverage: a BATNA, tit-for-tat, warnings, and bluffs.

Strengthen leverage   Below are four tactics for strengthening your leverage:

A *BATNA* is the *best alternative to a negotiated agreement*. Fisher and Ury first introduced the concept of a BATNA in their best-selling book, *Getting to Yes*. The purpose of a BATNA is to have at least one viable alternative when you enter into a negotiation. For example, when people ask me how they should ask for a raise, I tell them to get an offer in writing from another company for a job that pays more money than they are currently making. This offer is a BATNA and it provides leverage. Without a competing offer, people who ask for a raise have little leverage and their employer has most of the leverage.

In media selling, an example of how to acquire a BATNA would be for KAAA-AM, being aware of the interest of the acquisitive beer advertiser, to offer sponsorships to several other beer advertisers in order to generate interest in its baseball broadcasts before talking to the acquisitive beer company. If KAAA-AM drums up sufficient interest to be certain of an order from another beer advertiser, the station has a BATNA, which increases its leverage considerably with the acquisitive beer company.

Rule: Always go into a negotiation with a BATNA, if possible.

The *tit-for-tat* tactic means that you reciprocate the tactics, behavior, and style of the other side by matching them with your tactics, behavior, and style. For example, if the other side pounds the table and threatens to walk out, you pound the table and threaten to walk out. In order to understand the power of tit-for-tat, warnings, and bluffs, let us return to game theory that was introduced in Chapter 9.

You will recall that John von Neumann invented game theory in 1928 after watching a bluff in a poker game. He reasoned that in order to win in poker it was important not to play according to the probabilities of a certain card being dealt, but to play according to the moves of competitors. Twenty-two years later, in a program that was funded by the US Government at the Rand Institute in California, mathematicians, physicists, and other scientists studied, within the context of game theory, the strategic implications of two major world powers, the United States and the Soviet Union, each possessing the horrible destructive power of the atomic bomb.

One of the scientists invented a game called the Prisoner's Dilemma. The game was set up so that the punishments the two prisoners, who were isolated from each other, would receive were a great deal less if they turned in evidence that the other prisoner broke the law (whether the evidence was true or not). The scientists called turning in evidence defecting. The temptation to defect was so strong because of the way the punishments were weighted. Each turned in evidence that the other broke the law and both prisoners wound up in jail for 10 years. While in jail, the prisoners met and realized that if they had not defected and had said nothing, in other words if they had silently cooperated, they would have each received a minor punishment.[9]

When two scientists played a computerized version of the game repeatedly, they found that the best strategy was for each player to cooperate and settle for a smaller reward rather than being greedy (defecting) and going for a big reward. However, occasionally, one of the players would get greedy, and get a bigger reward. The players learned that when this defection happened the best strategy on the next move was to defect, or to use the tit-for-tat tactic, which taught the other player to cooperate again on subsequent moves and settle for smaller, but dependable, rewards. The US Government adopted the tit-for-tat tactic as the basis for its policy of deterrence based on the credibility of massive retaliation. In other words, if the Soviet Union built an ICBM with a nuclear warhead, the US would do the same – tit-for-tat.

Eventually, the tit-for-tat policy worked and the Soviet Union, virtually bankrupt from spending on a massive nuclear war machine, agreed to a program of mutual disarmament – cooperation. These lessons from the Cold War and from game theory are the foundation for another fundamental rule of negotiating.

Rule: Use tit-for-tat to teach the other side to cooperate.

A *warning* is an implied threat. The difference between a threat and a warning is that a warning is a relatively polite statement about what *might* happen. A threat is a more aggressive statement that communicates, "If you do X, I will retaliate by doing Y." Warnings and threats are effective only if they are credible. The other side must share your assumption that carrying out the warning or threat will make them worse off and believe it is not a bluff. President Bush's threat of war against Iraq became credible when Great Britain's Tony Blair strongly supported the war, and when 150,000 troops were mobilized and put on alert in the Middle East. Unfortunately, Bush's credible threat did not accomplish its purported purpose of motivating Saddam Hussein to disarm, rather it back-fired and caused Iraq to intensify its resolve to resist. The war in Iraq is an excellent example of the danger of making credible threats; that they often lead to destructive escalation.

People usually respond with hostility and anger when threatened. In business negotiations, warnings are much more effective than threats. Author Richard Shell writes that "Using threats in most negotiations is . . . like playing with fire – dangerous for everyone involved."[10] If you have a strong leverage position, your confident demands can become implied warnings. As an example, station KAAA-AM can tell the acquisitive beer sponsor, "This is our price. We have several offers on the table. The decision is up to you if you want to pay our price and agree to our terms. We'd really prefer to do business with you, but in fairness to everyone, we can't turn down the highest offer." When you warn that you might use your BATNA, be extremely careful and do so politely, self-effacingly, and almost apologetically in order to avoid unintended consequences and escalation.

Rule: Never threaten, politely warn instead.

A *bluff* is when you act as though you have a strong position when, in fact, you have a weak position. It takes a great deal of confidence to pull off a successful bluff. Beginners should not bluff. However, in negotiating, just like when you play poker or a team sport such as football, a bluff, or a fake, is an acceptable and sometimes effective tactic. But to pull it off, you must understand the subtleties and proper timing of a winning bluff. We must once again turn to game theory for answers on how to bluff successfully.

Game theory researchers discovered that the best strategy in playing many games, including the Prisoner's Dilemma, is a mixed strategy of bluffing or defecting occasionally and on a random basis. The logic of this strategy is that if you never bluff, you are too predictable and the other side will take advantage of you because it knows you will be consistent and never retaliate. On the other hand, if you bluff on a regular, predictable basis, the other side will eventually figure out your bluffing pattern and your bluffs become as predictable as Rich Gannon's fakes were in Super Bowl XXXVII. Therefore, the best way to keep the other side on the defensive is to bluff occasionally on a purely random basis so the other side never knows what to expect.

An example of a bluff in a media selling situation would be to set your initial offer higher than you are actually willing to accept. If you are dealing with a buyer with whom you regularly negotiate, you must have walked away from business in the past. By doing so, your current bluff becomes credible. Two things can happen in this bluffing situation, either the buyer pays the highball rate or the buyer may call your bluff and say that your price is too high. In which case, you can back down, lower your price and get the business. However, you can only back down on rare occasions, because the buyer will learn that your bluffs are just that, bluffs, and not believe them

Rule: If you bluff, use a mixed strategy and occasionally bluff on a random basis.

If you bluff on an occasional random basis, a buyer will never be certain whether or not you are bluffing. Bluffs are only for experienced negotiators, not for rookies.

After you have assessed the leverage of both sides and decided which of the above leverage tactics are best suited for your leverage situation and which leverage tactics the other side is apt to use, fill out the Leverage section of the Negotiating and Closing Planner.

2.5   Estimate the ballpark, commit to walk-aways, and set anchors

Estimate the ballpark   A *ballpark* is the difference between a buyer's initial offer and your highest legitimate expectations (HLE). Your HLE includes not only price but also terms and conditions. Rarely are media negotiations about price alone; they include many other elements such as contract terms, non-cancellation clauses, added value, favorable ad positions, options for renewals, favored-nations clauses, or competitive ad separation. Some of these conditions are often more important than price, and one or more of these elements might be deal breakers for both

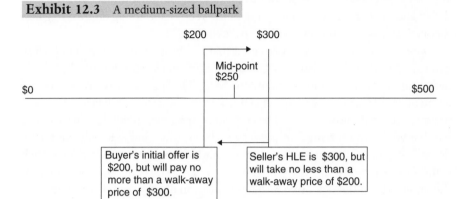

Exhibit 12.3 A medium-sized ballpark

sides. It is important to know what your deal breakers are and estimate what the other side's deal breakers might be, and then to plan accordingly.

Just as in Major League Baseball, negotiating ballparks come in different sizes. You want to negotiate in the smallest ballpark possible because it is easier and quicker to reach agreement. The size of the ballpark is determined by the other side's initial offer. Exhibit 12.3 shows an example of a medium-sized ballpark.

One end of the ballpark is your walk-away ($200 in Exhibit 12.3) and the other end is the buyer's walk-away ($300 in Exhibit 12.3). Note that the mid-point of the ballpark is $250, which is the potential agreement point – one that would satisfy both sides.

Rule: Most settlements are close to the mid-point.

You can gain knowledge of the other side's probable initial offer through careful research or by an understanding of the other side's past tendencies and approaches. For example, in Exhibit 12.3 we will assume the buyer has paid $250 in the past after making a lowest legitimate expectation (LLE) initial offer of $200, so you can assume that the buyer will open again with $200, but will pay more as in the past. Therefore, you should set your HLE at $300 to make sure you arrive at the $250 mid-point, at the minimum.

You will not always find that a buyer's initial offer is a reasonable, legitimate LLE, but is a lowball offer. Many buyers have a rule of negotiating that states: The lower price you initially ask for, the lower price you will wind up with. Therefore, many buyers open with an unreasonable lowball offer rather than with an LLE, and the lowball is way below your walk-away. No matter what the other side's initial offer is, you must clearly define and stick to your walk-aways.

Commit to walk-aways Without a walk-away, or a firm downside position, you will be nibbled away at by clever negotiators, which is like getting pecked to death by ducks; it takes a long time and is very painful. Walk-away means just that – you will walk away from a negotiation rather than settle for anything less. Your walk-aways must be absolutely firm; you must be committed to them, because having a soft downside position is a prescription for disaster. Read Appendix A, "Selling Magazines to Agencies" for an example of a disaster that occurred to a salesperson who was not committed to a walk-away.

Rule: Always go into every negotiation with a commitment to your walk-aways.

Even though it is vital to have walk-aways, do not focus on them during negotiations. Research shows that inexperienced negotiators have a tendency to focus on their low-end walk-away rather than their high-end HLE because of their aversion to loss. This tendency brings us to another rule of negotiating:

Rule: During negotiations, you must focus on your highest legitimate expectations (HLE), not on your walk-away.

Set your anchor Your HLE, which in Exhibit 12.3 is $300, should be not only what you must focus on and expect to get, but also the starting point in determining your opening offer. Your opening offer is your *anchor*. In negotiating when buyers first hear a high or low number, they unconsciously adjust their expectations accordingly. Therefore, it is vital that your initial offer anchors the other side's perception of your walk-away and that you open reasonably high. An unreasonably high initial offer can kill a deal or destroy your credibility if you drastically reduce your offer later.

It is crucial that you invest time in determining what your optimal anchor should be, as it is the most significant decision you will make in preparation and will be critical to a successful outcome. Anchors include price as well as terms and conditions, so your anchor should include a price that is high enough to give you room to come down to your HLE and include givebacks of terms and conditions that you are willing to concede. By carefully planning your price concessions and givebacks, you can prepare for some effective concession and closing techniques. Exhibit 12.4 shows the middle-sized ballpark with an anchor of $350.

In the ballpark in Exhibit 12.4 the mid-point is $250. By setting your anchor, your initial offer, at $350, you move the mid-point between your anchor and the buyer's initial $200 offer up to $275, a 10 percent increase over a $250 mid-point. Ten percent may not seem like much in these examples, but in media deals that involve millions of dollars, 10 percent is substantial. For example, in a $300 million deal, 10 percent would amount to $30 million dollars.

Since the other side's initial offer is the basis for your anchor, a lowball initial offer by the other side increases the size of the ballpark because you must increase the relative size of your anchor. Exhibit 12.5 shows an example of a large ballpark.

Exhibit 12.4　A medium-sized ballpark with anchor

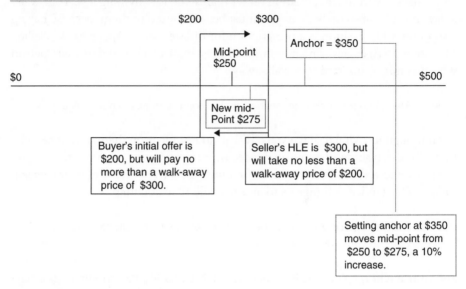

Exhibit 12.5　A large ballpark

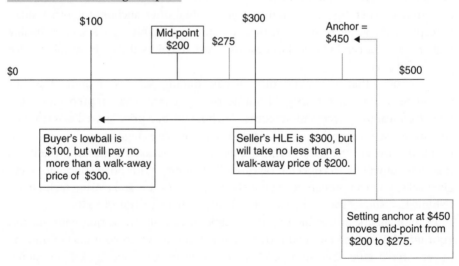

In Exhibit 12.5, your HLE has remained the same as it was in the middle-sized ballpark in Exhibit 12.4, but because the buyer's initial unreasonable lowball offer was only $100, the mid-point moved to $200, your walk-away price. Let us assume you don't know what the buyer's upside walk-away ($300) is. Nevertheless, your HLE is $300 and you would like to get close to that if possible. In order to do so,

Exhibit 12.6   A small ballpark

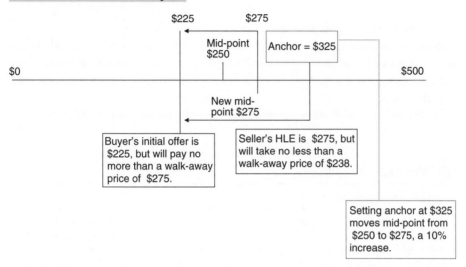

you must raise your anchor to an equally unreasonable $450 – tit-for-tat – in order to move the mid-point to $275, near the settlement you prefer.

Lowball offers often come from inexperienced or unreasonable negotiators or from new customers who are not familiar with your regular pricing, terms, and conditions. In such situations, let the other side open first, remain calm and polite, and set your anchor to move the mid-point close to your HLE.

On the other hand, initial offers from experienced negotiators and regular customers who are familiar with your pricing, terms, and conditions will often be reasonable and be close to current market prices and conditions – a tacit coordination situation. These types of offers will create a small ballpark, as shown in Exhibit 12.6.

In the small ballpark example in exhibit 12.6 the buyer's initial offer is a reasonable $225. Let us assume you deal with the buyer often, are familiar with the buyer's patterns and tendencies, and know that the buyer will not pay more than 10 percent over what was paid on the previous buy, which was $250. Thus, you estimate that the buyer's walk-away is $275 and, therefore, you set your HLE at $275. The mid-point between the buyer's initial offer of $225 and your HLE of $275 is $250, the potential settlement. The chances are that the buyer is counting on a $250 settlement, expecting to match the previous buy. However, by setting your anchor at $325, you move the mid-point up to $275, or a 10 percent increase over the previous price of $250, and a price the buyer is more than likely willing to pay. As you can see, setting a precise, well-thought-out anchor is crucial to help you achieve you objectives, targets, and HLE.

Rule: Always have a well-thought-out anchor.

2.6 Determine bargaining tactics

The literature on negotiating identifies a number of bargaining tactics that negotiators use to their advantage. Some are reasonable and acceptable; others are unfair, unreasonable, and unacceptable. Never use the unacceptable ones and learn to recognize them. Also, learn how to recognize both acceptable and unacceptable tactics.

There are several rules suggested in the bargaining tactics in Exhibit 12.7.

Exhibit 12.7 Bargaining tactics

Acceptable bargaining tactics

Tactic	Description/purpose	When to use	When used against you, your best response
Auction	Create an auction of competitive bids for a scarce resource – either a buyer for an advertising budget or a seller for a high-demand product.	When you have strong leverage – inventory or a product in high demand. Create a fear of losing in the other side.	Focus on your HLE, never go lower than your walk-away, and signal to the other side that you will walk away and not get into a competitive auction.
Cherry-pick	Pick only the best, most desirable elements of a product or package.	To pick apart a package offering; to negotiate for the most desirable individual elements separately, not as a whole.	When a buyer tries to cherry-pick you, show high prices for the individual units and a lower price for the overall package.
Crunch	Respond to an offer by saying, "It's not good enough," but don't give a number. Objective is to get the other side to respond with a number that is lower than you hoped for because of the other side's fear of losing.	In response to a low offer. The rule is, "Whoever gives a number first, loses."	Don't give a number. If a buyer says, "You're too high," respond with "What do you have in mind?"
Flinch	A sudden, physical reaction that tries to elicit a feeling of guilt, like, "You've got to be kidding!" response to an offer.	In response to a lowball offer. Only use occasionally.	Remain calm. Do not react. The other side is trying to get a rise, shock you. Don't respond.

Exhibit 12.7 Bargaining tactics (cont'd)

Acceptable bargaining tactics

Tactic	Description/purpose	When to use	When used against you, your best response
Good guy/bad guy (Good cop/bad cop)	The bad guy makes highly unreasonable demands and threats; the good guy's low requests seem reasonable in comparison – the contract principle at work.	In major, complex negotiations. Use your lawyers or management as bad guys (that is what they get paid for); as a salesperson, you be the good guy and offer a reasonable solution.	Make the right comparison. Don't compare the good guy's offer to the bad guy's offer; compare the good guy's offer to your HLE. Keep focused on your HLE.
Limited authority	To indicate that a negotiator has limited authority, cannot make a final decision, and has to check with a higher authority – a hint of a pullback in order to gain further concessions.	Use to stall for time, to think over an offer and craft a counteroffer, even if you have the final authority.	Agree to a break in the negotiating process while the other side checks with their higher authority and say, "That's a good idea. I have to check with my boss, too, because I may have gone too far." Hint at a pullback.
Nibble	A negotiator will indicate a strong readiness to settle, but will ask for just one more very small concession . . . then another, then another.	In the last stages of negotiations after many agreements and the other side is overcommitted. Nibble at the last remaining issues. "Can you give me just a dollar more?"	Stop the nibbling with a pin-down close. "I can't give you an additional 2% discount, but I will give you a half-percent discount if you give me the order right now with no further requests or changes." Give a small concession you were willing to give anyway to pin down a close.

Exhibit 12.7   Bargaining tactics (cont'd)

Acceptable bargaining tactics

Tactic	Description/purpose	When to use	When used against you, your best response
Price tag	To set a price limit. A buyer might say, "I like your proposal, but I only have $10,000, not the $15,000 you're asking for."	Price tags are buyers' LLE or sellers' HLE, not their walk-aways. Based on the rule that you never get anything you don't ask for, so why not ask for your LLE or HLE?	A price tag is a starting point, not a walk-away. Always challenge a price tag and treat it as an opening offer, not a final, walk-away.
Red herring	To negotiate hard on an unimportant issue, get concessions, then ask for reciprocal concessions on an important issue.	With multiple issues, feign the importance of a minor issue to you, receive concessions and then transfer those concessions to an important issue. Set a reciprocity trap.	Don't fall into reciprocity traps. Don't transfer concessions. Compare apples to apples – concessions on one issue do not apply to concessions on another issue. Commonly used tactic by media buyers.
Silence	To respond to an offer with silence.	Silence, like a crunch, is an attempt to get the other side to respond with concessions – bigger ones than you might have asked for.	The rule is: The first one to talk loses. Respond to silence with silence.
Split the difference	To offer to settle at the mid-point.	To get a quick settlement when the two sides are not far apart. Split the difference sounds like a fair offer, even if it isn't.	Often buyers will make a lowball offer and then offer to split the difference. Never split the difference when it is in the other side's favor or is not close to your HLE – have patience and keep negotiating.
Take-it-or-leave-it	An ultimatum and refusal to continue negotiations. Forces the other side to make a yes/no decision.	To signal a final offer; often used with the phrase, "A fair, final offer. Take it or leave it."	Leave it unless it is above your walk-away, which it usually isn't. Often a take-it-or-leave-it offer is a bluff, so always call the bluff.

Exhibit 12.7 Bargaining tactics (cont'd)

Acceptable bargaining tactics

Tactic	Description/purpose	When to use	When used against you, your best response
Throw-aways	Issues, terms, conditions, and added value that are part of an initial offer but are intended as concessions later in a negotiation.	Always have throw-aways in complex negotiations. Throw-aways should be issues, terms, conditions, and added value that are of relatively low importance – elements that you would normally give up. By including them in your initial offer, you set them up as concessions later to get the other side to give you concessions you want – the reciprocity principle at work.	Don't fall into reciprocity traps and give away something important to you when the other side makes a concession of minor importance to you. Always work on the fairness principle – trade concessions of similar value or importance.

Unacceptable bargaining tactics

Tactic	Description/purpose	When to use	When used against you, your best response
Big bait	Make a large initial offer in an attempt to find your bottom and walk-aways.	Never, because it's a hollow bluff or a lie. Users of big bait have no intention of making good on their initial, implied promise, but are just looking for the other side's rock bottom.	Recognize the tactic and name it. Call the other side's bluff. Say, "This sounds like a big bait to me. Are you willing to sign a firm, non-cancelable contract for the full amount?"

Exhibit 12.7 Bargaining tactics (cont'd)

Unacceptable bargaining tactics

Tactic	Description/purpose	When to use	When used against you, your best response
Blackmail	A threat meant to instill fear of loss. Usually a bluff.	Never, because it's unethical.	Recognize the tactic and name it. Call the bluff. Never give in, because it will make you vulnerable to future blackmail and larger and larger demands. Blackmail will continue regardless of what the other side promises. By giving in, you train the other side to blackmail you.
Change of pace	Bring some close to an agreement with a false promise, then back off, then promise again and get the other side so frustrated it will say yes to anything just to get closure.	Never, because it's unethical.	Recognize the tactic and name it. Have patience. Remain confident in the fairness of your proposal and in your HLE. Never respond with anger.
Deliver garbage	Insult the other side, its product, its management, and everything to instill a fear of losing on the other side. Lowers confidence and expectations.	Never, because it's too competitive and destroys relationships.	Don't catch the garbage. Pay no attention to it. Do not respond, and most important, do not lower your confidence or HLE. Smile and remain silent.
Renege	To take back a previously agreed-upon element in a negotiation. Objective is to instill fear of losing even more.	Never, because it breaks a promise, destroys trust, and leads to escalation – tit-for-tat reneging.	Recognize the tactic and name it. Flinch and say, "That's not fair! I have been negotiating in good faith and now you're taking something back." Never agree to reneging by the other side.

Exhibit 12.7 Bargaining tactics (cont'd)

Unacceptable bargaining tactics

Tactic	Description/purpose	When to use	When used against you, your best response
Starvation	Keeping food and water away from the other side in a lengthy negotiation in order to try to force a favorable settlement. For example, the side that controls the turf (location) will eat and drink before a negotiating session that begins at 11:00 a.m. and will last for several hours and then will not provide food or refreshments to the other side.	Never, because it destroys trust and shows lack of respect for the other side. Manipulative.	Name the tactic. Say, "I think you're trying to starve me, so I'm taking a break for an hour to go get something to eat and drink." If the other side objects, say, "Then order in some food. I'm much more agreeable on a full stomach."
Threats	To threaten to take a competitor's offer or to walk-out of the negotiation. A threat is like blackmail, often a bluff.	Never, because it destroys trust and discontinues fair negotiations.	Recognize the tactic and name it. Call the bluff and never give in because it will lead to more, larger threats.
Walk-out	To walk out of a negotiation before an agreement is reached; to refuse to negotiate further. Usually accompanied by an accusation of not being fair. Used to instill fear of losing. Invariably a bluff.	Never, because it destroys trust and prolongs negotiations unnecessarily.	Recognize the tactic and name it. Call the bluff. Let the other side walk out. Do not respond emotionally. The other side wouldn't resort to this tactic if it didn't want a deal; therefore, increase your HLE after a walk-out with confidence.

Rule: Never split the difference when it is in the other side's favor or is not close to your HLE; have patience and continue negotiating.

Rule: When faced with unacceptable and unethical bargaining tactics, name them and tell the other side the names so the other side knows you are not fooled.

Rule: Never respond emotionally; respond calmly, politely, and firmly.

After you have done the following: (1) assessed the situation, (2) assessed both side's negotiating styles, (3) identified interests, set objectives, and determined your targets, (4) assessed both side's leverage, (5) estimated the ballpark and committed to your walk-aways, and set your anchors; the next step, number 6, in the planning process is to determine the most appropriate bargaining tactics from the list of acceptable tactics in Exhibit 12.7. Write the tactics you select in your Negotiating and Closing Planner.

We have now covered six of the 10 preparation steps. We will pause for a while in the discussion of the negotiating planning process so you can acquire an understanding the last four steps of preparation: (7) decide when and how to open, (8) determine frames, (9) determine concessions and trade goals, and (10) plan your closes.

3   Maneuvering for Dominance and Control

Maneuvering for dominance and control is the second element in the negotiating planning process. Each side wants to gain a perceived power advantage so as to be perceived as dominant, and often maneuvers accordingly; its goal is to make the other side submissive. The most common maneuver is for one side to use the authority principle to impress the other with its status, authority, power, titles, and overall importance. Because most people tend to defer to authority and are impressed with status, if one negotiator is perceived to have more status, a more impressive title, or more power, that negotiator has an edge, it becomes dominant.

Rule: The other side only has the power you give it.

Because experienced negotiators, especially agency media buyers, will usually try to lower your confidence and expectations to gain an advantage, confidence is vital in negotiating: confidence in yourself, your proposal, your company, and your medium. Experienced negotiators will often try to get you to fall for an *authority trap* and indicate that they have the power to give you an order (and, therefore, affect your income). Other authority traps occur when buyers try to lower your expectations and remind you that their media plans and instructions from their clients will not allow them to pay your asking price. Buyers will also try to instill in you a fear of losing by reminding you that they can get lower prices from competitors or that they can buy another medium. In the face of these maneuvers, you must maintain your confidence and never lower your expectations; always keep your focus on your HLE.

Other maneuvers that crafty buyers often use to lower your confidence, reduce your expectations, and get you frustrated and angry (so you will make an emotional, not rational, decision) are: interruptions, hurry-up, delay, keep-you-waiting, and bring-in-the-boss.

Interruptions

Some buyers will continually interrupt a sales discussion or negotiation by taking phone calls, going for coffee, or even making quick calls. Buyers make these maneuvers in order to get you flustered, frustrated, and furious. Buyers know that if you let your ego and your emotions highjack your rationality, you will try to settle too fast just to get it over with and make a bad deal (for you).

Hurry-up

When buyers call for avails or give you a request for a proposal (RFP), they will often indicate they need it "immediately, if not sooner" in an attempt to hurry you up. Such a request is often followed by, "E-mail me the information by 1:00 p.m.. I don't have time to see you," or something similar. This maneuver is to hurry you up so that you do not have time to prepare adequately and to instill in you fear of losing if you do not meet their timetable. Of course, if you meet a hurry-up deadline, a buyer will rarely make the buy immediately. They typically use the delay maneuver.

Delay

Once you have made a presentation or submitted your avails or RFP, buyers often delay making a buy for as long as possible. They use this delay maneuver to make you worry about losing the order, hoping you will lower your price to avoid a loss. It is to counter this delay maneuver that you should always put a deadline on your offers. Another way to counter the delay maneuver is to call or e-mail the buyer who uses it and say something like, "I just wanted to let you know that we're filling up fast and those avails (or position) you wanted may not be available after today. Please give me an order ASAP, because I'd hate to see your client miss out on this opportunity and not be able to run its advertising."

Keep-you-waiting

Often buyers will keep you waiting, knowing that you will become frustrated and angry. Sometimes they will schedule appointments early and make you wait in a reception area with competing salespeople. Buyers use this maneuver because they know that salespeople often put competition on a personal level and, therefore, will lower their expectations and prices in order to avoid losing to a competitor waiting in the reception area. Remember that fear of losing can be a powerful influence, so do not let fear overcome you when you see a competitor. Be friendly, and increase your resolve to achieve your HLE. When you are waiting in a reception area with competing salespeople, it is sometimes a good idea to psyche them out by making a call on your cell phone to the office (no one has to be receiving the call) and say something like, "Hi. I'm stuck here waiting for the buyer. Would you please make sure to book all those orders I got yesterday and call me back when you're through, because I might have to tell the buyer we have so much business we can't fit in any more." Boost your confidence and lower the confidence of your competitors.

Bring-in-the-boss

In the middle of a negotiation, sometimes buyers call in their boss and say, "We're getting nowhere; I'm calling in my media director who will make sure you know that you will lose the business if you don't accede to our demands." This is an authority trap; do not fall for it. Do not lower you confidence or expectations. This is a good guy/bad guy tactic designed to intimidate you. Focus on your HLE and keep in mind that the buyer is admitting a desire for the deal by calling in the boss to help.

> Rule: Check you ego at the door and don't let your fear or emotions get the better of you; patience wins.

It will help you maintain your confidence and keep your expectations high if you realize that the other side's maneuvering for dominance and trying to appear to have a power advantage is nothing more than a thinly disguised bluff. After all, who has the power in today's media-dominated world, advertising agencies and their clients or the media? The media are the most powerful communication force in the world. Without advertising carried by the mass media, companies trying to sell their products and services to mass audiences would have to sell them one-on-one to individual consumers. Without advertising, there would be no mass distribution and no mass consumption of products. Modern marketing warfare is conducted by the forces of advertising on the battlefield of the media; this central position gives the media enormous power. As mentioned previously, companies must advertise and agencies must invest their clients' money in advertising, and the media provide advertisers access to both mass and targeted audiences. Media salespeople provide this access, so advertising agencies and their clients are dependent on salespeople in order to gain access to consumers. Therefore, as a media salesperson, never forget who has the power – you. Use this knowledge to boost your confidence in the face of threats and bluffs.

Experienced negotiators will also try to control the negotiating agenda. They will often come to the negotiating table with a printed agenda and demand that you stick to it. The reason for this is simple, and is expressed by the following rule:

Rule: Whoever controls the negotiating agenda controls the outcome.

The concept is straightforward. If you can control the items you will negotiate about, you can control the shape of subsequent agreements. For example, a media-buyer's one-sided agenda might be as follows:

1   Discussion of price
2   Discussion of discounts
3   Discussion of added value
4   Discussion of positions
5   Discussion of terms and conditions

This agenda will not lead to a discussion, but to a series of demands, beginning with demands on reduced or discounted prices. Once a buyer gets a discounted price, demands for add-ons at no cost will follow. When faced with such a lopsided agenda, do not begin negotiating. Instead, discuss the agenda and do not start negotiating until you have reached consensus on a fair, balanced agenda. It is best to hammer out an agreement on an agenda several days before a major negotiation begins.

Or, you can anticipate an agenda similar to the above, especially if you have previously negotiated with someone. You can anticipate that price will be the first item on their agenda. The first question will be, "What does it cost?" You can reply by saying, "In my price, I factored in the schedule of advertising you requested, our standard terms and conditions, the premium position you asked for, and the added value you requested, so the total, packaged price is $125,000." If the buyer asks for individual cost breakdowns for the premium position and the added value elements, make sure that you have priced them so that they add up individually to more than $125,000, otherwise the buyer will try to negotiate on each item in the hope of lowering the overall price. By packaging in this way, you take away much of a buyer's negotiating power.

Therefore, as opposed to the buyer's agenda above, an agenda that would be favorable to you would be as follows:

Agenda

1 Discussion of terms and conditions
2 Discussion of position
3 Discussion of added value
4 Discussion of price

This agenda is better because the final element, price, will depend on agreements on the preceding items. For instance, if a buyer wants a favorable position or a great deal of added value, then the price should go up. Price is not a single element, but is inextricably linked to the other parts of a deal – the more extras, the higher the price. Just like when you buy a car, the final price you pay depends on many factors such as terms (loan), conditions (insurance), and extras (trim, radio, and so forth).

> Rule: In order to avoid negotiating on each element individually, package all the elements in a deal so that the prices of the individual elements always add up to more than the packaged price.

Following are several more rules that apply to the pre-bargaining maneuvering for dominance and control phase of negotiating. They are divided into When Rules, Who Rules, Where Rules, and How Rules.

When Rule

> Rule: Negotiate only after you've created value, early in customer's planning cycle, and well before your imposed deadline.

Who Rules

> Rule: Negotiate at the highest level possible – only with the buying decision maker.

The bigger the deal, the higher in the organization you should go, because as deals get bigger the decision making authority level increases and you always want to negotiate with the final decision maker if at all possible – with the boss. The converse of this rule applies to you.

> Rule: Don't negotiate with your boss present if you can avoid it.

If your boss is present when you negotiate, the buyer will not talk to you, but to your boss, and you not only lose control of the discussion, but you will also lose control of the account, because the buyer will want to continue to deal with the boss. Furthermore, when bosses (a sales manager, an ad director, a general manager, or a publisher) are present at a negotiation with a salesperson, too often they do not want to look bad or lose the business and will make a bad deal. Some of the worst deals in the media are made by bosses who want to show off to salespeople that they can close and to clients to demonstrate that they have the authority to change terms and lower prices – it is a power trip.

On the other hand, there are times when it is desirable to have a boss present in a negotiation. For example, often on a big deal, the other side will want to negotiate at high levels in an organization. Sometimes, you might want to use the boss as the bad guy so you can play the good guy in a negotiation. Often, the boss can impress the buyer and put the buyer in an authority trap.

However, whenever the boss is involved in a negotiation, it is critical to come to an agreement beforehand as to the exact role the boss will play. When you negotiate with an account that is assigned to you, you should take the lead in recommending a negotiating strategy. For example, if a boss wants to accompany you on a call on a buyer and you understand the buyer well enough to know such a call is not appropriate, you might say, "I don't think it's a good idea for you to come on this call. The buyer is very defensive and is intimidated by managers; she thinks they put too much pressure on her. We have a great relationship and she might think you don't trust me. I'll take you on a call next week on a buyer with whom you can be a great help."

An effective use of bosses is to ask them to make a call with you on a buyer or customer to create value and not to discuss price. Managers can talk effectively about a company's philosophy, upcoming promotions, or new content – things that enhance your company's image and create value. When the buyer asks about price, your boss should say, "I'm not the person to talk about price. I think our product is so terrific that I'll ask too much. You deal with Jane. She will look after your best interests and get you the best deal we can offer. Also, she knows your needs better than I do." This is an ideal one–two approach that uses a boss effectively and keeps the negotiation under the control of the salesperson.

Where Rule

Rule: Negotiate on your own turf if possible.

As professional football, basketball, and baseball teams know, it is always better to have a home-field advantage. If you negotiate in your offices, you control the environment and the room set-up, you can be sure that you have the right equipment, and you have access to your management, to experts, and to information that can help you. Also, there is a subtle advantage to negotiating on your turf – it is your meeting and your chances of controlling the agenda are better. This rule particularly applies if you have nice turf, if your offices are attractive and reek of glamour (people love the glamour of the media), power, and authority. If you have shabby, unglamorous offices, go to customers' offices.

If customers prefer to negotiate on their turf, which is usually the case with media buyers, do not hesitate to go to their offices. If you go to a buyer's office, take advantage of the opportunity to read the room and learn as much as you can about the buyer's personality, needs, tastes, and preferences. Sometimes you can move the venue from a buyer's or customer's office to neutral turf. Suggest a meeting at a restaurant over a meal; dinner is best because negotiations can usually be stretched out, which reduces the pressure for a fast settlement.

How Rules

Rule: Negotiate face to face whenever possible.

A lot of media business is conducted on the phone or by e-mail. But when you negotiate like this, you are at a disadvantage. You cannot see the body language or non-verbal behavior of the prospect, thus substantial communication goes unnoticed and is lost. It is easier to be tough, mean, and competitive on the phone or in e-mails than face to face where a buyer has to look you in the eye and deal in person with your potential retaliation (tit-for-tat). Also, it is more difficult to establish rapport and empathy and build a solid relationship with a buyer on the phone or in e-mails than it is in person. Negotiating face to face gives you an advantage over competitors who do business on the phone or by e-mail.

If you have to deal with a distant buyer on the phone, always be the caller so that you are prepared. And if a buyer calls and wants avails or to place a buy, tell the buyer that you will call back. Do not sell or negotiate on an initial call or inquiry. Return the call as promptly as possible, but not before you are thoroughly prepared.

Rule: If you have to negotiate on the phone, you be the caller.

4   Bargaining

Bargaining is the hand-to-hand combat of the negotiating process; it is where the final agreement or settlement is determined. There are five steps in the bargaining process:

4.1   Warm-up
4.2   Open and frames
4.3   Signaling leverage
4.4   Making concessions
4.5   Building agreement

4.1 Warm-up

The warm-up is the opening skirmish in which you test your assumptions about the other side's style, strategy, and tactics. During the warm-up, you listen and observe carefully and do not give away any information that could be useful to the other side.

> Rule: Listen and get information 66 percent of the time, give information only 33 percent of the time.

While you are listening, look for gestures, body, language, and grooming that indicate low self-esteem and lack of confidence. Look and listen for clues as to whether the other side is competitive or cooperative. During the warm-up conversation, start with a positive, complimentary approach. Compliment the other side, its organization, and its advertising, but do not go overboard and be wildly enthusiastic. For example, after listening to opening remarks, you might say, "Because you are a reputable company, we look forward to doing business with you. We would like to have your advertising on our Web site because it makes us look better, and I always enjoy negotiating with you because I learn so much." Do not go overboard, but be positive and complimentary to set the tone for cooperation and an amicable bargaining process.

This approach works particularly well with cooperative negotiators because it signals a desire to be cooperative and to improve the relationship. Use this approach even with highly competitive people because it will put them off guard and make them over-confident. They will learn how tough you are when they make their first bombastic, outrageous, threatening demand and you use tit-for-tat and counterattack with equal force. When competitors discover that their initial assumptions about you were incorrect, they often become confused and make mistakes. When bullies are challenged, they often give in easily.

Also, before you begin bargaining and during the warm-up, you should have a discussion to verify what you are negotiating about, to get all of the issues on the table. It is important that you observe the following rule:

> Rule: Get the other side to state what they want at the beginning, and you tell them what your issues are – get most relevant issues on the table.

When the other side tells you what it wants, repeat the requests (or demands) and get agreement. For example, "You would like to run a 52-week schedule of ads in my newspaper at the bulk rate of 30,000 inches and would like top left position on page two and top right position on page three. Is that correct?" If you get agreement, then you tell them what your issues are. For example, "We'd like your business very much, but those positions you ask for will be difficult to deliver. So, let us see if we can work something out." In Chapter 9 I recommended that it was important to "put important terms and conditions that are different from standard media contract terms that advertisers are used to in your presentation and sell them aggressively because you want prospects to know what your terms and conditions are before you get into negotiations." By selling in deal terms and conditions in your presentation, you can set up this discussion about issues at the beginning of the negotiation.

In larger, more complex deals there might be some terms and conditions that are so vital to you that they are deal breakers – if you do not get them you will walk away from the deal. In these situations, it is important to tell the other side what issues are important to you. When you do so, it is best to include, in addition to the important terms, several throw-away terms you can use as concessions later in the negotiation. If you have crucial deal terms that are potential deal breakers, raise the price of your initial offer and then give concessions on those prices – lower them to your HLE – in order to secure those vital deal terms. If you do not have throw-away deal terms and corresponding price concessions, you will appear to be inflexible and the deal terms will be seen as unreasonable demands, which could stall and even sink a negotiation.

The other reason for this rule is that you will negotiate based on the other's side's initial requests. If the other side puts additional requests or demands on the table later in the process, it is unfair to you because you have been negotiating in good faith based on the assumption that all of the issues were on the table. You have been hoodwinked if the other side asks for more later on. If this should happen, your response should be, "Oh, I'm sorry. I didn't know you wanted a full-page bonus ad every month. You didn't tell me up front. I was basing my negotiating based on what you originally put on the table. Now we'll have to start all over again based on this new request."

Before you make an opening offer it is vital to get all the issues on the table so you know the size of the pie you are trying to divide up.

4.2   Open and frames

We will return now to the 10 steps in preparing for a negotiation. Step seven was to determine when and how to open. When you plan your opening strategy, there are two initial questions you have to ask yourself, "Should I open first?" and "Should I open optimistically or realistically?"

Open first?   Yes. In almost every situation in media selling, you should know what the other side's offer will be. In the identifying problems and qualifying step of selling, you have discovered customers' advertising budgets and have some sense of what they will pay and what terms they want. In the case of selling to agencies, buyers typically send an RFP or call for avails that lists the parameters of a buy: price, ratings, demos, dayparts, and so forth.

The only occasions in which you should let the other side open are: (1) Those in which you are not familiar with the style or demands of the other side or when you do not know them at all, and (2) when the other side are novices and are unfamiliar with media prices.

> Rule: Open first to set an anchor except when you don't know anything about the other side.

When you open, open with an effective anchor. An example of an effective anchor was in 1996 when NBC Television carried the Super Bowl. Traditionally, television networks announce their prices, their anchor, for the upcoming Super Bowl in July. For three prior years each network that carried the Super Bowl had raised the anchor price it announced in July approximately $100,000. In 1995, the price for a 30-seond commercial had been $850,000, so the expectation was that NBC would announce $950,000. However, NBC, in a good tactical move, announced that its price for Super Bowl commercials would be $1 million, *but* the price for the last three sold would be $1.3 million. Agency buyers rushed to buy Super Bowl spots for $1 million and NBC announced the first week in December that it had sold all of the available spots in the Super Bowl.

The following year, in 1996, the first year that Fox Television carried the Super Bowl, it announced in July that its price for the upcoming Super Bowl would be $1 million. Fox did not raise the price from the previous year because it did not have as extensive market coverage as NBC had. Fox also did not announce that it would raise the price for the last few commercials it sold. The result was that agency buyers waited to place their orders in hopes that Fox would lower its prices. Fox did lower its prices, and wound up selling spots late in December for $750,000 or less. By not having an effective anchor, Fox left several million dollars on the table.[11]

Open optimistically or realistically? In general, open optimistically. In the majority of situations you should open optimistically with the highest price and terms for which there is a supporting standard or explanation that would allow you to make a plausible case for it. In other words, if you can reasonably justify a price and terms, such as basing it on high demand, ask for it. A good rule of thumb is to open at least 15 percent above your HLE price, which gives you room to give concessions and still have the potential for getting your HLE. Also, include at least three throw-away terms in your initial offer for the same reason.

In some situations, where you are not dealing with an experienced media buyer or regular customer, you can use the contrast principle and open for up to 50 percent higher and then come down to your HLE, which will seem low in contrast. This tactic works best when you are making a presentation that has three proposals, as covered in Chapter 10. For example, if the largest of your proposals is for $75,000, then the second proposal for $50,000 seems much lower than if you opened with the $50,000 proposal.

Opening optimistically brings us to two more fundamental rules of negotiating:

Rule: When in doubt, open optimistically and have room to come down.

Rule: You never get anything you don't ask for, so ask for more than you hope to get.

Optimistic openings work best in transaction negotiating and when you do not know much about the other side.

There are several situations when optimistic openings are not a good tactic and *realistic openings* are better, which leads to the following rule and three corollaries:

Rule: When you know the buyer well, open realistically.

Corollary: Also, open realistically when you have no leverage, when in a tacit coordination situation, and when people say they won't negotiate and mean it.

When you have no leverage, an optimistic opening does not work. When you have a weak position, an overly optimistic open leads buyers to conclusions that you are either bluffing or not too smart – both bad signals to give. When dealing in a tacit coordination situation, you should be realistically optimistic, or close to your highest legitimate expectation. When you are dealing with a person who says, "I won't negotiate, bring me your best price," and you know from experience that the person is telling you the truth, it is best to open realistically with a fair initial offer just above the mid-point in your settlement range.

Experienced media buyers and negotiators, who have read books and attended seminars on negotiating, know the fundamental rules and understand the power of high expectations. Therefore, experienced agency and client negotiators, especially when negotiating for broadcast and cable, will try to lower your expectations every chance they get. They will lower your expectations when they call for avails or send out RFPs. They will say, "I'm in a hurry and have to make the buy today, e-mail me your avails and give me your lowest rates. You have only one shot." In such cases, if you do as instructed, buyers will call back and say something like, "You're too high, lower your rates or you won't get the business." So they lied, in a sense, and are in fact giving you a second shot. Therefore, it is imperative to know your buyers, know what their negotiating tendencies are, and respond accordingly with you opening offers.

When you open, remember the following two rules:

Rule: Get the bad news out of the way early.

Rule: Don't include most of the other side's requests in your initial offer.

The first rule above comes from the advice of Richard Chase and Sriram Dasu in their *Harvard Business Review* article, "Want to perfect your company's service? Use behavioral science." The authors write: "Behavioral Science tells us that, in a sequence of events involving good and bad outcomes, people prefer to have undesirable events come first – so they can avoid the dread – and to have desirable events come at the end of a sequence – so they can savor them."[12] Recency effects indicate that people tend to remember the last events or experiences in a series of events, so it is effective practice to save the best, most favorable experiences until last. For example, if your company requires unusual or onerous terms and conditions, such as asking for cash up front, it is best to introduce these items at the beginning of the bargaining process and get them out of the way.

The second rule above, about not including most of the other side's requests or demands in your opening offer, is based on the notion that you want the other side to ask for them so you can bargain for each request. If you give the other side all they ask for initially, you lose the opportunity to get something in return during the subsequent bargaining and concession-making process, but include a few of their requests in your initial offer to signal some degree of cooperation. Make the other side ask for most of their demands and requests because in that way you control your give-backs and concessions.

After you determine when to open and the most effective way to open, fill out that section of the Negotiating and Closing Planner.

The eighth step in the planning process is to determine frames. When you open, *frame* your initial offer positively, as you learned in Chapter 5 ("Free throws win ball games"), and during the bargaining process continue to frame all of your offers positively. Emphasize the value of your offers and their benefits that give the other side a good deal. For example, "The $125,000 package is the best deal we are offering currently. It is a 25 percent discount on the individual elements in the package if purchased separately." Positive framing provides the other side with justifications for making concessions. If you have prepared properly and have a needs portrait of your buyer and a Benefit Matrix, you will know the best way to frame your offers. With competitive negotiators who want victory, frame your offers as gains and wins for them – really good deals. With negotiators who fear losing, frame your offers as a way to avoid a loss and emphasize the pain and shame of losing.

Rule: Always frame all of your offers appropriately.

When you have determined how you are going to frame your opening offer and important subsequent offers, fill out that section in the Negotiating and Closing Planner.

4.3 Signaling leverage

After you frame and present your initial offer and before you begin trading concessions in the bargaining process, you want to signal your leverage, if you have leverage. Exhibit 12.8 shows how you should act when your leverage is strong and when it is weak.

Exhibit 12.8   Signaling leverage

Your actual leverage situation (as you see it)

	Strong	*Weak*
Firm	Make confident demands and credible threats. Display your alternatives and leave the decision up to the other party.	Emphasize the uncertain future Bluff (act strong when you are not).
Flexible	Show the other party you are investing in the relationship. Be generous.	Acknowledge the other party's power and stress the potential gains from future cooperation. Appeal to the other party's sympathy. What would they do in your position?

How you want to act

Source: G. Richard Shell. 1999. *Bargaining for Advantage.* New York: Penguin Books, p. 149.

As you can see in Exhibit 12.8, when you see your leverage as strong and want to act firm, make confident demands, lay out your BATNAs, and leave the decision up to the other side. A particularly strong BATNA will communicate that you have buyers who will pay higher prices for smaller chunks of a package you are offering and want to buy soon in order to get first-mover advantage. If you want to be flexible, show the other side that you are willing to invest in the relationship and be reasonably generous and cooperative. If you see yourself as having a weak leverage position and want to be firm, emphasize the uncertain future – that someone else, even a competitor, could buy your offering and the rates might go up. In this situation, making an early, small concession might be advisable to show your willingness to do a deal. If you want to be flexible when you have a weak leverage position, acknowledge the other side's advantage and frame your offers positively. Appeal to the other side's sympathy and call in some relationship chits. Ask what they would do in your position, and, in effect, throw yourself on the mercy of the court, as lawyers say.

The best way to signal leverage is to show and maintain a high level of confidence. At no time in negotiating can you communicate a fear of losing or a need to close fast. You must be calm, patient, and, most of all, confident. As in a gunfight in the old Western movies, the following rule applies:

Rule: Confidence is everything; whoever blinks first, loses.

4.4   Making concessions

Step nine in the preparation process was to determine concessions and trade goals. After you open and anchor the other side's perception of your walk-away, after you frame your initial offers to appeal either to their desire for a win or to increase their fear of losing, and after you have signaled your leverage and firmness or flexibility, you are ready to make concessions, or, better, to make trades. The first three rules of making concessions in the bargaining process are as follows:

Rule: Never begin with a major concession.

Rule: Don't just concede, try to trade; if you give up something, always try to get something in return.

Rule: Give the first concession on an unimportant issue, and then get a concession from the other side.

These rules are important because they remind you to begin with a small concession; they also indicate that is acceptable to give the first concession in order to break the ice and get things started, but give a small, unimportant concession. The second rule also reminds you that when you give a concession, always try to get a reciprocal concession before you move on. Sometimes you have to ask for reciprocation by asking, "I gave up on my request for a 13-week commitment. Can you give me a little higher rate?"

The third rule is important to remember because it gives you a clue as to what is important to the other side. Your first concession will be on an unimportant issue, so you must assume the other side's first concession will be on an issue that is not important. Trading concessions at the beginning of the bargaining process is like bidding in the game of bridge; you are giving the other side signals as to what cards you hold and how strong your position is. Your goal in bargaining is not just to concede, but to trade – to get something in return. If you plan your concessions properly, you can trade small, unimportant concessions for ones that are more important to you. Remember that media buyers usually have to invest all of their client's money, so even though they ask for a lower price initially, it is often not their most important issue.

As you proceed in the process of trading concessions, follow these rules:

Rule: Make small concessions and give them slowly.

Rule: Make the other side work hard for everything; they will appreciate it more.

These rules are based on the principle, "What we obtain too cheaply, we esteem lightly."[13] For example, if you open with a price of $100 in the demographic a buyer requested and the buyer says, "That's a little high, but can you give me some added value?" you know price is not the most important issue. The buyer virtually conceded on price and you know added value is more valuable. In this situation, switch from discussing price to making concessions for added value, starting small and working up slowly to a Clincher Close, which I will discuss later in the chapter.

As you go through the exchanging of concessions, make sure to continually invoke the principle of reciprocity. For example, "OK, I gave you the promotion you wanted, will give me the price I originally asked for?" Use the reciprocity principle as often as you can. If you feel what you are getting in return for a concession is not fair, say so. As in, "I gave you a valuable promotion and you are not going to give me the price I asked for. That's not fair!" A little outrage in the right places can be quite effective.

As you proceed with bargaining and trading concessions, use an effective concession pattern, which you have planned in advance. Exhibit 12.9 shows six concession patterns.

Look at Exhibit 12.9 and let us assume you have planned to give a 15 percent discount in four steps and have some throw-away terms you are willing to concede. But, just considering price, the first pattern is ineffective because all the concessions are of equal value, so buyers expect the pattern to continue because you have given no signal that you are close to your walk-away. The second pattern is equally ineffective because you say no, then give a big concession, so your buyers expect this pattern to continue and will not believe your no after the last 50 percent concession. The third pattern is awful because you say no several times, and then give a huge concession, so buyers will extend the negotiating interminably because they expect another large concession. The next pattern is also disastrous because you give a huge first concession and then stonewall, so buyers will extend the negotiation and insist on more concessions equally as large. The fifth pattern is bad, too, because with each larger concession you raise buyers' expectations, which extends negotiating. The most effective concession pattern is the final one.

Because you are willing to give a total of 15 percent, your concessions would be (1) 3.75 percent (25 percent × 15 percent), (2) 6 percent (40 percent × 15 percent), (3) 4.5 percent (30 percent × 15 percent), and (4) 0.75 percent (5 percent × 15

Exhibit 12.9   Concession tactics

Which tactic is most effective?

1	25%	25%	25%	25%
2	0%	50%	0%	50%
3	0%	0%	0%	100%
4	100%	0%	0%	0%
5	10%	20%	30%	40%
6	25%	40%	30%	5%

percent). All of these concessions are small and you are giving them slowly in four steps. You are beginning with a concession that is 25 percent of your planned total concession, then you move to 40 percent, but from there your concessions get smaller – 30 percent and finally only 5 percent, which signals that you have reached your limit. When you give this final concession, you should say something such as, "Well, I can lower my price by $3, but you will have to give me another week on the schedule" (assuming a price of $40). If the buyer cannot give you another week, keep probing until you get something – a larger share of their budget, for example.

As you go through the bargaining process of trading concessions, get small, easy issues out of the way first. If you run into a big issue, set it aside by saying you will come back to it later and move on to settle smaller issues. This tactic uses the commitment principle. As the other side invests increasingly significant amounts of time, energy, and other resources in the negotiating process, they become more and more committed to closing the deal for fear of losing it and wasting their time and energy. As an example, "OK, we've agreed on a promotion and on last position in the commercial pod, but we're still a little bit apart on price. Let us put the price issue aside for now and see if we can't reach agreement on how long your promotion will run."

Finally, as you progress through bargaining, keep your eye out for what tactics the other side is using. Be aware of all of the tactics in Exhibit 12.7. As Sun Tzu writes, "Do not swallow bait offered by the enemy."[14] Of course your customers are not your enemy, but they will often use tactics, or bait, to try to get an advantage. When you recognize a tactic, name it, do not fall for it, keep your confidence up, and move on.

When you determine the most effective concession pattern for an upcoming negotiation and determined your trade goals, fill out that section in the Negotiating and Closing Planner.

> Rule: Develop an effective concession pattern that signals when you get close to your walk-away.

4.5 Building agreement

Finally, as you go through the process of bargaining, follow the next rule:

> Rule: Summarize agreements and restate the other side's position on a regular basis.

Frequently restate the other side's positions during bargaining because, "If they understand you're hearing what they're saying, it reduces stress levels," according to Victoria Ruttenberg, a successful Washington, DC lawyer and mediator.[15] You are trying to build agreement brick by small brick; you are trying to get the other side to invest time and effort on a series of small agreements so their commitment to the process increases. Perhaps you have put off major issues earlier in the bargaining process; come back to them after you have reached a number of smaller agreements. You will find that large issues are easier to settle after smaller agreements have been reached – the other side's commitment is at its height. During this final stage of the bargaining process, do not get impatient:

> Rule: Be patient – with patience and hard work in exploring alternatives, you can make the deal better for both sides.

When you finally deal with the major issue, have patience and explore alternatives – be creative in finding solutions. As soon as you have reached agreement on the major issue, transition smoothly and calmly into your close. Stay cool.

5   Closing and Gaining Commitment

The tenth step in the planning process is to plan your closes. When you plan, keep in mind the first rule of closing:

> Rule: Expect to close.

You have planned well, you have bargained intelligently, and your confidence should now be at its peak. You must act as though you deserve the order, as though there is no doubt in your mind that you have the best offer, so ask for a decision. Close.

The closing phase can be smooth or a time of high anxiety. It is important to remain cool and confident during the closing phase and not show any worry or anxiety, regardless of the circumstances. Often experienced negotiators save their most powerful tactics for the closing phase. You may think you have reached agreement on all of issues under discussion and have asked for the order, but buyers will introduce tactics they have not used before – a crunch or a nibble (see Exhibit 12.7). It is common in the closing phase for both sides to use the scarcity principle.

Sellers will use the limited-number approach, the act-now-before-a-competitor-buys-it approach, or the get-in-before-the-deadline approach. Buyers will use the your-competitors-want-a-big-share-and-are-going-much-lower approach and attempt once more to lower your price. This threat may be a bluff or it may be true. According to Richard Shell in *Bargaining for Advantage*, scarcity is an emotional issue; both sides use it to attempt to create the fear of losing in the other side. One side can increase the other side's fear by warning that others are competing for a scarce resource (the seller's offering or the buyer's money). It is always a matter of judgment whether to hold firm or yield to an attempt to push your panic button. Your judgment will be informed by your understanding of the leverage situation at the moment when you must decide.[16] If you know your buyer's tendencies, you will know if they tend to bluff or not and, therefore, whether to hold firm or yield. However, in no circumstances should you go below your walk-away.

If a buyer's apparent final offer is below your walk-away, then always walk away, but do so nicely and not in anger. Say, "I'm sorry I can't go any lower. I'll take your offer back to my management, but I'm not sanguine about their agreeing," which leads to the next rule:

Rule: When you walk away, always leave the door open.

When such a walk-away occurs, you and your management can decide, outside the heat of battle, whether to go back with another offer. But make sure you wait at least a day – the buyer may call or e-mail you and meet your terms during that day.

In many situations the close will go smoothly, especially if you have used *trial closes* throughout the bargaining phase.

5.1 Types of closes

There are five types of closes:

5.1.1   Trial closes
5.1.2   Choice closes
5.1.3   Clincher closes
5.1.4   Last-resort-closes
5.1.5   Bad, never-use closes

5.1.1   Trial closes   There is on old saying in selling, "ABC, always be closing." The phrase comes from the old-fashioned, hard-sell school of selling, but as in many rules of thumb, there is a kernel of wisdom in the phrase. In modern selling and negotiating techniques, the always-be-closing concept translates into "use trial closes throughout your presentation and negotiating." Trial closes are an indirect method of testing buyers' temperature. Are buyers cold and need more information, or are they warm and ready to buy? The only way to know for certain is to ask. The worst that can happen is that you discover that they are not ready and they raise another objection. Actually, the main purpose of a trial close is to bring objections to the surface so you can deal with them. If there are no more objections, then you have a deal. Following are several trial closes you can use throughout your presentations and negotiations to test the water.

The Direct Close. Simply ask for the green light. Always avoid using the words *buy* or *order*. Do not ask, "Will you buy this?" Do not say, "How about it? Could I have the order?" Those words may frighten buyers. "I'll book this right away so you can get on the Web site by Monday, OK?" or "We'll agree on this price, then. Isn't that fair enough?" are better direct closes.

The phrase "Isn't that fair enough?" is one of the strongest closing phrases you can use. Nobody wants to be accused of implying that someone else is unfair and so people will go to great lengths to answer this question positively. Also, never ask a closing question that can be answered with an unambiguous no. The phrase, "I'll book this right away so you can get on the air by Monday, OK?" was used previously. If the buyer says no, then this is an ambiguous no and you make the assumption that they do not want to start on Monday, but do not make the assumption that they do not want to give you the order.

For example, suppose a buyer asks, "Could I run Wednesday through Saturday?" Do not respond with, "If I can schedule it this way, will you give me the order?" because you have, in essence, created an objection when before only a question about how to run the order existed. Instead, say, "Absolutely," thank them for the business, shake hands, and leave. If you cannot run the schedule as requested, say "I'm sorry we can't," explain why and use another close.

The Assumption Close. This close is particularly powerful because it is so painless for both a buyer and a salesperson. When you sense that the time has come, that a buyer has shifted gears from desire to conviction, you simply assume that the buyer has made the decision to buy and proceed accordingly. Talk and act as though the buyer has given you the green light. If you are correct in your assumption, the buyer will not stop you, in which case you have the order. If the buyer says, "Hold on. I haven't bought anything yet," then proceed with some probes to find out why the buyer is not ready.

The Summary Close. This close is an excellent trial close and should be used often. On a regular basis, summarize all the benefits to which a buyer has agreed. Emphasize those benefits in which a buyer has shown the most interest. Present an overwhelming weight of accepted evidence of superiority in your summary. Follow your summary with a statement such as "Can we go ahead with this plan?" You can also use the Silent Close that follows.

The Silent Close. Ask for the order with a direct close, with a Summary Close, or with any appropriate close and then shut up. There is an old rule used by many salespeople that says after a strong close "the first one who speaks, loses." You do not have to fill a void with words. Give buyers time to think. Let them become uncomfortable and start talking; if you do not speak, they surely will. When they finally say something, you will either get the green light or an objection, which gives you another opportunity to present a benefit that solves a problem. If you speak first, you let buyers off the hook.

The Pin-Down Close. This closing technique should be used judiciously. After prospects have expressed an objection, pin them down by asking if you can have the go-ahead if you can overcome their objection. For example, if a prospect says, "I don't like those early news spots," your response would be, "If I can get my manager to agree to move them to the late news, may I book the schedule?" You have used a Pin-Down Close. Be careful, though; avoid using this close too often or too early because a prospect might understand what you are doing and use the same tactic against you to get a string of concessions. If a prospect tries to extract another concession from you after a Pin-Down Close, a good tactic is to say, "Hey, let's be fair. You said we could go ahead if I moved those spots."

A good time to use the Pin-Down Close is when prospects try to put off a decision. When prospects say they want to think it over or that they will call or e-mail you later, quickly isolate their reasons for the stall and use a Pin-Down Close. The *let-me-think-about-it* excuse is the most common one you will encounter, and you must learn to overcome it quickly or you will lose sales. When you get this excuse, pin down the reasons for the excuse, narrow the objection, and then try a Pin-Down Close or a Clincher Close (which you will learn about a little later in this chapter).

Another time when Pin-Down Closes work well is when buyers try to nibble you (see Exhibit 12.7). A Pin-Down Close stops a nibble by saying, "OK, if I can get half of your spots moved to the late news, do we have a deal with no further changes?" After a nibble, do not give the other side their full demand, cut it in half, then if you want to, you can go all the way on their demand if half does not work.

The T-account Close. Use a lined tablet or any sheet of standard-sized paper and draw a line down the middle of the paper and then cross the T across the paper near the top. Next, in the left top section, write down a buyer's objections and in the section underneath write a list of all the reasons supporting the buyer's objections. Next, write in the right top section your off-setting benefits. Your list should be longer than a buyer's; if it is not, do not use this technique.

For example, if a buyer wants to put off making a final commitment until next month, put "Start Next Month" on top of one column and "Start Now" on top of the other column. With a prospect's help, write all of the objection in the left column and then write all of the reasons to start now in the right column. This technique is dramatic and graphic; it is particularly effective with precise, fact-oriented people. It also gives buyers the perception that you are being objective and fair ("Isn't that a fair list?").

Rule: Use trial closes throughout the negotiating process.

5.1.2 Choice closes Choice closes are especially powerful because they build commitment through choice. Chase and Dasu report on an interesting study that found that blood donors perceived significantly less discomfort when they were allowed to select the arm from which their blood would be drawn. The authors write that the lesson from this study is clear: people are happier and more comfortable when they believe they have some control over a process, particularly an uncomfortable one such as giving a salesperson an order. In some cases, the control given over is largely symbolic (as in the choice of arm), or it can be a meaningful, high-stakes decision. The medical profession has long recognized the value of allowing patients to make an informed choice about alternative treatments for cancer and heart disease. Doctors realize there is enormous value in involving the patient in these important decisions. Patients feel less helpless, less hopeless, and, most important, more committed to making the process work.[17] For this reason, increase commitment through choice by offering not just one proposal but possibly as many as three and let the other side choose.

The Choice Close. The Choice Close is one of the easiest closes to use. It is probably used more than any other close, and should be. You have already set up this close by providing three or more proposals in your proposal or presentation. Then, you simply ask prospects which of these options they prefer. When you have the answer, you have the order. "Do you prefer the first, second, or third package I offered, Mr Franklin?" "The third." "Great, an excellent choice! Thank you. I'll run right back to the office and get this scheduled and e-mail you the confirmation." The buyer might never say yes or "I'll buy it," but the buyer has given assent by making a choice.

When buyers are given a choice, they can make a decision without feeling forced into a corner. Buyers have the reassurance and confidence of asserting their free will and of expressing themselves. Furthermore, after they make the choice, you have the opportunity to reinforce their final decision. Always compliment prospects on their wise judgment.

The Minor-Point Close. This is another popular, effective, and easy close. With the minor-point close, you attempt to get buyers to chose and approve one or more minor details in an offer; if they agree, you have made a sale. The more minor points on which you can get agreement, the better. "We'll start the schedule next Tuesday so we have time to get the creative in, OK?" or "Instead of billing this to you the first week of the month, we'll send the bill to you a week early so you can be reimbursed more quickly from your client, OK?" When buyers agree to a minor point, they are saying yes the easy way. For example, a buyer who might hesitate if you ask whether you can go head with the $200,000 order for sponsoring baseball broadcasts will probably find it a snap to agree to provide you with artwork for a sponsorship ad in the stadium program booklet.

5.1.3 Clincher closes A Clincher Close is a well-planned close in which you make a final concession on a major request, on an important issue, or on substantial added value – you hold it back until the end and offer it to clinch the deal. From the beginning, you have your concession or improved offer in your back pocket but bring it out at the end only if you need it to close the deal. For example, you might be negotiating for a major 52-week buy on your Web site. The agency, on behalf of its client, has requested a low rate in return for giving you a firm 52-week commitment, wants four event promotions (one each quarter), as well as merchandising support for the client's sales force (prizes such as golf clubs and golf balls for sales contest winners). As you have progressed through the negotiation, you have agreed to the merchandising but are 10 percent apart on rate. The agency's final offer has been $225 cost-per-thousand and they are not budging. You are holding out for $250, the mid-point in the initial ballpark. However, you have not offered the four event promotions even though the other side has continually asked for them, even though you have been prepared to give the promotions. The Clincher Close would be to say, "OK, we seem to be stalled. What if I give you the four event promotions, which will cost us a great deal, and you give me my rate of $250? That seems like a win–win, fair agreement, doesn't it?"

Using Clincher Closes requires detailed planning before the negotiation and great discipline during the process – you lose the power of a Clincher Close if you introduce it too early in the process. Also, use Clincher Closes the first time you negotiate with someone, but not the second time. If you consistently use Clincher Closes with people with whom you regularly negotiate, they will expect them, always hold out for a major concession at the end, and when they receive the concession, they will not appreciate it but instead feel it is their due. With people with whom you regularly negotiate, use Clincher Closes only on an occasional, random basis – use a mixed strategy.

5.1.4 Last-resort closes When the above closing maneuvers do not work, try some of the following closes:

The "Make-Me-An-Offer" Close. Real estate and automobile salespeople fully understand the power of this closing technique – it gets prospects to express verbally their commitment to buy. When buyers make you an offer, they are not only committing to buy but they are also giving you the parameters of the final barriers to a sale. This is one of the last techniques you should employ because it typically results in a concession. Even though it is somewhat tricky to do, the best way to handle this close is to get buyers to make you an offer on terms other than price alone, instead, such as on added value. You might say: "I know that you want to be with us and that what I am offering is right for you. Make me an offer that contains an adjustment on something other than price and I'll see what I can do."

The "What-Will-It-Take?" Close. This is a more desperate version of the "Make-me-an-offer" close. With this close you are vulnerable to lowballing, but often, as a last resort, you will see if the other side goes below your walk-away and how much lower, which is information you can use in your next negotiation, after you walk away. Sometimes you might use this close on a small piece of business when the offer is low and you can walk away to give the other side a clear signal that you will walk away from low offers; it makes your anchor in subsequent negotiations credible.

The "What-Did-I-Do-Wrong?" Close. Finally, when you have failed to reach an agreement, pack your briefcase, say "Thank you for your time," and get up and head for the door. Just as you are going through the door, turn to the buyer and say, "Do you mind if I ask you one more question? I respect you and your opinion and feel I could learn something from this experience. Would you mind telling me what I did wrong? Where did I lose the sale?" The chances are good that your prospect will tell you; then, of course, you are in a position to start over (at that instant or on another call, whichever is appropriate).

5.1.5 Bad, never-use closes   Following are some closes not to use because they will ruin relationships.

The Poor-Me Close. Salespeople have been known to beg for orders by saying that they will lose their job if they do not get an order or that they must have the money to pay for their child's organ transplant. Do not try to heap guilt on buyers and do not beg to get an order; do not lower yourself or diminish your own dignity. Confidence and self-esteem are vitally important in the selling and negotiating process; do nothing to lessen yourself in the eyes of prospects. Customers admire strength. Begging also puts you in an awful negotiating position.

The Now-You-Have-It-Now-You-Don't Close. Some unscrupulous salespeople will promise anything just to get an order, knowing full well that they cannot deliver what has been sold. Their strategy is to take an order and then go back to buyers later and say they cannot deliver. They then try to switch buyers into other, lower-rated time slots (in broadcasting and cable), in less desirable positions (in print), or into paying higher rates. This maneuver has a narcotic temptation because it can shut out competitors; however, buyers are not dumb enough to let this work more than once. Nothing destroys your credibility faster than this bait-and-switch technique.

The For-You-Only Close. Some weak salespeople try only one close and then immediately rely on giving big concessions to make a sale. They promise prospects, "If you give me an order right now, I'll give you the lowest price possible, lower than anyone else." Salespeople who use this approach sound as though they just came in from an alley where they were peddling pornographic postcards, and buyers tend to show them about that much respect.

Whichever appropriate close you decide to use, do not close too aggressively, especially on bigger deals. You can create a sense of urgency with deadlines and limited-supply maneuvers, but the timetable has to be the other side's. Too much pressure can kill a prospective deal. Pressure on your part to close will make the other side suspicious – you will appear too eager for a deal and cause the other side to push for more concessions. As indicated earlier in this chapter, people want to buy, to make a choice. People do not like to be sold or pressured; they are much more comfortable in choosing and controlling the timing of their buying decision.

Also, pressure to close often strains a relationship, so you must be particularly careful about pressuring people with whom you regularly negotiate.

Rule: Don't close too aggressively; always keep the relationship in mind.

Sales managers, sales trainers, and many sales textbooks often overemphasize closing. You should close only when you are convinced that your customers are committed to your proposed solution and negotiated agreement and that you are convinced it is a fair deal that is right for the other side. Never push people into buying. Remember, you are managing a relationship for the long haul, and it would be counterproductive to close too aggressively and jeopardize a relationship. However, people have a natural tendency to avoid saying yes, from fear either of losing or of not getting a good deal, so you must maintain your confidence that your deal is the right one for them and not signal anything that would give them pause or give them an excuse to hesitate.

Rule: When closing, confidence is vital – you cannot signal in any way your fear of losing or your need to close fast.

Confidence is vital throughout the negotiating process, but even more so in the closing phase. Following are several things to keep in mind that will enhance your confidence.

5.2   Give the other side a "good deal"

People have their own unique definition of a good deal – it is an individualized perception. Your task before or during a negotiation is to discover your customers' personal definition of a good deal and then see that they get it.

Exhibit 12.10 shows a list of some customers' definitions of a good deal and how to respond:

Note in Exhibit 12.10 that all of the tactics involve complimenting people on their ability to get a good deal and to reinforce their perception of a good deal. When you negotiate, you have the power to give people a good deal, only if you know what their definition of a good deal is; plan your tactics in advance to make sure you give them a good deal as they define it.

Rule: Have confidence that you can give the other side a "good deal" – their definition of a good deal.

Finally, it will give you confidence and power in a negotiation if you have no fear of walking away. Good BATNAs vastly increase your confidence to walk away. Signal your confidence in how you act, walk, sit, and talk. Confidence does not

Exhibit 12.10 Types of good deals

Definition	Description	Tactic
Got a low price.	The perception of a low price is always relative. Remember the salesperson's father's advice, "never pay retail?" Some people will go to enormous lengths in time and effort to get what they perceive to be a lower price. Often such bargain hunters are called bottom fishers. They will take risks on quality and preemptability (not running an ad and replacing it with another, higher-priced one).	Offer bottom fishers low-priced packages of less-desirable, remnant, or preemptable inventory. Identify and keep a list of bargain hunters and call them when you have last-minute, reduced-price inventory. These are people who often know the price of everything and the value of nothing and, thus, will buy hard-to-move inventory. Make sure you emphasize the bargain, low-priced nature of your offering. When you get the order, compliment them on getting such a good bargain.
Got something someone else wanted.	The scarcity principle at work. Competition for scarce resources often gets people over-committed and makes inventory more desirable. Price, discounts, quality are not important, all that counts is that someone else wants it – especially if a hated competitor wants it. Fear of loss and envy are involved.	During negotiations, make sure people who have a tendency to be envious are aware of your BATNAs and know that their competitors are interested or have made an offer. Be honest, but on the other hand, do not fail to communicate such information. When you make the sale, compliment them for snatching it away from their competitors.
Got high quality at a reasonable price.	Many buyers are concerned with quality and service, and do not mind paying for it. For example, many people pay much more for a Mercedes or a Lexus than for a Ford or Chevrolet because of their perception of quality.	Create value from the beginning for these people and continually mention the word quality. When you reach agreement, compliment them for having the excellent judgment to recognize quality.
Got the last one.	The scarcity principle at work again. Fear of losing a scarce and valuable resource is involved.	The limited-supply maneuver works well here. Be honest when you let buyers know that there is only one left and create a sense of urgency due to the competition for it. Price is never the issue, so raise the price for the last one. When you close the deal, compliment them on their ability to make a fast decision.

Exhibit 12.10 Types of good deals (cont'd)

Definition	Description	Tactic
Got a warranty or guarantee: low risk of dissatisfaction	Some people with low self-confidence, who are risk-averse, and, especially, those who fear making a mistake, feel much more comfortable with guarantees or warranties. Ratings for upfront buys on network television and impressions on Interactive buys are typically guaranteed.	Emphasize the safe, low-risk nature of guarantees. Because guarantees are more important than price, buyers will generally pay more for guarantees. When you get agreement on a deal, compliment them on being such good, smart negotiators.
Got a discount.	To people who crave discounts, the actual price is not as important as the perception that they got a discount. Goods on sale appeal to these people; they will buy more than they need because they cannot resist a "50 percent discount."	Going in to a negotiation, raise the price on your initial offer by 20 percent, negotiate, and then as a Clincher Close, offer a 20 percent discount. When you make the sale, compliment them on being such a good negotiator and being able to get such a large discount.
Got something else free thrown in.	There are some people who love to get something for nothing, something free. They will pass up a "50 percent discount" offer, often feeling that is damaged or undesirable goods, and snap up an offer of "buy one and get one free." Same price, different frame.	With people who you have identified as those who like something else free thrown in, like with those who crave discounts, planning is the key. During negotiations, do not concede on price, even though you are willing to come down 15 percent but as a Clincher Close, say, "OK, if you'll give me my price, I'll give you 15 percent more inventory – a bonus of 15%." When you reach an agreement, compliment them for getting something free.
Got a win; feel like they won something important to them.	Many competitive buyers and negotiators care more about winning than anything else. In fact, they will not make a deal unless they feel like they have won.	Good planning will do the trick. Use a red herring, such as an event promotion that the other side insists on. Say no repeatedly, then as a Clincher Close, say, "OK you win, I'll give you the promotion if you'll give me the order now – before I change my mind." When you get the order, compliment them on winning. Make sure you tell them they have won.

Exhibit 12.10   Types of good deals (cont'd)

Definition	Description	Tactic
Got good results from advertising.	Many experienced advertisers view advertising as an investment, so it is not how much it costs that matters, but what their return on investment is. Interactive advertising is especially good at showing ROI.	With people who care most about results and ROI, it is vital that you control their expectations from the beginning and always under-promise and over-deliver. By lowering their expectations from the start, you can help ensure results. When you make the sale, compliment them for their sophisticated approach and deep understanding of the ultimate purpose of advertising, and reassure them that your primary objective as a salesperson is to get results for your customers.
Got a good deal compared to other media.	In today's media-saturated environment, buyers have a multitude of choices for placing advertising. If they select one over another or in combination with another medium, they typically want to feel that they got a good deal.	When you are in a selling or negotiating situation in which other media are being considered, stress the benefits of your medium – based not solely on price but on a wide variety of dimensions. A T-Account Close works well in these situations, where you compare the benefits of your medium to other media. When you reach agreement, compliment buyers on their insight and professionalism.

mean arrogance, bluster, or threats, but it reflects a firm resolve to make a deal that is fair to both sides.

You are now ready to complete the negotiating planning process by planning your closes. Select several of the above closes that are appropriate for your upcoming negotiating session and fill in the last section of the Negotiating and Closing Planner.

5.3   Get commitment

When you call on media buyers who are examining a number of competitive proposals, it is sometimes difficult to close a deal on a call or with an exchange of e-mails. If you find that one of the many closes above is not appropriate because the buyer has to evaluate more proposals, then it is important that you get some kind of commitment from the buyer (1) to recommend your proposal to a client or (2) to let you know where you stand so you can adjust your proposal if necessary. It is in these types of situations that having a strong personal relationship with a buyer is vitally important. If buyers know you and trust you, then they are more likely to give you some kind of verbal commitment. So, if you can't close, push for a verbal commitment of some kind.

On the other hand, when one of your closes is successful and you get an agreement, do not be satisfied with just an agreement – get a formal commitment. The objective of every negotiation is to secure commitment, not merely agreement. Commitment in closing a deal gives you a deal that sticks and that has incentives or penalties to ensure that both sides perform. Different kinds of negotiating situations call for different types of commitment. In some simple, familiar situations, both sides' word and a handshake is good enough, but in other, more complicated situations such as dealing with unfamiliar people or on large deals, legal contracts and other types of commitment are necessary.

According to Richard Shell in *Bargaining for Advantage*, there are four degrees of commitment:[18]

Social ritual. The commitment process begins with a simple social ritual such as a handshake, a bow, or an exchange of calling cards. In most buyer–seller relationships in the media both sides feel that their word is their bond, and that they would face loss of self-esteem and their reputation if they went back on their word or did not follow through on a commitment.

Public announcement. As the size of the deal increases, social rituals are often not enough to secure adequate commitment and it helps to make a public announcement. Once a public announcement is made, it is much more difficult for either side to back out. These announcements can be made in the form of a press release or a press conference. Just as you increase your commitment to your walk-away by telling your boss and others about it, public disclosures of a big deal increase commitment and bind both sides to an agreement.

Accountability. Accountability also enhances commitment. One way to finalize accountability is to put an agreement in writing. This type of accountability is commonly accomplished with an exchange of insertion orders (IO) and confirmations between buyer and seller. IOs and confirmations can be by mail, fax, or e-mail. Once IOs and confirmations of the IO are received, an agreement becomes legally binding. Some crafty buyers will reach a verbal agreement then send an IO at a lower price than agreed on, either hoping receiving salespeople will not notice or that they will go along with it to avoid a loss at that late date. Do not fall for this ploy, send back a confirmation that shows your original prices, and then wait for the buyer to respond.

Another type of accountability agreements are non-binding letters of intent (LOI). There might be several details left to be worked out after you have reached an agreement on major points at the end of a negotiation for a big deal. In such a situation, you might ask the other side for a letter that says that they will go ahead with the deal based on the assumption that the final, minor terms can be ironed out. Such a letter is not legally binding, but it significantly increases the other side's commitment to work out the remainder of the issues. Another type of agreement are exchanges of next-step agreements – a list of things both sides must complete to implement an agreement.

Simultaneous exchange. In some large, complicated deals, sending back and forth letters of agreement, IOs, or next-steps is not solid enough to secure a firm commitment. In such situations, it might be a good idea to use a simultaneous exchange to seal the deal. In the case of the sale of a home and the subsequent formal closing, the two sides typically exchange the title for the property and a certified check for the required amount at the same time. With extremely large, complex media deals, simultaneous exchange is a good practice.

Whichever form of commitment you use, always follow this rule:

Rule: Once you get commitment, say "thank you," shut up, and leave quickly.

Buyer's remorse usually sets in after someone buys something. You do not want to be present when buyer's remorse occurs. One of the biggest mistakes inexperienced salespeople make is to hang around and chat after they have made a sale or reached an agreement. They are afraid of being considered impolite and ungrateful by rushing off. Forget about being impolite, leave fast. You might want to make an excuse for your quick exit and say, "You've got an excellent deal. Thank you so much for the business. Now I have to run back to the office and book this order before someone else buys the great inventory you just invested in. Good bye." There is an old saying in sales that the jaw-bone of an ass slew a thousand Philistines and as many sales have been lost for the same reason because salespeople talk too much after making a sale.

6 Putting It All Together:
Create a Negotiating and Closing Plan

You should fill out the Negotiating and Closing Planner at http://www.mediaselling.us/downloads.html whenever you are going into a major negotiation and for dealing with the 20 percent of your customers who give you 80 percent of your business. Also, see the Negotiating and Closing Outline on www.mediaselling.com that summarizes all of the strategies, tactics, and rules. You can download this onto a PDA so you can review it before important negotiations.

Once you have created a thorough negotiating and closing plan, and before you enter into a major negotiation, rehearse. An excellent way to rehearse is to get a colleague (salesperson or sales manager) to rehearse with you. You should play the other side's role and your colleague should play your role. Rehearsing in this manner is the best way to refine and perfect your plan.

Rule: Always rehearse your negotiating and closing plan.

After you have rehearsed your plan, commit to it – carry it out just as you have rehearsed it. Rehearsal will give you confidence and increase your commitment.

Finally, just as when you make major presentations, debrief after negotiating. Practice makes perfect and debriefing makes it even better; which leads to the final negotiating and closing rule:

Rule: After every negotiation, debrief.

Many of the concepts and the strategies used in this chapter are those recommended by Richard Shell in *Bargaining for Advantage*, an excellent book that is applicable to media negotiating and one I recommend you read.

Test Yourself

1   What are the five elements in the negotiating process?
2   Why is knowing the other side's cultural background important?
3   What are the 10 preparation steps in negotiating?
4   What third style do you occasionally find in media negotiating?
5   What are the four negotiating situations?
6   What are the two basic negotiating styles?
7   What is a BATNA?
8   What is the purpose of the tit-for-tat tactic?
9   What is negative leverage?
10   What is an HLE?
11   What is a ballpark?
12   Name six acceptable bargaining tactics.
13   How can you avoid negotiating on each element in a package individually?
14   What are the five steps in the bargaining process?
15   Should you open first?
16   Should you open optimistically?
17   Give an example of a frame.
18   How should you give concessions?
19   Name three trial closes.
20   Give an example of a Clincher Close.

Project

Pretend a rich aunt can afford to buy you a new car and that you are going to ask her for a BMW roadster. Prepare for your request by filling out the Negotiating and Closing Planner, downloadable from http://www.mediaselling.us/downloads.html.

References

Richard B. Chase and Sriram Dasu. 2001. "Want to perfect your company's service? Use behavioral science." *Harvard Business Review*. June.

Jay Conger. 1998. "The necessary art of persuasion." *Harvard Business Review*. May–June.

Danny Ertel. 1999. "Negotiation as a corporate capability." *Harvard Business Review*. May–June.

Roger Fisher and William Ury with Bruce Patton. 1991. *Getting to Yes*, 2nd edition. New York: Penguin Books.

Michael Maccoby. 2000. "Narcissistic leaders: The incredible pros, the inevitable cons." *Harvard Business Review*. January–February.

László Mérö. 1998. *Moral Calculations: Game Theory, Logic, and Human Frailty*. New York: Copernicus.

Gerard I. Nierenberg. 1973. *Fundamentals of Negotiating*. New York: Hawthorne Books.

William Poundstone. 1992. *Prisoner's Dilemma*. New York: Doubleday.

Linda L. Putnam and Michael Roloff. 1992. *Communication and Negotiation*. Newbury Park, CA: Sage Publications.

Howard Raiffa. 1982. *The Art and Science of Negotiation*. Cambridge, MA: Harvard University Press.

James K. Sebenius. 2001. "Six habits of merely effective negotiators." *Harvard Business Review*. April.

Thomas C. Schelling. 1980. *The Strategy of Conflict*. Cambridge, MA: Harvard University Press.

G. Richard Shell. 1999. *Bargaining for Advantage*. New York: Penguin Books.

Sun Tzu. 1983. *The Art of War*, edited by James Clavell. New York: Dell Publishing

Bob Woolf. 1990. *Friendly Persuasion*. New York: Berkley Books.

Notes

1. Gerard I. Nierenberg. 1973. *Fundamentals of Negotiating*. New York: Hawthorne Books, p. 27.
2. Sun Tzu. 1983. *The Art of War*, edited by James Clavell. New York: Dell Publishing, p. 82.
3. Ibid., p. 7.
4. G. Richard Shell. 1999. *Bargaining for Advantage*. New York: Penguin Books, p. xiii.
5. Danny Ertel. 1999. "Negotiation as a corporate capability." *Harvard Business Review*. May–June, p. 6.
6. Ibid., p. 13.

7 Bob Woolf. 1990. *Friendly Persuasion.* New York: Berkley Books, p. 129.

8 Stefan Fatsis. 2003. "Small ball: NBC Maps a future without the big leagues." *Wall Street Journal.* January 31, p. A1.

9 William Poundstone. 1992. *Prisoner's Dilemma.* New York: Doubleday.

10 G. Richard Shell. 1999. *Bargaining for Advantage*, p. 95.

11 Personal conversation with Perry Stein, ex-VP of NBC Sports, November, 2000.

12 Richard B. Chase and Sriram Dasu. 2001. "Want to perfect your company's service? Use behavioral science." *Harvard Business Review.* June, p. 82.

13 Shell. *Bargaining for Advantage*, p. 169.

14 Sun Tzu. *The Art of War*, p. 35.

15 Hal Lancaster. 1998. "Most things are negotiable: Here's how to get good at it." *Wall Street Journal.* January 27, p. B1.

16 Shell. *Bargaining for* Advantage, p. 184.

17 Chase and Dasu. "Want to perfect your company's service?" p. 83.

18 Shell. 1999. *Bargaining for Advantage*, p. 197.

13

Skills: Servicing

Charles Warner

In Chapter 1 you learned that "There is only one valid definition of a business purpose: to create a customer." In Chapter 2 you learned the definition of selling: "Selling in the media is about creating customers and keeping them." Up to this point, this book has focused on how to create customers. This chapter emphasizes the importance of the last step of selling, servicing, in order to keep the customers you create, because as you learned in Chapter 2, "Customers require outrageous service that will make them raving fans."

The terms "outrageous service" and "raving fans" come from a book titled *Raving Fans* by Ken Blanchard and Sheldon Bowles, and these terms reflect the increased expectations of consumers for excellent service in addition to a quality product.[1] Before 1990, the 4 Ps of marketing (product, price, place, and promotion) were taught in colleges and written about in marketing textbooks. But in the 1980s consumers became fed up with shoddy quality and service from many American manufacturers. Japanese, German, and a few American companies saw a marketing opportunity and began emphasizing the excellent service that accompanied the purchase of their quality products. The best-selling business book, *In Search of Excellence*, published in 1982, urged companies to be close to the customer, and this phrase became the mantra of many companies. Improvement in service by the 1990s raised the expectations of American consumers and post-purchase service became the fifth P of marketing. Today, service is an inextricable attribute of most products, especially with intangible services such as advertising, where the media salesperson's service is the tangibilization of the advertising product.

Servicing in the Sales Process

The sales process involves creating customers and keeping them. You know that you have kept your customers when they come back, when they renew. Exhibit 13.1 shows the Renewal Cycle and how it fits into the sales process.

Note in Exhibit 13.1 that all of the steps of selling are the same in the renewal process except the first, Prospecting. Prospecting, the act of finding people to sell to, was accomplished when you received your first order from an account, but, as you learned from the Money Engine in Chapter 9, advertisers do not become customers until they renew. Therefore, always sell for the second order, not the first. Prospecting is hard, often frustrating work and it is easier to get a renewal for a $100,000 schedule than to prospect and sell a new $100,000 account.

Effective servicing can accomplish the third primary sales objective, to retain and increase current business. Your current customers are your best prospects, and it is easier and more efficient to get an increase of 25 percent (from $100,000 to $125,000, for example) from a current account than to prospect and sell a new one for $125,000. When you sell for a renewal, you have to go through the other five steps of selling because issues and challenges always arise when an advertising schedule runs and you must address them with new solutions. And even while your customers' schedules run, your competitors in your own and in competing media are

Exhibit 13.1 Creating customers and keeping them: The Renewal Cycle

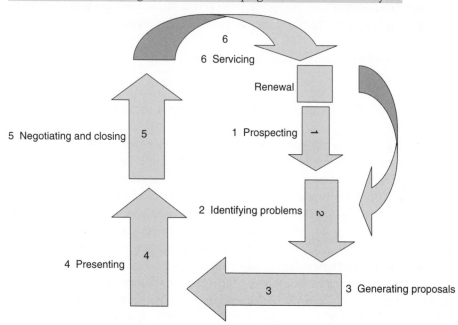

monitoring your media and trying hard to steal your customers. Your best defense against competitors' attacks is to give your customers outrageous service.

What is outrageous service? Ken Blanchard and Sheldon Bowles define "outrageous" as "substantially exceeding customers' service expectations." Your customers' expectations are determined by three factors: (1) What service they want; (2) what service they get from your competitors (your medium and other media); and (3) what service they have received from your organization in the past. Let's look at each of these factors separately.

What service your customers want

Just as you asked Discovery Questions before you got an order, you must ask Servicing Questions after each order you get from a customer (not just after the first one because their needs may change). The first step in providing service that substantially exceeds your customers' expectations is to find out what kind of service your customers want. You already have a good idea, in general, what they want from the surveys listed in Chapters 2 and 8 (you might want to look at them again. They are on pages 38–39 of Chapter 2). But those surveys are several years old and are based on the views of television and radio media buyers and advertising agency executives. The best thing to do is to ask your customers what they want and for them to give you a list of items that they believe constitutes ideal service. Asking customers what kind of service they want is an excellent idea for two reasons: (1) It lets them know up front that you care about them; and (2) it identifies a standard, or measure, of expectations so you can know what you have to do to substantially exceed them in order to provide outrageous service.

Rule: Find out what kind of service your customers want.

What kind of service your competitors give

Immediately after you ask your customers what service they want, the next step is to ask them which media salesperson gives them the best service and what makes their service the best. The reason you ask this question is because the first question will probably produce an extremely high, or even impossibly high, level standard of service – a wish list. The second question about your competitors' best service lowers the bar of their expectations from perhaps impossible heights to a reasonable height. So, just as with presentations, with service you will know how good you have to be – just good enough to win.

As you learned from game theory, your servicing strategy depends on the servicing strategy of competitors. To defend against their inevitable attacks, your strategy must be better because customers will judge your service against the best service they get from competitors, not on an absolute basis compared to their own highly optimistic wish list. By asking customers about the best service they get, you anchor their perception of good service at a reasonable level that you have a good chance of exceeding, providing there are no institutional constraints on your ability to provide competitive service, such as extravagant gifts and lavish entertainment. If you discover that your customers' expectations include these types of gifts and entertainment, it is best to control their expectations immediately rather than try to compete inadequately. You might say, "I'm sorry I can't match the entertainment or gift budget of my competition; it's against company policy. But I will try to make up for it with faster response and by providing you with more and better research and promotion ideas." If you are honest and sincere, and follow up on your promises, your customers, except for the few corrupt ones, will be pleased and satisfied.

Rule: Find out which competitor gives the best service and what kind of service it is and then exceed it.

Your past service level

Your customers' level of expectation is not only set by your competitors, but also by the level of service they have received in the past from your organization. After asking about the best service they receive from your competitors, ask them about the service they have received in the past from your organization. If you are lucky, you will not have to ask this question if a customer answers the question about the best service they get with a reply that it is from your or from your organization. In this case, you have a clear, measurable standard to meet and exceed. If you are not lucky and customers answer the question about your company's service with "Awful" or worse, you have a serious problem that promises will not even begin to solve. When you run into this problem, all you can say is, "I understand how you feel and I'm sorry for any inconvenience it has caused you. I know the only thing that will change your opinion is action and consistency, not words, so I'll say no more. I'll make no promises except that I will check in regularly to see how I'm doing. Let me try to get off on the right track by asking you what I can do for you right now – in the next few days?"

Rule: Find out what kind of service customers have received from your organization in the past.

Exceeding expectations

As you learned in Chapter 8 about creating value, if you want a happy customer, you under-promise and over-deliver in terms of what results they expect. It is the same with service; you must control your clients' expectations. Do not make any promises about what kind of service you will deliver; action always speaks louder than words. Also, as in negotiating, in servicing, start out small and increase the level of service slowly. If you start out with big perks and entertainment, you raise your customers' expectations. Your level of service must be good enough to be considered superior to your competitors', but it does not have to be extravagant or lavish, especially at first.

Also, the vast majority of customers value consistency more than extravagance. The same, consistent, high-level of service with every order, every schedule, every week, every month, and every year is what they prize most.

Rule: Consistency, consistency, consistency.[2]

Systems

Companies that have great reputations for excellent service are driven by excellent systems: mission statements; institutional service attitudes; service standards and policies; service tracking and measurement systems; and service feedback and reward systems. Without a service culture and systems that contain all of these elements, excellent service does not become an institutional priority, but an individual and inconsistent chore.

Mission statements   Many media companies have mission statements. Some are sincere, but many are public relations documents. Virtually all media companies' mission statements mention customers in one way or another, but rarely do they put their customers (advertisers) as a top priority; most of them, understandably, put their audience first.

ESPN is one media organization that gets its priorities right in its mission statement. Note in the last paragraph of ESPN's mission statement in Exhibit 13.2 that employees, customers, community, and shareholders are the order of its priorities (viewers are assumed to be the top priority because of the opening paragraph).

Why are organizational mission statements included in a chapter about servicing advertisers? Because if your company does not have a mission statement or has one that does not indicate or imply that being fair and responsive to customers is important, then you must write a personal mission statement that delineates what kind of a salesperson you want to be and what kind of service you want to provide to your customers. It is more than just setting a goal of providing excellent service. Writing a personal mission statement that includes superior service is making a promise, a commitment, to yourself and to your customers that you will provide service that is better than your competitors' and that exceeds your customers' expectations. And by writing it down, you increase your commitment.

Exhibit 13.2

ESPN
OUR MISSION

ESPN is committed to enhancing its position as the premier sports programmer in the world by delivering a superior product to its viewers, affiliates, and advertisers. We seek to attract and retain the most talented people by fostering an environment for them to thrive in their work efforts as they develop the finest sports program distribution system for both domestic and international markets.

People are the most valuable resource at ESPN. We believe in treating every employee with respect and dignity. We endeavor to support and reward our people for their efforts and we will strive to make ESPN a caring company, cognizant of each employee's personal and professional needs.

Our success has always been dependent upon people working together as a team. To sustain our success and competitive advantage, we must communicate with one another openly and honestly, assist each other in time of need, and vigorously support the team building effort.

From the start, aggressive thinking and risk taking have been at the heart of our success. We must constantly practice and encourage these qualities to secure our future. We must feel free to honestly disagree with one another while knowing when to treat mistakes as learning opportunities. In our competitive environment, creative risk taking can net us huge rewards.

We will continue to maintain our reputation for excellence while insuring our levels of profitability, as we look for creative ways to deliver the best programming and services within cost effective practices.

As an organization, we will strive to abide by these values. We believe that by embracing them, our EMPLOYEES will be enriched, our CUSTOMERS will be better served, we will have a positive impact on our COMMUNITY, and our SHAREHOLDERS will enjoy a healthy return on their investment.

Institutional service attitude   Many media organizations have a culture, an attitude about providing excellent service that is inculcated throughout the organization. Time Inc., Condé Nast, and some broadcast and cable television networks, are examples of these. Some retailers, such as Nordstrom and Stu Leonard's grocery stores, are widely acclaimed for their outrageous service. Wal-Mart is famous for having greeters at the doors who pleasantly welcome shoppers. As Sam Walton said, "The way you treat your associates is the way they will treat customers." Unfortunately, the majority of media organizations have neither an institutional service attitude nor a management that treats salespeople the way they want salespeople to treat customers.

What do you do if you work in a media company that does not have an institutional service attitude but practices the do-as-I-say-not-as-I-do, get-the-order-regardless style of management? Write a service-oriented personal sales mission

Exhibit 13.3   Sam Walton's Rule #8

Exceed your customer's expectations. If you do, they'll come back over and over. Give them what they want – and a little more. Let them know you appreciate them. Make good on all your mistakes, and don't make excuses – apologize. Stand behind everything you do. "Satisfaction guaranteed" will make all the difference.

Source: www.refresher.com/walton.html. April, 2003.

statement and vow never to treat your customers as management treats you. You cannot change your corporate culture, but you can change your own culture and attitude. Help yourself to change your attitude and remind yourself of your commitment to outrageous service by pasting Sam Walton's Rule #8 (in Exhibit 13.3) over your desk. It is also available on www.mediaselling.us so you can download it and print it out.

Service standards and policies   Some companies have service standards and policies that are based on a customer-oriented approach such as Stu Leonard's, "Our Policy: Rule 1: The customer is always right! Rule 2: If the customer is ever wrong, re-read rule 1."[3] If your company does not have written standards, guidelines, or policies for service, use the Servicing Checklist in Exhibit 13.4 (also available on www.mediaselling.us) as your personal guidelines for servicing.

Service tracking and measurement systems   Most media companies have Sales Force Automation (SFA) software programs that track sales calls, including service calls. Management rarely examines these tracking reports, especially reports that track service calls, except in some large, national media companies. And when media sales managers peruse call reports, they are usually more interested in the quantity rather than quality. Typically, media salespeople must develop their own system for tracking, measuring, and evaluating all calls, including service calls. These systems will be covered in Chapter 24.

Service feedback and reward systems   If you set servicing standards and goals and attempt to carry them out, how do you know if your customers believe you are providing the best service? You must have a feedback system. You can ask on a regular basis, "How am I doing?", but you will rarely get a candid answer because most people do not like to tell others people that they are not doing well. The typical answer to the how-am-I-doing question is, "fine," which does not give you much useful data. Many companies, including IBM and some premium automobile dealers, have third-party research organizations conduct customer satisfaction surveys immediately after a service encounter or on a regular basis with on-going customers. Some national media companies, and a few local media companies,

Exhibit 13.4 Servicing checklist

1	Ask customers what they want.	Ask what service they would consider perfect.
2	Ask customers what competitors do.	Ask what competitors are best at servicing and what they do that is so good. Use the answer as a benchmark and deliver better service.
3	Set servicing objectives.	After you discover what your customers' expectations are, set specific objectives for giving outrageous service.
4	Always say "thank you."	As soon as you get an order, compliment your customers on their good judgment, thank the person who gave you the order, and, of course, leave quickly. When you return to the office, send a brief handwritten note saying "thank you" again. Handwritten notes are much more personal than e-mails, but send an e-mail at the minimum.
5	Review your account list regularly.	Some salespeople review their account list every three days. Do not let a week go by when you do not review all the accounts on your list. Do not rely on your memory because you will forget to call on the grumps and over-call on the sweetie pies.
6	Presell	Servicing is selling, so always take the opportunity to sell a new benefit or advantage. Your preselling will serve you particularly well when a customer or buyer is under pressure to make a buy in a hurry.
7	Make copy, ideas, and schedule improvement calls.	In situations where advertising copy can be changed easily, as on Web sites and in medium- and small-market radio, make a copy call, suggest creative be revised, and recommend a new angle or another banner execution. This recommendation can be welcome in situations where a client has been running the same creative over and over again and may be boring everyone.

Furthermore, poor creative is often the cause of poor results for a client. Keep on top of how customers are doing. Is the advertising creating traffic, sales, or other results? If not, is it the creative? Is it the schedule? Change both if necessary, but do not hide your head in the sand and just hope for things to improve. Do something to help your customer.

Improvements in schedules, such as moving spots to a new time slot (for example, from daytime to early fringe in television), often allow customers to reach a new audience. Making unsolicited improvements for your customers can be a wonderful relationship builder. This service should be used rarely (on an occasional and random basis), though, or customers come to expect it.

Exhibit 13.4 Servicing checklist (cont'd)

8	Handle complaints immediately and honestly.	Fast response to client complaints is a must. If your medium has made an error of some kind, customers are probably upset; do not add fuel to the fire with a slow response. If you have made an error, admit it, apologize, and set about correcting the situation immediately. Problems tend to make customers impatient, so do not put them off. Give them status reports if a complaint takes longer than a day or two to be resolved. Do not allow clients to think you have let it slip your mind.
		Be quick to admit your own errors. If clients have to tell you first, you lose some trust. If you tell them first, you maintain your credibility. Also, if you tell customers first, you are more in control of the proposed solution. For example, if the reproduction of a client's magazine ad is off register, call the client immediately and offer a suitable make-good. Your chances of getting approval are much greater with this method than if a customer calls you.
9	Ask for referrals.	There is no better endorsement of you and your medium than a thrilled customer. After you are assured that customers are delighted with their campaign and their results, ask them to refer you to someone else for whom you might be able to solve some advertising problems.
10	Develop case studies.	Case studies are more effective than client success letters. Case studies can give specific details on how you solved marketing and advertising problems. Case studies can be used to demonstrate how an organization can marshal its resources and expertise to help customers achieve their specific marketing objectives. In addition, if you develop good advertising success case studies, you will hone your skills of defining and solving advertising problems – the perfect solution-selling approach. Finally, if you develop a case study with current customers, you will find not only that you will cement your relationship with those customers but also that you will come up with additional ideas for them. See "How to Write an Advertising Success Case Study" on www.mediaselling.us.
11	Ask for feedback.	Third-party surveys are best; customer polling by management is next best. If you cannot get either of these, then always ask customers, "How am I doing? Is there anything I could do to give you better service?"
12	Adjust and improve.	When you get feedback, use it to adjust your approach and improve your service until it is outrageous.

conduct yearly, third-party customer satisfaction surveys and these surveys give invaluable feedback to management about the level of service they provide so they can correct problems and learn what their competitors are doing right and wrong.

If your company does not conduct third-party customer satisfaction surveys at least once a year, then you should encourage your sales manager or ad director to conduct such a survey personally and informally on all of your accounts to see how you, your company, and your competitors are doing. If all else fails, you might consider sending out a survey yourself under the name of a fictitious research company and to a sample of at least 100 customers and agencies (fewer than 100 will give you an unreliable sample because your return rate will probably be around 20 percent). Include a self-addressed return envelope with postage included to the fictitious company's mail box number (which you have rented) or do the survey by e-mail. This process will ensure you remain anonymous and will give you invaluable feedback. Be prepared for the worst – that you and your management might not be perceived to be the best. But it takes courage to find out and face up to your weaknesses. You will find a sample Customer Satisfaction Survey at http://www.mediaselling.us/downloads.html in case you want to conduct one. Make sure you have your sales manager or ad director's approval. If they ask you not to send out a survey, do not send one out; you do not want your management to think you are trying to make them look bad.

More and more global companies have added an incentive payment to their sales compensation plans based on customer satisfaction ratings; 35 percent of IBM's incentive package is based on customer satisfaction. Media companies have generally lagged behind this trend and, unfortunately, few of them include rewards for excellent customer service. However, you can institute your own reward system – a high percentage of renewals at increased rates from raving fans.

Test Yourself

1 What is the purpose of selling?
2 What do customers require?
3 What step of selling does the renewal cycle eliminate?
4 What is the first rule of servicing?
5 Give two reasons for finding out what kind of service your competitors give.

Project

Project #1: If you are not a media salesperson, contact a local advertising agency media buyer or executive and ask if they would complete a customer satisfaction survey. If you get approval, customize the Customer Satisfaction Survey appropriately for your market, make an appointment, and fill out the survey along with the agency person. Analyze the survey and see what the importance of price, ratings, or Web traffic are in your market.

Project #2: If you are a media salesperson, write a mission statement for yourself that includes exceeding your customers' service expectations.

References

Kenneth Blanchard and Sheldon Bowles. 1993. *Raving Fans: A Revolutionary Approach to Customer Service.* New York: William Morrow and Company.

Thomas J. Peters and Robert H. Waterman, Jr. 1982. *In Search of Excellence.* New York: Harper & Row.

Notes

1   Kenneth Blanchard and Sheldon Bowles. 1993. *Raving Fans: A Revolutionary Approach to Customer Service.* New York: William Morrow and Company.

2   Ibid.

3   www.chartcourse.com/articlegoodservice. html

Part III

Knowledge

14

Business and Finance

William Redpath

Why Business and Finance in a Sales Book?

When you sell directly to a major advertiser, you should have some understanding of its financial condition as well as its marketing strategy, which you learned when you asked the Discovery Questions as outlined in Chapter 9. If you have a basic knowledge of financial terminology, you can talk to a company's CEO, CFO (chief financial officer), or CMO (chief marketing officer) more knowledgeably, which will give you an edge over the vast majority of competing salespeople.

On the other hand, when you sell to advertising agencies, it is important to talk their language – CPMs, CPPs, CPCs, reach, and frequency – not necessarily financial language.

Also, the majority of top managers in the media industry come from sales – general managers of radio and televisions stations and publishers of magazines and newspapers, for example. If you aspire to get into management, you should be familiar with the accounting principles and financial statements outlined below.

Accounting Systems

Business systems such as accounting are important to understand because once a salesperson completes a sale, data from that sale are input into a medium's operations system. Data flows from this system into an organization's accounting system. The importance of the proper handling of insertion orders (IOs), scheduling of advertising, and monitoring the pace of sales and unsold inventory cannot be overstated, for a medium's financial health is at stake. All media organizations must comply with legal requirements such as reporting for tax purposes and financial reporting for publicly traded companies; last, but not least, it is vital for the career health of sales managers and salespeople.

I know of a sales manager of a television station who was dismissed after the manager's station ran three Public Service Announcements (PSAs) during a Super Bowl telecast. Unsurprisingly, the station's general manager was watching and was less than amused.

Computers have revolutionized operations, production, and traffic systems. I remember working at radio stations during the 1970s at which traffic was done manually using long, thin cardboard-like strips that had advertisers' names and commercial lengths typed on them; these were then inserted in chronological order into metal holders. Once the metal holder was filled, it was photocopied and the result was a program log listing the program to be aired and the commercials to be aired in those programs.

Today's systems and the reports they generate make that system look barbaric. Not only do current computerized systems manage data, they analyze it to help sales management maximize revenue. Revenue management is the application of mathematical and analytical techniques (now done by yield management software) to determine prices in order to maximize revenue. Yield management is considered a branch of revenue management and has been used in the airline industry since the 1970s but is now used in many media industries, including broadcasting, cable, and Interactive.

Comprehensive data systems that interconnect traffic and operations to the accounting or business office are standard in media companies today. An accounting system supports all of the other departments of a media organization, including sales, and this accounting system manages accounts receivable, billing of advertising sold, and collections.

The importance of accounting should be obvious. While many people get involved in the media industries for reasons other than the bottom line, a media company, like any other business enterprise, must earn a profit in order to survive. The purpose of a sales department is to bring in the revenue that makes profitability possible. But, without accounting, one would not know if the quest for profitability were successful – profits come after subtracting expenses from revenue, and the accounting department keeps track of the revenue that salespeople generate.

Financial Reports

While some small media companies may report their historical financial performance using cash basis accounting, the vast majority of companies, including all that have to report their financial results to government agencies, such as public traded companies, or financial institutions to which these companies are indebted, use Generally Accepted Accounting Principles (or GAAP). While cash basis accounting is acceptable, but not mandatory, for tax reporting purposes, it is unacceptable for financial reporting purposes.

GAAP are set by the Financial Accounting Standards Board (FASB), a private organization based in Norwalk, Connecticut. GAAP change over time, as several new accounting principles are usually issued each year.

GAAP mandates use of accrual accounting, which means that revenues must be recognized when actually earned – in the case of the media, when advertising runs – not when cash is collected. Expenses are recorded when services or goods are used, not when they are paid for.

The General Ledger, which lists all accounts in an accounting system, feeds into a company's financial statements. A complete set of financial statements will include the following:

1 A balance sheet, sometimes referred to as a Statement of Financial Position
2 An income statement
3 A statement of cash flows
4 A statement of stockholders' equity

Because of its relative unimportance to having a basic understanding of how businesses operate on the financial side, I will not address the statement of stockholders' equity.

Balance sheet

Exhibit 14.1 shows an example of a balance sheet. This is the balance sheet for Ajax Communications, Inc., a fictitious publicly traded radio company.

A balance sheet is always a financial snapshot at a single point in time. On a balance sheet, assets always equal the sum of liabilities and owners', or shareholders', equity. If that does not make sense offhand, think of it this way. If you have something – an asset – either someone else owns it, and thus, it is a liability, or you own it, and, thus, it becomes equity.

Assets are listed at the top of the balance sheet in Exhibit 14.1 and liabilities and owners' equity are at the bottom. Assets start with Current Assets, which include Cash and Cash Equivalents, which are stable value instruments with a maturity date less than 90 days into the future.

Accounts Receivable are current assets, as are Prepaid Expenses, assuming the service that was prepaid will be used within one year. Assets are also not supposed to be stated at more than their Net Realizable Value. Therefore, a reserve needs to be estimated for Accounts Receivable that are not likely to be collected.

While inventory is certainly a term used in media selling, it is not inventory in the usual sense of the term (i.e., merchandise currently owned by a retailer that

Exhibit 14.1 Balance sheet

AJAX COMMUNICATIONS, INC.
CONSOLIDATED BALANCE SHEETS
(in thousands, except per share amounts)

	December 31,	
	2007	2006
ASSETS		
Current Assets:		
Cash and cash equivalents	$1,765	$778
Accounts receivable, net of allowance of $719 and		
$403 at December 31, 2001 and 2000, respectively	9,772	10,639
Other current assets	642	595
Total current assets	12,179	12,012
Property and equipment, net	25,817	20,716
Intangible assets, net	266,420	217,897
Other assets, net	1,940	2,108
Total assets	$306,356	$252,733
LIABILITIES AND STOCKHOLDERS' EQUITY		
Current liabilities:		
Accounts payable	$2,044	$1,672
Accrued compensation	1,000	932
Other current liabilities	3,010	2,298
Total current liabilities	6,054	4,902
Long-term debt, less current portion	87,019	45,010
Other long-term liabilities	75	84
Deferred taxes	4,870	4,317
Total liabilities	98,018	54,313
Stockholders' equity:		
Common stock	369	352
Treasury shares	(6,757)	(7,063)
Additional paid-in capital	270,694	259,386
Retained deficit	(55,968)	(54,255)
Total stockholders' equity	208,338	198,420
Total liabilities and stockholders' equity	$306,356	$252,733

is for sale) in the current assets section of a balance sheet. When inventory is accounted for on a balance sheet, it is usually accounted for using the FIFO (First In, First Out) or the LIFO (Last In, First Out) method in terms of recognizing which items to expense and which to retain in inventory. Inventory accounting is usually not an issue for businesses in non-inflationary times.

Long-term assets are those that are expected to be used over a period longer than one year, and they usually start with Property, Plant and Equipment (PP&E), also known as tangible assets. PP&E is stated at cost less depreciation and amortization over the course of its life. Over the lives of tangible assets, the depreciation and amortization systematically reduce the assets' net values. Land is not depreciated for either financial reporting or tax purposes because it is not a depreciating asset like printing presses are, for example, which wear out. Land does not wear out and need to be replaced.

Sometimes companies list intangible assets as long-term, non-current, assets. In the media industries, the most valuable intangible assets include FCC licenses, cable franchises, network affiliation agreements, and customer mailing and subscriber lists.

Program rights are a major intangible asset category for television companies. As with PP&E, program rights are booked when they are purchased and amortized as they are used, when the programs are aired.

Intangible assets are recognized, or booked, only if they are acquired alone or as part of a going concern business. Self-created intangible assets are not booked if they are developed internally. That is, if a salesperson develops a relationship with a particular advertiser or advertising agency that leads to revenue, that is not recognized as an asset on the books of the station. There can be many valuable self-created intangible assets with a company, but they are never explicitly recognized on the balance sheet. This is part of the tenet of conservatism of financial statements, to be addressed later in this chapter.

After intangible assets are acquired, they are amortized, almost without exception, in a straight line over 15 years for tax purposes (assuming they are acquired as part of an ongoing business in an asset transaction). For financial reporting purposes, intangible assets that have a finite life are amortized (decreased in value), with that amount recognized as an expense on the income statement, year by year, over the useful lives of the assets. Intangible assets that have an indefinite life are not amortized but are reviewed each year to make sure that their values on the financial statements, also known as book value or carrying value, is not greater than their fair values. If an asset's fair value is less than its book value, its book value must be reduced to be equal to its fair value, with the difference recognized as an expense on the income statement in that year.

Other Assets are other long-term assets that may have significant value; sometimes well above their book value. I once heard a business appraiser at a valuation conference state that he just about signed a valuation report valuing the equity of a closely held corporation when it dawned on him to inquire as to what was included in the Other Assets of that corporation. The book value of Other Assets was quite low and the assets, therefore, appeared minor in nature at first glance. What he learned was that it was Wal-Mart Stores stock that had been acquired many years earlier. In the interim, the stock had appreciated many times over, so his valuation would have been wrong if he had just assumed that the book value of Other Assets was the fair market value of Other Assets.

Historical Cost and Net Realizable Value are used in financial statements because of the concept of conservatism in historical financial statements. With the exception of certain marketable securities, assets are booked at cost and never increased in book value, even if they increase in fair market value. Conservatism is supposed to be an essential tenet of financial statements, even though one might not know it from recent financial scandals involving major corporations. Conservatism brings greater credibility to financial statements so that people using financial statements can know that claims made on financial statements are reliable and not overstated.

Looking at the bottom part of the balance sheet in Exhibit 14.1, Current Liabilities are liabilities such as Accounts Payable or Accrued Expenses, goods or services used that have not been paid for yet and that are to be paid for in less than one year. That also includes the portion of long-term debt that is payable in less than one year, if any. Current Assets minus Current Liabilities equals Working Capital.

Long-term debt consists of loans, notes, and bonds that have maturity dates more than one year into the future. Program payments to be paid in the future are also listed as liabilities, with payments to be made within the next year listed as a current liability. Prepaid magazine and newspaper subscriptions are also considered a liability because subscribers are owed magazines or newspapers in the future.

The shareholders' equity section of the balance sheet is on the bottom of Exhibit 14.1, and it lists the various types of equity including preferred stock, if any, and various classes of common stock. The book values of some of these items may not be even close to the fair market value of those securities. The book value of shareholders' equity can be negative, but, of course, the market value of an equity security cannot go below zero.

In terms of order of interests to be paid off upon liquidation of a corporation, debt has priority over preferred stock, which has priority over common stock. That is why preferred stock is called preferred, even though returns for holders of common stock have been higher over time. Common stock is the residual, or last, claimant on a liquidated corporation and is, therefore, considered riskier than other securities of a corporation.

Income statement

An income statement, which can be seen in Exhibit 14.2, covers a period of time such as one month or one year. Exhibit 14.2 is the publicly reported income statements for Ajax Communications, Inc. for fiscal years 2005, 2006, and 2007.

Exhibit 14.2 Income statement

AJAX COMMUNICATIONS, INC.
CONSOLIDATED STATEMENTS OF OPERATIONS
(in thousands, except per share amounts)

	Year ended December 31,		
	2007	2006	2005
Gross broadcast revenues	$59,339	$48,324	$25,613
Less agency commissions	5,594	4,217	1,759
Net broadcast revenues	53,745	44,107	23,854
Station operating expenses	38,530	30,173	18,325
Depreciation and amortization	13,436	8,602	3,368
Corporate general and administrative expenses	4,857	4,501	2,773
Operating (loss) income	(3,078)	831	(612)
Interest expense	(3,279)	(4,229)	(5,249)
Gain (loss) on exchange/sale of radio stations	4,444	17,504	(602)
Other (expense) income, net	(465)	860	163
(Loss) income before income taxes and extraordinary items	(2,378)	14,966	(6,300)
Income tax benefit	665	0	0
(Loss) income before extraordinary items	(1,713)	14,966	(6,300)
Extraordinary loss from debt extinguishment, net of taxes	0	(1,114)	(471)
Net (loss) income	(1,713)	13,852	(6,771)
Loss applicable to common shares			
Net (loss) income	(1,713)	13,852	(6,771)
Preferred stock dividend requirements	0	(629)	(5,205)
Preferred stock accretion	0	(26,611)	(17,221)
Loss applicable to common shares	(1,713)	(13,388)	(29,197)
Basic and diluted loss per common share:			
Loss before extraordinary items	($0.05)	($0.39)	($119.69)
Extraordinary items	0.00	(0.03)	(1.96)
Net loss per common share	($0.05)	($0.42)	($121.65)

In internal financial statements, the income statement style I prefer shows revenue and expense categories down the middle, with the past month's actual results, past month's budget, with plus or minus variance percentage, and past month for the previous year, with plus or minus variance percentage, on the left. On the right, there should be year-to-date actual results, a year-to-date budget, with plus or minus variance percentage, and year-to-date for the previous year with plus or minus variance percentage. This style is seen by going to www.mediaselling.us and clicking on "Chapter 14, Internal Income Statement."

With an income statement, revenues are, of course, listed at the top. Revenues are usually listed by category such Local, Regional, National, Network Compensation, Political, Trade, Production, Equipment Leasing.

Subtracted from gross revenues in media industry financial statements are advertising agency commissions and commissions paid to national sales representative firms. This reporting is somewhat incongruous, in my opinion, because advertising agencies are agents of advertisers, while national sales representative firms work for the media companies. Local salespeople also work for local media companies, but their commissions are included in sales department expense, which is an expense that is listed below net revenues. Nevertheless, this has been the standard industry accounting treatment of national sales representative expenses for a long time and there is little prospect of that changing.

Be careful when looking at reported or estimated market revenues in the media, and in radio and television in particular. You need to know if they include trade revenues or not; generally, they do not, but sometimes they do. It is particularly important to know when you are estimating the revenue share of a radio or television station within its market. As with anything else, you do not want to compare apples with oranges. Expenses are best listed by functional departments in income statements, with a more detailed list of expenses by category within functional departments below the list of functional departments.

It is important to know exactly what someone means when they use the term Operating Income. In the media industries, that term is frequently used to mean either Operating Cash Flow (OCF), which is the case most of the time, or Earnings Before Interest Taxes, Depreciation, and Amortization (EBITDA). However, in financial statements among most non-media businesses, the term Operating Income is synonymous with Earnings Before Interest and Taxes (EBIT). Therefore, depreciation and amortization is treated as an operating expense in the financial statements. If depreciation and amortization expense is not given its own line in the income statement, it will have a separate line in the Statement of Cash Flows. It is a reconciling item between Net Income and Cash from Operating Activities, because it is a non-cash expense. Adding depreciation and amortization expense back to EBIT will give you EBITDA.

To get from EBITDA to OCF, corporate overhead expenses, sometimes called management fees, which are charged, for example, by a corporate headquarters office to each of its owned media properties, must be added back. The only expenses that should be deducted from revenues in arriving at OCF are operating expenses of an operating unit, such as a television station, excluding corporate management expense and depreciation and amortization expense. Historically, OCF has been the most recognized profitability measure in the media industry.

It is very important to know what OCF is not, however. It is not a measure of true cash flow in the literal sense of the term. OCF is not a profit measure that is recognized in Generally Accepted Accounting Principles (GAAP) and it is not equivalent to Cash Flow from Operations that is seen in the Statement of Cash Flows, which is part of a complete set of financial statements.

Operating Cash Flow may be defined differently by different people. I know someone whom I greatly respect who defines OCF without including trade revenues or trade expenses. Including them in calculating OCF may change OCF in a given year due to timing differences of revenue and expense recognition, but inclusion of trade revenues and trade expenses is part of GAAP.

There are other problems associated with OCF and EBITDA, so it should definitely not be used as the only measure of earnings of a business. Among the problems is that EBITDA and OCF never take into account either depreciation or amortization of a business' assets, capital expenditures for new equipment, or expenditures for purchases of other businesses. EBITDA and OCF also ignore additions to working capital and overstate cash flow in periods when growth of working capital is necessary to sustain a business and nurture its growth.

In analyzing media company financial statements, besides knowing whether they are cash or accrual basis financial statements, one should know how trade revenue is treated. In the media industries, advertising time is frequently traded not for cash, but for goods or services. In television, sometimes programs are purchased for a station with no cash outlay, but the program supplier gets to keep a certain number of commercial availabilities to sell to local advertisers within the program. Other radio or television stations may trade the use of a new car for the general manager in return for commercials on the station, without any cash actually changing hands. Trade deals are also often referred to as barter deals. Financial Accounting Standard (FAS) 63 states that all trade and barter revenue should be recorded at the estimated value of the goods or services received. FAS 63 also states that, as with cash transactions, trade revenue is recognized when earned and trade expense is recognized when a good or service is used. If goods or services are received before commercials are aired, a liability for the advertising must be recognized until the commercial is aired. If the commercial is broadcast before the goods or services are received, an asset must be recognized until the goods or services are used by the station.

Frequently in these financial statements, trade revenues and expenses are listed separately, below the line – below the determination of OCF and EBITDA on the income statement. Some income statements will list trade revenues among the gross revenues and list trade expenses among the regular operating expenses. Still other income statements, although a small minority, will make no distinction between cash and trade revenues on the income statement, simply including trade revenues with cash revenues in the appropriate category of gross revenues. Some financial statements (although not GAAP compliant) do not recognize trade revenues and trade expenses at all. Because trade revenues and expenses can be much higher in the media industry than in other kinds of businesses, it is important to know how they are accounted for.

Even though it seems obvious that trade involves no exchange of cash, it is important that the terms of trade deals struck by stations with various advertisers are understood by station executives. I know of a program director of a television station that did not use all of a trade with a local department store. The trade was advertising time in exchange for clothing for news anchors and other on-air personnel. There was a time expiration on the clothing side of the trade. When asked why some of the trade credit went unused, the program director said, "I thought I was saving the station money." Instead, the station was shortchanged some clothing. If you're in charge of effecting either side of a trade deal, be sure you know all the parameters of the deal, as well as how the accounting for the trade is to be handled.

Because trade deals can be easily abused (e.g., merchandise received in a trade can be stolen, or services can be diverted to personal, rather than business, use), internal management controls must be in place in the approval process, and to make sure the trade deals are implemented and executed properly.

There is a lot of chatter and slang used about margins, profit margins, or cash flow margins, especially in the media industry. A margin is a percentage, or a ratio, with a numerator and denominator. If you do not know for sure what the numerator and denominator are, and I mean not what the numbers are specifically but what they represent, ask. Is the ratio Operating Cash Flow divided by gross revenues or something else? What you may find is that the person dispensing the margin information does not know what constitutes the ratio.

Statement of cash flows

The Statement of Cash Flows, as seen in Exhibit 14.3, is a very important financial statement, because this shows the actual cash flows of a business entity. Remember, the term Operating Cash Flow is a misnomer and should not be relied upon for flows of actual cash.

The Statement of Cash Flows is divided into three sections: Cash Flows from Operating Activities, Cash Flows from Investing Activities, and Cash Flows from Financing Activities. Operating activities are the operation of the business; investing activities include things such as capital expenditures; financing activities include the raising of cash through the sale of debt and equity securities, or the buyback of those securities, interest payments and dividend payments. It is in the Statement of Cash Flows that one really sees the true cash flows in a business or an entity

Exhibit 14.3   Statement of Cash Flows

AJAX COMMUNICATIONS, INC.
CONSOLIDATED STATEMENTS OF CASH FLOWS
(in thousands)

| | Year ended December 31, | | |
	2006	2005	2004
Cash flows from operating activities:			
Net (loss) income	($1,713)	$13,852	($6,771)
Adjustments to reconcile net (loss) to net cash provided by (used in) operating activities:			
Depreciation and amortization	13,436	8,602	3,368
Provision for doubtful accounts	822	725	390
Non-cash interest expense	283	1,579	1,576
Non-cash charge for debt extinguishments	0	1,114	471
Non-cash charge for compensation	491	0	0
(Gain) loss on sale of radio stations	(4,444)	(17,504)	477
Loss on sale of fixed assets and other	160	0	0
Changes in operating assets and liabilities, net of acquisitions:			
Accounts receivable	(328)	(6,249)	(1,481)
Other assets	(107)	(358)	(36)
Current and long-term liabilities	(803)	(2,940)	(372)
Deferred taxes	553	4,317	0
	8,350	3,138	(2,378)
Cash flows from investing activities:			
Acquisitions of radio stations, net of cash acquired, and escrow deposits on pending acquisitions:	(63,450)	(148,940)	(27,533)
Capital expenditures	(3,161)	(1,719)	(1,978)
Net proceeds from sale of radio stations	13,393	2,000	13,999
Proceeds from sale of fixed assets	27	0	0
	(53,191)	(148,659)	(15,512)
Cash flows from financing activities:			
Proceeds from issuance of redeemable convertible preferred stock	0	0	41,754
Proceeds from issuance of common stock	4,068	156,939	0
Proceeds from long-term debt	60,500	48,500	16,500
Principal payments on long-term debt	(18,491)	(28,824)	(26,704)
Payment of notes payable	0	0	(7,500)
Payment for deferred financing costs	0	(1,904)	(427)
Payment of issuance costs	(249)	(11,606)	(2,802)
Treasury stock purchases	0	(7,063)	0
Dividends paid on all series of preferred stock	0	(8,153)	0
Redemption of Series B preferred stock	0	(5,000)	0
	45,828	142,889	20,821
Net increase (decrease) in cash and cash equivalents	987	(2,632)	2,931
Cash and cash equivalents at beginning of period	778	3,410	479
Cash and cash equivalents at end of period	$1,765	$778	$3,410

that owns a business. Cash, after all, is the true lifeblood of a business. Regardless of other assets, revenues, or profitability, if a business does not have cash, or cannot raise cash, it cannot function.

One of the most important parts of a full set of financial statements are the footnotes. You should be able to read and understand footnotes because they amplify and elucidate other portions of the financial statements. If you do not understand what you read in financial footnotes, ask the entity's management or their investor relations department. Do not be satisfied with vague explanations that do not make complete sense. Any questions about the financial statements, including the footnotes, should be answered clearly and forthrightly for you, assuming you have a right to know or a need to know. If you are a salesperson looking at financial statements to see if a company is creditworthy or has enough money to be a good prospect, you can ask someone in your own business or accounting department, or ask your company's accounting or auditing firm to help you.

Financial Information

Historical financial information on all companies that file reports with the Securities and Exchange Commission (SEC) can be found through numerous online services, and through the SEC's Web site at www.sec.gov.

Many radio and television stations voluntarily participate in market revenue compilations. In many, but not all, radio and television markets, an accounting firm or some other entity is hired to survey all the radio or television stations in that market regarding the amounts of their respective revenues. The survey taker keeps each station's submission confidential, but adds the data for all stations together and then sends the market totals to every station, along with the overall rank number for that station, and its rank in various revenue categories. This information illuminates the market revenue situation for everyone and allows management to see objectively how their station(s) stack up versus intramarket competition. The National Association of Broadcasters (NAB) publishes an annual book on television market revenues for many surveyed television markets, and it can be purchased from the NAB.

Other historical broadcasting data, including radio and television market revenues, is estimated and published by several firms. BIA Financial Network, Inc. (Web site: www.bia.com) publishes several reference books on the radio and television industries, including a unique software reference source called *Media Access Pro*. BIA plans to publish reference books and software on other media and telecommunications industries in the future.

The Interactive Advertising Bureau (IAB) publishes revenue information on its Web site, www.iab.net/resources/ad_revenue.asp. *Advertising Age* magazine every year publishes magazine revenue, number of advertising pages sold, and circulation for the top 300 magazines and the information can be found on www.adage.com.

Types of Financial Statements

Financial statements are always the product of management, but are compiled, reviewed, or audited by outside accountants. There are essentially four types of financial statements:

1 Internal financial statements. These are statements that are produced by management. These are usually done on an accrual basis but are sometimes done on a cash basis, particularly in smaller companies.
2 Compiled financial statements. These financial statements are developed by an outside accountant or accounting firm based on information supplied by a client. The data is accepted essentially without review or questioning by the outside accountant.
3 Reviewed financial statements. These are financial statements for which an accountant performs some analytical and review procedures trying to identify major problems that need correction, if any. These procedures are far less than those employed in a full audit.
4 Audited financial statements. This is a full set of financial statements, including footnotes, that include an audit opinion from an outside, independent accounting firm as to whether the financial statements are in accordance with GAAP. Audits are performed in accordance with Generally Accepted Auditing Standards (GAAS). Audited financial statements are mandated by the SEC for any annual financial statements that are filed with it. Companies that have any publicly traded debt or equity must file with the SEC, except for certain very small companies. Also, it is a standard covenant in loan agreements that the debtor give annual audited financial statements to the creditor as long as the loan is outstanding. Business partners or shareholders in closely held companies sometimes demand audited financial statements as a condition of their investment.

Test Yourself

1 What is the full name of the accounting rules in the United States?
2 Does GAAP mandate cash or accrual accounting?
3 What are the three types of financial statements reviewed in this chapter?
4 Assets always equal what plus what?

5 Gross revenues minus what two items equals net revenues?

6 Name some major intangible assets for media companies.

7 What is the difference between OCF and EBITDA?

8 What is the difference between EBITDA and EBIT?

9 What is the difference between Operating Income (as usually defined in the media industries) and Operating Income in most other industries?

10 Why is the term "Operating Cash Flow" a misnomer?

11 Is trade revenue and trade expense included in revenues and expenses in GAAP?

12 What are the three sections of the Statement of Cash Flows?

13 What are the four types of financial statements?

Project

Go to the Web site of Viacom at www.viacom.com. Click on the "Investors Relations" link and then on the "Financial Announcements" link. Look at the Earnings Releases and click on "4th Quarter '08." Does Viacom report EBITDA? What does it report?

Resources

www.adage.com/datacenter. (*Advertising Age* magazine's Web site and its Data Center contain a wealth of information)

www.bia.com. (Media industry data, including industry financial data)

http://investing.businessweek.com/research/company/overview/overview.asp. (BusinessWeek's Company Insight Center provides detailed stock information and trends for publicly traded companies)

www.iab.net/resources/ad_revenue.asp. (The IAB's revenue reports)

www.kagan.com. (Information about the media industry)

www.nab.org. (The National Association of Broadcasters (NAB) produces some of the best industry financial data among all trade associations)

www.sec.gov. (US Securities and Exchange Commission.)

15

Marketing

Tim Larson and Ken Foster

Media salespeople no longer can think of themselves exclusively as print, broadcasting, cable, or Internet sales professionals. They are media representatives or marketing communicators, who, although they may work in a specific medium, must have the knowledge and ability to integrate competing media and the 5 Ps of marketing – product, price, promotion, place, and post-purchase service – in order to find, satisfy, and retain customers while making a profit for those customers and their companies.

It is important to understand that all 5 Ps in the marketing mix communicate messages to consumers and customers, not just the marketing promotion P represented by such tactics as advertising, public relations, sales promotion, event marketing, the Internet, and personal selling. As a media salesperson primarily focused on the marketing promotion P, which includes advertising, you still need to know which of the other 5 Ps need attention when serving customers and understand that marketing promotion tactics are not always exclusively the answer to clients' marketing problems.

The McDonald's Corporation represents an example where marketing promotion (which includes advertising) was not the answer to its marketing problem. In 2003, McDonald's was facing a crippling decline in revenue growth and profit for the first time in four decades. Top executives were called together with the creative managers of 10 global advertising agencies, and the group was charged with creating some new advertising ideas. "A great brand like McDonald's deserves great advertising," said McDonald's global chief marketing officer. "If you come up with a great idea, you'll have the chance to see it adopted globally."[1] This quote makes clear that executives at McDonald's saw the company's problem as primarily involving advertising.

Several marketing experts strongly took issue with that supposition, saying that McDonald's had to reassess its whole business model and positioning, that the company's problem was not anchored in its advertising, and better advertising was not the solution. Its problem was its product, a product that faced considerable consumer dissatisfaction. In other words, the problem was not with the *promotion* P but with the *product* P, not with the sizzle but with the steak (or hamburger).

If you were the media salesperson calling on McDonald's, or on any client experiencing a similar marketing problem, you should be knowledgeable enough about the 5 Ps and the marketing mix so you could advise your customers that advertising cannot increase the customer's bottom line if the product itself is the problem. You would make this point carefully and diplomatically, of course. Resist the natural urge to go immediately tactical with your own advertising ideas for a client when the problem lies with one of the remaining 4Ps of the marketing mix.

Throughout this chapter, we use the IMC acronym, which stands for Integrated Marketing Communications. IMC is a customer-focused, data-driven, and technology-facilitated marketing communication process easily integrated into the AESKOPP sales system, and IMC provides a universal framework for coaching, planning, and evaluating sales thinking and action.

Also, for efficiency's sake, the word *product* is used broadly in this chapter, referring to a service, an idea, a destination an institution, an organization, an individual (such as a politician running for office) or anything else that can, generally speaking, be marketed.[2]

Integrated Marketing Communication Planning Model

In today's business-to-business (B2B) or business-to-customer (B2C) marketplace, it is important to use integrated marketing communications (IMC) strategies to manage profitable relationships. Relationship management involves knowing your customers and your customers' consumers. Exhibit 15.1 shows an IMC planning model, which synthesizes the Northwestern University IMC model and marketing author M. Joseph Sirgy's systems approach. It provides a template for you to plan, audit, and monitor a client's marketing communications mix and encourages relationship building up and down the marketing chain.

Each of the seven parts of the IMC planning model in Exhibit 15.1 is discussed below.

Database

The key insight into the database is: Information is power and the database empowers you as a media salesperson. IMC planning begins with research. In order to develop and strengthen a relationship with your customers, you must

Exhibit 15.1 Integrated marketing communications planning model

Database	Purchase history	Demographics	Psychographics	Category network
Segmentation/ classification/ positioning	Differentiation or positioning by: • Product • Price • Service • Place • Promotion • Low price • Cost leadership			Focus related/ segmentation by: • Customer benefit/ problem • Use or application • User or customer image • B2C • B2B
Contact management	Manage all information-bearing experiences a customer or prospect has with the brand, the product category, or the market that relates to the marketer's product or service.			
Strategies, objectives, and tactics	See Exhibit 15.2 for a systems approach to analyzing marketing strategies and corresponding objectives. See Exhibit 15.3 for applicable marketing communication tactics and their relative effectiveness in achieving steps in the selling process.			
Marketing communications mix (5 Ps)	Product, Promotion, Place/distribution, Price, Post-purchase service			
Marketing communications tactics	Mass-media advertising, direct marketing, sales promotion, public relations, event marketing, Internet, word-of-mouth (WOM), personal selling, others			
Monitoring and control	Evaluated from the viewpoint of the media representative, any negative deviations from performance objectives require reassessment and adjustment.			

Source: Adapted from Don E. Schultz, Stanley I. Tannenbaum, and Robert F. Lauterborn. 1995. *The New Marketing Paradigm*. Lincolnwood, IL: NTC Books; M. Joseph Sirgy. 1998. *Integrated Marketing Communications: A Systems Approach*. Upper Saddle River, NJ: Prentice Hall.

first collect data on your customers' consumers. Data are collected in at least four areas: purchase behavior, demographic, psychographic, and category/brand networking, with purchase behavior considered the most useful. This is because conventional wisdom and practice indicate that the best predictor of a future purchase is a past purchase, both of which are quantifiable.

It has always been relatively easy to capture purchase information in business-to-business markets, but now it is nearly as easy in such business-to-customer markets as groceries where mass produced goods are scanned to keep track of purchases made by a large numbers of individual buyers over a long period of time. Demographic, psychographic, and brand/category data are, in turn, collected to better inform the purchase behavior data.

A database is designed to meet the media client's marketing requirements. There is no one type of database that fits all, but, generally, databases fall into one of three overlapping categories.[3]

1   *Historical data management system.* This involves passive data collection, usually including name, address, lead/sales activity, and promotion effort information. These data are used to develop lead and direct marketing lists. This is the simplest database form, and one not very useful by itself to a media salesperson.
2   *Marketing intelligence database.* This data gathering system builds on the historical system by adding purchase data information that allows the marketer to make detailed marketing decisions about future customer purchasing behavior. A media salesperson could productively use this type of database, but the next type may be superior.
3   *Integrated business resource.* This type of database drives your customer's business. All customer information sources and functions are integrated, and every aspect of the business is involved. This type of database provides your customers with valuable information about their business and drives brand value by helping customers manage relationships, including consumer relationships.

Technology has made database management possible, but there are still a variety of means for managing a database that range from low-tech to high-tech. On a small scale, a business card file of historical data is a good start for a database, but should probably be enhanced with additional behavioral information. The larger the list is, the more likely the need for technology to track the information.

Whatever system you use, a database helps you divide your customers' customers into meaningful segments and gives you specific information about who to target in order to achieve a profitable return-on-investment (ROI) for your customers' marketing efforts.

Segmentation

The key insight into segmentation is: It is more important to reach the people who count than to count the people you reach. Using meaningful information from the database, you can identify profitable segments through return-on-investment (ROI), lifetime-customer-value (LCV), or other purchase behavior analyses. Segments can be identified by using various positioning factors or by using any number of business-to-consumer and business-to-business variables, but the most meaningful segments are derived from purchasing behavior data. Important information about buyers might include quantities purchased, price sensitivity, seller loyalty, amount of service required, and of course, susceptibility to advertising, and promotional messages. Using these data, consumers might, for instance, be grouped into such descriptive buying segments as: Programmed Buyer, Relationship Buyer, Bargain Hunter, and The Chiseler.

Of course, you would have to have a critical mass in any one of these segments, but an ROI analysis, for instance, could reveal the most profitable segments. For example, your behavioral analysis might find that The Chiseler segment is very large, but that the buyers in that segment are so price conscious it is not a profitable segment to market to; that it would cost more in advertising and promotion efforts to attract customers in this segment than you could recoup in sales.

You could discover and test any number of purchase behavior segments using an integrated database system. Purchase or buyer behavior segments could be further delineated by customer demographic, psychographic, and category/networking data.

Contact management

The key insight into contact management is: Every contact a consumer has with your customer's product is an important information-bearing experience. The database also is important in this part of the IMC planning process. You identify all the contacts – also called "moments-of-truth" – the consumer has with the product. This gives you a good indication about how to customize messages for each of the consumer segments.

For instance, if you have a customer who is recruiting students to its college, contacts – "moments-of-truth" or information-bearing experiences – might include parents, peers, and school counselors, all of whom may advise or inform a student's choice. Messages to each of these contacts or segments from your college customer would have a one-look-and-feel component – superb education, fun, great professors – but each message would also be customized to satisfy the specific informational needs of each segment. For example, the students get party information, the parents get safety and financial assistance information, and the school counselors get congratulations for directing the students to the college.

Each time you make contact with your customer or your customers' consumers using the mix of the 5 Ps and marketing communications tactics, it is a moment of truth, and you either put money in the brand-equity bank, or you withdraw it, and your relationship (balance) with your customer and your customers' consumers is positively or negatively affected. Inherent in managing contacts is the timing and orchestration of the customized messages you send to each segment. In our college example, orchestration would involve determining which messages to send, to which segments, using what timing, and in what order.

Strategies, objectives, and tactics

The key insight into this step is: Do not play Alice in Wonderland. If a company does not know where it is going and does not have the knowledge to achieve its marketing communications objectives, it is Alice. You may remember in the story that Alice comes to a fork in the road and asks the Cheshire cat which path she should take. The cat asks Alice where she wants to go, and Alice responds she does not know. With a smile, the cat advises her that it makes no difference which path she takes.

Do not be Alice. Before going tactical with marketing-communications, a company needs to know where it is headed and what it wants to accomplish. Remember the McDonald's example at the opening of this chapter. What are your customers' marketing and marketing communications goals and objectives, and what marketing communications mix involving all of the 5 Ps might be employed strategically to achieve them?

In many cases, your clients may not know where they want to go but also may not know where they are. Suppose you ask a frozen yogurt shop, "Who is your target audience?" The customer replies, "Everyone." Clearly, the shop does not know where it is or who its customers are. Suppose you ask, "How is your frozen yogurt different from any other frozen yogurt?" The shop owner replies, "Frozen yogurt is frozen yogurt." Again, the client has not identified a niche, positioning, or unique selling proposition.

Marketing strategies, objectives, and tactics   Exhibit 15.2 provides a marketing compass to guide a company to Alice's tea party and the best mix of marketing strategies, objectives, and tactics to use. The model shows that marketing planning involves selecting among three primary strategies: differentiation, cost leadership, and focus.

Concentrating on a unique and valued one of the 5 Ps is referred to as positioning.

The differentiation or positioning strategy involves a synergy of the 5 P marketing mix (product, price, place, promotion, and post-purchase service), but with emphasis on a single P. Exhibit 15.2 shows several possible positioning variables for each of the 5 Ps.

Utilizing a cost leadership strategy involves designing an entire marketing campaign around the single element of price in the marketing mix. Exhibit 15.2 shows that if a marketer contemplates positioning by low price, it must conduct price research.

The focus strategy is used when a marketer wants to segment by customer benefit or problem, by user or customer image, or by product use or application.

Which of the three strategies a marketer uses depends on the marketer's overall business goals and objectives, the nature of the product, and which combination of the 5 Ps in the marketing mix are of primary concern.

Exhibit 15.2 Marketing strategies and corresponding objectives

Marketing strategies

Differentiation (positioning)		Cost leadership	Focus related (segmentation)
• **Product**	• **Promotion**	• **Low price**	• **Position by**
• Class	• Celebrity	• Conduct	• Customer benefit
• Attribute	spokesperson	pricing	or problem
• Intangibles	• Lifestyle/	research	• User or customer
• Competitors	personality	• Set price to	image
• Country of		value level	• Use or application
origin		• Communicate	
		to target	• **B2C Segmentation**
• **Place**	• **Price**	consumer	• Demographics
• Distributor	• Relative price		• Psychographics
– Tie-ins			• Sociocultural
– Location			• Motivational
– Service			• Consumption
• **Post purchase service**			• **B2B**
• Toll free number or Web contact			• End use
center			• Customer size
• Seamless and uniform customer			• Geographic
interaction			• Motivational
• Customize services and			• Consumption
communicate			• Channel type

Marketing Objectives
Brand awareness   Brand learning/association   Brand trial/purchase
Repeat purchase   Brand attitude

Source: Adapted from M. Joseph Sirgy. 1998. *Integrated Marketing Communications: A Systems Approach.* Upper Saddle River, NJ: Prentice Hall.

Marketing communications strategies, objectives and tactics   After determining a marketing strategy, objectives, and tactics, a marketer can use the system of analysis in Exhibit 15.3 to determine the best marketing-communications tactical mix to achieve the highest return-on-investment from its advertising and promotion efforts.

There are four marketing communications strategies: informative (thinker), affective (feeler), habit formation (doer), and self-satisfaction (reactor). These are borrowed from the ubiquitous Foote-Cone-Belding (FCB) advertising planning

Exhibit 15.3 Marketing communications strategies, objectives and corresponding tactics

Marketing communications strategies and objectives			
Brand awareness	*Brand learning/association*	*Brand trial/ purchase/repeat purchase*	*Brand attitude*
Generate maximum awareness and learning	Generate maximum awareness and positive attitude (liking)	Induce trial purchase and learning from product use (first timers) and reinforce learning (repeat users)	Induce trial purchase and brand liking from product use (first timers and reinforce positive attitude (repeat users
		Marketing communications tactical mix	
• Advertising (mostly print) • Reseller support (training, trade shows) • Public relations (press releases and publicity) • WOM (stimulate WOM through advertising and sampling referral system)	• Advertising (mostly broadcast) • Reseller support (cooperative advertising) • Public relations (press conference, corporate ads and event sponsorship) • WOM communication (stimulate WOM through advertising)	• Advertising (mostly print and interactive) • Direct marketing (direct mail, newsletter, direct response advertising) • Sales promotion (coupons, sampling, refunds and rebates, bonus packs, and price-off deals)	• Ad (outdoor and specialty) • Direct marketing (catalogs, direct response advertising, telemarketing and direct selling) • Sales promotion (premium and contests, sweepstakes) • Reseller support (contests and incentives, POP and personal selling) • Public relations (corporate ads, event sponsorship, product placement in movies and TV

Source: Adapted from M. Joseph Sirgy. 1998. *Integrated Marketing Communications: A Systems Approach.* Upper Saddle River, NJ: Prentice Hall.

model. The informative (thinker) strategy is used when a marketer wants to educate and inform a customer about important costs or benefits and generate maximum awareness and learning. Print and Interactive are good media for this strategy. The affective (feeler) strategy is used when a marketer wants to generate maximum awareness and a positive attitude or liking toward a branded product. Television and radio are excellent media for this strategy. The habit formation (doer) strategy is used to induce product trials and learning-from-use for first-time buyers, and to reinforce learning for repeat buyers. Sampling promotions are good for this strategy. The self-satisfaction (reactor) strategy is used to reinforce positive attitudes of repeat users. Television, radio, print, Interactive, and outdoor are all good media for this strategy.

The strategic mix of advertising, reseller support, public relations, word of mouth (WOM), direct marketing, point of purchase, sales promotion, and the other marketing communications tactics appropriate for each of the four marketing communications strategies are also shown in Exhibit 15.3.

Not discussed above is a marketer's overall business strategy. It is assumed in using the above marketing and marketing communications models that a marketer's goal is to grow its business and that marketing and marketing-communications can facilitate that goal. If a marketer's overall business goal is to harvest or divest, marketing functions are probably not involved. The objective of a harvest or divest business strategy is usually to maximize profits while minimizing costs. Marketing represents a business expense and takes resources away from this objective. It is important that you clearly identify your customers' overall business goals before you make marketing and marketing communications recommendations for them.

The 5 Ps of the Marketing Communications Mix

The key insight into this step in the marketing communications process is: If you change one, you change them all. If you have ever broken a rack of pool balls, you know you cannot move one ball without moving all the others. The same holds true for the marketing mix. Granted, each marketing-communications tool and tactic in the mix has intrinsic value, but the each of these values in the marketing mix changes when one changes.

The use-ratio of the 5 Ps, including marketing-communications tactics, known as the marketing mix, varies for each organization. For example, Mrs. Field's, the cookie maker, emphasizes place (distribution) and product in its mix, with very little attention given to promotion or pricing. If you changed the Mrs. Field's use-ratio, you would change the communication value of the entire marketing mix. Mrs. Field's locates its stores in high traffic locations and blows the exhaust of its ovens into the mall or street to tempt customers with the smell of baking cookies.

The 5 P marketing mix of Mrs. Field's is first and foremost place (location, location, location), then product and, finally, price, with little or no attention given to post-purchase service.

Change that mix and you change everything. For instance, the marketing mix for a typical bank is quite different. A bank also emphasizes location or place, but gives primary consideration to its service, product, pricing, and promotion. Change the bank's use-ratio to match the Mrs. Field's mix where distribution is emphasized over the other 4Ps, and you may have a run on the bank. Marketers should experiment with the marketing-communications mix to observe which use-ratio of tactics works best and produces a result greater than the sum of the individual parts.

As was made clear in the McDonald's case at the beginning of this chapter, it is important to remember that all Ps in the marketing-communications process communicate, not just the marketing promotion tactics. The following explains this assertion more fully.

Product communicates

The product lifecycle (PLC) model is grounded in what is called hierarchy-of-effects theory, in that the PLC principle suggests that every product, service or idea, goes through a series of steps or phases from birth to death, the first being an *introduction* phase. If it survives *introduction*, the product goes through a *growth* phase where different marketing-communications strategies, and tactics are implemented. Eventually, the product will *mature* to where still other strategies are required in order to maintain competitiveness. Most products eventually die, but the majority also experiences a *decline* phase, where still other unique strategies apply.[4]

The typical lifecycle of a product and the strategies relevant to each phase in the lifecycle are shown below. You should note how critical mass-media advertising and promotion are in each of the product lifecycle phases.

When a product is first introduced, heavy advertising and promotion efforts are required to keep the product before the public. If a product is successful, then competitors become an issue in the growth phase, and again advertising and promotion are required to differentiate the product from its competition.

Tide detergent, for instance, was introduced in 1948. Since that time it has been marketed as a "new and improved" product every few years in order to elongate its lifecycle. So just as in the *introduction* phase, Tide's advertising and promotion reintroduces the "new" Tide product to the marketplace in the *maturity* phase. Only during a product's *decline* phase is advertising less critical. During this last phase, marketers milk the cash cow by cutting expenses related to advertising and promotion. This is done to maintain some profit margin while product demand dwindles.

Exhibit 15.4   Product lifecycle

Introduction	Growth	Maturity	Decline
• Raise awareness • Sell into distribution chain • Target early adopters	• Continue awareness campaign • Relationship sales • Distribution chain coverage • Possibly reduce advertising and promotion • R&D on product innovation	• Innovation • Include advertising and promotion • Price to meet competition • Line extensions	• Harvest profits • Limit distribution • Less price sensitivity • Less advertising and promotion

Another marketing model related to how product communicates is Rogers's *diffusion of innovation model*. Sometimes called the adoption model, this model helps marketers strategize with regard to how consumers adopt new products over a period time.[5] In Rogers's model, only a small segment (2.5 percent) of a target population, labeled *innovators*, is willing to try radically new products. A slightly larger group (13.5 percent), the *early adopters*, lets the innovators experiment for a period of time before they adopt a product, while a two-thirds majority, the *early majority* and the *late majority* of the population (68 percent), represent a critical mass of potential consumers after a product has developed and been branded. Finally, a smaller group (16 percent) of *laggards* is the last segment to adopt a new – maybe at this point old – product.

A database should contain consumer information indicating where in the diffusion of innovation model consumers reside, helping marketers customize messages targeted at the most profitable segments, keeping in mind that the return-on-investment from the people in the *innovator* and *early adopters* segments may be less than the marketing-communication expenditures used to attract them. Marketers may nevertheless have to market to these segments, initially by charging higher prices and selling at a loss, in hopes of creating loyal customers when people in these segments move to the *majority* stages of adoption.

To better achieve success, several other general principles are important when introducing a new product or marketing an existing one.

- Heavy and effective advertising and promotion are critical for new brands.
- Besides promoting the brand, effective advertising is also important to promote the distribution method.
- Effective advertising increases the likelihood of success threefold.

- New products deliver incremental volume for both the manufacturer and the retailer, so the likelihood of co-op advertising and promotion is strong.
- Long-term support is essential: think "introductory" for at least two years.
- All products decline, plan for it.

Price communicates

As discussed earlier, price in the communications mix has more duties than simply generating revenue for a marketer. It also communicates. Listed below are some major pricing strategies and how they are likely to be impacted by marketing-communications tactics such as mass-media advertising. Salespeople should be knowledgeable about these strategies in order to advise clients and provide solutions to them.

Pricing strategies

Skimming. Skim the cream from the consumers who can afford a higher price. Lower the price over time. A skimming strategy will utilize targeted advertising and promotion to reach consumers with high incomes.

Prestige. "You get what you pay for." Set price high to communicate higher quality. Though prestige pricing is not usually advertised, make sure all the other variables of the marketing mix are consistent with a prestige approach. On occasion, prestige pricing is advertised to screen nonqualified consumers and to add to the value of the product.

Loss leader. Keep margins low on an item to pull customers into the store. The loss leader approach requires heavy advertising and is commonly used in the retail business. It is important to integrate in-store signage wherever the loss leader approach is used.

Full-line pricing. Keep margins low on a brand's products in order to sell the rest of the line.

Volume pricing. Keep prices low to generate more dollar volume rather than dollar margin.

Off-pricing. Communicate the previous price to show savings of the new price.

Odd-pricing. Odd numbers communicate a more real or precise price, lending price some credibility. Volume pricing, off-pricing, and odd-pricing also require advertising support.

Penetration. Cover the market with price oriented product and blitzing promotion. Penetration pricing requires an advertising blitz. It is commonly used with roadblock or other means of obtaining rapid reach. A roadblock is the purchase of all of available advertising on a particular time period, such as at an 11:00 p.m. break on a local television station, thus blocking out competitive advertising and potentially reaching everyone watching TV at that time.

Competitive pricing. Set prices to match or surpass competition.
Customary pricing. Priced based on custom, or what it has always cost.

Some marketers may fall into a category of regulated pricing, that is, they do not have control over what the price should be. State colleges and universities are examples: they advertise many of their educational programs and degrees but do not have control of tuition. It is important to ensure that the pricing strategy is consistent with all other variables of the marketing mix. For example as indicated above, if a pricing strategy is prestige, then promotional material must look and feel prestigious. It makes common sense for all variables of the marketing mix to be consistent all of the time.

Place communicates

At first glance, distribution methods may not appear to be associated with advertising and promotion, but it makes sense to consider the marketing-communications tactics that can be used at all levels in the distribution process. Simply speaking, distribution means to get the product or service from the marketing organization to the consumer in the B2B and B2C distribution chain.

Marketers may be any one of the businesses in the distribution chain – manufacturer, agent, wholesaler, or retailer. Each distribution channel has different needs, different relationships with its suppliers and clients, and different laws and rules governing its part in the distribution process. But each channel partner may be inclined to support advertising and promotion to meet its unique needs. All channel members communicate, not just the retailer. Place communicates and is fertile ground for strategic marketing-communications employment.

For some media such as newspapers and television, it is important to keep in mind that circulation or signal propagation may reach geographic areas that extend beyond a customer's travel range. However, businesses can increase their draw from distant areas if the customers are loyal or are destination purchasers. This is especially true for higher priced items such as automobiles, furniture, and appliances.

Marketing promotion communicates

And, of course, marketing promotion communicates. The possible mix of marketing-communications tactics is very broad. However, it is important to know the strengths and weaknesses of each tactic and how each is useful and effective depending on a marketer's goals and objectives. Exhibit 15.5 shows how marketers can employ marketing-communications tactics to move a buyer through the five mental steps in the buying process beginning with *Awareness*, followed by progressively more personal tactics to move the buyer through the last several steps,

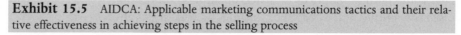

Exhibit 15.5   AIDCA: Applicable marketing communications tactics and their relative effectiveness in achieving steps in the selling process

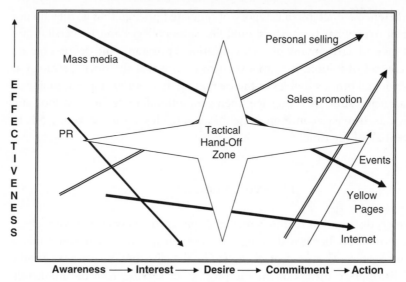

Interest, Desire, and *Commitment* to *Action.* This model is known by the AIDCA acronym.

You can see in the AIDCA model that mass-media tactics, with their potentially higher reach, are effective at creating *Awareness* and less effective in creating *Action* (purchase), where more personal tactics are usually needed. On the other hand, note that personal selling, with its fewer contacts and limited reach, is considerably less effective in creating *Awareness,* but more effective in creating *Action.* Several of the other marketing communications tactics and their relative effectiveness at each step are also shown in Exhibit 15.5. Note that PR helps to create *Awareness* but is of little effectiveness as you move toward the *Action* end of the five mental-step process. Likewise, sales promotion has little effect on the *Awareness* end of the process but is helpful in creating *Action.*

While mass-media tactics involve sellers who are looking for buyers, the Yellow Pages or, often, Google involve buyers who are looking for sellers. (When was the last time you browsed the Yellow Pages with no product in mind?) As such, mass-media advertising and promotion are used to create *Awareness,* and the Yellow Pages are used to produce behavior more on the *Action* end of the continuum. The effectiveness of event marketing at any AIDCA step depends on the size and purpose of the event.

An important point to be gleaned from Exhibit 15.5 is that there is a "Tactical Hand-Off Zone" in the AIDCA model. Because no marketing-communications tactic is totally effective at every mental-step in the buying process, an integrated

mix of tactics must be employed. As such, as a media salesperson you might recommend using mass-media tactics to create *Awareness* at the beginning of a schedule or campaign and then recommend handing off the responsibility of creating
Action (purchase) to more personal tactics, such as sales promotion or personal
selling.

A salesperson's knowledge of the strengths and weaknesses of each marketing
communications tool and tactic and its strategic mix is put to a test in the "Tactical
Hand-Off Zone." Some basic knowledge of the effectiveness of each medium, not
only the one(s) you sell, will go a long way in helping you develop a relationship
with your clients and create brand value for your client's product.

Listed below are some common marketing strategies that affect the marketing-
communications tactical mix.

Seasonality. Seasonal products affect advertising and promotion placement. Though
seasonality is often obvious, such as skis going on sale for winter, there are
some products and services for which seasonality is less apparent. Exactly how
far in advance of the buying season media should be placed is product specific
and often debatable. Working with your client, you will know when this strategy is applicable. The best way to find out seasonality is to ask your client
during the Discovery Questions.

Competitive strategies. Some advertisers often run campaigns head-to-head with
competitors. Others choose to fight the competition and "hit them where they
ain't" by using media in which competitors do not advertise.

Market share. To grow market share, you can either steal from the competition or
stimulate the entire market to buy more of what you are selling. However,
stimulating the entire market may benefit competition as well and can be quite
costly. To steal from the competition requires targeted advertising and an effective message.

Geographic targeting. Marketing that requires geographic targeting, whether
national, regional, or local, has a direct effect on which marketing communications tactics a marketer will use. For instance, if a marketer is targeting a small
geographic area, possibly a zip code, it might not use mass media. On the other
hand, it is important to realize that today's population is extremely mobile. A
small advertiser might well benefit from mass-media placement with extensive
reach simply because consumers can buy online.

Product strategies. When introducing a new product or innovating an existing
product, advertising and promotion support is required. Salespeople should
watch for new product introductions or innovations that are candidates for their
medium.

Branding strategies. There are two major strategies for branding: the so-called
Ford and General Motors approaches. The Ford approach suggests naming
every product line after the Ford brand – Ford Explorer, Ford Mustang, and
Ford Focus. General Motors's products utilize the secondary umbrella, such as

Chevrolet Impala or Pontiac Grand Prix, and generally ignore the General Motors brand.

Rule of thumb: If the sub-brand benefits from the umbrella brand, use it – Fox News or Sara Lee pastries, for example. When the umbrella brand is not a match, do not use it – Sara Lee luggage is not a match. In either event, marketers must determine the assistance advertising and promotion can provide branding and recognize the importance of the mass media in the branding effort, especially if the product is new.

Packaging strategies. New labels, a new functional design, a more convenient pouring spout, for example, all require mass-media assistance to inform the consumer of package changes.

Sales promotion support. As a media salesperson, you recognize already that the more a potential customer knows about your product, the better your chance of making a sale. You can also use mass-media advertising and sales promotion tactics to inform clients about your product.

Event marketing. Events are designed to meet specific needs of targeted consumers and have the capability of demonstrating products and developing brand loyalty. Advertising and promotion support can drive a lot of traffic to an event.

Merchandising. Integration with in-store signage and point-of-purchase (POP) displays can improve turnover rate and retail sales. It is important for salespeople to work backwards, that is, to go into the store to check out merchandising and then attempt to sell mass-media advertising and promotion support to their clients. Many studies have shown advertising increases turnover rate for retailers, and the higher the turnover the better the ROI for retail space.

Public relations and publicity. Many marketers depend on public relations and publicity to promote their products. However, advertising and promotion can go a long way to leverage the effect of PR and publicity efforts. Since marketers tend to provide public relations just prior to breaking a mass-media campaign, public relations can be an indication of a pending advertising expenditure.

Market research. Many marketers engage in market research prior to initiating a major campaign. It may be wise to provide assistance, perhaps even free public service announcements for the research, so you keep a foot in the door for the campaign roll-out based on the research.

Common sense and good IMC practice dictate that all 5 Ps in the marketing-communications mix communicate and that they must be integrated. The products marketers develop communicates (their color, size, sound – listen to a Harley or a Coke), smell (Mrs. Field's), and function ("Nothing runs like a Deere"), all communicate. The price you charge communicates – higher price is usually associated with higher quality; lower price with lesser quality and prestige. The place where a marketers distribute its product communicates – Nordstrom's versus Wall-Mart versus the Internet. Certainly, a marketer's post-purchase service communicates and either creates a loyal customer and repeat business or drives customers to the competition. And, of course, marketing promotion communicates – mass-media advertising, PR, personal selling, sales promotion, events, the Internet, word of mouth, matchbook covers, whatever, all communicate and have relative strengths, weaknesses and levels of effectiveness when integrated.

Monitoring and Control

The key insight here is that monitoring and control are not actually steps in the marketing-communication planning process. Monitoring and control are ongoing, carried on from start to finish of a marketing effort to assess whether the marketing-communications plan is meeting a marketer's performance objectives.

Negative deviations from stated corporate, marketing, and marketing-communications performance objectives require ongoing reassessment to discover weaknesses and failures in the plan as it is executed. This allows marketers to make adjustments at any point in the execution of the plan.

Failure to meet objectives at any level – corporate, marketing, or marketing communications – does not necessarily mean a marketing plan is a poor one. In reassessing the plan, marketers may discover the objectives were not realistic, the budget was too small to accomplish stated objectives, or the time allotted to achieve the objectives was too short. With close monitoring and control, timely and salient adjustments can seamlessly be made to the errant objectives, and the execution of the plan can continue uninterrupted.[6]

Test Yourself

1   What are the 5 Ps in the marketing-communication mix?
2   Identify and briefly explain each of the seven steps of the IMC planning model?
3   List and briefly explain each of the three marketing planning strategies.
4   List and briefly delineate the four marketing-communications strategies.
5   Discuss the concept of the Tactical Hand-Off Zone in the AIDCA model.

Project

As a media salesperson, assume you have a hybrid car dealer as a client. What useful purchase behavior and other data would you collect on your client's customers? Using that data, identify and describe four meaningful buyer behavior segments. Next, suggest and support the best pricing strategy your hybrid car dealer client could use to sell product to people in each of the four segments. Finally, identify the key insight to understanding each segment and write a one-sentence, customized message targeted to each of the segments.

References

Gary Armstrong and Philip Kotler. 2003. *Marketing*, 6th edition. Upper Saddle River, NJ: Prentice Hall.

George E. Belch and Michael A. Belch. 2001. *Advertising and Promotion: An Integrated Marketing Communications Perspective*, 5th edition. Boston: McGraw-Hill.

Alvin C. Burns and Ronald F. Bush. 2003. *Marketing Research*, 4th edition. Upper Saddle River, NJ: Prentice Hall.

Clarke L. Caywood. 1997. *The Handbook of Strategic Public Relations and Integrated Communications*. New York: McGraw-Hill.

Stuart Elliott. 2003. "McDonald's stung by a loss, summons a high-level meeting to rework its marketing." *New York Times*, February 4.

James G. Hutton, and Francis J. Mulhern. 2002. *Marketing Communications: Integrated Theory, Strategy and Tactics*. Hackensack, NJ: Pentagram.

Rob Jackson and Paul Wang, P. 1994. *Strategic Database Marketing*. Lincolnwood, IL: NTC Books.

Everett M. Rogers. 1983. *Diffusion of Innovations*, 4th edition. New York: Simon & Schuster.

Don E. Schultz, Stanley I. Tannenbaum, and Robert F. Lauterborn. 1995. *The New Marketing Paradigm*. Lincolnwood, IL: NTC Books.

M. Joseph Sirgy. 1998. *Integrated Marketing Communications: A Systems Approach*. Upper Saddle River, NJ: Prentice Hall.

Notes

1   Stuart Elliott. February 4, 2003. "McDonald's stung by a loss, summons a high-level meeting to rework its marketing," *New York Times*, Internet Business/Financial Desk: NYTDirect@nytimes.com.

2   James G. Hutton, and Francis J. Mulhern. 2002. *Marketing Communications: Integrated Theory, Strategy and Tactics*. Hackensack, NJ: Pentagram, p. 4.

3   Rob Jackson and Paul Wang, P. 1994. *Strategic Database Marketing*. Lincolnwood, IL: NTC Books, p 27

4   Gary Armstrong and Philip Kotler. 2003. *Marketing*, 6th edition. Upper Saddle River, NJ: Prentice Hall, p. 337.

5   Everett M. Rogers. 1983. *Diffusion of Innovations*, 4th edition. New York: Simon & Schuster.

6   M. Joseph Sirgy. 1998. *Integrated Marketing Communications: A Systems Approach*. Upper Saddle River, NJ: Prentice Hall.

16

Media Research

Roger Baron

Your job as a salesperson for a radio or television station, a magazine, an Internet Web site, or any other medium is to sell time or space to display an advertiser's message. But what you are really selling is an estimate of the number of people who will be exposed to that message. The more people who see the advertising, the more money you get. Media sales is one of the few professions where the product you are selling is made by someone else – the research company that produces those estimates. To be an effective salesperson, you need to understand what the numbers mean, where they come from, their strengths and weaknesses, and the simple math that drives how you use them.

This chapter begins with research concepts that apply to all media – the general principles of media research that media planners and buyers use when they talk about a media plan. Then we will see how these concepts apply to each of the major media. We will take a brief look at the five "impossible" questions that every salesperson encounters in the course of their work – questions that media research cannot definitively answer. The chapter wraps up with an annotated list of media research resources available free on the Internet.

General Principles of Media Research

Target audience

All media planning begins with a statement of the target audience, which is a description of the people an advertiser is trying to reach. The target audience is the most important marketing decision an advertiser will make because it drives all of an advertiser's subsequent decisions, and all of your decisions as you sell your medium. Which programs have the largest audience for this target audience? Which programs have the greatest percent of the target audience among its viewers? When is the best time to reach them? What promotional materials, what colors, what style will be most appealing to this target group?

This core marketing decision is not always obvious; an advertiser may need your help. For example, everyone with a house needs carpets, but the carpet store's target audience is usually the person who makes the purchase decision. Customer research you have access to may reveal that women are the first to notice that the old carpet needs replacing, but it is a joint decision between husband and wife about which store to go to and which carpet to buy. The same research may find that the majority of carpet buyers are between the ages of 35 and 54. So the primary target audience for this advertiser might be adults between the ages 35 and 54, expressed in media shorthand as A35–54.

Geography

When we think about where people live, it is usually in political or even postal terms: states, cities, counties and perhaps zip codes. For media sales, what matters is the geographic area where the advertising can be seen or heard, although for research purposes, that area must be adjusted to reflect the counties reported in the US Census. For national television on the broadcast networks, cable or syndication, the coverage area is the entire country. For local radio it is the counties that are covered by a station's signal, generally the Standard Metropolitan Statistical Area (SMSA). For local television, it is the counties in the Designated Market Area (DMA), which Nielsen defines as all the counties where the stations of a given city get the plurality of viewing. More about DMAs later.

Target audience universe

Media coverage areas are defined in terms of counties because we need the census data to tell us how many people live there. This Universe Estimate (UE) is the denominator that will be used to calculate ratings. Knowing that 75,000 people watch the early news on a television station is interesting, but to be meaningful for comparison purposes, it must be expressed as a percentage of the people living in the area. Rating services such as Nielsen and Arbitron report this UE for every age/sex demographic. So, for instance, in 2007 there were 2,027,006 men between the ages of 25 and 54 living in television households in the Chicago television market (DMA). The age breaks are defined by the Census Bureau, so, for instance, there is no UE (and, therefore, no rating) for men age 27 to 42 – a group not defined by the Census Bureau. The television UE is expressed as the number of people living in households with a TV set because most, but not every, home has one.

Advertising impressions

An advertising impression is a single exposure of a message to one person in the target audience. This sounds simple, but the exact meaning of exposure is different for each medium, and is governed by the way the medium is measured by the research companies. For television, it can mean the people who push a button on Nielsen's People Meter to indicate they are watching television. But are they paying attention to the set? Do they watch every minute? Do they remember to punch out of the meter when they go to the bathroom or put the kids to bed? Do they continue watching during commercials? These are the kind of questions that are discussed at industry conferences, but the only thing that matters to you as a salesperson is the number reported by Nielsen.

In smaller markets, a television impression means the viewer wrote in a time-formatted diary that he/she was watching a channel during a given quarter-hour of the day. The diary cannot hope to accurately reflect the channel surfing usually associated with TV viewing, but this is the best Nielsen can do for smaller markets that cannot afford the expensive people meter methodology.

Radio is measured by the Arbitron company with a quarter-hour formatted diary where listeners record the station they were listening to. Over the next few years, the radio diary will be replaced by the Portable People Meter that detects an inaudible code to identify the station. Note that the definition of impression will change from "listening to the radio" to "being within earshot of the loudspeaker."

Gross impressions   Just as cooks never talk about one bean or one pea in a recipe, advertisers never talk about one impression. The concept of gross impressions begins with the total number of people watching a television program or listening to a radio station at a given moment. This can easily number in the millions. In the average minute of the 2007 Super Bowl, 24.3 million men age 25–54 were watching the action. Thus, a single commercial in the Super Bowl was seen by 24.3 million men 25–54 and that commercial received 24.3 million impressions.

But the concept of gross impressions is more than that. It is the simple addition of the impressions every time an ad is displayed.

GROSS IMPRESSIONS = the simple addition of impressions every time
an ad runs

In the 2007 Super Bowl, a Bud Light commercial ran six times. Each time it was watched by 24.3 million men age 25–54. By the end of the evening, Bud Light had accumulated 145.8 million gross impressions ($6 \times 24{,}300{,}000 = 145{,}800{,}000$). Note that this does not account for duplication. Surely some of the men saw the commercial several times, but gross impressions reflect the total *media weight* for the game. The same concept applies over any period of time and any number of programs. Planners typically think in terms of weekly media weight.

Rating

Talking about hundreds of millions of impressions is mind-boggling. It is much more meaningful to think of the impressions as the percentage of the target audience universe. This percentage is called a rating. To calculate it, simply divide the impressions by the target universe and multiply by 100 to get the percentage.

> RATING = the percentage of the universe that is watching or listening to
>   a given program

According to the Nielsen national UE, 60.4 million men age 25–54 live in United States television households. And we know that 24.3 million of them watched the average minute of the 2007 Super Bowl. So, 24.3 million divided by 60.4 million = 40.3 percent. Ratings are always expressed in terms of the appropriate demographic, so a salesperson might say that the Super Bowl got a 40.3 rating against men 25–54. Expressed more precisely, 40.3 percent of men age 25–54 were watching (had their People Meter button pushed) during the average minute of the 2007 Super Bowl. This is the Average Minute or Average Audience (AA) rating.

Note that this 40.3 rating is for the Super Bowl, which is about the only program on television to get such a high rating. The rating of most primetime network TV programs is less than 5, and cable ratings are generally less than 1.

The same concept works in a local television market; although, because of the way a diary is formatted, ratings are expressed as an average-quarter-hour (AQH) audience instead of the average minute. As noted earlier, the Chicago DMA has 2.03 million men age 25–54. According to Nielsen, 951,000 of them watched the average-quarter-hour of the 2007 Super Bowl. So 951,000/2.03 million is a 47 rating. Expressed as a sentence, 47 percent of Chicago men age 25–54 watched the average-quarter-hour of the 2007 Super Bowl. Since the Bears were playing, it is not surprising that the Chicago rating was higher than the national rating.

Because radio is still measured with a diary in most markets, a radio rating is also expressed as an average-quarter-hour (AQH) audience. Also, because local radio is sold by daypart instead of by program, a rating refers to an average-quarter-hour of the broad time period. So if a Chicago radio station gets a 1.3 AQH M18–34 rating in morning drive time, it means 1.3 percent of the men age 18–34 who live in the Chicago metro area have written in their diary that they listened to that station during the average-quarter-hour (the average of the 80 quarter hours) Monday–Friday from 6 to 10 a.m. Because radio advertisers buy spots that are evenly rotated through all the days and times in the daypart, the average is the most practical measure of a station's audience.

Magazine advertising is sold issue by issue, but there are several different ways of measuring how many people will see the advertising. Mediamark Research, Inc. (MRI) shows its respondents a black-and-white rendering of the magazine's logo and asks if they are sure they have "read or looked into" it during the last publication period (a week for weeklies, a month for monthlies, and so forth). Because this question can apply to any particular issue of the magazine, the result is a measure of how many people read the average issue – called the Average Issue Audience or AIA. Newspaper readership is also defined in terms of AIA (weekday or weekend/Sunday), but the measure is less important as a sales tool because newspapers are primarily evaluated in terms of the geographic area they serve. Although the math of an AIA is the same as for a rating, the word "rating" is reserved for broadcast audiences. Another word for a magazine or newspaper's Average Issue Audience is its coverage.

The concept of a rating is different when it comes to the Internet. When an advertiser runs a commercial in a television program, instantly millions of people see the ad. By contrast, Internet advertising is bought one impression at a time at a price often based on cost-per-thousand impressions. An advertiser may decide to buy 500,000 impressions on ESPN.com. That can be divided by the universe to get the same thing as a rating, but unlike broadcast, an Internet Web site's rating is determined by how many impressions the advertiser wants to buy, not by the medium.

Unlike broadcast, where advertisers must use a sample to estimate how many people are exposed to an ad and then what effect it has on sales, Internet advertisers know with great precision how many times an ad was served, how many times an ad was clicked on, and how many times people bought something after clicking on an ad, even if they do not know who saw or clicked on it. Internet advertising is sold based on two different models, as you will learn in Chapter 20 – an impressions model and a performance model. For the time being, the term that has the most meaning for Internet advertising is gross impressions.

Gross rating points

For planning purposes, advertisers add the ratings of all the programs where the advertising appears to get gross rating points or GRPs. This is the same concept as gross impressions, only expressed as the sum of the rating points.

GROSS RATING POINTS = the addition of rating points every time an ad runs.

Gross rating points are typically used to describe the message weight per week or per month, although it can be used for any period of time. Following is an example of a schedule that will deliver 120 gross rating points a week:

Three commercials, each with a 15 rating	=	45 GRPs
Five commercials, each with a 10 rating	=	50 GRPs
Five commercials, each with a 5 rating	=	<u>25 GRPs</u>
Total weekly GRPs		120 GRPs

Is it possible to have more than 100 GRPs? Sure. Since GRPs are the simple addition of the ratings, there is no limit to the number of points that can be scheduled. Quick-serve restaurants, movies, and other heavy promotional advertisers typically run at least 250 GRPs in a week. Occasionally a television advertiser will run four or five hundred GRPs a week, giving viewers the feeling that they see the commercial every time they turn on a television set.

Although it would be nice, no advertiser is going to buy all the planned GRPs on one station. As a salesperson, you are concerned with getting your share of the buy. You will probably not be told how many total GRPs are being bought or what the total budget is. But those numbers exist, and are at the top of the buyer's mind as she works to buy the required GRPs for the budget she has been given.

The GRP concept can be extended to other media such as radio, magazines, and newspapers. In magazines, for example, gross rating points equals the average issue audience multiplied by the number of ad insertions. For example:

People magazine's average issue audience (coverage) of women age 18+ = 25.4%
    Number of ads to be placed in *People* = 5, thus gross rating points (GRPs) = 127.0

An advertiser who runs a single insertion in several magazines would calculate gross rating points by adding the target audience coverage of each insertion.

W18+ coverage of *People*	=	25.4
W18+ coverage of *Reader's Digest*	=	19.6
W18+ coverage of *Shape*	=	4.5
W18+ coverage of *New Yorker*	=	<u>1.7</u>
Gross ratings points		51.2
		(rounded to 51 GRPs)

For many years the Outdoor Advertising Association of America has used a showing as its basic unit of sale for the outdoor industry. A showing is defined as the number of poster panels needed in a market to produce a daily effective circulation (daily vehicular traffic past any of the boards) equal to a certain percentage of its population. So a 100 showing would equal the number of billboards needed so that the daily effective circulation is equal to the market's population, 100 percent, or 100 GRPs per day. Other units of sale would be expressed as fractions of this basic unit: a 75 showing is 75 gross rating points daily, a 50 showing is 50 gross rating points daily, and so on.

The outdoor industry is working to replace the showing concept with impressions based on the number of people passing each billboard in a market every day. This would allow outdoor to be planned in the same way as other media; however industry observers expect it will be several years before such a fundamental change is implemented.

Reach and frequency

It should be obvious that gross rating points do not account for duplication. In the magazine example, a reader of both *People* and *Reader's Digest* would be exposed to the ad twice, while a reader of all four magazines might see the ad four times.

> REACH = The percentage of a target audience that is exposed to an ad at least once
>
> FREQUENCY = The average number of times that a person who was reached sees an ad

These three concepts are bound together with the equation:

GROSS RATING POINTS = Reach × Frequency.

For example, a television schedule of 200 W25–54 GRPs in primetime is a collection of spots whose W25–54 ratings add up to 200. Computer models based on Nielsen data tell us this schedule will be seen by (will reach) 61 percent of these women an average of 3.3 times (61 × 3.3 = 200). Some will see the commercial only once, others will see it many times, but the average woman who was reached will see it 3.3 times. Conversely, 39 percent will never see the commercial.

Exhibit 16.1 illustrates the concepts of reach and frequency using a hypothetical schedule of four television programs in a market with 10 households; thus when a program is seen in only one home, it gets a 10 rating.

Reading across Exhibit 16.1, the first home has received two impressions ("Two and a Half Men" and "CSI Miami"), but is counted only once toward reach. The second home did not see any of the telecasts or commercials. The third home was exposed once, the fourth home three times, and so on. By the end of the week, the four telecasts have accumulated 110 GRPs, reaching 60 percent of the homes one or more times, and the average home that was reached saw the commercial 1.83 times. Other terms that are sometimes used to describe net reach are cumulative audience (referred to as cume), net unduplicated audience, or net reach. Each is correct, but in popular usage media buyers are more likely to say, "The reach of these four programs is 60 percent." Note how GRPs and reach increase with each telecast. Frequency is calculated as GRPs divided by reach. So, in the last row of the table, 90/50 = 1.8 and 110/60 = 1.83.

Exhibit 16.1   Reach/frequency of a one-week television commercial schedule – four commercials

Home	"American Idol" 6/22 8:05 p.m.	"Two and a Half Men" 6/24 8:27 p.m.	"CSI Miami" 6/28 9:15 p.m.	"Boston Legal" 6/29 10:22 p.m.	Total impressions
#1		X	X		2
#2					0
#3				X	1
#4	X	X	X		3
#5	X			X	2
#6					0
#7			X		1
#8					0
#9	X		X		2
#10					0
Ratings	30	20	40	20	0 = 40%
GRPs	30	50	90	110	1 = 20%
Reach	30%	40%	50%	60%	2 = 30%
Frequency	1.0	1.25	1.8	1.83	3 = 10%

The numbers at the lower right of the table show the percent of homes exposed different numbers of times (a frequency distribution). Four homes (40 percent) never saw the commercial – were never reached. Two homes (20 percent) saw the commercial only once. Three homes (30 percent) saw it twice. And one home saw it three times.

The sales unit and media efficiency

Everything that is sold comes in some kind of unit. Meat is sold in pounds, gasoline in gallons, fabric in yards, and so forth. In television and radio the unit of sale is typically the 30-second commercial; in magazines, the page; and in newspapers, the column inch. But the unit itself is meaningless without the associated audience that tells us how many people will see it. By long-standing convention, advertisers use cost-per-thousand impressions as the measure of media efficiency. It is calculated by simply dividing the cost of the ad by thousands of impressions. Here is an example:

A 30-second spot on "Boston Legal" costs $160,000

The average minute W25–54 impressions = 2,800,000

Cost-per-thousand (CPM) W25–54 = $160,000/2,800 = $57.14

At the same time, another channel is running "Law & Order: Criminal Intent." A 30-second spot on this show costs $152,000 and is watched by 2,221,000 W25–54. This is less money but proportionally even fewer target viewers. The CPM for this spot is $152,000/2,221 = $68.44. The program has a higher CPM and so is less efficient in reaching W 25–54 than "Boston Legal."

Broadcast planning with cost-per-rating-point (CPP)

CPM is useful for comparing the efficiency of different programs, schedules, or media, but for planning purposes the cost-per-rating-point (CPP) metric is more practical. CPP is used when planning spot television or radio. As we saw earlier, the 2.221 million W25–54 impressions for "Law & Order: Criminal Intent" can be expressed as a rating. There are 62.1 million women age 25–54 in the United States. The show's rating among this group is 2.221 million/62.1 million = 0.0357, or expressed as a percent, or rating, 3.57.

So the CPP of this network program is $152,000/3.57 = $42,577. This seems like a lot of money, but for perspective, a 30-second commercial in the 2007 Super Bowl cost $2.4 million and was watched by 33 percent of W25–54, giving a CPP of almost $72,300. But that's the Super Bowl, and as they say, "If you have to ask how much it costs, you can't afford it."

Local market cost-per-rating-point information is provided by SQAD Inc (www. sqad.com), as seen in Exhibit 16.2. Household CPPs are reported by market and

Exhibit 16.2 Cost per TV household rating point

		First quarter 2007: 30 spot ($)		
Ranked DMAs	*Daytime*	*News average*	*Primetime*	*Fringe average*
1 New York	700	1,142	4,149	1,191
2 Los Angeles	827	1,295	4,478	1,352
3 Chicago	284	683	1,874	485
4 Philadelphia	174	598	1,784	328
5 Boston (Manchester)	195	362	1,662	478
6 San Francisco–Oakland–San Jose	268	616	1,985	637
7 Dallas – Ft. Worth	181	359	884	253
8 Washington, DC (Hagerstown)	268	487	1,826	389
9 Atlanta	108	322	796	230
10 Houston	181	450	921	279
Total top 10	3,186	6,314	20,359	5,622

Source: SQAD Inc. 10/2006 Issue, Level = Average, Target = Household CPP, first quarter 2007. Used with permission.

by daypart in *Brandweek*'s annual *Marketer's Guide to Media*, a low-cost, handy reference to common media statistics that is for sale online at http://www.brandweek.com/bw/directories/mgm_index.jsp.

The household CPP gives a general idea of the cost of a schedule, and is used here for illustration, but most planning is based on demographic costs-per-point that SQAD sells to its subscribers.

In Exhibit 16.2, using Chicago as an example, primetime costs $1,874 per household GRP. A schedule of 200 GRPs per week for four weeks costs $1,499,200 (200 × 4 × $1,874).

Note that the cost varies by market size. This is because there are more people in 1 percent (one rating point) of New York than there are in 1 percent of Atlanta. Although the CPM may be similar, the CPP reflects this population difference.

Also note that the cost varies by daypart. Primetime programming has broad appeal and sets the tone for popular culture in America. Daytime television has a narrower range of program types. The audience is much smaller and demographically less diverse. As a result, the cost-per-rating-point is lower. This is not unlike differences in the cost-per-pound for different cuts of beef.

Research Accuracy:
Understanding Where the Numbers Come From

Research accuracy is determined by the size and representativeness of the sample and the methodology that is used to gather the data. As we consider these, we should keep in mind that research companies are first and foremost businesses. They must find buyers for their products and at the same time make a reasonable profit for their investors. This forces them to balance quality with cost as they determine the size of the sample, the way the sample is recruited, and the way the data are collected. To a large extent, research is as accurate as the suppliers' customers can afford.

The sample

Since a census (counting everyone) is not affordable or practical for marketing purposes, research companies take a sample and project the findings to the entire population, or the universe. This is totally acceptable as long as the sample is representative of the universe, that is, as long as the people in the sample behave in the same manner as the universe to which they are being projected. There are three broad types of samples, presented here in order of their cost.

The *random sample* is the most expensive. It is used as the basis for ratings that serve as the currency for radio, television, and magazines. It is the only type for which researchers can calculate a statistical margin of error. In a random sample, ideally everyone in the universe has an equal chance of being included – light viewers, heavy viewers, young, old, men, women, rich, poor, city, suburban, rural – people from all parts of the universe have an equal chance of being a respondent.

Conceptually, a random sample could be obtained by getting a list of everyone in the universe (the sample frame), sorting them by a random number, contacting every Nth name and then asking for their participation. But getting an all-inclusive list is difficult, and then making contact is even more of a challenge these days with answering machines, gated communities, do-not-call lists, and general hostility to market research. Companies such as Nielsen Media Research use especially trained membership representatives who make multiple attempts to contact selected homes and convince them to join a sample. Detailed rules govern the selection of alternate homes if the first randomly chosen home continues to refuse.

Despite all the care taken to recruit a random sample, its final composition may still not look like the universe, because peoples' willingness to participate in a survey varies by age, income, ethnicity, and other factors. Young adult males are especially hard to recruit. To correct for this problem, research companies weight the results to bring the sample demographics in line with the census. If the sample has a smaller percentage of young adults than is found in the general population, each person who does agree to participate will be given a larger weight (will count for more people). At the same time, easily recruited older adults, who are over-represented, will be given a smaller weight. The sum of all the weights is the number of target audience people in the universe.

The *representative sample*, sometimes called a quota sample, is a less expensive alternative to the weighted random sample. From the Census, the researchers know what percent of the sample should fall into each demographic cell. The cells (quotas) for older adults are easy to fill. But the quota for young men is extremely difficult and may require contacting hundreds of candidates before enough are found. Although the demographic cells may match the proportionality of the US Census, the shortcoming of a quota sample is that those people who quickly agree to participate may have different viewing/listening habits from those who only agree after multiple attempts to gain their cooperation.

The least expensive, and least accurate, sample is the *volunteer* or *convenience sample*. It is made up of people who respond to a mass mailing, are intercepted in a mall, or respond to an Internet solicitation. Recruitment attempts are generally accompanied by some form of reward or payment for their participation. Because of its low cost, the Internet is becoming a popular convenience sample for research that does not require the discipline and accountability of research that will be used as currency for media sales.

Error in media research

There are two kinds of error in survey research: sampling error and non-sampling error.

Sampling error   Sampling error exists solely because the research uses a sample instead of a complete census. It is based on statistics and the mathematics of probability. The margin of error can be precisely calculated for surveys that take a random sample and project audience estimates to a universe. By projection, we mean that if 5 percent of the women age 25–54 in a Nielsen sample watch "Boston Legal," then Nielsen will report that 5 percent of all the 25–54 year-old women in America watch "Boston Legal."

The sampling error does not depend on the size of the universe (the market) being measured. Just as a nurse does not need to draw more blood from a tall man than from a short one to identify their blood type, a researcher does not need to talk to more people in a large market than a small one to know how many watch a given television program. From a statistical point of view, a sample of 5,000 people in Missoula, Montana, has the same margin of error as a sample of 5,000 people in New York City. This is true as long as the samples accurately reflect the population.

Sampling error is also affected by the size of the rating being measured. For surveys with a given sample size, the relative margin of error (the margin of error divided by the rating) is smaller for high rated programs than for low-rated ones.

Sampling error can be reduced by recruiting a larger sample – the more people in the sample, the smaller the margin of error. But it follows the square root law – it takes a sample four times as large to cut the sampling error in half. Since most of the cost of research is in recruiting the sample, this can be a costly option. Sampling error can also be reduced by averaging the rating over a longer time period or more telecasts. The more measurements there are, the smaller the margin of error. The least accurate rating is for a single low-rated broadcast.

Researchers acknowledge the statistical margin of error, but in practice it is viewed as a simple fact of life. Although the theoretical true rating can be larger or smaller than what is reported, it is of little day-to-day concern because the resulting rating estimate is satisfactory for media planning and buying purposes.

Non-sampling error   Non-sampling error is much more important because its bias, while understandable, cannot be quantified. It is caused by the messy reality of the research process. Evaluation of research suppliers focuses on how well they control the four kinds of non-sampling errors.

① *Sample frame bias*. The sample frame is a list with the name, address, phone number or other way of contacting anyone in the universe from which the sample is drawn. Bias exists if some members of the universe are not listed, and so have no chance of being selected for the sample, and if their behavior is different from the average person. For example, not so long ago researchers commonly used the list of numbers in a telephone exchange (the phone book) as the sample frame. That is no longer acceptable because it excludes cell-phone-only households that tend to be younger, have higher income, and are more technologically sophisticated. Because of these consistent demographic differences, people in cell-phone-only homes are likely to have different media habits from those in wired homes, and as a result, the survey will undercount programs that appeal to that group.

Sample frame bias can be overcome by using an Area Probability Sample that divides a market into groups of addresses – perhaps one or two city blocks. These areas are numbered and randomly chosen. Than an interviewer goes to the neighborhood and literally walks door to door in an attempt to recruit every Nth home. Alternatively, letters are sent to every address in the selected area. With an Area Probability Sample, selection does not depend on the characteristics of the household. This methodology is used by Nielsen, MRI, and other research services whose reports are used as currency for media sales.

② *Non-response bias.* This bias results from households that have been selected at random but are unable or unwilling to cooperate with the survey. It results from simple refusals, language barriers, long-term not at home, access barriers such as apartment buildings or gated communities, unsafe neighborhoods, and incomplete questionnaires. As with sample frame bias, non-response bias is important to the extent that the non-responders are different from the people who do cooperate. By definition, it is impossible to know the demographics of people who refuse to provide that information, though researchers can get an idea by comparing the behavior of people who readily cooperate with those who require multiple visits from the recruiter before they will join. There is an industry campaign to improve response rates, but it is an ongoing challenge.

③ *Response bias.* This bias results from answers that do not reflect true behavior, and there is a systematic effect. Examples are inaccurate diary keeping, channel confusion, magazine title confusion, and poor memory. Modern electronic systems like Nielsen's people meter are subject to response bias if people fail to punch out when they leave the room, and if there are differences between demographic groups. Another example of response bias is seen in respondent's reluctance to accurately report their income, race, or education. Like the other forms of non-sampling error, this type of bias is impossible to quantify.

④ *Processing errors.* These errors occur during the mechanical processing of the data. They include data entry errors, editing mistakes, and errors in the software when calculating or printing the reports. These errors occur more frequently these days as a result of new calculations that account for the effect of TiVo and other types of digital video recorders (DVRs) on the ratings. An example of processing error occurred after Hurricane Katrina with the failure of the telephone system that transmits viewing data to Nielsen's Technology Center in Florida. In another now classic example, a research company double printed one page of the report book and omitted the next. The embarrassing error was discovered at a sales call as the research sales rep was showing the rating report to a client.

The Media Rating Council

This discussion of research errors is not to imply that the ratings are deeply flawed, but to demonstrate that nothing is perfect. The research suppliers take great pains to minimize non-sampling error. Their efforts are audited in detail by the Media Rating Council (www.mediaratingcouncil.org). The MRC is a non-profit industry organization that was established at the behest of Congress in 1964 to maintain standards in media ratings through the oversight of methodologies and implementation. Its mission is to "secure for the media industry and related users audience measurement that is valid, reliable and effective." It accomplishes this mission by setting standards and conducting detailed audits that are performed by an independent CPA firm to verify compliance. Membership includes more than 100 broadcast and cable networks, magazine publishers, radio station groups, radio networks, advertising and media buying agencies, and other users of research data. The research firms themselves are not allowed to be members.

The key to the MRC's success is its stringent policy of non-disclosure. The audited research companies, Nielsen, Arbitron, and MRI, for example, allow complete access to their proprietary processes with the understanding that they will remain secret. Upon completion of an audit, the MRC will only report that the service is accredited or not. In the latter case, no reason is given for the denial. The mere existence of the MRC and its accreditation process gives the industry assurance that the research is being conducted properly.

Media Research Concepts Specific to the Major Media

Up to now we have presented audience and research concepts that are common to all media. But in addition to these generalizations, each medium has its own research that salespeople will use every day as the tools of their trade.

Television

The broadcast ratings industry has been evolving for more than 75 years. In the early 1930s, radio advertisers decided they needed to know how many people were listening to their commercials, so they formed the Cooperative Analysis of Broadcasting (CAB). This group commissioned the Crossley Company to conduct a survey of station listening. Crossley used a telephone recall methodology in which randomly telephoned individuals were asked to recall the stations that people in their household listened to over the past day. In the 1930s, most radio listening occurred in a household or family setting; today's radio ratings are calculated for individuals and not households.

In 1942 the A.C. Nielsen Company announced it would begin measuring commercial network radio audiences with a mechanical device, the Audimeter, which purportedly removed human error. The result was the Nielsen Radio Index. This device used a stylus to make a scratch on a moving roll of film that was mailed back to Nielsen's headquarters, then in Skokie, Illinois. The original Audimeters are on display today in many Nielsen offices.

The Nielsen Television Index began in 1950 using paper diaries. The Recordimeter, a mechanical device similar to the Audimeter, was introduced in 1956 to supplement the diary and record which channel the set was tuned to. This combination of a television set meter to record what program was playing, and a diary to identify who was watching, continues to this day as one of the three ways Nielsen measures television audiences.

Television geography: The Designated Market Area (DMA)   The most commonly used geographic area for local television is the Designated Marketing Area (DMA). There are 210 DMAs in the United States. Each is made up of all the counties that spend the plurality of viewing hours tuned to the TV stations of a given market. Exhibit 16.3 shows a map of the Chicago DMA.

The majority of DMAs consist of whole counties, though some are split if a topographic feature such as a mountain range creates different viewing patterns. For instance, the Sierras split El Dorado County between the Sacramento, CA, and the Reno, NV, DMAs. County assignments to DMAs are updated annually, resulting in minor revisions, mostly in the fringe counties where a few viewers can swing the audience.

The *Total Survey Area* (TSA) counts all viewers to the stations in a market, including viewers who live in counties outside the DMA. For local television sales, stations typically report DMA ratings and TSA (000) thousands of viewers.

Television time is sold either by program or by time periods know as dayparts. The most commonly used dayparts are shown in Exhibit 16.4.

In Exhibit 16.4 the Cume % Homes shows that almost every household (97 percent) watches primetime, while a little over half watch television after 11:30 p.m.

Nielsen methodology   Nielsen uses three methodologies to measure television viewing:

• Nielsen People Meter (NPM) for national television and the largest local markets

Exhibit 16.3   Chicago DMA

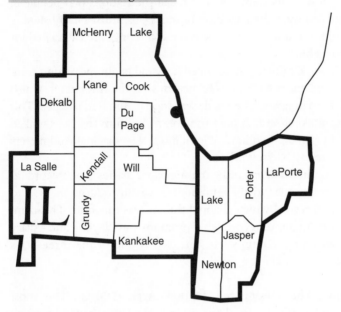

Source: Nielsen Media Research. Copyrighted information of The Nielsen Company, licensed for use herein.

Exhibit 16.4   Television dayparts cume % homes

Daypart	East/West Time Zone	Central/Mountain Time Zone	Cume % homes
Early morning	Monday–Friday 7–9 a.m.	Monday–Friday 7–9a.m.	70
Morning	Monday–Friday 9 a.m.–noon	Monday–Friday 9 a.m.–noon	72
Afternoon	Monday–Friday noon–3 p.m.	Monday–Friday noon–3p.m.	72
Early evening	Monday–Friday 5–8 p.m.	Monday–Friday 5–7p.m.	90
Primetime	Monday–Sunday 8–11 p.m.	Monday–Sunday 7–10p.m.	97
Late news	Monday–Friday 11–11:30 p.m.	Monday–Friday 10–10:30p.m.	88
Late fringe	Monday–Friday 11:30 p.m.–1 a.m.	Monday–Friday 10:30–midnight	52

Source: Nielsen Station Index, *Chicago Viewers in Profile*, Oct, 2007. Copyrighted information of The Nielsen Company, licensed for use herein.

- Integrated set meter/diary – mid-size markets – due to be replaced by the People Meter
- Diary only – small markets.

The Nielsen People Meter (NPM) is the most precise and accurate method for measuring television audiences, and is used for broadcast network, cable, syndication, and spot TV in the top ten DMAs. The NPM consists of two parts. The human interface is a small box that sits on top of each set in the house that has a screen five inches or larger. Household members use this to record who is watching. A row of lights on the front blinks red when the set is first turned on. Each person is assigned a button, and there is space to identify the age/sex of visitors. Go to the *Media Selling* Web site, www.mediaselling.us/NielsenPeopleMeter.htm, to see a picture of the Nielsen People Meter.

Household members are instructed to push their button if they are "watching television." So if Dad is watching the football game, he would punch his button and his light would change from red to green. Mom, who may be in the room but is doing something else, would not punch hers. Her looking up from time to time, and even watching a commercial, would not be recorded. From the moment when someone's button is pushed, every channel the set is tuned to is recorded and sent by telephone to Nielsen's computers. The meter reports viewing in one-minute increments, allowing Nielsen to report the number of viewers in the average minute of the program (the AA rating).

The second part of the People Meter is another, larger box off in a closet somewhere that identifies to which channel the set is tuned and sends the data by telephone line to Nielsen's computers in Florida. This is a challenge in today's 500-channel television environment. The Active/Passive or A/P meter identifies the station being watched with an inaudible code embedded in its audio signal (the "active" part). A wire carries the signal from each set's loudspeaker or audio output jack to the meter. Passive digital signal matching is used to identify channels that are not encoded. Together they achieve almost 100 percent accuracy in identifying what the viewer is watching. The A/P meter was specifically designed to handle today's digital environment, including cable boxes, satellites, digital video recorders (DVR) like TiVo, high definition television (HDTV), video games, PC viewing, and other forms of video delivery that have not even been invented.

The largest DMA's below the top ten are measured by a combination of a meter (the Recordimeter) that electronically records how long the set is turned on and what channel it is tuned to. Respondents write down who is watching in a diary. This meter/diary integration is the same methodology that has been used since 1956, and is scheduled to be replaced with the A/P meter in 56 markets (70 percent of US TV households) by 2011. Although they are known popularly as Local People Meter (LPM) markets, the hardware and all of the procedures are identical to the way Nielsen measures national television – the only difference is that the sample is weighted to represent the local market's population instead of the nation's. The LPM has minute-by-minute granularity that would allow reporting the average minute (AA) audience, but by long-standing practice all spot markets, even LPM markets, continue reporting the average-quarter-hour (AQH) audience.

Nielsen is working on simpler, less expensive versions of the A/P meter for markets rank 57 to 125. But until it is released, and indefinitely for markets ranked 126 and above, all viewing will be captured in a diary. Respondents write down what station/program they are watching in quarter-hour increments, causing ratings to be defined in terms of the number of viewers during the average-quarter-hour (AQH) of a program or daypart.

While researchers are quick to admit that Nielsen's diary is the least accurate methodology, especially in today's world, it is also the least expensive. Like all media research, the bulk of the cost is borne by the media that use the data to support their sales efforts. Buying agencies pay relatively little. As markets get smaller, the fixed cost of research becomes a bigger burden on stations that have limited ability to raise their ad rates. So, while the diary methodology is deeply flawed, it is all that stations in the smaller markets can afford.

On the other hand, the diary has the advantage of providing a direct link to the viewers in the form of written comments on the last page. These are a popular source of information for station managers who make an annual visit to specially provided reading rooms in Nielsen's Technology Center near Tampa, Florida.

Research in support of selling television Television's unit of sale is the 30-second spot, but what you are really selling is an estimate of how many people will watch a program at some time in the future. Television sales are all about predicting future ratings and coming to an agreement between the buyer and seller. The following describes the process, the research, and the judgments that go into that prediction. The core arithmetic is:

RATING = HUT×Share

Homes Using Television (HUT): By convention, the following refers to the HUT which would be used to calculate a generic household rating. The same logic and arithmetic applies to Persons Using Television (PUT) which is used to calculate a demographic target (persons) rating. Almost all media sales are based on persons ratings. (e.g., W25–54).

HUT = the percentage of homes using television

It turns out that the percentage of homes or persons watching television on a given day and time is relatively stable from year to year. Changes, if any, are slight, as seen in Exhibit 16.3.

Exhibit 16.5 Nielsen diary

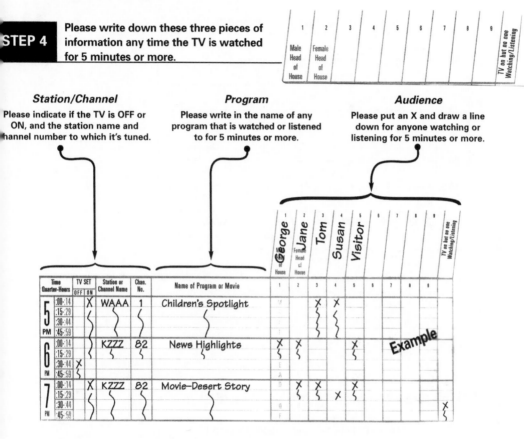

Source: Nielsen Media Research. Copyrighted information of The Nielsen Company, licensed for use herein.

The HUT level does change from month to month, especially in primetime and early fringe when people are out of the house in the early evening hours of summer. Daytime and late fringe are much less affected, as seen in Exhibit 16.7.

Each market has its own pattern of HUT level changes. In Phoenix, for instance, the HUT level goes up in the summer when people stay indoors to avoid the extremely hot weather. But whatever the market, buyers and sellers generally agree on what the future HUT will be for any given daypart and month.

Share and rating: In Exhibit 16.7 we see that 61 percent of homes were watching primetime television on the average night in November, but their viewing was divided across the 100+ channels available in the average home. That division of the pie is quantified as each station's share.

Exhibit 16.6   Yearly trends in homes using television (HUT)

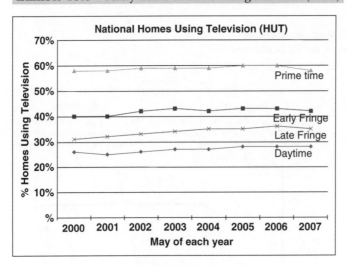

Source: Nielsen Media Research – *Total US Households Using TV Summary Report – 2000–2007*. Copyrighted information of The Nielsen Company, licensed for use herein.

Exhibit 16.7   Monthly trends in homes using television (HUT)

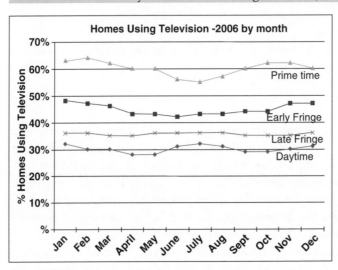

Source: Nielsen Media Research – *Total US Households Using TV Summary Report – 2006*. Copyrighted information of The Nielsen Company, licensed for use herein.

Exhibit 16.8 Hypothetical HUT, shares and ratings

Station/network	Program	Household share	Household rating
WLS-ABC	"Desperate Housewives"	18%	12.4
WBBM-CBS	"Cold Case"	13%	9.0
WMAQ-NBC	"Sunday Night Football"	17%	11.7
WGN-CW	"America's Top Model"	1%	0.7
WGBO-Univision	"Cine Especial"	2%	1.4
WCPX-ION	"Sunday Night Movie"	1%	0.7
WTTW-PBS	Various	2%	1.4
Cable	All channels combined	46%	31.7
	Total share/HUT	100%	69.0%

SHARE = the percentage of HUT/PUT that are tuned to a given program

You know from the earlier discussion that a rating is the percentage of the homes or persons in a market who are watching a program. The sum of the ratings from all the programs on air at a given time equals the HUT. And the sum of the shares is 100 percent. Exhibit 16.8 shows what that might have looked like one Sunday in November in Chicago from 8:00 to 9:00 p.m. Central Standard Time.

Sunday is a heavier-than-average night for viewing television. On this particular Sunday, 69 percent of the homes were watching television from 8 to 9 p.m. Eighteen percent of the homes using television were watching "Desperate Housewives," or 12.4 percent of all homes were watching the program (69.0 × 0.18). The same logic applies for all the programs on air at that time. These metrics are reported for national television in the Nielsen Television Index, and for each market by the Nielsen Station Index "Viewers In Profile" report. They are available for purchase in hard copy or from online systems provided by Nielsen and other suppliers.

Projecting next year's ratings: If a spot on this November "Desperate Housewives" telecast in Chicago cost $32,000, the cost-per-rating point (CPP) would be $2,580 ($32,000/12.4). Note that this is more than the $1,874 average CPP for Chicago primetime reported earlier. "Desperate Housewives," as a high-rated appointment viewing program, carries a higher-than-average CPP. How much should the station charge for that spot next June when the primetime HUT is 56.0 percent?

It comes down to a judgment of how well the program will perform next year – that is, what share it will get. If the share stays the same, the rating will be 56 × 18% = 10.08. At the same CPP, the station should charge $26,006 (10.08 × $2,580). But it is a judgment call to suggest that the share will stay the same.

The Chicago ABC station salesperson would point to the growing success of the program in Chicago, the introduction of exciting new characters, and the weakness of the competition. "Our research people project "Desperate

Housewives" will get a 20 share next year – well worth the $28,896 we will charge" (56 HUT × 20 share = 11.2 rating × $2,580 CPP = $28,896).

The buyer, of course, sees it differently. "Oh, give me a break! By next June "Desperate Housewives" will have gotten tired. The show may have new talent, but that's because they're replacing two of the favorite characters who are leaving to make a movie. And besides, next June the show will be in reruns. I do not think it will do better than a 14 – it will not be worth more than $20,227" (56 HUT × 14 share = 7.8 rating × $2,580 CPP = $20, 227).

This example is simplistic in the sense that advertising is sold as packages of spots that are evaluated against the bottom-line cost and target audience GRPs. But the concept and the math are the same, and a judgment must be made about the future share and rating of each program in the package.

Radio

In all but the smallest markets, radio audiences are measured by Arbitron, Inc. (www.arbitron.com). Rural America is surveyed by Eastlan Ratings (www. eastlanratings.com) which provides low cost radio ratings based on a telephone survey. Unlike the television DMA whose composition is determined by viewing patterns, the geographic unit of radio ratings is the Metro Survey Area. This is a commercial construct that generally corresponds to the US government's Metropolitan Area. As a convenience to marketers who plan television on a DMA basis, Arbitron will report the number of listeners in counties that make up the DMA, but the primary geographic unit for radio is the Metro.

Listening estimates are obtained from a one-week Arbitron diary placed in households by way of a random sample, as seen in Exhibit 16.9.

Unlike a Nielson television diary that is formatted by quarter-hour, an Arbitron radio diary is unformatted. Nevertheless, audiences are reported as an average-quarter-hour (AQH) rating. This is the same rating concept that was discussed earlier. A 1.0 M18–34 rating of a Chicago radio station in morning drive time means that during the average-quarter-hour of that time period, the station is listened to by 1 percent of the men age 18–34 who live in the Chicago Metro Area.

In addition to AQH estimates (rating, persons, and share), Arbitron reports each station's cumulative audience – the estimated number of people who listened to the station during one or more quarter-hours over the days included in the daypart listed in the rating report. These two estimates, the AQH rating and cume are the principal metrics of radio research. Although Arbitron reports the audience for each season, buyers generally use a four-book average because radio audiences are far more stable than television programs. Exhibit 16.10 shows a partial page from a Radio Market Report as delivered on Arbitron's Web site – the company no longer prints hard-copy reports.

Exhibit 16.9 Arbitron diary

You count in the radio ratings!

No matter how much or how little you listen, you're important!

You're one of the few people picked in your area to have the chance to tell radio stations what you listen to.

This is *your* ratings diary. Please make sure you fill it out yourself.

Here's what we mean by "listening":
"Listening" is any time you can hear a radio – whether you choose the station or not. You may be listening to radio on AM, FM, the Internet or satellite. Be sure to include all your listening.

Any time you hear radio from Thursday, Date 1a, and Wednesday, Date 1b, write it down – whether you're at home, in a car, at work or someplace else.

When you hear a radio, write down:

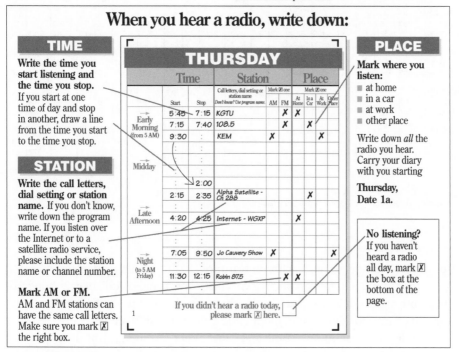

TIME

Write the time you start listening and the time you stop.
If you start at one time of day and stop in another, draw a line from the time you start to the time you stop.

STATION

Write the call letters, dial setting or station name. If you don't know, write down the program name. If you listen over the Internet or to a satellite radio service, please include the station name or channel number.

Mark AM or FM.
AM and FM stations can have the same call letters. Make sure you mark ☒ the right box.

PLACE

Mark where you listen:
■ at home
■ in a car
■ at work
■ other place

Write down *all* the radio you hear. Carry your diary with you starting

Thursday, Date 1a.

No listening?
If you haven't heard a radio all day, mark ☒ the box at the bottom of the page.

Questions? Call us toll-free at 1-800-638-7091. Visit our Web site: www.arbitronratings.com

© 2007 Arbitron Inc.

Source: Arbitron, Inc. Used with permission.

Buyers divide the cume persons by the AQH persons to get an indication of the station's audience turnover. For WAAA, an all-news station, listeners tune in for a few minutes to get the latest headlines, weather and sports, and then move on. The M–F 6 a.m.–7 p.m. 4-book turnover is 14.3 (10521/735) compared to 9.8 (2100/215) for WCCC, a soft music station, that has much longer time spent listening, a lower cume compared to the AQH, and so less turnover. It takes more

Knowledge

Exhibit 16.10   Arbitron Radio Market Report

Radio Market Report Summer 2007	Anytown, USA

Target Listener Estimates

Persons 12+

	Monday-Friday 6AM-7AM				Weekend 6AM-MID				Saturday 6AM-10AM				Saturday 6AM-3PM				Saturday 3PM-7PM			
	AQH (00)	Cume (00)	AQH Rtg	AQH Shr	AQH (00)	Cume (00)	AQH Rtg	AQH Shr	AQH (00)	Cume (00)	AQH Rtg	AQH Shr	AQH (00)	Cume (00)	AQH Rtg	AQH Shr	AQH (00)	Cume (00)	AQH Rtg	AQH Shr
WAAA-AM																				
SU '07	733	10650	.9	5.0	364	6529	.5	4.2	742	2640	1.0	7.5	384	1874	.5	2.8	333	1275	.4	3.3
4-Book	735	10521	1.0	4.8	403	6754	.6	4.6	717	2710	1.0	7.2	420	1910	.6	3.0	313	1291	.4	3.1
WAAA-FM																				
SU '07	434	9512	.6	3.0	286	6002	.4	3.3	172	1019	.2	1.7	512	2457	.7	3.7	436	1617	.6	4.3
4-Book	435	9510	.6	2.9	312	5996	.4	3.6	240	1112	.3	2.4	529	2334	.7	3.8	442	1774	.6	4.3
WBBB-FM																				
SU '07	62	1123	.1	.4	41	581	.1	.5	46	180	.1	.5	91	263	.1	.7	49	158	.1	.5
4-Book	68	1124	.1	.5	47	700	.1	.5	42	171	.1	.4	92	281	.1	.7	66	206	.1	.6
WCCC-FM																				
SU '07	237	2143	.3	1.6	42	552	.1	.5	81	219	.1	.8	81	168	.1	.6	41	96	.1	.4
4-Book	215	2100	.3	1.4	39	600	.1	.5	68	197	.1	.7	78	215	.1	.6	63	174	.1	.6

© 2008 Arbitron Inc.

Source: Arbitron, Inc. Used with permission.

spots per week on stations with high turnover (shorter time spent listening) to achieve its cume potential. Note that Arbitron reports radio audiences in hundreds (00) compared to television audiences shown in thousands (000). The time spent listening varies for different demographic groups and different seasons.

In addition to the AQH, Cume and Time Spent Listening, Arbitron reports an Exclusive Cume (people who only listen to a single station for the whole week), place of listening (home, work, car, other), the audience duplication between stations, and the demographic/ethnic composition of each station's audience.

As it is for television, the diary is an imperfect methodology to report radio listening due to frequent dial switching and human error in reporting to what station the radio is tuned. After many years of testing, Arbitron has developed the Portable People Meter (PPM), a cell-phone sized device that "hears" an inaudible code in the audio signal. A motion detector ensures the device is being worn. At night, the respondent puts the device in a docking station that charges the battery and at the same time transmits the day's data to Arbitron's computers.

The PPM changes the definition from "listening to the radio" to being within earshot of the loudspeaker. It has been in used as the currency in Philadelphia and Houston since 2007 and has been accredited by the Media Rating Council in

Houston. Arbitron plans to replace the diary with the PPM in the top 50 markets, but there have been bumps in the road that may delay these plans. Any change in methodology changes the numbers produced. Stations measured by a PPM report fewer average-quarter-hour listeners but more cumulative listeners than were recorded in the diary. This difference is due to listening picked up by the PPM that a respondent may have failed to enter in a diary.

Since a station's price is based mainly on the AQH audience, the lower PPM numbers are causing stations to scrutinize the sample's age, sex and ethnic composition compared to the census, and the respondent's compliance with Arbitron's rules. The station's reaction is a reminder that media research is a bread and butter issue for them.

Local radio is sold by daypart in each market. National radio (network radio) is sold by both daypart and program. The network radio audience is reported by Arbitron in a service called RADAR (Radio's All Dimension Audience Research). The report is essentially a roll-up of the local diaries from each market. RADAR reports the audience to individual networks for the daypart AQH, the audience to all commercials aired on network-affiliated stations, and the audience to commercials broadcast within network programs. Aside from these differences, the core metrics of network radio are the same as local.

Magazines

The currency of consumer magazine media sales is circulation, or the number of copies printed. While not every magazine has subscribers, all the major books (industry jargon for a magazine) are audited by the Audit Bureau of Circulations (www.accessabc.com). The ABC was created in 1914 by advertisers, advertising agencies, and publishers as an industry organization to independently verify circulation. Its audits provide detailed information about how many copies are sold and the characteristics of those sales. The ABC pink sheet publisher's statement is a standard element in the media kit of every audited magazine.

Guaranteed circulation may be the basis for rates, but advertisers want to know how many people read the magazines and their demographic composition. A number of research companies provide this information, but the two largest (and intensely competitive) services are Simmons (www.smrb.com) and MRI (www.mediamark.com). Both survey a random sample of 25–30,000 people per year – Simmons by mail, MRI by personal interview. These single source surveys capture media exposure, product use, attitudes about a wide variety of subjects, and a broad range of demographics for each respondent. See their Web sites for methodological details.

Agency buyers use research to determine which magazines should carry the advertising of a given product. The key concepts for magazines are coverage and composition. Coverage is analogous to the broadcast rating – it is the number or

Exhibit 16.11   *People* magazine reader composition

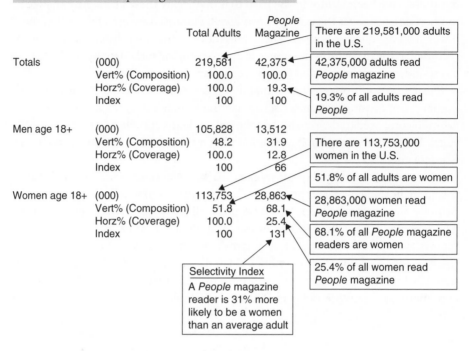

		Total Adults	*People* Magazine	
Totals	(000)	219,581	42,375	There are 219,581,000 adults in the U.S.
	Vert% (Composition)	100.0	100.0	42,375,000 adults read *People* magazine
	Horz% (Coverage)	100.0	19.3	
	Index	100	100	19.3% of all adults read *People*
Men age 18+	(000)	105,828	13,512	
	Vert% (Composition)	48.2	31.9	There are 113,753,000 women in the U.S.
	Horz% (Coverage)	100.0	12.8	
	Index	100	66	51.8% of all adults are women
Women age 18+	(000)	113,753	28,863	28,863,000 women read *People* magazine
	Vert% (Composition)	51.8	68.1	
	Horz% (Coverage)	100.0	25.4	68.1% of all *People* magazine readers are women
	Index	100	131	
				25.4% of all women read *People* magazine

Selectivity Index

A *People* magazine reader is 31% more likely to be a women than an average adult

Source: 2007 MRI Spring, weighted by population. Copyright © Mediamark Research & Intelligence LLC. Used with permission.

percentage of the target audience that is exposed to the medium – in this case, the percentage of the target universe that reads the magazine. Composition is the percentage of the magazine's readers who fall into various demographic groups. The surveys are accessed with standard industry software that yields the report shown in Exhibit 16.11.

This example shows that *People* magazine is read by 19.3 percent of all American adults (42,375 /219,581). It is read by 12.8 percent of men and 25.4 percent of women (28,863/113,753). The magazine covers 25.4 percent of all women age 18+ which is the same concept as a rating. Those 28,863 female *People* readers are 68.1 percent of all adult readers (28,863/42,375).

These numbers are interesting, but they are only meaningful when put in the context of total adults. This is the value of the Selectivity Index. 51.8 percent of all adults in America are women, but 68.1 percent of *People*'s readers are women. If you see someone on the street reading *People*, chances are that person is a woman. Put another way, a selectivity index of 131 means that a *People* magazine reader is 31 percent more likely to be a woman than the average adult (68.1/51.8). Conversely, the reader is 34 percent less likely to be a man.

This example used simple demographics, but the same concept applies to product users. For example, instead of gender we could have used medium-heavy users of bottled water. A research report would tell us that 48 percent of all adults are M-H users of bottled water. Of *People* magazine readers, 55 percent are M-H users. And so, *People* magazine readers are 15 percent more likely to be M-H bottled water users than the average adult.

The Selectivity Index is a key metric. It tells a buyer how well the magazine delivers against a target audience compared to the base of total adults. This, in combination with the magazine's ABC circulation analysis, coverage and composition, its CPM target audience, and the magazine's contribution to total schedule reach/frequency form the primary research considerations in a magazine buy.

Specialized research services (national base only) MRI and Simmons are broad single-source services that have been characterized as a mile wide and an inch deep. While they cover virtually every product and service used by American consumers, they do not go into much detail, and they do not report on niche markets that take a special effort to recruit a sample. Other services are available that focus just on narrow target audiences.

- Monroe Mendelsohn surveys homes with $85,000 household income (www. mmrsurveys.com)
- IPSOS US Business Elite surveys corporate senior management (www.ipsos. com)
- KMR-Group's MARS studies the media behavior of persons with various ailments for pharmaceutical advertisers (www.kmr-group.com/americas/gateway.asp)
- Erdos & Morgan's Opinion Leader study reports the media behavior of opinion leaders classified by industry such as immigration, the environment, healthcare, and aerospace (www.erdosmorgan.com).

Qualitative measures: engagement In addition to the previously mentioned metrics, research services publish a wealth of data on various *qualitative* aspects of a magazine's circulation and the reading experience. The Audit Bureau of Circulations (ABC) reports newsstand versus subscription sales, the number of copies sold at full price versus at a discount, the number of copies sold for one year versus longer terms, copies distributed to public places, and many other characteristics of the circulation that *may* be related to the value that a reader places on the magazine. One assumption is that the more a magazine costs readers, the more likely they are to be engaged with it, and presumably the more likely they are to be influenced by its advertising.

MRI offers a number of measures of reader quality, including: number of issues read out of four; place of reading; actions taken as a result of reading the magazine; time spent reading; interest in advertising; and overall evaluation of the magazine as "one of my favorites."

While all of these are *plausibly* related to involvement/engagement, there have been virtually no studies that connect these measures to the effectiveness or memorability of the advertising. The few studies that do exist have failed to show any consistent relationship. At the most, these measures of engagement should be used as tie-breakers between publications that are comparable on the key metrics.

Newspapers

Readership of the national newspapers (the *Wall Street Journal*, *USA Today*, the *New York Times*) is reported by MRI and SMRB using the same measures as national magazines, their natural competitors. Local newspapers are typically chosen on the basis of their coverage of a local advertiser's sales territory. However, in addition to geography, advertisers want to know how well papers reach people who shop at certain stores, visit local malls, or attend home games of the city's professional sports teams.

Scarborough Research (www.scarborough.com) provides this information in 81 DMAs. It uses a 16-minute telephone interview followed by a mailed self-administered questionnaire and TV diary. Another local service, Media Audit (www.themediaaudit.com), competes with Scarborough, but uses a telephone interview exclusively. Exhibit 16.12 shows an example of a Scarborough report. Note that it is in the same format as the MRI example except that Scarborough reports the audience in hundreds (00), not thousands (000).

Internet

The currency of print advertising is circulation. For the Internet, advertisers buy a certain number of ad impressions that are served to a user's computer browser. For example, one element of an online campaign may be 500,000 impressions served to visitors to www.espn.com. These impressions might be purchased at a CPM of $20.00 per thousand. A total ad buy is often tens of millions of impressions scattered over literally hundreds of Web sites. Delivering those impressions is the job of companies that are referred to as third party ad servers, such as DoubleClick, that keep track of which sites should get how many impressions. The ad-serving companies deliver (serve) ads as they are requested by users' browsers, and then bill an advertiser when the required number of impressions has been reached.

Just as circulation does not tell a print buyer about the demographics of a magazine's readers, a count of impressions does not say anything about the demographics of the people who are moving the mouse – the Web site's visitors.

Two research companies provide this information: Nielsen NetRatings, a division of Nielsen Online (www.nielsennetratings.com), and comScore (www.

Exhibit 16.12 Chicago Scarborough report

		Total Chicago adults	Daily/Sunday Chicago Tribune combo	Daily/Sunday Chicago Sun-Times combo
Total adults	Unwgt	4,285	1,785	1,028
	(00)	72,918	27,696	18,064
	Vert%	100.0	100.0	100.0
	Horz%	100.0	38.0	24.8
	Index	100	100	100
Attended Chicago Cubs baseball game last 12 months	Unwgt	717	326	190
	(00)	13,665	5,740	3,755
	Vert%	18.7	20.7	20.8
	Horz%	100.0	42.0	27.5
	Index	100	111	111
Attended White Sox baseball game last 12 months	Unwgt	816	371	232
	(00)	15,197	6,358	4,288
	Vert%	20.8	23.0	23.7
	Horz%	100.0	41.8	28.2
	Index	100	110	114
Attended Chicago Bears football game last 12 months	Unwgt	272	119	81
	(00)	5,139	2,113	1,563
	Vert%	7.1	7.6	8.7
	Horz%	100.0	41.1	30.4
	Index	100	108	123

Source: Scarborough Research, Chicago Local Market Study, Release 2 2007 Used with permission.

comscore.com). Both use a panel of respondents who agree to allow the research companies to put tracking software on their computer. The respondent logs into the computer when first sitting down, then every keystroke is recorded and included in the tabulations.

A visitor to a Web site can go in and out many times, even in the same session. Each time will be recorded as an impression to the site, yielding a very large but inherently useless number. Web publishers such as www.espn.com use NetRatings or comScore to show the number of unique visitors, or simply uniques, over a 30-day period, counting each visitor only once. This is roughly comparable to a cume in other media.

Unlike other media where the base is essentially the total population in the geographic area served by the medium, an Internet rating can be calculated from three different bases:

1   Total US population. This base should be used when comparing an Internet rating to other media.
2   Internet Universe. Persons age 2+ who had access to an Internet-accessible computer, whether or not they actually went online in the last month – roughly 85 percent of US population.
3   Active Universe. Persons age 2+ who have used an Internet-accessible computer in the last 30 days – roughly 65–70 percent of the US population.

Typically Web publishers will report their audience in terms of the Active Universe in order to show the largest percentage.

Exhibit 16.13 shows an example of a NetRatings NetView report and the many ways of looking at the visitors to a Web site. These include the number of page views (screens) seen by each unique visitor, the number of sessions over the month, the time spent with the site per person, and other metrics. Note that the report can be broken down by home and work samples. Active Reach is computed against the Active Universe. Universe Reach is computed against the Internet Universe. NetView does not calculate reach against the total US population.

By clicking on the Web site name, you can see the demographic composition of those visitors, as seen in Exhibit 16.14.

These reports give the buyer a complete picture of the size and demographics of a Web site's visitors, but there is a big difference between this information and a television rating. When a commercial appears on a television program with five million viewers, we know that when it is finished, five million people will have seen it (or at least will have had the commercial displayed on their television set).

The Internet is different. Using the report on www.espn.com as seen in Exhibit 16.14 as an example, over the course of a month, 20,184,000 different people will have visited the Web site at least once. But that number is meaningless to the Internet advertiser who decides to buy only one million impressions. And, unlike television that delivers the impressions all at once, it takes time for the impressions to be delivered on the Internet. As each browser requests a page of content from www.espn.com, the third-party ad server sends it an ad. But the server handles many advertisers, so those one million impressions do not all go to the first million browsers. It takes time, days or even weeks for less popular sites, before there will be enough requests for pages that the server can deliver the one-million impressions an advertiser wants. In short, television exposures are immediate; Internet exposures are delivered over a period of time, possibly several weeks.

The proper evaluative metric of a Web site for an advertiser is determined by the number of impressions that are bought, not by the total number of visitors. Media buyers use the NetRating's WebRF program or comScore's PlanMetrix Reach/Frequency system to show the net reach of an Internet campaign across many Web sites. Note that as a salesperson, you probably will not be privy to what other sites an advertiser is buying or how much the advertiser is paying.

Exhibit 16.13 Nielsen Online, NetView

Nielsen/NetRatings NetView

United States

UPDATES   DICTIONARY   HELP   LOGOUT

Last update: Dec 05

| Sites | Category | Demographic | All Sites | Search |

Audience: Entertainment - Sports (Subcategory) Edit

Formats: Site Metrics Demographics Audience Summary

Control: Latest Month (Oct 2007) Home and Work

☑ Include Internet Applications   ☐ Ad-Supported Only   ☑ Include Adult Sites

☐ Include Domain/Subdomain

Site Metrics: Standard Metrics

RUN REPORT

28 rec found

Report: Category (Internet Applications Included) – Brand or Channel **Period:** Month of October, 2007
Panel Type: Home and Work **Country:** United States
Category: Entertainment **SubCategory:** Sports

■ Brand = Channel

SAVE REPORT   ADD SITES()   PRINT   EXPORT (XLS)   EXPORT (CSV)

Brand or Channel	Unique Audience (000)	Active Reach (%)	Universe Reach (%)	Rank	Total Sessions (000)	Sessions Per Person	Total Minutes (000)	Time Per Person (hh:mm:ss)	Total Web Page Views (000)	Web Pages Per Person
☐ **Sports**	**71,884**	**45.23**	**33.13**	**n/a**	**675,080**	**9.39**	**5,484,741**	**1:16:18**	**8,549,280**	**119**
+ ☐ ESPN	20,184	12.70	9.30	1	142,911	7.08	910,557	0:45:07	1,277,051	63
☐ Yahoo! Sports	19,730	12.41	9.09	2	156,960	7.96	987,131	0:50:02	1,956,480	99
+ ☐ FOX Sports on MSN	14,002	8.81	6.45	3	85,221	6.09	336,077	0:24:00	506,496	36
+ ☐ CBSSports/CSTV Network	13,206	8.31	6.09	4	89,139	6.75	774,609	0:58:39	1,076,625	82
+ ☐ NFL Internet Network	13,047	8.21	6.01	5	50,261	3.85	384,869	0:29:30	526,129	40
+ ☐ MLB.com	11,358	7.15	5.23	6	45,487	4.01	223,134	0:19:39	246,335	22
☐ eBay Sports	8,987	5.65	4.14	7	28,479	3.17	136,879	0:15:14	271,610	30
☐ AOL Sports	7,304	4.60	3.37	8	25,422	3.48	130,033	0:17:48	77,642	11
☐ SI.com	6,290	3.96	2.90	9	31,303	4.98	155,899	0:24:47	236,704	38
+ ☐ Fantasy Sports Ventures Network	4,754	2.99	2.19	10	24,008	5.05	143,318	0:30:09	212,724	45
+ ☐ Turner Sports New Media	3,808	2.40	1.76	11	17,773	4.67	88,103	0:23:08	96,452	25
☐ JumpTV Sports	3,356	2.11	1.55	12	8,756	2.61	31,960	0:09:31	37,131	11
☐ USATODAY.com Sports	3,233	2.03	1.49	13	9,726	3.01	30,266	0:09:22	29,179	9
☐ Cabela's	3,060	1.93	1.41	14	6,119	2.00	44,102	0:14:25	83,393	27

Source: Nielsen Online, NetView, October 2007, US Home and Work. Used with permission.

Exhibit 16.14 Nielsen Online, NetView demographics

Nielsen//NetRatings

Detail Demographics for Brand: ESPN

Month of October , 2007, Home and Work

Category	Target	Unique Audience (000)	Unique Audience Composition (%)	Composition Index by Unique Audience	Web Page Views Composition (%)	Composition Index by Web Page Views	Coverage (%)
ALL	Total	20,184	100.00	100	100.00	100	12.70
GENDER	MALE	13,724	68.00	140	85.88	166	17.76
	FEMALE	6,460	32.00	62	14.12	29	7.91
PERSONS - AGE	2 - 11	551	2.73	30	0.46	29	3.76
	2 - 17	1,803	8.93	44	8.39	95	5.61
	6 - 11	539	2.67	36	0.43	29	4.52
	12 - 17	1,252	6.20	56	7.93	110	7.15
	12 - 24	2,215	10.97	58	12.52	105	7.41
	12 - 34	5,480	27.15	85	36.48	135	10.80
	18+	18,381	91.07	114	91.61	100	14.50
	18 - 24	963	4.77	61	4.59	97	7.78
	18 - 34	4,228	20.95	100	28.55	144	12.73
	18 - 49	12,989	64.36	135	77.73	132	17.08
	21+	17,954	88.95	117	91.00	102	14.92
	21 - 24	536	2.65	71	3.98	154	9.02
	21 - 34	3,801	18.83	112	27.94	158	14.19
	21 - 49	12,562	62.24	142	77.12	136	18.05
	25 - 34	3,265	16.18	123	23.96	159	15.67
	25 - 49	12,027	59.58	149	73.14	135	18.90
	25 - 54	14,395	71.32	142	80.21	121	18.06
	35+	14,153	70.12	119	63.06	88	15.13
	35 - 49	8,761	43.41	161	49.18	126	20.47
	35 - 64	13,206	65.43	131	61.24	93	16.69
	45+	8,116	40.21	96	23.01	51	12.15
	55+	3,023	14.98	69	6.81	34	8.72
	55 - 64	2,076	10.29	81	4.99	35	10.25
	65+	947	4.69	52	1.82	31	6.56

Source: Nielsen Online, NetView, October 2007, US Home and Work. Used with permission.

In the example shown in Exhibit 16.15, an advertiser is buying 50 million page views (impressions) against a target of M18–34, focusing on sports Web sites. Note the reported number of page views for each site in Exhibit 16.15 and the number that the advertiser is buying (Page Views Required). The computer system tells the reach of that number of impressions on each site and the combined campaign statistics in terms of GRPs, reach and average frequency (OTS = Opportunities To See) to the base of the Active Universe.

Exhibit 16.15 IMS Media Solutions report

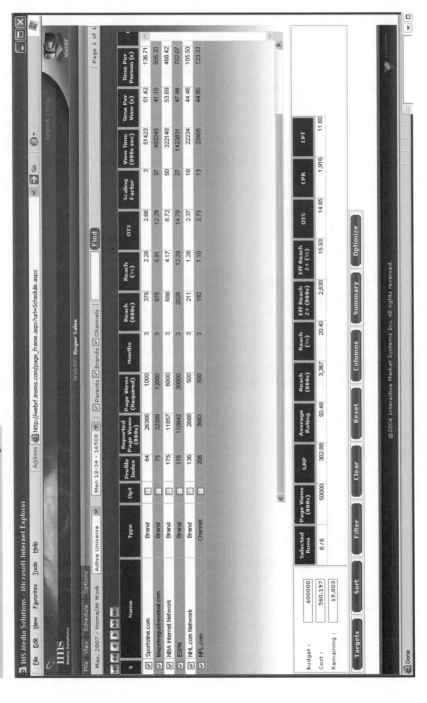

Source: Nielsen Online, IMS WebRF. Used with permission.

Measuring the audience of emerging media platforms   It seems every day there is an article in the trade press about a new media form that has the potential to revolutionize electronic communications. We hear about video-on-demand, mobile advertising on cell phones, ads in cell phone video, advergaming (ads in video games), streaming video on the Internet, podcasting, advertising walled gardens on digital video recorders like TiVo, and others that will likely be developed after this book has gone to press. All of these (yes, *all* of these) have research and developmental issues that go beyond the non-sampling errors discussed earlier. The particulars differ from medium to medium, but they include:

- Irregular geographic coverage
- Privacy concerns
- Need for regulatory approval
- Technical limitations
- Copyright restrictions
- Competitive conflicts among similar services
- Lack of demographic data (impressions counted by the hardware, not by the person using it)

Salespeople cannot expect the definitive sort of research for these emerging media that is available for the traditional media. The research that is available can be used to *imply* advertising exposure, but most advertisers would not accept it as a currency measure.

As noted earlier, research companies are businesses that must deliver a profit to their investors. As each new medium appears, a research company's first consideration is whether it will draw enough advertisers to be successful. Only then will the research firms begin the long process of developing a service to measure its audience.

The Top Five Impossible Questions that Media Research Cannot Answer

Up to now we have discussed the general concepts and methodologies of media research and the concepts that are unique to each of the major media. The methodologies that are based on a random sample have a statistical margin of error. All methodologies have non-sampling error caused by the real world challenges of producing research. But these sources of error can be identified and accounted for.

In the course of a salesperson's work, other questions come up for which there is no simple answer. These are the most important questions in media because they involve subtle judgments about what is best.

The following frequently asked questions cannot be definitively answered because they depend on what is happening in the mind of each consumer. They are presented here to characterize them as "impossible" questions, to sensitize salespeople to the inevitable day when one of them comes up in the course of their work, and to provide something to say and ways to think about helping the advertiser make a reasonable judgment.

How much is enough?

This is the most common question, and it takes many forms. What is the least I can spend and still have an effective campaign? If I have X number of GRPs against my primary target, am I delivering enough weight against the secondary target? My last campaign was wildly successful. I ran XX number of GRPs and actually had to turn away customers. Next time, how much weight can I cut back and still be successful?

There are several approaches to answering the question that will put the advertiser in the ball park. If the advertiser has competitive sales and spending information, it is common to match the share of voice to the share of market. An advertiser with a 10 percent share of a market should be spending at least 10 percent of the media dollars spent in that industry. Certainly an advertiser should look back at the experience with comparable products. For example, some industries have an historic advertising to sales ratio. Go to www.mediaselling.us/downloads/adsalesratios.xls to see the ad-sales ratios for 200 industries as published by *Advertising Age*.

An industry rule of thumb is that an ad must be seen three or more times to be effective. While this sounds like a reasonable prescription, it finesses the question, "How many people can I afford to reach 3+ times?" In the end, and unfortunately, many advertising budgets are simply what remains after all other costs have been accounted for.

Which medium is most effective?

Effective at doing what? Different media have different strengths. Effectiveness is heavily dependent on the creative quality. Many people think television is the most effective medium, but the question comes up when television is not appropriate or affordable. There are virtually no independent, public domain studies of cross-media effectiveness. Advertisers who do conduct these studies treat the results as highly confidential. What publicly available research does exist comes from industry associations whose studies are designed to promote the value of their medium. As they say, "Don't ask your barber if you need a haircut." The best advice is to ensure the advertiser has matched the strength of the media to the marketing objectives.

What is the best environment?

This question assumes there is a rub-off effect between the medium and the advertising message; however, as noted earlier, numerous studies have failed to quantify that effect, or even to confirm that it exists. We know that high-rated television programs attract more light viewers, but there is a heavy cost premium for these iconic programs. The first position in a commercial break has a larger audience than mid-break positions, but pod position is usually beyond a buyer's control.

In magazines, an ad on the back cover is more likely to be read than one inside the book, but advertisers pay a premium for that position. Some advertisers believe a magazine ad near the front of the book is preferable, but since most insertion orders request "Far forward, right hand page" these (assumed to be) desirable positions are more likely to be given to advertisers running a heavy schedule. At the least, salespeople should ensure that advertisers running multiple insertions are given a fair rotation.

Which is better: flighting or continuity?

This age-old question concerns how a limited advertising budget should be scheduled over the year: in short bursts of heavy media weight followed by hiatus weeks of no activity, or continuous advertising at low weight. If the budget allows the advertiser to buy 1,600 GRPs a year, should they be scheduled in four 4-week flights (total 16 weeks on-air) of 100 GRPs/week? Or would it be more effective to run for 40 weeks at 40 GRPs/week?

For products that are sold more or less evenly throughout the year, advertisers are guided by the "recency theory of advertising" that was proposed by media guru Erwin Ephron. In contrast to the theory that three exposures are needed, the recency theory is based on research that shows a single exposure close to purchase is most effective. Since there is a steady demand for non-seasonal products, the advertiser should maintain a continuous presence on-air. The goal should be to maximize the total weekly reach points (the annual sum of each week's reach points). This is achieved by continuity scheduling.

However, this ignores the effect of competitor's advertising that may be flighted. Also, there is a need for synergy between the advertising and seasonal consumer or trade promotions. Finally, there is a reluctance to go below a perceived minimal level of about 50 GRPs per week. Most advertisers appreciate the importance of continuity, but given this minimum, they find continuity scheduling to be an ideal that is beyond their brand's budget.

When is my commercial worn out?

It is hard enough to know what a commercial "does" when it is fresh. Commercial wearout is really a variation of the "How much is enough?" question. An industry rule-of-thumb is that a commercial is worn out when the heaviest viewers are exposed 26 times – somewhere around 1,000–1,500 GRPs. This has become a benchmark against which to judge a given situation, but many questions remain. Does that rule apply to a single execution or to an entire campaign of similar but different creative executions? Over what period of time? What is the effect of hiatus periods? Is that target rating points or household points which are usually larger?

One researcher sees a political agenda behind the question. The agency wants to make a new commercial and the advertiser does not, or vice versus. People who are closely involved with the lengthy creative process may be so close to the commercial that they will think it is worn out when in fact it has not even been on air.

It should be clear by now that there is no simple answer to these "How much is enough" questions of effective frequency, flighting versus continuity, minimum GRP levels, maximum hiatus weeks, media effectiveness, wearout, and so forth. Research can provide guidance, but in the end, it requires buyer and salesperson judgment to apply these general findings from the past to specific plans for the future.

Media Research Resources on the Internet

There is a wealth of information available on the Internet. The research companies, the media, and industry associations all have Web sites that offer helpful information about their service, methodology, and the media they cover. This is provided at no charge, although some require registration with name, company, and e-mail address. What they do not give is current information about the audience to specific media vehicles – television programs, magazines, radio stations, and so forth. This data, the product they sell, is password protected and limited to paying clients.

General media planning sites

Advertising Media Internet Center (www.amic.com). This site is produced by Telmar, a worldwide provider of media planning software. It provides links to media industry associations, media terminology, and a broad range of other planning services in the Ad Info section. The "Media Guru" accepts questions from site visitors. A searchable database provides his answers to over 7,000 questions since 1995.

MediaBuyerPlanner (www.mediabuyerplanner.com). This Web site is for professional media buyers and planners but it also provides up-to-the-minute news about the major media – invaluable for keeping up with industry news.

Mediapost (www.mediapost.com). This site is an online newspaper that covers the media industry. It has daily feeds of the latest developments from a cadre of more than 50 writers and reporters. Subscription is available for a no-charge registration.

World Advertising Research Center (www.warc.com). WARC.com provides the largest single source of intelligence for the marketing, advertising, media, and research communities worldwide, drawn from more than 40 international sources including the UK publication ADMAP, the Advertising Research Foundation, and other organizations. The Web site offers a trial membership, but there is a charge for long-term access.

Broadcast

Nielsen Media Research (www.nielsenmedia.com). The unprotected areas of the site offer an overview of the TV rating service, a description of how television audiences are measured, and occasional free reports on current topics. The password-protected section gives Nielsen clients access to virtually all of their resources, in PDF and Excel formats that were formerly only available in hard copy.

Arbitron, Inc. (www.arbitron.com). This service is the primary source of audience ratings for network and local radio stations throughout the United States. The company's Web site provides information about its reports, market populations, an overview of radio listening patterns, and a broad range of special reports that can be downloaded at no charge. The site offers a high resolution map of the entire United States down to the county level, with radio metro areas highlighted. This site is essential reading for anyone in radio sales.

SQAD, Inc. (www.sqad.com). SQAD is the primary source of local market radio and television costs per rating point in all 210 DMAs, as well as national television CPP. The Web site gives an overview of the company's methodology and tips on how to use the data, but usable cost information is only available to clients, or can be purchased online.

Cabletelevision Advertising Bureau (www.onetvworld.org). The CAB is a trade association that exists to promote cable television as an advertising medium. The Web site presents the strengths of cable television in comparison to broadcast network and syndication. Numerous reports and special tabulations are available, all at no charge. It also contains detailed audience information, program schedules and other material about more than 95 advertiser supported cable television networks.

Television Bureau of Advertising (www.tvb.org). The Television Bureau of Advertising is the not-for-profit trade association of America's spot television industry. TVB provides a diverse variety of tools and resources to support its members and to help advertisers make the best use of local television. The Web site provides a broad range of information about the television industry, viewing trends, advertising expenditures in all media (not just television), and useful facts about the television market. Because the TVB is supported by local stations, there is only limited information about cable and network television. Some areas of the site are limited to TVB members. This site is essential reading for anyone in local television sales.

Radio Advertising Bureau (www.rab.com). The RAB is a trade association that exists to promote radio as an advertising medium. The Web site has extensive information on radio listening habits and the strength of the medium compared to other broadcast and print alternatives. The *Radio Marketing Guide and Fact Book for Advertisers* is especially valuable. Like the other association Web sites, it contrasts the strengths of radio to the weaknesses of other media.

National Association of Broadcasters (www.nab.org). The NAB is the principal trade association of the television industry. Its work focuses mostly on the business of broadcasting and governmental relations. The Web site contains reports on current events in the industry, regulatory issues, and technical advances. Although there is only limited information about advertising sales, the site provides useful background information.

Print

Mediamark Research & Intelligence, LLC (www.mediamark.com). This Web site describes the MRI service and provides audience information for magazines and Internet Web sites. It is mostly useful to MRI subscribers.

MRI Plus (www.mriplusonline.com). This site provides rates, circulation information, top-line MRI readership estimates, editorial calendars, and promotional media kits for more than 5,500 consumer magazines and business publications. The Web site includes audience composition information for more than 90 cable networks. This massive amount of information is provided for free (with no-cost registration) by the publications. The only drawback is that information from some copyrighted reports is a few years old. This is a useful Web site for all media professionals.

Audit Bureau of Circulations (www.accessabc.com). The Audit Bureau of Circulations verifies the circulation statements made by major consumer magazines and newspapers. Although the audit data is password protected to subscribers, the site contains free reader profile reports for dozens of magazines, and other useful data. The Industry Resources tab contains links to numerous media-related Web sites.

BPA Worldwide (www.bpaww.com). BPA Worldwide is the global industry resource for verified audience data and media knowledge. After no-cost registration, users can get audit reports for more than 2,500 media properties in more than 25 countries. These include business publications that are supported by advertising and distributed free to qualified subscribers, Web sites, events, e-mail newsletters, databases and other advertiser supported media.

Magazine Publishers of America (www.magazine.org). The MPA exists to promote the value of magazines as an advertising medium. The Web site provides a wealth of free information about the magazine industry and how people read magazines. Because it is an industry group, however, it does not have data on individual titles that might be used to sell one over another. The annual *Magazine Handbook* in the Resources/Research section provides especially useful information for salespeople about the medium.

Newspaper Association of America (www.naa.org). The NAA is a non-profit organization that represents over 1,800 newspapers in the US and Canada. The Web site Information Resource Center provides information about newspapers and readership. The "Resources Toolbox" contains dozens of articles that help sell the value of newspapers, all offered at no charge, without registration.

Outdoor

Outdoor Advertising Association of America (www.oaaa.org). The OAAA is the lead trade association representing the outdoor advertising industry. Founded in 1891, the OAAA is dedicated to promoting, protecting and advancing outdoor advertising interests in the US. With nearly 1,100 member companies, the OAAA represents more than 90 percent of industry revenues. The Web site's "Marketing Resources" section presents information about the medium and various creative units available. Links to outdoor companies can be used for local market information and to request price quotes.

Eller Media Company (www.ellermedia.com). Eller is one of the largest outdoor companies in the US. Its Web site has links to suppliers of all media including television, radio, interactive, and many different forms of out-of-home media.

Internet

Interactive Advertising Bureau (www.iab.net). Founded in 1996, the Interactive Advertising Bureau represents over 300 leading interactive companies that actively engage in and support the sale of interactive advertising. The Web site provides general information about Internet advertising, industry standard ad sizes, and tools to aid in selling online advertising.

Technology news services. Three companies compete to provide detailed news of the emerging media platforms: Jupiter (www.jup.com), Forrester (www.forrester.com) and eMarketer (www.emarketer.com). All three provide strategic analysis and insight about commerce on the Internet. They track industry trends, make forecasts of future business activity, and provide useful background information for sales. The Web sites list the titles of all the studies they have conducted, but a subscription is required to access the full reports.

Advertising publications

Advertising Age (www.adage.com). *Advertising Age* is the weekly trade publication of the advertising industry. It covers all phases of advertising, media, creative, and Internet communication. Current feature stories are displayed online, but past articles and detailed information requires a subscription.

Adweek (www.adweek.com). *Adweek* is a weekly trade publication that covers the advertising industry. The company's Internet Web site, Adweek Online, provides daily headlines and excerpts from its trade magazine. Subsidiary publications include *MediaWeek* and *BrandWeek*.

Advertising terms/glossaries

Advertising terms (www.knowthis.com/general/marketing-terms-and-definitions.htm)

Internet terms (www.matisse.net/files/glossary.html)

Internet glossary (www.adglossary.com)

Test Yourself

1 What is the difference between a rating and a share?
2 What is a DMA?
3 What is a HUT level?
4 How are gross impressions and GRPs calculated?
5 What is a cume?
6 What is the difference between reach and frequency?
7 What is the major rating company in television? In radio?
8 What is more important in determining the accuracy of a rating, the size of the population sampled or the size of the sample?
9 How do you calculate campaign CPM and CPP?
10 What is a unique?

Project

Using Exhibit 16.2, "Cost per TV household rating point," create two network televison schedules of 12 spots each, distributed in all four dayparts. One 12-spot schedule should be for Chicago and one 12-spot schedule should be for Atlanta, and both schedules should show cost-per-spot and total schedule costs. Assume the following ratings for each daypart: Daytime = 2.0, News Avg. = 4.0, Primetime = 8.0, and Fringe Avg. = 2.0. Go to "Chapter 16 Project Format" in the downloads area of www.mediaselling.us to see an example of how the schedules in this project should be formatted. You can distribute the 12 spots among the four time periods any way you want.

Reference

Jack Z. Sissors and Roger B. Baron. 2002. *Advertising Media Planning*, 6th edition. New York. McGraw-Hill.

17

Advertising

Charles Warner

Advertising is selling (mass selling), so the purpose of advertising is the same as the purpose of personal selling – to get customers and keep them. The way advertising gets and keeps customers is also similar to the way personal selling does it, which is to create value, present effectively, get customers to take action, and then get them to repurchase. In advertising the creating value function is referred to as building brand image, or brand attitude as Tim Larson and Ken Foster call it in Chapter 15. Getting customers for a national consumer package goods advertiser or a local department store simply means selling products. So the *purpose of advertising is to build brands and sell products.*

Media consultant Erwin Ephron estimates that approximately 80 percent of national advertising dollars in broadcast television networks are invested for brand building, or reminding and reinforcing consumers about brands they are familiar with.[1] This high percentage of ad dollars invested for reminding indicates the importance national advertisers place on building brand image. Great advertising both builds brand image and sells products, good advertising does one of these things well, and poor advertising does neither. But even well-written and well-produced advertising cannot build an image for or sell a bad product, as you learned in Chapter 15.

Advertising and Promotion

Both advertising and promotion are marketing communications and part of the third P of marketing – promotion. However, the objectives of advertising and promotion are different: Advertising tells you why to buy a product, promotion tells you when to buy a product. Advertising creates value and builds brand image for the long term and, therefore, consumers will pay more for brands they like and trust. Promotions, as you learned in Chapter 8, are designed to get people to take action and buy a product immediately, usually because of a price reduction, rebate, or discount. Promotions have a short-term effect and in the long run hurt sales and profit margins. Therefore, as you learned in Chapter 8, it is more profitable to invest $1 in advertising than to promote a $1 reduction in price in an attempt to increase volume.

How Advertising Works

Advertising has both a long-term and a short-term effect on sales because well-crafted, consistent advertising takes consumers up an Advertising Ladder similar to the Sales Ladder you learned in Chapter 11. Exhibit 17.1 shows the Advertising Ladder.

In order for advertising to work, it must take consumers, step-by-step up the Advertising Ladder. Every advertising message should have an objective based on the five steps in Exhibit 17.1 that lead up to the sixth step, repeat purchase. As a media salesperson, you must know what advertisers' objectives are (or help them figure them out) in order to recommend an effective solution and an advertising schedule in your medium. In terms of solutions, you must define the problems that accompany the steps on the Advertising Ladder: consumers' lack of awareness, lack of information about a product, a marketer's low share of market, declining sales, low-level of repurchase, and so on.

The types of schedules that you will recommend will depend not only on your customers' advertising objectives but also on their media plans. If you are selling to national advertisers, they will most likely have an advertising agency that creates

Exhibit 17.1 The Advertising Ladder

Advertising	Corbett*	Marketing**	Sales
Repeat purchase		Repeat purchase	Repurchase
Reinforce and remind	Reminding	Brand attitude	Satisfaction
Adoption/purchase	Persuading	Brand trial and purchase	Action
			Conviction
Induce trial	Informing	Brand attitude	Desire
Communicate information		Brand learning/association	Interest
Create awareness		Brand awareness	Attention

* Michael Corbett with David Stilli. 2002. *The 33 Ruthless Rules of Local Advertising*. New York: Pinnacle Books, p. 53.
** Tim Larson and Ken Foster, Chapter 15 of this volume.

their media strategy and media plans. If you are selling direct to local advertisers who do not have agencies, you must advise them on the best media strategy and plans that will help them meet their marketing and advertising objectives.

National Advertising

National advertisers invariably retain advertising agencies to do two things: create and place their advertising.

Creating advertising. Advertising agency creative departments are responsible for writing and producing advertising in the three top national media – television, the Internet, and magazines. Newspapers and radio are primarily local media, so large, national advertising agencies do not create a lot of advertising for newspapers and radio. And highly paid creative people generally do not like to create newspaper ads or radio commercials because they believe these media are dull compared to television and magazines, especially television. Copywriters and agencies do not show prospective clients newspaper ads they have created, they only show their television commercials, or commercial reels as they are called. An agency's, creative director's, and copywriter's resumé is their commercial reel, and you will never, ever hear an agency say, when showing a reel to a client or a prospective client, "And here is a commercial we did that came from an idea that a salesperson brought us." A media salesperson selling to a national agency does not call on the creative department or creative people at an agency, as it is generally a waste of time.

Placing advertising. Agency media departments are responsible for placing advertising. The two basic functions of a media department are planning and buying media. Media consultant Erwin Ephron writes that "The purpose of media planning and buying is to enhance advertising's positive effects on sales."[2] In this chapter you will learn how media planning works, because when you call on media buyers, they will be buying according to a media plan that has been put together by a media planner. In some smaller agencies, the media planning and buying is done by the same person, but in larger national agencies the two functions are separated.

Media planning

Media planning is essentially deciding which media to buy and how much of each medium to buy in order to reach an advertiser's target audience while staying within a budget. It sounds relatively simple, but, in practice, it is complicated. Let us look at each of these decisions separately.

Which media to buy? First, media planners analyze which media reach an advertiser's target audience most effectively and most efficiently. The effectiveness criterion is based on the execution the creative department has decided upon. For example, for a mass-marketed cosmetics product that appeals to teenage girls, a creative department might decide that a four-color ad featuring a glamorous teenage model might be the best creative execution, so magazines would be the most effective medium.

Once the most effective media have been selected, planners then consider efficiency. The efficiency criterion is based on media costs, primarily on cost-per-thousands (CPM), except online where other efficiency measures might be used – online efficiency criteria are covered in Chapter 20 "Interactive." CPM is used to judge the comparative efficiency of network television (broadcast and cable), network radio, and magazines. Spot radio, television, and cable and local radio, television, and cable are evaluated based on comparative cost-per-point (CPP) data. Spot means buying on a market-by-market basis. For example, a spot television campaign might include buying the top 100 markets out of a total of 212 television markets in the US.

The next step in the planning process is to figure out how much media can be purchased based on an advertiser's budget. Advertising budgets are determined according to a percentage of sales. Industries have different advertising-to-sales ratios, as seen in Exhibit 17.2, which shows just 10 industries out of 190 industries that are reported on.

The ad-to-sales ratios are available at www.adage.com in the Data Center, in the Marketing/Advertising link, and under the title of "Advertising to sales ratios by industry." In Exhibit 17.2, you can see the wide variance by industry from a low of 1.6 percent to a high of 16.8 percent of advertising dollars spent as a percentage of sales. Therefore a typical auto rental and leasing company that had $2

Exhibit 17.2 Advertising-to-sales ratios of selected industries

Industry	Ad dollars as a percentage of sales
Auto rent and lease, no drivers	2.1
Beverages	7.8
Biological products, excluding diagnostics	1.6
Blank books, binders, bookbinders	5.5
Books: publishing and printing	7.6
Bottled and canned soft drinks, water	2.9
Building material, hardware, garden-retail	3.1
Cable and other pay TV services	1.9
Commercial printing	7.2
Distilled and blended liquor	16.8

Source: http://adage.com/datacenter/article?article_id=109934. Accessed July, 2007.

billion sales would allocate $42 million dollars (2.1 percent) for advertising, whereas a beverage company that had $2 billion in sales would allocate $156 million dollars (7.8 percent) for advertising.

If we take the auto rental company with $2 billion in sales and an annual advertising budget of $42 million dollars as an example, a media planner might go through the following thought process: "I know the client likes television and the creative department believes it has a memorable creative execution. However, because network television is so expensive, we cannot buy enough network television to make an impact. Also, the creative is targeted to business travelers and the majority of business travelers are concentrated in the top 25 markets. I think I'll recommend 70 percent of the budget be spent in television in the top 25 markets and 30 percent of the budget in cable in those markets on ESPN and the Golf Channel." Let us assume the auto rental client approves this portion of the media plan.

The next step would be for the planner to look at CPPs in the top 25 markets for television and cable and estimate how many weeks and how many spots per week in each medium to buy. These two factors will depend on advertising objectives. So, the planner might go through the following thought process: "The auto rental brand is well known, so I don't have to have a big, short burst of commercials to create awareness or to induce trial. The commercial is persuasive, so I need to reach and persuade business travelers on a continuous basis because business travel is not particularly seasonal. I need to reach them when they are planning a business trip and, therefore, are most receptive to my message. I will recommend a 39-week continuous schedule that runs March through November, I will optimize on reach for $42 million, and I will look at several media mixes."

The above paragraph introduces six concepts into planning considerations: reach, frequency, recency, continuous scheduling, optimization, and media mix. As you learned in Chapter 16, reach is the number of different people an advertising message reaches over a designated period of time, and frequency is how many times the average consumer is reached by an advertising message over a designated period of time. Recency in terms of media planning is a little more complicated.

Recency   Recency in media planning is a concept that Erwin Ephron introduced to media planners in 1994 based on the research of John Phillip Jones. Jones's research was published in his book *When Ads Work*. Up to that time, it was assumed by the media planning community that frequency is what drove sales because people tended to forget advertising messages, so the messages needed to be repeated often. However, Jones's research indicated that a single exposure could strongly influence which brand consumers purchased if those consumers were ready to buy. Recency is the last message consumers are exposed to before they buy and is, therefore, the most effective. Thus, the objective should be to expose advertising messages when consumers are receptive. Ephron wrote that if there is a window of opportunity for the ad message preceding each purchase, media's job is to put the message in the window.

Since the introduction of the recency planning concept, it has gradually replaced frequency as the favored planning model, especially with package goods advertisers and their agencies. Recency planning means that reach becomes the most important criteria, not frequency.

Continuous scheduling   Jones's and Ephron's research concluded that, because of the concept of recency, it is more effective to advertise continuously than to start and stop with heavy schedules and then cut back for several weeks or months (referred to as flighting) or to heavy-up regular schedules from time to time (referred to as pulsing). The point of continuous scheduling is always to be present in the window of opportunity when a consumer is receptive and in the market for a product.

Optimization   Optimization means trying to find the best combination that provides the most reach for either the lowest CPM or for a given budget amount. Most of the larger and many mid-sized agency planners use optimization computer programs called optimizers into which they input all the data and parameters of a media plan. According to Erwin Ephron, "TV optimizers were a response to three powerful forces – *recency planning, fragmentation and sharp increases in prime time pricing.*"[3] Optimizers produce printouts, called flow charts, that show the best combination of dayparts and media that will provide the optimum reach that is either the most efficient (CPM) or within the limits of a specified dollar amount.

Media mix   Media mix modeling is also referred to as marketing mix modeling. Optimizers will always show that the cost of additional reach after a certain reach level has been attained in any one medium is expensive and that a combination of media is the best way to achieve maximum reach at the minimum cost. Exhibit 17.3 shows an example of how expensive it is to add incremental reach to a network television schedule.

This example shows that achieving a 30 percent reach level has a CPM reach of $15, which more than doubles to $33 for just 5 percent more reach, and an additional 5 percent reach costs an additional 34 percent. Erwin Ephron writes, "Marketing mix modeling finds diminishing marginal response to media weight. As more dollars are spent in any medium, the sales response per-dollar for that medium tends to do down. That's why mixing media is seen as the key to greater advertising effectiveness."[4]

These concepts are explained more fully in Erwin Ephron's booklet, *From Recency to Fusion: Seven Ideas that Nudged the Business.* This enlightening book is a recent history of media planning by the subject's foremost expert and I recommend that you download it from www.ephrononmedia.com and read it, especially if you are now calling on or hope to call on large agencies that have media planning departments and use optimizers.

Exhibit 17.3 The cost of incremental reach

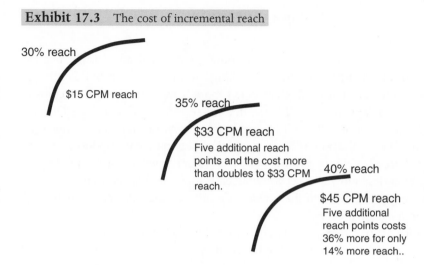

30% reach

$15 CPM reach

35% reach

$33 CPM reach

Five additional reach points and the cost more than doubles to $33 CPM reach.

40% reach

$45 CPM reach

Five additional reach points costs 36% more for only 14% more reach..

Source: www.charleswarner.us. Media Mix presentation.

Selling to media planners

If you are a broadcast network television salesperson, there is little reason to call on media planners because most major national advertisers, especially consumer package goods advertisers, spend approximately 80 percent of their advertising dollars in television (network and spot) and you would not want to do anything to derail this gravy train. However, if you are selling Interactive, cable, magazines, or radio, you should call on planners and show them media-mix presentations, demonstrating that by adding your medium both reach and efficiency can be increased. In February 2003 the *Jack Myers Report*, a widely read media industry newsletter that often identifies trends, featured a headline that read, "Sellers Shift Focus From Buyers to Planners."[5] The accompanying article indicated that many national sales organizations had realized the benefits of calling on media planners. Several national sales organizations, such as Turner Broadcasting, are armed with their own optimization programs that show that their medium can add reach and efficiency to a broadcast network television schedule. The only way to get a medium (other than broadcast network television) added to a media plan is to call on planners with credible research information that shows how your medium can add efficient reach to a television schedule. Do not sell against television, but sell with it – in combination with television – and sell your medium to planners, not to buyers. By the time the media plan gets to a buyer, it is too late.

Local Advertising

The purpose of local advertising is the same as national advertising, but the emphasis locally is generally more on selling products than on building brand image, which means that local advertisers generally evaluate the effectiveness of their advertising based more on sales results and return-on-investment (ROI) than on ratings, circulation, CPMs, CPPs, reach, frequency, or branding. Bringing up the concept of optimization, recency, or diminishing marginal response to a local retailer will usually get you nothing but a blank stare as will a discussion of brand image or branding. However, as you will learn soon, branding is as important in local advertising as it is in national advertising and is an important concept for you to teach to local advertisers.

The other major difference between national and local advertising is that sales-people often have to be responsible for creating advertising – writing copy and either producing or supervising the production of ads or commercials.

The best book about local advertising is Michael Corbett's *The 33 Ruthless Rules of Local Advertising*. I will give you some of those rules in this chapter, but the best way to learn about them is to buy, read, and study the book.

Corbett's Rule #6: Know what a new customer is worth to you.

Corbett writes that determining the value of a new customer allows local busi-nesses to manage their advertising expenditures accurately. To calculate the value of a new customer a business must know several things: (1) How much does the typical customer spend on an average purchase? (2) What is the net profit on an average purchase? (3) What is the average patronage lifetime? (4) How many repeat sales does a customer make? (5) How many prospects will a typical cus-tomer refer? (6) How often will that customer base turn over, or how many times will new customers be needed to replace those who leave? (7) What has been invested in advertising to get the current customer base? (8) What is a new cus-tomer worth? A business may discover after making all of these calculations that it will be investing more in advertising than will be realized from a customer's first purchase. However, the future profits from repeat purchases and referrals might well compensate for an initial loss on the first purchase.

Corbett's Rule #7: Understand the purpose of advertising.

According to Corbett, "The purpose of advertising is to create an equity position in a target market and to reach and motivate a sufficient number of consumers so that a business can realize a specific growth objective."[6] An equity position is branding. So, branding is of critical importance to local advertisers, because, as Corbett writes, "The objective of advertising is to first have an impact on the mind of the consumer followed by or accompanied simultaneously with an impact on the spending of the consumer."[7]

Corbett's Rule #9: Use the most powerful tool in local advertising.

According to Michael Corbett, the most powerful tool in local advertising is a Unique Selling Proposition (USP) or, what Corbett calls, a Preemptive Advantage. The idea of a USP was developed by the legendary advertising executive Rosser Reeves in the 1950s. In his book, *Reality in Advertising*, Reeves defines a USP in three parts: "(1) Each advertisement must make a proposition to the consumer. Not just words, not just product puffery, not just show-window advertising. Each advertisement must say to each reader: 'Buy this product and you will get this specific benefit.' (2) The proposition must be one that the competition either cannot, or does not, offer. It must be unique – either a uniqueness of the brand or a claim not otherwise made in that particular field of advertising. (3) The proposition must be so strong that it can move the mass millions, i.e., pull over new customers to your product."[8]

Corbett claims that most local businesses have not developed a USP, are not aware of the USP concept, and that without a USP a local business is just one of many similar businesses, "just another store front."[9] But a USP cannot be stated in a worn-out cliché such as "the lowest prices in town" or "the best service in the city" because everyone uses these phrases and nobody believes them. A USP must be a truly unique and different positioning statement and promise.

Corbett's Rule #10: If your doors are open, you should be advertising.

And by advertising, Corbett means advertising all the time, not just occasionally, for five reasons: (1) People shop all the time, not just when a business decides to advertise. (2) People move; in some markets as many as 25 percent of the population moves out of the area every year. (3) People forget, mainly because they have been exposed to thousands of advertising messages a day. (4) People often take their time buying. (5) To establish an equity position in the consumer community. So, what Erwin Ephron taught media planners about continuous scheduling works for local advertisers, too, only the words are different. Continuous scheduling means advertise all the time.

Corbett's Rule #12: Think long term.

The notion of a local business saying, "I'll try this for a month and see how it works," will not work. Corbett writes, "Using the media for infrequent, short term advertising schedules will not get you the same growth benefits you'll get when you advertise with consistency, frequency, and impact. If you advertise from week to week, idea to idea, promotion to promotion, you're usually going to end up disappointed."[10]

Corbett's Rule #26: Use a proven scheduling formula.

By a proven scheduling formula, Corbett means several things; here are two: "(1) Choose a medium you can dominate. (2) Determine if your chosen medium for domination reaches a sufficient number of your target consumers."[11]

If an advertiser cannot dominate an entire medium such as television, then the advertiser should try to dominate a daypart or a particular type of programming. Corbett recommends radio schedules that run every week for sixteen weeks and three out of four weeks thereafter with a minimum level of average frequency of three. In television he recommends a schedule of 250 gross rating points (GRPs) per week and a schedule of two weeks out of every month. Corbett also writes that "If you're advertising with a dominant, consistent schedule, it doesn't matter on which days you run your ads."[12]

Finally, two of Corbett's rules are closely related. I have used only nine of Corbett's 33 rules of local advertising because I want to give you just a sample of the wisdom that permeates his book in an attempt to entice you to read it.

Corbett's Rule #30: Sell something more profitable than low price.

Corbett's Rule #31: Avoid the "sale" syndrome.

The same principle of creating value applies to advertising as well as to media selling – if you create value by emphasizing high quality and excellent service before mentioning price, you can get a higher price. Local businesses that try to compete with national discount chains such as Wal-Mart by offering lower prices are bound to lose in the long run because they can never consistently beat Wal-Mart on prices and they certainly cannot out-advertise huge corporations. The only hope local businesses have against big national chains is to create a Unique Selling Proposition that positions their businesses on something other than price, on elements such as quality, selection, service, and convenience.

Corbett's rule to avoid the sale syndrome, or habit, is closely related to the notion that competing on the basis of low prices is unprofitable. Sales can be useful if used sparingly. Consumers are assaulted by sale advertising day after day in the media and have, therefore, become suspicious of retailers who invent excuses to have a sale. Traditionally, Nordstrom, which is known for high-quality merchandise and excellent service, has only two sales a year, which they do not advertise heavily because they do not have to – their shoppers know about them. Regular Nordstrom shoppers eagerly await these bi-annual sales and crowd the stores trying to get a bargain. Nordstrom's increased volume makes up for price reductions. Having a sale means discounting the price of goods, which, in turn, means lowering profit margins. *To make up for a price reduction of just 15 percent, a retailer has to increase its volume by 80 percent to attain full-price profit levels.* This idea is so important that I'm going to repeat it: To make up for a price reduction of just 15 percent, a retailer has to increase its volume by 80 percent to attain full-price profit levels. To get that kind of increase in volume, a retailer would have to invest in much more advertising, which would wipe out the profit margin of the increased volume. To attempt having sales on a regular basis would merely increase these losses.

Many local retailers say they have no choice but to compete on the basis of price, especially in slow economic times. But of course they have a choice, which is to develop a compelling USP. This is where intelligent, informed, solutions-focused local media salespeople can help.

By understanding the advertising objectives of both national and local advertisers, media salespeople can offer solutions to advertising problems – both creative solutions (to local advertisers) and media scheduling solutions.

Test Yourself

1 What is the purpose of advertising?
2 What is the difference between advertising and promotion?
3 What are the six steps on the Advertising Ladder?
4 What are some of the differences in selling national advertising to large agencies and selling local advertising to businesses that do not have an agency?
5 What is an optimizer?
6 Why is continuous scheduling important?
7 What is a USP and why is it important?

Project

Project #1: Select commercials for five different products that you see on local television and identify which step on the advertising ladder they address.
Project #2: Go to the Web site www.mediabuyerplanner.com, subscribe the RSS feed, and read the posts sent to you for a week and see if you understand the jargon and the points made.

References

Michael Corbett with David Stilli. 2002. *The 33 Ruthless Rules of Local Advertising*. New York: Pinnacle Books.

Erwin Ephron. 2003. *From Recency to Fusion: Seven Ideas that Nudged the Business*. www.ephrononmedia.com

John Phillip Jones. 1995. *When Ads Work: New Proof that Advertising Triggers Sales*. New York: Lexington Books.

Resources

www.adage.com (*Advertising Age*'s Web site)

www.charleswarner.us (the author's Web site with case studies, articles, and presentations)

www.ephrononmedia.com (Erwin Ephron's Web site and newsletter)

www.mediabuyerplanner.com (*Media Planner and Buyer* Web site and newsletter)

Notes

1 Personal conversation with Erwin Ephron. October 2002.

2 Erwin Ephron. 2003. *From Recency to Fusion*. www.ephrononmedia.com, p. 38.

3 Ibid., p. 14.

4 Ibid., p. 3.

5 Jack Myers. 2003. *The Jack Myers Report*. February. 3, p. 1.

6 Michael Corbett with Dave Stili. 2002. *The 33 Ruthless Rules of Local Adver-tising*. New York: Pinnacle Books, p. 31.

7 Ibid.

8 www.emediaplan.com/admunch/Biographies/Rosser.asp. Accessed April 2003.

9 Corbett and Stili. 2002. *The 33 Ruthless Rules of Local Advertising*, p. 43.

10 Ibid., p. 51.

11 Ibid., p. 125.

12 Ibid., p. 127.

18

Television

J. William Grimes and Ron Steiner

Broadcast Television

The history of broadcast television

The watershed year of 1939 had a number of milestones that marked both the beginning and the end of lives and trends that would change the world of geo-politics, business, and popular entertainment:

January 1 – Two engineers start Hewlett-Packard in their garage.

March 3 – Mohandas Karamchand Gandhi begins fasting to protest British auto-cratic rule of India.

April 1 – Dictator Fernando Franco captures Madrid and the Spanish Civil War ends.

April 9 – Singer Marian Anderson sings before 75,000 people on the Lincoln Memorial after the Daughters of the American Revolution deny her access to Constitution Hall.

April 30 – President Franklin Delano Roosevelt gives a speech to open the New York World's Fair and become the country's first president to appear on televi-sion. The National Broadcasting Corporation (NBC), owned by RCA, broad-casts the ceremony, thus becoming the first television network in the US to begin regular broadcasting.

May 1 – Batman makes his first appearance in comics.

June 12 – Major League Baseball opens its Hall of Fame in Cooperstown, NY.

July 4 – Future Hall of Famer Lou Gehrig, suffering from a terminal disease that would be named after him, gives a moving farewell speech in Yankee Stadium.

August 2 – Albert Einstein writes President Roosevelt about developing an atomic bomb and the idea for the Manhattan Project is born.

August 17 – *The Wizard of Oz* opens to rave reviews at the Capitol Theater in New York – a movie that symbolized Hollywood's Golden Age and the greatest single year in film history – at a theater that would eventually close because of the debilitating effects of television on the motion picture industry.

September 1 – Nazi Germany invades Poland, beginning World War II in Europe.

September 23 – Sigmund Freud dies.

October 30 – Gracie Slick is born and later becomes the lead singer in the pioneer psychedelic rock band, Jefferson Airplane.

December 15 – *Gone With the Wind* opens at Lowe's Grand Theater in Atlanta – another theater that would close because of television's impact on the motion picture industry. *The film* would go on to win nine Oscars.[1]

NBC's telecast of the opening ceremony of the New York World's Fair was watched by viewers on TV receivers inside the RCA Pavilion at the fairgrounds as well as on TV sets installed on the 62nd floor of the RCA building in Rockefeller Center. NBC programming in 1939 consisted of operas, cartoons, cooking demonstrations, travelogues, and fashion shows. RCA's chairman was David Sarnoff, whose primary interest in television was the same as it was in radio – selling receivers. RCA was in the manufacturing business and it mounted radio and television programming in order to create demand for radio and TV sets.

Radio roots   KDKA-AM in Pittsburgh was the nation's first regularly programmed commercial radio station. Beginning on November 2, 1920, it broadcast the US presidential election returns from a shack on the roof of a Westinghouse building in Pittsburgh. WEAF-AM in New York aired the first commercial in 1922 for the Jackson Heights real estate company in Queens – it was referred to as a "talk" and lasted 10 minutes.

In the 1920s radio station transmitters popped up randomly and chaotically like daisies in America's yard, broadcasts interfered with each other's frequencies, so in 1927 the government established the Federal Radio Commission (FRC) to bring order out of the chaos and assign specific frequencies to current stations and to new applications. In 1934, the FRC became the Federal Communications Commission (FCC) and Congress assigned it the mission of regulating the exploding number of radio stations. The FCC regulated radio station licenses, not networks, as it still does today. It gives licenses to stations to "serve the public interest, convenience, and necessity." Therefore, it can only regulate programming on stations, not programming produced by program distributors and suppliers such as networks and syndicators.

NBC, established in 1926 by RCA, was the first radio program distributor, sending its programs through telephone transmission lines to stations across the country. In 1927, William S. Paley's Columbia Broadcasting Company (CBS) began to compete with NBC in the radio network business.

The FCC kept licensing new radio stations to a point that NBC had so many stations, several in the same city, that it divided its stations into two networks, the Red and the Blue. In 1943, the FCC felt that NBC has too big and potentially too influential, and forced a sale of their Blue network to Edward Noble, who formed the American Broadcasting Company (ABC) as a third radio network.

TV's early growth   The first licensed commercial television station was WRGB-TV in Schenectady, NY, operated by General Electric (GE). GE's basic business was manufacturing appliances and it was a leading producer of radio receivers, competing with RCA. GE saw television as a new opportunity to make television sets for America's living rooms. Other television station transmitters quickly poked holes in the American sky as the technology advanced and as the government became more interested in providing this new video service to everyone. Established media owners, such as the three radio networks, radio station owners, and newspapers saw television not only as a major competitor, but also as a potentially valuable asset.

All of the early television stations operated on channels 2 through 13, known as VHF (Very High Frequency). It was not until 1952 that the FCC approved UHF (Ultra High Frequency) stations, using channels 14 through 83. In the early days of broadcast television, VHF was technically far superior to UHF. That advantage has vanished in the modern era due to improved technology and the distribution of television signals by means of cable television.

The first television stations produced live local entertainment, news, and kids' programs. They needed additional programming and looked to the same companies that provided radio programming – the networks – to fill out their broadcast day. The new television networks were the same three companies that produced programming for radio stations: ABC, CBS, and NBC. These three radio networks cobbled together television networks in 1948 and became the program providers for local television stations. In return for the programming that the networks provided, local stations became affiliates and provided an audience for the networks in local markets. This audience was quite valuable because the networks, along with the local stations, relied on advertising as their sole source of revenue. CBS had a slight head start on NBC for supremacy in television. ABC was far behind the older, more-established NBC and CBS networks in attracting successful local stations as affiliates, primarily because of CBS's and NBC's lineups of popular personalities and movie stars. The networks provided programming, while affiliates provided local audiences – a win–win for both.

The three network program providers were also television station owners. CBS, NBC, and ABC each owned stations in the country's largest markets, New York,

Los Angeles, Chicago, Detroit, and other top markets, which provided huge local audiences and, therefore, large national audiences for their networks' programming. These stations owned by the three network companies were then, and still are, known as O&O stations – owned and operated – although in November, 2007, NBC changed the name of its station group from the NBC Owned-and-Operated Stations Group to the NBC Local Media Division. According to an NBC press release the name change reinforces its mission: "Our stations produce local content for a multitude of platforms beyond their primary channels. NBC Local Media better reflects the full scope of our capabilities, as well as our ability to offer clients a fully integrated, local media solution across the full portfolio of our assets."[2] This announcement reinforces the trend of integrating online media with traditional media and selling them in a cross-platform package.

The competition to have the most popular local affiliates was keen among the three networks. In order to keep the local stations in the fold, the networks asked stations to sign affiliation contracts that laid out the terms for paying the stations compensation for network option time – the times that stations had to run network programming. Network compensation was a fee based on a station's hourly advertising rate. The amount of compensation varied from station to station and was based on market size and local station ratings. Network compensation became an important revenue stream that supplemented a station's local advertising revenue. Affiliate contracts varied in length from one to five years, and at the end of each contract, strong affiliates had the bargaining power to negotiate an increase in their compensation, reinforced by the potential treat of switching network affiliations if a network was unwilling to increase its compensation.

Explosive growth   By 1980, most cities around the country had three affiliated television stations, each aligned with one of the three networks. In smaller cities there may have only been one or two stations licensed by the FCC. During the 1970s and early 1980s, the FCC continued to grant more and more television licenses. When the FCC licensed a fourth or fifth television station in a market, those stations had no network affiliation and were, therefore, known as independent stations. Independent stations had to program their entire broadcast day without the aid of network programs and, therefore, they relied heavily on syndicated programming. Most new stations, operating without network programming and network compensation, were not in a financial position to produce significant news programs or other local productions. Without highly popular network shows and without local news programming competitive with affiliated stations, independent stations struggled to achieve financial solvency, especially in markets outside the top five.

In 1985 News Corporation, an international media company controlled by Rupert Murdoch, paid $250 million dollars for a 50 percent stake in the 20th Century Fox movie studios. In May of that year, News Corp. paid $1.55 billion to acquire television stations in six major US media markets (New York, Los Angeles, Chicago, Dallas, Houston, and Washington DC) from Metromedia. By September of 1985, Murdoch's company had bought the rest of 20th Century Fox and the stage was set for Murdoch to launch a new television network. With a program production capability from 20th Century Fox, a nucleus of local television outlets, and an increasing number of independent stations thirsting for programming, Murdoch created the Fox Television Network and began to challenge broadcast television's establishment – ABC, CBS, NBC, and their affiliates.

By the fall of 1986, FOX had established a list of 96 local stations that became the foundation of the Fox Television Network. The fledgling network was competing with the three older networks, each with more than 200 affiliate stations, and by the end of the 2007 season FOX became the number-one network with adults 18–49, largely because of its mega-hit "American Idol."

Encouraged by the success of FOX, other networks were created, each trying to secure a slice of the lucrative broadcast television advertising pie. UPN, the WB, and Paxton all joined the fray, along with the Univision and Telemundo Spanish language networks, in seeking audience and ad revenue. UPN and the WB combined in 2005 to become the CW network, and Paxton became the Ion network.

In 2006, NBC, owned by GE, purchased the motion picture company Universal Entertainment from Vivendi and became NBCU.

TV station programming

Local television stations' programming is a combination of locally produced programs, network programs, and syndicated programs. There are two types of syndicated programs, off-network and first-run. Off-network programs are those that previously ran as primetime shows on one of the national networks. Once a program accumulates approximately 100 episodes, it becomes a candidate for sale on an exclusive and market-by-market basis to individual stations. Programs such as "Seinfeld," "The Simpsons," and "Everyone Loves Raymond" are examples of programs that have had successful runs on a network and have then been put into syndication.

The second type of syndicated programming, first-run, is original programming produced specifically to sell to stations, that never has had any network exposure. Programs, such as "Oprah," "Inside Edition," and "Wheel of Fortune" are examples of first-run syndicated programs.

Both off-network and first-run syndicated programs are sold on an exclusive station-by-station, market-by-market basis. The companies that syndicate television programs are typically the same movie studios that are most active in producing network shows, such as Warner Brothers, Paramount, Sony Pictures, and 20th Century Fox.

Networks, local stations, and syndication companies rely on advertising as a primary source of revenue, which means that there are sales positions and opportunities in all three areas of broadcast television.

Stations

In 2007, there were 1,372 commercial television stations in the United States, 585 VHF stations (a signal radius of about 60 miles for Very High Frequency) and 787 UHF stations (a signal radius of about 35 miles for Ultra High Frequency).[3] You may want to check these numbers, as they are updated yearly on the Television Bureau of Advertising's Web site (www.tvb.org, in the Research Central link, in the Market Trends Track link, under TV Basics). The majority are network-affiliated stations.

DMAs

Broadcast station licenses are issued by the FCC and are licensed to cover a particular area or market. Markets define a trading area surrounding a city or group of cities. Nielsen Media Research calls local television markets Designated Market Areas (DMAs). DMAs include a cluster of counties that are covered by the local television signals in the market area. Every county in the United States is assigned to one and only one DMA. Each DMA is usually named after the biggest city in the market area, such as the Chicago DMA (#3) or the San Antonio DMA (#37); although, there are several multi-city DMAs such as San Francisco–Oakland–San Jose (#6) or Tampa–St Petersburg–Sarastoa (#13).[4] Each county is assigned to that DMA in which the television stations most watched in the county in question are located.

In addition to these formal uses of the term market, there are several other uses for the term market in the television business. Some of the common uses are the African-American market, the Hispanic market, or an upscale market, for example. These markets are market segments that are of interest to advertisers. In all its usages the term market indicates a consumer segment that can be targeted by an advertiser.

Advantages of broadcast television

There are many advantages of broadcast television. First, television has enormous reach. TV reaches more people each day than any other medium – 89.9 percent of all adults every day. There were 111,348,100 TV homes in the United States in 2007, according to Nielsen, in 210 DMAs – the largest being New York, with 7,391,940 TV homes, or 6.664 percent of the homes in the country and the smallest, #210, being Glendive, MT, with 3,980 homes.[5] All of those homes in all of those DMAs watched TV an average of 8 hours and 11 minutes per day during the 2004–2005 season, up ten minutes over the previous season.[6]

Exhibit 18.1 Jack Myers' ad spending estimates

Medium	2007 ($ million)	% share	2008 ($ million)	% share
Broadcast television[1]	48,083	21.0	52,271	21.0
Broadcast network	18,936	39.0 of TV	19,542	37.0 of TV
Cable television[2]	24,048	10.0	25,701	10.0
Cable network	17,702	74.0 of cable	18,941	74.0 of cable
Newspapers	45,763	19.8	44,665	18.1
Magazines[3]	23,669	10.0	24,448	10.0
Radio[4]	20,934	9.0	21,632	9.0
Online/Internet	16,708	7.2	20,717	8.4
Total advertising	**215,843**		**227,917**	

[1] Includes broadcast network, broadcast syndication, and local and national spot television.
[2] Includes cable network and local/regional cable television.
[3] Includes consumer and business-to-business magazines.
[4] Includes terrestrial and satellite radio.
Source: http://www.jackmyers.com/commentary/media-spending-forecasts/9805012.html. Used with permission.

Second, advertisers and their agencies believe TV is the most powerful advertising medium, and, therefore, invest more money in broadcast television than any other medium – see Exhibit 18.1. A very large percentage of what we learn, we learn through sight. The visual aspect of television is exciting and dramatic and, thus, a major reason that TV skyrocketed in popularity when it was first introduced. And because advertising is all about informing, persuading, and creating brand equity in a product or service, the sensual aspects of sight, sound, motion, and color make television exceptionally compelling as an advertising medium.

In addition to providing sight, sound, motion, and color, television also provides a means to demonstrate and dramatize a product's use, function, and appeal. Print advertising can be attractive by using vivid colors, but it is static. Television can provide the same colorful scene, plus the images move. Sight, sound, motion, color, drama, and high-definition also evoke emotion, and engaging people's emotions is one of the most powerful ways to stimulate them to take action.

Television commercials can be as short as five seconds, called billboards, which lead into and out of a program, to 10 seconds, to 15 seconds, to 30 seconds, to 60 seconds, and all the way up to half-hour and hour-long programs. These long-form program-length commercials are commonly referred to as infomercials.

Television is also attractive to marketers for its nation-wide coverage through network and syndicated programming. In the current highly fragmented media world, broadcast television still has the broadest reach – 99 percent of American households – and the ability to have impact on the greatest number of people at any one time. Television events and programs such as the Super Bowl, the Academy Awards, "American Idol," and "CSI" are unmatched in their ability to amass enormous audiences.

When people are surveyed, they select television as the "most influential," the "most credible," the "most authoritative," the "most exciting," the "most persuasive," their "primary news source," and the medium that they spend the most time with, as seen in Exhibits 18.2 through 18.8.

One of the disadvantages of broadcast television is that it is not highly targeted. Some advertisers are more interested in a smaller geographic area or in households

Exhibit 18.2 Time spent with media

% of total daily media hours (2006)

Television	58.28
Radio	22.8
Newspapers	4.44
Internet	12.44
Magazines	2.04

Source: www.tvb.org . Used with permission.

Exhibit 18.3 Television news

Primary sources of news (adults 18+)

Broadcast television	43.5%
Cable news networks	23.8%
Newspapers	11.2%
Radio	9.3%
Internet	9.4%
Public TV	3.4%

Source: www.tvb.org. Used with permission.

Exhibit 18.4 Television as a medium

Most authoritative (adults 18+)

Television	51.0%
Newspapers	23.5%
Radio	9.6%
Magazines	11.4%
Internet	4.5%

Source: www.tvb.org. Used with permission.

Exhibit 18.5   Television as a medium

Most exciting (adults 18+)

Television	76.5%
Internet	5.4%
Radio	6.3%
Magazines	8.1%
Newspapers	3.7%

Source: www.tvb.org. Used with permission.

Exhibit 18.6   Television as a medium

Most influential (adults 18+)

Television	81.8%
Internet	3.7%
Newspapers	6.6%
Radio	4.5%
Magazines	3.5%

Source: www.tvb.org. Used with permission.

Exhibit 18.7   Television as a medium

Most persuasive (adults 18+)

Television	66.5%
Newspapers	11.8%
Radio	8.0%
Magazines	9.0%
Internet	4.7%

Source: www.tvb.org. Used with permission.

Exhibit 18.8   Television as a medium

Learn about products (adults 18+)

Television	52.2%
Magazines	20.8%
Newspapers	11.1%
Internet	11.0%
Radio	5.0%

Source: www.tvb.org. Used with permission.

with high income and education levels. Other media, such as Interactive, may be more effective in reaching a desired target audience more precisely. Some advertisers believe broadcast television is expensive. It can be costly on a unit cost basis or when it comes to creating award-winning commercials, but for reaching a mass audience, broadcast television is usually the most efficient medium and is certainly the most effective one in terms of the impact of and engagement with its advertising messages.

Another disadvantage of television advertising is that it is not tangible and is fleeting. While a print ad can be read, studied, re-read, and passed along, once a television commercial is over, it is gone until the next airing or until someone replays it (and watches it) on a digital video recorder (DVR).

Furthermore, the short length of most television commercials does not allow for a lot of detail. A print ad can include many more facts and information, while a 30-second television commercial is restricted to the presentation of dramatic headlines and emotion-arousing appeals.

How local broadcast television is sold

Because broadcast television's audiences are measured continually in the majority of markets, the audience of any program or time period is known with a reasonable amount of precision, as you learned in Chapter 16. Not only is total audience measured, but also its demographic components. Advertising rates in local television are based primarily on five elements: (1) The size of the audience; (2) the demographic makeup of that audience; (3) the supply of available inventory; (4) the current demand for that inventory; and (5) reach. Sales management of a local station, not a station's network or national sales representative firm, controls local television station pricing.

Local television stations generally price and sell their inventory by dayparts, as seen in Exhibit 18.9.

Special programming such as sports and news specials are priced at levels that are not tied to traditional daypart pricing, but are driven by demand – in

---

Exhibit 18.9 Local television dayparts

Late night (Monday–Friday)
Early morning (Monday–Friday)
Daytime (Monday–Friday)
Early news (Monday–Friday)
Early fringe (Monday–Friday)
Primetime (Monday–Sunday)
Late news (Monday–Friday)

Source: www.tvb.org. Used with permission.

high-demand sporting events such as the Super Bowl, a 30-second commercial can be priced as high as $3 million.

Regular daypart pricing is based in large part by audience levels and demographics in those dayparts. Thus, Late Night is the least expensive because television's audiences are smallest at that time. Primetime is the most expensive because television audiences are the highest during primetime (8:00–11:00 p.m. Eastern Standard and Pacific Standard Time, and 7:00–10:00 p.m. Central Standard and Mountain Standard Time), and, more important, the huge reach of primetime commercials makes them more desirable and in higher demand by large national advertisers whose products have mass appeal.

In local television a very large percentage of an affiliated station's revenue comes from news programming – early morning news, early news, and late news, which can add up to as much as three and a half or four hours of news programming. Local television stations can only sell commercials between network programs during the daytime, primetime, and late night. The time between network commercial programs is referred to as a break and there are only between five and seven breaks in three hours of primetime programming. These breaks total no more than, perhaps, a total of eight minutes of commercial time during primetime, thus limiting the amount of revenue stations receive when network programming runs. When local programming such as news or syndication airs, a station makes much more money because a half-hour of news programming can carry as much as eight minutes of commercial time.

Both local and network television is bought and sold based on negotiating. When rates are negotiated, an advertiser pays based on audience delivered and on current supply and demand. Therefore, if you are considering a career as a television salesperson, you are urged to pay particular attention to the section on negotiating in Chapter 12 of this book, as it will serve you especially well.

Local television station sales managers often evaluate salespeople based on what share of an advertiser's television budget they get when they make a sale. Even though the strategy of selling for share is prevalent in local television, it is not the most effective strategy for maximizing revenue. See Chapter 1, "Strategy," in *Media Sales Management*, available free at www.mediaselling.us.

Account lists   Television stations assign salespeople account lists that contain the names of prospects and advertisers. Sales managers usually attempt to balance accounts that are prospects into three levels: excellent, good, and fair, often referred to as A, B, and C prospects respectively. Often new, inexperienced salespeople are assigned account lists that are mostly prospects and are evaluated on how well they turn these prospects into revenue-producing customers. Typically experienced salespeople are assigned an account list that has revenue-producing accounts and agencies. In large markets the most prized account lists contain big agencies with large accounts that invest a lot of money in television.

When experienced salespeople interview for an open job at a local television station, or even at a network, the first question they usually ask is, "What agencies are on the open list?" Because the vast majority of local television station salespeople are paid on some sort of commission basis, having a list that produces a lot of revenue is of vital importance. Agency-oriented salespeople are farmers, and as such they know their success depends on good seed and fertile ground.

In local television, sales staffs are typically organized by agency and direct account lists based on a salesperson's established relationships and experience. Often they are divided into agency/transactional staffs and retail/development staffs. Occasionally a station will organize its staff geographically, but this type of structure is more typical with national reps who are often organized geographically. Some local stations use a category structure, in which salespeople are assigned accounts by category or vertical, such as automotive, retail, or financial. For more information about sales department structure, see Chapter 2 of *Media Sales Management* at www.mediaselling.us.

Selling local broadcast television to advertising agencies   A local television station's advertising revenue is divided into local sales and national spot sales. The revenue for local sales is also split into two types: missionary/development selling and service/transactional selling. Missionary selling is typically calling direct on marketers by hunters. Service selling is typically calling on agencies by farmers, as described in Chapter 2.

Advertising agencies represent and advise local clients about how to use media, about creative approaches, about production of commercials, and about placing commercials in the media. A television station's salespeople in large and medium-sized markets sell primarily to an advertising agency's media department and do transactional business. An agency's media department is commonly made up of a media director, media planners, and media buyers. Large agencies with many clients will have several people in each of these positions. A small local agency may only have one person handling all of the media planning and buying functions.

Television stations' service salespeople call on agencies to inform buyers and agency personnel about their station's programming, special promotions, Nielsen ratings, and advertising rates. Usually a single station salesperson is assigned to an agency and attempts to do as much business as possible with that agency's clients. Much of the interaction by a salesperson is with media buyers, and salespeople try to keep buyers up to date on a station's special opportunities and new programming. More often, a media buyer contacts television station salespeople, alerting them that a client is planning to use television advertising and requesting information about available time, rating information, and costs per unit, known as a request for avails. Sometimes, a request for avails comes in a more formal format known as an RFP (request for a proposal), typically sent by e-mail to a station salesperson.

When a salesperson receives a request for avails or an RFP, the salesperson typically fills out an online form containing all the RFP information. A station automated, computerized system then computes and returns to the salesperson a proposed schedule, sometimes referred to as a package, containing available spots.

Because television is commonly sold by negotiating, it is salespeople's job to create value with the agency and client, as described in Chapter 8, while at the same time maximizing revenue for a station – often a delicate balancing act. During the buying process, it is the job of media buyers to purchase the best value for their clients. Hence, the negotiating process takes place with an agency outlining the parameters of its needs and stations' salespeople responding with their best possible match to agency specifications. Stations often submit their rates at a high level, while media buyers' initial offers are typically at a relatively low level. The two sides negotiate the price along with other factors of value for a client – just like the negotiating process covered in Chapter 12.

Factors other than price that can be negotiated are commercial spot placement, rotation of commercials in a schedule, product separation, help in production of commercials, payment terms, and added value. Added value can take the form of anything that adds value to a commercial schedule, such as merchandising materials, additional exposure on the station in talk shows or with promotion spots, or tickets to local attractions and sporting events that agencies can pass along to their clients. Often stations create packages that can include a commercial schedule as well as added-value elements such as merchandising, sponsorship of special programs, and tickets to big events, especially if an advertiser is buying commercials in an event, such as a sporting event, that a station is airing.

Selling to advertising agencies requires skills in using Nielsen rating information advantageously, in using other research information, in presentation skills, in negotiating, and in excellent customer service. Salespeople assigned to agencies also need to be adept at meeting and dealing with people at the agency other than just the media buyers. The most successful salespeople make it their business to contact media planners, in order to make sure that broadcast television is included in campaign plans, and account executives, who deal with the agencies' clients, to suggest special uses of television by those clients.

Selling local broadcast television direct to marketers   In large markets (the top 50), the primary source of local television station revenue comes through advertising agencies. As market size descends, the percentage of agency-placed business decreases and the percentage placed directly from marketers increases. A top-50 market television station may do 85 percent of its business with agencies. A station in a market below the top 50 may do 85 percent of its business directly from local clients.

Although a local salesperson who calls directly on local marketers needs proficiency in using ratings information, ratings are not usually of critical importance because clients are usually more interested in return on investment (ROI) than in ratings. Missionary salespeople who sell successfully on a direct basis usually are better at fostering relationships with decision makers, providing creative ideas on how to use television advertising, understanding a prospect's business (see Chapter 14), selling on an ROI basis, and providing customer service. There is usually less negotiation involved in direct selling than there is in selling to media buyers, but sometimes negotiating skills are important, especially with retailers who are often skilled negotiators. Much of the negotiation in direct selling involves elements other than Nielsen ratings that can be negotiated, such as commercial placement, added value, and help in producing commercials.

When calling on local retailers, salespeople should understand how cooperative advertising, commonly referred to as co-op, works. To gain a basic understanding of co-op advertising, see the Co-Op advertising section in Chapter 19, "Newspapers," p. 423.

Sales compensation   The most prevalent compensation method for local salespeople is straight commission, although some stations use a combination of salary, bonus, and incentives. Often service selling to advertising agencies earns a lower commission rate than business stimulated by the salesperson who sells direct. Therefore, if you are interested in being more highly compensated as a television salesperson, learning the skills of missionary/development selling is advisable – hunters usually make more money.

Two rules of thumbs to remember: (1) Agencies care about ratings and responsive service; therefore, knowing the personal needs profile of an agency buyer is vital. (2) Marketers care about results and ROI; therefore, knowing a customer's business and marketing objectives and strategies is vital.

Selling non-traditional revenue   In recent years, there has been increased pressure on local television station management for annual revenue increases, while at the same time audiences to local television stations have been declining as cable viewing and Internet usage have eaten into the time people spend with broadcast television. Advertising dollars follow eyeballs, so growth in local television advertising dollars has been slow and station management looks for other revenue streams for growth.

Television station revenue other than advertising revenue is referred to as non-traditional revenue (NTR), which has become a significant source of additional revenue for local television stations. Selling sponsorships of parades, station promotions and contests, and community affairs projects are examples of NTR, and virtually all such NTR is sold on a sponsorship basis, not on a CPM or CPP basis. Selling these sponsorships requires creating value, selling at higher levels (usually at the client level), and taking a more creative approach and a longer time than selling avails on a commodity, CPM or CPP, basis. For more information about selling NTR, see Chapter 21, "Radio."

National/regional selling

Local television stations sell to advertising agencies and direct clients within a station's DMA. Stations generally divide agencies and clients outside a station's DMA into two categories: national and regional. The definition of what is considered a national account or a regional account is typically negotiated with a station's national sales representative company (covered in the next section of this chapter) and covered in a contract between a station and a national rep firm.

In most local television stations a national and/or regional sales manager deals with national and regional business. For example, a station in Austin, Texas, might define all agencies and most clients in the state of Texas as regional business and have a regional sales manager travel to Dallas and Houston to call on agencies and regional clients. On the other hand, another station in Austin might have a contract with its national rep firm that designates all agencies in Dallas as national accounts but those in Houston as regional.

A national rep firm, which typically has offices in all major advertising centers, services accounts designated as national. A station's national sales manager is responsible for all national business and for calling on national accounts along with national rep salespeople who service those accounts.

Typically, local stations control pricing, not a rep firm or a network. Station sales management continually assesses demand for a station's inventory from both national and local accounts and determines time–period pricing, which can change daily in busy months such as November and May. See Chapter 1 of *Media Sales Management*, at www.mediaselling.us, for more information on pricing strategy.

National representative selling

Selling broadcast television advertising on behalf of a number of stations around the country to major advertising agencies is another type of selling. National representative firms sprang up in the newspaper and radio industry because papers and stations realized that it was much more efficient to hire a national sales organization with offices in large advertising centers than to bear the cost of sending their own salespeople to distant cities to call on advertisers and agencies. When television stations were first licensed, companies that also owned newspapers and radio stations owned many of the original television stations that went on the air; therefore, these companies followed the tradition of using national rep companies.

There are two types of national rep firms: O&O and independent. O&O organizations represent stations owned and operated by the major networks, such as ABC, CBS, FOX, or NBC. Independent reps, such as the Katz Television group and Blair Television, represent stations not owned by the networks.

As pointed out earlier in this chapter, national rep firms establish offices in cities around the country that are major advertising centers. National reps may have as many as 20 offices, some in large cities such as New York, Chicago, Los Angeles, Detroit, and Atlanta, and in these offices, the reps will employ a large number of salespeople, perhaps as many as 70 in New York. A smaller office in Minneapolis or Charlotte may have only two or three salespeople.

In large-market offices, a major rep, such as Katz Television Group's Continental Television Sales, might have 100 television station clients, but it splits the sales staff in large offices into teams that represent smaller groups of stations. For example, one team might represent large markets and another team might handle smaller markets, or teams might be divided by network affiliation – all ABC, CBS, FOX and NBC stations in a separate group. The volume of business in the top media centers dictates that reps structure themselves in this manner in order to give better attention to each station and to give salespeople a consistent story to tell buyers. In smaller-market offices, staffed with just a few people, the salespeople are required to sell a rep's entire list of stations.

Selling for a national rep is quite different from selling locally. Local selling requires contact with both agencies and clients. In national rep selling, salespeople have very little contact with clients and they have little opportunity to stimulate business or do missionary selling, because they respond to requests from agencies to present available programs, ratings, and rates for the stations they represent. Therefore, a national sales job is much more reactive than local selling and it is more ratings- and numbers-oriented than local selling.

Agencies use cost-per-point (CPP) as their criteria for efficiency and for planning purposes when buying local markets. A typical agency request for avails might consist of a market budget of $25,000 a week for four weeks for 30-second commercials, a target audience of women 18–49, and 300 gross rating points (GRPs) a week in early morning, daytime, prime access, and late night. The request might include ten of a rep's market with different budgets for each market. Buyers evaluate reps' submissions, which are generally in the form of different packages of spots, and buyers generally select offers based on the lowest CPPs. Rep salespeople typically do not have an opportunity to change their offers once they submit packages unless a salesperson has a particularly good relationship with a buyer.

National rep salespeople must understand Nielsen ratings and have good negotiating, relationship, and servicing skills. Because most media buyers who work for national agencies are very busy, the transactions between a buyer and a salesperson are less about understanding the business of an advertiser and more about negotiating a current buy, getting it done quickly, moving on to the next buy. The process also includes trying to minimize the administrative details that come with changes in the delivery of commercial schedules. These back-office administrative changes have traditionally been referred to as paperwork, but because the majority of communication today is done by e-mail, the term paperwork is outdated.

Changes often occur when a local station misses commercials, runs the wrong version of a commercial, or moves a commercial for some reason. When such changes happen, station sales management will offer substitute positions for missed commercials. These substitute positions are called *make-goods*, and a vast majority of a rep salesperson's administrative details involves dealing with make-goods.

Rep salespeople are farmers who facilitate transactions; there is not a great deal of selling or creating value involved. Being a rep salesperson is a good entry-level sales job for learning the television business, but it is not a sales job that is highly paid (until you get into management) or that is likely to lead to a management job at a television station or network.

Spot television

One of the major appeals of national spot for advertisers and agencies is the flexibility of buying individual markets – that is what spot television means, buying market-by-market. Later in this chapter, we will discuss network selling and you will learn that buying networks gives marketers the opportunity to cover the entire country with just one buy. However, with national spot, marketers have the flexibility to run schedules in selected markets to cover a specific region of the country, to cover just the top markets, or to cover a number of markets that are strategically important to their business growth. An example of strategic market selection would be if a marketer wanted to protect its market share in markets in six Southern states; it would choose to use spot television in markets in those six states. Rather than select the top 50 Nielsen DMAs, where 68.9 percent of the nation's TV households are, marketers can select markets based on such criteria as current sales, market share, ethnic makeup, or as a test market for a new product. For example, a fishing boat company may find that Tampa–St Petersburg, FL (Nielsen DMA ranked 13th)[7] may be much more important than New York City, the number-one market. If a marketer's distribution is not truly nationwide, a selective spot television buy in the Tampa–St Petersburg market would be much more effective and much less costly.

National reps sell in the spot television marketplace.

Broadcast television network selling

Each national broadcast television network has a sales staff devoted to calling on advertisers and advertising agencies. Like other television salespeople, network salespeople try to promote their medium by encouraging the use of nation-wide networks and by selling the fact that advertisers place the largest share of their total television advertising dollars in network television. According to Jack Myers'

Exhibit 18.10　Network television dayparts
Early morning (Monday–Friday)
Daytime (Monday–Friday)
Primetime (Monday–Sunday)
Early evening news (Monday–Friday)
Late evening (Monday–Friday)

Source: www.tvb.org. Used with permission.

2007 and 2008 ad spending estimates, broadcast television networks' share of all broadcast television dollars was 39 percent.[8] Furthermore, according to the Jack Myers' estimates, broadcast television represented 21 percent of total advertising investment in America for 2007 and 2008 (see Exhibit 18.1, p. 377).

Unlike local television and national spot television, which is bought, planned, and, thus, sold on a cost-per-point (CPP) basis, network television is planned, bought, and sold on a cost-per-thousand basis (CPM). And television networks sell dayparts that have different nomenclature from local TV stations. See Exhibit 18.10.

Upfront and scatter markets　Furthermore, networks sell their inventory in two different markets, or frames of time, during the year: in what are called the *upfront market* and the *scatter market*. The upfront market takes place each spring, with advertising schedules purchased to start with the networks' upcoming fall season. There is no exact date for the start of the upfront market, but it usually breaks in May. Networks jockey for position and try to get off to a fast start in order to capture as much money as they can before the other networks begin selling their inventory. Typically, primetime inventory is the first to be sold and then other day parts follow.

During the upfront market, which lasts only a few weeks, each network decides what percentage of the next season's inventory it will sell. Networks establish their upfront CPM pricing based on projected ratings and then negotiate with agencies to determine final pricing. Because networks sell CPMs based on estimated ratings for the upcoming season, they guarantee an advertiser's schedule will achieve an estimated rating level. For example, if an agency buys an upfront schedule consisting of 100 points a week for Verizon Wireless on ABC, ABC will guarantee the schedule achieves 100 rating points. If the schedule underdelivers by, say, 30 rating points, ABC owes Verizon make-goods worth 30 rating points. These make-goods are referred to in the business as audience deficiency announcements (ADAs) or audience deficiency units (ADUs). Therefore, one of a network salesperson's jobs consists of monitoring schedules that have been placed in the spring, watching to see if purchased programs do not achieve projected ratings, and arranging for ADAs.

A network tends to overestimate rating levels of its upcoming season programming in order to maximize the upfront dollars it receives. It is better to underdeliver and give make-goods than it is to underestimate ratings and, thus, overdeliver rating points which means its inventory has been priced too low.

A broadcast network that is enjoying strong ratings may sell as much as 80 percent of its inventory during the upfront market. If a network experiencing weak ratings anticipates that the economy and business climate will be strong in the coming broadcast year, it might sell a lower percentage of its inventory, in the range of 70 percent, in the upfront market, hoping to get a higher price later in the scatter market. Traditionally, the upfront market will generate commitments from advertisers of around $9 billion for ABC, CBS, CW, FOX, and NBC.

The broadcast networks sell the inventory that was not purchased in the upfront market as the season progresses in the scatter market. The scatter market tends to break in late August or early September and agencies purchase schedules for the upcoming fourth quarter. There are four scatter markets, one for each quarter. Scatter market prices are usually higher than in the upfront market, and the networks tend not to give ratings guarantees for schedules purchased in the scatter market, although rating guarantees are always subject to negotiation, especially by lower-rated networks and those with less favorable demographics. Scatter market buying has less guesswork and more stable pricing because current supply, demand, and actual ratings dictate prices.

Broadcast network sales structure   Broadcast networks have sales offices in only the largest media markets of New York, Chicago, and Los Angeles. Network salespeople must be excellent communicators and prodigious entertainers, and have solid, established relationships with the top-level agency and client executives.

If a network has contracts for major sports programming, its sales organization will typically have a dedicated sports sales team. Salespeople who sell network sports work hard during the sports seasons and frequently entertain clients and agency personnel at sporting events seen on their network. Most networks also have separate teams dedicated to selling daytime, primetime, and news programming.

While the salespeople who sell for television networks spend a lot of their time dealing with advertising agencies, they also contact and sell directly to marketing managers and advertising directors at major advertisers. For example, the VP of Advertising for a major automotive company would typically be involved in creating strategy and setting parameters for network ad campaigns; networks expect their salespeople to be comfortable and expert at dealing with these top advertising executives and their agencies. Broadcast network salespeople are the kings and queens of media selling – highly paid, with large expense accounts, each responsible for, perhaps, as much as $500 million in advertising revenue.

Program selling

Companies that produce programs for television, such as Warner Brothers and Paramount, sell to two types of customers: original programming to networks (broadcast and cable) and re-runs to television stations as syndicated programs. Top executives (the President or Executive Vice President, for example) of the television divisions of these production companies typically sell to the networks. For example, Les Moonves, the CEO of CBS in 2007 was previously the President of CBS Entertainment, the division of CBS that selects and schedules programs for the network, as the entertainment divisions of all networks do. Prior to that, Moonves was President of Warner Brothers Television, which produced such programs as "ER" and "Friends" when he was President, and he was involved in selling these programs to the networks.

High-level production executives pitch the networks the concept of a new program in hopes that a network will like it well enough to order a pilot episode. A broadcast network might order as many as 30 pilots for an upcoming season and might eventually select four or five to run in its primetime schedule. If a show that a network has selected achieves good ratings, the network will probably order up to 13 episodes to run over the 22-week network season. Often production companies will spend more money producing a primetime program than it receives in license fees from a network in hopes that the program will be a hit, remain on the network for at least 100 episodes, and, therefore, have a good chance of going into syndication. A production company can recoup its investment in a hit show many times over when the program's episodes go into syndication. When syndicated, a mega-hit like "Seinfeld," which ran for nine years on NBC, can produce hundreds of millions of dollars in profits for its production company, as "Seinfeld" did for Castle Rock Entertainment, which Warner Brothers owns.

Syndicated program selling   Earlier in this chapter, you learned about the two types of syndicated programming, off-network and first-run. Television production companies usually have three divisions, a production division that creates and produces programs, a distribution division that employs salespeople to sell both types of syndication programs to television stations, and a barter division (covered later in this chapter). Selling syndicated programming is a multi-billion-dollar business. To get an idea how big it is, carefully examine television program listings and look at all of the programming on the local television stations in your market. Can you tell how much of a FOX affiliate's programming is syndicated?

Salespeople who sell syndicated programs are very well paid, and must have extensive knowledge not only about their own products but also about the strengths and weaknesses of every station in every market that they call on. Territories of syndicated distribution salespeople are generally assigned regionally. For example, a syndication company may have an office in Atlanta, where one or two salespeople call on all of the stations in all of the markets in the southeast quadrant of the country.

Syndicated salespeople must be excellent negotiators. If they are selling a particularly high-rated program or package of programs, they can often use the scarcity principle and create an auction – competitive bidding from different stations that crave the program, especially if they know other stations in the market want the same program. It takes a skilled negotiator to deal with auction bidding from customers with whom they must maintain good relationships.

Syndication advertising selling   Another type of selling in the syndication business is selling advertising inside syndicated programming on local stations, which is done by the barter division of a syndication company. In the first quarter of 2007, according to an *Advertising Age* report, national syndicated revenue amounted to $986.6 million.[9] When television stations sign a contract with a syndication company for the rights to air a program, they do so for a certain number of runs over a specified number of years. As an example, station KAAA-TV may buy the rights to the off-network show "Will & Grace." Typically, the station would purchase the license to air each episode of that show five times, over a period of, say, six years.

A station can pay for syndication rights in three ways: cash, barter, and a combination of cash and barter. When stations purchase a license for cash, they buy the rights to all of the commercial inventory within the program. Generally, a half-hour program that runs in prime access time contains seven minutes of commercial time. Therefore, if a station buys the rights to "Will & Grace" for cash, it would have available seven minutes (fourteen 30-second spots) during each airing of that program.

"Will & Grace" has 124 individual episodes, which have all run in primetime on the ABC Television network. When sold on a cash basis, the total rights fee is based on a price per episode multiplied by the number of episodes. For example, if a station agreed to pay $4,000 per episode for "Will & Grace," it would pay a total of $4,000 times 124 episodes, or $496,000 for the rights to air the program five times during a six-year period. The per-episode price is negotiated based on a station's market size and the program's estimated ratings.

Stations have a second method of paying license fees for syndicated programming – barter. When a station buys the rights on a barter basis, the seven minutes of inventory within each episode are typically split between the station and the syndication company on a 50/50 basis, each receiving three and a half minutes of commercial time. The station makes no cash payment when it buys a program on a barter basis and can sell its half of the inventory. The syndication company can sell its half of the inventory to national advertisers at favorable rates that are generally lower on a CPM basis than broadcast network programming but with nationwide reach if a popular show such as "Wheel of Fortune" is sold in a total number of markets that contain over 90 percent of the country's population.

The third way that a company can sell syndicated programs is through some combination of cash and barter. In a cash/barter arrangement, a station pays a reduced license fee in cash and gives up, for example, one and a half minutes of inventory and retains five and a half minutes to sell locally. A syndication company uses its portion of the inventory to sell to national advertisers.

Syndication advertising sales is similar to network sales, with salespeople calling on advertisers and advertising agencies. Salespeople show potential buyers a list of stations on which the programming appears, a list of markets, and projected ratings for the syndicated program on a multi-market, or national, basis. Also, as in network selling, syndicated inventory is priced on a CPM basis and ratings are guaranteed to an advertiser. Syndication barter salespeople must have the same negotiating skills and understanding of Nielsen ratings as national rep and network salespeople have, but must also have extensive knowledge of television programming, both past and present.

Jobs in broadcast television

This chapter indicates that there are jobs in local television sales, national spot television sales, network television sales, and syndicated television sales. Many jobs are available, many opportunities to make an extremely good living, and many opportunities to forge a career in television.

The easiest route to getting a job in broadcast television is to start at a local television station. Every commercial television station has a sales force consisting of from one to four sales managers and from four to fifteen or more salespeople. Because there are several broadcast television stations in every market, there is access to television sales jobs throughout the USA. There is also great mobility from station to station and market to market as well as many opportunities to move from local sales, to national spot sales as a rep, to syndication sales, and, eventually, to network sales.

Preparation for a career in broadcast selling should include courses in sales, such as one that uses this textbook, courses in business, courses in advertising, courses in marketing, and courses that enhance your overall communications skills. A sales job in the broadcast television industry places salespeople in the important role as a key link between marketer and medium, and offers the opportunity to be part of the exciting, high-paying, and glamorous television industry.

Cable Television

The history of cable television

In 1948 in the small town of Mahoney City in central Pennsylvania John Walson, who owned the only general store in town, lamented that he could not sell to his customers the hottest new electronics product in America. Throughout the country, television sets were flying off the shelves in large cities and suburbs. Television with its "sight, sound, and motion" programming from the three networks, ABC, CBS and NBC, was exciting people who lived within the reach of the networks' affiliated stations' local broadcast signals. But John Walson in Mahoney City had little hope of selling this profitable new product because people in his community could not receive signals from television stations. The reason was that Mahoney City was too far from the nearest city that had a television station – either Pittsburgh to the west or Philadelphia to the east. A contributing factor to this lack of television reception in Mahoney City was the hills and small mountains surrounding the community that blocked TV signals. Such technical and geographic barriers throughout rural America were excluding millions of people from receiving this new entertainment and information medium in 1948.

It occurred to this entrepreneurial storeowner that if he could somehow access the television signals from either Pittsburgh or Philadelphia and then retransmit them into the households of his community, he could begin to sell television sets in his store. To realize his dream, he built a large receiving antenna (later called a master antenna) on the top of a high hill in the Allegheny Mountains 30 miles east of Mahoney City. Next, he purchased cable wire that connected his antenna to a small building in town. This cable wire, called coaxial cable, was capable of transmitting infinitely more content (text, audio, and video) than normal telephone wires were. From this location, the system head end, as a cable company's central offices are called today, additional coaxial cable trunk wires were strung on telephone poles. Next, separate coaxial wires from the trunk lines on the poles were strung into each cable system subscriber home, thus enabling the distribution of the television signals of the three Philadelphia television network stations. This new method of distributing distant signals of television stations via cable wires into small, usually rural, American towns became known as Community Antenna Television (CATV). Today, it is simply called cable television, or cable.

The vendors of the new coaxial cable, in their sales presentations to cable system owners, stressed an important benefit that at that time had no immediate economic advantage for the cable operators. That benefit was that cable wires had substantial unused capacity, or bandwidth, to deliver more than three channels of television programming into subscribing households. In fact, the earliest coaxial cable had the capacity to deliver 12 channels of video programming. Since there were no other channels except the three networks' stations and because the cable owners were rapidly building new systems in new communities, negotiating with local telephone companies for access to their telephone poles (pole attachment), and working with banks to obtain the necessary financing, the thought of additional channel capacity or any additional applications was mostly overlooked.

John Walson, the rural Pennsylvanian storeowner, soon stocked up on RCA television sets that he sold to his customers and simultaneously sold them CATV for $3 per month so they would have something to watch on their new sets. The biggest expense for the new customer of cable television was the one-time $125 upfront connection fee. Some observers called this subscription television because it was the first time that people actually paid money to receive television programming. Similar to the magazine industry, where most people paid to receive magazines and were referred to as subscribers, so, too, were those who paid the new cable system companies for their television.

During those early years of the cable television industry, no advertising was sold by the local cable systems. The systems retransmitted the network television stations' programming in its entirety, meaning that the stations' network and local advertisers' commercials were seen by cable subscribers – thus increasing audience outside stations' broadcast coverage areas. The most significant implication of the growth in cable television subscribers across the country was that the three broadcast networks and their affiliated stations were delivering additional viewers to both their network and local advertisers.

The cable systems paid no compensation to the networks for their programming nor did the broadcasters pay the cable systems anything for their incremental audience resulting from cable system carriage. In later years, these economic issues and other issues would lead to divisiveness between the broadcasting and cable television industries and to legal initiatives and new government regulations.

Regulation and legislation   Regulation of the cable television industry evolved differently from that of broadcast television. Soon after John Walson's cable system began operating in Mahoney City, scores of other entrepreneurs were constructing master antennas and laying cable wires to build systems throughout rural America. Small-town governments, which are always seeking new tax revenues, soon saw an opportunity to create new income for their communities by taxing cable systems' monthly subscriber revenues. These taxes created a small but continuous stream of revenue for these small towns.

City governments soon realized that there was a much larger economic opportunity when they observed that more and more individuals and small companies wanted to wire their community and become the town's cable operator. (It was assumed from the inception of the cable industry that only one cable system could financially operate successfully in a town or city because of the substantial capital expense of building out the plant – or buying the equipment and wiring the community.) City governments soon created franchising committees, which would evaluate the merits of competing proposals and then award to the selected applicant the community franchise to build and operate a cable system.

Thus, the regulation of the nascent cable television industry began at a local level. It was not like the FCC system that regulated the broadcast industry. There were people in both Washington and the cable and broadcast industry who objected to local control of the cable industry and petitioned the FCC to intervene. In 1956, the FCC decided that cable systems were not common carriers and therefore the Commission had no jurisdiction over the industry.

Later, both the FCC and the courts held that cable companies could operate in any market, and that cable systems were not in violation of copyright infringement because cable system subscribers were paying for the connection to the content and not for the content itself. Broadcasters had wanted to restrict cable operations to rural areas without access to broadcast over-the-air signals, but their request was denied. The ruling allowed cable systems to have a chance to succeed economically and enabled millions of people with no previous access to television programming to receive it.

In the ensuing years, the cable industry fended off both legal and congressional lobbying efforts by the telephone, broadcasting, entertainment, and sports industries, which all tried to capture a part of the growing cable system subscription revenues. Many in the cable industry credit the personality and power of one of the great cable television pioneers and characters, "The Mouth from the South," Ted Turner, for turning the industry around.

The Superstation   The year 1975 will be remembered as the year that changed forever the media industry in the United States and, eventually, throughout the world. Prior to that, only the US government was using satellites orbiting thousands of miles above the globe. The Radio Corporation of America (RCA) had won approval from the FCC to launch the first commercial satellite – a space station geosynchronously orbiting 23,400 miles above the earth with the capability of sending 24 channels of television programming back to earth. Each channel was called a transponder. RCA successfully launched this first satellite in 1975 with one customer, a small pay channel that mailed videotapes of movies leased from the Hollywood studios to a few cable systems that charged their subscribers an additional monthly fee for the service. The company was called Home Box Office (HBO) and it agreed to lease one of RCA's satellite transponders for the life of the satellite, which was 10 years.

For this new system of satellite distribution to succeed, a significant amount of capital was required for equipment to send the programming from HBO studios up to the satellite and downlinks at cable systems to receive the programming. In 1975, cable systems were mired in bank debt borrowed to build their systems and few could afford to pay for downlinks at their headends. HBO, owned by the profitable Time, Inc., devised a financial method to fund the cost of downlinks for the cable systems, thus enabling the systems to receive HBO programming from RCA's satellite and to market the movie channel to their subscribers for $5 per month. HBO's business strategy was to share subscriber revenue equally with the systems and not to accept advertising.

Two years later, in 1977, HBO was still RCA's only customer and its $200 million investment in its communications satellite was looking extremely bleak. Around this time Ted Turner, then the owner of a money-losing UHF television channel, WTBS, in Atlanta, was desperately seeking ways to increase revenues. His station's ratings were continually the lowest in the market and he could not afford to outbid his competitors for quality syndicated programming. The production of competitive local news was also too expensive. The station, however, did have one valuable programming asset: it had purchased the rights to televise the Atlanta Braves baseball games. Despite the games' high ratings, the station still ranked fifth overall and the Atlanta market's television revenues were too low for all five stations to be profitable.

At about this time, Turner agreed to meet with a young cable operator from Florida who claimed to have an idea that would increase WTBS' ratings and revenues. The idea was for Turner to lease a transponder on the satellite, uplink the station's programming and downlink it into cable systems that were now serving nearly five million homes. Not only did this plan eventually achieve Turner's financial hopes for his station, soon referred to as the Superstation, but its success also encouraged other programming entrepreneurs to create new and original cable networks. ESPN, USA Network, CNN, MTV, and others soon followed. Cable systems now had access to a growing supply of non-broadcasting programming. Suddenly new cable subscriptions were growing at a record pace and Wall Street was courting the cable television industry.

While the Superstation sold all of its advertising to local and regional advertisers and, increasingly, to national or network television advertisers, the other new cable networks followed the advertising commercial inventory model created by the broadcast networks with their affiliated stations. That was to provide two minutes of commercial time each hour for the cable systems to sell advertising in their local communities.

Primarily because the early cable system owners and operators were engineers with little understanding of marketing or advertising, and because of the significant costs associated with advertising insertion equipment and salespeople, few cable systems took advantage of the local advertising sales opportunity. By the early 1980s, however, with the continuing increase in the number of cable networks, the improvement of these networks' programming, improvement in audience measurement techniques, and growing advertiser acceptance of cable as a medium, cable systems began to address this important new revenue stream. During the last two decades in the twentieth century, cable system operators increased their investment in capturing local adverting revenues. In the last few years, local ad revenues have represented the highest percentage of revenue growth for cable systems, and in the national television market, cable networks now rival the broadcast network in ad revenues.

Advertiser acceptance   In the early years of the cable industry, ad-supported networks' struggle for advertising revenues was difficult. The most serious drawback was that Nielsen's National Television Index (NTI) did not measure the cable networks. It would not be until late 1983, after significant negotiations, that Nielsen agreed to measure cable networks. Nielsen indicated that if a cable network were available in 12 million cable households it would then qualify for

NTI audience measurement. The broadcast networks vigorously opposed this decision and quietly threatened Nielsen with reprisals. Advertisers, and particularly their ad agencies, also used the poor quality (in their view) of cable's programming, its relatively small universe of subscribing households, and a lack of budget for the new medium as an excuse not to advertise.

Nonetheless, cable, with Turner's networks, ESPN, and MTV leading the way, gradually overcame these objections. When the first Nielsen ratings measuring WTBS, ESPN, and USA were released, the audiences were tiny and the combined cable networks' share of viewing was less than 1 percent. But a measured audience it was.

Equally important, the cable system business was now in favor with Wall Street and large institutional lenders and the pace of new cable system construction rapidly increased. With more new cable networks, each town and city in the country was now clamoring: "I Want My Cable TV," a clever takeoff of the successful advertising campaign used by MTV to tell kids to exhort their parents to sign up with the cable system for MTV.

Both ad-supported and premium pay (without commercials, like HBO) cable networks were also attracting new investment and they began to upgrade the quality of their programming and to schedule more original programming. The impact of the new programming was that cable networks' share of television viewing was increasing nearly as fast as households with cable were. By 2005, there was more total viewing to cable networks than to broadcast networks, primarily because there are many more cable networks than broadcast networks, as seen in Exhibit 18.11.

Industry structure and consolidation By the late 1970s the cable system industry, which was comprised of hundreds of different owners, was beginning

Exhibit 18.11 Long-term US household share trend

	Total day shares (US households)	
	1985/86	2006/07
Ad-supported cable	10.0	51.4
ABC affiliates	19.7	7.5
CBS affiliates	21.6	8.1
NBC affiliates	21.6	7.3
All other TV*	27.1	25.7
Total non ad-supported cable	90.0	48.6

* All other TV includes independents, pay cable, FOX/WB/UPN/PAX affiliates, PBS, all other cable and Hispanic broadcast.

Source: *CAB 2008 Factbook*. New York: Cabletelevision Bureau of Advertising, p. 32. Used with permission.

to consolidate. New companies were being formed to acquire existing systems and to petition for new city franchises. As these companies acquired more systems they were referred to as Multiple System Operators (MSOs). Among the consolidators were Time Warner Cable, Comcast, now the largest MSO, Telecommunications, Inc (TCI), now owned by Comcast, and Cox Cable.

As in any industry, the key factor driving cable system consolidation was scale economics, meaning the larger a company was (scale) the lower the per unit cost of necessary goods and services would be (economics), and today the ten largest MSOs control more than 85 percent of all US cable subscribers.

By the mid-1980s the cable networks, while still not profitable, were being viewed by larger industry companies as valuable assets. Cable network consolidation began with ABC acquiring ESPN from the Getty Oil Company; Viacom acquiring MTV, Nickelodeon and The Movie Channel; and NBC acquiring the USA Network, as examples.

Carriage fees   Scale economics was a key driver of the consolidation described above. The idea was that the more networks a company owned the better its bargaining position with the MSOs for programming carriage fees would be. Carriage fees – money paid by cable systems to the networks for the carriage of the networks' programming – were a major change for the industry and would have lasting impact not only on cable systems and cable networks but on broadcast television as well.

When the cable networks were first formed in the late 1970s, the business models they employed were identical to those used by the broadcast networks. They would acquire and produce programming and provide it to their affiliates, cable systems, and MSOs, which would distribute it to their subscribers. Both would promote the programming and, importantly and similar to the model of broadcast television, the cable networks would compensate the systems for their distribution and generate all their revenues from the sale of advertising. By 1982, it became apparent to the cable networks that their advertising revenue estimates were greatly exaggerated and not achievable. The result was increasing operating losses with little hope of ever reaching profitability.

In 1982, ESPN, led by CEO Bill Grimes, would change the system and save the cable television network business model. ESPN charged MSO companies 10 cents per month, or $1.20 per year, per subscriber. At this time, MSOs were charging an average of $15 per month for only 12 channels of television programming while not paying anything for the programming and collecting monthly fees from the cable networks. The MSOs charged subscribers a minimum fee that included cable delivery of local television stations, WTBS, and a group of advertising-supported cable networks such as ESPN, MTV, CNN, USA, and Lifetime. This minimum was referred to as basic cable, the basic tier. Pay or premium cable referred to the channels, like HBO and Showtime, in another tier that subscribers paid an additional monthly charge to receive. These premium channels were commercial-free.

After 18 months of intense and often heated negotiations with each MSO, all agreed to pay ESPN a monthly subscriber fee averaging 5 cents per subscriber per month. The actual monthly fee was a bit higher, but ESPN provided a discount to systems that agreed to advertise ESPN programming on other channels using local advertising inventory of other cable networks. This new business model, or partnership, changed the industry forever because as other networks followed ESPN's lead in charging the systems a carriage fee, all the cable networks' subscriber revenues greatly increased and were soon exceeding their advertising revenues. Much of the new profits that the networks were generating was reinvested in new programming, which enabled the networks to increase both the quantity and the quality of their programming.

The subscriber fees paid by the MSOs to the networks led to better programming, which, in turn, created the rationale for cable operators to raise prices to their customers and to add new subscribers. The result was a substantial increase in revenues and profits for both MSO and cable networks. Furthermore, this new partnership motivated the MSOs to begin upgrading their system facilities, thus creating more channels for new cable networks and making substantial investments in people and equipment to sell local advertising aggressively. Thus, in the mid-1980s the MSOs embarked upon a concerted effort to challenge newspapers, radio, and television stations for their share of local advertising. It has taken the systems much time, investment, and effort, but today local advertising revenues represent local cable systems' fastest growing revenue stream, and they are continually taking share of market from local television stations.

Cable network programming   There are two basic types of cable networks: ad-supported (e.g., ESPN, MTV, and CNN) and premium pay (e.g., HBO and Showtime that have no advertising). From now on in this chapter when we mention cable networks, we are referring to ad-supported networks, because they are the ones that sell advertising. These ad-supported cable networks gathered and analyzed reams of market data and subscriber programming preferences. First, they looked at what movie titles were available. There were libraries of movies not only from Hollywood but also from around the world, and, better yet, the broadcast networks had licensed only a small percentage of these films. USA Network was being successful, in part, by programming feature films, for example. Networks could always produce more news with investments in bureaus and reporters, as CNN, MSNBC, and FOX News did. Thousands of college sporting events were not being televised by broadcasters, and fishing, auto racing, and yacht racing were available – a fact ESPN and the regional sports networks took advantage of. Films about animals, history, and geography existed in large quantities, which the Discovery Channel and A&E took advantage of. The list could continue, but the point is that a large supply of programming did exist and not all of it was expensive.

Having learned that the programming existed and could be acquired, the cable networks next learned that to differentiate from and to compete with the broadcast networks it would be strategically smart to have a programming theme for each channel – such as sports, news, or animals. Such a theme would provide the viewer with a clearer understanding of the networks' programming position and allow networks to promote themselves more effectively. More importantly, the networks would be able to approach advertisers with whom their target audience was compatible, as MTV did with Pepsi. Most importantly, the networks could offer to many advertisers an audience delivery that had a high composition of a desired target audience. This targeting meant that if an advertiser was seeking to buy men 18–34 and a sports event on ESPN had one million total viewers, as many as 60–70 percent of those viewers might be men 18–34. The same advertiser could buy a similar type program on CBS, which might deliver two million viewers, but a lower percentage would be men 18–34. Thus, ESPN's audience composition would be better – less waste – making ESPN, in this example, more competitive with a broadcast network even when its total audience was much smaller.

The confluence of the programming strategy – scheduling programs of the same type so that viewers know that the channel will always be providing some kind of sports (ESPN), news and information (CNN), or youth lifestyle (MTV) – and the advertising sales strategy of selling audience composition created a great deal of economic value for the cable networks.

Satellite direct-to-home competition   The great growth for the cable television industry began in the early 1980s, driven by access to capital that enabled the operators to build new system franchises and cable networks to produce original programming. Even as new cable systems were being built throughout America, there were many rural areas that lacked sufficient population to justify the investment in a system. These areas lacked the level of density of homes that was financially necessary for the cable systems to extend their services. However, people in these remote areas had no less desire for television than their distant neighbors did.

The companies that manufactured the satellite-receiving antennas for cable systems recognized that if they could produce a receiver dish that people without cable television could purchase and locate on their property, these companies would have access to a new market. Soon they produced a consumer satellite antenna receiver and, although these new dishes were 6 feet in diameter and often an obtrusive sight on a property, people were soon buying this new direct television product. Despite the equipment's high installation cost and the fact that local television stations could not yet be offered, by 1990 over two million large dishes were a feature of the landscape of rural America.

In 1994, Hughes Aircraft Company launched four high-powered satellites 22,300 miles above earth. The power of these geosynchronous satellites (this term refers to the fact that as the world turns so do the satellites thus enabling the continual reception of the television signals to the same geographic receiver antenna dishes) was such that more than 200 video channels could be downlinked into 18-inch receivers.

Today the direct-television industry has two major players, DirecTV and the Dish Network, and they provide serious competition to the cable system industry by providing lower prices than cable and access to multiple channels to homes in rural areas that cable companies cannot afford to wire. In 2007 they reached 30 million homes. As competition is intended to do, companies work harder to supply new services that customers want at increasingly lower real costs while simultaneously improving their customer service. The winner is the consumer.

Advantages of cable television

Advertising on cable television has many of the benefits of other broadcast media and certain unique advantages.

First, it has the sight, sound, and motion of television, which of course it is. For most consumer products, the unmatchable power of sight, sound, and motion is acknowledged to drive sales more than any other medium.

However, unlike broadcast television, the audience of which declines during the summer months, cable television audiences tend to be consistent the year around, as seen in Exhibit 18.12.

Like magazines, cable's segmented programming attracts viewers with highly desirable demographics. ESPN, as an example, has a high percentage of men viewers in its audience. This high male audience composition results in less waste audience for an advertiser for whose products men are the primary buyers.

Similar also to many magazines in delivering highly targeted audiences, cable shares radio's ability to add frequency inexpensively to an advertising schedule.

Exhibit 18.12 Consistent ad-supported cable ratings throughout the year

	US households average audience share (%), fourth quarter 2005	US households average audience share (%), first quarter 2006	US households average audience share (%), second quarter 2006	US households average audience share (%), third quarter 2006
Total day (Monday–Sunday, 6 a.m.–6 p.m.)				
Ad-supported cable	19.4	19.8	19.4	20.1
(index to full year)	98	101	98	102
ABC/CBS/FOX/NBC*	12.5	12.7	10.8	9.9
(index to full year)	109	110	94	86

* Average share of ABC/CBS/FOX/NBC affiliates' audience across the US.

Source: *CAB 2007 Factbook*. New York: Cabletelevision Bureau of Advertising. Used with permission.

Increased frequency occurs because audiences remain loyal to the narrow genre of the programming. As a schedule of commercials airs on that channel, frequency builds because many of the same people view for longer periods of time and then return the next day and the next week to the same channel. Cable channels tend to have more loyal and demographically narrower viewers than broadcast television networks do.

Cable advertising also adds reach to an advertising campaign on broadcast television. There are still some advertisers who spend most of their advertising dollars in broadcast television, but because a broadcast-television-heavy campaign would underdeliver in cable homes, the broadcast campaign would likely reach a lower audience than planned. Furthermore, the audience of a broadcast-only schedule would reach, in general, lower income levels than a similar schedule on cable would, as seen in Exhibit 18.13.

An advantage of cable television advertising that only weekly newspapers or direct mail can match is the delivery of an audience in a small geographic area or trading zone. In most markets there are more than one cable system head ends, which means that the television commercial can be distributed to subscribers in more than one smaller geographic subsets of a market. Thus, in New York City an

Exhibit 18.13   Cable *vs.* non-cable household income characteristics

Upscale profiles	Cable HH vs. US average (index)	Non-cable HH vs. US average (index)	% advantage cable HH
Education: graduated college plus	107	89	20.2%
Home value $500,000+	120	69	73.9%
Occupation: professional and related occupations	108	88	22.7%
Downscale profiles	*Cable HH vs. US average (index)*	*Non-cable HH vs. US average (index)*	*% advantage cable HH*
Education: not graduated from high school	83	126	−34%
Household income less than $20,000	86	122	−29.5%
Home value less than $50,000	74	139	−46.8%
Occupation: natural resources, construction and maintenance occupations	92	112	−17.9%

Source: *CAB 2007 Factbook*. New York: Cabletelevision Bureau of Advertising. Used with permission.

advertiser who wants to reach only consumers in Queens County can do so without having to buy advertising on the cable systems in the four other boroughs. The result is that the advent of these smaller trading zones is providing cable television with a new competitive advantage for advertisers. Also, smaller geographic audience delivery is enabling cable systems for the first time to compete effectively with small weekly newspapers, direct mail, and penny savers (free weekly newspapers).

Another more generic advantage of cable as an advertising medium is that its commercial unit cost is invariably lower than that of its broadcast competitors. This is particularly true in smaller cities where the systems have not attracted nearly the share of advertising revenue that their share of viewing would dictate. Therefore, not only is the cable system's commercial price significantly lower than the market's television stations on a dollar basis, but also its cost-per-thousand viewers delivered to the advertiser are much lower than broadcast stations.

Cable television reaches households with higher incomes than broadcast television does. This advantage translates into a cable household spending more money on virtually every advertised product and service, making cable much more attractive to advertisers, especially an advertiser of upscale products such as Mercedes, financial services, or premium wine.

How local cable television is sold

Local cable systems have sales staffs of similar sizes to local television stations in markets and they sell in much the same way as local broadcast television is priced and sold and to the same customers. In fact, local cable, after newspapers, is the largest competitor to local television.

Local cable salespeople typically do more missionary/development selling than local broadcast television station salespeople do, especially in medium- and small-sized markets.

Local cable salespeople have much more inventory and more targeted inventory to sell than local TV salespeople do. Local cable salespeople not only sell by dayparts but also by cable networks.

Interconnects In many large markets there are is more than one cable company that has a franchise because there is more than one city in a DMA. For example in the country's largest DMA, New York there are several companies that have cable systems, such as Time Warner Cable, Cablevision, and Comcast. To make it easier for marketers to invest in advertising on cable and not have to deal with multiple cable system sales forces, in most markets the cable systems have cooperated to set up a joint venture to sell advertising or make an arrangement with the largest MSO to sell for all cable companies in the DMA. These sales organizations are called interconnects and serve the function of a local rep firm. Exhibit 18.14 shows the interconnects in the top ten markets.

Exhibit 18.14	Major market interconnects

DMA	Interconnect/system
New York	Time Warner Cable Media Sales
	NY Interconnect/Rainbow Media Sales
Los Angeles	Adlink
Chicago	Comcast Spotlight
Philadelphia	Comcast Spotlight
Dallas–Ft. Worth	Comcast Spotlight
San Francisco–Oakland–San Jose	Comcast Spotlight
Boston–Manchester	Comcast Spotlight
Atlanta	Comcast Spotlight
Washington, DC	Comcast Spotlight
Houston	Time Warner Cable Media Sales

Source: *CAB 2008 Factbook*. New York: Cabletelevision Bureau of Advertising. Used with permission.

Selling for an interconnect or for a local cable system is similar to selling for a local television station – to agencies in the larger markets and direct in smaller markets. The types of selling are similar (missionary and service) and account lists are generally similar.

How national cable television is sold

National spot cable is sold by the national sales organizations of the large MSOs and cable companies such as Comcast Spotlight and Time Warner Cable Media Sales, which have offices in the major advertising centers and function much like national sales representative firms do in broadcast television.

Cable television network selling	When cable networks were getting a foothold in the 1980s, cable salespeople emphasized to advertisers the significant CPM differential between broadcast and cable networks. Each cable network during the early days was forced to price their audience at CPMs much lower than their broadcast competitors because of a smaller household universe, lower viewing levels, and a greater supply of commercial inventory.

However, today many of the 116 national, 41 regional news, and 13 regional sports cable networks[10] receive higher CPMs than broadcast networks do because the advantages of cable television make cable audiences more desirable to advertisers.

Unlike broadcast television networks, cable networks account for a majority – 74 percent – of all cable revenue (see Exhibit 18.1, p. 377). Although cable networks generally sell the same dayparts as broadcast networks do (see Exhibit 18.10,

p. 388), because cable has more targeted programming, advertisers often buy specific programs rather than dayparts – ESPN "Sports Center" or "The O'Reilly Factor" on FOX News, for example.

Upfront and scatter markets   Advertisers and agencies buy cable networks in the same two markets as they buy broadcast networks, although in the upfront market, primetime broadcast generally breaks first because ABC, CBS, FOX, and NBC are still in the greatest demand because of their larger reach. However, the big four broadcast network affiliated stations (which reflect the audience of the broadcast networks) collectively do not have as large a total viewing audience as the 116 ad-supported cable networks do, as you can see in Exhibit 18.11 (p. 397). The 27.1 percent share of viewing that All Other TV has in Exhibit 18.11 includes pay cable, PBS, and Hispanic broadcast and cable viewing so, by interpolating, you can see that there is more viewing to ad-supported cable networks than there is to five broadcast networks (currently ABC, CBS, CW, FOX, and NBC).

Cable networks also sell in the four scatter markets similar to the way broadcast networks sell. However, cable networks tend to do better than the broadcast networks do in the third quarter scatter market (summer) because cable networks' share of viewing tends to increase during the summer months when the four major broadcast networks are programming re-runs and trying out new programs (see Exhibit 18.12).

Cable network sales structure   Cable networks have a similar sales structure to the broadcast networks, with sales offices in only the largest media markets. There is virtually no difference between the skills and types of relationships needed for cable network and for broadcast network selling. On the other hand, because cable networks generally have consistent programming genres during the day, they typically do not have separate teams for selling daytime, sports, and other program types like the broadcast networks do.

Even though some companies such as Viacom and Time Warner own multiple cable networks (see Exhibit 18.15), each network generally has its own sales staff. Some of the multiple cable network owners, such as Viacom, have a small group of high-level salespeople who coordinate large investments, typically over $5 million, by advertisers across several networks.

Cross-platform selling

Many of the media conglomerates, such as Time Warner, Viacom, News Corp., and Clear Channel Communications, have a small group of experienced salespeople who sell across all of a company's media assets – television, cable, interactive, radio, magazines, and outdoor – and do what is referred to as cross-platform selling. This means that salespeople in these groups can sell a combination of

Exhibit 18.15 Multiple US cable network owners

AETN*	NBC Universal	Time Warner	Viacom	The Walt Disney Company
A&E	Bravo	Adult Swim	BET	ABC Family
Biography	Sci Fi	Cartoon Network	Comedy	Channel
Channel	USA	CNN	Central	The Disney
Crime &		CNN Headline	MTV	Channel
Investigation		News	MTV2	ESPN
Channel		CNN International	Nickelodeon	ESPN2
History Channel		Court TV	Nick at Night	ESPN News
Military History		HBO (premium)	Spike TV	ESPN Classic
Channel		TBS	VH1	ESPN
		TCM	VH1 Classic	Deportes
		TNT		ESPNU

* The A&E Television Network (AETN) is a joint venture of the Hearst Corporation, ABC, Inc., and NBC Universal.

Source: www.aetn.com, www.nbcuni.com, www.timewarner.com, www.viacom.com, and http://corporate.disney.go.com. Accessed October 27, 2007.

several or all of a company's assets in one package to an advertiser or agency. An advertiser can deal with one salesperson, can place one order, and receive one invoice, which simplifies the process. The opportunity to do this type of synergistic selling had great appeal in 2001 when AOL and Time Warner merged, and was one of the reasons given at the time for the merger.

However, the dream of synergy soon disappeared in the AOL Time Warner merger when it became obvious that walking the walk was much more complex and difficult than talking the talk of cross-platform synergy. The reason for the disconnect was that AOL Time Warner thought the ease and benefits of one-stop-shopping were worth a premium price, but the agencies and advertisers thought that if they bought a bundle of several media, which would mean a fairly large order, they should get a discount. AOL Time Warner did a few successful cross-platform deals, but overall the efforts were and are still not as significant a part of its revenue stream as was anticipated.

The disconnect still plagues cross-platform selling in 2008, as this book is being written. Some large cross-platform deals are negotiated today between major advertisers who are willing to shift their share of ad dollars and media conglomerates who are willing to give discounts for a reasonable increase in share. However, such deals cannot continue over a long period, because no advertiser is willing to continually increase its share of spending with one company, because it would eventually have to give that company 100 percent of its ad dollars – an unreasonable expectation. Thus, cross-platform selling by media conglomerates to large advertisers will only continue in specialized situations.

Salespeople who do cross-platform deals must be knowledgeable in all the media a conglomerate offers, especially Interactive, which is the most complicated media to sell, and must be excellent communicators and relationship builders at high levels in the corporations to whom they sell and whom they service.

Jobs in cable television

There are numerous entry-level sales jobs in cable television at local cable systems, at interconnects, and in the national sales offices of MSO sales organizations. As in broadcast television, it is often easier to start in a market outside of the top ten and work up rather than trying to break into sales at a cable network headquartered in New York. On the other hand, one of the best ways to get a selling job in a cable network is to start out in a sales-support job and work into a higher-paying sales job.

Other good job opportunities are in the affiliate marketing area. Because cable television networks have two revenue streams – subscriber revenue from MSOs and advertising revenue, with subscriber revenue being the largest source of income – there are two types of selling jobs: affiliate marketing and advertising sales. An affiliate marketing salesperson calls on cable system operators and MSOs for a network and manages the affiliation relationship with these cable systems. The job involves negotiating contracts that set the per-subscriber fees MSOs pay for carriage of a network's programming, the channel position of a network on a cable system, the tier a network will be on (a basic tier if a network is ad-supported), and promotional and event arrangements that benefit both the network and the cable operator.

Affiliate marketing jobs require a great deal of travel but they are the best jobs in which to learn the cable business from the ground up. George Bodenheimer, the CEO of ESPN and ABC Sports, came up through the ranks of affiliate marketing to have the top job at cable's most profitable network.

Both broadcast and cable are different delivery systems of television programming – now being joined by the Internet – but they are both television, an exciting, competitive, rewarding, creative, and glamorous business that attracts people who are drawn to this type of business culture and to the corresponding challenges.

Test Yourself

1 What was the first television station licensed by the FCC?
2 In what year was the FOX Television Network founded? And by whom?
3 What are the major dayparts sold in local television stations?
4 What are the major dayparts sold in broadcast and cable network television?

5   Give two examples of off-network syndicated programs and two examples of made-for-syndication syndicated programs.

6   What is the upfront market?

7   What are makegoods?

8   How many commercial television stations are there in America?

9   What is a DMA?

10 What medium is second to television as being perceived to be the most persuasive?

11 What does CATV stand for and why is it important in the history of cable?

12 Who was the "mouth of the South" and why was he important?

13 What programming service was the first to go up in 1975 on the RCA satellite?

14 What is an MSO? An interconnect?

15 How many cable networks were there in 2006?

Projects

Project #1: Look at a current issue of *TV Guide Magazine* and choose three local TV stations to examine. One should be an ABC, CBS, or NBC affiliate; one should be a FOX affiliate; and one should be an independent station. Try to identify how many hours of syndicated programming each of the three types of stations run. What type of station runs the most syndicated programming? What do you think the financial implications are of being the station that runs more hours of syndicated programming than the other two types?

Project #2: Go to www.adage.com, click on Data Center and then on the 100 Leading National Advertisers & Other Spending Data section and download the "Leading National Advertisers Marketers Profiles Yearbook." Examine the Yearbook and see where the top advertisers invest their advertising dollars. Is most of it in TV? Newspapers? The Internet? What did you learn from examining the Yearbook? How might you use it if you were a television salesperson?

References

CAB 2007 Factbook. New York: Cabletelevision Bureau of Advertising.

CAB 2008 Factbook. New York: Cabletelevision Bureau of Advertising.

Resources

www.adage.com (*Advertising Age* magazine)
www.broadcastingcable.com (*Broadcasting and Cable* magazine)
www.jackmyers.com (media financial information, TV and cable programming)

www.mediapost.com (*Media News* magazine, media information)
www.mediaselling.us/media_sales.html (*Media Sales Management*)
www.nielsenmedia.com (Nielsen ratings information)
www.onetvworld.org (Cabletelevision Advertising Bureau)
www.sbca.com (Satellite Broadcasting and Communication Association)
www.tvb.org (Television Bureau of Advertising)

Notes

1   1939, http://en.wikipedia.org/wiki/1939. Accessed September 23, 2007.

2   http://www.broadcastingcable.com/article/CA6500592. Accessed November 15, 2007.

3   http://www.tvb.org. Accessed October 25, 2007.

4   Ibid.

5   www.nielsenmedia.com. Accessed October 25, 2007.

6   www.tvb.org. Accessed October 25, 2007.

7   www.nielsenmedia.com. Accessed October 25, 2007.

8   www.adage.com/datacenter/article.php?article_id=117203. Accessed October 18, 2007.

9   Ibid.

10 *CAB 2007 Factbook*. New York: Cabletelevision Bureau of Advertising.

19

Newspapers

Thomas J. Stultz

The History of Newspapers

Newspapers have been a leading source of local advertising since April 26, 1704, when Postmaster John Campbell first published his weekly *Boston News Letter*. The paper's first advertisement was a real estate announcement that sought a buyer for an Oyster Bay, Long Island, estate.

Surprisingly, the advent of newspaper advertising did not prompt a rapid spread of newspaper publishing in the United States. There were only 70 weekly newspapers in 1790. By 1820, that number of weekly newspapers grew to 422. The number of daily newspapers also rose during that period, increasing from 24 in 1800 to nearly 400 in 1860; however, the biggest push for newspapers came in 1833 when Benjamin Day published *The New York Sun*, the first successful penny newspaper in New York. In four years, circulation of *The Sun* reached 30,000, making it the world's largest newspaper. These penny newspapers were sold by newsboys for a penny instead of the customary 6 cents on street corners in major cities across the United States. Many of these papers relied on sensational articles to appeal to readers and stand out from the other papers being sold on the same street corner. By making the newspaper affordable, circulation began to grow as did the number of newspapers published.

Newspapers in the age of the Internet

In 2006, a total of 1,437 daily newspapers were published in the US.[1] Unlike television, which is dominated by four major networks, newspapers remain a local medium – an attribute that both helps and hinders advertising sales efforts. Advertisers like having the ability to target local markets and, in most cases, newspaper circulation covers the primary retail trading areas most important to retailers. Although dealing with over 1,400 newspapers can be cumbersome for national advertisers, the Newspaper Association of America manages a Newspaper National Network (NNN) whose core strength is its ability to work with national advertisers and their agencies to find ways to make multi-market newspapers work in support of their marketing strategies. The NNN plans and places ads in over 9,000 newspapers – see www.nnnlp.com for details.

Half a century ago, daily newspapers were primarily published in the afternoon. Of 1,772 daily newspapers published in 1950, more than 80 percent (1,450) were published in the afternoon. In 2006 there were 1,437 newspapers with 614 (43 percent) published in the afternoon. The number of Sunday newspapers has grown from 549 in 1950 to 907 in 2006. While daily circulation of all US newspapers declined from 53.8 million in 1950 to 52.6 million in 2006, Sunday circulation actually increased from 46.5 million to 53.1 million, respectively.[2] Consumers spend $10.9 billion annually to read daily newspapers, including the advertisements.[3]

Part of the decline in circulation can be attributed to the increased costs of subscribing to daily and Sunday newspapers in most cities, and to selective reductions in delivery to areas outside the paper's primary retail trading zone as part of cost-cutting measures to increase profits. In addition, the merger of morning and afternoon newspapers in previously competitive markets has reduced both the number of newspapers published and total newspaper circulation. These mergers are typically in the form of joint operating agreements (JOAs). In 2007 fewer than 45 cities had more than one daily newspaper and 11 of those were operated under common ownership. In addition, 12 of the multi-newspaper cities operated under Joint Operating Agreements (JOA) made possible by the Newspaper Preservation Act of 1970.[4]

JOAs were created to preserve a diversity of editorial opinion in communities where the market no longer supported two competing daily newspapers. Under a JOA, editorial operations remain separate while advertising, printing, delivery, and business operations are combined. The elimination of competition in newspaper markets typically results in higher advertising and circulation rates. One reason for these increases is because duplication of newspaper readership in a market is reduced through consolidations and closings, which makes advertising more efficient in single newspaper markets, even though the single remaining newspaper's rate might be higher.

Of course, a major reason for declines in newspaper circulation, readership, and advertising revenue is because of increased competition from weekly newspapers and, especially, the Internet.

There are thousands of weekly newspapers (paid and free), alternative weeklies, advertising shoppers, and local magazines and coupon packets competing for print advertising dollars. In the face of this competition and in order to offer advertisers increased market penetration, many daily newspapers publish Total Market Coverage (TMC) products that are distributed free to non-subscribers on one or more days per week.

Newspaper executives and advertisers are concerned about both the competition and the declining newspaper readership. Average weekday readership of daily newspapers in the top 50 markets has declined from 77.6 percent in 1970 to 48.4 percent in 2007 while Sunday readership has gone from 72.3 percent to 55.4 percent, in the same period.[5] Exhibit 19.1 shows newspaper readership trends from 1998 to 2007.

Newspaper executives are also concerned about the industry's steady decline in total yearly newspaper advertising expenditures which have dropped from $48.67 billion in 2000 to an estimated $43.843 billion in 2007, a drop of 10 percent, as many advertisers switch their ad dollars to online media.

Rather than fight the competition from the Internet and the proliferation of news Web sites and blogs, newspapers have embraced the Web and are migrating their content to their own Web sites. Such robust Web sites as www.nytimes.com and www.washingtonpost.com attract many millions more readers than their printed versions do and bring in substantial revenue, although not yet nearly enough to make up for the loss of advertising revenue in their print editions.

Exhibit 19.1 Daily newspaper readership 1998–2007

Average weekday readership adults (000)

Year	Total adults	% of adults	Men	% of men	Women	% of women
1998	79,046	58.6	40,442	62.2	38,624	55.2
1999	77,680	56.9	39,860	60.6	37,821	53.4
2000	76,596	55.1	39,330	58.8	37,267	51.7
2001	76,367	54.3	38,998	57.5	37,369	51.3
2002	79,638	55.4	40,318	58.2	39,321	52.8
2003	79,094	54.1	40,030	56.8	39,064	51.5
2004	78,285	52.8	39,727	55.5	38,558	50.2
2005	77,673	51.6	39,428	54.1	38,245	49.2
2006	76,088	49.9	38,693	52.3	37,395	47.6
2007	74,714	48.4	38,246	51.0	36,467	45.9

Source: *Scarborough Research Top 50 Market Reports 1998–2007*. Prepared by NAA Business Analysis & Research Dept. Used with permission.

Exhibit 19.2 Annual advertising expenditures 2003–2007

Year	Total print $ millions	% change	Total online $ millions	% change	Total of print and online	
					$ millions	% change
2003	44,393.12	1%	1,216.42	**	45,609.54	*
2004	46,702.00	5%	1,541.26	27%	48,243.26	6%
2005	47,408.08	2%	2,026.52	31%	49,434.60	4%
2006	46,601.34	–2%	2,664.06	31%	49,265.40	–0.3%
2007**	42,703.81	–8%	3,223.06	21%	45,926.87	–7%

* Online was not calculated in 2002.
** Author's estimates.
Source: Prepared by NAA Business Analysis & Research Dept. Used with permission.

Exhibit 19.2 shows overall newspaper advertising revenue trends, including newspapers' Web sites' revenue.

Newspaper Content

Each of the 1,437 daily newspapers is unique in its content because newspapers generally serve different markets, readers, and advertisers. And the newspapers are written, edited, and produced by local news organizations. Newspapers are unique because they totally recreate their products every single day in print. Each day's newspaper is completely different from the one published the day before and from the one to be published the day after.

The content of individual newspapers varies based on the markets served and the size of the newspaper. National newspapers, such as *USA Today* and the *Wall Street Journal*, focus on major national and international news. Metropolitan newspapers like the *Chicago Tribune* and the *Los Angeles Times* offer very broad coverage with an emphasis on state and national news, politics, and college and professional sports, while de-emphasizing local, community news. Suburban and community newspapers offer highly localized content featuring news about local city and county governments, high school sports, civic group activities, and other information not available in the larger newspapers. Each newspaper offers its own version of business and entertainment news, and features geared to the broad national, metropolitan or local audiences they serve. In order to appeal to everyone in a household, newspaper editors produce a wide variety of material beyond simply covering the news. For example, sports and financial pages are believed to have the most appeal to male readers, while lifestyle, social news, shopping columns, fashion, and food news are produced to attract female readers. Comic strips, school news, high school sports and entertainment news are produced to appeal to younger readers while also appealing to a much wider audience.

In the process of gathering and publishing the news, newspapers serve as a daily record of events. While other media may compete with national and metropolitan newspapers for major political or crime stores, mid-size and smaller newspapers almost exclusively cover the local city council meetings, public hearings, and other local events. The publication of this information contributes to an informed electorate which helps democracy work. And the presence of reporters in cities and towns across America provides a safeguard against political corruption and abuse. Newspapers present news of the preceding day and provide a record of that day's news, business, and sports activities. Newspapers provide information on upcoming events and provide entertainment. Newspapers carry strong opinions written by the newspaper's editorial writers or syndicated columnists. These opinions help establish a dialogue on important local, state or national issues and prompt responses from readers who submit letters to the editor, so their viewpoints can be published. This entire process helps unite communities, promote greater understanding, and inform the citizenry in ways that often move them to action.

The typical newspaper is divided into themed sections. While these sections vary from market to market, the most common include main news, state/local, national/international, lifestyle, business, sports, and entertainment. Specialized sections are also published on topics such as home and garden, books, theater, movies, music, automotive, real estate, and careers. These sections make it easier for the reader to work through a newspaper and provide targeted opportunities for advertisers.

The role of newspapers in society has changed very little since Harrie Davis wrote in 1906,

> It is the vigilant sentinel of the masses, the guardian of their rights, the voice of their thoughts and the bulwark of their liberties. It binds the human race together with a link of friendship, tells men of their fellows, and records the progress of the world in the making.[6]

Today, newspapers are compiled and edited by trained reporters and editors who are charged with selecting and chronicling the day's most important, useful, or entertaining happenings. By doing this work for consumers, the newspaper then becomes a random-access database that offers readers easy, non-linear access to the world's events in a format that they can use at their own convenience. Unlike television, which is often viewed passively, a newspaper is an active medium, requiring the reader to physically hold it and turn its pages to read and use it. Also, television is linear, real time, non-random access, which means that television content (radio, too) comes in linear form, one piece after another, and you cannot skip ahead or turn back. You take the content in the order and in the time frame that it is sent.

In order for a newspaper to be influential and successful, it must be trusted by its readers. As a result, newspapers traditionally operate with a strict code of ethics for their journalists. Policies regarding potential conflicts of interest, fairness, independence and objectivity are found in most newsrooms. In addition to avoiding conflicts brought about by close association with political action groups or acceptance of gifts from news sources, news personnel operate independently of the newspaper sales and marketing departments. The separation is necessary in order to avoid being asked to provide favorable news coverage for the newspaper's top advertisers. While such a favorable article might offer a short-term benefit to the newspaper financially, it is commonly believed that such coverage would damage the editorial integrity, reputation, and credibility of the newspaper over the longer term. As a result, a higher premium is rightfully placed on the newspaper's credibility than its short-term financial needs. While advertising sales representatives are often asked by advertisers for special news treatment, the separation of church and state policy allows the sales representatives to remove themselves from any potential controversy surrounding advertisers and editors. And it best serves the needs of readers. See Chapter 3 for a more detailed discussion of media and sales ethics.

How Newspapers Are Sold

Newspapers are "sold" in two ways: to readers (consumers) and to advertisers (customers). Unlike broadcast television, which has only one revenue stream – advertising – and like cable, newspapers have two revenue streams: circulation revenue and advertising revenue, which includes revenue from inserts. Circulation revenue is further broken down into two types: subscription sales and single issue sales.

Circulation revenue

Daily newspapers are sold to consumers either by subscription or on a single-issue basis. Subscribers receive their papers via home delivery, either through "little merchant" walking carriers or adult motor route carriers. Single issues are purchased out of vending machines or over the counter at various news outlets including, but not limited to, newsstands, street hawkers, grocery stores, and so forth. A number of papers are also available to businesses, hotels, and motels on a bulk-purchase basis. Regardless of how consumers receive a newspaper, an individual newspaper's circulation is the combined total of paid subscriptions, single-copy sales, and bulk sales. Circulation revenue traditionally amounts of 20–25 percent of newspapers' total revenue.

Advertising revenue

Unlike other media that base audience projections on sampling techniques, as described in Chapter 16, newspapers base their advertising rates on average weekly circulation and the size and placement of an ad.

Newspapers rely on outside circulation auditing firms to provide independent verification of their circulation numbers. Most daily newspapers are audited by the Audit Bureau of Circulation (ABC), which was established in 1914. The ABC has rules and requirements that all of its members must follow in order to obtain an acceptable audit. Two other newspaper auditing firms, Certified Audit of Circulations, Inc. (CAC), and Verified Audit Circulation (VAC), are also recognized by most advertisers. These audit firms are used primarily by smaller newspapers and weekly publications. In addition to auditing paid circulation newspapers, CAC and VAC also audit free newspapers and advertising publications. The standardization of the auditing process gives advertisers a high level of confidence in a newspaper's circulation claims and the numbers presented to them by newspaper sales representatives. In addition, the audits provide advertisers with a consistent format that merges with their own customer databases for more convenient market analysis.

Audits not only provide average paid circulation figures but also record how many of the papers were purchased through discount programs and at regular price. Circulation data available for newspapers include the number of copies delivered by various methods – newspaper carriers, dealers or agents, street vendors, over-the-counter, and vending machine sales and by the US Postal Service – for the newspaper's city zone, retail trading zone (RTZ), and areas outside the RTZ. Audit reports typically report circulation by community and by zip code. An audit report will also provide advertisers with an estimate of occupied households within each of the newspaper's circulation measurement areas to enable advertisers to easily calculate the newspaper's household penetration in the communities or zip codes most important to an advertiser. Go to www.nytimes. whsites.net/mediakit/newspaper/circulation/index.php to check out the latest *New York Times* weekday and Sunday circulation.

Newspaper salespeople need to know and understand their newspaper's circulation patterns in order to advise advertisers on how best to utilize their newspaper. Sales representatives should also know their competition's coverage in their key zip codes and be able to talk about duplication of reach and readership.

Newspaper Readership

People with higher education and older people are more likely to read a newspaper. See Exhibit 19.3 for details.[7]

Exhibit 19.3 Average daily newspaper readership by education and age demographics

	Education			
Year	Attended high school	Graduated high school	Attended college	Graduated college
2007	36.6%	46.0%	49.6%	53.6%
	Age			
Year	18–24	25–34	35–54	55+
2007	33.9%	33.7%	48.0%	63.7%

Source: *Scarborough Research Top 50 Market Report, 1998–2007.* Prepared by NAA Business Analysis & Research Dept. Used with permission.

Of course, newspaper readership varies from market to market and depends on the demographics of each market, literacy rates, ethnic composition of the market, and competitive alternatives. For that reason, most large and mid-size newspapers conduct their own readership studies on a periodic basis. These studies, conducted by independent research companies that follow established standards of measurement, provide individual newspapers with an excellent look at their readers, non-readers, and users of competitive media including television, radio, weekly newspapers, shoppers, and direct mail. The data collected in these studies are used internally by newspaper managers to identify areas for improvement in content, service, and sales. The data are also used externally with both existing advertisers, to reassure them of the value of newspaper advertising, and with potential advertisers, to demonstrate the size of the audience the advertiser is missing by not using the newspaper.

This readership research breaks down the market in ways that enable advertisers to analyze the newspaper's reach among various demographic groups. These ways include household income, age, sex, race, education, home ownership, marital status, and, probably most important, shopping preferences. The studies also track shopping patterns for various shopping centers and malls as well as for individual stores and services. By measuring these variables consistently on a periodic basis, newspapers help advertisers identify trends or market changes that may impact their businesses in positive or negative ways.

Most newspapers provide this proprietary readership data along with other syndicated market demographic information and census data to help advertisers better understand local market trends and conditions. By being a primary provider of this useful information, newspaper advertising representatives become an extension of the advertisers' marketing departments. This information allows the sales representatives to help advertisers develop successful programs that grow their businesses. Because a salesperson is involved in the planning and develop-ment of these programs, they often benefit by making sure their newspaper is a significant part of a new or expanded advertising program.

One important finding of practically all market research studies is that consum-ers read newspapers for both news and advertising information. The fact that readers regularly, and habitually, look at newspapers to learn what is on sale at their favorite stores or what special item they can find in the newspaper's classified adver-tising section makes a compelling argument for newspaper advertising. Readers regularly shop the ads in newspapers whether they are looking for a new home, a new job, or a new stereo system, in order to keep up with local price trends.

In many ways, readers look at newspaper advertising as a shopping mall of information and store news to help them decide where and when to shop.

Newspaper Advertising

Newspaper advertising comes in all shapes and sizes. An effective newspaper ad might consist of only three lines of carefully worded copy, placed in the Merchan-dise for Sale category in the classified section, or it could be a multi-page section printed behind the main news section. Newspapers are organized to accommo-date all types of advertising from both big and small advertisers. Advertising in newspapers is typically divided into four categories – classified, classified display, display, and preprinted inserts.

Classified advertising

Even though classified advertising in newspapers has been hurt significantly by free Internet services such as Craig's List (www.craigslist.com) for general classi-fieds, Monster.com (www.monster.com) for jobs, job-specific Internet services such as HigherEdJobs.com (www.higheredjobs.com), and individual sites by real-tors, auto dealers, auto manufacturers, and boards of realtors, classifieds is still an important source of ad revenue for newspapers. Classified advertisements, also called want ads, appear in small type under indexed headings which identify the type of product or service advertised. Many newspapers also offer bold headlines, color type, and logos in classified to help improve the readership of individual ads. These small ads, often numbering more than one million per year for large met-ropolitan newspapers, provide strong newspaper readership and interactivity with readers. Classified ads are usually sold on a per-line basis and appear in the classi-fied sections of the newspaper. Generally, these sections have 10 columns per page. Some papers have six, eight, or nine columns. These small ads inform readers where yard sales are being held, what used cars are for sale, and who is trying to sell their exercise equipment. A number of service businesses also use these classified ads because they can afford to advertise every day. This increased frequency enables consumers to know where to look for contact information when they are in need of someone to trim their trees, mow their lawns, or clean their gutters.

Classified display ads

Classified display advertising differs from regular classified in several ways. The copy usually occupies more space. It is surrounded by a bold border and often features product illustrations, bold type and headlines, and/or company logos. The most common users of classified display advertising are automobile dealers, realtors, and employers or recruiters. By placing these similar advertisements in one section of the paper, newspapers make it easy for readers to comparison shop for services such as these. At the same time, the shopping environment works for advertisers because consumers know where to look for the market's most comprehensive compilation of ads of interest to them when they are in the market for a new or used car or truck, a new home, or a new job. Research shows, for example, that new car buyers are very likely to read automotive ads in their newspaper before buying to get information on the models and prices that interest buyers most. These same buyers continue to read the automotive ads for several weeks after making their purchase just to make sure they got the best possible deal. Consumers have been trained through years of consistent advertising to rely on newspapers for such information. As a result, advertisers know they need to be represented in the newspaper marketplace on a consistent basis if they wish to be successful.

Display ads

Display advertising (often called ROP – run of paper or run of press) is the term used to describe the bold advertisements found in sections of the newspaper other than the classified section. These display ads usually occupy fairly large spaces, but can vary in size from one column inch (1 7/8 inches wide by 1 inch deep) to a 126 column-inch-page, six columns or 12 inches wide by 21.5 inches deep. Display ads are surrounded by bold or graphic borders and are not placed under specific headers, similar to the classified display ads. These display ads may be promotional, offering price and merchandise information, brand or image building, or a combination of these styles and formats. Advertisers like display ads because they can squeeze a lot of product and price information into each ad. This gives consumers more product options to consider. And, it increases the likelihood that one or more of their advertised items will appeal to potential customers.

Display advertising is often divided into two major categories – local, also referred to as retail, and national, often referred to as general. Newspapers rely heavily on local retail advertising which is usually sold via bulk annual contracts at the paper's most attractive rates. Local display advertising is sold by the newspaper's sales representatives through direct sales calls on local store owners or managers or at regional and national chain store offices. In most cases, an advertiser is treated as a local account if it operates a retail or service outlet within the newspaper's market area. National display advertising has been a declining segment for newspapers. Much of the traditional national display advertising, which consisted of manufacturers' product coupons, has shifted away from display ads to coupon ads in the Sunday coupon supplements. These supplements are produced by national firms such as Valassis and News America. They are distributed primarily through Sunday newspapers across the US.

Newspaper representative firms   National ads are usually sold by newspaper representative firms. Newspapers charge higher rates for national advertising which typically comes from manufacturers, wholesalers, service organizations, or political action committees. Publishers justify the rate differentials by explaining that national advertising is usually commissionable to advertising agencies while local display ads are usually non-commissionable to advertising agencies. Also, national advertising representative firms usually take a percentage of each sale, which also increases the newspaper's costs for each national transaction. Furthermore, publishers feel they should reward local advertisers with the most attractive rates because of the consistency of their advertising programs with the newspaper and because most local advertisers do not serve as wide a geographical area as most national advertisers do, and, therefore, do not have as large a potential market. Many advertising executives believe the national rate differential has contributed significantly to the industry's loss of national advertising. However, newspapers that have reduced national rates individually have not typically seen an increase in volume from national accounts. It is more likely that a switch to television advertising by most national advertisers is the culprit and cause of this decline. Broadcast competitors generally do not charge different rates to local and national advertisers.

In addition to local display and national display, newspapers also offer category rates for market segments, such as movies and entertainment, electronics, automotive dealer associations, and so forth. To see an example of different rate categories, go to www.nytimes.whsites.net/mediakit/newspaper/rates/ad_rates.php to see the categories offered by the *New York Times*.

Newspaper pricing

Unlike the broadcast and cable media, newspapers are not constrained by limitations on advertising inventory availability – they have what economists call elastic supply. Newspapers can usually add more pages or reduce the number of pages to deal with increases or decreases in advertising volume. While broadcasters sell spots at rates that reflect current market supply and demand economics because of their fixed-inventory constraints (inelastic supply), newspapers charge established advertising rates that reward advertisers for contractual commitments based on frequency and/or volume (in advertising space or dollar investment).

Newspapers, unlike broadcasting and cable, want to encourage advertisers to buy more and more space. Newspaper advertising contracts are usually sold on an annual basis, although most newspapers reserve the right to adjust advertising rates with 30 days written notice.

A typical newspaper advertising rate card is designed to encourage advertisers to make significant commitments to run well-planned, consistent advertising programs with the newspaper, rewarding them with lower advertising rates based on increased levels of volume or frequency, see www.nytimes.whsites.net/mediakit/newspaper/rates/ad_rates.php for an example. A newspaper rate card allows advertisers to know in advance what their advertising will cost every time they advertise during the life of the contract. This means that advertisers in the same business, running identical advertising schedules, can generally expect to pay the same rates and have similar opportunities for lower rates based on increases in advertising, although in recent years, because of declining revenue, newspapers are more willing to negotiate rates than in the past.

Advertisers also like knowing that their advertising rates are consistent throughout the year, unlike in television and radio. This way, they can better plan and budget their regular advertising and promotion programs. They do not have to worry about costs increasing during the advertiser's most important seasons and can adjust the size and frequency of their ads to reflect current business trends and seasonal patterns. Larger advertisers negotiate aggressively for preferred positioning within the newspaper with back pages, color positions, and page three among the more popular positions.

A typical newspaper rate card will offer non-contract open rates for occasional advertisers, annual bulk rates and/or dollar volume contracts for larger advertisers, and various small space frequency contracts for smaller stores and services. Newspapers often offer special introductory rates to entice non-advertisers to try newspaper advertising. And many newspapers offer special incentives to advertisers who agree to increase their total investment with the newspaper by significant amounts. Exhibit 19.4 shows a typical newspaper annual bulk rate structure for display ads in a daily and Sunday newspaper with 65,000 circulation.

As you can tell from the rate structure seen in Exhibit 19.4, newspapers offer contract rates for small, mid-size, and large advertisers. To determine what rate an advertiser should be paying, a salesperson will need to know either the average ad size and frequency or the advertiser's annual budget. For example, an advertiser who wants to run a quarter-page ad every week, 52 weeks a year, would be running 1,638 column inches per year. To determine the number of annual inches in this case, the salesperson would need to know that a full page ad is 126 column

Exhibit 19.4 Display advertising annual bulk rates.

Inches per year	Rate per column inch	Minimum annual dollar volume
Non-contract open rate	$49.60	
126 inches per year	$35.40	$4,460
200 inches per year	$32.70	$6,540
500 inches per year	$30.90	$15,450
1,000 inches per year	$30.10	$30,100
2,000 inches per year	$29.70	$59,400
4,000 inches per year	$29.30	$117,200
6,500 inches per year	$28.90	$187,850
9,000 inches per year	$28.40	$255,600
12,000 inches per year	$28.00	$336,000
15,000 inches per year	$27.60	$414,000
20,000 inches per year	$27.20	$544,000
25,000 inches per year	$26.60	$665,000
30,000 inches per year	$26.20	$786,000

inches, 6 columns wide by 21 inches deep. Thus, a quarter-page ad is 31½ column inches, 3 columns by 10½ inches. The salesperson would then multiply the ad size, 31½ inches, by the number of weeks in a year (52) to determine the minimum annual commitment. To be on the safe side, a sales rep could have the advertiser sign a 1,000-inch bulk rate contract which would earn the advertiser a contract rate of $30.10 per column inch.

Newspaper salespeople will typically discuss special holiday programs or major sales events when an advertiser might want to increase ad size or frequency. As a result, a more aggressive approach would be to seek a 2,000-inch bulk contract which would earn an advertiser a contract rate of $29.70 per column inch. By signing a larger contract, an advertiser earns a lower rate and gets the benefit of nearly 400 more column inches to help with major sales events. At the same time, the newspaper gets another $10,000 in advertising revenue from this customer. In this way, the bulk contracts serve as a valuable sales tool to help salespeople increase the business they receive by helping their advertisers earn lower rates through increased advertising volume.

Newspapers also offer discounts to encourage advertisers to repeat the same ads within a limited time frame. These pick-up rate discounts typically range from 20 percent to 50 percent off the regular price of the ad for increasing the frequency of the ad schedule. Newspapers establish rules for such repeat ads that limit the number of copy changes and the time frame to earn the discounts. Other discount programs encourage advertisers to run ads every day, every other day, weekly or in large multi-page units. Many newspapers also offer remnant or stand-by advertising rates. A limited number of remnant ads are sold at lower than normal rates and may be scheduled or not scheduled at the newspaper's convenience. Newspapers use these remnant ads to boost advertising on slower days, fill sections that need to be printed in advance of the main news sections, and balance out the mix of editorial and advertising in the paper's makeup on any given day. A newspaper advertising sales representative should be familiar with all the rate options in order to recommend the most effective program to advertisers.

Color rates and positioning

Advertisers also have a variety of color and positioning options with newspapers. Color ads are available in one color plus black, called spot color; two colors plus black; and process color, or full color. Because the color ads consume more of the newspaper press capacity, newspapers have surcharges that are added to the cost of the advertising space to pay for the additional color ink and loss of press capacity. Because of the uncertainty regarding the number of pages printed on any given day, newspapers usually do not guarantee advertising placement requests from advertisers unless the advertiser is willing to pay a premium rate or negotiates a prime position as part of a regular (usually very large) display advertising contract. Whenever possible, newspapers do try to accommodate positioning requests within the various sections of the paper.

Co-op advertising

Co-op advertising is another source of revenue for newspapers. Each year national manufacturers set aside billions of dollars to pay for local promotion of their products. Retailers who meet the requirements of the individual co-op programs earn total or partial reimbursement of ad costs from the manufacturers, usually based on the value of the products retailers purchase from the manufacturers. Newspaper reps help retailers identify sources of co-op advertising dollars which can then be used by retailers to increase their advertising exposure without increasing their costs. Because manufacturers set aside the co-op advertising dollars when retailers buy their products, the retailers need to use the money they have already invested to increase their store traffic and turn more merchandise through the use of larger, more effective ads. Many newspapers have co-op specialists to assist salespeople in finding and capturing co-op dollars for retailers. Co-op advertising has changed in the past few years. Today many advertisers are taking co-op in the form of discounts on merchandise or in-store placement allowances instead of building up co-op media advertising dollars.

Newspaper inserts

Newspaper preprints or inserts are advertising circulars that are not printed as part of the daily or Sunday newspaper but are distributed through the newspaper. Many advertisers, particularly national chain stores, use inserts because they can gain economies of scale by printing millions of copies at a time and shipping them in bulk to the newspapers they select to distribute their advertising messages. Preprints also provide advertisers with more options for running full color advertisements and for choosing higher grades of paper. Preprint advertisers can usually print and distribute more pages of advertising through this method. In addition, preprint advertising enables advertisers to zone their distribution to targeted areas, usually zip codes, around each of their stores or service areas. By maximizing the space available for product display and targeting the distribution, advertisers feel they can make their advertising investment more effective and more efficient. One weakness, however, is the lead time required for producing these preprinted inserts. For example, a typical display ad can be scheduled on Thursday for a Sunday newspaper, while a preprinted insert often must be designed, printed, and shipped weeks ahead of its distribution date. The loss of lead time can make it difficult for advertisers to respond to changing competitive environments. In addition, efforts to centralize and standardize these preprints in order to avoid printer charges for makeovers and changes often result in a loss of autonomy for individual stores or regions which may face different market pressures and preferences.

Newspaper preprint rates typically charge advertisers based on the size of the preprint or number of papers; quantity distributed, or thousands of pieces to be delivered; and the annual frequency, or number of times advertisers plan to distribute preprints per year. These factors are calculated into a cost-per-thousand rate for each size preprint.

Elements of Effective Newspaper Advertising

Little has changed over the years since 1923 when Dr Daniel Starch, a Harvard professor, noted that:

> [the] functions of an advertisement are fivefold: To attract attention (the advertisement must be seen); to arouse interest (the advertisement must be read); to create conviction (the advertisement must be believed); to produce a response (the advertisement must be acted upon); and to impress the memory (the advertisement in most cases must be remembered).[8]

To make their advertising more effective, advertisers often need help with designing their advertising, especially in smaller and middle-size accounts. They need help from their newspaper sales representative to help them find better ways to promote their products and services more effectively. Salespeople should remember that their accounts are not usually experts in advertising. Thus, their job is to educate their customers so their advertisements produce better results. A salesperson's number-one objective is to get results for their customers, as you learned in Chapter 2, and an important factor in generating more results from newspaper ads is finding ways to increase ad readership by using effective layouts and writing good copy.

A professional newspaper salesperson should understand the fundamentals of good advertising copy and layout, so they can advise their clients and potential clients. Often a newspaper sales representative may eventually be the person responsible for writing the copy and laying out the ad, especially at smaller newspapers. At larger newspapers, a creative department usually produces the ads.

One good sales technique is to invest the time to produce a sample ad, or spec ad, which can demonstrate to the advertiser what the newspaper is capable of producing for them. Spec ads also show advertisers that the sales rep is interested in their business and is attempting to share expertise to help advertisers grow their business. While developing spec ads, either alone or with assistance from a creative services department, takes some time, it is usually very productive in terms of selling advertising campaigns with multiple insertions. If the spec ad helps make the sale, it can turn into months or even years of regular advertising. A number of new digital art and graphics services enable newspaper reps to create spec ads quickly by reviewing successful ads from other markets and accessing creative artwork that can be customized for their clients.

Each newspaper should offer training in copy and layout in general with specific procedures for processing advertising materials at that newspaper. For general information, the NAA 2007 *Newspaper Advertising Planbook* recommends the AIDA Formula for creating effective ads. This formula claims that good ads have four things in common: They create attention, interest, desire, and action.

A = Attention	Grab the reader's attention with headlines, type, white space and visuals.
I = Interest	Make the copy interesting and benefit-oriented.
D = Desire	People read ad copy to find out how a product or service benefits them. So make sure the copy answers this reader's question: "What's in it for me?"
A = Action	Urge the reader to act now – and make it easy to do so.

These four elements translate into successful ad layouts and designs by using attention-grabbing headlines and key benefit statements, dominant illustrations or graphics, readable and complete copy, a compelling offer, and an attractive, recognizable company logo complete with store locations, hours, telephone numbers, and Web site URL. Such ads give consumers the information they need to make intelligent shopping decisions.

Establishing advertising budgets

Newspaper sales representatives who have earned the trust of their customers will often be asked to help customers develop their advertising budget. Whether helping prepare an actual budget or simply advising when, what, and how much to advertise, a salesperson needs to understand how to prepare and plan advertising. This planning is another process that takes time at the front end in working with clients, but reduces the time a salesperson spends with that account on a regular basis, because ads and budgets are planned for the upcoming months.

The budget planning process begins with an overview of how advertisers' business has performed over the past 12 months and how they expect it will perform in the upcoming year. Wise advertisers should attempt to match their advertising investments with their monthly sales trends or expected sales. The newspaper industry publishes an annual *National Advertising Planbook* that helps salespeople advise their clients on when and what to advertise and how much they should be investing each month based on that industry's sales patterns.

The advertiser and salesperson should record the monthly sales and identify what percent of the entire year's sales were made each month. In another column, the salesperson should record how much the advertiser invested in advertising each month and what percent of the entire year's advertising dollars were invested each month. Theoretically, those two items – sales and advertising – should be approximately the same percent of the year's totals for both categories. For example, an advertiser who receives 8 percent of sales in January should invest 8 percent of the annual advertising in January as well.

This formula makes sure that advertisers have a consistent advertising presence in the market while also placing the heaviest advertising investment in the months with the greatest sales potential. In theory, it is similar to the notion of fishing when the fish are biting.

By establishing the budget amounts, a salesperson and an advertiser can work together to plan the best items to place in each ad, the days to run the ads, and how to track the results of each ad. A salesperson may also want to recommend setting aside some additional dollars for special promotions or opportunities. And a salesperson may want to advise an advertiser to increase spending ahead of the sales curve to build momentum before the biggest shopping seasons.

If newspaper salespeople can become involved in clients' planning and budgeting, they can actually become an extension of the client's marketing and advertising department. Such a relationship places the newspaper sales representative in the best possible position to help clients grow their business and to secure a fair share of clients' advertising for the salesperson's newspaper.

Newspaper Sales Organizations

Newspaper sales departments are organized to serve their different customers and represent their different products. These products include classified, classified display, local or retail display, national display and preprints. Because each sale involves a different pricing and marketing strategy, most newspapers are organized along these advertising product lines. Naturally, a larger newspaper will have more layers of senior executives and mid-level supervisors than a small paper will. The basic structure, though, will be similar in newspapers of all sizes. The key sub-departments in a typical advertising sales department include:

The Advertising Director or Vice President of Advertising is the top advertising executive at the newspaper – a position that usually reports either to the Publisher or General Manager. The Advertising Director directs all advertising sales, creative and customer service departments, usually including classified, national, and retail departments.

The Retail Advertising Manager manages the local display advertising sales staff and sales, including hiring and supervising direct reports. The Retail Advertising Manager will plan local sales promotions, have input on key pricing decisions, coordinate special advertising sections, conduct training, and often handles many of the newspaper's major accounts. Depending on the size of the newspaper, retail managers may have local sales supervisors and co-op advertising coordinators reporting to them instead of the local sales reps. The retail manager also works with the Advertising Director to establish annual revenue and expense budgets and sales initiatives.

The Classified Advertising Manager organizes and supervises the inside telephone sales staff and customer service functions in classified, and works with inside and outside salespeople selling and servicing existing display accounts and developing new business. Automotive, real estate, recruitment, commercial line ads, and private party ads usually fall under the supervision of the classified manager. At larger papers, there may be additional inside telephone sales managers, category specialists for recruitment, automotive, and real estate, and supervisors for the outside sales teams for each category of classified display advertising. Classified managers recruit, hire, train, and supervise personnel for their departments. They also work with the advertising director to establish budgets, sales goals and quotas, and implement pricing and marketing programs.

Major Accounts Manager, National Advertising Manager, Co-op Advertising Manager are positions you find at larger newspapers. Major accounts managers direct a team of sales representatives that works with the newspaper's largest accounts, which often include many national and regional retail chains. These accounts demand more attention and a higher level of professional service and sales pressure from newspapers. As a result, the major accounts department attempts to surround these accounts by presenting the newspaper's story and benefits to everyone involved in the advertiser's decision making process. This intense coverage means calling on local store managers, district managers, regional advertising directors, and corporate officers, for example, to make sure everyone involved in recommending advertising purchases is aware of the newspaper's benefits and its position in its market. The national manager works with the newspaper's national sales representative firm. The co-op manager works with local display salespeople and retailers in an effort to find co-op dollars so retailers can stretch their advertising.

The newspaper's sales structure provides the organizational support to care for each type of customer. It also provides excellent career opportunities for professionals who are hired at one level and progress through the ranks. Of all the media reps in the market, newspaper reps consistently spend the most time with retail clients and decision makers. As a result, they have an excellent knowledge of what is happening in the local market and become a valuable source of information and ideas for all their clients. Generally, newspaper salespeople are the most knowledgeable marketing professionals in their markets.

Account assignments   Newspaper sales managers have a variety of ways of assigning accounts to salespeople. Newspapers may assign account lists, account categories, or geographic territories to outside sales representatives. Each method has it pluses and minuses. Account list assignments give outside salespeople freedom to cover the entire market prospecting for accounts. Once they make a sale, the account goes on their account list indefinitely. This method makes sure that someone is calling on the best potential accounts because commissioned salespeople aggressively pursue the biggest spenders. However, the account list method often results in duplication of effort as multiple salespeople are calling on the same accounts. In the process, many smaller accounts often get overlooked.

Category assignments make sense when special knowledge or expertise is necessary or where there is a common buying structure in place. Typical category salespeople would serve automotive, real estate, recruitment, entertainment, ad agencies, chain stores, department stores, and grocery stores, for example. The advantage of having category specialists is that salespeople develop a depth of category knowledge and expertise that serves advertisers well. Category specialists do not work as well with small local accounts because there are too many of them to effectively cover without wasting a lot of time driving around the market. That's where territorial salespeople come into the picture.

Territorial salespeople are assigned specific geographic areas and every account in their territory is theirs to sell, with the exception of any major or category-excluded accounts. The purpose of the territorial sales structure is to make it efficient for salespeople to park their cars and go door to door soliciting advertising and servicing clients. Because newspapers offer advertising programs for all size businesses and budgets, territorial salespeople consider practically every business in their area a prospect for advertising in the newspaper.

The purpose of all of the various sales structure options is to make sure the newspaper is surrounding as many of its potential advertisers as possible with the right amount and type of sales expertise necessary to properly sell and service each type of account. Because the needs of each advertiser vary for a multitude of reasons, most newspapers utilize a combination of the possible sales structures. Regardless of how a newspaper operates, it is a salesperson's job to seek more business from existing accounts, while at the same time increasing the number of active accounts by prospecting for and convincing businesses to begin advertising in their newspaper. With slightly more than one half of the typical newspaper salesperson's compensation based on commissions and bonuses, they have a strong incentive to increase revenues for their newspapers. Newspaper salespeople must also have incentives for signing new accounts since there is usually some turnover with smaller businesses.

The Future of Newspapers

With every major new entrant into the media landscape, many observers have predicted the imminent demise of the newspaper industry. First it was radio, then television, then direct mail, then audiotext and videotext, and now the Internet. All of these entrants were expected to replace newspapers because of the unique characteristics and competitive advantages these up-and-comers offered that news-papers could not – sight, sound, motion, instantaneous access, depth and breadth of coverage. However, in spite of these threats, newspapers remain an important source for news and advertising information and the dominant source for local news and information.

In addition, newspaper executives are struggling with what to do about declin-ing circulation and market penetration. Many are wondering if the traditional paid circulation model will remain intact or if new measurements for audience penetra-tion and readership might not be more appropriate in the quest to serve both readers and advertisers. These issues are especially sensitive as information becomes more commoditized with increasing amounts of news and information now avail-able free from sources other than daily newspapers, especially the Internet.

Newspaper executives are also searching for ways to make their popular Internet sites financially successful. Newspaper Web sites are among the most popular on the Internet and their rapidly increasing revenue is helping newspapers but, unfor-tunately, not enough to stem a steady decline in overall newspaper profit margins.

In spite of these challenges, newspapers should remain a viable business and an important medium for the foreseeable future. The industry is learning how to reduce and control costs through consolidation, automation, out-sourcing, and resource-sharing. Newspapers are using technology to provide better and more efficient customer service. And, most important, newspapers remain the primary vehicle for local news and advertising information.

Test Yourself

1 What is the significance of penny newspapers?
2 How many daily and weekly newspapers are there in the United States?
3 What is a JOA and how are they usually organized?
4 In the newspaper industry, what do the following sets of initials stand for: ABC, CAC, VAC?
5 Which demographics read newspapers (1) the least and (2) the most?
6 What are the two possible meanings of the term ROP?
7 In newspapers what are bulk rates?
8 Name four benefits of newspaper advertising.

Project

Imagine that you are the owner of a local furniture store that is preparing to open a new store. Your new store will be 50,000 square feet and you know that most furniture stores located in neighborhood shopping centers generate and average sales per square foot of $178.33 annually. You've learned that most household furniture stores invest 9.7 percent of sales in advertising and that sales in the fourth quarter typically make up 28.7 percent of the annual total with 8.6 percent of total sales in October, 9.5 percent in November, and 10.6 percent in December. Given that information, how much should you budget for newspaper advertising in the fourth quarter, assuming an average amount of sales per square foot? Prepare an advertising budget and then use the advertising rate card for display advertising annual bulk rates (Exhibit 19.4) to determine how many column inches of advertising and how many full-page ads you can purchase and stay within your proposed budget (assume an annual dollar volume of $336,000 on the rate card in Exhibit 19.4 and 126 column inches in a full page).

Resources

www.naa.org (The Newspaper Advertising Association)
www.nnnlp.com (The National Newspaper Network sales organization)
www.editorandpublisher.com (*Editor and Publisher* magazine)
www.snpa.org (Southern Newspaper Publishers Association)
www.inlandpress.org (Inland Press Association – for progressive newspapers)

www.readership.org (Northwestern University's Readership Institute research center)

References

Editor & Publisher International Year Book 2002. New York: Editor & Publisher.

Albert Wesley Frey. 1953. *Advertising.* New York: The Ronald Press Company.

Inland Press Association. 2002. *National Cost and Revenue Study for Daily Newspapers.* Des Plaines, IL: Inland Press Association.

Inland Press Association. 2002. *Newspaper Industry Compensation Study.* Des Plaines, IL: Inland Press Association.

International Newspaper Marketing Association. 2002. *Outlook 2003: Positioning Newspapers for Uncertainty.* Dallas, TX: International Newspaper Marketing Association.

Mack Hanan. 1989. *Key Account Selling.* New York: American Management Association.

Mack Hanan. 1999. *Consultative Selling.* New York: American Management Association.

Otto Kleppner. 1941. *Advertising Procedure.* New York: Prentice-Hall.

Philip Kotler. 2000. *Marketing Management.* New York: Prentice-Hall.

Newspaper Association of America. 2007. *NAA 2007 Newspaper Advertising Planbook.* Arlington, VA: Newspaper Association of America.

Newspaper Association of America. 2007. *Circulation Facts, Figures, and Logic.* Arlington, VA: Newspaper Association of America.

Newspaper Association of America. 2007. *Competitive Media Brochures.* Arlington, VA: Newspaper Association of America.

Newspaper Association of America. 2007. *Why Newspapers?* Arlington, VA: Newspaper Association of America.

New York Press Club. 1906. *Journalism Illustrated.* New York: The New York Press Club.

Ohio University-Scripps Howard News. 2002. *Newspaper Readership Survey Results.* Athens, OH: Ohio University Press. June.

Daniel Starch. 1926. *Principles of Advertising.* Chicago: A.W. Shaw Company.

Notes

1 http://www.naa.org/Trendsand-Numbers/Total-Paid-Circulation.aspx. Accessed November 26, 2007.

2 Ibid.

3 http://www.naa.org/trendsandAnumbers/Circulation-Expenditures.aspx. Accessed November 26, 2007.

4 *Editor & Publisher Yearbook.* 2002. New York.

5 http://www.naa.org/docs/Research/Daily_National_Top50_1998–2006.pdf. Accessed November 26, 2007.

6 *Journalism Illustrated,* 1906. New York: New York Press Club.

7 http://www.naa.org/docs/Research/Education_Daily_National_Top50_98–07.pdf. Accessed February, 2008.

8 Daniel Starch: 1926. *Principles of Advertising.* Chicago and New York: A.W. Shaw Company, p. 7.

20

The Internet

Vincent Thompson and Paul Talbot

As an advertising medium, the Internet is complex and measured differently from traditional media. Also, online advertising buys are often difficult to execute and to implement. So why are marketers switching billions of dollars to the Internet? Because the Internet is one of the most disruptive innovations of our time and represents the most fertile environment ever for marketer–consumer interaction. Disruptive technologies transform societies – the way people live, think, and conduct business – and the Internet has been as disruptive and transformative as movable type, the telegraph, airplanes, and the computer.

The History of the Internet

Most historians agree that the birth of the Internet occurred in 1969 when computer scientists from the government and universities linked large mainframe computers together with the objectives of sharing data and distributing information over a network. This groundbreaking work came from a desire to ensure the safety of government data during natural disasters or war and to allow university researchers the ability to share information. Prior to this project, networks were set up like phone systems with information traveling through vulnerable central-ized hubs. With the invention of the distributed network, information could be simply routed along any of the networks' many connections until it found its way to its final destination. Aiding this concept was the use of packets. Packets allow small chunks of digital data to be sent into the network independently and then reassembled at their final destinations. Once the initial computers at UCLA and Stanford universities were connected in 1969, other universities followed suit and with each addition the network gained more power and provided more value to its users.[1]

Over the next five years scientists developed cornerstone technologies such as e-mail, the ability to access the network remotely, and the ability to host multiple chat sessions. Born as the Arpanet, the main long distance backbone was paid for and maintained by the National Science Foundation (NSF). The NSF had an Acceptable Use Policy limiting any commercial use of the Internet and encourag-ing researchers to only exchange e-mails or share files with persons in their fields of expertise.[2]

It was e-mail that first demonstrated the value of the Internet. Suddenly phone tag was decreasing and the challenges that time zones played were falling by the wayside. Researchers were communicating more via e-mail, and the benefits were obvious. Some within the research community argued that the Internet should be commercially available so that business could share in these new efficiencies, but computers were still extremely expensive and the Internet needed another wave of innovation before their case for increased use became apparent.[3]

That time did come, however, in 1993, when Tim Berners-Lee, a researcher at the CERN atomic research center in Switzerland, developed protocols which allowed computers to better communicate over the Internet and allowed any computer on the network the ability to browse another's content. Soon a Web browser followed and the World Wide Web was born. At the University of Illinois a student named Marc Andreessen, who later co-founded Netscape, and his friends took the Web to a whole new level by introducing a browser they called Mosaic which had the ability to view graphics while running on the ubiquitous Microsoft Windows platform. This innovation combined with other factors, such as the rising popularity and falling price of personal computers and the US government's decision to lift the Acceptable Use Policy and stop subsidizing the Internet, created tremendous momentum. In 1994, the Internet became a commercial medium and entrepreneurs sprung up to harness its power and the opportunities it provided. Internet Service Providers (ISPs) that provided telephone dial-up connection to the Internet grew out of small fan clubs or non-profit endeavors and morphed into large-scale businesses. Between 1993 and 1996, the number of Web sites one could visit grew from 130 to over 150,000.[4] In Robert Reid's book *Architects of the Web*, he profiles the core innovations that defined the World Wide Web in its earli-est days and still play a key role today.[5]

According to Reid, those core innovations were:

HTML and the Internet browser. Hyper text markup language (HTML) gave us the
language to program Web pages. Embedded HTML code uses commands,
called tags, that tell a Web browser how to display content, where to put
images, and what backgrounds should look like. Browsers recognize all of these
commands and bring the pieces together for us.

Java. Java technology from Sun Microsystems gave Internet surfers the opportunity to run little computer programs within HTML content. Java allowed programmers to animate many Web applications such as mortgage calculators,
registration forms, and the booking engines that travel and airline Web sites
use.

Streaming audio. A company named Real Audio provided a way for us to send
music and later video over the Internet in a stream of packets that assemble on
computers and provide users with a constant image or music stream.

VRML (Virtual Reality Modeling Language). VRML gave us the opportunity to
render 3-D images on the Web making visual applications more appealing and
powerful.

Advertising measurement. I-Pro was the first company to measure the Web in such
a manner that advertisers and programmers could understand it and how
people used it.

Content sites and merged media. Wired magazine and C-Net were the first to put up
Web pages with custom content designed to inform users and build a relationship with them. Users could not only read content but they could also participate in creating their own content through message boards and online chat
areas.

As the online world and the Internet gained popularity with consumers in the late
1990s, exuberance for the Web skyrocketed. Anyone coming in touch with the
medium could see the value of doing things online and see the impact that
this new medium had on business. Suddenly, everyone wanted a piece of the
action and investors began throwing their money at Web-based businesses. Pundits
spoke of "the new economy" and those involved felt they were at the epicenter
of a revolution. Each month, a new business category gained popularity online
and immediately followers jumped into the game. Businesses that originated
solely as online businesses were called pure-plays or dot.com businesses. Businesses that had physical locations and created online sites earned the moniker of
click-and-mortar businesses. On Wall Street investors made large bets that the
pure-plays would displace the traditional offline category leaders and bet against
traditional firms without Internet presence. It was the new economy against the
old and the old guard raced to join the game only adding to the Internet frenzy.
During this phase of incredible expansion, dot.com jobs and dot.com dreams filled
the heads of many recent college graduates and many mid-career employees

as they sought wealth in the form of valuable stock options from dot.com start-ups.

The birth of Internet advertising

It was the summer of 1994, and the Web had become a commercial environment. However, few knew about it and the controversy over how the Web should be used dominated the conversations of those who did. Should sites accept advertising? Should content be free? Time Inc.'s Walter Isaacson was rolling out Pathfinder, an assemblage of some of the prestigious and popular Time Inc. content on the Web and freely accessible to all. The *New York Times* launched @times.com and in San Francisco's South of Market district in the depths of *Wired* magazine's accounting office sat a cubby hole filled with designers cranking away on what would become HotWired.com.

HotWired.com would be a techno-savvy site that examined technology and its implications on society, just as its sister publication *Wired* had, but without moving content from the printed media online. HotWired.com would stay away from shovelware, as they called re-purposed content from print, and create its own fresh content for the Web. *Wired* founder Louis Rossetto, *Hotwired* CEO Andrew Anker, and their first hire, Jonathon Steuer, all knew that advertising was going to be the primary revenue stream in their business plan. When it came time to execute, none of them really had any preconceived ideas about what online advertising was. Prodigy had tried advertising on its online service and was vilified by its users – this was the Web, a pristine environment without advertising and without standards. But HotWired.com included advertising in their business plan and had to move ahead.[6]

Thinking about the relationship between advertising and editorial in the print world, the HotWired.com team decided that ads would ride along with content and that users who clicked on the ads would be directed to advertisers' websites. After some debate, they settled on what they believed to be their primary advertising vehicle, a 468 x 60 mega-pixel unit floating at the top of each page. They could have called it a spot, a billboard, or a Web click or many other labels; instead they called it a banner, and today it remains as the most common form of Internet advertising.

Today, many marketers believe that consumers simply move past banners, that standard-sized banners have become merely wallpaper, and that consumers do not stop to read them. Thus, larger and different size ad units have been developed that include interaction and moving graphics. These interactive, moving, or video ads are called rich media.

When it came time for the HotWired.com team to determine pricing, they decided to charge a set fee per banner per month. They did not charge for individual impressions. The idea of charging for impressions by the thousand came from traditional media buying practices and soon after became the standard Internet pricing model.

CompuServe, AOL, and Yahoo!

No Internet companies exemplified the new Internet economy, better than its earliest stars – CompuServe, AOL, and Yahoo!

CompuServe CompuServe was the first online service to offer Internet connectivity as early as 1989 when it connected its proprietary e-mail service to allow incoming and outgoing messages to other Internet e-mail addresses.[7]

In the early years of the 1990s, CompuServe was the most popular Internet service provider (ISP), with hundreds of thousands of users visiting its thousands of moderated forums, forerunners to the endless variety of discussion sites on the Web today. For example, in 1992, CompuServe and Eliot Stein's ShowBiz forum hosted the industry's first electronic movie press kit, for the Universal computer-themed feature film *Sneakers*.[8]

During the early 1990s, CompuServe's hourly rate fell from over $10 an hour to $1.95 an hour. In April 1995, CompuServe topped three million members, still the largest online service provider, and launched its NetLauncher service, providing Internet access capability via the Mosaic browser. AOL, however, introduced a far cheaper flat-rate, unlimited-time, advertisement-supported price plan in 1996 in the US to compete with CompuServe's hourly charges, which caused a significant loss of customers for CompuServe until it responded with a similar plan of its own at $24.95 per month in late 1997.

In February 1998, John W. Sidgmore, then the vice-chairman of WorldCom, and the former CEO of UUNET, devised a complex transaction in which World-Com purchased all the shares of CompuServe with $1.2 billion of WorldCom stock. Literally the next day, WorldCom sold the CompuServe Information Service portion of the company to AOL. AOL in turn sold its networking division, Advanced Network Services (ANS), to WorldCom and CompuServe became a division of its one-time competitor AOL.[9]

AOL AOL began life as a short-lived venture called Control Video Corporation, founded by William von Meister. Its sole product was an online service called Gameline for the Atari 2600 video game console. Subscribers bought a modem from the company for $49.95 and paid a one-time $15 setup fee. Gameline permitted subscribers to temporarily download games and keep track of high scores, at a cost of approximately $1 per hour.[10]

In 1983, the company nearly went bankrupt, and an investor in Control Video, Frank Caufield, had a friend, Jim Kimsey, brought in as a manufacturing consultant. That same year, Steve Case joined the company as a full-time marketing employee upon the joint recommendations of von Meister and Kimsey. Kimsey went on to become the CEO of the newly renamed Quantum Computer Services in 1985, after von Meister was quietly dropped from the company.[11]

Case rose quickly through the ranks; Kimsey promoted him to Vice-President of Marketing not long after becoming CEO, and later promoted him further to Executive Vice-President in 1987. Kimsey soon began to groom Case to become CEO, which he did when Kimsey retired in 1991.

Kimsey changed the company's strategy, and in 1985 launched a sort of mega-bulletin board service for Commodore 64 computers, originally called Quantum Link ("Q-Link" for short). In May 1988, Quantum and Apple launched AppleLink Personal Edition for Apple II and Macintosh computers. After the two companies parted ways in October 1989, Quantum changed the service's name to America Online. In August 1988, Quantum launched PC Link, a service for IBM-compatible PCs developed in a joint venture with the Tandy Corporation.[12]

In February 1991, AOL for DOS was launched using a GeoWorks interface. This was followed a year later by AOL for Windows. These changes coincided with a growth in pay-based online services, for example Prodigy, CompuServe, and GEnie. AOL discontinued Q-Link and PC Link in the fall of 1994.[13]

New CEO Case positioned AOL as the online service for people unfamiliar with computers, in contrast to CompuServe, which had long served the technical community. The PlayNet system that AOL licensed was the first online service to require use of proprietary software, rather than a standard terminal program; as a result it was able to offer a graphical user interface (GUI) instead of command lines, and was well ahead of the competition in emphasizing communication among members as a feature. In particular was the Chat Room concept from PlayNet, as opposed to the previous paradigm of CB-style channels championed by CompuServe. Chat rooms allowed a large group of people with similar interests to convene and hold conversations in real time.[14]

In March 1994, AOL added access to USENET to the features it offered. AOL quickly surpassed GEnie, and by the mid-1990s, it passed Prodigy (which for several years allowed AOL advertising) and CompuServe under Steve Case's leadership and vision. The subtitle of author Kara Swisher's book, *aol.com*, says it all – "How Steve Case Beat Bill Gates, Nailed the Netheads, and Made Millions in the War for the Web."

Originally, AOL charged its users an hourly fee, but under the direction of brilliant marketing whiz, Bob Pittman, and CEO Steve Case, the company dropped its hourly fee. On December 1, 1996, it announced a flat rate of $19.99 per month. Within three years, AOL's user base grew to 10 million people. During this time, AOL connections would be flooded with users trying to get on, and many canceled their accounts due to constant busy signals. But AOL's massive marketing program flooded the country with computer disks containing AOL access software as effective television commercials hammered home the message, "AOL – so easy to use, no wonder it's #1." Marketing turned the tide and AOL became syn-onymous with the Internet, as over half the traffic to the Internet in America came through AOL – truly America online.

AOL was entering its peak growth years, and according to Kara Swisher:

> In the second quarter of 1997, AOL had 153 million page views a day in content, 136 million in People Connection (essentially sex chat), 131 million in e-mail, and 62 million on the Internet. People were spending more than a half-hour a day on the service. There was growing proof, at least in a poll commissioned by AOL, that television usage was being affected by online activities of consumers.[15]

By January 2000, AOL's growth peaked when the total value of its stock (market capitalization) reached $164 billion – larger than General Motors, Ford, and Chrysler combined. This gigantic market cap made it possible for AOL to do the seemingly impossible – buy the world's largest media conglomerate, Time Warner. AOL paid a 71 percent premium for Time Warner's stock to acquire 56 percent of Time Warner, and when the deal was approved on January 7, 2000, it was the biggest corporate merger in US history, worth an estimated $183 billion.[16]

But, as the saying goes, "what goes up must come down." AOL top advertising sales executive Myer Berlow called the six months after the merger "the perfect storm" because over-aggressive cost reduction predictions and over-aggressive revenue increase predictions met a slowdown in advertising and the bursting of the dot.com bubble. When the AOL–Time Warner merger was announced on January 10, 2000, AOL stock on the New York Stock Exchange closed at $72.62 a share. Three years later, on January 12, 2003, when AOL Time Warner chairman Steve Case resigned, the stock closed at $14.83, confirming that the merger was not only the largest but also the most disastrous in the history of US business.[17]

Yahoo!   In January 1994, Jerry Yang and David Filo were Stanford University electrical engineering graduate students. They started a list of Web pages in a campus trailer in February 1994 as a way to keep track of fantasy basketball statistics on the Internet. The lists were published as a Web site named Jerry's Guide to the World Wide Web and grew large enough to require categories and subcategories organized in a hierarchy.

In April 1994, Jerry's Guide to the World Wide Web was renamed Yahoo. Filo and Yang said they selected the name because they liked the word's general defini-tion, which comes from *Gulliver's Travels* by Jonathan Swift: "rude, unsophisti-cated, uncouth."[18]

By the end of 1994, Yahoo! had already received over one million hits. Yang and Filo realized their Web site had massive business potential, and on March 1, 1995, Yahoo! was incorporated and a month later, on April 5, Sequoia Capital provided Yahoo! with two rounds of venture capital. "Yahoo" had already been trademarked for barbecue sauce and knives. Therefore, in order to get the trademark, Yang and Filo added the exclamation mark to the name[19] In April 1996, Yahoo! had its initial public offering (IPO), raising $33.8 million dollars, by selling 2.6 million shares at $13 each.[20]

Like many search engines and Internet directories, Yahoo! diversified into becoming a Web portal. In the late 1990s, Yahoo!, MSN, Lycos, Excite, and other Web portals were growing rapidly as primary entries to the Internet. Web portal publishers rushed to acquire other companies to expand their range of services in the hope of increasing the time a user stays with the portal, or in Internet industry parlance, to become "stickier."

In 1997, Yahoo! acquired online communications company Four11. Four11's Webmail service, Rocketmail, became Yahoo Mail. Yahoo! also acquired Classic-Games.com and turned it into Yahoo Games. Yahoo! then acquired direct marketing company Yoyodyne Entertainment, Inc. In March 1998, in an attempt to keep up with AOL's highly popular Instant Message (AIM) service, Yahoo! launched Yahoo Pager, an instant messaging service that was renamed Yahoo Messenger a year later. Digital video advertising was born with the sale of Mark Cuban's and Todd Wagner's Broadcast.com to Yahoo! in 1998 for the sum of $5.7 billion – that put digital video on the map. In 1999, Yahoo! acquired Web hosting provider GeoCities, once more trying to compete with AOL and its Digital Cities joint venture.[21]

The fierce (and often unfriendly) competition between Yahoo! and AOL led both companies to innovate, which was good for consumers, and led to battles for advertising revenue, which was good for advertisers. In the last two years of the twentieth century, the two companies commanded approximately 90 percent of all Internet advertising revenue. As a result, on January 3, 2000, at the height of the dot-com boom and of the AOL–Yahoo! competition, Yahoo! stock closed at an all-time high of $475.00 a share.[22]

In late 2002, Yahoo! began to bolster its search services by acquiring other search engines. In December 2002, Yahoo! acquired search engine Inktomi and in July 2003 it acquired Overture Services, Inc. and its subsidiaries AltaVista and All-theWeb. In February 2004, Yahoo! dropped Google-powered search results and returned to using its own technology to provide search results.[23]

In early 2005, Yahoo! continued acquiring companies to expand its range of services. For example, Yahoo Launchcast became Yahoo Music and in March 2005 Yahoo! purchased photo sharing service Flickr and launched its blogging and social networking service Yahoo! 360°. In June 2005, Yahoo! acquired blogs, a service based on real simple syndication (RSS) feed aggregation. Yahoo! acquired social bookmark site del.icio.us in December 2005.[24]

In February 2008 Microsoft announced an offer of $31 for all of Yahoo! shares in an attempt to buy the company and merge it with its own MSN network so it could compete more effectively with the behemoth Google.

The dot.com bubble

Business people bought into the premise that online made things more efficient. Retailers did not need stores. Banks did not need branches. Brokerage houses did not need brokers; you could trade your own stock. Everyone hates the car buying process right? Why not sell cars online? How about Christmas trees and hams? Why not sell them online? What about hardware or pet food or sports scores or the Yellow Pages? How about a bride from Russia? It seemed like any need that one could have suddenly had taken the form of a funded business plan and a destination on the Web. Many believed that Universal Record Locators (URLs), or domain names, such as Etoys.com, or Pets.com were prime real estate. Some well-respected Los Angeles entrepreneurs paid an estimated $7.5 million in stock for the rights to Business.com. As hysterical as things became, and as high as the valuations spiraled, the time came for reality to take hold. Many of the dot.coms imploded when the dot.com stock market bubble burst after the AOL–Time Warner merger in 2000. Short of cash, the dot.coms sold their assets and sent their employees home. Many hard lessons were learned during the dot.com bubble. While some of the lessons can still be argued, in general, entrepreneurs learned the following about consumers and the online universe:

Efficiency and price are not the only drivers of success. Adding convenience and cost savings does not guarantee success. Pets.com did not make it as pure-play Internet company. Consumers were not ready to abandon their habits. Some even enjoyed the process of shopping at the local pet store. Amazon.com, the Web's biggest retailer, has built a large brand and a thriving business, but it did not replace the bookstores entirely. What about the other thousands of dot. com sites? Most did not make it, and most failed to do what people in offline stores do every day by selling things to us and creating desire. The Web has yet to replace the salesperson who tells me how nice my sweater looks when I try it on. That said, clothing is a category that is working online. The Gap, Banana Republic, and Old Navy were among the first retailers that made their online business work, because they started with customers buying basic clothes they knew and understood and then the business built from there.

Consumers expect Web content to be free. With the Web came communities and the ability to find people with similar interests and passions. If you were a punk rocker in Utah you could connect with punks in Great Britain. Community sites flourished as users contributed to message boards and participated in social networks. Editors began to believe that e-zines, or online magazines, would allow them to publish content with lower costs and reach highly targeted groups. Thus, the content site was born and investors raced to support them. The value of these sites was measured by the number of visitors and by the potential to sell advertising. What publishers learned however, was that content was expensive to create. The typical dot.com content site was burning in the range of $500,000 to $1 million a month, and users were unwilling to pay for the content. At the same time, advertisers were not buying enough to fund the businesses.

For online marketers there quickly became a glut of advertising inventory and prices dropped accordingly, which meant these online publishers could not recover their costs and many folded.

The Google.com search disruption

Before the 2000 dot.com stock market bubble exploded and became the dot.com bust, AOL had purchased Netscape, located in the heart of Silicon Valley, for $4.2 billion in the fall of 1998. But Netscape employees were not thrilled about working for what they perceived to be arrogant, Eastern managers, so many of them left for Silicon Valley Internet start-up businesses. One of those new start-ups that was hiring was a new search engine named Google – a name many traditional business people thought was as silly as Yahoo!.

As was the case with Yahoo!, Google was started by two Stanford University graduate students. Larry Page and Sergey Brin argued vigorously when they first met at a Stanford indoctrination tour in 1995. Brin was the guide whom Page thought "was pretty obnoxious."[25] But the two obviously found each other intellectually stimulating and formed, to say the least, a productive relationship. By 1997, they had developed a highly efficient search engine based on an innovative and complex mathematical algorithm that they called PageRank, based on how many links a Web page had from other Web pages.

On September 7, 1998, Page and Brin incorporated Google, Inc. and began to determine the best business model for their efficient search engine. The two originally tried to license Google to other search engines rather than attempt to start their own competitive search engine company. At that time, Yahoo!, Excite, AltaVista, Infoseek, and HotBot were all in the search business, so Page and Brin made presentations to those companies to try to sell them a license for their new search technology, but with no success. The other search companies were wedded to their own methods and technology and saw no need to spend money on an unproven technology.[26]

This not-invented-here mindset is typical when established companies are faced with a disruptive technology, as Clayton Christensen points out in his book *The Innovators' Dilemma*:

> Disruptive technologies bring to a market a very different value proposition than had been available previously. Generally, disruptive technologies underperform established products in mainstream markets. But they have other features that a few

fringe (and generally new) customers value. Products based on disruptive technologies are typically cheaper, simpler, smaller, and frequently more convenient to use.
There are many examples in addition to the personal desktop computer . . . [t]ransistors
were disruptive technologies relative to vacuum tubes.[27]

Christensen writes that most disruptive technologies are adapted initially by the
least profitable customers in a market, and, therefore, most companies can rarely
justify adopting disruptive technologies until it is too late. Such was the case with
Yahoo!, Excite, AltaVista, Infoseek, and HotBot, all of whom, with the exception
of Yahoo!, Google eventually put out of business with more relevant, faster, and
easier-to-use technology.

But by 2000, Google had still not determined how to make money on its
superior search technology. It took the impetus of the dot.com stock bubble
bursting for Brin, Page, and Google's new CEO, Eric Schmidt, to figure out a
viable business model, with the help of an ex-Netscape sales executive, Omid
Kordestani. In October 2002, Google introduced its new automated advertising
service called AdWords, modeled after Bill Gross's GoTo pay-for-search-results
model, but which featured an automated online auction in which advertisers both
large and small could bid for keywords on a cost-per-click basis. Google's revenue
skyrocketed from zero to, as John Battelle writes, "a billion dollars, one nickel at
a time."[28]

Exhibit 20.1 shows how dominant Google had become in search by the end of
2007, as it was well on its way to accomplishing its mission "to organize the world's
information and make it universally accessible and useful" and, in fact, be "the
closest thing the Web has to an ultimate answer machine."[29]

This dominant position in Web searches led Google to be the most profitable
Internet business in the world, with a market capitalization on March 20, 2008, of
$135 billion, larger than the combined market cap of three other media conglom-
erates, Time Warner, Walt Disney, and News Corp. on that date. Market capitalization is the market value of a company that is calculated by multiplying the

Exhibit 20.1   US core searches by search engine

Core search entity	December 2007
Google sites	58.4%
Yahoo sites	22.9%
Microsoft sites	9.8%
Time Warner Network (AOL, etc.)	4.6%
Ask Network	4.3%

Source: http://searchenginewatch.com/showPage.html?
page=3618341. Accessed March, 2008.

Exhibit 20.2 Google financial comparisons (in $billions), full year as of December 31, 2007

	Google (GOOG)*	Time-Warner (TWX)**	Walt Disney (DIS)**	News Corp.*** (NWS)**
Market cap	$135	$50.75	$60.1	$18.4
Total revenue	$16,594	$46,482	$35,510	$28,655
Gross profit	$9,949	$19,056	$6,781	$10,010
Net income	$4,203.7	$4,387	$4,687	$3,426

* NASDAQ stock symbol.
** NYSE stock symbol.
*** News Corp. as of July, 2007.
Source: http://investing.businessweek.com/research/company/overview/overview.asp. Accessed March, 2008.

number of outstanding shares of a company by the price of a single share of stock. And in 2007, with about one-third of the total revenue of the world's largest media company, Time Warner, Google had approximately the same net income, as seen in Exhibit 20.2.

The MySpace.com social network disruption

Google was a disruptive technology that changed the way people found information. MySpace.com was a disruptive technology that changed the way people connected with each other. MySpace is a social networking Web site offering an interactive functionality, user-generated content, and a user-submitted network of friends, personal profiles, blogs, groups, photos, music, and videos.

After the 2002 launch of the original social networking Web site, Friendster. com, several eUniverse employees with Friendster accounts saw its potential and decided to mimic the more popular features. Within 10 days, the first version of MySpace.com was ready for launch. The project was overseen by Brad Greenspan (eUniverse's Founder, Chairman, CEO), who managed Chris DeWolfe (MySpace's CEO in 2007), Josh Berman, Tom Anderson (MySpace's president in 2007), and a team of programmers and resources provided by eUniverse, an Internet advertising services company.[30]

The first MySpace.com users were eUniverse employees and, aided by the considerable resources of eUniverse, the original founding team was able to promote the innovative new site to eUniverse's 20 million users and e-mail subscribers to jump start MySpace.com and move it to the top. A key architect of the site was tech expert Toan Nguyen who helped stabilize the MySpace.com platform. Shortly after its launch, team member Chris DeWolfe, in its first business plan, suggested that the site start charging a fee for the basic MySpace.com service. Brad Greenspan rejected the idea, believing that keeping MySpace.com free and open was necessary to make it a large and successful community and to attract advertising.[31]

Most of the original MySpace.com users were young people interested in music and bands who wanted to get exposure for their music. Users could create their own mini-Web sites on MySpace.com, upload pictures, contact other friends on the service, or use other functionality to hook up. The site's success was phenomenal and created a sensation among young people who now felt they could connect with their favorite bands, favorite comedians, or other young people with like interests. However, because of the user-generated content (UGC), the site was often chaotic and anarchical; its design seemed too cluttered and many users found it hard to navigate.

Many traditional national advertisers found that UGC did not give them the safe, clean (or bland, depending on your viewpoint) editorial environment they desired, so they did not flock to advertise on MySpace.com. Despite this, it succeeded dramatically, as you can see in Exhibit 20.6 (p. 451), which shows the top ten Web sites in March, 2008, MySpace.com is ranked number eight with over 46 million unique visitors a month.

MySpace.com was so successful that, as all highly successful businesses do, it spawned many competitors, with the most successful by far being Facebook.com. Facebook.com was started by Mark Zukerberg when he was a 20-year-old Harvard student. In 2007, *Forbes* magazine ranked Zuckerberg, Facebook.com's CEO, as, "on paper," the world's youngest self-made billionaire with a net worth of $1.5 billion.[32]

Facebook was launched on February 4, 2004, and as of March 2008, was a privately held company. The free-access Web site allows users to join one or more networks, such as a school, place of employment, or geographic region to connect with other people in the same network. The name of the Web site refers to the paper facebooks depicting members of a campus community that some American colleges and prep schools give to incoming students, faculty, and staff as a way to get to know other people on campus. In March 2008, as many as 14 million photos are loaded to Facebook.com every day and some young users spend as many as three hours or more a day on the popular site.[33]

Social networks such as MySpace.com and Facebook.com are the world's new coffee houses, soda fountains, and pizza parlors where people can hang out together, catch up, and join discussions with a variety of interesting groups. People can connect and make new friends. The phenomenon of social networks not only created a new kind of cyber meeting place but it has also created a new metric for measuring the advertising effectiveness of a Web site – time spent. The more time a person spends on a Web site, the more opportunities publishers have for serving ads, for making more ad impressions. Thus, a site that has traffic of four million unique visitors a month on which people spend an average of a half-hour a day more than likely serves as many ad impressions as a site with one-fourth as many unique monthly visitors – one million – on which people spend an average of two hours a day.

The YouTube.com video disruption

The major content Web sites such as AOL.com, Yahoo!.com, and CNN.com and the large social network sites such as MySpace.com and Facebook.com primarily used still photos because video was expensive to serve. However, in mid-February 2005, three former PayPal employees, Chad Hurley, Steve Chen, and Jawed Karim, created a video-sharing Web site where users could upload, view, and share video clips. The founders called their new Web site YouTube.com. The site used Adobe Flash technology to display a wide variety of video content, including movie clips, clips from television programs, and music videos, as well as amateur content such as videoblogging and short original videos.[34]

Thirteen-year-old boys in Peoria or Tuscaloosa, who are aspiring Steven Spielbergs, could mash-up videos or produce their own videos and post them on the Web free for all their friends to see in a place their parents were clueless about. The secret sauce was Flash, which by 2005 had been unobtrusively embedded and automatically updated on over 90 percent of all computers, as had Adobe's other universally available software product, Adobe Reader, which read Adobe PDF files. YouTube.com officially accepts uploaded videos in WMV, AVI, MOV, MPEG and MP4 formats and automatically converts them to FLV (Flash) files in a standard size and bit rate format for playback on the site.[35]

Political candidates for the 2008 US Presidential election used YouTube.com as an outlet for advertising and on November 28, 2007, CNN aired a debate among the Republican candidates in which the candidates fielded questions selected from a pool of questions submitted by users of YouTube.com. Because of the use of technology to aggregate questions from a wide range of constituents, the forum has been referred to as "most democratic presidential debate ever."[36]

Like the founders of MySpace.com and Facebook.com before them, the young YouTube.com founders did not have a business plan. They believed the often quoted exhortation from the 1989 movie *Field of Dreams*: "build it and they will come." Like the movie's hero, who built a baseball field in the middle of an Iowa cornfield, the founders of these Web sites built them on faith – faith that people would come in droves to their innovative Web sites and that if they had enough traffic, the money would follow.

And it did. In October 2006, Google announced that it had reached a deal to acquire YouTube.com for $1.65 billion in Google stock, making the three founders multi-millionaires, and leaving Google with the problem of how to monetize the wildly popular Web site, which by the third quarter of 2008 had become the fourth most popular site on the Web (see Exhibit 20.6).

Commerce on the Web

The concept of pure-plays, or businesses that exist only online, was introduced earlier in this chapter. Another type of online business is referred to as a click-and-mortar enterprise, or a business that has physical locations as well as an online presence.

Benefits the Web provides to businesses selling products or services online

1 The ability to inform, educate and transact with customer 24 hours a day, seven days a week (24/7).
2 The ability to collect data on customers' behaviors (observed via online activity).
3 The opportunity to test copy, offers, and products quickly and inexpensively.
4 The opportunity to offer better and faster customer service.
5 Low cost of entry.
6 Unlimited shelf space (see definition of the Long Tail below).

Successful commerce businesses online

E-commerce   Many of the original dot.com bubble pure-play online retailers have failed. However, many online e-commerce success stories are sites that are attached to big national brands such as Target.com, Walmart.com, and Gap.com. Other online retailers have been big success stories, such as Amazon.com and Buy.com. Both sites aggregate a large number of products and attempt to sell them at a discount. Many niche commerce sites are flourishing because they give consumers access to products that are hard to find in the stores. Websites of mass marketers such as Wal-Mart only sell hits – hit DVDs, hit records, hit books, hit products: they cannot afford to carry products that do not sell fast.

However, you can find slow-selling, unique items in narrow niches on a Web site out in the Long Tail. The Long Tail is a concept developed by *Wired* editor, Chris Anderson, in a book of the same title. Anderson writes that "The era of one-size fits-all is ending, and in its place is something new, a market of multitudes . . . Increasingly, the mass market is turning into a mass of niches."[37]

Anderson elaborates:

> The new niche market is not replacing the traditional market of hits, just sharing the stage with it for the first time. For a century we have winnowed out all but the best-sellers to make the most efficient use of costly [retail] shelf space, screens, channels, and attention. Now, in a new era of networked consumers and digital everything, the economics of such distribution are changing radically as the Internet absorbs each industry it touches, becoming store, theater, and broadcaster at fraction of the traditional cost.
>
> Think of these falling distribution costs as a dropping waterline or a receding tide. As they fall, they reveal a new land that has been there all along, just underwater. These niches are a great uncharted expanse of products that were previously uneconomical to offer. Many of these kinds of products have always been there, just not visible or easy to find. They are the movies that didn't make it to your local theater, the music not played on the local rock radio station, the sports equipment not sold at Wal-Mart. Now they're available, via Netflix, iTunes, Amazon, or just some random place Google turned up. The invisible market has turned visible.[38]

Community and commerce   eBay developed a site for collectible enthusiasts that has become a commerce Mecca. Today, the site participates in over $1 billion in transactions a month. If you need it, someone is likely selling it on eBay. eBay users have formed a self-governing community that has its rules and order established and maintained by the users.

News and content   The *Wall Street Journal* has over 800,000 people paying for its online version of the paper. The *New York Times* and the *Los Angeles Times* offer their content free as does CNN.com, one of the largest content sites on the Web. Why don't all sites charge for their content? Publishers struggle with this dilemma daily. First, the goal of the site must be determined. By offering content free, sites generally get more traffic, and more traffic usually means a greater opportunity to sell advertising and a larger forum to promote the offline version of their content. On the other hand, Epicurious.com has a different business model. It is one of the Internet's largest sites dedicated to food; it is free and houses thousands of recipes. Epicurious.com makes money by charging companies for the placement of their products within the recipes and on the site.

Online gaming   The gaming sector is exploding as are the games channels on major portals, such as AOL Games and Yahoo Games. Advergaming, or advertising within online games, provides new and innovative ways to advertise. Sites such as Microsoft's X Box Live and Sony's Everquest.com are building huge audiences. In addition to gaming for pure entertainment's sake, gaming-for-profit sites proliferate on the Web, especially the most popular gaming sites – poker and, above all, Texas Hold 'Em Poker – although, US government regulations have kept gambling for money offshore.

Financial services   In the financial sector you will find the Web used as a powerful customer service tool. People can do their banking 24/7 on sites such as Cititbank, and they can trade stocks without a broker on E-trade.com or Schwab.com. Internet users can also find sites that aggregate offers and facilitate transactions between buyers and sellers. Lendingtree.com will help people find the lowest mortgage by giving mortgage bankers the chance to compete for their business.

Matchmaking   The Internet has served as a good place for matchmaking. While eBay brings buyers and sellers together and Monster.com matches job seekers with employers, Match.com and eHarmony.com play matchmaking roles.

Travel   The Internet is not only a place for research but it is also a place to book flights and hotel rooms on travel sites such as Orbitz.com, Travelocity.com, and Priceline.com.

Auto   The automotive category has two types of online players: (1) manufacturers – GM, Ford, and Toyota, for example – who primarily use the Web to educate the public about their products and special offers and to send Web surfers to their dealer networks, and (2) lead resellers who usually provide product information and comparison tools while qualifying leads and sending them off to a local dealer. Lead resellers usually have a relationship with dealers in which the dealer pays the lead resellers for each qualified lead.

The Internet in 2008

At of the end of 2007, 75 percent of US adults accessed the Internet. See Exhibit 20.3, which shows the demographics of Internet users.

People surf the Web for a variety of reasons, with e-mail being the biggest reason. Exhibit 20.4 shows what people do on the Web.

Internet users have also learned to multi-task and use the Web while they are doing other activities, such as watching television, as seen in Exhibit 20.5.

And when they surf the Web, Exhibit 20.6 shows the top ten sites where they went in March 2008, according to Quantcast.com.

Exhibit 20.3 Demographics of US internet users

	Percentage who use the Internet at least "occasionally"
Total adults	75
Women	74
Men	76
Age	
18–29	92
30–49	85
50–64	72
65+	37
Race/ethnicity	
White, non-Hispanic	76
Black, non-Hispanic	56
English-speaking Hispanic	79
Geography	
Urban	77
Suburban	77
Rural	64
Household income	
Less than $30,000/yr	61
$30,000–$49,999	78
$50,000–$74,999	90
$75,000 +	93
Educational attainment	
Less than high school	38
High school	67
Some college	84
College +	93

Source: Pew Internet & American Life Project, October 24–December 2, 2007. http://www.pewinternet.org/trends/User_Demo_2.15.08.htm. Accessed March, 2008.

Exhibit 20.4 Internet activities

Internet activity	Percentage of adult users who report this activity
Send or read e-mail	92
Use a search engine to find information	91
Search for a map or driving directions	86
Look for info on a hobby or interest	83
Look for health/medical info	82
Look for info about a service or product they are thinking of buying	81
Check the weather	78
Get travel info	73
Get news	71
Buy a product	66
Visit a local, state, or federal government Web site	66
Buy or make a reservation for travel	64
Surf the web for fun	62
Go to a Web site that provides info or support for a specific medical condition or personal situation	58
Research for school or training	57
Watch a video clip or listen to an audio clip	56
Look for "how-to" or "do-it-yourself" or repair information	55
Look up a phone number or address	54
Online banking	53
Take a virtual tour of a location	51
Do any type of research for a job	51
Watch a video on a video-sharing site like YouTube.com or Google Video	48
Look for news or information about politics or upcoming campaigns	47
Look for info about a job	46
Get sports scores and info	45
Get info about a college, university, or other school they or a family member might attend	45
Download other files such as games, videos, or pictures	42
Get financial info such stock quotes or mortgage interest rates	41
Send instant messages	39

Source: http://www.pewinternet.org/trends/Internet_Activities_2.15.08.htm. Accessed March, 2008.

Exhibit 20.5 Online activities while watching TV

Online activity	Percentage of respondents
Checking e-mail	53
Surfing the Web for content that is not related to what they're watching	32
Surf the Web for content that is related to what they're watching	19

Source: http://emarketer.com/Articles.aspx?id=1006008. Accessed March, 2008.

Exhibit 20.6 Top 10 Web sites, March, 2008.

Website	Rank	US reach*
Yahoo.com	1	125,521,168
Google.com	2	123,801,224
AOL.com	3	56,302,230
YouTube.com	4	54,970,072
Microfsoft.com	5	51,984,456
MSN.com	6	48,355,650
eBay.com	7	48,300,664
MySpace.com	8	46,801,096
Wikipedia.com	9	44,648,500
MapQuest.com	10	43,071,116

* Reach is the number of different people who visit a site in a month, or unique visitors a month.

Source: http://www.quantcast.com. Accessed March, 2008.

The Advantages of the Web as a Marketing Medium

The Internet is more than a medium for advertising; it is a complete integrated marketing tool. Following are some advantages of the Web:

The ability to brand, inform, and sell within the same environment. Historically marketers used different marketing weapons to accomplish their goals. For instance, television was always considered the best branding medium, and brochures and newsprint the best way to inform. For selling products or services, marketers needed a sales force on the phone or in person. While the early Internet marketers were not recommending discarding the other channels, they were making the point that the online world seemed the best place to do it all.

The Internet has given marketers the ability to brand to the appropriate audience, inform them, and transact all on the same Web site, all at the same time. Furthermore, marketers pay $15 per thousand for branding, up to $3,000 per thousand to inform via a brochure or direct mail campaign, and several hundred thousand dollars per thousand to have salespeople sell cars in dealers' showrooms. Online marketers can do it all for as little as $15 per thousand. No wonder marketers are so excited about marketing on the Internet.

Pull vs. push. Until the Internet came along, all content was determined by producers, editors, directors, and publishers packaging up their best estimate of what the public's tastes were and pushing it out via a daily newspaper, a television station, a radio station, or a magazine. With the Internet, users are in charge. Web sessions are entirely controlled by users. They will pull up what they are interested in, either by browsing around or by using search engines such as Google or Yahoo!. So instead of waiting to watch a television special on the band U2, people can go online and download their music, read about their lives, watch their videos, and print pictures of the band. No longer are people sitting around and waiting for a particular part of a television program where a song they liked is played.

Online is a personal experience. Unlike television or radio where the ads need to scream at you to get your attention, online ads are literally 18 to 24 inches from your nose occupying a good part of your view. The Web is also a private place giving users the ability to look at products and ads they may be embarrassed to look at in print for fear someone could see what they are reading. The Web provides a whole new forum for sensitive health issues, research, or anything private.

Online allows users to customize their relationship with a brand. Scott Bedbury, known for his marketing roles at Nike and Starbucks and giving the World "Just do It" and "Frappuccino" has said "A great brand is a story that's never completely told."[39] As marketers work hard to give their brands meaning and create stronger connections to their consumer, the Web is a perfect incubator and laboratory. Consumers can download screen savers, take company logos and skin their music players with them as well as build fan sites, interactive chat areas with other fans, or Web pages on MySpace.com. For marketers this can be quite good or quite bad. When consumers are leading the brand story, they can take it in a direction that is good for profits or they can trash it in blogs, forums, chat rooms, on MySpace.com, or on YouTube.com in a matter of days. Should marketers take the risk? Most trend-oriented brands do and have found that the Web accelerates the inevitable.

Online and opportunity to view. Kent Volandra who worked at Prodigy in the online services early days and ran Interactive Advertising for Initiative Media in the late 1990s, illustrated for chapter co-author Vince Thompson the concept of "opportunity to view" within the online universe. Kent said that essentially all media is purchased on the concept of opportunity to view. When an advertiser buys advertising time on television, the advertiser is not guaranteed viewers, but rather is guaranteed the opportunity for viewers to see an ad. An advertiser can buy an ad in the newspaper on page four of section B, and, hopefully, the reader will turn to page four of section B and read the ad. The difference with online is that you only pay when your ad is served up on a page, and pages are only served up seconds after prospects click their mouse. For every ad they buy online, advertisers can be assured that prospects were staring into their screens waiting for the content and the ad to appear.

Leveling the field. On the Internet it is hard to tell the difference between Wal-Mart and Wall's Mart. Businesses of any size can look like equals. This leveling effect provides a great advantage to smaller businesses, provided they can out-market and out-service their larger competitors. Unlike traditional national marketing that gives an edge to large companies due to cost barriers, online can be purchased in small increments and, thus, give the smallest businesses the opportunity to compete.

Online extends customer relationships. In 1997 Martha Rogers and Don Peppers penned the bestseller *The One to One Future*. This book served as a lightning rod for the marketing community by demonstrating the value of focusing on share of customer as opposed to share of market, and by highlighting the methods leading-edge marketers were using to facilitate one-to-one marketing relationships with their consumers – relationships in which marketers, by gathering as much information as they could about their customers, could present the most appropriate and saleable opportunities. When customers are given relevant value, they are more willing to share information and marketers can deliver better products allowing the relationship to continue to grow. The Internet has become the perfect vehicle for one-to-one marketing.[40]

Customers can fill out their profiles, respond to offers, and share opinions while marketers can gather data and e-mail addresses, study customers' preferences and behaviors, and find ways to please them. Marketers can send e-mail newsletters with helpful tips and give customers incentives such as coupons and special offers.

However, for some types of products it is difficult to establish a relationship with customers. Other types of products might have users who desire a relationship. For example, young consumers might want to have a relationship with their Nike sneakers, but not with their Crest toothpaste. As marketers realized the potential of one- to-one marketing, the customer relationship management (CRM) business capability of the Internet has boomed.

Customer service. The Internet has enabled customers to gain information like never before. Running Windows? Get one of dozens of updates this year at Microsoft.com. Broke a piece on your baby stroller and the company is in Italy? No problem: order it online and download the schematic for installation. Many sites are now offering live support; simply log on, open a chat window, and begin typing. The company saves long-distance telephone charges and users can get a text record of conversations and instructions for later use as well as links for more information. The Internet has revolutionized customer service to the benefit of both companies and their customers.

The ability to measure and track. With increasing clutter and the overall effectiveness of advertising dropping, in the last decade marketers have been looking for proof of the effectiveness of their advertising. Early Internet pioneers quickly positioned the greatest benefit of the online medium as its ability to track consumers' actions. With the Internet, marketers know every impression served and every ad clicked on. By placing a cookie on a user's computer when an ad is viewed, marketers can actually see if users saw an ad and if they came later to visit the advertised site. Tracking was and still is very powerful for marketers. With an investment in online advertising, marketers can determine how many items they sold, how many accounts they opened, or how many people registered as a result of their online advertising investments. They can determine a return on advertising investment (ROAI), something they could never do with traditional advertising. The online medium is the most accountable of all the media.

This unique accountability has done a great service to the industry as well as a great disservice. The quality of measurement and the role it plays in determining the medium's value is central to any discussion on Internet advertising. Some believe that the medium's value is limited to that which can be measured. Others believe Albert Einstein's comment, "Not everything that counts can be counted, and not everything that can be counted counts."[41] The debate over the value of tracking metrics and ROAI still wages because executives of online advertising sites argue that an ad (banner or even text link) has branding value regardless of whether people click on it.

The Evolution of Banners
and Online Marketing Tools in 2008

Once the 468 × 60 banner was born, other size ad units followed, and the smaller units were referred to as buttons. Many of these buttons were 120 × 60 or 60 × 60. The numbers refer to the number of mega-pixels on a computer monitor that the ads covered. Units that did not contain graphics, but instead were lines of clickable text, were referred to as text links. Banners are also referred to as display advertising, as opposed to text links. Banners, buttons, and text links were quickly adopted by many sites and became the first standard units of the industry.

Uniform ad sizes have been an important part of the industry's growth, as they have allowed marketers to make one size ad unit for submission and viewing on multiple sites. But were these early standard units the best or just the first? As the industry struggled to determine the value of an online ad unit and how to best measure it, either by click-through, converted sales, or brand recall, the publishing community has continued to experiment with new sizes as well as new technologies, especially video, that will make online advertising more effective.

Online tools in 2008

Following is an overview of the most popular online marketing vehicles today.

Standard ad units. Standard ad units usually refers to units that are either static or animated and occupy spaces defined by pixel size such as 468 x 60, 234 x 30, or 160 x 600, for example. The current collective wisdom is that bigger is better. Exhibit 20.7 shows the Internet Advertising Bureau's (IAB) list of standard units in order of their current (March 2008) popularity.

Content integration. It is not always easy to tell what is editorial and what is advertising on the Internet. Some online publishers simply wholesale content slots to third parties. Sometimes these third parties supply the content. Sometimes the content is objective, other times it is pure advertising disguised as editorial. Most marketers have found that including advertising within the content is good for their business, yet at the same time understand that the force driving the effectiveness of these placements is users' trust in the content. Proper content integration includes good journalism and full disclosure. If the content a consumer is reading about Alzheimer's disease comes from a drug company, it is acceptable as long as publishers let consumers know. Consumers would hate to learn that there were some non-traditional treatment methods as effective that did not find their way into the content because the content was paid for and written by an advertiser.

Exhibit 20.7   Standard ad units*

Size	Name
728 × 90	Leaderboard
300 × 250	Medium rectangle (best for video)
180 × 150	Rectangle
160 × 600	Wide skyscraper
120 × 600	Skyscraper
468 × 60	Full banner
120 × 90	Button 1

* In approximate order of popularity with advertisers; measurement in pixels.
Source: http://www.iab.net/iab_products_and_industry_services/1421/1443/1452. Accessed, March, 2008.

Sites usually charge more for content integration and this integration may take several forms, such as: (1) *Integration* in an online article in the form of text links inside the editorial content or in a sidebar. These placements can be paid, free editorial, or part of a value-added offering in conjunction with an advertising buy. (2) *An integrated mini-site or information center* that is a sponsored content area that links from an editorial page and contains articles and utilities. (3) *The complete responsibility for programming an area or channel*; the company programming the channel typically receives the rights to sell or share in the sale of advertising and to create customer relationships with users.

Search advertising. The majority of online users do not browse the Web aimlessly, but rather actively search the Internet with the help of a search engine such as Google or Yahoo!. Users also use search engines within shopping destinations to find products or travel destinations. Search presents a powerful marketing opportunity because marketers of all sizes can place advertising in front of prospects while they are expressing an interest and potential need. Search advertising takes several forms. Google, for example, has paid search results at the top of the first results page and along the right side of the first and subsequent results pages. For instance, a dog food manufacturer can buy the keyword "pet food," and whenever this term is input by a user in the Google search box, the manufacturer's text link will appear on the search results pages. These links are known as sponsored links. If you would like to learn more about Google search advertising, visit www.google.com/ads. There you will find information about Google's AdWords program for advertisers who want to buy keywords on a cost-per-click basis via an automated online auction and Google's AdSense program for site owners who wish to run Google advertising links on their sites and receive payments from Google when visitors to their sites click on a link.

Pop-ups and pop-unders. In addition to the ads served within Web pages, Internet users are served ads that appear on their screens, either covering or appearing below content. These types of ads are highly intrusive and are the least favorite among online users. At the same time, some marketers find them to be powerful marketing devices. If the product or service being advertised is desired by the user, then the pop-up may actually be a welcome piece of content. Marketers using these more intrusive methods must consider users' reactions to the intrusion and the potentially negative effects. Most intrusive advertising is for products not looking to brand themselves with users or hoping to develop long-term relationships, but rather the intrusive advertising is from direct marketers looking to sell a product in a one-time-only transaction.

E-mail marketing. A huge industry has blossomed to help marketers sell their products via e-mail relationships with consumers. Consumers receive two types of e-mail: (1) Unsolicited e-mail referred to as spam, which is hated by everyone, and (2) opt-in e-mail where the user has requested it. This type of marketing is often referred to as permission marketing. In most cases, consumers receive opt-in e-mail either as an e-mail newsletter or as a single e-mail notification of product releases, events, or promotions. Contesting, access to Web sites, or special content is the most common way for marketers to get users to opt-in to an e-mail program. E-mail marketing is effective if properly targeted and executed.

Promotions and contests. Creating promotional events and contests is a powerful way to get users to be familiar with a brand and to take a specific action for reward or potential for reward. Often, if a promotion or contest is structured properly, marketers can get users to have several interactions with their brand. For instance, an auto manufacture may run a "Sightings Campaign" where users are encouraged to visit the auto company's Web site daily to see the car in a new environment. With each visit, a consumer can enter to win additional prizes. Promotions and contests can be as creative as a marketer chooses. The benefits of contests to marketers often extend for years if a marketer is wise in their collection of user data and re-markets to its data bank of customers' names.

Affiliate networks. Rather than paying for advertising and hoping sales will follow, many marketers have turned to offering bounties or commissions for referrals. Amazon.com has over 1,000 affiliates who agree to place an Amazon.com logo on their website. Each time a product is purchased by someone who clicks through to Amazon.com using the link, Amazon.com agrees to pay the Web site publisher a portion of the transaction. While it seems that everyone would do business this way, there are some drawbacks. For example, marketers such as Amazon.com have less control over the environment in which their ad appears. They must watch out for objectionable content, and some brands simply refuse to be marketed next to competitors or in cluttered environments with brands of less stature. Also, only a minority of the online universe is going to purchase in this manner. Therefore, while many companies have taken advantage of affiliate networks, few have looked to affiliate groups as their only source of Web traffic and sales. To learn more about affiliate marketing go to www.affiliate-program.amazon.com/gp/associates/join.

Rich media. This term generally refers to any advertising or content application that does more on the page than just lie there as a static placement. Rich media includes, but is not limited to, animation, 3-D treatments, video, and ads that have utilities built into them such as forms for submission or calculators. Rich media executions usually take one of the following forms: (1) *In-the-banner executions.* Ads where all the animation, video, or rich elements begin and finish within the constraints of the banner dimensions. (2) *Out-of-the-banner executions.* Ads that begin in the banner and then may expand the banner area when clicked on or rolled over, or ads that begin in the banner and then fly out over the page and return to the banner later. For example, a truck ad might show the truck driving out of the banner across the page of content and then driving back into the banner. (3) *Beyond-the-banner executions.* These executions do not occur in any set area and simply execute on the page. Sometimes the ads appear or float across pages and other times they cover entire pages until clicked on.

Rich media, especially video, has proven to have greater click-through rates and higher recall among users. When properly targeted and executed, users typically appreciate the technology. Like other ad vehicles, when rich media advertising is distracting and poorly executed, users get turned off. Rich media usually costs more to execute, approximately $1,000-$5,000 per creative unit, while more standard units fall in the $500-$1,500 range. Of course, online ad creation, like all ad creation, has a dramatic range in pricing based on the execution and the cost of talent involved. In addition to the creative costs, rich media usually involves higher advertising and serving costs. Websites almost always charge more to serve rich media, which usually needs to be served by a rich media provider who will charge a fee, which ultimately comes out to a small percentage of the overall ad costs.

While all online technologies are evolving at a fast clip, rich media is among the fastest. The best way to familiarize yourself with these technologies is to read online ad industry trades such as www.clickz.com and visit the sites of the rich media providers mentioned below. Most providers offer galleries of their work so you can see the technologies in action and conceptualize new opportunities.

Rich media sites

   www.viewpoint.com
   www.eyeblaster.com
   www.pointroll.com
   www.unicast.com
   www.eyewonder.com

Video. The tool in most demand by both advertisers and users is *video.* YouTube. com's explosion on the Internet scene as more and more consumers adopted broadband distribution demonstrated that short videos could be uploaded and downloaded by everyone. YouTube.com's traffic skyrocketed and videos became the rage, especially for young people. Major national advertisers such as P&G and Ford saw an opportunity in 2005 to test video advertising as a way to bolster their commercials' exposure because of the decline in broadcast network television viewing.[42]

In order to smooth the digital video advertising buying and selling process, the Digital Video Committee of the Interactive Advertising Bureau (IAB) has developed ad format guidelines and best practices for the most common current in-stream ad products, including linear video ads, non-linear video ads, and companion ads. Because these guidelines are continually changing as both video publishers and advertisers learn more about how to make online video more engaging and video advertising more effective, we will not publish these guidelines here, but urge readers to go to www.iab.net for the latest guidelines, standards, and information for digital video.

Measuring Online Advertising

Before initiating any online advertising campaign, clients, agencies, and publishers need to agree on the goals of the campaign and discuss expectations. With different goals come different types of measurement, such as:

Impressions delivered. The number of impressions actually served to an online user. Usually an ad is recorded as being served the moment a user's browser calls for an ad to be rendered onto a page.

Click-through. Of those impressions served, click-through is measured by how many users performed an action by clicking on a banner or link.

Conversion. Of those who click through on an ad, conversion is measured by how many completed an action desired by the marketer, such as the purchase of a product, enrollment for a newsletter, or participation in an online game. Conversion percentages are arrived at by matching a marketer's data with the publisher's data or relying on a third party to serve the ads and track users' behavior online. Third-party ad servers accomplish this tracking by using small programs called cookies. Cookies also allow for latent conversion tracking. By tracking latent conversions, marketers can ask the question "How many people viewed my ad, didn't click, but decided to visit my Web site later?" Marketers tracking latent conversion have found these numbers to be quite high. In some cases, as many as five people visited a site later for every one person clicking through immediately. This tracking technology has given some support to those arguing in favor of the Web's ability to brand.

Brand recall. While some products are best suited for direct marketing and direct marketing measurements, the majority of brands advertised rely much more heavily on brand metrics. You may buy Ron Popeil's Rotiseriee on television or buy it online with a call or a click, but it is unlikely you'll buy a Cadillac or decide to switch your homeowner's insurance that way. Because of these challenges, marketers look to brand recall research to measure if users saw an ad, if they remember the marketing message, and if they were influenced to the point of changing their buying intentions or taking action. Dynamic Logic is the leading firm for this type of research on the Web. Dynamic Logic conducts its research by showing an ad to users and then asking them several questions about their awareness of the brand and purchase intentions. Later, Dynamic Logic contrasts the users' answers against the answers of a control group who did not see the ad. By looking at the two sets of data, marketers can determine if the ad influenced their target consumers.

Online Pricing Models

While most advertising is sold on the basis of cost-per-thousand impressions (CPM), the Internet has allowed for experimentation with pricing models. With CPM, a publisher sells inventory for what the market will bear and advertisers take the risk that the investment will yield results. The other models are based on the premise that a publisher risks inventory and does not receive payment until the user performs an agreed-upon action. Following is a list of the most common *performance-based pricing models*:

CPC (cost-per-click). Marketers only pay for users who click on an ad or text link.

CPA (cost-per-acquisition). Marketers only pay for customers who are acquired after clicking on an ad or text link. Often a question is whether a marketer will pay the same rate for someone who is a new customer and for someone who is an existing customer. Another question that has to be worked out is if the payment to the publisher should be based on a one-time purchase or on a customer's lifetime value to the marketer. Lifetime values are difficult to calculate and are open to intense negotiations between buyer and seller.

CPR (cost-per-registration). Marketers only pay for customers who come to them as a result of clicking on an ad and then register at their site.

CPT (cost-per-trial). Marketers pay only for those people who agree to try their product.

Most major Web site publishers are not willing to assume the risk upfront that they will get paid on a performance-based deal, especially for high-demand inventory. However, many publishers have been willing to try performance-based models for low-demand inventory or for inventory on which they have established a marketer's response rate and, thus, can predict revenue with some certainty. Often marketers and publishers will agree on a *hybrid deal* in which a marketer guarantees a certain minimum to the publisher plus the opportunity to share in any upside if sales exceed baseline projections.

It is important to remember that pricing models are fundamental points of negotiation, and in negotiaton each party wants to increase the upside and limit risk. Once two parties are in business together they can, if willing, share results and negotiate with a solid base of knowledge.

How Internet Advertising Is Sold

Most online sales opportunities are with publishers. Others exist with networks, and Internet service providers.

An online publisher is not necessarily an offline publisher gone digital, such as *Sports Illustrated*'s SI.com. Along with magazine publishers that have staked out a presence online are broadcasters and cable operators, newspapers, radio stations, television stations, and television and cable networks. They are all online, and they all maintain sales organizations to maximize online revenue.

Alongside the usual suspects of the old world who have emigrated online is a collection of new online publishers. Some are bloggers, such as the *Huffington Post*, which have attracted large and desirable audiences.

Others may be more data driven or information-centric, such as WhitePages. com or Edmunds.com, Yahoo.com or Expedia.com. But whatever the publisher's content, the economic need to monetize this content and the audience of users it attracts provides opportunities for salespeople.

Content delivers users. Users create page views. Page views deliver impressions. And impressions are the currency of online advertising campaigns. In certain respects, they are dangerous for the salesperson, because impressions create a disadvantage in terms of the salesperson's site being commoditized. Salespeople need to create a differential competitive advantage and give planners and buyers good reasons why an impression on their site is preferable to an impression on a competitor's site.

There are two ways to create this differentiation. One is to help a planner understand exactly why users are on the site – the type of content they are looking for, how they find it, and how they use it. Because online is not an intrusive medium, the audiences are, by definition, in search of something. This does not mean they are necessarily using a search engine, but they may, for example, be on Boston.com looking for reviews of a seafood restaurant in a particular neighborhood. The quality of the content in terms of how well it will help a user answer a question, gather desired information, or in some way deliver a user benefit, will help salespeople create value for a site.

The second way to avoid the commodity trap is to use research. The two major online ratings services, comScore and NielsenNetratings, each provide qualitative research. Digging through this third-party data and creating relevant stories allows the salesperson to create value. Planners typically place a high degree of importance on qualitative research. They are particularly interested in audience composition.

For instance, let's say the target is W35–54 planning to buy an import car in the next six months. Three percent of Site A's audience delivers this target, and 6 percent of Site B's audience delivers the target. Therefore, Site B is twice as attractive to the planner.

The salesperson for Site B who has taken the time to research the audience can negotiate from a position of power and attempt to command a premium CPM. But what is the salesperson for Site A going to do?

Unless there is a compelling story buried in the research, such as the 45–54 cell of the demographic performing well, the soundest tactic will usually be some type of a content or integration play. For instance, Site A may have a "New Car Preview" section that can be sponsored. The salesperson needs to show the planner why this content is a good fit for the advertising messaging, and counter the deficiencies of the research with a compelling advertising integration concept. The salesperson needs to "get beyond the banner" and weave the prospect's messaging into the content in such an effective and innovative fashion that the problems created by the research data are diminished, if not eliminated.

But when all is said and done, a salesperson should understand that both projected and delivered impressions are essential to planners and buyers. Clients and their agencies need to have an understanding of how their campaign will perform. For some campaigns, reach is important. For others, reach is not nearly as essential as delivering a tightly defined audience, such as people who travel to Las Vegas more than six times a year. Sites that offer relative small audiences, perhaps less than two million monthly unique visitors, are typically inappropriate for campaigns that require reach.

These smaller sites need salespeople who inherently understand which marketers will make good partners, who the site can perform for, where long-term relationships can be created, and where win–win outcomes are the norm. To be successful, salespeople simply need to know, really know, their site, its content, and its audience.

What great online salespeople do

Many of the traits and behaviors that salespeople demonstrate in the offline world are essential in the online world.

From knowledge to persistence to persuasion, the set of skills is much the same, but naturally there are aspects of media sales in the online world that differ somewhat from those of the offline world. One is speed. Response times to planners and buyers are often measured in hours, not days. A salesperson who is accessible, who responds quickly, and who respects a planner's clock, is a step ahead of the competition. Another is math. Generalizations are dangerous, but with the exception of researchers, most people who enter the media business do not do so to give their natural math skills an opportunity to shine.

In online media sales, basic math skills are essential. Knowing how to calculate a share of voice for a campaign, knowing how to package different rates, how to blend and balance placements to help manage the site's inventory, how to work with impressions and delivery data, all are important aspects of the everyday world of the online salesperson. While many of these tasks may be delegated to an administrative assistant or a support team, a salesperson conversant with and comfortable with online math competes with an advantage.

A related skill is knowing how to work with Microsoft Excel. The electronic spreadsheet is a vital means of communication between an online buyer and an online salesperson. A salesperson with shaky Excel skills is as disadvantaged as the salesperson with superficial product knowledge or poor communication skills. The ability to quickly complete an RFP without having to depend on an assistant is a plus.

Meticulous follow-up after the sale has been made and the schedule has been booked is vital. In some online media sales organizations, special teams are designated to manage the campaign and ensure proper delivery. Other publishers may split this task between sales and traffic. No matter what the structure, it is ultimately the salesperson's responsibility to monitor and manage campaign performance. Tracking impression delivery, communicating shortfalls, arranging alternate placements and dealing with performance are each items on a campaign checklist. As with all sales issues, it is best for the salesperson to be dealing with problems early in the game. The great salesperson will not only communicate problems to the client, but will simultaneously suggest solutions.

How online deals get done

Online hunters develop high-level relationships on the client side, learn about business issues, and develop an understanding of their client's marketing objectives and personal needs. They take ideas to clients, steer these ideas through agencies, and turn these ideas into revenue. Deals may unfold independently of a client's measured media budgeting process, and could be cross-platform deals blending online with offline media offered by the same firm.

Online farmers work in a more reactive environment, where they are responding to RFPs. This process typically begins with a budget. The client and the client's agency identify a campaign's objectives, define the demographic targets, assign a budget, and carve up this budget allocating specific amounts to each medium that will play a role in the campaign. Somewhere in this process an online budget is determined.

The online agency, or the online team housed in a client's lead agency, will then start to identify the sites that might best be a part of the media plan. This process typically starts with the use of a planning tool from comScore or Nielsen. The planner will enter the quantitative and qualitative criteria, and the application generates a list of sites which, to differing degrees, meet the criteria. Depending on what the planners are looking for, this list of possible sites, or prospects, can be extremely long or extremely short.

At this point, an RFP is sent to the Web sites the planners believe will be appropriate for a campaign. An RFP is typically an Excel document which summarizes the objectives of a campaign, provides information on the target, the ad units which are going to be used, any requirements for rich media or third-party serving, a budget range, flight dates, and other considerations. In many instances, agencies will use an online application such as Atlas or SiteDirectory, where these data are available to the publisher on a password-protected site. The publisher is notified of the RFP by e-mail, then goes to the site indicated for the campaign information, and completes an RFP online.

When an RFP is completed by the publisher and submitted, an evaluation process ensues. Planners will look not only at pricing, but at the appropriateness of the content in which ad units are placed. In some instances, a publisher will offer some type of sponsorship or integration that goes beyond the banner.

These types of integrations can reflect any appropriate content a publisher offers that helps advance an advertiser's goals. For instance, a New Homes area of a real estate section would offer ideal customer integration for a homebuilder.

Great online salespeople will not just understand an advertiser's objectives as outlined in the RFP, they will demonstrate the creativity and the product knowledge to build a bridge that results in a win–win outcome. This is why the first thing salespeople need to do when receiving an RFP is to read it thoroughly and have a precise understanding of what is being requested. All too often the only information considered is the budget and the flight dates.

There are a number of issues with the RFP that salespeople will manage. These issues could range from a request for geo-targeting (serving the ad units into designated geographies), to frequency capping (placing a limit on the number of times a user is exposed to an ad unit).

Knowing how a client or an agency will judge the results of a campaign is another important piece of information for salespeople. There may be certain sections of a site that perform better than others when it comes to click-through. If a specific CTR, or click-through rate, is a stated objective in an RFP, salespeople should make sure placements reflect the desired CTR. Every online planner is different, but most will welcome an appropriate question from salespeople concerning an RFP. A salesperson may have a suggestion that falls outside the scope of a RFP. For example, there may be a special package that differs slightly from the flight dates and budget specified that a salesperson believes would align well with the campaign criteria. Rather than simply including this information in the response, it is best to check with a planner beforehand. Planners value salespeople who respond accurately, thoughtfully, and on time. They also value salespeople who understand both the online property they represent and what a client is trying to get done.

An RFP is a bit like the proverbial double-edged sword. While an RFP often forces salespeople to follow a predetermined structure which does not allow for much selling, it allows the planner to gather and manage a lot of information in a relatively simple process. This is why the great salesperson should always include a succinct and specific buy rationale with the submission. In most instances, this rationale can be a single-page document. Screenshots and URLs which help a planner understand exactly where a placement will appear not only are helpful to an agency, but give salespeople an opportunity to differentiate a site's content. Relevant qualitative research data points offer proof and help the planner feel more comfortable with what is being proposed. Over time, the better a planner knows and understands a site, the more comfortable he or she will be including it on a plan.

Effective communication with online buyers   Online planners are deluged. New sites appear daily. Existing sites regularly unveil new capabilities. The workload can be heavy and the online agency's media department is typically fighting off a torrent of unreasonable deadlines. Planners and buyers may not have the time they would like to spend with salespeople. The preferred means of communication is e-mail. A great salesperson will understand the planner's world and manage both communication and the relationship accordingly.

The role of networks

When an advertiser needs to reach a defined audience and is not terribly concerned about the specific sites the campaign includes, a network is often used. Online ad networks are simply a collection of sites represented by an independent firm. Networks such as DoubleClick typically include a large number of sites reaching different types of people.

Networks often address a specific segment. There are contextual networks, which place ads into content areas that are relevant to the advertiser. For instance, the online media planner working on a life insurance firm's campaign may tell a network it wants clearance solely in business content. The network may represent a business site such as *Forbes*, a newspaper such as the *Los Angeles Times*, and others that offer content appropriate for the campaign. This inventory will be bundled into a media plan. An advertiser will know flight dates and impression levels and demographics but may not know exactly which sites the campaign will run on.

Along with the contextual networks, there are behavioral networks. These firms also represent a number of publishers. The key difference is that the ads are served only to users who demonstrate specific behaviors, based on user data that has been collected, often from an ISP such as AOL that collects data for its behavioral network, Tacoda. For instance, the life insurance company ad may be served to a user who has spent a lot of time in financial planning content when that user is checking out college basketball scores.

Other networks serve different purposes, such as the sale of video units, text links, or remnant inventory. A publisher's unsold inventory is often given to a network such as Drive to sell at low rates. Blogs often use networks to sell their inventory. Blog publishers typically perform better for low-cost products such as apparel, food and beverage, and entertainment.

The role of search and social media

The role of search, and increasingly, mobile and local search is significant. In an ever-shifting landscape of financial data, the revenues constantly change, but what remains constant is the significant share of total online revenues generated by search campaigns.

Search underscores one of the fundamental differences between online and offline marketing. Offline marketing typically requires more of an attention-getting, intrusive quality. It needs to stand out and grab a prospect's attention.

Online messages can appear in an environment where the prospect is actually looking for this information. Someone who does an online search for "Zurich Hotels" is probably a pretty good prospect for a Zurich hotel.

Search is often considered an ideal marketing tool. Advertising appears in places where potentially qualified prospects prepared to transact are looking for information. From the marketer's perspective, search falls into two buckets. One is organic and one is paid. Organic search results are a result of a site's SEO or search engine optimization. These results appear in the search engine's actual listings in the center of the page. Paid search campaigns are typically based on bids advertisers make to have their text messages appear on the pages where search results are listed. These results typically appear on the right hand side of the page, in the right rail.

The major search firms such as Google do not use salespeople to market these paid listings, but rather an online auction-based system. Google bases cost-per-click (CPC) fees on a combination of the actual bid and the amount of click-through the ad receives. The actual position of an ad is also partially based on both factors.

To help marketers manage search campaigns, a number of specialized agencies offer search engine marketing and optimization. Firms such as iCrossing, 360i and Efficient Frontier manage literally millions of keywords. Other major digital agencies such as Avenue A/Razorfish include search as a capability.

As search evolves, and increasingly embraces areas such as mobile platforms along with video and local results, marketers will have an increasing number of tools. Social media, from wikis and widgets to branded social networks, are generating rapidly increasing revenues. Mobile and niched social networks may have the potential to replace more broad-based models such as MySpace.com. Established global media brands such as ESPN.com are offering marketers the opportunity to place messaging in community content. Social networking tools are incorporating content from offline publishers.

Video

Video content has quickly evolved from a quirky novelty to mainstream online content, and marketers are eager to embrace it. But there are a few challenges. First, the intrusive nature of television advertising does not translate well to the online medium. Marketers who run an instream ad or a pre-roll unit prior to a news report or an entertainment clip risk generating resentment from online users predisposed to immediate content gratification. To try and avoid this backlash, some sites actually play the commercial video elsewhere on the page.

The standard 30-second television commercial seems to drag on for an eternity online, thus a stampede to 15-second units. And the actual content and construction of ads produced for broadcast and cable do not always translate well to online. Add a less than ideal technology, in terms of load times and resolution, and you have an environment ripe for innovation, experimentation, and upheaval.

Salespeople in the digital world who have video content to offer clients should understand that there is a significant migration of video from the offline to the online world. Scripted shows such as webisodes are appearing. Segments of news programs are readily available. In a throwback to the days when network radio and television sponsors had a hand in the production of content, major marketers such as McDonald's are involved with the creation of video programming, which provides innovative brand integration.

Making a Living Selling Online Advertising

There are many opportunities today to sell online advertising, and with the industry projected to grow, there will be many more online sales jobs to come. Many online sales jobs do not come with the security of traditional media sales jobs, yet many do come with the opportunity to earn substantially more money. Many believe online media to be the fast track for learning and career growth.

Following are some typical jobs in an online sales department. You will find these titles vary company to company but responsibilities are similar.

Account executive/ sales representative. These roles are for media sellers dealing directly with clients and agencies. Some companies have inside sales forces selling on the telephone such products as online directories and search. Most account executives receive a base salary plus a commission based on attaining a revenue goal. Account executives need to be much more than ad peddlers. It is essential that they are students of marketing and provide real expertise in helping their partners achieve their marketing goals.

Account manager. Account managers exist in organizations that support servicing of customers above and beyond the normal service of a sales representative. Account managers take responsibility for ensuring that agreements are met and that online schedules are implemented and tracked properly. The online medium is extremely complex; getting banners up and running and served properly, and checking click-throughs daily and weekly to see that partners get agreed-upon results are huge tasks. Account management personnel work very hard to make customers happy. Most account management people are not paid based on commission, but many do have bonus plans.

Sales coordinator. These roles are usually entry-level positions designed to provide assistance to sales representatives, account executives, or account managers. Coordinators usually help in the creation of advertising plans, sales presentations, scheduling, and much more. A sales coordinator's role provides a tremendous opportunity to learn the business by getting a broad view of the organization and the sales process while playing a key role on a sales team.

Planner/sales strategy/solutions. In some sales departments the role of creating advertising packages and ideas for clients is staffed with media experts, called planners. In some companies this task is done by a group called sales strategy. In other companies, the system for pulling together media plans is automated or the role of strategy is left to the manager and salesperson. The creation of media plans and ideas is an extremely important role because effective, creative plans differentiate a company in the market. Planning and sales strategy are rewarding positions for creative people with a knowledge of media planning and strategy.

Operations specialist. The role of operations specialist can consist of processing contracts, trafficking ad copy, implementing campaigns by scheduling impression, and pulling reports or it can be defined more narrowly with other job titles dedicated to this process. Regardless, there exists a great opportunity for those who like working with systems and supporting sales organizations in a non-selling role.

Test Yourself

1   What is purpose of the browser?
2   How does Java help us?
3   What are the nine advantages of online advertising?
4   What is rich media?
5   Why is it important to agree on how success will be measured with your client?
6   What are the various pricing models for Interactive advertising?
7   What is an RFP?
8   What is the difference between AdWords and AdSense?
9   Explain what an online ad network is.

Project

Go to www.quantcast.com and find the current rankings for the top ten Web sites. Also, find the reach and rank of your favorite blog.

References

Chris Anderson. 2006. *The Long Tail.* New York: Hyperion.

John Battelle. 2005. *The Search: How Google and Its Rivals Rewrote the Rules of Business and Transformed Our Culture.* New York: Portfolio.

Scott Bedbury. 1997. "What Great Brands Do." *Fast Company*, August.

Clayton Christensen. 1997. *The Innovator's Dilemma: When New Technologies Cause Great Firms to Fail.* Boston: Harvard Business School Press.

Ward Hansen. 2000. *Principles of Internet Marketing.* New York: South-Western College Publishing-Thomson Learning.

Sam Hill. 2002. *60 Trends in 60 Minutes.* New York: Wiley.

Jay Conrad Levinson. 1993. *Guerrilla Marketing,* 2nd edition. New York: Houghton Mifflin.

Robert Reid. 1997. *Architects of the Web: 1000 Days that Built the Future of Business.* New York: Wiley.

Martha Rogers and Don Peppers. 1997. *The One to One Future: Building Relationships One Customer at a Time.* New York: Doubleday.

Kara Swisher. 1998. *aol.com: How Steve Case Beat Bill Gates, Nailed the Netheads, and Made Millions in the War for the Web.* New York: Times Books.

Resources

www.alwayson.goingon.com (Always On is a media company tracking the digital economy and ranking the top 100 new startups)

www.cj.com (Commission Junction is an online advertising company that delivers performance-based solutions)

www.clickz.com (ClickZ is a Web site that has news and articles about digital advertising)

www.eyeblaster.com (Eyeblaster is a digital advertising management company that allows marketers to manage online ad campaigns that include streaming video)

www.eyewonder.com (a rich media and streaming video ad management service)

www.google.com (the search giant)

www.iab.net (The Interactive Advertising Bureau's Web site that includes standard banner sizes and up-to-date research and online revenue numbers)

www.imediaconnection.com (IMedia is a newsletter and events company dedicated to educating users about online advertising)

www.linkshare.com (Linkshare helps companies manage online advertising campaigns)

www.paidcontent.org (Paid Content is a newsletter and business media company tracking the digital economy and content)

www.pewinternet.org (The Pew Internet and American Life Project Web site that contains statistics and reports on Internet usage by many demos)

www.pointroll.com (PointRoll is the leading company that creates banners that users can interact with)

www.quantcast.com (a Web site on which you can get traffic information by multiple demographics on most Web sites – monthly reach and rankings)

www.searchenginewatch.com (A Web site that provides update information and rankings of the search engine business and traffic.)

www.techcrunch.com (Techcrunch is a newsletter and blog covering startups and Silicon Valley.)

www.unicast.com (Aids advertisers manage rich media advertising campaigns, especially streaming video.)

www.viewpoint.com (Video streaming platforms and technologies that provide rich images)

Notes

1 John Cassidy. 2002. *dot.con: The Greatest Story Ever Sold*. New York: Harper Collins.

2 Ibid.

3 Ibid.

4 Ibid.

5 Robert Reid. 1997. *Architects of the Web: 1000 Days that Built the Future of Business*. New York: Wiley.

6 Ibid.

7 http://en.wikipedia.org/wiki/CompuServe. Accessed March, 2008.

8 Ibid.

9 Ibid.

10 http://en.wikipedia.org/wiki/AOL#Histor. Accessed March, 2008.

11 Ibid.

12 Ibid.

13 Ibid.

14 Ibid.

15 Kara Swisher. 1998. *aol.com*. New York: Times Books, p. 279.

16 Ibid., p.141.

17 http://money.cnn.com/2003/01/13/news/companies/aol/index.htm. Accessed March, 2008.

18 http://en.wikipedia.org/wiki/Yahoo! Accessed March, 2008.

19 Ibid.

20 Ibid.

21 Ibid.

22 Ibid.

23 Ibid.

24 Ibid.

25 John Battelle. 2005. *The Search*. New York: Portfolio, p. 68

26 Ibid.

27 Clayton Christensen. 1997. *The Innovator's Dilemma: When New Technologies Cause Great Firms to Fail*. Boston: Harvard Business School Press.

28 Battelle. *The Search*, p. 95.

29 http://www.google.com/corporate/. Accessed March, 2008.

30 http://en.wikipedia.org/wiki/MySpace. Accessed March, 2008.

31 Ibid.

32 http://en.wikipedia.org/wiki/Mark_Zuckerberg. Accessed March, 2008.

33 http://en.wikipedia.org/wiki/Facebook. Accessed March, 2008.

34 http://en.wikipedia.org/wiki/YouTube. Accessed March, 2008.

35 Ibid.

36 Ibid.

37 Chris Anderson. 2006. *The Long Tail*. New York: Hyperion, p. 5.

38 Ibid., p. 6.

39 "What great brands do." 1997. *Fast Company*. August, p. 96.

40 Martha Rogers and Don Peppers. 1997. *The One to One Future: Building Relationships One Customer at a Time*. New York: Doubleday.

41 http://aolsearch.aol.com/dirsearch.adp?query=Albert%20Einstein's%20quotes.

42 http://www.iab.net/iab_products_and_industry_services/1421/1488/DVPlatform?o12499=. Accessed March, 2008.

21

Radio

Paul Talbot

The History of Radio

New York City, August 28, 1922: Rains the night before had broken the heat wave. Fans at the Polo Grounds watching the first place Yankees play the Saint Louis Browns were sent home early. But tonight there would be an even more dazzling sporting event. Johnny Dundee would defend his world Junior Lightweight Championship against Pepper Martin. Neither the ballgame nor the fight would be heard on the radio. But on that cloudy evening something never before heard would crackle through the city. Something that would launch thousands of new careers and indelibly change American business. Shortly after dark on an otherwise uneventful Monday night in 1922, while Johnny Dundee was going the full 15 rounds with Pepper Martin, the world's first radio advertisement was broadcast.

The advertisement was on radio station WEAF and lasted 10 minutes. A real estate development firm had bought a 10-minute block of time to promote its apartment buildings. The program started like this:

> Let me enjoin upon you as you value your health and your hopes and your home happiness, to get away from the solid masses of brick, where the meager opening admitting a slant of sunlight is mockingly called a light shaft, and where children grow up starved for a run over a patch of grass and the sight of a tree. Friends, you owe it to yourself and your family to leave the congested city and enjoy what nature intended you to enjoy. Visit our new apartment homes in Hawthorne Court, Jackson Heights, where you may enjoy life in a friendly environment.

WEAF had been on the air only a few months when the world's first commercial was broadcast. The station was owned by the American Telephone & Telegraph Company. But it was not America's first radio station. That distinction can be claimed by a number of broadcasters including Pittsburgh's KDKA which broadcast federal election returns in 1920.

When the first advertising was broadcast, the radio itself, the receiver, was hardly the type of device you would expect to find in millions of homes within a few years. You could not plug it in. The early radios required battery power. You could not simply turn a dial to tune in a station. This required the maneuvering of a thin wire called the cat's whisker over a crystal. Radios did not have speakers; they required earphones and an antenna had to be strung up.

On the night its first advertisement was broadcast, radio was the domain of the hobbyist. In the explosion of interest in the device after restrictions of technology were lifted following World War I, broadcast bedlam blotted the airwaves. Stations did not have assigned frequencies.

Five years later the federal government made its first attempt to bring regulatory order to the dial with the establishment of the Federal Radio Commission (FRC) in 1927. The FRC assigned frequencies, established a broadcasting band between 500 and 1,500 kilocycles, and gave the best-funded stations with the most powerful transmitters the best dial positions which allowed signals to travel farther at night and more clearly during the day. Out of radio's awkward birth, two men emerged who laid the foundations of the broadcasting business that largely remain intact. One was a gruff Russian immigrant who looked like he slept in his clothing. He placed his bets on tubes and transmitters. The other was a debonair American tobacco heir with hundreds of suits in his closet. This man placed his bets on crooners and comedians. Each built a radio network. Each was a visionary.

Each was a fierce competitor. And each can take credit as being a founding father of today's media business.

The immigrant was David Sarnoff. Sarnoff's journey from a village in southern Russia to the executive suite of NBC lead through the tough New York City neighborhood of Hell's Kitchen where he delivered telegrams. He learned Morse code, made a name for himself reporting the details of the sinking of the *Titanic*, and in 1916 sent a memo to the president of the Marconi Company suggesting that radio could be used, as he put it, as a "music box." A few years later Sarnoff was the guiding force behind the establishment of the National Broadcasting Company (NBC), and the nation's first radio networks that appeared in the fall of 1926.

The tobacco heir was William S. Paley. After graduating from the Wharton School of Finance and Economics at the University of Pennsylvania in 1922, he went to work for his family's Philadelphia-based cigar business, the Congress Cigar Company. Every day the Paley factories manufactured a million and a half cigars, most notably the popular La Palina. In 1927 Paley was a Vice President of the Congress Cigar Company when United Independent Broadcasters, a ramshackle radio network which included Philadelphia's WCAU, approached his family for an investment. Paley's father was skeptical. But the family had seen the impact on sales attributable to the "La Palina Hour" broadcast on WCAU.

A deal was struck and in September, 1928, William Paley showed up for work at the UIB offices in New York's Paramount Building. The company had 16 employees. Within a year there was a new name, the Columbia Broadcasting System, and enough new affiliates – radio stations in different markets linked together into one network – for Paley to tell advertisers that his fledgling network was the nation's largest.

Paley and Sarnoff battled through the 1930s and 1940s to attract the mass audiences that would interest national advertisers. They raided each other's talent and courted each other's clients. Americans loved what these two men put on the air. The first radio show to attract a national audience to tune in at a specific time was "Amos 'n' Andy." It began a 19-year run on NBC in 1929. Radio programmers and producers swept through the nation's vaudeville theaters searching for talent. They found people like Ed Wynn, Burns and Allen, and Jack Benny. In 1900 there were more than two thousand vaudeville theaters. By 1930, fewer than a hundred remained. The audiences had gone to radio.

Comedy was served up in the easily duplicated structure of the variety show, which featured an announcer, an orchestra, a straight man, sketches, stand ups, puns, punch lines, and characters who captured the flavor of the audience's diverse ethnicity with exaggerated accents. Every show had a sponsor. Performers wove the name of the product into their scripts. Jack Benny launched every show with the invocation "Jell-O, again."

While radio's largest audiences were delivered by comedians, everything from opera to boxing filled the airwaves. Americans were enthralled. In a landmark 1935 study funded by the Rockefeller Fund, *The Psychology of Radio* found that for every telephone in the country there were two radios. Seventy-eight million Americans were regular listeners. Women liked music, men liked sports, the poor listened more than the well-to-do, and 95 percent of the people surveyed said that they would rather listen to a man's voice than a woman's.[1]

Radio geared itself up to deliver the news in the late 1930s. There was fierce opposition and intense political pressure from newspaper publishers. But as World War II unfolded, an infrastructure was built to report on the war. Edward R. Murrow's broadcasts from London, air-raid sirens blaring in the background, brought the war into America's living rooms. News became a staple of radio.

World War II was radio's last big story. In 1946 there were nine television stations in the United States. Eight years later there would be 354. By 1950 common wisdom suggested that radio was an unnecessary medium. The popular programs and their stars left radio for television. Radio networks were, for the most part, dismantled. Television captured the nation's fancy, created new stars, and crafted new definitions of leisure.

But radio stations did not go the way of vaudeville. The opposite took place. In 1948 there were 1,621 AM stations. By 1960 that number had more than doubled to 3,458.[2] Radio still mattered because the medium struck out on a different path from television. Television was a national, mass-appeal medium. Radio evolved into primarily a local medium with segmented audiences. Stations chose formats to deliver well-defined audiences. Television owned the living room but radio owned the kitchen, the bedroom, the car, the backyard, and eventually the beach. The dawn of the transistor in 1954 turned radio into a portable medium. Audiences grew. Revenues rose. And shifting social patterns dealt the medium strong cards as young people and African-Americans turned to radio for entertainment they wanted but could not find on television.

Radio has been sold to advertisers since 1922. It has never lost its importance. It has been a vital platform for marketers for more than 80 years. Today the people who sell radio advertising enjoy remarkable opportunities.

Today's Radio Industry

Radio is primarily a local business; only 5 percent of radio's total advertising dollars in 2007 went to national wired radio networks and only 17 percent went to national spot radio, according to the accounting firm of Miller, Kaplan, Arase & Co.[3] Local radio stations tend to be locally operated, with management, sales, and programming, by and large, rooted in the local marketplace. Ownership usually is not. A number of large companies such as CBS, Clear Channel, Cox, Emmis, Citadel, and Cumulus own and operate large numbers of radio stations. Some of these groups own large numbers of small stations in small markets. Some have a smaller number of larger, higher-billing stations clustered in major markets, and some companies have a blend of each. In terms of the number of stations owned and operated, Clear Channel, in 2007, was the largest radio company with 1,182 stations.[4] This concentration of ownership is largely a result of two events that unfolded at roughly the same time during the mid to late 1990s.

The first was the deregulation of federal restrictions on broadcast ownership. This ruling paved the way for a business entity to own multiple stations in one market and lifted limits on the total number of stations that one company could own. This deregulation spurred the rise of interest of the investment community in radio. As in other industries where deregulation encouraged economic consolidation, the radio industry, with its emerging economies of scale, became attractive to Wall Street investors. What had been a highly fragmented business quickly became consolidated. And the consolidation of radio has created significant changes and opportunities for salespeople.

Opportunities for salespeople

The greatest of these opportunities is the possibility that a salesperson may be selling more than one station. Because one company may often own more than one station in a single market, the deployment of salespeople and which station or stations they sell results from a strategy set by management. While the tendency is for individual stations to maintain individual staffs, there are situations where management may assign a salesperson to a specific account with responsibilities for generating revenue for more than one station. This could be a result of a special relationship the salesperson enjoys with the client, a request from clients to have a single salesperson from the group call on them, or a decision based on a strategy put in place by management.

The degree to which salespeople communicate and cooperate with their counterparts at sister stations differs significantly. This depends, again, on management strategy. In some situations there is a high degree of internal competition where the salesperson treats a counterpart on a sister station as an actual competitor for revenue. In other situations there is a greater degree of cooperation, to the point where a salesperson will share information about a client and work with the sister stations' salespeople to develop plans to either secure or grow the business for all of the stations involved. Station-based strategies and market-based strategies for maximizing revenues are common.

The consolidation of the radio industry has impacted more than structure. It has prompted organizations to experiment with ways of packaging a number of media assets into one bundle to make potentially attractive offerings for advertisers. It has encouraged the emigration of programming from one market into another. Contests, a hallmark of radio promotion, are now often run in a number of markets simultaneously. And behind the scenes, operating expenses are being more aggressively managed as economies of scale are brought to bear on what has historically been a decentralized business.

Radio Station Structure

You will find much the same structure in most radio stations. As a salesperson you will report to a sales manager. This may be either a local or a general sales manager. The local sales manager's responsibilities are exactly what they sound like; supervising the local sales department, which in a typical station delivers the majority of the station's revenue. The single most important task a local sales manager performs is to hire the best and most knowledgeable people possible, so you may want to bring this up and sell yourself a bit when you're interviewing. Also, it might be a good idea to bring along a well-thumbed copy of this book with you to an interview.

Other responsibilities include training the sales staff and growing its collective skill level, managing and pricing the inventory of commercial availabilities that is available to sell, reporting activities and progress toward sales objectives to senior management, evaluating the performance of the sales staff, gathering information from the sales staff to effectively monitor the marketplace and the competition, developing new products to sell, and working with other departments within the station in order to communicate a station's value to the salespeople.

The local sales manager may report to a general sales manager, who would typically oversee both the local and the national sales efforts. In situations where there are a number of stations owned by one company in a single market, the sales managers may report to a director of sales who oversees the sales of the group of stations and sets strategy for all of the company's stations in the market.

The national sales manager works with the station's national sales representative firm. National sales managers spend most of their time on the telephone working on pieces of business that are being negotiated by national salespeople on the station's behalf in offices such as New York, Chicago, or Los Angeles. The national sales manager will travel to these markets to keep the rep firm and important clients informed of the station's activities, such as events and promotions, competitive and format changes, and market conditions.

The sales department may have a support staff. Sales assistants help salespeople prepare presentations and print out research reports. Some stations have research directors who work with the salespeople on presentations that are ratings intensive.

The sales department works closely with two other departments. One is traffic, the other production. It is the responsibility of the traffic department to make sure that a log is produced each day. The log is a legal document that serves as a record of when advertisements and other program materials are broadcast. Because it is vital that the advertising is broadcast at the time of day the salesperson has told the client it will be on the air, accurate and ongoing communication between the sales department and the traffic department is essential. Account executives quickly learn that next to their boss, the person in the station who can best help them manage their business and their success is the traffic director.

In some stations, a continuity director reports to the traffic director. It is the function of the continuity person to make sure that advertising copy or produced commercials are in the station before the appointed deadline, that it is properly coded and in the hands of the production department to be ready for broadcast. Campaigns can often be a bit complicated, with different commercials for different days of the week, or in different rotations. Continuity people make sure that the advertising runs properly.

The production department typically has three responsibilities, two of which involve the sales department. One responsibility is making sure that advertising produced outside the station is transferred to the medium used to broadcast the commercials, such as a tape cartridge machine or a hard drive. The other is the actual production of advertising that originates with the station and has been produced at the direction of the salesperson. The production director will round up all of the necessary elements, ranging from the voice of on-air talent, to sound effects, to music in order to produce a professional piece of advertising. The production director's other responsibility, which tends not to involve the sales department, is producing the station's own advertisements or promotion announcements, referred to as promos. The promos may deal with anything from a station contest to a weekend's special programming.

Everything that is broadcast by the station is the responsibility of the program director. Commonly known as the PD, this person decides which disk jockeys or personalities will be on the air and when, what music will be played or what kind of talk or news will be aired, what promotions will be run, and what kind of an image the station portrays. It is the PD's objective to get as many people as possible to listen for the longest period of time possible and to have the station positioned in the minds of the listeners so that they will remember it if they are ever surveyed for the ratings.

Depending on the size of the station, PDs may or may not be performers on the air. PDs may or may not have a music director and a promotion or a marketing director reporting to them. The music director decides which songs will be played and how often, based on their popularity or other criteria set up by the PD.

The business manager tends to all of the financial functions of the station. From managing receivables to processing invoices and preparing month end profit-and-loss statements and other financial reports, the business manager's day is spent immersed in numbers. Salespeople work with the business manager on two tasks; a new advertiser's creditworthiness and collections. Good radio account executives know how to read an aging list (a list of accounts that are past due on their payments) and take the proactive steps necessary to make sure that the station's invoices are paid in a timely fashion.

The chief engineer has limited interaction with salespeople. The chief engineer is responsible for making sure the station's transmission is in legal compliance, that the transmitter is performing at optimal technical specifications, that the sound of the station is properly processed, and that the studios are properly equipped and maintained.

At the helm of the station is the general manager (GM). The GM works with all department heads to ensure smooth and profitable operations. The GM's most important task is the protection of the license granted by the Federal Communications Commission (FCC) entitling the station to legally broadcast. Without a license there is no station.

The Radio Business Is Competitive, not Complex

For different reasons, there is no radio station without salespeople. The sales staff is a cornerstone of a station. Most new radio salespeople are daunted by what they perceive to be a formidable learning curve. In particular, they're overwhelmed by the apparent complexities of the ratings, which you learned about in Chapter 16. But in reality, the business is relatively simple.

As a new salesperson, you should remember that you're part of a mature industry where the hardest work is figuring out people, not figuring out industry buzzwords or ratings. It is important to know about the technical aspects of the ratings. But it is essential to know about the people you're calling on. You need to understand their desires, their motivations, their perceptions, and their needs. If you build your career paying more attention to your client's character than your station's cume, if you focus on a prospect's behavior more than focus on your station's broadcast signal pattern, you will prosper. Your true complexities come into play in understanding the type of people you're selling to, not in what you're actually selling. This is hardly the exclusive province of radio. So when you apply the AESKOPP formula and develop your skills in establishing and maintaining relationships with your prospects and customers, identifying and solving advertising and marketing problems, and getting results for these people, you're covering all the bases. Do not be overwhelmed by the imagined complexities of the radio business.

You also need to be aware of the highly competitive nature of the radio business. Just as radio programmers compete for ratings and the loyalty of listeners, radio salespeople compete for business. This competitive environment is unrelenting and is fueled by savvy media buyers who, when negotiating with salespeople, will be quick to remind them that they, the buyers, can buy essentially the same product cheaper from the competition. This threat puts you in a position where you need to know as much about your competitors as possible. When you know their pricing and their inventory situation, you can make more intelligent negotiating decisions. The trap to avoid falling into is thinking the worst of your competition and believing that they will always undercut you on price. We are all somebody's competitor. If we all undercut on price, we would all be giving our product away. A healthy respect for the competition and an understanding of what is really happening across the street will benefit you.

With the high degree of competition comes a high degree of fun. Remember that selling radio is more fun than selling newspaper advertising and harnesses more of your creativity than selling television. Your job in radio is inherently more interesting than your competitor's selling job is in another medium. This concept leads to the notion that when it comes to business, you are not just competing against other radio stations, you're competing against other media. You need to understand why radio is inherently better.

The Advantages of Radio

While you should never use negative selling against another radio station, because you are attacking your medium, you should know how to communicate the weaknesses of the media you are competing against for budgets. Newspapers, broadcast television, and cable television are each plagued with problems for an advertiser. They are also the home of the budgets you want to target for your station. The temptation to move dollars from a competing station onto your station is always present, and this occasionally might be acceptable even though it does not increase the size of the radio advertising pie in your market. You should remember that in most instances larger financial opportunities present themselves when you work to move dollars from a competing medium. Targeting budgets placed with the newspaper, broadcast television, and cable television is exhilarating, profitable, and something many of your radio competitors are not very good at. It is also hard work. You need to be patient and prepared. You need to understand the weaknesses of your competitors. Let's start with newspapers.

Radio versus newspapers

About six times more money is spent on newspaper advertising than is invested in radio advertising. The local newspaper is your primary competitor and it is pockmarked with shortcomings, ranging from unattractive demographics to pricing inefficiencies. Circulation has been on a downward skid for 50 years. So has the amount of time people spend reading the paper. The typical American adult spends 5 percent of his or her annual time spent with consumer media with a newspaper, but more than 22 percent with radio.[5] Just slightly more than half the people who read the paper read only the first section, which happens to be the strongest section in terms of readership.[6] Less than half the paper's readers even notice a full-page ad. Newspaper advertisers face imposing clutter problems – 68 percent of the Sunday paper is advertising.

And then there is pricing. As circulation declines, rates increase, and advertisers grow resentful and feel trapped by what they often perceive as the only game in town when there is newspaper monopoly. There are not too many beloved newspaper salespeople working the streets.

Radio versus broadcast television

Broadcast television also has a special knack for upsetting media buyers. Television commercials are often bumped, or preempted, and not run as scheduled. This can happen for a number of reasons, ranging from being preempted by political advertising to being moved aside to make way for a client willing to pay a higher rate.

But even if every schedule ran exactly the way it was booked, broadcast television has a significant problem with advertisers. In the last 15 years, ABC, CBS, and NBC have lost half their viewers. The three networks commanded a 61 percent share of primetime household viewing in the mid-1980s. Today it is only a 24.7 share.[7]

As broadcast network shares have gone down, unit commercial loads have gone up. Television clutter is highly problematic with as much as a 24-unit spot load every hour.

Television is having trouble connecting with busy people. Forty percent of all viewers are considered light viewers who watch television less than 90 minutes a day. Remember that the average American adult spends more than three hours a day with radio.

And then there is the quality of the broadcast television audience. The more money people make, the less broadcast television they watch. Conversely, the more money people make, the more likely they are to be radio listeners.

You might want to remind your clients that the median cost of producing a national television commercial is more than $350,000, and that to effectively compete against these messages on a somewhat level playing field, low budget production will not cut it. Radio, on the other hand, offers highly discrete audiences and highly affordable production.

Sometimes television gets the credit for the job the radio has performed. I remember telling one of my retail clients as we prepared to launch her campaign and put her on the radio for the very first time that some day, one of her customers would come in and say "I saw your ad on TV" when in fact the radio campaign was the only advertising in the market. My client smiled and shook her head in disbelief. But sure enough, a month or so later, she gave me a call. "You wouldn't believe what just happened." Naturally, I did.

Radio versus cable television

Cable television is one of the big reasons why broadcast television is being relegated to the media choice of the downscale consumer. But it is not the sole reason. Cable television ratings are largely driven by programming such as wrestling and cartoons, perhaps not the most appropriate environments for an advertiser looking to connect with an interested, affluent consumer.

Cable television audiences are small and they are splintered. There are more choices for the viewer on the cable set top box than there are for the listener on the radio dial. Ad clutter is even more extreme than in broadcast television, with some cable networks running up to 28 units an hour.

Great radio salespeople who understand human nature know that we never want to launch a frontal assault on competitive media, essentially telling an advertiser that they're stupid for spending their money in such a squalid, cluttered environment. The disadvantages need to be carefully communicated so as to create doubts, and in a fashion that sets the stage for a shift in the media mix so that radio can be brought into the plan.

National Advertising

I mentioned the role of the national sales manager and the rep firm. Let's revisit this and find out exactly what these people do. Let's say that today is Monday and that on Friday American Airlines is going to cut all of its domestic fares to $99. Suppose the marketing people at American Airlines know from their market research that 80 percent of their business comes from the top ten markets, so that is where they'll run 100 percent of their advertising. Because the advertising must be produced and distributed quickly, they decide to use newspapers and radio to advertise the new low fares. The American Airlines marketing people call their advertising agency, give them a budget, and tell them to get radio schedules launched in the top ten markets on Friday.

Rather than getting in touch with 100 stations, ten leading stations in each of the top ten markets, for rates and clearance information, media buyers at American's advertising agency will call a rep firm. The rep firm is a sales organization that sells advertising for a number of stations that are its clients. These stations are typically in different markets. The rep firm has salespeople, just like a radio station, that call on the media buyers at large advertising agencies and media buying firms that place business nationally and regionally.

The American Airlines scenario is typical. The rep firm knows the latest rate and clearance information, which in some instances can change quickly, for all of its stations. So rep salespeople will present the American Airlines' agency's media buyer rates and clearances for their stations in the markets that are "up," or being bought. The buyer and the reps then negotiate, and when a deal is struck the reps send the order out to their stations and the business is booked.

A rep's primary contact is the national sales manager, who at some stations may also double as the general sales manager or even the general manager. The national sales manager needs to make sure that the rep firm is well informed on the station and the market and that the rep gets quick and accurate information pertaining to specific pieces of business being negotiated.

National business can also be placed on networks. Essentially, there are two types of networks. One is a wired network and the other is an unwired network. An unwired network is a collection of stations in different markets with only one common denominator; its stations broadcast a client's advertising. The rep firm manages this group of stations to make sure that the inventory clears, that the rotations are proper, that the creative is being properly trafficked, and that the invoicing is correct.

Network Radio

As in television, there are also several radio networks, such as CBS, ABC, ESPN, and Westwood One (owned by CBS). Radio stations affiliated with these networks do not have traditional, exclusive affiliate contracts, as most television stations do, but radio stations agree to carry network programming, such as news or talk programs. Typically radio stations are not compensated for carrying programs that include network commercials, but they receive free programming and are allowed to insert local commercials in the programs they carry.

Often radio stations carry programs from more than one network. For example, a station might carry CBS news programs, "The Osgood File" and "The Jim Bohannon Show" from Westwood One, and, perhaps a talk show such as the Premiere Network's "The Rush Limbaugh Show."

Radio networks have sales staffs that sell to national advertisers that are represented by agencies, so the type of selling is similar to selling for a cable network.

Local Advertising

Local advertising falls into one of two categories, agency and direct. Direct business is created by working directly with an advertiser – no advertising agency is involved in handling the creation of the advertising or the scheduling strategy of the campaign. These tasks are a salesperson's responsibility. Skilled salespeople who understand that the most important order they receive is the second order, since this signifies the creation of a customer, will do everything possible to ensure the success of the campaign that has been sold through the first order.

Local advertisers have needs. Typically, they are business needs. A restaurant client might tell you that "Dinner business is fine but I need to get more people in here for lunch."

As a skilled salesperson, the only things you need to bring to your first meeting with a direct prospect are a strong sense of curiosity and a business card. You will ask a lot of intelligent Discovery Questions similar to those you learned in Chapter 9, you will identify the business need of the prospect, and you will schedule a follow-up meeting to present your solution.

A great first sales call will have you only talking about your station 10 percent of the time and developing an understanding of the customer's marketing issues 90 percent of the time.

When you ask questions to identify these marketing issues, keep in mind there are two schools of thought on taking notes. One says ask for permission and then take copious notes. The other says listen attentively and do not take notes because prospects may feel uncomfortable. They may feel that something they say may be later used in a manipulative fashion to get them to do something they do not want to do. Furthermore, on the first call it is more important to develop rapport with your prospects and show them that you care about them and their business than it is to record their every word on a piece of paper. Whatever the case, you cannot sell a solution unless you understand what you're selling a solution to and have developed enough rapport so that prospects look forward to having you back.

On your first call you may want to hold off on presenting a media kit or a ratings report. But it is a good idea to have these materials tucked in your briefcase so you can pull them out to discuss them if the client asks.

Local direct advertisers do not care as much about ratings, or programming formats, or air personalities as much as they care about making a profitable investment in advertising. They do not have a high degree of price sensitivity. They do have a high degree of results sensitivity.

Radio Programming

Just as magazines target specific audiences by the nature of their editorial content, and just as television networks reach different types of audiences with different programs, radio uses formats to deliver specific audiences.

A 2007 study of formats conducted by M. Street Corp. revealed that the most popular format is Country, followed by News/Talk.[8]

Radio salespeople should have an understanding of what types of audiences the different formats deliver. All News and Classical Music attract listeners with the highest median incomes. Adult Standards and All Sports attract the highest concentration of homeowners. For broad reach, Adult Contemporary and Country deliver the highest reach of adults 18+. To reach young adults in the 18–34 demographic, Contemporary Hit Radio is the leading format.

Regional tastes come into play with format preferences. Country, for instance, has historically failed to deliver sizable audiences in urban markets outside the south, western, and north central states.

You should also know that variety within a format is commonplace. Some Country stations play music designed to appeal to women in their thirties while others play music for men in their forties. Some of the songs they play may be the same, but there will be musical-mix differences within the same format, and there will also be differences with the image the station portrays, the style of its announcers, the objectives of its contesting, and all the other elements that go into the positioning of a station.

The first week on the job, every new radio salesperson should take their station's program director out to lunch, ask a lot of questions, and learn exactly what the program director is attempting to do. When you have a detailed understanding of the station's programming, how it competes, and the exact niche it is attempting to occupy in the market, you will benefit in two ways. First, you'll be better informed. This information translates into a greater degree of confidence. Secondly, you'll know exactly what kind of people listen to your station and in turn what kinds of advertisers you can deliver great results for and in what business category you should be prospecting.

How to Get Results for a Client

There is nothing theoretical about results. Advertising must work. It must deliver at least the results the client expects and, preferably, exceed those expectations. So, a sensible first step in ensuring results is a discussion with the client on what can reasonably be expected from a radio advertising campaign.

It behooves a salesperson to carefully manage expectations, as you learned in Chapter 8.

The first thing to keep in mind is that advertising is a risk. Not just radio advertising, but any advertising is as far as one can get from the proverbial sure thing. Smart business people understand this fact. Therefore, never make promises.

Next, have a conversation with a client in which the two of you set some benchmarks for success. If your client is a mortgage broker and makes $2,000 for every new loan processed, a radio schedule that costs $2,000 and generates just two new clients is probably a pretty good deal. You do not want to be the radio salesperson who goes back to the client when the campaign is over, learns that the station created just two pieces of business and rushes to the conclusion that the results were unacceptable. Only by knowing in advance what defines a win for the client, only by understanding the metrics of the deal, will the salesperson have the knowledge necessary to move forward, renew the business, and create a long-term, satisfied client.

By the way, a good radio salesperson knows that it is a mistake to visit with a new client after the campaign is over and only then to ask how things are going. The better move is to check in after the first week. And do not sell one- or two-week campaigns if you can help it, sell 26- or 52-week campaigns, because continuity is the best strategy for long-term success.

Aside from managing expectations, there are a number of things a good radio salesperson will do to stack the deck in favor of good results. There is nothing wrong or deceitful about stacking the deck. Good results constitute a win for the salesperson and a win for the client.

First comes understanding exactly what the client wants the advertising to do. Results are typically linked to specific objectives. You cannot tell how the advertising is working when all the client says he wants to do is to "Get my name out there." This leads us to the notion that in a somewhat simplified context, there are only two kinds of advertising. One is strategic and the other is tactical. The *strategic advertisement* is designed to get the listener to believe something. The *tactical advertisement* is designed to get the listener to do something. Know which kind of advertising you're working with.

The ad cannot be conceived, let alone scripted or produced, unless you and the client agree on its purpose. This concept sounds simple. In reality, it can be difficult. The client may rely on a salesperson to suggest an ad's purpose. Only by understanding the client's business can a salesperson make a thoughtful recommendation. It may be as simple as getting a listener to call the business to learn about the benefits of refinancing a mortgage.

Creating radio commercials

Take note of the word *benefits*. You have already learned in the material on media sales skills that you do not want to be in the business of selling features. You want to be selling benefits. It is exactly the same with advertising. If you are writing a commercial for an appliance store that is trying to sell refrigerators, do not talk about urethane door insulation. Talk about "Built to use less electricity and save you money." So make sure that commercials are wrapped around benefits, not features.

There are five styles of radio ads: jingles, testimonials, drama, humor, and straight information. Each, when properly developed, is effective. The use of jingles prompted one advertising wag to remark, "When you've got nothing to say, sing it." But good jingles have an uncanny ability to penetrate the mind and leave an enduring impression, which is often a good feeling about a product or store. If you have a client interested in a jingle, the production director or the program director at your station can suggest a good producer.

Testimonials are extremely powerful, but only when there is a good fit between the spokesperson and the product. Credibility is important, as is the ability of the listener to see in his mind the spokesperson using and knowing something about the product. Word of mouth is perhaps the single most influential factor when it comes to motivating people to try a product, and well-crafted testimonial campaigns capture the essence of word of mouth.

Drama is often little more than conversation. We have all heard these commercials. A woman asks her husband if he has heard about the new restaurant in town. He says no. She then proceeds to tell him all about it. But realistic conversations are hard to write. Commercials like this are easy to write if the goal is anything short of excellence. But with a few clever twists, a good ear, production that puts real people and not staged announcers into their roles, these ads are intriguing, informative, and often quite effective.

Humor is hard work. Humor is also a risky business because if the joke falls flat, the attempt at humor will cast the advertiser in a bad light. To the listener, it is not just a stupid joke, it is a stupid business whose image is impaired by that stupid joke. But just as we all have a primal need for a good story, we enjoy a good laugh, and in the rarified environments where advertising and humor intersect, great results can be achieved with a clever, memorable, and truly funny commercial.

Then there is the commercial that is straight information. You have heard these and if they strike you as a collection of points hastily strung together to last 60 seconds you're probably correct. Lists of facts about a business, where a benefit is never suggested, rarely stimulate a response. That is because these lists of features rarely penetrate our minds. We never really hear radio commercials like this – they do not penetrate our consciousness. For a piece of radio advertising to work, it needs to push whatever we are thinking about right now out of the way so it can command our attention. Only then will the listener consider the message, evaluate its benefits, and be in a position to do business with your advertiser.

One afternoon I was driving back to my station through a hardscrabble part of the city when I noticed the sign that every radio salesperson yearns to see, "Opening Soon."

I had time, so I stopped, went into a trailer and started chatting with the owner. He had leased a vacant lot surrounded by chain link fencing and was starting an auto auction. He had a very limited budget. I learned that one of his auctions would take place each Sunday night. I knew that we could give him a great rate on Sunday afternoons when demand on our inventory was relatively light. So I suggested that he run a campaign with us just to support the Sunday night auction. He understood the benefit of the focus and the immediacy. He also said he would give away a car every Sunday night to one of the registered bidders.

The ad I wrote started and ended with the phrase, "Tonight you can win a free car." The copy was built on the platforms of immediacy, a call to action, and a significant benefit. There was nothing artistic about it. I knew it would never win an award. This piece of advertising was simply a workhorse. The ad ran four times each Sunday between 3:00 and 7:00 p.m. I never changed the copy. And, of course, it worked like a charm.

The time you take to develop a great piece of advertising is time well spent. You will discover that success is largely a matter of building up a list of active advertisers. The single best way to do this is to get results for advertisers. Developing an advertising campaign is a wonderful creative exercise, and a perfect and profitable means of showcasing your creativity. See Appendix B "Writing Copy" for more information about the art and science of writing effective advertising copy.

Selling to Agency Buyers

Most media buyers at agencies usually want to make good buys. They are receptive to learning more from salespeople about how a station performs in delivering specific audiences. But sometimes they are restricted in how they can make their buy. Whatever the case, it is essential that radio salespeople know their station's audience, understand the strengths and weaknesses of their station, know their station's audience composition, and how the competitors fare with their audience delivery. But knowing the station and the market is just a start. Knowing the buyer is what matters most.

Great radio salespeople love their buyers. They know exactly how their buyers like to work, and they are highly attentive to both the personal and the business needs of the buyer. They know that there are some common themes in what media buyers want from a salesperson; superb communication skills, integrity, candor, quick turnarounds, accuracy, and consistently flawless execution of booked schedules.

But there is more. Media buyers need to be understood. They need to be respected. They need justification and they need to know why. And a media buyer needs to know that if there is ever a problem the salesperson is going to accept responsibility and fix the problem.

Rate negotiations between a media buyer and a salesperson can be tough and fraught with tension. But the relationship can be wonderful. The relationship is not defined by the tension of the occasional rate negotiation but by a genuine willingness of the two parties to work together, to partner in an effort to do work that benefits the radio station, the agency, and the client. Skilled buyers who are self-confident understand this relationship. Less skilled buyers will be hesitant to work toward this type of a relationship.

How Radio Is Sold

Radio is sold by dayparts, as seen in Exhibit 21.1.

When it comes to pricing, radio is a highly negotiable medium. Part of this is attributable to the notion that most radio salespeople are woefully trained in negotiating if they have not read Chapter 12 in this book. But the economics of supply and demand come into play as well.

Most stations in larger markets use some type of a yield management strategy, with the help of software programs, to price their inventory. The higher the demand, the higher the rate; and, conversely, the lower the demand, the lower the rate. Great sales staffs create demand.

Great sales managers in turn understand exactly how their product should be priced. They use pending business reports to have a grasp of what is being offered for sale that has not yet been closed. (See the Business Pending Tracker form, available for download at www.mediaselling.us/downloads.html.) From an analysis of historical data, they understand that there will be greater demand during the middle and final weeks of a month so they will quote higher rates for these weeks. They may also know that more advertisers would like to be on the air Wednesday through Saturday so these days of the week will be priced higher if advertisers insist on running only on those days. Different times of day, or dayparts, will attract different levels of demand. They will be priced differently.

The goal of the station is to sell the highest possible percentage of all available inventory at the highest possible rate. It is the responsibility of the sales manager to anticipate demand, set pricing, take special considerations into account, and help the sales staff maximize revenue.

The tactic most commonly used to support a yield management strategy is packaging. The station wins by building schedules for clients that blend inventory from different dayparts, days and even weeks to achieve its objectives. The client wins by being in a position to reach broader segments of the station's audience and to enjoy pricing efficiencies.

Exhibit 21.1 Radio dayparts

Daypart name	Time
Morning, or AM, drive time	6:00–10:00 a.m., Monday–Friday
Daytime	10:00 a.m.–3:00 p.m., Monday–Friday
Afternoon, or PM, drive time	3:00–7:00 p.m., Monday–Friday
Night time	7:00 p.m.–midnight, Monday–Sunday
Weekends	6:00 a.m.–midnight, Saturday and Sunday
Overnight	Midnight–6:00 a.m., Monday–Sunday

How to Use Radio Research

Once you start working as a radio salesperson, it will not be long before somebody tells you, "If you live by the ratings, you'll die by the ratings." Ratings are important because in terms of raw dollars most decisions on where to place advertising schedules are primarily based on ratings. The system is simple. The higher a station's ratings, the more business it will attract, the higher the rates it can charge and the higher the levels of revenue it can generate. Another important function of ratings is to help programmers make decisions on their content. Poorly performing dayparts often mean the on-air personality who hosts those hours may be replaced, the music may be adjusted, or some other change made in hopes of attracting higher ratings.

Agency buyers are not interested in listening to radio salespeople whine about the shortcomings of Arbitron and the integrity of the data. At the end of the day, blemished as it is, the Arbitron numbers represent the best data for agency buyers and radio salespeople to use.

In a negotiation, agency buyers will use the data to make a station look worse than it is so they can try to negotiate a lower rate. The salesperson will do the opposite. There is an abundance of tactics each side in the negotiation will use to support their positions. A skilled radio salesperson needs to know how to mine stories from the raw data, how to establish value from this data, how to rebuff anticipated ratings-based attacks from agency buyers, and in general to have an understanding of the strengths and weaknesses of a station.

When a salesperson calls on an agency and a buyer says "You went down in the ratings," the salesperson needs to be able to respond with information that counters this negative slant on the new data with something positive. "Yes, our average quarter hour numbers were off a little, but our cume was up . . . we're actually reaching more people now than in the last survey, and look at our weekends, our shares there are up more than 20 percent." Crafting statements like this takes time but you should never put yourself in a position where an agency buyer can get away with establishing a one-sided story as the truth. And the truth is that virtually every ratings survey, even those that create ghastly carnage for a station, contains data that a salesperson can use to establish something positive. Optimism is vital – the glass is always half full.

So far we've been talking about the type of ratings that tell us how many people listen, their age, and their sex. This rating information is called *quantitative ratings*. But in many markets there's an entirely different and additional type of ratings. These ratings tell us about the characteristics of the audience – the educational attainment and household income of a listener, what kind of car they own and plan to buy next, their marital status, even whether they prefer to shop at Target or Wal-Mart, and how much money a week they spend on groceries. These ratings are called *qualitative ratings*.

Because many stations deliver essentially the same numbers of listeners, and because it is the job of the salesperson to create a differential competitive advantage for a station, using qualitative data, if it is available, can make a big difference. If you and your competitor are each trying to get an agency piece of business for a bank where the desired demographic is adults 25–54 and your audience delivery is basically the same, and you can use qualitative data to show that your listeners have higher incomes and higher net worth, thus representing more value to the bank because they will place larger deposits and grow the bank's assets more quickly, you will win. You should also be able to use this qualitative data to secure a higher rate.

If you spend your career looking at ratings to see only how your station ranks against the competition, you squander a wealth of data that can get you onto pieces of agency business you otherwise would lose. But keep in mind that if you spend your career talking to direct clients about ratings, you're squandering something entirely different, the opportunity to identify a business problem that can be solved by advertising.

Selling Sports on Radio

You do not hear this sort of thing on the radio anymore. But on October 3, 1951, it was all that mattered if you were a baseball fan.

> So don't go away. Light up that Chesterfield. Stay with us and we'll see how Ralph Branca will fare against Bobby Thomson. Thomson against the Brooklyn club has a lot of long ones this year. He has seven home runs. Branca pitches and Bobby takes a strike called, on the inside corner. Branca throws, there's a long fly, it's gonna be, I believe. The Giants win the pennant, The Giants win the pennant, The Giants win the pennant, The Giants win the pennant, The Giants win the pennant.[9]

Russ Hodges made the call as the New York Giants came from behind to beat the cross-town Dodgers and win the National League pennant. His play-by-play descendants are not inviting their listeners to light up Chesterfields or anything else today. But the fans of every baseball team in America know that just as the book is inevitably better than the movie, the radio broadcast is better than the television broadcast. If you pursue a career in radio sports sales and if you are sufficiently adept at reminding advertisers of this axiom, you will have a lot of fun and you will make a handsome living.

Today the sport we almost never hear on the air was the genesis of radio sports broadcasting – boxing.

On July 4, 1923, in Shelby, Montana, Jack Dempsey defended his heavyweight title against Tom Gibbons. Minutes after the last punch, fight fans in New York heard a detailed report of the bout on WOR. This was not blow-by-blow, round-by-round live coverage, but the Dempsey–Gibbons fight is regarded as the first sporting event broadcast on radio.[10]

Today there are stations that broadcast nothing but sports. The first was New York's WFAN, which launched an all-sports format in 1987. ESPN has a radio network. Opinionated sports-talk show hosts abound.

The economics of running a sports franchise are closely linked to the economics of broadcasting sports. Today a single play-by-play broadcast may have more than 50 different advertisers. Rights fees have increased dramatically so the amount of inventory sold has expanded commensurately. For years, there would be a single minute of advertising during a basketball time out. Demand has increased this time to a minute and a half. Baseball has gone from one- to two-minute breaks between innings. Between 1955 and 1966 the New York Yankees had two sponsors; Ballantine Beer and Camel Cigarettes.[11]

Over the past 20 years sports programming has been a source of significant economic growth for the radio business. Advertisers have demonstrated a strong thirst for sponsorship opportunities. In the 1980s Anheuser Busch went on a spending spree securing a large number of local sponsorships in order to more effectively compete against Miller and Coors. The strategy worked as Budweiser and Bud Light each gained market share at the expense of the competition.

If you are selling radio sports, you are obviously competing against television. You probably have a number of advantages, the foremost of which would that the package you are offering consists of broadcasts of every game. On television the rights are typically split between cable, network, pay per view, and local stations. An advertiser's investment in radio broadcast rights often provides a bond with the announcer, which approaches something of an implied endorsement. Promotions are easier to execute on radio. Promos the station runs before the broadcast, inviting listeners to tune in, can include the sponsor's name. And on the radio, tune out during commercial breaks is less of a problem for advertisers than on television, where zapping is virtually endemic on sports broadcasts.

Selling radio sports is largely a matter of selling the benefits of affiliating a product with the respective team. There is a historic spillover of loyalties from a fan of his team to a product that sponsors the team's broadcasts. In smaller markets, radio salespeople know that finding business owners who are ardent supporters of a team means they have found a good prospect for advertising. The packages that a station or a local network builds will typically include value above and beyond in-game, pre-game, or post-game placements. These packages could range from stadium signage and desirable tickets to awards banquets and team golf tournaments. In any event, advertisers who make a marketing investment in a sports franchise or program are doing much more than making a ratings-driven media buy. They are making an investment in improving the public perception of a business by a positive affiliation with what is hopefully a well-liked sports franchise.

Selling Events

An event might be a concert; it might be a pumpkin patch. Whatever the event, there are opportunities for a radio station to get involved. The station's involvement often leads to sponsorship sales to third parties.

This type of business typically falls into a category that radio broadcasters refer to as non- traditional revenue, or NTR. The structure of a deal and the extent of a radio station's involvement determine the economics and the sponsorship opportunities.

Just as sports franchises have developed a lucrative revenue stream by selling signage at stadiums they own or control, radio stations have attempted, with differing degrees of success, to sell on-site exposure at events they produce or promote. This effort can range from a banner inside a concert venue to a booth at a crafts fair. The benefit to an advertiser is the opportunity to have direct contact with a prospective customer in a positive environment and exposure to, hopefully, large numbers of people who fit a particular demographic profile.

There are two major challenges involved with selling events. One is financial and is the amount of money a sponsor believes is justified in investing. Measuring the return on this investment is difficult for an advertiser. The second is time. There is both the limited amount of time a sponsor will enjoy exposure during an event, and the often extraordinary amount of time the radio station invests in planning, producing, and selling an event.

Hispanic and Urban Radio

Nothing has changed the makeup of radio in the past few years to the extent that Hispanic radio has. There are eight times the number of Hispanic stations than there were 20 years ago. The reason: dramatic shifts in demography.

Hispanics account for about 13 percent of America's population. Looking at this from a different vantage point, America's Hispanics represent the world's fifth largest Spanish-speaking country. Naturally, Hispanics are served by radio and advertisers look for effective ways of making a connection with this increasingly vital audience through radio.

Because Hispanic population tends to be concentrated in the major markets, so do the radio stations serving them. The audiences are large: the leading stations in Los Angeles, San Francisco, Dallas, and New York are often Hispanic.

Programming is tailored to address different cultural and regional nuances. For the melting pot of New York City, a bilingual format works well. Regional Mexican formats perform well in California and the other border states. Tejano formats target multi-generational Texans, Tropical formats target Caribbean Hispanics, and Romantica formats provide an international, mass-appeal.

The people who manage Hispanic radio stations suggest that the significance of their medium for advertisers is not as much about language as it is about culture and the links America's Hispanics choose to retain with their cultural roots. They would also point out that Hispanics tend to be heavier users of radio than other media.

America's large African-American population is also served by radio. There are more than 300 urban-formatted stations and a number of formats designed to appeal to different segments. Contemporary Hit and Urban Contemporary target teens. Alternative reaches young adults and older adults prefer Urban Adult Contemporary, Urban Oldies and Smooth Jazz.

Unique Qualities/Competitive Advantages of Radio

Radio offers advertisers a number of advantages. The most significant of these is the medium's ability to target specific segments of the population. While this can also be achieved on cable television and the much more static, low-impact medium of magazines, the specific characteristics of the audiences radio can deliver to an advertiser can often be more narrowly defined.

For instance, an advertiser who needs to reach a working mother of two young children would be an ideal candidate for radio. Because this woman needs to help get her children ready to leave the home in the morning, she's not watching television, although the television may be turned on and is used as background noise. She does not have time to read the paper, if one comes to the house. But once in the car and on her way to work she is alone with the radio. She may listen to the radio at work, but she's certainly not watching television or reading the newspaper. The radio remains on in her car as she leaves the office to pick up her children and take them to soccer practice. Radio is typically the last medium she is exposed to before making the largest purchase of the day. Advertisers can study ratings to determine which types of station deliver the largest audience in their targeted demographic. In the case of the working mother of two small children, the target would probably be a woman between 25 and 44. One common mistake advertisers make when determining which radio station(s) to use to deliver a desired audience is in defining the audience too broadly. Advertisers who target audiences with adult 18–49 or adult 25–54 demographics, a fairly common practice, often reach too broad an audience. The advertiser who buys radio against an adult 25–54 demographic should remember that the consumer characteristics of a 25-year-old woman and those of a 53-year-old man, both of whom are within the defined target, tend to have little in common.

Radio salespeople can help advertisers make more intelligent decisions on which station(s) to include in a campaign, and help ensure stronger results, by suggesting that the advertiser look at the demographic epicenter of the target. In the case of a media buy where the advertising agency says it wants to reach an adults 25–54 demographic, intelligent questions on the part of the salesperson may identify the heavy user of the advertised product as being in a 25–34 cell of the demographic. It may turn out that 80 percent of all the purchasing activity within an adult 25–54 demographic takes place in this adult 25–34 cell. This fact means that a good media buy will concentrate on this demographic target cell.

Along with the ability to reach very specifically defined audiences, where radio is surpassed only by direct marketing, online and offline, radio offers an advertiser other significant advantages. One of these is often perceived as a disadvantage by some prospective advertisers. That is the fact that radio lacks a visual component.

Radio salespeople are often left with the feeling they have been given an insurmountable objection when an advertiser touts television because of its ability to show a picture of the product. But radio can take on this assignment quite nicely. By writing effective copy and by using sound effects and music, a radio commercial can easily engage the imagination. A good radio commercial will actually put listeners to work creating a unique and personal image in their own mind. A television viewer who is in the market for a new sofa may see a furniture store's advertisement. None of the sofas viewed may be appealing. But the radio listener who is in the market for a sofa will hear the selection of sofas described. The image of the sofa the listener wants will take shape in the listener's mind. The listener will associate this image with the advertiser and as a result will go to the store and look at the sofas.

When radio advertising is carefully written and well produced, this type of theater of the mind often takes place. But when cliché-riddled copy is carelessly thrown together just to get something on the air, radio has been cheated out of an opportunity to do the job it has been performing capably and consistently for more than 80 years.

Local advertisers often believe that "getting my name out there can't hurt." However, in some instances, people exposed to a business's advertising are less likely to buy its product if they did not like the commercial than people who have not been exposed to the advertising at all. Therefore, in radio, like in any medium, good advertising works and bad advertising does not work.

Radio is a mobile medium. When transistor radios came along in the 1960s, radio suddenly left the living room and went to the beach. Walkmans took this mobility to a new level in the 1980s. Today, radio reaches us everywhere. Thirty-seven percent of listening takes place at home, 43 percent in the car, and 20 percent elsewhere.[12]

Radio is arguably the most intimate medium. It is alone with a listener in the dark. It is the sole companion for a commuter. Because of the warmth of the human voice and its ability to communicate with intimacy, radio is an extremely powerful marketing tool when the proven fundamentals of advertising strategy are properly applied.

Just as radio can be intimate, it also has the ability to intrude. When someone is alone in their car, driving to a job they do not really like, a radio commercial for a firm which is hiring employees will prove more effective in reaching this potential candidate than a newspaper ad in the help wanted section. The people who go to the help wanted section are looking for a job. Employers know that the best candidates for the positions they have to fill typically are not looking for a job. Instances such as this underscore the importance of intrusiveness. While other media such as television are arguably intrusive, radio's ability to intrude with intimacy and to intrude on a well-defined demographic target gives it special value to the savvy advertiser.

Radio in the New Economy

If we think about radio as most of us know it, something that is on either the AM or FM band, it is probably safe to say that the medium will largely remain as vibrant, as relevant, and as meaningful a part of Americans' media diet as it has been for the past 80 years. Certainly, it will change. Driving the change will be the insurmountable surges of demographic shifts and relentless advances in technology. Radio has traditionally been a harbinger of leading-edge media change. Radio is where middle-class white teenagers discovered black music on what were called "race stations" in the 1950s. In the 1960s many of the economically undervalued and overlooked stations on the FM dial captured the feelings of a generation whose emerging viewpoints and tastes were all but ignored in virtually every other medium. The 1980s provided substantive media platforms for talk-show hosts whose brand of conservative politics paved the way for organizations such as the FOX News Channel.

Radio has a history of being the medium that is in the vanguard of change. But that, too, has changed because of the Internet. A radio station no longer requires a transmitter.

HD or high definition technology allows stations to broadcast digitally. It is available to 80 percent of the US population. At the end of 2007 there were more than 1,500 HD stations on the air.[13] Listeners need to purchase a special radio to receive these signals. Broadcasters believe benefits such as expanded programming choices and enhanced audio quality, where FM stations will offer CD audio quality and AM stations will offer FM audio quality, will help grow their audiences. Scrolling text on receivers provides data ranging from song title and artist to traffic reports.

Satellite Radio is a subscription service. The industry's two major firms, Sirius and XM, have proposed a merger which has been approved by shareholders but awaits regulatory approval as of the writing of this chapter (March, 2008). Each offers music, news, sports, and a variety of spoken-word formats.

Satellite radio operates in an environment of uncertainty. The exact subscriber base of Sirius and XM is not publicly available, but believed to total approximately 13 million. One of the reasons for this is usage similar to the churn experienced by wireless phone companies. One example of this: a potentially high share of subscribers who receive the service on a six-month free trial do not renew when they purchase a new car with the in-dash equipment.

XM offers advertising opportunities via show sponsorships and segment sponsorships on some of its channels. Sirius offers limited advertising across its 65 channels as well. Each firm attempts to limit advertising so as not to alienate paying subscribers who have a low tolerance for commercial interruption.

When the merger between XM and Sirius has been completed, the two programming services will be combined with a new channel lineup.

Making a Living Selling Radio Advertising

Radio salespeople work in a medium that offers a variety of rewards. The financial opportunities are potentially lucrative. So are the opportunities to demonstrate creativity and to learn firsthand the lessons of marketing, human nature, and business.

Radio salespeople typically enjoy the opportunity to manage more pieces of the sales and marketing process, from developing a promotional concept to producing the actual advertising, than their counterparts in other media, especially in markets below the top 25, where most of the business comes from agencies. The sales process itself may often rely more on the salesperson's creativity than a more quantitative and numbers-oriented type of sale that tends to exist elsewhere in the media world, especially in television.

One of the benefits of a career in radio sales is the ability to work with a variety of different businesses. This is stimulating, educational, and a virtual guarantee that boredom and complacency will rarely enter into your world. It is not unusual for a radio salesperson to call on a car dealer in the morning, have lunch with a furniture retailer, call on a homebuilder in the afternoon, and stop by a night club client in the evening.

With tenacity, determination, and a sense of purpose, your first radio sales job may not be hard to get, and it may well be a business more difficult to leave than to enter. You may discover that the friendships you make, the pace at which your business both runs and evolves, and the sense of enjoyment and satisfaction you derive make the radio business one that will stimulate and support you for the rest of your career.

Test Yourself

1 Why did radio evolve from a national to a local medium?
2 What does a program director do?
3 How does selling to an advertising agency differ from selling to a direct client?

4 What do media buyers expect of the salespeople who call on them?
5 If a prospective advertiser told you that television was better than radio because it reached more people, how would you respond?
6 Why is Hispanic radio experiencing such robust growth?
7 What benefits does sports marketing provide an advertiser?

Project

Browse through your daily newspaper and find a large ad. Write two 60-second radio commercials. Write one of the commercials so that a radio listener is *encouraged to do something* (a tactical commercial). Write the other ad so the listener is encouraged *to develop a belief* about the advertiser (a strategic commercial).

References

Susan J. Douglas. 1999. *Listening In*. New York: Times Books.

David J. Halberstam. 1999. *Sports on New York Radio*. Lincolnwood, IL: Masters Press.

Radio Advertising Bureau. 2002. *Radio Marketing Guide and Fact Book: 2002–2003*, New York: Radio Advertising Bureau.

Resources

www.clearchannel.com (Clear Channel Radio Web site)
www.rab.com (Radio Advertising Bureau)

Notes

1 Susan J. Douglas. 1999. *Listening In*. New York: Times Books.
2 Ibid.
3 Radio Advertising Bureau. 2007. *Radio Marketing Guide and Fact Book: 2007–2008 Edition*. New York: Radio Advertising Bureau.
4 www.clearchannel.com. December, 2002.
5 Veronis Suhler Stevenson *Communications Industry Forecast 2007–11*.
6 Media Audit. March 2001.
7 *CAB 2008 TV Facts*. New York: Cable-television Advertising Bureau, p. 25.
8 M. Street Corp., 02/07.
9 David J. Halberstam. 1999. *Sports on New York Radio*. Lincolnwood, IL: Masters Press, p. 285.
10 Ibid.
11 Ibid.
12 Radio Advertising Bureau. *Radio Marketing Guide 2007–2008*.
13 Radio Advertising Bureau HD Radio White Paper 2007.

22

Magazines

Phil Frank

Magazines and newspapers, together, represent two of the oldest media in the world. Going back to the 1860s, magazines and newspapers have played a vital role in the history of advertising. Since that time, magazines have been documenting the events, opinions, and cultures of the world.

Magazines are incredibly personal, with 19,419 magazines dedicated to a wide variety of interests in 2006.[1] If you have a hobby or an interest in something, there is a magazine for you. When a reader and a magazine come together, it is a different relationship than a person has with a television program, a radio personality, or a Web site.

Magazines arrive in people's mailbox, on the doorstep, or in their shopping cart because people have made an effort to get the magazine and to pay for it. The fact that readers pay for magazines is a fundamental difference between magazines and most other media. This transaction creates a relationship built on trust. Readers trust that the editors of a magazine will provide them with a quality product that appeals to their tastes and interests and is worthy of their investment.

Selling advertising in a magazine can be fulfilling because, if you enjoy reading a particular magazine, you will have conviction and a sense of satisfaction when you sell advertising in it and you will be among the group of salespeople regarded as the best in media – magazine sales representatives.

The magazine business is also quite challenging because it is highly competitive. Marketers are selective when they invest their money and they choose only a limited number of magazines in which to buy advertising. Most marketers cannot afford to surround a reader with ads in multiple publications, and, thus, competition for limited advertising budgets is intense. Therefore, it is imperative that good magazine salespeople position their books to have top-of-mind awareness in an advertiser's mind to get their fair share of limited budgets. Also, because of the competitive sales environment, it is vital for a successful magazine salesperson to have a strategic understanding of an advertiser's business and to cultivate strong personal relationships.

The people who work in magazine sales need to be more than effective, smart negotiators, they need to be creative in how they position their product to a variety of advertisers. They need to think strategically to develop winning ideas that distinguish themselves and their product in the marketplace, and they need to flexible enough to alter their approach as many marketers face the challenge of multiple advertising alternatives, especially online opportunities.

The History of Magazines

In the late 1800s magazine were read by only a few people because magazines at the time were expensive to produce and expensive to distribute – there was no mass transportation at the time – so they appealed primarily to an upper-class audience.[2]

Magazines at that time were small, soft-cover books that carried stories of limited appeal because they had a European, aristocratic approach. The masses were reading newspapers and weekly tabloids. The magazine production process was expensive in the 1800s and technologically limited; printing 100,000 copies took a very long time. And, until the United States Congress created second-class mail in 1879, the Post Office would only carry magazines a short distance, and it was quite expensive.[3]

In 1883, a Scotsman named S.S. McClure dropped the price of his magazine, *McClure's*, a general-interest magazine, to only 15 cents. It became very successful and widely read. Not long after, a rival publisher lowered the price of his magazine from 25 cents to 10 cents. This set off a new age in magazine sales, as everyone realized that dropping cover prices could lead to increased circulation.[4]

However, magazines still looked like and read like books. There were no headlines or continued stories; pictures were confined to small sizes, but design and production of magazines would soon change. In the 1890s, sketch artists were employed by magazines and assigned to cover events and stories. The artists sent back dramatic and romantic interpretations of the world. As one historian pointed out, the drawings of the Civil War were far from the reality of gruesome events.[5]

In the early 1900s, the first photo interview was conducted and started what would later lead to significant changes in editorial approach and design. New technology also was developed, which changed the look of the printed page, and advertising agencies now saw real possibilities for new forms of advertising layouts.[6]

In the late 1800s magazines carried mostly small-sized classified advertising. But new magazine and advertising designs and layouts were suddenly attractive to advertisers, and the economy of producing magazines underwent massive changes. By the 1930s, magazines were starting to bring in more and more advertising dollars, and this surging revenue made it possible to sell magazines to readers at below production costs. Thus, publishers could lower cover prices and increase readership. Magazines were no longer selling merely to readers; they tried to attract a steady and returning audience for advertisers.[7]

Advertisers soon realized that full-page ads with slogans, headlines, and logos allowed for a different language in selling their products and services. The best magazine designers came from advertising agencies, and they reshaped editorial content to bring readers to the ads. From the 1930s on, advertising continue to strengthen its grip on publishers.[8]

The design revolution continued in 1940s and 1950s, led mostly by fashion magazines. Bleed photographs were developed – photographs or art that extend to the edge of the page. Several influential art directors refined design using big pictures, experimented with headlines, and jumped the gutter – ran pictures or headlines across the centerfold of a two-page spread. In the early 1970s, Time Inc.'s *People* magazine launched and positioned itself as a general-interest magazine that lionized celebrity – it was one of the greatest launches in magazine history.[9]

Since the 1970s, there have been continual changes in magazine design and technology, and the medium has grown because of its innovative approach to finding more and more areas of interest so that people continue to justify paying for more magazines than ever before – there was a 9 percent jump in the number of magazines between 2000 and 2006 (17,815 vs. 19,419).

The current state of magazines

New trends are developing in the way magazines are produced and delivered. Production is getting more sophisticated, thus allowing advertisers to insert two or three different versions of an ad in selected editions, such as regional editions, of a magazine. New editorial segments continue to be developed, and readers are still intrigued by attractive, up-to-the-minute design. Publishers and editors are being continually challenged in their approach by other media, and are looking for ways to stay original, unique and relevant, including moving their magazine's content to the Web, as *The New Yorker* and *The Atlantic* did in 2007.

Editorial

Editorial diversity

The primary differences between magazines and other media is that there is a magazine for the diverse interests of a huge number of people. It's hard at first to realize the vastness of the editorial universe, but think about the working mother for a moment and the many different aspects of her life. How many different magazines might be of interest to such a woman?

- She works and has an interest in the business world: a *business magazine*
- She likes to get away from her job and travel: a *travel magazine*
- She's a parent: a *family magazine*
- She shops for many things for her home: a *home magazine* and a *food magazine*
- She likes to keep up with the world: a *news magazine*
- She likes to take in a movie or music: an *entertainment magazine*
- She takes her appearance seriously: a *fitness magazine*, a *fashion magazine*, and a *beauty magazine*

That makes ten areas of interest that she spends time and energy on each week, and there are many magazines to help satisfy those interests. Magazines offer readers information in subjects and areas of their life that reflect their values and aspirations, which is one reason that the average reader spends 45 minutes reading each of issue of a magazine.[10] There is literally a magazine for everyone. Exhibit 22.1 shows the number of consumer magazines from 1997 to 2007.

Exhibit 22.1 Number of magazines

Year	Total magazines
1997	18,047
1998	18,606
1999	17,970
2000	17,815
2001	17,694
2002	17,231
2003	17,254
2004	18,821
2005	18,267
2006	19,419
2007	19,532

Source: Magazine Publishers Association. 2008. *The Magazine Handbook 2008–2009*. http://magazine.org/advertising/handbook/Magazine_Handbook.aspx.

Exhibit 22.2 New magazine launches by interest category, 2007

38 Metropolitan/regional state	4 Men's
27 Crafts/games/hobbies/models	4 Pop Culture
15 Automotive	3 Sex
13 Fashion/beauty/grooming	3 Fishing/hunting
13 Special interest	3 Dogs/pets
12 Entertainment/performing arts	2 Science/technology
11 Black/ethnic	2 Military/naval
10 Home/home service	2 Comic technique
8 Health	2 Gay/lesbian
8 Sports	2 Nature/ecology
7 Children's	2 Teen
7 Women's	2 Literary/reviews/writing
6 Arts/antiques	2 Politics/social topics
5 Camping/outdoors	2 Fitness
5 Computers	2 Travel
5 Business/finance	1 Gardening
4 Epicurean	1 Gaming
4 Motorcycles	1 TV/radio/communications/electronics
4 Bridal	1 Media personalities
4 Music	1 Horses/riding/breeding

TOTAL 248

Source: Magazine Publishers Association. 2008. *The Magazine Handbook 2008–2009*. http://magazine. org/advertising/handbook/Magazine_Handbook.aspx.

As readers crave to be entertained and informed, magazine editors and publishers look for opportunities to fulfill these needs. Each year the magazine industry works to bring new magazines to the market, filling the narrowest of interests and the broadest of topics. In 2007 there were 248 new consumer magazines introduced to satisfy the need people feel to be informed and entertained. The launches spanned 40 different interest categories, as shown in Exhibit 22.2.

Some launches quickly become regular features on the newsstand, *ESPN – The Magazine, O, In Style, Maxim*, and *Teen People*, for example. Some launches get a lot of publicity, but eventually fold for one reason or another, *Rosie, Talk, Yahoo! Internet Life*, and *Industry Standard*, for example. The success or failure of a magazine often has a direct link to general psyche of the country, the economy, people's current tastes and fads, and the rise and fall of certain industries.

Editorial is the brand, the product

For an advertising salesperson, a magazine's editorial, combined with the audience it attracts, is the product they have to sell. The editorial content (referred to as just editorial from now on) is the beginning and end of a magazine's success. It's the editorial that distinguishes one magazine from its competitors. *Time* magazine's editorial is far different from that of *US News & World Report*. It is the editorial that readers pay to have delivered to their homes or purchase on a newsstand. It's the editorial that draws a certain type of reader to a magazine, thus creating a demographic profile that salespeople use to attract advertisers interested in reaching that particular demographic.

The editorial of a magazine can be the catalyst of a successful magazine or the cause of its downfall. Editorial becomes the brand of a magazine, and editorial is the stimulus for growth in readers and, in turn, advertising pages. Marketers who want to reach those readers will want to be associated with the magazine's brand. And, in time, certain advertisers and their brands become so closely associated with a magazine that the brands seem to meld together. Think of sports magazines and a beer advertiser or beauty magazines and a cosmetics advertiser. This close association leads to some sensitive issues regarding editorial and advertising.

Advertising to editorial ratio

Nearly all magazines contain both editorial and advertising. It's advertising that keeps subscription and newsstand prices reasonable. While editorial and advertising both inform and entertain, magazine staffs work hard to keep a reasonable ratio between these two elements. If editorial and advertising are not in a suitable balance, it can have one of two effects on readers: (1) It will alienate readers because of too much advertising or (2) it will not deliver enough revenue to keep the magazine alive because of too much editorial. In 2006 in consumer magazines, the percentage of advertising to editorial was 53 percent editorial to 47 percent advertising, a ratio that has remained relatively stable for a decade.[11]

Balancing editorial and advertising is a science and an art, and there are times that there are exceptions to the average 53/47 ratio. The exceptions are all over the newsstands, but when executed in an intelligent way, an imbalance is hardly noticeable. In bridal magazines, car magazines, and computer magazines, the advertising-to-edit ratio can swing all the way to 80/20 because readers are often as interested in the ads as they are in the editorial.

In developing and maintaining the correct ad-to-edit ratio, magazine editors and magazine publishers, who run the business side of a magazine, tend to work quite closely together and focus on readers' interests. However, they fall on different sides of the fence when it comes to final editorial control.

Edit and advertising: church and state

"Church and state" is the phrase magazine people use to describe the line that exists between the editorial side of a magazine and the business and advertising side. The separation can be fuzzy at times, but it boils down to maintaining the integrity of the relationship between the editors and the readers of a magazine. Just as church and state should be independent, as laid out in the US Constitution, so should the editorial and the advertising sides of a magazine.

As an example, imagine if you're reading an article in *BusinessWeek* about home mortgages and inside the story there is a favorable mention of a particular bank; then, smack in the middle of it, there is an ad for the same bank mentioned in the story.

Finally, imagine that this bank is one of the magazine's largest advertising clients; would you think the mention in the story was a coincidence? Could the editor have been influenced to write a favorable story about the advertiser in the magazine? If you, or readers in general, perceive that the editorial of the magazine is not objective, you might stop reading the magazine.

The issue of the integrity and credibility of the editorial is where editors and publishers are in agreement. Editors need to maintain the objectivity and credibility of the magazine by keeping the reader's faith that the writers are independent. Publishers occasionally become angry when editors write critical articles that involve advertisers, but a responsible publisher realizes that this objectivity is the very reason readers trust the magazine's editorial.

The biggest outcry comes from advertisers. It's not uncommon for an advertiser to ask a salesperson if some editorial pieces can be created that would frame their advertising in a beneficial way. This response to such a request should be an automatic "no" from the salesperson, but often money clouds a publisher's judgment, and there is a face-off with the editor. In the end, editors typically win, and, hopefully, advertisers understand.

This issue hits at one of the two core responsibilities of the editors, which are not to compromise on editorial integrity and always to keep readers' best interest in mind.

Audience

An audience for a magazine starts with its circulation and grows as original readers pass an issue along to other readers. This second part of a magazine's audience is aptly labeled the pass-along audience. Circulation comes from two sources, subscriptions and single-copy, or newsstand, sales.

Subscribers

A magazine gets subscriptions when readers agree to pay an upfront fee to a magazine in order to have the magazine sent to an address. Consumers usually receive a discount over the price they would pay if they were to buy the same number of issues one at a time at a newsstand. In addition, with a subscription, consumers have purchased the convenience of having the magazine delivered to their home or office. For the magazine, there are two advantages: (1) They have made a guaranteed sale of their magazine well into the future; and (2) they grow their audience in a way that creates greater stability over time.

In 2007, 87 percent of all consumer magazines were sold by subscription, a percentage that has been growing steadily over the last 10 years. Also, there hasn't been a major change in the last ten years in the total number of consumer magazines sold.[12] Therefore, as media planners wonder where to invest their dollars, they can consider magazines' stability, particularly in light of the media fragmentation that has occurred over the last ten years, led by cable television and the Internet. Stability is an important consideration for someone charged with the responsibility of investing millions and millions of dollars in advertising.

Single-copy, or newsstand, sales

While subscriptions represent the stable part of a magazine's circulation, single-copy sales demonstrate the vitality and an ongoing gage of interest in a magazine. Single-copy sales are an important measure for a media buyer to study, as this piece of data provides a gage of a magazine's editorial strength, the appeal of its graphic design, the relevancy of its cover story, and its overall ability to compete in popularity with other magazines in a similar category of interest.

Good magazine media buyers take many other factors into consideration as they evaluate the health and strength of a magazine's total circulation. For example, magazines that are more established should not have to rely too much on newsstand sales to keep their circulation strong. On the other hand, a successful launch of a new magazine should result in a high number of newsstand sales, should demonstrate that it is gaining momentum early in its life, and should help to convert many of these single-copy purchasers into subscribers over time.

Qualified circulation

The practice of qualified, or controlled, circulation takes place more in business-to-business and trade magazines. This is a circulation strategy in which publishers actually give a magazine away free but only to people who meet certain qualifications. A magazine being written about the software industry may want to give its magazine away to product engineers, for example.

By limiting the number of readers, because readers have to qualify in order to receive the magazine, the magazine creates an attractive audience for advertisers who want to reach qualified buyers.

Establishing and growing a rate base

Advertisers and media buyers establish an agreement that a magazine must deliver a guaranteed number of readers on an issue-by-issue basis. This guarantee on the actual number of people who receive a magazine, either by subscription or by buying a single copy, is known as a magazine's rate base.

Magazine publishers use the rate base to set their advertising rates on the basis of CPMs, and these CPMs become guarantees of the number of readers that an advertiser will reach. Magazines set and adjust their own rate base and, naturally, they try to grow their rate base so they can, in turn, raise their advertising rates.

Additionally, a magazine's circulation is affected by its age. As I mentioned above, a magazine that has been published for 50 years or so, such as *Sports Illustrated*, will probably not see huge changes in its audience size or rate base because the audience has matured and leveled off. In fact, magazines that have been around for many years and that are consistent in maintaining their rate bases demonstrate that they maintain their relevance to their readers. However, for a younger magazine that is still developing and has yet to achieve its potential audience level, rate base increases are common and actually cheered on by media buyers as a sign of popularity.

Magazine publishing companies are experts at pricing their magazines. They decide on the price of a single copy of a magazine based on several factors, which include: (1) The frequency of the publication – weekly, as in the case of *People*, or monthly, as in the case of *Architectural Digest*; (2) the editorial category and the audience it will attract, such as an upscale or mass appeal audience; (3) the number of competitors – in other words, does the consumer have a lot of choices in a magazine category? and (4) the perceived value to a reader.

Circulation managers at magazines continually look to build and grow their audiences. They typically look for interesting promotional opportunities. Some magazines will give away merchandise such as clothing, appointment books, or chances to travel in order to induce people to subscribe. Or they may look to partner with a retailer such as a grocery store, a pharmacy, or a more specialized store, that will bundle the sale of a subscription with that of their own goods.

This practice of building circulation and raising rate bases has recently undergone scrutiny and some challenges. For example, recently, a consumer advocate group was able to stop a publisher's clearing house from selling subscriptions to potential readers via sweepstakes. Sweepstakes and contests were a consistent source for new subscribers, and recent restrictions of these practices have put even more pressure on circulation managers to replace those subscribers no longer available through the use of sweepstakes by using other methods.

Rate base audits

To avoid any questionable practices, magazine publishers and agency planners and buyers have gone to a third party to monitor the rules by which a magazine can raise its circulation, and thus its rate base and its rates. The monitoring entity is known as the Audit Bureau of Circulation (ABC). One of the ABC's most important jobs is to question any suspicious activity in rate base growth. Suspicious activity can include continuing to send issues to people who have cancelled, or counting as full-price subscriptions those have been sold at deep discounts.

Revenue from circulation

The average magazine draws 55 percent of its revenue from advertising and 45 percent from circulation. It's easy to see how publishers see their advertising sales team and their circulation sales team as equally important. This 55/45 split hasn't changed much in the last few years, and even as the economy leaps and dives, the ratio has remained steady. The ratio of 55 percent advertising revenue, 32 percent subscription revenue, 13 percent single-copy sales revenue has remained roughly the same for the years 2004–2006.[13]

The circulation business is a $10 billion industry in its own right. Circulation managers are facing many challenges and circulation departments are continually looking for openings on the newsstands and the opportunity to develop new magazines. Good circulation directors tend to be aggressive with both new and old magazines, and will often run a series of short-term promotions to increase single-copy as well as subscription sales. They know that if they can recruit subscribers, there is a good chance that the magazine will be able to hold them for a long time, which will help sustain and grow revenue far into the future.

Circulation

There is a saying in the real estate industry, "Location, location, location." Many advertisers would say that for media companies it should be, "Circulation, circulation, circulation." While decisions on where to spend media dollars are not always one-dimensional, circulation does play a big role.

For the most part, advertisers want audiences to be both targeted and large. Magazines deliver in both ways. With one issue of a magazine, advertisers can reach tens of millions of consumers, and magazine readers have demographics that are much more desirable than television audiences or even consumers on the Internet.

Magazine reach

Many media planners and buyers make the argument that network television is the best medium for reach; however, with the fragmentation of audiences and programming successes by subscription-only cable networks, this argument is not as airtight as it used to be.

There are a large number of magazines that can compete with top-rated network television programs on the basis of audience accumulation and reach. There are many magazines that deliver larger audiences than most cable networks and top-ranked Web sites.[14]

Pass-along audience

You may be wondering how magazines can achieve this reach, particularly if the circulation numbers of the top 25 magazines are, for the most part, under five million.

Magazines are portable and consumers can read them at home or away from home. Additionally, most issues of most magazines are read by more than one person. This extra audience is referred to as the pass-along audience, as I mentioned previously. Depending on the quality of the editorial and the interest category, some magazines have a pass-along audience that reaches over ten readers per copy. More specifically, the way this works is that a magazine is delivered either at home or at work and several different people pick it up and read it. When you go some-where – a doctor's office, a friend's home, a barbershop, or a library – how many people are actually reading an issue of a magazine? This is largely how magazines accumulate the massive reach that makes them very competitive with other media. Exhibit 22.3 shows the many locations in which magazines are read.

General profile of magazine readers

Magazines, in general, offer an audience that is younger, more affluent, better educated, and more empowered than other media do. Additionally, heavy maga-zine readers are a very loyal group, and consume less television than the general population. These characteristics make the average magazine reader very desir-able for advertisers, especially when compared to the average television viewer. For example, a cross-media comparison conducted by leading media agency, Carat,

Exhibit 22.3	Magazine reading by place	
In own home		81%
Out-of-home		76%
doctor/dentist office		37%
in someone else's home		26%
at a newsstand/store		26%
at work		25%
in a beauty salon/barbershop		14%
at a library/club/school		8%
on an airplane		7%
in a business reception room		7%
during other travel		2%
traveling to/from work		2%

Source: Magazine Publishers Association. 2008. *The Magazine Handbook 2008–2009.* http://magazine.org/advertising/handbook/Magazine_Handbook.aspx.

found that, in reaching teens 12 to 17, the top 25 magazines lead versus the top 25 primetime television programs.[15]

Production of a Magazine

Magazine production is an art unto itself. First, there is the physical production of the book, then the quantity produced, and finally the frequency of publication.

In terms of the physical production, there are two methods of binding. The first is called saddle stitch. In this method, the pages are laid on top of each other over an arm, the way a saddle lies on top of a horse, and then fastened together, or stitched, with staples. The second method is called perfect bound. This method employs gluing the pages to a spine, much the way many books are. Perfect-bound production is largely used for magazines that carry a substantial number of pages in one issue, because staples are not large or sturdy enough to pierce and hold a large number of pages. It is typically easier for perfect-bound magazines to handle advertising on heavier paper stock than it is for saddle-stitch magazines. However, saddle-stitch magazines offer publishers a more efficient way to customize different versions of the same issue to reach specific subscribers.

Pricing

Magazines are largely priced the same way other media are. Pricing is based on cost-per-thousand (CPMs) and is measured on the basis of circulation. Magazines that have mass appeal tend to have lower CPMs, typically in the range of $7.50 to $25.00. Other magazines, which reach special-interest audiences, have higher CPMs. The CPMs of some of the smaller, more specialized magazines are usually in the range of hundreds of dollars, and can easily surpass $500. Yet media buyers and advertisers know that other media have a lot of waste coverage and cannot put advertising in front of special interest and highly desirable demographic groups in the pinpoint manner magazines can. In contrast, the CPMs for *direct mail catalogues* can be as high as $3,000, so a $500 CPM for a highly targeted magazine seems like a bargain.

For an example of the importance of pricing in selling and negotiating magazines to agencies, read Appendix A "Selling Magazines to Agencies."

Research

There are several syndicated research companies that provide vital information to magazine sales teams and media buyers alike. These include Mediamark Research, Inc. (MRI) and Monroe Mendelsohn Research (MMR), which produce data similar to the Nielsen ratings in network television, which you learned about in Chapter 16.

To give you an indication of how important research is and how it can be used to pinpoint a target audience, following is an example of how I used research when I was a media supervisor at Ammirati and Puris, an advertising agency. I once had a client who produced a product that kept fruit fresh for a long time and was good for either canning, preserving, or serving fruit. The product worked well and prevented fruit salad from getting a brown tinge on it in an hour. Through research we found that our target audience was primarily women in the southeast of the United States. We used research to find women in the southeast who canned more than 15 jars of fruit each month – a small audience of heavy users – and we were able to find several magazines that reached just this target audience.

Buyers look at demographic research and psychographic research. There are many studies that help a buyer understand the psychographics, or lifestyle, of their target audience, for example, aspiring vs. comfortable, or settled vs. adventurous; and their interests, for example, cars, jazz, local politics, or nature hikes. Magazines are particularly suited to delivering desirable demographics in an environment that addresses the interest and psychographics of a target audience.

Positioning an ad in a magazine

Media buyers are often taught to find the medium that reaches their target audience, and then buy it at the best price they can negotiate. Once a buyer has selected a magazine on those two parameters, the next discussion is typically about the position an ad will receive inside the book. Depending on how image conscious an advertiser is, this part of the discussion can play a major role in negotiations.

Publishers realize the importance of position and charge extra for the most desirable positions inside their books. The most desirable positions are determined according to two main factors: (1) Visibility, which has to do with the way that readers actually read a magazine, and the assumption is that most read from front to back; and (2) adjacency to desirable editorial.

There are three or four positions in a magazine that are considered more visible than other positions. These positions are: (1) The first ad inside the front cover, referred to as the second cover; (2) the page on the inside of the back cover, referred to as the third cover; (3) the back cover itself, referred to as the fourth cover; and (4) the page opposite the table of contents (TOC).

Other key positions are based on how close to the front of the magazine an ad is positioned. Ads that are positioned more forward are more likely to be seen, simply because most people read a magazine from front to back. For the most part, the front of the book is read more than the back. Good publishers and editors work hard to spread the more widely read editorial throughout the magazine in an attempt to have readers go through the entire book.

Finally, another desirable position is having an ad adjacent to specific editorial that may have particular interest to a certain part of a magazine's audience or ties well into an advertiser's creative execution. For instance, in a sports-oriented magazine, a financial advertiser may remark how they are the leader in performance among their competitors, and the magazine may list statistical leaders in a sport. Thus, an ad and the editorial have some synergy and may provide added exposure for an ad.

Another desirable editorial position occurs when single copies of magazines are bought largely on what appears on the cover. In those cases, an advertiser may want to secure a position adjacent to the editorial of the cover story, thinking that readers will spend time in that part of the magazine which would give an ad there greater exposure.

Ad units

There are many different types of ads that appear in magazines; currently there are 22 ad sizes that are measured for effectiveness. These range from a single page in black and white to an ad using color. The position of an ad, the appearance of an ad, and the size of an ad are reasons why some ads seem to be more ubiquitous and remembered more than others. Exhibit 22.4 shows the impact of magazine advertising by type of unit, color, position, and paper stock.

Advertisers continue to find new size and shapes of ads that they can put in magazines. Larger ads and more creative size and shapes help advertisers'

Exhibit 22.4   The impact of magazine advertising by type of unit, color, position and paper stock

Type of magazine advertisement		Recall index
Unit	**Full page**	**100**
	Inside front cover	107
	Inside back cover	105
	Back cover	117
	Multiple-page units	115
	Two-page spread	109
	Less than full page	80
Color	**Black and white**	**100**
	Spot color(s)	96
	4-color*	106
Position	**Second half of issue**	**100**
	First half of issue	102
Paper stock	**Regular**	**100**
	Heavy**	118

* Four color (incl. fifth color or metallics), two color, and black and white.
** "Heavy" defined as any paper weight heavier than run-of-book stock (Source: Affinity Research VISTA Print Rating Service, 2008).
Source: Magazine Publishers Association. 2008. *The Magazine Handbook 2008–2009*. http://magazine. org/advertising/handbook/Magazine_Handbook.aspx.

messages achieve greater impact. The various sizes tend to be given interesting names that are a challenge for the production people to try and understand. These include French Doors, Double Dutch, ½ Page Flap, ⅓ Page Gate, and Tabs, for example.

Marketing extensions

More and more advertisers are asking publishers to provide some kind of strategic extension for their advertising campaign or marketing strategy. These extensions can either be included in the cost of the advertising, or for larger scale extensions, a publisher may ask for and receive incremental revenue.

These marketing extensions are referred to by several names, including merchandising and added value. In the current competitive magazine marketplace, publications will often give advertisers 1–2 percent of their advertising spending for marketing extension. These extensions can include anything from reprints of their ads, to be used for direct marketing to customers or prospects, to collateral sales material for an advertiser's own sales force.

What's happening more often is that magazines are creating larger and larger extensions, including hosting seminars, setting up entertainment events, and conducting sweepstakes, for example. These programs are usually offered to the advertiser for an incremental investment, which is often highly discounted from the true value of the extension.

Giving advertisers marketing extensions is becoming more and more prevalent in the current magazine marketplace. As clients and agencies undergo downsizing, and the window of opportunity for a truly groundbreaking and successful product launch is getting smaller and smaller, so marketers are continually looking to their media partners to develop concepts to cover a wide spectrum of marketing responsibilities.

This increased demand for media companies to develop broader and broader marketing extensions and cohesive programs has been spurred on by the impact of a slow economy and its effect on both marketers and advertising agencies.

Marketers are reducing their staffs and, thus, are reducing both manpower and intellectual capital in their organizations. Additionally, marketers are reducing the number of agency relationships and consolidating the work with, typically, one or two agencies as opposed to having specialists work on different aspects of their marketing communications.

Advertising agencies are consolidating their buying functions, which is providing them with greater and greater clout in negotiating for lower prices; thus, magazines must develop ideas for which they can charge premiums. Agencies are being pressured by their clients to deliver efficient costs, a strong return on investment, and new, high-impact creative ideas. Simultaneously, agencies have to reduce their staff size, and this reduction lessens their ability to provide marketing support, which, in turn, results in a rising demand for media companies to provide additional services and more in the way of added value.

Working with Both Advertising Agencies and Clients

Good magazine salespeople cover both agencies and clients because they can learn a great deal from both about how to craft the most effective solution. And combining the information that they get from each and using it wisely typically results in the good salespeople being distinguished from the rest of the pack.

Agencies are paid to analyze media and make investment recommendations based on the overall marketing objectives and strategies of the client. The clients magazine salespeople typically call on are brand managers and they are paid to keep their product fresh in the minds of the consumer and help build equity in a brand and the product. It's this equity that creates and sustains long-term loyalty among their customers. In other words, agencies have a great deal of information about specific advertising campaigns, while clients have large-scale information about the overall marketing direction of a brand and know about market conditions, strategies and the competitive landscape.

It has been a traditional practice in the magazine-selling field to call on clients. Brand managers, advertising directors, senior vice presidents of marketing, and even CEOs will see salespeople from major national magazines, particularly those that cover their industry: *Car and Driver*, *PC World*, and *Travel and Leisure*, for example. Over the years, no other media, with perhaps the exception of the major television and cable networks, have had access to top management, and this access is one of the great advantages of selling for national magazines.

Magazine Advantages Over Other Media

One of the reasons magazines have access to top management at both agencies and clients is that magazines are not only important national media but also they are unique in many ways, ranging from the physical characteristics of magazines to the way that their readers respond to advertising.

Effectiveness of print advertising

Magazine advertising is a core resource to some of the world's largest marketers. Magazines have the reach, the demographics, the immediacy, the efficiency, the creative platform, and the ability to both communicate with a mass audience and target a narrowly defined group of people. Marketers find this combination of reach and targetability appealing. Magazines have proven effective for both brand building and selling products.

For generating awareness and building momentum for a brand, magazine advertising is more relevant and targeted – creates more consumer engagement – than television or online advertising, according to a 2007 Dynamic Logic Ad Attraction survey, as seen in Exhibit 22.5.

In terms of targetability by interest, magazines are highly competitive with the Internet and cable television. The Internet currently has in the neighborhood of five billion Web sites, and growing daily, compared to about 19,500 consumer magazines. There are often thousands or even millions of Web sites on one topic. For example, a Google.com search on the term "interest rates" returned 50,290,000 results. This fractionalization makes it exceptionally difficult to place advertising in order to achieve reach quickly. Even though search advertising on Google.com using AdWords is highly targeted, is also extremely fragmented.

With cable television, there are more than 300 channels currently available. Even the most popular channels typically average only a 1.0 rating in primetime. Magazines provide not only the diversity of cable, but also greater reach.

Exhibit 22.5 Consumers enjoy magazine advertising and agree "Advertising adds to the enjoyment of the following":

Reading magazines	48%
Listening to radio	36%
Watching cable TV	32%
Watching network TV	32%
Using the Internet	21%

Source: Magazine Publishers Association. 2008. *The Magazine Handbook 2008–2009*. http://magazine.org/advertising/handbook/Magazine_Handbook.aspx.

Exhibit 22.6 Magazines improve marketing and advertising ROI

Recommendations for reallocation of media spending*

Magazine	69%
Online	44%
TV	19%

* Percentage of studies where spending should increase for medium, based on a marketing evolution study.
Source: Magazine Publishers Association. 2008. *The Magazine Handbook 2008–2009*. http://magazine.org/advertising/handbook/Magazine_Handbook.aspx.

Magazines and ROI

There is an old saying in advertising, "I know my advertising is working, but I'm just not sure where my advertising is working." In the late 1990s and early part of this century, more than in any other time in recent history, marketers began to stress that advertising needs to generate a return on investment (ROI). The Internet was a major catapult for ROI because it provided specific feedback, immediately, on the productivity of an ad in terms of response rates.

Now, it's common for marketers to hold their ad agency to ROI goals, and in turn ad agencies are trying to hold media companies to ROI goals as well. ROI has become such an important element of advertising that marketers are now having their finance departments attend meetings in which ad agencies are trying to win a company's advertisement assignments, for example.

Therefore, media has to show, in one form or another, that they can help with sales and produce ROI on the dollars they receive. Many studies have shown that, dollar-for-dollar, magazines produce a 23 percent more effective return on investment than other media at comparable budget levels, as summarized in Exhibit 22.6.

Relationship with readers/audience involvement

Consumers pay for magazines and newspapers on a regular basis. No one pays to watch the Super Bowl or "Late Night with David Letterman" on television.

You may pay your cable company to get 300 channels, but not specific programming. No one pays to listen to his or her local radio station; you simply get a radio and turn it on. No one pays to surf CNN.com or Yahoo.com; you pay your cable company, or telephone company, or an Internet service provider (ISP) to get access to the Internet, but, for the most part, you are not paying to go to a specific non-porn site.

With print, magazines and newspapers, consumer are turning over money for every magazine or paper they want to receive and for every issue they want to read. This transaction is fundamental to understanding the relationship magazines hold with their readers. It is not uncommon to hear someone ask, "What are your favorite magazines?" The variety or lack of variety in their magazine choices can be an interesting insight into someone's interests. The answer may be, "I subscribe to magazines X, Y and Z, and on occasion I'll pick up Magazines A, B, C." Magazines are very personal for their readers, providing the information and entertainment that is most relevant and interesting to them.

The relationship between a reader and a magazine, represented by the transactional nature of the relationship, is very much built on trust. When readers pay for an issue, they expect value. If the value they expect is delivered, then readers return and pay again, expecting the magazine to deliver again. If that trust is broken on a consistent basis, readers do not return.

For advertisers, this relationship is certainly an excellent context in which to communicate. Readers of magazines are committed to their decision on what to read and what not to read. They carry issues of magazines to work, while they commute or travel, even while they are on vacation. Because of this relationship, readers tend to interact with advertising in a very different way as well.

Advertising in magazines grabs consumers' attention and motivates them to purchase the products, brands, and services advertised. Additionally, a reader of a magazine has to be actively engaged with a magazine for advertising even to be seen. If a reader is not turning the pages of a magazine, nothing happens. However, if a television viewer or radio listener wanders away losing all interaction with a broadcast, the broadcast continues, and advertising runs with nobody there to receive it.

Unique creative

For several reasons, magazines offer the copywriters and art directors of advertising agencies a rare opportunity – to tell a story or explain something in more than 60, 30, or 15 seconds. There is no limit on the time someone can spend accessing the contents of a magazine. This type of access is referred to as random access because readers can access a page as often as they like and whenever they want, on a random basis. Radio and television are linear access because listeners and viewers cannot go back or skip forward to hear or view just those parts of the programming that interests them. Because of this type of access, print ads have the opportunity to expand the way they communicate with a reader.

Try to explain, or sell, something to a friend in 30 seconds – the average length of a television commercial. It is difficult. Thirty seconds is not a long time; you cannot give much information in that time, so copywriters for television concentrate on trying to get viewers to make an emotional connection with a brand by making them laugh or cry or lust for the brand. Magazines give copywriters more liberty to explain product benefits, to make competitive comparisons, to give more information, and to define a brand. Also, magazine advertising can be fun. There are many entertaining, creative platforms for an ad. Whether it is putting a sticky note on an ad, creating suspense with consecutive pages, or using pop-ups, magazines offer much more than a one-dimensional piece of paper to work with. On the other hand, a straightforward full-page ad in a magazine provides the space to tell a good, informative brand story.

Context for advertising

Magazines provide excellent opportunities for marketers to take advantage of having their ad appear in an environment that is relevant to, complementary to, and in harmony with their advertising message. This concept is referred to as context. Having an ad appear in an environment that is relevant to the advertising message or to the product is good context.

Because there are a multitude of magazines that cover a vast array of interests, marketers have a wonderful opportunity to take advantage of the special, complementary context that magazines can provide for their messaging.

Magazines in the New Economy

Many magazines are fighting to maintain their profitability levels, or to maintain any profit at all. New magazines are being launched, and while some fail, others are quite healthy and are putting their older competitors in a position of high risk. The competition of one title versus another is always healthy and keeps editorial staffs sharp and up to date on how consumers digest information and what information they want.

As magazines face competition from television, the Internet, and other media, the cooperation between these different media is also on the rise and will help minimize many of the competitive threats. For example, Time Warner-owned CNN.com drives traffic to the online Web pages of Time Warner-owned *Money* and *Fortune* magazines, which opens up the possibility of cross-platform selling.

Jobs Selling Magazine Advertising

Most magazines have a similar structure in their sales operations, and this structure offers different types of jobs for different types of people. The various departments and the jobs inside of them are:

Sales

Sales, the frontline of any media company, can be the most rewarding role, but sales is also the most demanding. Typically, the entry level for a magazine salesperson coming right out of school is either to start as a sales assistant or a junior account executive at an advertising agency. Generally, the sales organization for a magazine consists of the following jobs, starting at the top: publisher, associate publisher, regional manager, office manager, senior account executive, junior account executive, and sales assistant.

As people enter and move up the ranks of a sales division, they will find they are spending time with fewer and fewer clients and spending more time on managerial issues. However, publishers and their primary associates are not sitting in their offices all the time. Publishers will often travel across the country to call on a magazine's largest accounts.

Account executives, which in this book we refer to as salespeople, are typically making multiple sales calls each day. Most will start with a breakfast meeting, then schedule other calls throughout the day. In the span of a week, a salesperson will make between 10 and 25 calls depending on the location and availability of their clients.

Magazines are very dependent on relationships. The medium is not commoditized, as much of television and radio is, and it faces fierce competition every day. Therefore, it is important to be in synch with clients every step of the way and to build and maintain very close relationships with these clients.

Sales development

The Sales development group works very closely with sales to create strategically oriented proposals that capitalize on the inherent assets of a magazine and how it can help elevate a marketer's message. People in this group need to have a strong marketing background, be able to understand advertising objectives, and translate all of these elements into creative solutions that can sell a client's products.

In recent years, sales development teams have been spending more time on sales calls with salespeople. It is important that this group understand the opportunities and priorities of their clients, and they are often asked to help sell the architecture and core elements of the proposals they develop, including cross-platform opportunities.

A sales development job has less pressure than a sales job does, as typically compensation is not tied to achieving a sales goal and, therefore, salaries and total compensation are usually lower than those of salespeople.

Marketing

In some magazines, sales development and marketing teams are combined. However, the responsibilities are distinctly different. The focus of marketing/events is on making sure a magazine and its editorial and audience are well understood by the advertising marketplace.

Marketing people work directly with their research departments to help understand the makeup of the magazine's audience. They also work directly with editors to help position the magazine's content in a unique way. People in marketing also help develop a positioning story and value proposition for a sales team that will help salespeople position the magazine in a way that maximizes their opportunity to sell ad pages.

Research

Research departments at magazines are taking on more diverse responsibilities than ever before. The Internet has been a primary cause of this change. Historically, research departments would study data being delivered by syndicated research firms, but now they are more proactive and are being asked to provide their analysis not only of a magazine's audience, but also of the direction and trends of the marketplace and of their advertisers' businesses.

Research departments work closely with the sales department to study historical trends of individual advertisers or categories of advertisers. They look for positive momentum or downward trends, either of which can signify opportunities for growing revenue. Additionally, these departments are now developing capsules of information on advertising prospects that provide salespeople with the opportunity to approach their clients with knowledgeable background information on their company and their industry.

If a magazine has just been launched and its audience is too new and too volatile to be measured by syndicated research, it is the responsibility of a research department to develop a prototype of its audience. The prototype is developed by selecting other magazines that have similar editorial, circulation, and demographic appeal. Prototyping a magazine's audience can be very interesting as it involves trying to create a personality for a magazine based on what little available data there is.

Finance

The finance group at any magazine is important to every salesperson because this department helps to develop the pricing component of every sales proposal. The finance department has an interesting perspective on a magazine. Because finance people work with every salesperson, they know the ins and out of each deal that is put together and can be extremely helpful and even creative in pricing a deal. Often, pricing is not as simple as studying history to see what prices an advertiser has paid in the past or forecasting future growth from certain accounts. Pricing also involves figuring out the production costs that a magazine may assume for special creative units as well as other production costs. Overall, this team makes sure that every proposal that goes out the door is bringing revenue to the bottom line of the magazine.

In conclusion, a career in magazine sales is one of the most interesting, rewarding, creative, and satisfying of all media sales. Whether you sell for a city magazine, a trade magazine, or a national mass-consumer magazine, you will find selling for one of the oldest advertising media is both highly competitive and extremely satisfying because you can find a magazine that fits your greatest interests and passion and can therefore sell a product that you love to intelligent, interesting people.

Test Yourself

1   When was the first mass-appeal magazine sold for 15 cents?
2   Give an example of how many different magazines, by interest category, that a working mother who has an interest in her business, the world, her family, her children, travel, and her appearance might subscribe to.
3   Approximately how many different magazine titles were there in 2007?
4   How many new magazine launches were there in 2007?
5   What is the advertising to editorial ratio in the average consumer magazine?
6   Explain what is meant by the phrase "church and state" as it applies to the magazine business.
7   What percent of the total revenue of an average consumer magazine comes from subscriptions?
8   Explain the difference between a saddle-stitch and a perfect-bound magazine.
9   Give three reasons for magazine's effectiveness as an advertising medium.

Project

Purchase a copy of *Teen People* magazine and read it carefully, noting all the editorial features in the magazine and the advertising. Then, create a PowerPoint presentation that will be given to Pepsi-Cola, recommending that it make a major, year-long investment in *Teen People*, which will require shifting some dollars out of network and cable television. Do not be concerned with or present any cost figures; your task is to get Pepsi-Cola to reduce its television expenditures and invest in *Teen People*. Rely heavily on information about magazines' effectiveness that you will find in *The Magazine Handbook*, available at www.magazine.org.

References

Samir Husni. 2002. *Guide to New Consumer Magazines*. New York: Bowker.

Art Kleiner, 1979, "A history of magazines on a timeline," *Co-Evolution Quarterly*.

Magazine Publishers Association. 2008. *The Magazine Handbook 2008–2009*. New York: Magazine Publishers Association.

Oxbridge Communications. 2003. *National Directory of Magazines*. New York: Oxbridge Communications.

Resources

www.adage.com/datacenter (*Advertising Age* magazine's data center)

www.magazine.org (Magazine Publishers Association Web site – lots of useful information)

www.mediafinder.com (Media Finder – the largest database of US and Canadian periodicals)

Notes

1. Magazine Publishers Association. 2008. *The Magazine Handbook 2008–2009*. www.magazine.org/resources/research.html
2. Art Kleiner. 1979. "A history of magazines on a timeline." *Co-Evolution Quarterly*.
3. Ibid.
4. Ibid.
5. Ibid.
6. Ibid.
7. Ibid.
8. Ibid.
9. Ibid.
10. Magazine Publishers Association. *The Magazine Handbook 2008–2009*. www.magazine.org/advertising/handbook/Magazine_Handbook.aspx.
11. Ibid.
12. Ibid.
13. Ibid.
14. Ibid.
15. Ibid.

23

Media Comparisons:
Advantages and Disadvantages

Charles Warner

As you learned in Chapter 9, one method of prospecting is to approach current advertisers in other media. Because there are few businesses that do not advertise in one medium or another, the vast majority of your prospecting will be conducted by monitoring other media to find advertisers who use another medium and then attempting to switch them to your medium by selling its advantages. Also, because your best prospects are your current customers, you will encourage them to invest less in other media and to invest more in your medium. In this process, you have to be careful not to disparage customers' judgment for buying another medium.

It is best to focus on the concept of media mix and how your medium can add reach, frequency, improved targeting, impact, or all of these elements to a customer's advertising campaign. But while recommending a media-mix strategy, you should not knock the competition, either in your medium or in other media. Instead of knocking the competition, you should sell the advantages and synergies that can come from combining other media with your medium.

With the increased fragmentation and segmentation of media – more cable channels and networks, more Web sites, the decline in newspaper circulation and broadcast television viewing – mixing and combining media is the best way for advertisers to get more for their advertising dollars, especially more reach. To understand the media mix concept more thoroughly, go to www.charleswarner. us/indexpresentations.html and read the presentation "Media Mix and the Natural Laws of Advertising by Erwin Ephron."

Cross-platform selling will steadily increase in the coming years, and in order to participate in this trend, salespeople will have to be experts in all media and sell them bundled together as an effective advertising mix. Many media conglomerates such as Viacom, Time Warner, CBS, NBCU, and Clear Channel are currently practicing a cross-platform selling approach.

Following are lists of advantages and disadvantages of the media covered in this book. When you view the lists, keep in mind that you should not focus on the disadvantages of other media, but on the advantages of your medium and how it can add to the effectiveness of a media mix. To give you some ideas of which media to go after, see Exhibit 23.1.

As you can see from Exhibit 23.1, television gets the largest share of adults' 18–49 and 18+ time and the largest share of total advertising dollars. Newspapers

Exhibit 23.1 Media time spent (in hours) by age and household income and advertising expenditures

Medium	Percentage of time spent yesterday, age 18–49*	Percentage of time spent yesterday, age 18+*	Estimated percentage of total advertising expenditures, 2008**
Television	46	51	31.7
Newspapers	4	6	18.1
Radio	27	24	8.8
Magazines	3	3	10.0
Internet	20	16	8.4

Medium	Percentage of time spent yesterday, HH income $25–50K*	Percentage of time spent yesterday, HH income $100K+*	Estimated percentage of total advertising expenditures, 2008**
Television	57	40	31.7
Newspapers	5	6	18.1
Radio	23	24	8.8
Magazines	3	4	10.0
Internet	12	26	8.4

Exhibit 23.1 (cont'd) Media time spent (in hours) by education and advertising expenditures

Medium	Percentage of time spent yesterday, education (high-school grad)*	Percentage of time spent yesterday, education (college grad+)*	Estimated percentage of total advertising expenditures, 2008**
Television	56	45	31.7
Newspapers	4	7	18.1
Radio	26	22	8.8
Magazines	3	4	10.0
Internet	11	22	8.4

Sources: * TVB, Nielsen Media Research Custom Survey 2006. http://www.mediainfocenter.org/television/competitive/time_reach.asp. Accessed March, 2008.
** Jack Myers Media Spending Forecasts. http://www.jackmyers.com/commentary/media-spending-forecasts/9805012.html. Accessed March, 2008.

receive a substantially higher percent of total dollars than time people spend reading them (18.1 percent versus 6 percent). This disparity indicates that newspapers are vulnerable to competitive media attacks, using the reasonable argument that media dollars should be allocated according to how much time people spend with each medium.

Some media, such as television, are considered to have more impact than other media. However, given that television has greater impact and reach, and is more memorable, if you are an advertiser that appeals to consumers in higher income and education demographics, you have to ask if you should be shifting some of your ad dollars online, as evidenced in Exhibit 23.1.

On the other hand, radio gets 24 percent of adults' time but only 8.8 percent of ad dollars, according to Exhibit 23.1. Therefore, radio, using time-spent dollar allocation logic, should get a considerably higher share of advertisers' dollars. The same rationale holds true for the Internet, with only 8.4 percent of dollars and 16 percent of time spent with adults, 26 percent in higher-income households, and 22 percent in higher-education households.

Newspapers

If you sell for a medium other than newspapers, be careful not to criticize newspapers too much, especially to local retailers, who for years have been relying on newspaper advertising for their survival and growth. However, newspaper circulation is in decline and many retailers are switching – to some degree on another –

Exhibit 23.2 Newspapers

Advantages	Disadvantages
Credibility: One of the oldest, most highly regarded media. Loyal readers, high degree of credibility, familiarity, and acceptance.	*Decreasing circulation:* In most cities circulation reaches less than 50 percent of all households. Newspaper circulation nationally has been declining steadily for decades.
Visuals: The combination of text, graphics, and pictures can show products and create a visual appeal that reinforces a message.	*Increased CPMs:* As circulation has declined, newspaper rates continue to increase, thus increasing CPMs, which are among the highest in the media.
Mass audience: Newspapers reach a large audience in a market with one exposure.	*Passive:* Newspapers provide information once a consumer is in the market for a product, but they do not build awareness, aid in branding, or create product demand. Used mainly for price comparisons.
Ad variety: Newspapers offer a variety of ad sizes that allows advertisers to match budgets to ad sizes.	*Clutter:* A typical daily newspaper is over 60 percent ads, not counting free-standing inserts. Ads often appear next to or on top of competitive ads, encouraging price comparisons. Little or no product separation.
Upscale audience: Newspapers generally reach an older, upscale audience, including homeowners.	*Page browsers:* Most people do not read all sections of a paper every day, only those they are interested in. Even the most read sections are seen by only one-half of the people who buy a newspaper.
Long copy: Newspaper ads have the ability to communicate lengthy, complex or detailed information and descriptions.	
Couponing: By use of coupons, advertisers can track responses.	*Low ad readership:* Even if people read a newspaper section, on the average only 42 percent of readers will recall noting a full-page ad.
Random access: Readers can access an ad when they want to, at their convenience, and pour over it. Readers control the amount of ad exposure.	*Older readers:* People in younger demographics rarely read newspapers, especially 18–24.
	Increased competition: Interactive is attacking one of newspapers' stronger ad categories, classifieds, especially recruitment advertising. eBay is now the country's largest used-car dealership.
Portability: Newspapers can be read anywhere, on a train, on the beach, in any room in a house.	*Low targetability:* Difficult to reach many high-potential target segments efficiently.
Shelf life: Newspapers can hang around for days or weeks and be accessed again and again.	*Poor production:* Even with the addition of new and improved newspaper color printing technology, it is difficult to make some products, such as food and new cars, appealing in newspaper advertising.
Lead time: Advertisers can place orders with a relatively short lead time – not as long a lead time a magazines, outdoor, or television.	*Declining couponing:* Despite increased coupon face values, coupon redemption has been declining for years – too many coupons, too little interest.

Source: www.naa.org/TrendsandNumbers.aspk. March, 2008.

their advertising dollars to other media, especially to the Internet. The best way to go after newspaper money is to sell the ROI benefits and efficiency of your medium, and to use updated figures from Exhibit 23.1, especially, if you sell for television, radio, or the Internet.

Broadcast Television

Both American viewers and advertisers are in love with television, and with good reason. Television moves products and services, it embeds brands in people's minds, and it creates an emotional bond between consumers, advertisers, and ideas. Television garners the biggest share of major national advertising dollars because it works, or at least these major advertisers and their agencies are convinced that it works. Changing their minds is like pushing a huge rock uphill; it is incredibly hard work and it takes a long, long time. The best way to get a piece of a television advertising budget is to go slowly and to try to get a little bit at a time. Cable television struggled for 15 years before it made significant inroads on broadcast television, especially network, budgets. If you are selling against television, you have allies such as radio, newspapers, magazines, and online, and all of them make television their primary target. Use a media-mix approach and show advertisers that, despite television being an excellent reach medium, it is quite expensive to add reach after about 35 percent is achieved because of diminishing marginal response to media weight. See www.charleswarner.us/indexpresentations.html, "Media Mix and the Natural Laws of Advertising by Erwin Ephron."

Radio

Radio continues to slog along unglamorously as an efficient advertising workhorse. Radio is efficient, builds frequency, and is a great medium for consistently reminding people about their favorite brand, retailer, or bank. It is also an excellent hamburger helper – radio can beef up impact, efficiency, and reach when combined with another medium. Radio's greatest advantage is its recency – the last advertising consumers are exposed to when they are ready to make a buy and before they make a purchase. For more information on how radio can work effectively with other media, go to www.rab.com, click on "Get the Facts," and see the "Radio Marketing Guide and Fact Book," also click on the "Competitive Media" tab to compare see how radio works well in combination with other media.

Exhibit 23.3   Broadcast television

Advantages	Disadvantages
Sight, sound, motion, emotion: The most powerful medium. Combines visual appeal with the ability to touch viewers' emotions. Well-executed television commercials can grab and hold attention like no other medium. Excellent for creating awareness, branding, and reminding.	*Declining audience shares:* In television's most watched time period, primetime, ratings and share of viewing have been steadily declining, thus decreasing the medium's reach.
Reach: Television is ubiquitous; 98 percent of American homes have a television set. Television, especially primetime TV and big events such as the Super Bowl and Academy Awards, can reach over half the homes in America with a single program. No medium has the reach of television.	*Increased CPMs:* As ratings have declined, rates have not been lowered correspondingly. Television requires large budgets to make an impact – not for the small businesses or the faint of heart.
Mass audience: Television is the most mass of all the mass media. It reaches virtually everyone.	*Linear access:* Unlike print, viewers cannot go back or forward to view a commercial again, when it is gone, it is gone. Commercials have no shelf-life, unless recorded on a digital video recorder (DVR), such as a TiVo.
Time spent: People spend a great deal of time with television. The average home watches over eight hours a day, on the average.	*Clutter:* Commercial clutter has increased substantially in recent years. Some television commercial and promotional pods contain as many as 17 individual units, thus chasing people to record programs so they can skip commercials.
Young audience: Baby-boomers (45–65 year olds) and 18–34 year olds grew up with television, watch it, and love it. The medium continues to attract young viewers, who are desirable targets for most advertisers.	*High production costs:* The average national television commercial costs over $350,000 to produce. Small advertisers cannot compete.
Competitive separation: Television provides more competitive separation than newspapers, the Yellow Pages, and the Internet.	*Channel surfing:* People watch TV with a remote in their hands and surf when commercials come on. DVRs, such as TiVo, also make it easy to skip commercials.
Intrusive: The most intrusive of all media. Viewers have to make an active effort to avoid commercials.	*Viewing decreases as income increases:* The lightest television viewing households are in the top third of incomes in the US. Heavy viewing is in lower-income households and by older people (65+).

Source: www.tvb.org/nav/build_Frameset.aspx. March, 2008.

Exhibit 23.4   Radio

Advantages	Disadvantages
Personal, the "theater of the mind": Even though radio is only a sound medium, it is a very personal medium. Radio can involve and excite people's imaginations with scenes and stories that would be impossible to put in a television commercial. Radio is second only to television in its ability to emotionally involve people.	*Sound only:* You cannot show or demonstrate a product or its package and label on radio. Although the human voice is personal and warm, many advertisers believe they need a picture of their store, product, or themselves to sell their products.
Frequency and reach: Radio is an inexpensive medium and frequency can be purchased efficiently. Also, radio is even more ubiquitous than television. Because of radio's extensive penetration, it can extend the reach of any other medium.	*Increased clutter:* Though not as cluttered as television, radio has become increasingly more cluttered with not only more commercials in an hour but also with more commercials appearing in a single commercial break, which limits a commercial's impact.
Low production costs, fast closing: Lowest production costs of all media. Some of the most effective commercials cost nothing and are read by on-air personalities. Commercial copy can be added or changed on a same-day basis if need be.	
Efficient: In terms of CPMs, radios are the lowest of any medium except for outdoor. Radio offers both reach and frequency efficiently.	*Linear access:* Unlike in print, listeners cannot go back or forward to hear a commercial again, when it is gone, it is gone. Commercials have no shelf life.
Imagery transfer: Studies show that by airing the audio portion of a well-crafted television commercial, radio can stimulate the mind to recreate the visual image originally placed there by television, which costs a lot less than on a television screen.	*Fragmentation:* In some markets there are more than 60 radio signals competing for listeners' attention and advertisers' money. Even though radio as a medium can deliver reach, in many markets to match the reach of a newspaper or a television station, ten or 20 radio stations have to be purchased, making it difficult to buy.
Competitive separation: Radio provides more separation than newspapers, the Yellow Pages, and the Internet.	
Intrusive: Not as intrusive as television, but more intrusive than print or outdoor.	
Targetability: Similar to magazines in ability to target a wide variety of age, interest, life-style, and gender groups. Especially effective at reaching hard-to-reach teens, minorities, and ethnic groups.	*Declining listening:* For the last several years, total radio listening has declined, especially among younger people as listening to iPods, non-commercial radio, satellite radio, and Internet radio has increased dramatically.
Portable: Radio is everywhere. There is more radio listening in cars than there is at home. You cannot read a newspaper or magazine, or watch cable or broadcast television, or surf the Internet while driving a car, but you can listen to radio and look at billboards – an excellent combination of media.	

Source: www.rab.com/public/MediaFacts/Factbook.cfm. March, 2008.

Cable Television

In 2007 cable television networks had a larger audience in primetime than all of the broadcast television networks combined.[1] Cable offers more targeted programming to a more affluent audience than broadcast television, as detailed in Exhibit 23.5.

Exhibit 23.5 Cable television

Advantages	Disadvantages
Sight, sound, motion, emotion: The same qualities as broadcast television, the most powerful medium. Combines visual appeal with the ability to touch viewers' emotions. Well-executed television commercials can grab and hold attention like no other medium. Excellent for creating awareness, branding, and reminding.	*Small audiences:* Because cable gives viewers so many choices of channels, cable audiences are fragmented and smaller than those on broadcast television networks.
Continued growth: Cable now reaches 87 percent of US television households and continues to take audience from broadcast television.	*Inaccurate local numbers:* As many as 15 percent of homes get television programming from satellite TV or other delivery systems and so local cable ratings are not as stable as cable network ratings.
Inexpensive: Compared to broadcast television, cable CPMs are low.	
Targetability: Cable can subdivide its audience into more easily targeted segments than broadcast television. Most homes have a choice of over 200 channels, and that number is growing. Cable is the choice medium: Sports, music, news, food, travel, and more.	*Clutter:* Commercial clutter has increased substantially in recent years. Some cable television commercial and promotional pods contain as many as 15 individual units, thus chasing people to record programs so they can skip commercials.
Upscale, suburban: Because cable in a subscription medium, it tends to reach up-scale households in major markets and their suburbs. Cable household generally are better educated and have higher incomes.	*Linear access:* Unlike in print, viewers cannot go back or forward to view a commercial again, when it is gone, it is gone. Commercials have no shelf-life, unless recorded on DVR, such as TiVo.
Competitive separation: Like broadcast television, cable provides more competitive separation than newspapers, the Yellow Pages,	
Intrusive: Television is the most intrusive of all media. Viewers have to make an active effort to avoid commercials.	

Source: *CAB 2008 TV Facts.* 2008. New York: Cabletelevision Advertising Bureau.

Magazines

Magazines are a highly targeted medium, with magazines devoted to almost any human endeavor you can think of. However, with increased time spent on the Internet and other media, time spent with magazines has declined in recent years, and of the major measured media has the lowest time spent (see Exhibit 23.1.). For national media such as broadcast television, cable, and radio networks and, especially, Interactive, magazines currently are a vulnerable target.

Exhibit 23.6 Magazines

Advantages	Disadvantages
Wide readership: According to the 2008 MRI study, 84 percent of adults say they read one or more magazines.	*Competition:* There are nearly 18,000 magazines, which creates too many choices for consumers. Many magazines do not survive their first year of publication. Established magazines are expensive for this reason.
Targetability: There is a magazine for every conceivable interest. Advertisers can target by product affinity, lifestyle, interest, hobby, or demographically.	
Portability: Magazines are even more portable than newspapers because they are smaller. Magazines can be read anywhere except, hopefully, the car.	*Time:* The average person spends only 3 percent of media time weekly with magazines.
Content relevance: Advertising can be placed near relevant editorial material to heighten the interest and readership.	*Expensive:* Magazines are the most expensive of the major media on a CPM basis. And even though magazines can be purchased on a regional or spot (market-by-market) basis, to do so is extremely expensive.
Regionalizing: Magazines can be purchased on a regional, city, or even ZIP code basis.	
Advertorial: An in-depth advertising message can be created to appear more like editorial copy than an ad and can present complex information.	*Inflexible:* Because lead times of six weeks or more are common, ads must be prepared long before publication dates, which limits flexibility to adapt to market conditions.
Production: Most magazines are printed on glossy stock that can reproduce four-color advertising beautifully. There are many exciting and arresting creative opportunities in magazines.	

Source: www.magazine.org/content/Files/magHandook07_08.pdf. March, 2008.

The Internet

Interactive will have the highest percentage growth over the next decade of any medium, as its share of advertising dollars continues to grow and its share of time spent grows compared to other media.

Exhibit 23.7 The Internet

Advantages	Disadvantages
Direct response: On the Internet advertisers can reach highly educated, affluent, and younger consumers who can purchase with a mouse click.	*Low awareness:* Internet users pay less and less attention to banners every year as they become wallpaper to frequent users.
Interactivity: Interactive allows customers to communicate directly with advertisers and tell them what they like and do not like, and what they will buy.	*Inexperience:* Many advertisers and agencies have yet to learn the intricacies of the Internet – how to use it, how to buy it, and how to design effective creative.
Information: Advertisers can provide information to consumers before they buy a product. Over 70 percent of the people who buy a new or used car, research it on the Internet.	
Immediate: Consumers do not have to wait for a brochure to be sent to get information. Advertisers can change offers and prices in real time in response to competitive pressure.	*Spam and pop-ups:* Spam has severely hurt the effectiveness of e-mail advertising. Software can block annoying pop-ups, which makes them ineffective with users who have the software – mostly younger, Internet-savvy ones.
Tracking: Interactive technology allows advertisers to measure exactly how many people saw which ad and how they responded or whether they made a purchase. Consumers' online behavior can be tracked and ads served accordingly.	
Optimization: Internet ad serving technology can serve demographically, geographically, and life-style targeted ads to specific consumers.	*Hard to buy:* Difficult for many advertisers to understand. Hard for agencies to make a profit buying Internet advertising. Some online companies, are difficult to do business with.
Branding: New research indicates that the Internet is not only an excellent direct-response medium but is also good for branding. New interactive, rich-media and video ad technologies make branding more effective than ever before.	

Exhibit 23.7 The Internet (cont'd)

Advantages	Disadvantages
Efficient: Online CPMs are generally lower than other media, except out-of-home. And cost-per-click search advertising is extremely efficient.	
Added reach: Advertising dollars invested online can add reach to any other media investment. Along with radio, the ideal media-mix component.	
Search advertising: Small advertisers can purchase keywords on Google on a cost-per-click basis by using Google's AdWords automated auction system. Google search advertising is a low-cost, performance-based ad model affordable for even the smallest advertiser, and search advertising is highly relevant to most users.	

Source: www.iab.com/ resources_admin_downloads_IAB_comScoreExecPreso.ppt. March, 2008.

Outdoor

Billboards reach everyone who can read – they are highly visible and virtually inescapable, and new technologies are making outdoor advertising more noticeable and exciting. Never a high-growth medium, out-of-home advertising will continue to be an important medium, especially on the highways and for tobacco and liquor advertisers.

Yellow Pages

In the third edition of *Media Selling* the Yellow Pages were included as a major advertising medium; there was even a separate chapter for Yellow Pages. Since then, Yellow Pages advertising has migrated to the Internet, to a large degree, to such Web sites as www.craigslist.com, www.google.com, www.yellowpages.com, and www.yellow.com. Therefore, the Yellow Pages are not included in this fourth edition of *Media Selling*.

Exhibit 23.8 Outdoor

Advantages	Disadvantages
Brevity: Outdoor is effective for conveying brief messages and simple concepts.	*Brevity:* Message capacity is limited to five or seven words at most – cannot deliver more than a simple message and cannot show benefits or advantages.
Low cost: Out-of-home's CPMs are significantly lower than any other medium by a factor of 10 or more.	
	Low recall: Commuters are behind the wheel and other potential customers are exposed very briefly, and such conditions as rain and fog can limit readability and recall.
Directional: Billboards can be used to point directions to businesses.	
Geographically targeted: Billboards can be placed in high-traffic areas and transit ads in places where people commute. Also, an inexpensive way to reach minorities or ethnic groups that might be grouped in certain locations.	*Lack of effective measuring tools:* Unlike other media, out-of-home has no reliable method to measure its audience or effectiveness. CPMs are based on street or highway traffic, not on exposure.
Bonus showings: Billboard operators do not pull down a board when a contract is up or until the board is sold to another advertiser, so sometimes a free showing can last for months.	*Inflexible:* Ads must be ordered 28 days before they go up, and once up cannot be changed, in most cases.
	Ugly image: Because of growing environmental concerns, many communities have limited the volume of out-of-home advertising.

Source: www.oaaa.org/outdoor/research/. March, 2008.

Test Yourself

1 What are six advantages of newspapers?
2 What are four advantages of broadcast television?
3 What are five advantages of radio?
4 What are four advantages of cable television?
5 What are four advantages of magazines?
6 What are five advantages of Internet advertising?
7 What are five disadvantages of outdoor?

Project

Assume you are selling advertising for a local Web site in your market. Write a presentation to a local advertiser who invests all of its advertising dollars in the local newspaper and recommend a switch of some percentage of that budget onto your Web site. Use the data in Exhibit 23.1 and in the media-mix presentation on www.charleswarner.us/indexpresentations.html in the presentation "Media Mix and the Natural Laws of Advertising by Erwin Ephron" to craft your recommendations.

Resources

www.onetvworld.com (The Cabletelevision Bureau of Advertising's Web site)

www.charleswarner.us (the author's Web site where presentations referred to in this chapter are located)

www.ephrononmedia.com (media buying and planning expert Erwin Ephron's Web site)

www.iab.net (The Interactive Advertising Bureau's Web site)

www.magazine.org (The Magazine Publishers Association of America's Web site)

www.oaaa.org (The Outdoor Advertising Association of America's Web site)

www.rab.com (The Radio Advertising Bureau's Web site)

www.tvb.org (The Television Bureau of Advertising's Web site)

Note

1   *CAB 2008 TV Facts*. 2008. New York: Cabletelevision Advertising Bureau.

Part IV

Opportunities, Preparation, and Persistence

24

Opportunities, Organization, and Time Management

Charles Warner

Opportunities

The fifth element in the AESKOPP system of selling is Opportunities. If you have the proper attitude, the emotional intelligence (EI), the right skills, and sufficient knowledge to make a sale in your chosen medium, you will *not* get an order unless you create opportunities to use your attitude, EI, skills, and knowledge.

You create opportunities by using the Money Engine system you learned in Chapter 9 and, especially, the prospecting element within that system. Now might be a good time to review the Money Engine system as a way to reinforce the vital importance of prospecting and developing new business in pursuing a successful career in media selling.

Preparation and Persistence

There is an old joke that you have heard 1,000 times, but it bears repeating in this chapter about preparation and persistence. A young person stops a passerby on Fifth Avenue in New York and asks, "How do I get to Carnegie Hall?" The stranger answers emphatically, "practice, practice, practice." Notice the passerby did not say "practice" once, but three times, which emphasizes the need not only to practice in order to become highly skilled, but also to be persistent. Preparation and persistence, the last two elements in the AESKOPP system, go together hand-in-glove.

The twist in the above joke is that the passerby thought Carnegie Hall was a goal rather than a destination. However, to either achieve a goal or arrive at a destination, you need directions. You need a plan for your journey toward your goal of being a successful media salesperson, perhaps even being a world-class champion salesperson.

Tiger Woods set a goal when he was a young boy of being the greatest golfer who ever lived, and he eventually achieved that goal. How? Practice, practice, practice. Tiger's practice routines are legendary. He will practice a six-foot putt 100 times; not just the putt, but 100 times without missing. In a *Time* magazine article, Dan Goodgame wrote:

> He has become, over time, eerily calm under pressure and an obsessive student of the game who reviews videotapes of old tournaments for clues about how to play each hole. He works hard at building his strengths and honing his shots. But what is most remarkable about Woods is his restless drive for what the Japanese call *kaizen*, or continuous improvement. Toyota engineers will push a perfectly good assembly line until it breaks down. Then they'll find and fix the flaw and push the system again. That's *kaizen*. That's Tiger. It's also Tiger's buddy, Michael Jordan, who worked as hard on defense as offense and in his later years added a deadly fall-away jumper to his arsenal. No matter how good they say you are, Michael tells Tiger, "always keep working on your game."[1]

Later in the same article, Dan Goodgame writes about how Tiger Woods decided to rebuild his swing after he won the Master's tournament in 1997. His coach, Butch Harmon, told Tiger that it would not come quickly, but, as Goodgame writes, "Woods didn't hesitate. He and Harmon went to work in a *kaizen* sequence of 1) pounding of hundreds of practice balls, 2) reviewing tapes of the swing, and 3) repeating both the above."[2]

The above *kaizen* sequence emphasizes the importance of creating a Spiral of Disciplined Preparations that you can repeat over and over again – with persistence – to achieve more and more success, as shown in Exhibit 24.1.

Note in Exhibit 24.1 that, as you go along the path, beginning at the center, and implement the elements of Plan, Organize, Perform, Measure, Evaluate, and Adjust that lead to Set Objectives, each Set Objectives element is larger – you are raising your performance bar each time in a continual spiral of improvement.

Because of all you must try to get done in each of the six steps of selling, as a media salesperson, you have to keep a lot of balls in the air. To help you manage this juggling act and keep everything straight, you need well-organized systems for each of the elements in the Spiral. You will learn in the remainder of this chapter a number of systems and rules that will help you.

Exhibit 24.1 The Spiral of Disciplined Preparation.

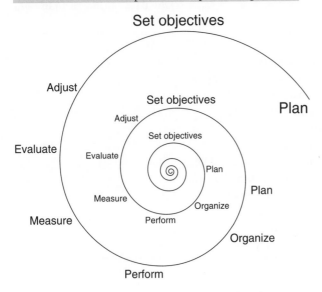

Preparation

Set objectives

Remember that goals have a longer time horizon than objectives: goals are set for longer than a year in the future, objectives for a year or less. The first objective you must set is how much you want to earn in the coming year. Then, work backwards to see how much revenue you must generate to achieve your income objective. In most radio and television stations, salespeople are paid based on some sort of commission system, so there is a direct relationship between their income and how much revenue they generate. In most television and cable network, magazine, newspaper, and online sales organizations, salespeople are paid on the basis of a salary plus an incentive for reaching an individual or an organizational revenue goal. But whatever the makeup of your compensation system, you must estimate the revenue you need to generate in order to achieve your desired income level. To arrive at that income, you must set objectives for activities in each of the six steps of selling. When you have set your objectives, you must then develop plans to achieve them.

Plan

Yearly plan Begin each year with a yearly plan, as shown in Exhibit 24.2, which is a yearly sales plan for a radio station salesperson, as are all the examples in this chapter because there are 50 percent more radio salespeople in the country and,

Exhibit 24.2 Planners

Yearly planner

Priority	Yearly objectives Year: 2008	Due date	Date of follow-up
A	Increase billing by 15% to $2,543,000	12/31	
A	Select 7 new target accounts	1/15	
A	Spend more time on A and B accounts	12/31	
A	Increase average order size by 25%	6/31	
B	Improve closing skills – up to 33%	6/31	
B	Improve prospecting skills – contact/ appointment ratio up to 70%	4/1	
B	Get Torres Cadillac on 52-week schedule	3/15	
B	Get 20% more money from Davis Toyota	2/15	
B	Get 25% more money from Coca-Cola	5/1	
C	Improve research knowledge	3/1	
C	Write a retail presentation	2/1	
C	Practice presentation delivery skills	5/15	

Monthly planner

Priority	Monthly objectives Month: March	Due date	Date of follow-up
A	Write J. C. Penny presentation	3/9	
A	Set up J.C. Penny breakfast meeting	3/2	
A	Work out with PD details of Coca-Cola promotion	3/5	
A	Write Coca-Cola presentation	3/9	
B	Take Torres to basketball game	3/16	
B	Make baseball presentation to Davis Toyota	3/23	
B	Collect from Sub Shop, Jones Motors	3/28	
B	Follow up on Men's Shop promotion	3/30	

Weekly planner

Week: 3/3–7

MONDAY	TUESDAY	WEDNESDAY	THURSDAY	FRIDAY
9:30 – Quincy's – pitch baseball	8:30 – Sales meeting	8:30 – Finalize and rehearse Coca-Cola presentation	7:30 – Breakfast – Coca Cola marketing group – pitch renewal	9:00 – In office – prospecting on the phone
10:30 – Torres Cadillac – presentation – renewal	10:00 – BBB Agency – presentation	10:30 – Martin Motors – service	10:30 – Torres Cadillac – presentation	10:00 – Prospecting
11:45 – Sub Shop – collection	11:45 – Engine Re-builders – qualify	11:00 – Cutler Cutlery – discovery	11:45 – Sub Shop – collection	11:00 – Prospecting

Exhibit 24.2   Planners (cont'd)

Week: 3/3–7

MONDAY	TUESDAY	WEDNESDAY	THURSDAY	FRIDAY
Lunch: Davis – baseball sponsorship	**Lunch:** John Doe – promotion idea	**Lunch:** CCC Agency – pitch baseball	**Lunch:** Mary Martin – get Kolb's buy parameters	**Lunch:** Open
2:15 – Smith Honda – pitch news	2:00 – Black Ford – new schedule	2:15 – Doobie Bros. – spec spot	2:30 – Henry's Harley"s – renewal	2:15 – Open
3:00 – The Mall – service-results of weekend sale.	3:00 – Bower Jewelers – service	3:00 – The Mall – renewal	3:30 – Newbie's – discovery	3:00 – Rill's Restaurant – pitch weekend package
4:00 – Morton's – spec spot	4:00 – Able Agency – spec spot	4:00 – Open	4:15 – PermaPress – pitch copy idea	4:00 – On phone – make appointments for next week
5:00 – Jones Agency – pitch movie schedule	5:00 – Harry the Hat – pitch baseball	5:15 – Fletcher Furniture – pitch special weekend package	5:00 – Jones Agency – close on movie schedule	5:00 – On phone – make appointments for next week
	7:00 – Dinner BBB Agency – pitch baseball		7:30 – Dinner Widmer Brothers – pitch special weekend package	6:00 – Office – paperwork and week's wrap-up.

Daily planner

Priority	**To Do** Monday, March 3	**Deadline**
2	Make McDonald's appointment for 4:00 Wed.	12:00
1	9:30 Quincy's baseball pitch	9:30
2	Work out with PD details of Coca-Cola promotion	5:00
1	10:30 Torres Cadillac – renewal pitch	10:30
1	12:30 Lunch: Les Escargot – Davis – baseball	12:30
1	2:15 Smith Honda – news pitch	2:15
1	3:00 The Mall – check results	3:00
1	4:00 Morton's – spec spot	4:00
1	Jones Agency – pitch movie schedule	5:00
3	Write Barney's IO	6:00
3	Check on Doobie Bros. spec spot for Wed.	6:00
3	Write Mall renewal pitch	7:00

thus they are applicable to more sales jobs. However, all of the examples are applicable to all media selling situations and can easily be adapted for any medium.

Note in the Yearly Planner in Exhibit 24.2 that the yearly objectives are prioritized A, B, and C. There are no D priorities; if a priority is not an A, B, or C, you should not bother with it.

Monthly plan   Begin each month by filling out a Monthly Planner, as shown in Exhibit 24.2. Set your monthly objectives so that: (1) You keep on track to accomplish your yearly goals and their due dates and (2) you keep your Money Engine heated up. As you remember, the Money Engine has four sections: Prospects, Pending Accounts, Active Accounts, and Renewals (see Exhibit 9.1 on page 150). The example that was used in Chapter 9 for keeping the Money Engine fueled was out of 100 accounts on your list, 80 should have reasonable potential, 40 should be bona fide prospects, 20 should be pending, 10 should be active accounts if you consistently have a 50 percent closing ratio, and you should be working on renewals for all ten active accounts if all ten are legitimately renewable.

You must look at your account list, decide which type of account in the Money Engine needs attention, enter the activities into your Monthly Planner, and then prioritize them.

Weekly plan   The most important element in your planning system is your weekly plan (see the Weekly Planner in Exhibit 24.2). Weekly Planners are much more effective than call reports because they focus on the future rather than report on past activity. Call reports are typically exercises in writing fiction used as policing systems by management, which does not sit well with or motivate salespeople (they get the message that management does not trust them). Planners, on the other hand, focus on planning. During the week, you must continually work to set up appointments for the next week, or weeks, so by the end of the week, your Weekly Planner for the next week is 90 percent full. This system forces you to be organized and to be conscious of how many calls and what type of calls you will be making.

On Friday evening or over the weekend, go through the following steps in filling out your Weekly Planner for the upcoming week:

1   Examine your previous week's Weekly Planner to see if there is any unfinished business to be carried forward.
2   Fill in information about any additional calls you made during the previous week.
3   Fill out the Key Account Call Tracker (see Exhibit 24.3) based on the calls you made the previous week.
4   Look over your appointment calendar and schedule all of your appointments for the coming week in your Weekly Planner. Always include the purpose of

Account	3/1	3/8	3/15	3/22	3/39	Month	4/5	4/12	4/19	4/26	Month	5/3	5/10	5/17	5/24	5/31	Month	Qtr
Abbey	R*		S		I	3												
Bud	S	S		I	U	3												
Cartier	U	S		U	I	4												
Denny's	I			I	U	3												
Eckert	IP		I			2												
Ford	N		NG		S	3												
GM	NG		S			2												
Hoyt	R			I		2												
IHOP	R					1												
Jack's	S		I		R	3												
K&K	S			N	NG	3												
Liberty	S		U			2												
Mazda	U			NG		2												
Nissan	I		R		S	3												
Orrey	N					1												
PepBoys	NG		U			2												
Quill	S		U		S	3												
Royal	NG			U		2												
Sam's	S			NG		2												
Turbo	R		S	S	S	4												

* Call type: I = Idea, IP = Identify problems (every six months), N = New schedule, NG = Negotiation, PE = Presenting, R = Renewal, S = Service, U = Up-sell.

Monthly analysis
1 Too many calls on Turbo and Cartier, not enough on Orrey and IHOP.
2 Too many service, not enough idea calls.

the call or type of call in the Weekly Planner. Never make or schedule calls that do not move a sale forward or have a specific servicing purpose.

5 Look over your Monthly Planner and see what type of accounts need attention and what activities need to be undertaken and put both on your To-Do list (To-Do lists will be covered later in the chapter).

6 Examine your To-Do list and enter items that need to be accomplished during the upcoming week on the appropriate day on your Weekly Planner.

7 Give a copy of your Weekly Planner to your sales manager or ad director, and keep a copy for yourself.

8 Keep all of your Weekly Planners in a folder and evaluate them at the end of the month.

In the Weekly Planner in Exhibit 24.2, notice that the 32 calls that have been scheduled (including lunch and dinner) are of different types: pitching copy ideas and spec spots, pitching baseball sponsorships and a special weekend package, pitching for renewals, collecting, discovery, and qualifying. Notice there are open slots so the unscheduled times can be filled in when new opportunities occur during the week. The week is not over-scheduled – a good practice to follow. Also, note that a whole morning has been set aside for making prospecting calls and part of Friday afternoon has been left unscheduled so that calls can be made and e-mails sent to set up appointments for the following week.

Daily plan As you make appointments during the week for upcoming weeks, enter them into your appointment calendar system. Most media salespeople use PDAs or cell phones, such as a BlackBerry, or an appointment booklet. But whatever system you prefer, have only one system and use it not only to guide you each day but also as the basis for filling out your Weekly Planners and Daily Planners. See the Daily Planner in Exhibit 24.2. Follow these steps when you fill out a Daily Planner each morning before 9:00 a.m. After 9:00 a.m., you should be doing scheduled tasks or on the street making scheduled calls:

1 Look at your weekly planner and enter all appointments for the day in your Daily Planner.

2 Look at your appointment calendar and enter any new appointments you have made that are not in your Weekly Planner.

3 Look at your To-Do list and transfer items that need to be completed that day to your Daily Planner.

4 Fill out any Business Opportunity Reports and Disposition Reports you need to because of the calls you made or information you received the previous day (see Exhibit 24.4). Update your Business Pending Tracker (see Exhibit 24.5) with information from the Business Opportunity Reports. It is important to do these three tasks daily, because if you let them slide, you will never catch

| **Exhibit 24.4** Business opportunity report |

BUSINESS OPPORTUNITY REPORT

Account: XYZ Toyota
Product: Autos
Agency: K&K
Buyer: Mary Smith
Salesperson: Charles Warner

Date of request: 9/23
Rating service: Arbitron

Primary target audience: A 25–54   Secondary target audience: W 25–49
Schedule starts: 10/28   Schedule ends: 12/1
Evaluation basis (Metro, DMA, TSA): Metro
Number of weeks: 5   Weekly reach goal: 30
Weekly market budget: $5,600   Weekly frequency goal: 4
Market CPP target: $95   Dayparts: AM, PM, WE
Target number of spots per station: 15   Target number of stations: 5

Other: (Merchandising, promotions, co-op, affidavits, contests): Request merchandising, will buy without it.

DISPOSITION

Won: ☺ Lost:

Order ($/spots/dayparts): $1,500; 15 spots, AM, PM, WE

CPP: $100   Share of budget: 25%   Avg. Rate: $100

Stations ($/spots) CPP, Share of budget:

WBBB – 18%
WCCC – 17%
WDDD – 20%
WEEE – 20%

---

up. Be disciplined and get in the habit of filling out Business Opportunity and Disposition Reports (at the bottom of the Business Opportunity Report) and updating your Business Pending Tracker daily.

5 Do not over-schedule yourself – no more than 12 To-Do items or appointments in a day.

Exhibit 24.5 Business pending tracker

Business Pending Tracker Charles Warner
10/7/2008

Account	Wk$	Demo	Wks	Up Date	AM	Day	PM	WE	NT	10/14	10/22	10/28	11/4	11/11	11/18	11/25	12/2	12/9	12/16	12/23	12/30	1/5	W/L	Reason
							Daypart																Disposition	
Warner Bros	$1.0	A12–34	2	9/30	1	1	1	1	1	1	1												L	Demo
20th Cent Fox	$2.0	M18–34	1	9/30	1	1	1	1	1	1	1												L	Demo
ABC Ford	$10.0	A25–54	8	9/23	1		1	1					1	1	1	1	1	1	1				W	
XYZ Toyota	$28.0	A25–54	5	9/23	1		1	1				1	1	1	1	1							W	
Courtsy Chev	$12.0	A25–49	6	9/16	1		1	1	1			1	1	1	1	1							W	
Dixie Lexus	$6.0	M25+	4	9/23	1	1	1	1				1	1	1	1	1							W	
Big Wheel Tires	$4.0	A25–54	3	9/30	1		1		1		1	1	1										W	
Joe Cadillac	$5.0	A25+	9	9/16	1		1	1				1	1	1	1	1	1	1	1	1			W	
Mary Mattress	$2.0	W25–49	4	9/30	1	1	1	1	1			1	1	1	1								W	
Belk's	$5.0	W25–54	1	9/30	1	1	1	1	1														W	
Total $ '03 = 390 * Total $ '02 = 305 *					10	5	9	8	5	1	4	5	7	6	6	5	2	2	2	2	0	0		Won '03 = 8, Lost = 2 (80%W)
Total # '03 = 10 Total # '02 = 7																								Won '02 = 5, Lost = 2 (71%W)

Av. # Wks '03 = 4.3 Av. # Wks '02 = 6.4

* Weekly $ × No. Wks.

When you schedule your Daily Planner be tough on yourself. Do the hardest things first if you can. If you have several top-priority calls to make during the day, begin with the most difficult ones and save the easiest ones for later in the day if you can. If you do the task that is most fun last and reward yourself, you will have something pleasant to look forward to.

Organize

Organize your accounts   You have two types of accounts on your account list: *assigned* and *unassigned*. Assigned accounts and agencies are those given to you by your management and those for which you are responsible; unassigned accounts are those you develop yourself through prospecting. Both types of accounts should be classified as A, B, or C accounts. Accounts classified as A are *key accounts*, or those 20 percent of your active accounts that generate 80 percent of your billing. Accounts classified as B are *target accounts*, or accounts that you have not yet sold but that have the potential of being key accounts. Accounts classified as C are medium-sized accounts that are currently active or have reasonable potential. You must have a system for organizing the information on your accounts in order to prospect, sell, and service them. Systems can vary from simple index cards to complex computerized systems, but whatever system you use, it must be an easily accessible database that contains the information as seen in the Account File in Exhibit 24.6.

Organize your desk   It is vital to keep your internal materials well ordered and accessible. When you are in a hurry, and salespeople are often in a hurry, you do not want to have to shuffle through a pile of randomly arranged papers to find the latest rate information or a copy of a sales presentation. You should be able to see the top of your desk every morning when you come to work. Put information in folders that you can reach easily when you are on the phone. I prefer colored folders with a different color for each subject such as: Active Accounts, Weekly Planners, Prospects, Management, and so forth. The Management folder is for notes of things you want to talk to your sales managers about. Do not waste time and interrupt yourself and your management with each individual question that might come up (unless it is urgent). Save items so you can talk to management about several items at one time. Put your phone, if it has a cord, on your left, if you are right-handed, so you can hold the phone with your left hand and write with your right hand and the phone cord is not trailing across the desk as you try to write. Have an 8½ × 11 inch spiral notebook on your desk to keep notes in when you talk on the phone and take it with you to meetings to take notes. Put the following information in separate folders:

Sales promotion material and presentations. These are the tools of your trade. Make sure you keep them up to date and in folders near by so you can get to them

---

Exhibit 24.6   Account file

Account: J. C. Penny	**Agency:** BB & B	**Products:** Various
	Buyer: Jane Doe	
Address: 700 Main St.	**Address:** 333 Oak St.	
Fairfield 20202	Fairfield 20202	
Phone: 322–8000	**Phone:** 433–7654	

Decision maker: Harry Hoyt, Store manager (X – 8001, harry@jcp.com), Mary Sanders, Advertising Manager (X – 8002, mary@jcp)

Needs portrait: Harry – Personal/Business: Achievement, competition, control, impulsiveness, order, risk-taking

    Personal/Non – business: Conservative, nurturance, play, recognition,

    Mary – Personal/Business: Risk avoidance, defensiveness, recognition, control, autonomy, contrariness

    Personal/Non-business: Affiliation, novelty, recognition, deference, play, nurturance

Business needs: Huge newspaper schedule. Use radio as supplement. Demos: Adults 18+, women 25–54. Sale and promotions oriented

Competition: Wal-Mart, Target, Sears. Wal-Mart and Target outspend substantially in TV, Sears outspends substantially in newspapers. None uses much radio.

$Potential: $200,000   **Type:** B (Target account)

Contact date	Contact type	Pending	Order
1/17	PO*		
1/20	IP		
1/30	IP		
2/8	IP		
3/2	PE		
3/9	PE	$150,000	
3/16	NG		$145,000

* PO = Prospecting, IP = Identifying problems, PE = Presenting, NG = Negotiating and closing, S = Servicing.

---

in a hurry when you are preparing a proposal or presentation, rushing out to make a call, talking to someone on the phone, or sending an e-mail.

Rate information and special packages or sections, which must be kept current on a daily basis. Check with your sales manager or ad director regularly to see if new inventory has become available, rates have changed, or new packages, Web pages, or sections have been designed and released.

Inventory records, which also must be continually maintained. Put the latest information in a folder and keep it at your fingertips for quick reference when you are on the phone or e-mailing people. Develop a good relationship with the operations department so you can always find out the latest information on what is available to sell. Your income is dependent on how much you sell, which, of course, depends on what is available to sell.

Active account information, which must also be current. Keep a copy of the current Insertion Order (IO) or contract for each account in a three-ring binder or accessible in an automated, computerized system. When you fill out an IO or contract, put a copy in the binder or enter it into an automated computerized system. Enter new IO or contract information daily.

Organize your briefcase   Carpenters and mechanics have their toolboxes; you have your briefcase. It is as important to you as any worker's toolbox. Your briefcase is not only a necessity but it also has become a symbol of a salesperson, so make sure your symbol reflects the image you want to convey to your customers. Equip yourself with an attractive, functional case. It should contain a laptop computer with a mobile Internet connection so you can send and receive e-mail from anywhere. Keep several copies of current research information, sales promotion material, and success case studies in your briefcase, also, extra batteries for your cell phone, laptop, and other electronic devices.

Organize your laptop   I strongly recommend that you invest in a light, portable laptop, not only to use as an appointment calendar and address book, but also to store important documents that you can review before making calls. While you are waiting in a reception area to see a buyer or a client, it is handy to be able to fire up your laptop and review your Negotiating and Closing Planner, or when you are in a prospect's office to refer to the Discovery Questions.

Organize your laptop so that you can easily find presentations that you show to buyers and customers. I recommend that you keep all of your presentations on your desktop and not in separate files that you have to search for then open. Also, download onto your laptop the documents, presentations, and forms such as "Advertising Strategies in a Slowdown," the Checklist for Presentations, and blanks of the forms in this chapter. All of this material is available on www.mediaselling.us.

Organize your knowledge acquisition   You should keep folders on your computer or three-ring binders on your desk for each competitor in your medium and for each competitive medium. In these folders or binders, you should place the latest rate information (if you can obtain it), sales promotion material, and research information. You can usually pick up this material from clients and agencies if you have managed relationships with them properly. Keep these competitive folders updated. When you are on the telephone with customers who inform you that they are considering buying from one of your competitors, it helps enormously to have an abundance of information about that competitor at your fingertips; it aids you in creating a differential competitive advantage. You should regularly monitor the content of your major competitors and put brief notes into the proper folders about any major shifts in programming, content, advertising strategy, and management. You want to be a market expert in order to gain source credibility with your accounts, so you must keep your information current.

You should also have folders in your computer or binders for the following knowledge areas:

1 Market information such as population, demographics, business conditions, demographic trends, and the like.
2 Customer-helpful information such as relevant material from general business publications like *Business Week, Fortune, Forbes, The Jack Myers Report*, and *Advertising Age*.
3 Publications specific to your key accounts' industries, such as *Automotive News*.
4 Publications specific to your industry such as *Editor and Publisher, Folio, Radio, Inc* or *Television Week*.

You should always have your computer on your desk turned on and connected to the Internet so you can go to a company's Web site when you talk on the phone to a customer. When you are on the phone with an account, you should have its account file on your screen, either in a file generated by an automated software system or in a file you have generated (blank available on www.mediaselling.us).

Organize your community activities   It is not only good citizenship but also good business practice to become involved in community activities. It is helpful to become part of a network of relationships with business executives, community leaders, and consumers. Get involved in organizations such as Rotary Club, League of Women Voters, Kiwanis, Knights of Columbus, Boy Scouts and Girl Scouts, or various church organizations.

Manage your money   The two most important resources you have are *money* and *time*. You must set up systems to organize and manage both. First, keep track of where your money goes. Buy a good record-keeping system for appointments and expenses if your organization does not supply you with such a system. If you do not write down your expenses daily, you will forget most of the details about them and will not be able to get full credit for them. If you are ever audited by the Internal Revenue Service, you will need to produce a *daily expense record* in addition to receipts as proof.

Second, budget your expense money. Then, look over your *weekly expense record* to see if you are on budget. Be stingy with yourself; save your money for important clients and plan your calls geographically to save both time and gas. Even if your company allows you to use some of its trade deals with local restaurants, treat these trade deals as though they were cash, and do not waste lunches on friends or other salespeople. Also, take prospects and customers to lunch and dinner at nice restaurants. It is better to invest your expense money in fewer but more memorable, quality meals (you are creating value at meals and entertainment, too).

Next, always fill out expense reports weekly. If you let them go longer than a week, they will become ever more burdensome and time-consuming. If your organization does not reimburse you for your business and entertainment expenses, you must know exactly how much of your own money you are spending so you can budget for it, spend it in the most effective manner, and get proper deductions for your expenses when you pay your taxes.

If your company reimburses you for all or part of your expenses, keep the same accurate weekly records as you would if it were your own money and submit your expense accounts weekly. The longer you wait to fill out your expense reports and turn them in, the more interest-free money you will be lending to your company. It is best to handle your expenses in cash rather than on credit cards unless you have two credit cards, one for business and one for personal use. If you have just one credit card that charges interest on unpaid balances and you put business expenses on it, you will invariably wind up paying interest on business expenses.

Another tip based on my personal experience: Do not get in the habit of taking cash advances from your company to finance your business expenses. You will regret it. You will more than likely spend the cash not only on business expenses but also on other things, unless you can possibly remember to keep your own money in one pocket and the business's in another pocket; then when you go to bed, you remember to put the money from one pocket on the left-hand side of the dresser . . . forget it. Do not take cash advances for expenses or you will find yourself paying back money to the company for which you cannot account – a painful experience.

Manage your time   The other resource you must control is your *time*. Time is a salesperson's most important resource, even more important than money, because you must have time to make the calls and presentations that result in sales. It is easy for salespeople to find a million excuses to have coffee with acquaintances, to linger longer than is necessary with friendly customers, or to knock off early to get back to the office to do paperwork. After several days of rejections without getting an order, it is a natural tendency to want to hang around the office and not to go out and face prospects and more rejections. Remember: no opportunities, no sales; no objections, no sales; no rejections, no sales. You must organize your days, weeks, and months to take advantage of every minute of the workday. You must manage your time to maximize face-to-face contacts with prospects and customers.

The first rule in time management is:

Rule: Develop the proper attitude about time.

Just as you must learn to control and manage your emotions, attitudes, and money, you must learn to control and manage your time. Restructure your thinking so that you see time as an opportunity to gain a competitive edge. Time is a finite, non-expandable resource of which everyone has exactly the same amount. Every salesperson on your staff and on every sales staff in every medium has a maximum of 24 hours a day, not a millisecond more or less, so no one has an edge in the amount of time available to use. You create your competitive edge by how well you manage the time available to you and to everyone.

Because time is finite and ticks away at the same rate for everyone, when you say to yourself something like, "I didn't make that call on Coca-Cola today because I didn't have enough time," stop and think how illogical you are being. There cannot be "enough" or "too much" time – everyone has the same amount. The problem is not that there is not enough time; the problem is that you did not effectively manage the finite amount of time available to you. Furthermore, once time passes by, it is irreplaceable. It cannot be saved, made up, or overspent; so, you must use what you have wisely.

Rule: Time can only be used or wasted.

The next rule in managing your time is:

Rule: Know how much your time is worth.

Calculate how much your time is worth to you. As we did at the beginning of this chapter, figure out how much you want to earn in a year and then break that amount down into weekly, daily, and hourly amounts. Put a note with the hourly figure (such as "$68 per hour," which is $136,000 yearly) in plain view at your office desk so you can see it daily, particularly when you are on the phone, to serve as a reminder of how much in income it costs you each hour you spend in the office not making calls.

The next rule of managing your time is:

Rule: Know where your time goes.

Peter Drucker wrote that managing time is a three-step process: Recording time, managing time, and consolidating time.[3] In order to know where your time goes, you must record your time by keeping a minute-by-minute log of everything you do for three days every six months. Keep your notebook with you at all times for these three days and write down absolutely everything that you do. It is imperative

Exhibit 24.7   Time log

Time	Activity	Time used	Priority	Improvement
8:00 am	Read paper	20 min.	2	Read at home.
8:20 am	Got coffee	10 min.	3	Bring it with me.
8:30 am	Planned day	15 min.	1	Do night before.
8:45 am	Did paperwork	30 min.	1	Do in the evening.
9:15 am	Drove to call	15 min.	1	Start earlier.
9:30 am	Called on Coca-Cola	45 min.	1	

that the time log be complete and accurate. The reason to keep a time log is that the perceptions we all have about how we spend our time are incredibly inaccurate. Things that we like doing seem to go fast, and things that we dislike doing seem to go slowly, so we invariably misjudge how much time we spend on each type of task. It is impossible to estimate how much time you spend on each activity in your daily routine, so you must write it down. If you are going to manage your time effectively, you must first know how you spend it, and the time log is the only useful tool to use for recording activity.

Your time log should have five columns and should look like the example in Exhibit 24.7.

When you have finished your time log, analyze it to see if you are doing the right things. Fill in the Improvement column on your time log after you have asked yourself the following questions:

1 Am I doing the right things at the right time? Did I do things I did not need to do? Could they have been done outside the office?
2 What could be done better, faster, simpler, in less detail?
3 What interrupted me? How often, how long, and how important were the interruptions? How long did it take to recover and get back on track?
4 What contacts did I make with others? How important were the people? Were the communications important? How long did they take?

Most time logs reveal that interruptions are the biggest time wasters and that the biggest source of interruptions is ourselves. We interrupt ourselves because we allow our attention to wander, we want to be friendly, we need to socialize, and we tend to place a low value on our own time. Analyze your time log carefully and then use the following tips to help you manage your time more efficiently.

Rule: Consolidate your activities.

Here are more time management rules. The next is the primary time management rule.

Rule: Do one thing until it is finished.

The most important lesson you can learn about time management is to do one task at a time and not to leave it until you are finished. Concentrate and do not interrupt yourself; do not get up and go for coffee or talk to your friend at the next desk. When people interrupt you, tell them you will get back in a few minutes when you are finished with what you are doing. If you are interrupted by someone you cannot put off, make sure you go back to the task you were working on immediately after the interruption. Go back, and back, and back until you finish it.

Rule: Use chunking.

Set aside large chunks of time in which to do your non-selling tasks, preparations, and follow-ups. Part of the trick to sticking to a task until it is finished is to plan your time efficiently. It is very inefficient to stop and start tasks. It takes you a few minutes to get mentally prepared, organized, and into the task you are doing; for example, you line up your pens, arrange the stapler, rearrange your desk top, find paper clips, turn on your computer, think about how to start, think about how to begin, and think about how to commence. If you are interrupted, you have to begin the mental process all over again, and that wastes time. A job that takes 15 minutes to do working straight through without interruptions will take half an hour if you are interrupted for only one minute, three or four times while you are working. Thus, it is vital that you plan your time so that when you have tasks that take large blocks of time (15 minutes or more) you set aside chunks of time to do these tasks during parts of the day when you are least likely to be disturbed.

For instance, if you have to complete the paperwork on several orders, estimate how long this task will take you (say, half an hour) and set time apart in tomorrow's schedule for half an hour of uninterrupted time. Before or after normal office hours is best for paperwork. You should be calling on customers between 9:00 a.m. and 5:30 p.m. Most salespeople find they can maximize their selling time by doing their paperwork and generating presentations at home at night or in the morning before they get into the office and by planning for large chunks of continuous time in which to do their work.

Rule: Write everything down.

Write down the important details of every conversation you have at your desk in your spiral notebook (I prefer spiral notebooks because I can keep them on file and refer back to them). Never trust your memory for anything, and write down everything you have to do. At the end of the day (at home is best), you can look over your notes and transfer information to your To-Do list. You can transfer the notes on accounts onto your To-Do list, into your Account Files, or into a folder if the notes are extensive and important for future reference. Taking good notes is a major timesaving device because you know where to find information and you will not have to rack your brain to remember things.

Rule: Plan every hour of your workday.

In no area of selling is self-discipline more important than in planning your time. You must plan every hour of your working day, every week, every month, and every year. Time management experts estimate that every hour you spend in planning saves you three or four hours in execution. By failing to plan, you plan to fail. Do your daily plan for the next day the evening before or in the early morning of that day. Indecision and procrastination are huge time wasters. The best way to overcome a natural tendency to be indecisive about what to do, and to avoid procrastinating about doing it, is to plan carefully every hour of your day and then to work this plan unrelentingly.

Rule: Set priorities for everything and do first things first and second things not at all.

When you make a plan, put a priority on everything according to its importance. As Peter Drucker said in his book *The Effective Executive*, "Do first things first and second things not at all."[4] Set priorities on the basis of the 20/80 principle. In time management, this means that 20 percent of your activity will produce 80 percent of your results. Set priorities to concentrate on your key and target accounts.

Rule: Set a deadline on everything.

When you fill out your Daily, Weekly, and Monthly Planners, you must put a deadline on every task (you probably remember the importance of deadlined goals from Chapter 5). Unless you have a deadline, your tasks are unmeasurable intentions instead of measurable objectives. The classic example of an indefinite, unmeasurable, and useless objective is the use of the phrase "as soon as possible." "As soon as possible" may mean the next hour, the next day, or the next week depending on who defines what is possible and whose priorities are being used. Plans and To-Do lists are virtually worthless unless they contain specific deadlines for each activity.

Rule: Do not attempt to do too much.

We all tend to be unrealistic about how much we can get done; we tend to be optimistic. You are probably aware of Murphy's first law, "If anything can wrong, it will." Murphy's second law is "Everything takes more time than you think."

Salespeople are especially optimistic by nature and in their overall outlook, which is good for most things. However, this tendency can work against you when you are planning your time. Not only does over-planning mean that you will not get some things done but it also means that you are apt to get discouraged and depressed about how much you are not getting done. Just as you must control your customers' expectations, you must control your own expectations about how much you can get done so you will not feel frustrated and unsuccessful. When you hear people say, "I never have enough time and I'm always behind," it probably means that their expectations for what they can get done are too high. This condition can lead to stress and low self-confidence, which can be disastrous. As in any objective-setting situation, you want to set moderately difficult but achievable task-completion objectives to give yourself a sense of success and confidence when they are achieved.

Rule: Be flexible.

Your task-completion objectives and daily schedules must be flexible. Unforeseen opportunities will always occur, so you must be able to adapt. One way to build in flexibility is to purposefully avoid filling your schedule so that, in a sense, you are planning for interruptions and a little serendipity. If you have established your priorities properly, you will set four or five calls or tasks to be done in a day; therefore, if a top-priority item comes along unexpectedly, you can move some of your second-priority items to the next day.

Rule: Bunch your tasks.

Consolidate, bunch, your tasks so that you schedule a group of similar things together to be done at the same time. For instance, you might set aside 4:45–5:30 p.m. to return phone calls or set aside 7:45–8:30 a.m. on another day to get some reports and paperwork out of the way. You can bunch service calls by making six or seven in-and-out calls in a morning or you can bunch calls by geographic area. Always be on the lookout for efficient ways to bunch your activities and tasks, which is a way to execute the third of Drucker's steps in time management, consolidate time.

Rule: Remember Parkinson's Law.

"Work expands so as to fill the time available for its completion," economics professor C. Northcote Parkinson noted while observing large bureaucratic organizations in which everyone seemed busy but little was getting accomplished.[5] In other words, if there were seven people in a bureaucratic organization and the work that had to be done could be done by one person, the six other people would find ways to keep busy by inventing systems, controls, hierarchies, and paperwork.

Applying this principle to individual time planning reveals that it is temptingly easy for you to keep busy and to fill time. You can find a thousand tasks that have to be done in the office on a rainy day. The colder it is outside, the longer it takes to generate each presentation and the more time in the office it takes to rehearse them. The problem in time management is not filling time or doing things but doing the *right* things. When you make your daily plan and write down things to do, ask yourself, "Does this *have* to get done?" Be ruthless with yourself and eliminate all frivolous time wasters. Ask yourself, "How much money am I making by doing this?" and "Am I moving the sale forward on this upcoming call?" The most important time you have is face-to-face time with your clients and prospects; so, maximize it.

If you use this cost–benefit analysis technique in planning your time, when you come to items such as dropping by to see a friend or taking time off to pick up tickets for next Saturday's football game, you will know what the costs are (because you have figured out what an hour is worth to you) and you will be able to make an informed decision. By the way, workaholics often do not get a lot accomplished; they are dedicated to keeping busy, and so they tend to invent activities to fill time. Plan your time so that you *work smart* and get the right things done. If you manage your time properly, you can normally get your work done in eight or ten hours each day and have plenty of time to be a well-rounded person and devote time to community service and to your family and other interests.

Rule: Focus on activities that get results.

Too many sales planning and reporting systems focus on activity for its own sake, not on activities that get *results*. For example, a reporting system that only keeps track of the quantity of calls a salesperson makes focuses on activity, not results. Your job is creating customers and keeping them, and the outcome of creating customers is getting orders. Thus, you must focus on getting the right orders from the right customers (your key and target accounts that pay their bills).

Effective systems must include all of the selling elements that lead up to results, not just one or two activity elements. Some sales managers or ad directors still insist that salespeople fill out activity-oriented call reports. It is counterproductive to argue or to try to teach them how it should be done by saying, "Charles Warner says in his book, *Media Selling*, that activity-focused call reports are useless." Do not tempt fate or jeopardize your job; keep quiet and fill out the reports neatly and turn them in on time, two critically important factors for those who use call reports (they rarely read them, but they want them to be neat and on time). However, make sure you use your own results-oriented systems that you are learning about in this chapter:

Manage your To-Do lists   To-Do lists that contain a large number of things you intend to accomplish are virtually useless unless they are prioritized and deadlined. For To-Do lists to be useful, they must be part of a time management system that begins with yearly and monthly objectives and they must be updated on a weekly and daily basis accordingly. You may find that your initial To-Do list contains just your objectives and the immediate tasks that are required to achieve those objectives, and at the beginning of the year it may be two pages long on your appointment calendar or To-Do system on your computer. I do not recommend keeping To-Do lists in spiral notebooks because To-Do lists need to be updated at least weekly; this can be done easily in a software system such as Outlook, which saves time from having to hand-write an updated list every week.

Following are rules for To-Do lists.

Rule: Prioritize all To-Do list items.

People usually compile To-Do lists by adding items to the bottom of the list as they occur to them, and, therefore, the items are not ordered according to priority. Priorities should be set on a first-, second-, or third-level basis. If you have anything less important than a three, you should not be doing it. To make matters worse, most people cross off items on the list as they do them, thus making the list hard to read and even more disorganized.

Rule: The longer your daily list is, the worse it is.

When people look at a To-Do list, the longer it is, the more they get discouraged, so they play little unconscious tricks on themselves. To make themselves feel better and more successful, they choose a number of minor list items that they can accomplish in a hurry and for which they can give themselves feedback for achievement. To correct this tendency, you must do a Daily Planner and move only those items from your To-Do list and appointment calendar onto your Daily Planner that are important and that you know you can complete.

How you feel about how much you get done is not based on how hard you work but on how long your daily To-Do list is. If you put 10 items on your Daily Planner and complete 11, you will be happy and feel successful, as though you accomplished a lot. If you put 12 items on your Daily Planner and complete 11 of them, you will be depressed and feel unsuccessful, stressed, and as though you did not accomplish much. It is up to you how successful you feel; you can control it by the length of your daily To-Do list.

Rule: Do the nastiest, hardest things first.

People tend to select from their To-Do list the easiest or the most fun things to do. Picking the smallest, easiest, and most enjoyable tasks may satisfy our personal, short-term needs for achievement, but they are really excuses to procrastinate and put off harder and, often, more important tasks. These types of rationalizations disregard priorities and thus are self-defeating for achieving objectives.

Perform

The next step in the Spiral of Disciplined Preparation is to perform the daily tasks and activities on your Daily Planner. Do not waste time, stay on schedule. In his *Harvard Business Review* article, "The tests of a good salesperson," Saul Gellerman identified three factors that differentiated top-performing salespeople from medio-cre salespeople: Discussion focus, time management, and staying power.[6]

You learned about the importance of discussion focus in Chapter 11. Gellerman says that the top-performing salespeople he observed did several things to manage their time effectively. First, they did not wait more than 20 or 30 minutes for a scheduled appointment with a customer, as many salespeople did, because they realized it was a signal of low regard or low interest, or a negotiating ploy. Being kept waiting also signaled that a seller would willing to be put off in a like manner during future calls. Also, top-performing salespeople knew that they had to get on with their scheduled appointments and spend time with promising customers. By staying power, Gellerman meant that top-performing salespeople stuck to their schedule and slogged on relentlessly, regardless of multiple rejections or weather. These stars "hunted for a quick sandwich and then headed for the next customer. Weaker sellers lingered over lunch, cussed the fates that had ordained that day to be so unrewarding, and eventually reentered the fray with low expectations."

Gellerman's message is clear: When you perform your daily tasks, finish all of your scheduled tasks and do so with relentless discipline.

Measure   You must measure your performance so you can evaluate it, adjust it, improve it, and set higher objectives. Even though your revenue production, or billing, is certainly an important measure of your past performance, it is not the only one that tells you how well you are doing. There are several things other than billing that you should measure:

① *Key account contacts*, which you track with the Key Call Account Tracker Report in Exhibit 24.3. You do not need to track all of your calls because that would take too much time, but you need to focus on your 10 or 20 key accounts that give you 80 percent of your billing. Update this report daily and give a copy of it weekly to your management.

② *Pending business*, which you measure by filling out a Business Opportunity Report (Exhibit 24.4) daily (and giving a copy to management daily) and transferring the information from the Business Opportunity Report into a Business Pending Tracker (Exhibit 24.5). Give a copy of your updated Business Pending Tracker to manage-ment every week. Many media organizations refer to business pending reports as a pipeline. Some sales organizations want pipelines for all pending business, some just for pending business on target accounts, and some just on pending busi-ness over a specified amount, $100,000 for example. Regardless of organizational requirements, you should keep your own pipeline on all pending business. If your company does not have automated computerized programs that compile these pending business, or pipeline, reports for you, you should do them by hand.

③ *Business lost.* Once a month do a summary of your business disposition reports (at the far right of the Business Pending Tracker in Exhibit 24.5). Summarize why you lost any business and to whom. All salespeople hate to fill out business disposition reports and often fail to do so to avoid the pain. However, do not be defensive but be candid in this summary because you want to know the reasons for losses so you and, especially, management can make any necessary adjustments. Business disposition reports are like bad-tasting medicine, bitter to take, but it helps you get better. Exhibit 24.8 shows a monthly Business Disposition Summary (the information for which you get from the Business Pending Tracker).

④ *Business closed.* A business closed report is the most fun of any report; all salespeople love to fill them out and send them to management. Some companies call these reports business-booked reports. Up-date this summary daily and give it to management at the end of the week. These reports also measure your progress toward your two main objectives – your revenue and income objectives. The Business Disposition Summary (Exhibit 24.8) contains a weekly total as well as a monthly business-disposition analysis.

Evaluate

If you want to create more customers one month than you did the previous month, you are going to have to continually improve your performance – *kaizen*. The elements in the Spiral of Disciplined Preparation will help you improve. The next step toward *kaizen* is to evaluate the information (measurements) you have gathered, as Tiger Woods does when he watches video tapes of his golf matches and you do when you debrief after giving a major presentation or going through an important negotiation.

Exhibit 24.9 shows an evaluation schedule that indicates the performance elements you should evaluate and when (daily, weekly, monthly, quarterly, or yearly).

All of the forms and reports listed in Exhibit 24.9 are available as blank forms on www.mediaselling.us.

Adjust

The next step after evaluating all of your performance elements is to adjust, to correct any problems you have discovered – like Tiger Woods or a Major League baseball player, to adjust your swing and make it better. Your adjustment should include a set of improvement objectives, as show in the Improvement Opportunities Chart in Exhibit 24.10.

Exhibit 24.8 Business disposition summary

Salesperson:
Week:

Account	$	W/L	Share	Reason	Stations
Warner Bros		L		A12–24 demo ($1,000)	WBBB WCCC
20th Cent Fox		L		M18–34 ($2,000)	WBBB WCCC
ABC Ford	$2,000	W	20%		
XYZ Toyota	$7,000	W	25%		
Courtesy Chev.	$4,000	W	30%	Merchandising	
Dixie Lexus	$2,000	W	33%		
Big Wheel Tires	$800	W	20%		
Joe Cadillac	$5,000	W	100%	Baseball	
Mary Mattress	$1,000	W	50%	WE package	
Belk's	$1,000	W	20%		
Speedway		L		M 18–34 ($3,000)	WBBB WCCC
Pepsi-Cola		L		A12–34 ($30,000)	WBBB WCCC WDDD WEEE WFFF WGGG

Month: Analysis

Lost young demo business: Warner Bros., Fox, and Speedway.

Lost Pepsi – big piece of business. Bought six other stations that cut rates significantly. Do not pursue business or cut rates because we have lion's share of Coca-Cola business at higher rates.

Won Courtesy Chev. Due to merchandising – only cost 1% for merchandising.

Won Joe Cadillac because of baseball – only buys sports and pays good rates.

Won Mary Mattress becsue of WE package. The package worked well; need more special packages to pick up similar business.

"Is all this necessary?" you may ask. "Do I really have to go through these planning, organizing, measuring, and evaluating steps? Can't I just get out there and sell?" The answer is, no, you do not *have* to. You might be able to improve your performance without filling out all these reports and doing all of the analysis. If you are doing well and writing orders, you may feel you do not need help. On the

Exhibit 24.9   Evaluation schedule

Report	When you complete	When you give to management	When you evaluate
Yearly planner	Beginning of year	Beginning of year	Yearly
Monthly planner	Beginning of month	Beginning of month	Monthly
Weekly planner	End of old week	Beginning of new week	Weekly
Daily planner	Daily		Weekly
Key account call tracker	Daily	End of week	Monthly
Business opportunity report	Daily	Weekly	Monthly
Business pending tracker	Daily	Weekly	Monthly
Business disposition summary	Weekly	Monthly	Monthly
Time log	Every six months		Every six months
Core competencies	Quarterly	Quarterly	Quarterly
Improvement opportunity chart	Quarterly		Quarterly

other hand, even when things are going well, you might not know why you are being successful. It is wise to keep records so that if you have a slump you can compare what you are doing to when you were performing well.

Just as Tiger Woods looks at tapes of every hole he plays, constantly analyzing, evaluating, and making detailed improvement plans, so other champion athletes lift their performance with similar disciplined preparation. Champion salespeople are no different. Remember, sports performance is more dependent on natural talent than is sales performance. Thus, in sports, a talented Major League baseball hitter might be able to raise his performance by 15 percent from .280 to .322, or by 25 percent to a league-leading .350, by improving his techniques. However, a weak .230 hitter may have an impossible time trying to improve his performance 15 percent because of a lack of natural ability.

However, most salespeople can reasonably expect to improve their performance by at least 15 and perhaps 25 percent over the course of a year by using the systems in this chapter. If you can improve your performance by 25 percent each year for three years and are on a commission system, you can potentially double your yearly income.

By administering these systems, you will be more objective about your performance, something few salespeople are, and the systems will help you make a thorough evaluation of your sales activities. Administering these systems takes

Exhibit 24.10 Improvement opportunity chart

Performance measures	This month: September	Opportunities for improvement	Competencies to concentrate on
Average order size:	$3,000	Larger orders – pitch recency theory and continuity.	Preparation: Generating solutions (research).
Average number of orders per week:	6	Make more prospecting contacts to fill up the Prospecting section of the Money Engine to increase my pipeline.	Opportunity: Prospecting
Average length of schedules:	4.3 weeks	Pitch recency and continuity. Talk to sales manager about offering a 6-week discount.	Knowledge: Pricing
Average number of spots per order:	15	Pitch Week End Packages and bundle in more WE and nighttime spots in all proposals.	Preparation: Strategic thinking.
Average rate:	$100	Open higher in negotiations and ask for higher rates on proposals.	Skills: Negotiating and closing.
Average share of budget per order:	25%	See above to get higher rates. Don't lower rates to get a higher share – 25% is fine if rates are higher. Have BATNAs for all proposals.	Skills: Negotiating and closing.
Average number of contacts* per week:	45	Up contacts by 50%. Set aside more time during week.	Skills: Prospecting, getting appointments.
Average number of appointments* per week:	20	See above and below.	See above.
Contacts/ appointments ratio:	44%	Practice phone techniques. Write a new phone script and rehearse it.	See above.
Average number of presentations* per week:	10	If appointments go up, presentations will go up.	Skills: Presenting
Closing ratio (orders/ presentations ratio):	60%	Prepare more thoroughly for negotiations	Skills: Presenting, negotiating

* *Contacts* = prospecting call trying to set up an appointment. *Appointments* = A qualifying, identifying problem, or servicing call, not a call on which you expect to get an order. *Presentations* = A call on which you present something (an idea, a promotion, or a proposal) and on which you could possibly or expect to close a sale. A presentation call could be a negotiation.

about a half-hour each day, an hour at the end of each week, two hours at the end of each month, and three hours at the end of each quarter – less if you keep up with everything on a daily basis – all of which time is well invested considering the potential results. Your performance should improve slowly but steadily, and you could well become a top-billing professional. At least 80 percent of all media salespeople do not perform this type of detailed measurement and evaluation each month, but they are the ones who typically do only 20 percent of the billing. Be one of the few who manage their time well, who analyze their performance regularly, and who are invariably among the 20 percent who bill 80 percent of the revenues and make 80 percent of the money.

Persistence

The great hitters in Major League baseball know that when they are in a slump they must keep swinging the bat. A major factor in their success is their confidence. They know that they can hit, that their grips and stances are right, and that they will get their hits if they watch tapes of their at bats, adjust, and keep swinging.

These top performers also know that no player can be totally consistent all the time and that every player is subject to streaks. Top performers have longer hot streaks and shorter slumps than do other players, but they are still relatively inconsistent from day to day, although over a season they tend to perform close to their lifetime averages. Top performers are realistic about these streaks and have the mental discipline to wait them out, to be patient, and to keep swinging. Patience is not only a virtue but it is also a necessary ingredient of successful performance.

Salespeople are like Major League baseball players in that they are also subject to hot streaks and slumps. The way out of slumps is the same for salespeople as it is for baseball players, to keep swinging. Be persistent and disciplined in your work habits. Have confidence in your ability, and do not let negative thinking get the better of you. Give yourself positive feedback, practice visualization and mental rehearsal, take the high road by doing the right, ethical thing and your slumps will get shorter and shorter and you will be more and more successful.

Persistence means never giving up and continually slogging along on the journey toward *kaizen* and your ultimate goal to which the Spiral of Disciplined Preparation will take you.

Test Yourself

1 What are the seven elements in the Spiral of Disciplined Preparation?
2 What is the first objective you must set?
3 What are the four type of planners?

4   Which planner is most important?
5   What should you do with accounts classified as D accounts?
6   Give three areas for knowledge acquisition.
7   When should you file expense reports?
8   If you should do first things first, when should you do second things?
9   What is chunking?
10 What is wrong with long To-Do lists?

Project

Write a list of all of things you want to get done next month and then order these items according to priority on a one-, two-, or three-level basis and set deadlines for them. Next, prepare a daily planning guide for what you will do tomorrow, complete with priorities and deadlines.

References

Peter F. Drucker. 1966. *The Effective Executive*. New York: Harper & Row.

Alex McKenzie. 1975. *The Time Trap*. New York: McGraw-Hill.

C. Northcote Parkinson. 1957. *Parkinson's Law*. New York: Ballantine Books.

Stephanie Winston. 1983. *The Organized Executive: New Ways to Manage Time, Paper, and People*. New York: W.W. Norton.

Notes

1   Dan Goodgame. 2000. "The game of risk: How the best golfer in the world got even better." *Time*. August 14. www.time.com. Accessed April, 2003.

2   Ibid.

3   Peter F. Drucker. 1966. *The Effective Executive*. New York: Harper & Row, p. 25.

4   Ibid., p. 24.

5   C. Northcote Parkinson. 1957. *Parkinson's Law*. New York: Ballantine Books, p. 15.

6   Saul Gellerman. 1990. "The tests of a good salesperson." *Harvard Business Review*. May–June.

Appendix A
Selling Magazines to Agencies
Phil Frank

Media buyers are inundated with information. They have more data to consider and understand than ever before. The manner in which they digest this massive amount of information and utilize it to help make recommendations on which media vehicles they will invest in, is very personal. Each buyer's approach is unique.

The tools that buyers have are not just research, but also strategy and tactics. The best buyers try to balance all of these elements. They are also creative in finding ways to make research work in their favor.

Media buyers and salespeople tend to look at an advertising campaign from two different vantage points. Buyers look at a campaign as a composite, trying to satisfy their marketing objectives in a manner that takes good strategy, smart tactics, and their priorities into consideration. Sellers focus just on their medium, making sure that they get their fair share of a budget (and more).

The Buying Process

The buying process consists of three stages: (1) Studying data and determining which markets to buy (pre-buy analysis); (2) making a decision; and (3) placing orders (the buy). In studying and determining which markets to buy, a buyer takes many elements into consideration and analyzes them to figure out what magazines or media outlets are going to be must-buys and which ones will have to fight to get the business. In this analysis, buyers begin to sense where they have leverage.

Buyers have many tools in the early stages of a buy, and they try to use them to their advantage. Many buyers, particularly in recent years, rely more and more on objective data from syndicated research firms, and often put magazines with the largest reach on their short list of must-buys. However, experienced buyers consider that magazines add depth and texture to an advertising campaign; they believe these element can lift the creative execution, based on their own subjective interpretations of the market and a magazines' editorial content and environment.

Media buyers have a responsibility to make the best choices and to buy at the lowest rates they can find. But the best buyers are able to balance these two priorities and deliver effective advertising recommendations.

Studying the marketplace

Buyers will look at many facets of the media marketplace and look closely at individual magazines. They will look at information from syndicated research on the demographics of each magazine's audience (composition and coverage), as well as any information they can gather on the psychographics of all of the magazines being considered. Additionally, they will try to balance all this objective research with a certain amount of subjectivity.

Demographics

When they conduct an analysis of a magazine's demographics, buyers look at two measures: audience composition and coverage of the target audience. Composition is a percentage of a magazine's audience that is in a particular demographic (for example, 67 percent of *Sports Illustrated*'s audience is composed of men 24–39). Coverage is more of a quantitative measure of a magazine's audience. Coverage is a percentage of a particular demographic that is reached by a magazine (for example, *Women's Day* reaches 23 percent of women 25–34).

Buyers look at both sets of data and give each magazine a weighted average on composition and coverage. These weighted averages are applied to all magazines being considered, and then magazines are ranked according to these weightings. So, a buyer develops a list that shows, based on objective data, which magazines are strong performers and which are weaker, according to the criteria they have selected. The magazines low on the list will be expected to provide aggressive discounts if they want to be included on a buy.

Quantity versus quality

Buyers who are trying to promote a product, brand, or service to a large audience but also are interested in a particular type of people, will want to deliver reach against a large audience but also be sure that they are utilizing magazines that address the interests and tastes of their target audience. A good buyer tries to balance reaching a large quantity of prospects with reaching the highest quality prospects with a well-thought-out magazine plan.

Psychographics

Strategic buyers further differentiate magazines by looking into the psychographics of the audience they deliver. They will try to find a way to match the attitudes, interests, and lifestyles of their prospects to a magazine. Psychographics can be loosely defined and broadly applied, thus they tend to be used on a secondary basis in analyzing a market for an upcoming buy.

A marketer who sells a new European car may be trying to find a demographic segment of adults 25–49 with an annual income of over $75,000 and who are in a managerial position. And they may find through research that their customers are also people who like to hike, prepare meals at home more than three times a week, and own pets. Thus, once buyers have ranked books by their demographic performance; they may alter this list based on how books deliver on the psychographics of their audience. So, an epicurean magazine may have low composition and only above average coverage, but because its editorial carries a lot of recipes for home cooking, it would potentially be considered higher than other magazines with similar demographics.

Beyond conducting these standard analyses, there are differences in how one buyer may study a market versus how another buyer studies it. Some buyers tend to put more weight on these objective data while others are more subjective.

Subjective and objective analysis

To complete the exercise of balancing magazines that deliver quantity and ones that deliver quality, a planner has both objective resources, such as syndicated research, and subjectivity that is based on a buyer's awareness of trends.

Buyers will look at all the syndicated research they can get their hands on, and the objective data has a great deal of influence on the final purchase. However, there are other factors to consider when putting together a must-buy list. These are the more subjective aspects that help distinguish a solid plan.

In the area of more subjective considerations, a smart buyer will consider factors such as:

- whether or not a magazine is receiving criticism from a competitor, indicating the competitor is worried
- if the magazine provides a highly unique and untapped audience
- if the magazine is getting buzz from PR or strong word-of-mouth reference
- if the magazine has unique opportunities for different creative advertising executions
- if the magazine has unique editorial (special issues, for example)
- if the magazine has extraordinary ad positioning opportunities
- if the magazine as the ability to gain positive PR exposure.

Setting the Market

Once all the studying is completed, buyers have a sense of what books make sense to be considered and they must now set the market in a way that will make it highly manageable and provide buyers with several points of leverage. Setting the market is done in a fairly logical manner. It begins by utilizing research data to try to shrink the market by negotiating separately with magazines in different editorial categories, playing one magazine off against another and one category against another. For example, telling all of the seven sisters (the top seven women's magazines such as *Better Homes and Gardens*, *Good Housekeeping*, and the *Ladies Home Journal*) that the others in the category are all giving big discounts.

Buying criteria

Buyers will use their research and their judgment to create a first-cut list. The buying criteria used to make these decisions are based primarily on objective research, but with some subjective considerations.

Buying criteria are typically expressed in terms of minimum indices versus a specific target audience. For example, to make the first cut a magazine must deliver, at the minimum, a 130 index in composition and at the minimum a 120 index in coverage against adults 25–54, professional/managerial, and college graduate or more. A buyer is now setting the market, and all books that meet the criteria are able to participate in the later rounds of negotiations.

Segmenting the market

Next, buyers will take the shortened list of magazines and begin to divide it into smaller sections in order to continue to set the market. This phase is initiated by buyers so they can better compare and contrast magazines that have similar characteristics in either an editorial category or key audience delivery.

For example, buyers will segment the market so that three or four large-scale business books or four or five of the women's service books are grouped together for comparison. They will often create spreadsheets for a quick glimpse at how the competition looks in each segment. The key elements they will compare include:

- Audience Composition Index
- Composition Index rank inside of a segment
- the weight or value that composition holds in their evaluation process
- Coverage Index
- Coverage Index rank inside of this segment
- the weight or value that coverage holds in their evaluation process
- efficiency (CPM)
- CPM rank
- the weight or value that CPM holds in their evaluation process
- final weighted rank.

Weighting a factor simply means assigning a value of how important it is in the evaluation process. When creating this spreadsheet, the weights for each element of comparison are expressed as a percentage, and when all the weights are added together they should sum to 100 percent.

Depth of a buy in a segment

As buyers set the market, they can estimate what pricing will come in from the market, and begin to make preliminary estimates on how many books they actually will end up buying in the final version of the plan.

The factors that weigh on this decision are based on some of the following elements: editorial differentiation, efficiency, out-of-pocket costs, and strategic importance in reaching the target audience.

In the end a buyer will decide whether or not to buy one or two publications, or two or three publications in a segment. It is vitally important for the buyer to tell sellers this decision, because it will determine how aggressive sellers will need to be in negotiations.

Managing a Budget

Finally, buyers will put one more twist into setting the market and that is how they will manage their budget. This often comes down to strategic priorities and the objective of the advertising. Should this budget support a promotion and create very broad reach over a short period of time or does it need to convey a more intricate message over a longer period of time? This is where the marketing side of the buyer's mind comes into play.

Additionally, advertising tactics will help buyers decide how to manage their budget. Will they be launching with a high-impact, multi-page creative and then sustaining their presence with smaller and smaller units, or will their entire campaign be composed of a series of fractional pages running in a variety of magazines? These considerations leave the buyer with some decisions that can be made further into the negotiating process.

Making the Buy

Entering the more competitive rounds of negotiations that will ultimately lead to some sellers winning the business and some going home empty-handed, buyers and sellers become very tactical. Buyers will probably begin to slowly release some pieces of information that they have been holding on to that will make or break a seller's proposals.

Buying tactics

Smart buyers hold their cards very close to their chest, releasing just enough information to have the market stay as competitive as possible. Often, one seller can dictate the entire direction of a segment and not receive the business in the end. If a buyer sees a seller starting to substantially drop prices, the buyer will make this known to the seller's competition to see how they respond. Often sellers will trump each other and set a new bottom to the market. A smart seller realizes what is happening and will assess if buyers are simply riding the downward spiral, or if they would settle early with one or two books who submit best and final offers.

As a Media Director in 1993 I witnessed a segment of magazines compete for my business for three consecutive years. The segment contained three publications that were close in audience composition and coverage. One magazine had a unique editorial posture that gave it an advantage, although I was not going to disclose that early in negotiations.

All three magazines submitted their first proposals and they were offering aggressive discounts. All proposals ended up with very competitive CPMs. All of the magazines were told of their standings after this first round. One of the magazines took its discount much, much deeper than I expected and totally caught the others by surprise. The other two responded and deepened their discounts, but not as deep as their aggressive competitor.

I told the first book that the other two had responded with deeper discounts, I did not offer too many specifics, but said that once again the competition had tightened up. The first magazine dropped its rates again, now putting its discount at a level I had never witnessed before in this segment. I gave the other two books word of this second move by their competitor and neither one bit. They realized that the other book was willing take the business at a loss and they would not go there. They said they were done negotiating, having offered their best and final rates. In the end, I had to tell the book that went with the deepest discount that it had over-discounted, and if it was willing to drop their price so far, I could no longer see value in their product. The other two books realized that they had to respond to the first move, but not the second.

I, as the buyer, knew I was not going to buy the lowest discounted book, but the ploy had allowed me to gain leverage and drive the price lower in the other two books.

Tie breakers

Tiebreakers come into play when, after several rounds of negotiations, the competition is so tight that it is hard for buyers to make a decision. Therefore, buyers must look to elements of a proposal other than audience strength and price. Tiebreakers may be: what ad positions are promised (covers, opposite TOC, or far forward), the strength of marketing extensions, or the relationship a buyer has with a seller. It is rare that a buyer ends up negotiating with two books and having a dead heat, but it is not unheard of, and the intangibles, such as relationships, become very important – they are tiebreakers.

In the final analysis, after buyers have thoroughly examined all of the objective data, applied expert subjective judgment about editorial environment, and negotiated aggressively, in a tiebreaking situation the secret of success is not to look into the mind of buyers but into their hearts.

Appendix B

Writing Copy

Every ad or commercial should have four major appeals or powers, according to ERISCO (Emotional Response Index System Company), a research firm specializing in testing advertising copy:[1]

1 *Stopping power*, which is an ad's ability to grab attention immediately.
2 *Holding power*, which is the ability to keep attention throughout the body of the message.
3 *Going-away power*, which is the ability to leave the listener, viewer, reader, or user with a memorable image or impression of the main selling point.
4 *A promise* about the product.

Stopping Power

The elements that produce stopping power should be attention grabbing and dramatic and should be related to the major selling point. Attention grabbers not related to the main idea in an ad or commercial can be counterproductive and confuse the issue. Consumers might remember the attention-grabber rather than the product name.

Holding Power

Holding power is necessary to get the main selling message across. The selling message, or content, must be stated in terms of benefits to the consumer and must lead up to and connect to a specific or implied promise about the product that satisfies a pressing consumer need or want. Holding power combines the concepts of Interest and Desire in the Advertising Ladder/Sales in Chapter 17, "Advertising."

When writing radio or television commercials, repeat a store's or product's brand name frequently. This information is an important part of an ad's content and it makes sure the viewer or listener remembers the advertiser. Commercials should use simple language and short, uncomplicated sentences to get the message across. There is no time to build a long, difficult, logical argument for a product (print does this well), and viewers and listeners are unlikely to follow it anyway. Keep to a simple style; read the copy out loud and have someone else read it to you as well. Does it sound comfortable? Does it create the mood and elicit the emotional response you want?

Commercials are best when they are written to appeal to consumers' emotional needs. People tend to buy what they *want* and not necessarily what they *need* in a practical sense. To connect between needs and emotions, commercials must create an emotional involvement and an attitudinal harmony with the product and stimulate an emotional response.

There are four basic emotional appeals, according to ERISCO: money, affection, status, and security. Like leverage, each of these four appeals has two sides, positive and negative. The positive side is the desire to have more of the appeal; the negative side is the fear of losing it or the threat of not having it.[2]

Money

Virtually everyone wants more of it and feels insecure about being without it. People also want to get money with as little effort as possible. The word *free* has the strongest appeal of any word in advertising. Following are other powerful words associated with money:

Positive	Negative
Bargain	Expensive
Profit	Deficit
Economical	Extravagant
Savings	Loss

Affection

The desire for love, friendship, attention, belonging, and sex is common to all people. The affection appeal is almost as strong as the money appeal and, for some, even stronger. Fears involved in the affection appeal are as strong, if not stronger, than desires for affection. The attention-holding element in the affection appeal is more in the promise than in the fulfillment. Affection is a particularly strong appeal for young people.

Positive	Negative
Attraction	Rejection
Understanding	Misunderstanding
Friendship	Dislike
Love	Hate

Status

Status is the recognition appeal. It reflects the feeling many people have about being perceived as important. The status appeal can be quite powerful, as people seek approval and appreciation for their work, appearance, attitudes, and actions.

Positive	Negative
Advancement	Demotion, stagnation
Superior	Inferior
Exclusive	Common, run-of-the-mill
Suave	Sloppy
Beautiful	Ugly

Security

Security is the emotional appeal of self-preservation. Generally, the older people get, the more important security is to them.

Positive	Negative
Comfort	Pain, discomfort
Family, together	Alone, isolated
Healthy	Sick
Time-saving	Time-wasting
Secure, safe	Vulnerable

Going-away Power

Ads with *going-away power* stay in people's minds. The memorable aspect of a commercial should be related to the main selling point.

The Promise

To be effective, all advertising must contain a future promise: "Get clothes whiter than ever before," "Builds strong bodies twelve ways," "The ultimate driving machine." Even retailers who are promoting a sale can include a promise in their commercials: "Up to 40 percent off on all items," "Best savings of the year," "No credit refused." The promise is the benefit to the consumer, and the best way to present it is to link it strongly to the advertiser's name: "Always the lowest prices."

When you write advertising for customers, craft it to make sure it has stopping power, holding power, and going away power. Make sure it has at least one strong emotional appeal. Emotional appeals have two dimensions, positive and negative – people want it or fear losing it. And finally, all good advertising has a strong promise – explicit or implied. Always include a powerful promise when you write advertising.

Notes

1   Charles Warner and Joseph Buchman. 1991. *Broadcast and Cable Selling*, 2nd edition. Belmont, CA, p. 263. Adapted from ERISCO (Emotional Response Index System Company) promotional material.

2   Ibid.

Index